UNDERSTANDING THE BIBLE

UNDERSTANDING THE BIBLE

A READER'S INTRODUCTION

SECOND EDITION

STEPHEN L. HARRIS

CALIFORNIA STATE UNIVERSITY, SACRAMENTO

MAYFIELD PUBLISHING COMPANY

PALO ALTO AND LONDON

Library of Congress Catalog Card Number: 84-061924
International Standard Book Number: 0-87484-696-X

Manufactured in the United States of America
10   9   8   7   6   5   4   3   2

Mayfield Publishing Company
285 Hamilton Avenue
Palo Alto, California 94301

Sponsoring editor: Jim Bull
Manuscript editor: Marie Enders
Managing editor: Pat Herbst
Production editor: Jan deProsse
Art director: Nancy Sears
Cover and text designer: Nancy Benedict
Illustrator: Janet Ralston
Production manager: Cathy Willkie
Compositor: Publisher's Typography
Printer and binder: R. R. Donnelley

CONTENTS

PREFACE

The world's best known and most influential book, the Bible is also one of the least understood. Although three great world religions—Judaism, Christianity, and Islam—claim its authority for their beliefs, neither they nor any of the hundreds of lesser faiths that have developed from them can seem to agree on its fundamental message and meaning. Bewildered by contradictory interpretations, the modern reader may well hesitate to approach the Bible unaided but will be surprised how quickly understanding deepens once a few basic questions are answered about its origin, growth, historical background, and content.

The present one-volume text may be used with the Bible alone or as a supplement to a more comprehensive historical-critical text, such as W. Lee Humphreys's *Crisis and Story* (for the Old Testament) or C. Milo Connick's *The New Testament* (for the Christian Scriptures). Whether used alone or in conjunction with another textbook, however, *Understanding the Bible* aims to give the reader clear and convenient access to the Bible's basic teachings.*

Part 1 offers replies to questions commonly asked about the Bible, the questions grouped according to subject and theme. This simple format makes it easy for the reader to learn about such topics as the origin and growth of the Bible, how and when various biblical books became accepted as sacred, the meaning of the terms "Old" and "New" Testament, why Protestant and Roman Catholic Bibles differ in content, the importance of the Dead Sea Scrolls, how the Bible was translated from its

---

*The following translations of the Bible have been used for the biblical passages quoted in the text: Edgar J. Goodspeed, *The Apocrypha* (Chicago: The University of Chicago Press, 1966), for 1 and 2 Esdras; Samuel Sandmel, ed., *The New English Bible* (New York: Oxford University Press, 1970), for the New Testament and Prayer of Manasseh; and *The Jerusalem Bible* (Garden City, N.Y.: Doubleday, 1966) for the Old Testament and the rest of the Apocrypha.

ancient languages into modern English, and the relation of modern scholarship to biblical interpretation. Each subject is treated in a brief essay, many including references to further scholarly reading on the subject.

Providing background for both the Old and the New Testaments, Part 2 opens with a survey of the Bible's historical and geographical environment, including a discussion of archaeological discoveries that have helped illuminate the biblical world. After reviewing scholarly theories about their composition, Part 3 analyzes the Bible's first five books—the Torah (a Hebrew term meaning *law, teaching,* or *instruction*). Part 4 covers individual books among the Prophets, and Part 5 discusses the Writings. To acquaint the reader with the large body of extracanonical Jewish religious literature and its relation to the Bible, Part 5 includes summaries of the Apocrypha (books contained in the Greek Old Testament and the Roman Catholic and Eastern Orthodox Bibles) and the Pseudepigrapha (noncanonical writings of ancient Judaism). By including the Apocrypha and Pseudepigrapha with their evolving ideas on the Messiah, the Day of Judgment, and life after death, the text helps bridge the gap between Old Testament expectations and later Christian doctrine. Their presence illustrates both the continuity and diversity of Old and New Testament thought.

Discussions of biblical documents in *Understanding the Bible* typically include data about a book's date, historical context, authorship, and theological content. Because the sequence—Law, Prophets, and Writings—reveals much about the nature and growth of the Old Testament, the order of the original Hebrew volumes is followed. No doctrinal interpretation is presented, however. Each book is examined as a self-contained entity; themes linking it with other works written or edited during the same period or by the same school of religious thought are brought to the reader's attention; and a book's particular influence on Jewish or Christian beliefs is noted. Some readers may wish to begin their investigation of the Bible by familiarizing themselves with the material contained in Parts 3 through 6. Others will prefer to read the Bible first and then consult the critical discussions presented here. Whichever procedure is followed, the book-by-book analyses are designed to enable the reader to form a clear concept of each book's distinctive message.

Part 7 offers information about some significant historical and cultural developments in Judaism between Old and New Testament times; it also includes material on the Palestinian political situation in Jesus' day, a description of the leading Jewish religious groups, a brief survey of the types of literature appearing in the New Testament, and a new section on the continuing search for the historical Jesus.

Beginning with a review of current scholarly theories about the origins of the Gospels, Part 8 surveys each of the twenty-seven New Testament books, with emphasis on each work's thematic purpose, authorship, date, historical value, and theological concerns. Updated bibliographic references to authoritative studies on each book are included. For the convenience of those who use this text to study only the New Testament, allusions to Old Testament figures, terms, and ideas are explained when necessary. Additional definitions of both Old and New Testament concepts are found in Part 9.

In the concluding section the reader will find an alphabetized glossary that defines or identifies a representative selection of principal figures, concepts, historical events, and biblical terms from both Testaments and that cites the biblical passages in which the terms most significantly appear. No other guide or introductory text contains such a list of indispensable terms for quick reference.

Understanding the Bible is in no way sectarian or doctrinaire. Its purpose is to provide a direct and helpful means of learning what the Bible actually says—in addition to surveying what scholars, historians and other thoughtful commentators have said and written about it. Whenever possible, the text supplies historical background that explains why individual Bible writers speak in the terms they do. Although this book cannot attempt a complete analysis of the historical forces that brought the Bible into being or an exhaustive critical examination of its literature and textual transmission, it does endeavor to inform the reader of the scope and trends of modern scholarship, which have done so much to clarify the biblical record. Acquainted with some of the events and ideas that shaped ancient Israel and Christianity, informed of important scholarly discoveries about how and when various biblical books were written, both the general reader and the Bible student will find reading the Book of Books a clearer and more enjoyable experience.

A major purpose in undertaking the second edition of *Understanding the Bible* was to make the revised text as lucid and useful as possible to both students and instructors. To facilitate the reader's grasp of important biblical concepts, a number of new tables summarizing such topics as the Abrahamic, Mosaic and Davidic covenants, the chronological development of the prophets, and the Gospel writers' use of Old Testament scriptures have been incorporated into the text. The lists of recommended readings have also been expanded and updated.

The field of biblical scholarship is vital and growing, each year adding valuable information from the labors of archaeologists, historians, textual critics, theologians, and literary analysts. The new general bibliography reflects many of the current scholarly investigations that significantly increase our knowledge and appreciation of the biblical world. My debt to the experts represented in this list, as well as in the bibliographic references cited at the end of most sections, is vast and gratefully acknowledged.

Some comment needs to be made about an issue that troubles an increasing number of Bible readers: reference to the Judaeo-Christian deity as "he." Virtually all writers of both the Old and New Testaments employ the masculine pronoun when alluding to supernatural beings, whether gods, angels, or demons. (Significant exceptions include the prophetic denunciations of Ishtar, "Queen of Heaven"; Astarte, Baal's female consort; and other fertility goddesses worshipped by Israel's neighbors.) In discussing such passages, the author tries to avoid sexist language. When dealing with the idea of divinity, a moment's reflection reminds us that the Supreme Being cannot be limited by human gender. But the reader must distinguish between current beliefs about spiritual reality and the assumptions of a patriarchal society out of and for which the authors of Scripture wrote. Viewing the universal sovereign as male is indeed culture bound, but it is the practice followed in the texts transmitted to us. To respect the historical integrity of the biblical text and minimize reader confusion, this book employs the same pronouns that appear in the passages being discussed. In the broader world of church liturgy, theology, and philosophic speculation, the reader will recognize that the Being whom the Bible writers seek to communicate with is above and beyond merely human attributes, including gender.

Among those who have helped make the second edition a reality, I particularly wish to thank the reviewers who have used this textbook in class and were able to offer practical advice on improving its usefulness as a teaching tool. The reviewers are Claudia Camp, Texas Christian University; Frank Courneen, Canisius College; Marcus Gigliotti, Siena College; Robert Hann, Florida International University; William Kramer, California State University, Northridge; Richard Law, Washington State University; and Warner Sizemore, Glassboro State College. I am also grateful to Dr. Bob Platzner, my friend and colleague at California State University, Sacramento, for several helpful suggestions for revising the text, and to the Reverend James Townsend, who offered insight on several theological points.

I owe thanks to the late Barbara Pronin, who skillfully edited the first edition; to Marie Enders, who edited the manuscript of the second edition; to James Bull, the sponsoring editor at Mayfield Publishing Company; and to Alden Paine, now retired, who inaugurated the entire project and has continued to provide welcome assistance.

I am forever obliged to my sons, Geoffrey and Jason, whose questions about the Bible inspired several of the topics discussed in Part 1. Finally, I am grateful to those excellent students who for fifteen years have lightened and brightened the task of teaching the Bible to undergraduates. Their stimulating questions, perceptions, and challenges to accepted wisdom have sparked many a rewarding classroom discussion. To them and their future peers this new edition is directed.

PART 1

QUESTIONS READERS ASK ABOUT THE BIBLE

AGE, AUTHORSHIP, AND ORIGINAL LANGUAGES

1. *What is the Bible?*

Known as the Good Book, as if it were a single volume, the Bible is a collection or library of many small books written over a period of more than a thousand years. The Hebrew Bible, known to Christians as the Old Testament, is largely a record of the Hebrew deity's dealings with the chosen people, Israel. It contains twenty-four books (divided into thirty-nine in the Christian Bible) of narrative, legal material, poetry, and prophecy.

To the original Hebrew Bible Christians add the New Testament, consisting of four narratives of Jesus' life (Gospels), a theological account of the early Church (Acts), twenty-one letters, and an apocalypse (revelation of future history). Most Protestant Bibles contain sixty-six books (thirty-nine from the Old and twenty-seven from the New Testament). Roman Catholics, most Eastern churches, and some Protestants, however, include a number of additions to the Old Testament list, and these extra books are known as the Apocrypha.

2. *What does the word* bible *mean?*

The word *bible* means "little books." It is derived from the Greek term *biblion*, the diminutive form of *byblos*, which means "papyrus" or "book." That usage in turn comes from the ancient Phoenician city of Byblos, where the papyrus plant was cut and dried in strips for use as writing paper. The manuscript material thus produced was called after the place of its manufacture, Byblos.

3. *Who wrote the Bible?*

We do not know who wrote most of the Bible. The Old Testament authors did not labor for personal recognition but to convey their sense of Israel's god and his purpose for the world. Old Testament authorship was typically anonymous, although later traditions assigned important books to eminent figures of the past. In the last several centuries B.C.E. (before the common era), Moses was regarded as the author of the Bible's first five books, the Pentateuch, although most modern scholars believe that these books assumed their present form long after Moses' day. Most of the narrative books—Joshua, Judges, Samuel, Kings, and Chronicles—are the work of nameless priests, scribes, and archivists. None make direct statements about their origin or compilers. Scholars believe that the great prophets—Amos, Isaiah, Micah, and others—delivered their messages orally and that their words were collected and written down by later disciples whose names are unknown.

The same anonymity prevails in the New Testament. While late second-century Church traditions attributed various Gospels and letters to prominent early disciples and apostles, most of the texts make no claims of authorship. The conspicuous exceptions are Paul's letters, written between about 50 and 62 C.E. (of the common era) to newly founded Christian churches in such cities as Corinth, Thessalonica, Philippi, and Rome. Although the author of Luke-Acts may have been a Gentile (non-Jew), all other Bible writers were Jewish, members of the Israelite nation.

4. *When was the Bible written?*

Most scholars date the first connected written account of biblical history—from the creation to Israel's conquest of Palestine—at about the tenth century B.C.E. This document, which forms the oldest narrative strand in the Pentateuch, is characterized by its relatively consistent use of the personal name Yahweh for the Hebrew god and is usually called J, for *Jahveh*, the German form of the divine name.

Before J was written, Israel's history had been transmitted orally in the form of isolated songs, cultic recitations, and poetry. Stories concerning Israel's most famous ancestors—the patriarchs (tribal fathers) Abraham, Isaac, and Jacob—had been passed by word of mouth through many generations until they were incorporated into J. Early priests, prophets, and other national leaders also recited accounts of the central event in Israel's past—Yahweh's rescuing his people from slavery in Egypt and giving them his law on Mount Sinai—at public festivals and ceremonies. These creedlike recitals of the Moses-Sinai story, once isolated fragments of oral tradition, are now embedded in longer narratives (see 1 Sam. 12:7–15; Deut. 26:6–10; Josh. 24:1–13).

Certain poems celebrating decisive historical victories are thought to be older than the written context in which they now appear. A good example is Miriam's song of Yahweh's triumph at the Red Sea (Exod. 15), which may have circulated independently of other oral material and was included in the J narrative around 950 B.C.E. The last books of the Old Testament were composed only a century or two before the birth of Jesus; some of the Apocrypha were written even later.

While the library of the Hebrew Scriptures took approximately a millennium to complete, the New Testament was composed during a much shorter period, probably between about 50 C.E. (for Paul's earliest letters) and 150 C.E. (for the final form of 2 Peter). In all, biblical literature represents a time span of approximately 1,100 years.

5. *Is the Bible the world's oldest book?*

No. At one time biblical scholars believed that the Bible was the only significant literary production of the ancient Near East. During the past century, however, archaeologists have found remains of other ancient libraries, such as that of the Assyrian Emperor Ashurbanipal IV (668–627 B.C.E.), in the ruins of whose palace at Nineveh, capital of the Assyrian Empire, were discovered hundreds of clay tablets inscribed with a wedge-shaped writing known as *cuneiform*. Ashurbanipal's tablets were in Akkadian, a Semitic language used by Assyrians and Babylonians, but they seem to have included translations from the much older literature of Sumer, the first known high civilization of the ancient Near East. The Sumerians, later invaded by Akkadian-speaking peoples, were a non-Semitic group that built city-states along the southern Euphrates River near the head of the Persian Gulf in what is now Iraq.

For Bible scholars, perhaps the most important finds were eleven tablets recounting the adventures of Gilgamesh, a legendary king of Uruk, a leading Sumerian city. The *Epic of Gilgamesh* includes a vivid account of a great flood, which only a single man, Gilgamesh's ancestor Utnapishtim, survived. Directed by Ea, the god of wisdom, Utnapishtim built an ark (a box-shaped boat) on which he, his family, servants, and various animals were preserved. In numerous details, including the sending out of birds to find dry land and the offering of sacrifice after the flood waters receded, the Gilgamesh flood story remarkably parallels that in Genesis. Scholar Alexander Heidel believes that both the Sumero-Babylonian and biblical accounts go back to a single source, although the Gilgamesh version is clearly the older of the two.

Mesopotamia, as the Greeks called the Sumero-Babylonian area between the Tigris and Euphrates rivers, produced other counterparts to familiar Bible stories. The Mesopotamian creation account known as the *Enuma Elish* (meaning "When Above") is sometimes called the Babylonian Genesis. Old Testament laws and legal practices are also paralleled in Sumerian and Akkadian inscriptions, the most famous of which occurs on a black stone monument called the Stele of Hammurabi. Ruler of the short-lived Old Babylonian Empire, Hammurabi revised and codified preexisting laws about 1690 B.C.E. Carved in stone for public view, Hammurabi's code is reflected in several Mosaic laws of the Pentateuch. Like Moses, Hammurabi claimed to have received his ordinances from a god, in his case the Babylonian sun deity Shamash.

Although Sumero-Babylonian literature is polytheistic (presenting a world with many gods), works like the *Enuma Elish* and *Epic of Gilgamesh* did have an impact on the men who wrote the Bible. The common Mesopotamian belief in the divine creation of life and the gods' control of earthly events influenced the development of Israel's religious thought. According to Genesis and Joshua, Israel's ancestors had worshiped Mesopotamian gods. At a later period the Israelite captives in Babylon (587–538 B.C.E.) absorbed considerable Mesopotamian myth and folklore, some of which, refined by Hebrew monotheism, later appeared in Scripture. The priestly account of creation in Genesis 1 may have been a response to witnessing the splendid public performance of the *Enuma Elish* at the Babylonian New Year festival.

In addition to Mesopotamian influences, which were particulary intense during the Assyrian and Neo-Babylonian hegemony of the eighth through sixth centuries B.C.E., Egyptian and Canaanite ideas also affected Israelite religious thought. Among other Egyptian borrowings, Proverbs 22:17–23:11 contains what is virtually a Hebrew translation of passages written or compiled by Amenemope (Amenemophis), one of Egypt's leading wise men, while Canaanite motifs permeate almost the entire Old Testament.

After the Hebrews settled in Palestine (Canaan) in the thirteenth century B.C.E., they not only took over many older Canaanite shrines and urban sanctuaries, such as those at Bethel, Shechem, and Jerusalem, but they adopted Canaanite hymns, poems, and religious titles to apply to Yahweh's worship. Prayers and epic poems celebrating Baal, the Canaanite fertility god, and El, father of all gods, such as those found at Ugarit (Ras Shamra), supplied many of the terms and images that Bible writers characteristically use to describe Yahweh (Pss. 82; 50:2–3; Gen. 21:33; Ezek. 16:3; Judg. 5:4–5). Genesis 14:18–24 includes a brief narrative that shows how Abraham identified Yahweh with El Elyon ("God Most High") of the Canaanite city of Salem.

RECOMMENDED READING

Coogan, Michael David. *Stories from Ancient Canaan.* Philadelphia: Westminster Press, 1978. A paperback collection of Canaanite myths and their biblical parallels.

Cross, F. M. *Canaanite Myth and Hebrew Epic, Essays in the History of the Religion of Israel.* Cambridge, Mass.: Harvard University Press, 1973.

Heidel, Alexander. *The Babylonian Genesis.* 2nd ed. Chicago: University of Chicago Press, 1951. A paperback translation of the *Enuma Elish* with commentary.

_____. *The Gilgamesh Epic and Old Testament Parallels.* Chicago: University of Chicago Press, 1949.

Pritchard, James B., ed. *Ancient Near Eastern Text Relating to the Old Testament.* 3d ed., supp. Princeton, N. J.: Princeton University Press, 1969. Translations of relevant Egyptian, Babylonian, Canaanite, and other ancient literatures—the standard work.

_____. *The Ancient Near East in Pictures Relating to the Old Testament.* Princeton, N. J.: Princeton University Press, 1965. A companion volume.

_____. *The Ancient Near East: An Anthology of Texts and Pictures.* Princeton N. J.: Princeton University Press, 1965. A less expensive work containing excerpts from the two preceding books.

Sandars, N. K. *The Epic of Gilgamesh.* Baltimore: Penguin Books, 1972. A readable translation of the *Epic of Gilgamesh* with a scholarly introduction.

6. *In what languages was the Bible originally written?*

Most of the Old Testament was written in classical Hebrew, the Semitic tongue spoken by the Israelites. Certain later books were composed in Aramaic, an Aramean (Syrian) dialect closely related to Hebrew and probably also the language spoken by Jesus. The entire New Testament is in Koine Greek, the international language of the first-century workaday world, a tongue derived from the fusion of classical Greek with the commercial vernacular of Near Eastern peoples conquered by the armies of Alexander the Great. The blending of Oriental and Greek elements produced a cosmopolitan culture known as Hellenistic, arbitrarily dated as beginning with the death of Alexander in 323 B.C.E. Hellenistic ideas exerted considerable influence on the thinking of late Old Testament authors, and early Christian theologians as well. Merely phrasing age-old religious ideas in Greek, a language in which even the commonest terms were loaded with philosophical implications, subtly changed their religious meaning.

MANUSCRIPTS AND TRANSLATIONS

7. *When was the Bible first translated?*

The first translation of the Hebrew Bible was begun in Alexandria, Egypt, in the mid-third century before Christ, when leaders of the Jewish colony there found that the younger generation of Jews no longer understood classical Hebrew. According to legend, seventy scholars were appointed to translate the Scriptures into Koine Greek, and after laboring for seventy days, they produced seventy identical versions. According to historical fact, however, this landmark translation, known as the Septuagint (after the seventy or seventy-two elders who supposedly produced it), took more than two centuries to complete. The Pentateuch (Genesis through Deuteronomy) was translated first, followed gradually by the prophetic books and the Writings (poetic and wisdom literature), and eventually by works that later became known as the Apocrypha. A Hellenistic Jewish work, the *Letter of Aristeas*, gives a popular version of the Septuagint's origin (see pp. 224–225).

The Septuagint was extremely influential among Jews living outside Palestine and was the Bible adopted by the early Greek-speaking Christians. Most of the Old Testament passages cited in the New Testament are either direct quotations or paraphrases of the Septuagint Bible. Indeed, so completely did Christians take over this Jewish translation that the Jews were forced to produce another version for their own use.

The next great step in making the Bible available to a wider audience was St. Jerome's production of the Latin Vulgate. Commissioned by the bishop of Rome to render the Scriptures into the common tongue for the Latin-speaking Western church, Jerome, between 385 and 405 C.E., produced what became the official Bible of Roman Catholicism. Following the general decline in literacy after the fall of Rome in the late fifth century, no other major translation of the Bible was published for nearly a thousand years. Pre-Reformation translators at first merely rendered Jerome's Latin into the languages of modern Europe. Not until William Tyndale in the 1500s were translations again made from the Bible's original Hebrew, Aramaic, and Greek.

RECOMMENDED READING

Klein, Ralph W. *Textual Criticism of the Old Testament: The Septuagint after Qumran.* Philadelphia: Fortress Press, 1974.

8. *In what forms has the Bible's text been preserved?*

No original copy of any biblical book has survived. The oldest extant forms of Scripture are manuscript (handwritten) copies on papyrus (paperlike sheets made from the papyrus plant) and parchment (dried and treated animal skins). Countless ancient copies of the Old Testament, or parts thereof, were undoubtedly lost during the repeated destruction of Jerusalem and its temple, such as those by the Babylonians in 587 B.C.E. and by the Romans in 70 C.E. Wars, persecutions, and mob violence also account for the loss of many Hebrew manuscripts kept in synagogues (Jewish meeting places for instruction and worship) throughout the Greco-Roman world.

Before the Dead Sea Scrolls were discovered in 1947 and after, the oldest complete copies of the Hebrew Bible were those made in the ninth and tenth centuries. These manuscripts were largely the work of *masoretes* (from an Aramaic word meaning "tradition"), medieval Jewish scribes who added vowel symbols to the consonantal Hebrew script. The Masoretic Text (MT) is the standard form of the Hebrew Bible today. Although only the scroll of Isaiah was found complete, the discovery of the Dead Sea Scrolls produced at least fragments of every Hebrew canonical book (except Esther), some of which date from as early as about 150 B.C.E. and represent the most ancient surviving texts.

Although there are no complete New Testament texts earlier than the fourth century C.E., the oldest manuscript fragments date from the second century and include versions preserved in Greek, Syriac, Latin, Ethiopic, and other languages. Among the many New Testament manuscripts occur an estimated 400,000 textual variations, though the essential meaning of the text seems relatively clear in most cases.

Of the thousands of surviving Old and New Testament manuscripts or fragments, no two are precisely alike, which presents the textual critic or translator with a formidable challenge. He or she must compare variations among these thousands and try to determine which one, or combination of several, appears closest to the supposed original. Because all manuscripts differ from one another to some degree, a given text's exact relationship and fidelity to the (forever lost) original is virtually impossible to determine. The scholar's task of sorting out new manuscript finds and comparing them with previously known versions, thus to enhance the quality and reliability of the biblical text, is a continuously ongoing process known as lower (textual) criticism.

9. *How did our modern English translations come about?*

Although none of his work has survived, the first man credited with translating the Bible into his native English was the Venerable Bede, a Benedictine monk and historian of Anglo-Saxon England. In the 730s Bede rendered part of Jerome's Latin Vulgate into Old English. During the tenth and eleventh centuries a few other Bible books, including the Psalms and Gospels, also appeared in English, but it was not until the fourteenth century that the entire Bible would be translated into that language. Except to Church leaders and a few scholars, Latin had by then become a dead language and the Vulgate Bible incomprehensible to most Christians. To make the Scriptures accessible to the British, John Wycliffe, an English priest, translated both Old and New Testaments, completing the project around 1384. But the Church, fearing the effect of Bibles in the popular tongue, in 1408 condemned Wycliffe's version and forbade any future translations.

Two historical events, however, ensured that the Bible would find a larger reading public in English. The first was Johann Gutenberg's invention of movable type in 1455. The second was the Protestant Reformation, begun in 1517, when the German priest Martin Luther protested administrative corruption within the Roman Catholic church. A German translation of the Bible completed by Luther himself in the years 1522–34 was the first version in a modern European language based not on the official Latin Vulgate Bible but on the original Hebrew and Greek.

The first English translator to work directly from Hebrew and Greek manuscripts was William Tyndale, who, under the threat of persecution, fled to Germany, where his translation of the New Testament was published in 1525 (revised 1534). Tyndale's version of the Pentateuch appeared in 1530 and his Jonah in 1531. But intense persecution prevented him from completing his translation of the Old Testament, and in 1535–36 he was betrayed, tried for heresy, and burned at the stake. Although he did not live to finish translating the entire Bible, Tyndale's superb rendering of the New Testament and Pentateuch has influenced almost every English version since.

Although the Church forbade the reading of Wycliffe's or Tyndale's translations, it nevertheless permitted free distribution of the first printed English Bible—the Coverdale Bible (1535), which relied heavily on Tyndale's work. Matthew's Bible (1537), containing additional sections of Tyndale's Old Testament, was revised by Coverdale, and the result was called the Great Bible (1539). The Bishops' Bible (1568) was a revision of the Great Bible, and the King James Version was commissioned as a revision of the Bishops' Bible. The Geneva Bible (1560), which the English Puritans had produced in Switzerland, also significantly influenced the King James Bible.

By far the most popular English Bible of all time, the King James was authorized by James I, who appointed fifty-four scholars to make a new version of the Bishops' Bible for official use in the English church. After seven years' labor, during which the oldest available manuscripts were diligently consulted, the king's scholars produced in 1611 the Authorized or King James Version, which is one of the masterpieces of English literature. Made at a time when the language was at its richest and most creative in vocabulary, rhythm, and style, the King James version remains unsurpassed in literary excellence. Later English translations may be more accurate and have the advantage of being based on more recently discovered manuscripts, but none has phrased the Scriptures in so memorable or quotable a fashion.

The first Revised Version of the King James was published in England between 1881 and 1885; modification of this, the American Standard Revised Version, was issued in 1901. Utilizing the (then) latest studies in archaeology and linguistics, the Revised Standard Version appeared between 1946 and 1952. Modern scholarship continues to advance its knowledge of biblical languages and textual history, resulting in a number of new Bible translations that are sometimes more exact, if less beautifully worded, than the King James.

These include the Jerusalem Bible (1966), the New American Bible (1970), the New English Bible (1976), and the Doubleday Anchor Bible, the latter issued in a heavily annotated series of volumes beginning in the 1960s and not yet complete. Two relatively new translations in paperback—the Good News Bible and the Living Bible—are extremely popular with students. Readers should be aware, however, that while the former is a responsible paraphrase of the original text, many experts consider the latter a highly unreliable and misleading translation. There are, in addition, many recent translations by individual scholars or groups of scholars, such as those by Richard F. Weymouth, James Moffatt, J. B. Phillips, and Edgar J. Goodspeed and J. M. Powis Smith, each of which has its distinctive merits and drawbacks.

RECOMMENDED READING

Bruce, F. F. *History of the Bible in English.* 3rd ed. New York: Oxford University Press, 1978. A concise history and critical evaluation of all major English translations from Anglo-Saxon times to the present.

The Jerusalem Bible. Garden City, N. Y.: Doubleday, 1966. A vivid Roman Catholic translation in paperback that uses the name Yahweh throughout the Old Testament. The hardbound edition contains scholarly introductions and many informative notes.

The New English Bible with Apocrypha: Oxford Study Edition. Edited by Samuel Sandmel. New York: Oxford University Press, 1976. A clear, readable paperback translation with helpful footnotes.

THE OLD TESTAMENT CANON

10. *What is meant by* canon?

The term *canon* refers to the standard or measurement by which books were included or excluded from the final list of authoritative Scripture. In Greek, *canon* means a straight stick by which something is ruled or measured. The Hebrew word *qaneh* also referred to measurement or the norm by which something was judged.

11. *How did the biblical canon come into being, and which parts of the Bible were first accepted as canonical?*

Bible scholars emphasize that canonization occurs as a historical *process*, not by arbitrary decrees of a religious council or other authority. The Hebrew Bible grew by degrees, its contents expanding to incorporate new documents as Israel's writers over many generations recorded and interpreted their nation's political and spiritual experiences. The end result of a long period of development, canonization took place as the community of faith gradually accepted the religious authority of a book or books. As centuries passed, Israel's legal and prophetic writings grew ever more venerable and were quoted, debated, and read publicly in the synagogues until familiarity with their teaching and their recognized consistency with the Mosaic tradition made them by use and habit part of the Hebrew Bible.

By about 400 B.C.E. the Jews regarded the first five books of the Bible (the Pentateuch) as authoritative and binding. These five scrolls constituted the Torah, meaning the "law," "teaching," or "instruction" that Yahweh gave to Israel through Moses.

Next to be accepted were the prophetic books, which form the second major division of the Hebrew canon. By about 200 B.C.E. the Former Prophets (Joshua, Judges, Samuel, and Kings) and the Latter Prophets (the three Major Prophets, which occupy one scroll each, and the twelve Minor Prophets, which are encompassed on a single scroll) were regarded as sacred.

As early as the mid-second century B.C.E. a third category of Scripture was recognized. In the preface to his Greek translation of Ecclesiasticus (Wisdom of Jesus Ben Sirach), the translator speaks of "the Law and the Prophets and the *other volumes of the fathers*" (italics added). These "other volumes" are the Writings (in Hebrew, the *Kethuvim*), whose contents were not clearly defined for many generations. Not until after the Romans had destroyed Jerusalem in 70 C.E. did the Jewish community attempt to set a precise limit on the number of books comprising the Writings. Then the problem was not so much what to include as, considering the vast number of religious volumes available, what to omit.

Following the Roman destruction of the Jewish state, a group of distinguished rabbis (teachers of the Law) assembled at Jamnia on the Palestinian coast to define and consolidate the essential teachings of the Jewish religion, including a statement about which books of the Hebrew Bible were to be accepted as sacred and authoritative. The Jamnia assembly of about 90 C.E. was not the last such body to debate the issue, but it appears that the rabbis exercised their moral authority to favor usage of the following books and no others: Psalms, Proverbs, Job, the five scrolls to be read on major holy days (Song of Songs, Ruth, Lamentations, Ecclesiastes, and Esther), Daniel (the only fully apocalyptic work to be included), and the work of the Chronicler (1 and 2 Chronicles, Ezra, and Nehemiah). Some historians have suggested that the rabbis also acted to exclude the writings of the heretical new Christian sect as well as a number of books found in the Greek Septuagint Bible. Many of the latter were extremely popular among Greek-speaking Christians, however, and today are included in the Roman Catholic, Eastern, and Anglican canon as the Apocrypha.

RECOMMENDED READING

Freedman, David Noel. "Canon of the O.T." In *The Interpreter's Dictionary of the Bible: Supplementary Volume*, pp. 130–36. Nashville: Abingdon Press, 1976. A good introduction.

Pfeiffer, Robert H. "Canon of the O.T." In *The Interpreter's Dictionary of the Bible*, Vol. 1, pp. 498–520. New York and Nashville: Abingdon Press, 1962.

Sanders, James A. *Torah and Canon*. Philadelphia: Fortress Press, 1972. A concise and helpful introduction to canon formation.

12. *What are the Old Testament Apocrypha?*

The word *apocrypha* is the plural form of a Greek adjective meaning "hidden," a designation that may have applied to writings thought to contain some form of "secret" doctrine whose teachings would be "hidden" from ignorant or uninitiated readers. In this respect, however, they are not different from other books of the Bible, nearly all of which express difficult or obscure ideas.

Since the Bible of the early Church was not the Hebrew but the Greek, it is natural that the apocryphal books in the Septuagint were adopted by the Roman Catholic church and included in Jerome's Latin Vulgate translation. These were: 1 and 2 Esdras, Tobit, Judith, the Wisdom of Solomon, Ecclesiasticus, Baruch, the Prayer of Manasseh, 1 and 2 Maccabees, Additions to the canonical Book of Esther, and Additions to Daniel (the Prayer of the Three Hebrew Children, Susanna, and Bel and the Dragon). Of these, 1 Maccabees is excellent history, Ecclesiasticus and Wisdom first-rate examples of Hebrew wisdom literature, and Tobit a well-crafted historical romance.

Interestingly, Jerome himself first described books found in the Greek but not in the Hebrew Old Testament as Apocrypha, and his implied distinction of relative worth between the two was vigorously emphasized by many Protestant reformers. The latter argued that because the Old Testament is meant to illustrate the faith of pre-Christian Israel, Protestant Christians ought to include only books found in the original Hebrew Bible as defined by the rabbis at Jamnia; hence most Protestant translations contain books from the Hebrew canon only. One result of the Reformation, many leaders of which questioned or even denied the Apocrypha's religious authority, was the famous Council of Trent (1546) at which the Roman Catholic church reaffirmed its position that these books were "deuterocanonical" and therefore a "second canon" of sacred literature.

RECOMMENDED READING

de Lange, Nicholas. *Apocrypha: Jewish Literature of the Hellenistic Age.* New York: Viking Press, 1978.

13. *Is inclusion of the Apocrypha the only difference among Jewish, Protestant, and Roman Catholic Bibles?*

Unfortunately, no. To compound the confusion, both Protestants and Roman Catholics retained the Septuagint's general ordering of contents, which differs appreciably from the Hebrew (see Table 1-1). The threefold Hebrew division of Scripture into Law, Prophets, and Writings is in some respects a more logical (and chronological) arrangement than the Septuagint's interspersing of prophets with historical writings and poetic books.

TABLE 1-1 Order of Books in the Old Testament

Hebrew Bible (Masoretic Text)		Greek Septuagint Bible	Roman Catholic and Greek Orthodox Old Testament	Protestant Old Testament
Torah	Pentateuch	Pentateuch	Pentateuch	Pentateuch
Bereshith	(Genesis)	Genesis	Genesis	Genesis
Shemoth	(Exodus)	Exodus	Exodus	Exodus
Wayiqra	(Leviticus)	Leviticus	Leviticus	Leviticus
Bemidbar	(Numbers)	Numbers	Numbers	Numbers
Debarim	(Deuteronomy)	Deuteronomy	Deuteronomy	Deuteronomy
Neviïm (Prophets)		Historical Books	Historical Books	Historical Books
Former Prophets		Joshua	Josue (Joshua)	Joshua
Yehoshua (Joshua)		Judges	Judges	Judges
Shofetim (Judges)		Ruth	Ruth	Ruth
		1–2 Regnorum (1–2 Samuel)	1 and 2 Kings (1–2 Samuel)	1–2 Samuel
Shemuel (1–2 Samuel)				1–2 Kings
Melakim (1–2 Kings)		3–4 Regnorum (1–2 Kings)	3–4 Kings (1–2 Kings)	
		1–2 Paralipomenon (1–2 Chronicles)	1–2 Paralipomenon (1–2 Chronicles)	1–2 Chronicles
		1 Esdras*	1–2 Esdras (Ezra and Nehemiah)	Ezra
		2 Esdras (Ezra-Nehemiah)	Tobias (Tobit)*	Nehemiah
		Esther	Judith*	Esther
		Judith*	Esther (with additions)	
		Tobit*	1–2 Maccabees*	
		1–4 Maccabees*		
		Poetry and Wisdom	Poetry and Wisdom	Poetry and Wisdom
		Psalms	Job	Job
		Odes*	Psalms	Psalms
		Proverbs	Proverbs	Proverbs
		Ecclesiastes	Ecclesiastes	Ecclesiastes
		Song of Songs	Canticle of Canticles (Song of Solomon)	Song of Solomon
		Job	Wisdom of Solomon*	
		Wisdom of Solomon*	Ecclesiasticus* (Wisdom of Jesus Ben Sirach)	
		Sirach (Ecclesiasticus)*		
		Psalms of Solomon		

Latter Prophets	Prophetic Books	Prophetic Books	Prophetic Books
Yeshavahu (Isaiah)	Isaiah	Isaias (Isaiah)	Isaiah
Yirmevahu (Jeremiah)	Jeremiah	Jeremias (Jeremiah)	Jeremiah
	Baruch*	Lamentations	Lamentations
	Lamentations	Baruch (including the epistle of Jeremias)*	
	Epistle of Jeremiah*	Ezechiel (Ezekiel)	Ezekiel
Yehezqel (Ezekiel)	Ezekiel	Daniel (with additions; Prayer of Azariah and Song of the Three Young Men;* Susanna;* Bel and the Dragon*)	Daniel
	Susanna*		
	Daniel		
	Bel and the Dragon*		
Tere Asar (Book of the Twelve)		Osee (Hosea)	Hosea
Hosea		Joel	Joel
Amos		Amos	Amos
Micah		Abidas (Obadiah)	Obadiah
Joel		Jonas (Jonah)	Jonah
Obadiah		Micheas (Micah)	Micah
Jonah		Nahum	Nahum
Nahum		Habucuc (Habakkuk)	Habakkuk
Habukkuk		Sophonias (Zephaniah)	Zephaniah
Zephaniah		Aggeus (Haggai)	Haggai
Haggai		Zacharias (Zechariah)	Zechariah
Zechariah		Malachias (Malachi)	Malachi
Malachi			

Kethuvim (Writings)

Tehillim (Psalms)
Iyyob (Job)
Mishle (Proverbs)
Ruth
Shir Hashirim (Song of Solomon)
Qoheleth (Ecclesiastes)
Ekah (Lamentations)
Ester (Esther)
Daniel
Ezra-Nehemyah (Ezra-Nehemiah)
Dibre Hayamin (1–2 Chronicles)

*Not in Jewish or Protestant Bibles; considered deuterocanonical by Catholic scholars and relegated to the Apocrypha by Protestants.

In Christian Bibles, then, the distinction between the Prophets and the Writings is seriously obscured. The traditional Christian catalogue separates the Festival Scrolls, such as Ruth, Esther, and the Song of Songs, from one another, with the result that their devotional and cultic significance is no longer clear. The original arrangement is more meaningful, for some of these short books were probably adopted into the canon because of their long association with particular holy days on which they were read aloud. Their long-term familiarity to the Jewish community of faith may largely have determined their canonization.

14. *Are there any other Jewish writings that were not received into the Bible?*

Yes, late noncanonical Jewish books known collectively as the Pseudepigrapha because some of them were piously but inaccurately attributed to revered biblical figures of the distant past, such as Enoch and Moses. Dating from about 200 B.C.E. to 200 C.E., the Pseudepigrapha include a rich variety of legendary and apocalyptic material that significantly influenced Jewish and early Christian thought. Many pseudepigraphal works were found among the Dead Sea Scrolls, the Essene library from Qumran. (Individual books of the Pseudepigrapha are discussed in Part 6.) Manuscripts of some of these books show signs of reworking by Christian hands, which indicates that they circulated among, and were read by, members of the early Church.

RECOMMENDED READING

Charles, R. H., ed. *The Apocrypha and Pseudepigrapha of the Old Testament in English.* 2 vols. New York: Oxford University Press, 1913, reprinted 1963.

Charlesworth, James H., ed. *The Old Testament Pseudepigrapha.* Vol. 1, *Apocalyptic Literature and Testaments.* Garden City, N. Y.: Doubleday, 1983. A monumental scholarly edition of the Pseudepigrapha, with new translations and notes.

Eissfeldt, Otto. *The Old Testament: An Introduction.* New York: Harper & Row, 1965.

Nickelsburg, George W. E. *Jewish Literature Between the Bible and the Mishnah.* Philadelphia: Fortress Press, 1981.

Rost, Leonard. *Judaism Outside the Hebrew Canon: An Introduction to the Documents.* Nashville: Abingdon Press, 1976.

Soggin, J. Alberto. *Introduction to the Old Testament.* Philadelphia: Westminster Press, 1976.

15. *What are the Dead Sea Scrolls?*

Until about thirty years ago the oldest known extant manuscript copies of the Hebrew Scriptures were the Masoretic Texts, which dated from about the ninth and tenth centuries C.E. In 1947, however, according to a popular version of the story, a Bedouin shepherd boy threw a stone into a cave at Qumran near the Dead Sea and heard pottery shattering inside. Investigating later, he found hidden in the cave clay jars containing leather scrolls. On examining the site, scholars found an entire library of religious books dating from about the second century before Jesus to the first century after.

Many of these scrolls were copies of canonical Old Testament works—such as Isaiah, the Psalms, Deuteronomy, and Daniel—as well as commentaries on them. There were also original writings, apparently produced by a monastic group of Essenes, a Jewish sect that occupied the Qumran area over the three-century period during which the manuscripts were written. These original works included a Manual of Discipline for the Qumran community and a set of military instructions for fighting the cosmic battle between good and evil, the imminent War of the Sons of Light against the Sons of Darkness. Many other tracts, sermons, and biblical explications were found in various caves.

This find was significant in several ways. First, it provided copies of at least fragments of all Old Testament books (except Esther) that were almost a thousand years older than any other extant manuscripts. Second, it demonstrated that while many biblical texts contained numerous variations from the received copies, the Book of Isaiah, represented in a scroll twenty-four feet long, had been transmitted for nearly ten centuries with little appreciable change. Third, it revealed the existence of a monastic religious community, mentioned by the first-century Jewish historian Josephus, that was strikingly different from mainstream or rabbinic Judaism. Finally, it proved that the Qumran community apparently practiced certain rites, such as a form of water baptism and a covental meal, that strikingly resembled later Christian customs.

RECOMMENDED READING

Betz, O. "Dead Sea Scrolls." In *The Interpreter's Dictionary of the Bible*, vol. 1, pp. 790–802. New York and Nashville: Abingdon Press, 1962.

———. "Essenes." In *The Interpreter's Dictionary of the Bible: Supplementary Volume*, pp. 277–79. Nashville: Abingdon Press, 1976.

Cross, Frank Moore. *The Ancient Library of Qumran and Modern Biblical Studies.* Garden City, N. Y.: Doubleday, 1961.

Fitzmyer, J. A. *The Dead Sea Scrolls. Major Publications and Tools for Study.* Missoula, Mont.: Scholars Press, 1975. A bibliographic reference.

Gaster, Theodore H. *The Dead Sea Scriptures in English Translation.* Garden City, N. Y.: Doubleday, 1976.

Ringgren, Helmer. *The Faith of Qumran.* Philadelphia: Fortress Press, 1961.

Vermes, Geza. *The Dead Sea Scrolls, Qumran in Perspective.* London: Collins, 1977.

THE NEW TESTAMENT CANON

16. *What does the term* testament *mean, and how do the Old and New Testaments differ in respect to that meaning?*

In biblical terms, *testament* is a synonym for *covenant*, which means an agreement or promise. In the Hebrew Bible, Yahweh initiates a covenant with Israel that gives the Old Testament its name. At Mount Sinai, where Yahweh has brought the Israelites after rescuing them from Egyptian slavery, he promises to be their god, and they vow to obey him. Because this agreement was mediated through Moses, it is called the Mosaic Covenant or Testament, and this legal bond between Israel and Israel's god is the central theme of the Torah. But several of Israel's prophets felt that the people had so grievously broken their covenant obligations that a new, more spiritual agreement was called for. Jeremiah, in particular, predicted that Yahweh would make a new covenant with his people (Jer. 31:31).

Christians believe that Jesus inaugurated that new covenant at the Last Supper: "And he took the cup, and gave thanks, and gave it to them, saying, Drink ye all of it: For this is my blood of the new testament . . ." (Matt. 26:27–28; King James Version). (The adjective *new*, not present in the earliest manuscripts, was added later to emphasize the change in God's relationship with humankind. Both the Revised Standard Version and the Jerusalem Bible omit *new* and use *covenant* instead of *testament* in this passage.) To Christians, then, the Jewish Scriptures, dealing with the older Mosaic Covenant, came to be known as the Old Testament; the Greek writings about Jesus and his disciples were called the New Testament. The Christian community regarded both parts of the Bible as authoritative and suitable for religious instruction.

17. *How and when was the New Testament canon formed?*

The first official listing of the twenty-seven books that accord with the present New Testament canon was not issued until 367 C.E., more than three centuries after the deaths of most of Jesus' original followers. This important list appeared in the Easter Letter of Athanasius, bishop of Alexandria, who, though citing only the twenty-seven canonical books as authoritative, suggested that Christians would also profit from reading certain noncanonical works that, until the end of the fourth century in some areas of the Roman Empire, were regarded as almost on a par with what we think of as "genuine" New Testament books.

By what standards, then, were certain Christian writings accorded canonical status while others, once equally popular with early Christians, were denied it? Probably the chief criterion was a book's association with the apostolic tradition. Letters undisputedly by the Apostle Paul, for example, were probably the first part of the New Testament to be collected and circulated among various Christian congregations. By the mid-second century, as 2 Peter 3:15–16 testifies, Paul's letters were regarded as scripture. To the nine or ten Pauline epistles that modern scholars accept as authentically his—1 and 2 Thessalonians, 1 and 2 Corinthians, Romans, Galatians, Philippians, Colossians, Philemon, and (possibly) Ephesians—were gradually added the so-called Pastoral Letters, 1 and 2 Timothy, and Titus.

A number of memoirs of Jesus (Gospels) circulated in the Church before the four contained in the New Testament were recognized as superior to their competitors and canonized. These may have included the Gospel of Thomas, discovered in Egypt in 1945, along with fragments of other Christian-Gnostic books. (A heretical group, the Gnostics saw Jesus as pure spirit, not man, who revealed a secret *gnosis* or knowledge to a spiritual elite.) Thomas records none of Jesus' actions, only his purported teachings and sayings, some of which may be as authentic as those preserved in Mark or Luke.

The earliest reference to the four Gospels as authoritative occurs in a book called 2 Clement, falsely ascribed to Clement, bishop of Rome, which quotes a passage from Matthew as "scripture." At about the same time, Justin Martyr, a churchman executed in Rome in the 160s, cited the "memoirs of the Apostles" or "gospels" as though they were of equal status to the Hebrew Prophets. The books of Matthew, Mark, Luke, and John, which had hitherto circulated anonymously among Christians, were now being regarded as the work of apostles or attributed to individual disciples.

Up to the second century the Christian Bible consisted of the Old Testament, the Apocrypha, and the letters of Paul. The concept of Christian Scriptures as totally distinct from the Jewish Bible then received a strong impetus from a Gnostic Christian named Marcion, who rejected the entire Old Testament as presenting a barbarous image of God. Among the many Christian writings then extant, he accepted only the Gospel of Luke and the Pauline letters as morally authoritative. Although Marcion's extreme position was repudiated by the Church, his ideas nonetheless helped to formulate the concept of an altogether separate body of inspired Christian books—the germ of the New Testament.

The Muratorian Canon, a document that appeared toward the end of the second century, is probably typical of the mixed bag of canonical and apocryphal works that the second- and third-century Church recognized as sacred. Compiled in Rome, this canon lists the four Gospels, Acts, thirteen letters of Paul (including the Pastorals but not Hebrews), Jude, 1 and 2 John, the Wisdom of Solomon, Revelation, and the Apocalypse of Peter. In comparable lists made during this transitional period, the four Gospels, Acts, and letters of Paul are firmly entrenched in the growing canon.

Numerous other books, particularly those assigned to Peter, James, and Jude, as well as Hebrews and (usually) Revelation, remained in dispute, accepted by some but rejected by others. Certain Old Testament Apocrypha, such as the Wisdom of Solomon, and New Testament Apocrypha, such as the Apocalypse of Peter, mingled with what would later become canonical books. As late as the fifth century, a Greek manuscript known as the Codex Alexandrinus included 1 and 2 Clement (letters attributed to an early bishop of Rome) in the New Testament. Finally, some important Eastern churches, such as those at Alexandria and Antioch, resisted inclusion of Revelation, partly because of its dubious Johannine authorship. Although eventually accepted, it never attained the same authority as other New Testament books. The Syrian churches consistently denied it canonical status.

The New Testament canon developed gradually over three centuries through widespread usage and the common consent of leading Christian communities. As in the case of the Old Testament canon, generations of familiarity conferred a venerable and authoritative status to the books most influential in Church doctrine and practice. Because connection with apostolic times was considered necessary, "late" books, such as James and 2 Peter, took longer finding acceptance than did works written by the end of the first century. Even after Bishop Athanasius issued his definitive list in 367, the canon varied from place to place. Perhaps most conclusive in the completion and sealing of the New Testament contents was the Latin Vulgate, in which Jerome followed Athanasius' canon and included the seven Catholic ("General") Epistles as well as the disputed Hebrews and Revelation. Other Christian writings, some of which had once been considered inspired, were relegated to the status of Apocrypha.

RECOMMENDED READING

Grant, Robert M. *The Formation of the New Testament.* New York: Harper & Row, 1965.

von Campenhausen, Hans F. *The Formation of the Christian Bible.* Translated by J. A. Baker. Philadelphia: Fortress Press, 1972.

18. *What are the Christian Apocrypha?*

Books generally called the Christian Apocrypha are early writings that did not find a place in the New Testament but were nonetheless popular reading in some parts of the Church. These include the First Epistle of Clement, a sermon from the bishop of Rome to the Corinthian congregation. Dated about 95 C.E., 1 Clement is closer to genuine apostolic times than several later books, such as 2 Peter and the Pastorals, which were admitted to the canon. The Didache (Teaching of the Twelve Apostles), which contains moral instruction and regulations for the rites of baptism and communion, may be the first organized document on ecclesiastical policies produced by the Church. The Shepherd of Hermas (which was at times accepted as canonical) and the Epistle of Barnabas were influential as well. The Christian Apocrypha also includes variant Gospels, such as the Gospel of Thomas, a Gnostic document dating from about 130 C.E.

RECOMMENDED READING

Hennecke, Edgar. *New Testament Apocrypha.* Vol. 1, *Gospels and Related Writings;* Vol. 2, *Writings Related to the Apostles, Apocalypses, and Related Subjects.* Edited by Wilhelm Schneemelcher. Translated by R. McL. Wilson. Philadelphia: Westminster Press, 1963. This important work offers both a good translation of the New Testament apocryphal books and a discussion of their relation to the official canon.

Pfeiffer, Robert. *History of New Testament Times: With an Introduction to the Apocrypha.* New York: Harper & Brothers, 1949.

THE ISRAELITES AND THEIR GOD

19. *Who were the Israelites?*

In biblical terminology, the Israelites are descendants of the patriarch Jacob, whose name was changed to Israel. Chosen by their god to represent him among the nations, the Israelites formed a twelve- (later two-) tribe country that occupied Palestine from the thirteenth century before Jesus to the first century after, when they were dispersed by the Romans.

The anthropological origins of Israel, however, are much more complex and obscure. According to the national credo given in Deuteronomy 26:5, "a wandering [or 'perishing'] Aramean" was their "father" or progenitor. The Arameans (Syrians), with whom the Israelites were ethnically connected, were originally a nomadic people who migrated westward from the Arabian Desert. About 2000 B.C.E. a Semitic group known as Amorites or "Westerners" infiltrated Mesopotamia, the land between the Tigris and Euphrates rivers in what is now Iraq, and settled there. The Arameans may also be related to this group.

It is in Mesopotamia, home of the world's oldest known civilizations, that Israel's national traditions begin. In Genesis the Aramean family of Abraham, chief ancestor of the chosen people, is represented as moving northward from Ur, a major city in lower Mesopotamia, to Haran, 600 miles distant in what is now southern Turkey. (Some scholars place Abraham's original home in *northern* Mesopotamia, but most commentators identify it with the ancient Sumerian site.) From Haran, Abraham traveled southward with his flocks and herds to Canaan (Palestine). Recent archaeological excavations in the Haran area have confirmed the existence of practices and customs during the first half of the second millennium B.C.E. that are depicted in Genesis. Although the Genesis stories were not written until centuries after the tribal movements they describe, certain of their details were transmitted orally with impressive accuracy.

The Israelites belonged to, and eventually developed from, a larger group of Arameans known as the 'Apiru (or Habiru)—apparently less a racial or ethnic group than a class of "outsiders" who lacked a definite or accepted place in ancient Near Eastern society. Racially mixed, they wandered from place to place serving as shepherds, caravan drivers, mercenary soldiers, slaves, and outlaws. Although the term *'Apiru* may be equivalent to the biblical word *'ibri*, meaning "Hebrew," not all the 'Apiru were biblical Hebrews. The Israelites were Hebrews, but they were only one small part of a much larger class of nomadic 'Apiru who moved rootlessly throughout the ancient Near East. After the biblical Hebrews settled in Canaan to found the nation of Israel, they were known as Israelites, traditional descendants of Abraham, Isaac, and Jacob.

In Scripture, the word *Israel* has several meanings. As used by many prophets it denotes the collective descendants of Jacob, Yahweh's covenant people. In a political sense, it also refers to (1) the united twelve-tribe kingdom under David and Solomon and (2) the northern ten-tribe kingdom that split from Judah (the Davidic state) in 922 B.C.E.

RECOMMENDED READING

Albright, W. F. *The Biblical Period from Abraham to Ezra.* New York: Harper & Row, 1963.

_____. *From the Stone Age to Christianity.* Garden City, N. Y.: Doubleday, 1957.

Bright, John. *A History of Israel.* Philadelphia: Westminster Press, 1972.

de Vaux, Roland. *Ancient Israel, Its Life and Institutions.* London: Darton, Longman & Todd, 1961.

_____. *The Early History of Israel.* Translated by D. Smith. Philadelphia: Westminster Press, 1978.

Hermann, Siegfried. *A History of Israel in Old Testament Times.* Philadelphia: Fortress Press, 1981.

Jagersma, Henk. *A History of Israel in the Old Testament Period.* Philadelphia: Fortress Press, 1983.

Noth, Martin. *The History of Israel.* New York: Harper & Row, 1960.

Orlinsky, Harry M. *Ancient Israel.* Ithaca, N. Y.: Cornell University Press, 1960.

Wolff, Hans Walter. *Anthropology of the Old Testament.* Translated by M. Kohl. Philadelphia: Fortress Press, 1981.

20. *By what different names did the Israelites know their god, and what is the significance of these differences?*

Bible manuscripts contain a number of different names and titles for the Hebrew deity. Genesis 1, for example, uses the generic name *Elohim*, a plural form denoting "gods" or "divine powers," although this does not necessarily imply that the Hebrews believed in many gods. Even the most monotheistic prophets continued to use the name Elohim.

In Genesis 2:4b occurs the first appearance of the Tetragrammaton, a Greek term designating the four sacred letters (YHWH) of the Hebrew god's personal name. Because the Hebrew language was originally written without vowels, we are not certain precisely how the divine name was pronounced, although most biblical scholars agree that *Yahweh* is a close approximation. (The familiar English name *Jehovah* derives from a Latin rendition of the Tetragrammaton, to which the vowels from Elohim and Adonai were added. This version of the divine name can be traced to Petrus Galatinus, confessor to Pope Leo X, 1518 C.E.)

According to one widely accepted theory, the name Yahweh is derived from the Hebrew verb meaning "to be" or "to cause to be," as God reveals to Moses when he states, "I Am who I Am" (Exod. 3). God is here speaking in the first person; in the third personal singular, the phrase becomes *Yahweh* ("He is"). The divine name, occurring nearly 7,000 times in the Old Testament, expresses both Yahweh's eternity (He always is) and his purposiveness, his causing all things to be or happen. The meaning of *Yahweh* is thus closely tied to the Hebrews' view of their god as the lord of history.

To avoid profaning (taking in vain) the divine name, by the third century B.C.E. Jewish rabbis began to substitute the Semitic term *Adonai* (meaning "lord" or "master") when reading aloud passages containing the four sacred letters. Eventually the name was pronounced but once a year, by the high priest on the Day of Atonement. For centuries Protestant and Roman Catholic Bibles followed the Jewish practice of substituting "Lord" or "God" whenever the Tetragrammaton occurred, but recent scholarly translations, such as the Doubleday Anchor Bible and the Jerusalem Bible, have restored "Yahweh" to its rightful place in the English text. (The King James translators indicated textual occurrences of the Tetragrammaton by printing "GOD" or "LORD" in small capitals where "Yahweh" had originally appeared. The Revised Standard Version and the New English Bible also follow this practice.)

Other names and titles of God, confined chiefly to the Pentateuch and Job, include *El Elyon*, "God Most High" (Gen. 14:19–22), *El Olam*, "God Everlasting" (Gen. 21:33), and such terms as "the Shield of Abraham" (Gen. 15:1) and "the Fear of Isaac" (Gen. 31:42, 53). Particularly interesting is the term *El Shaddai*, which is usually translated "God Almighty," although some experts think that it means "God of the Mountain." Certainly it is on Mount Sinai that El Shaddai, who identifies himself as "the God of Abraham, the God of Isaac, and the God of Jacob," reveals that he is also Yahweh (Exod. 3 and 6) and commands Moses to bring Israel back to that mountain to worship him. Similarly, it is to Mount Sinai that El Shaddai descends when he reveals his law and makes his covenant with Israel.

Different names for the deity, particularly Elohim and Yahweh, are associated with distinct literary styles and theological attitudes in the biblical text. This realization first led scholars to discover in the biblical narratives different strata or literary strands that seemed to derive from different sources, each of which tended to use a distinctive name or names for God. For a fuller explanation of the major sources that experts have found in the first five books of the Bible, see Part 3, "The Law (Torah)."

21. *Is there a single "biblical view" of Israel's god? How do different Old and New Testament writers present their deity? What is the deity's relationship to humankind? Are human beings possessed of divine qualities?*

The reader will better appreciate the Bible's portrait of the deity by remembering that each individual writer of Scripture had a personal, and therefore necessarily limited, understanding of his god. Because the Bible authors also wrote from a variety of theological viewpoints and from an ever-changing cultural perspective during the approximately 1,100 years that it took the Bible to be completed, each gave a somewhat different emphasis to the divine nature. The scriptural portrait that emerges is thus extremely complex, even contradictory, a composite portrayal to which many different personalities contributed.

To some writers Yahweh was primarily strength; to others the deity was a military leader who gave victory to his people; to still others he was an unknowable intelligence, the mysterious creator and sustainer of the universe. The highest concepts of the biblical God, in which the Creator appears as supreme wisdom, love, and mercy, are found in the Prophets of the Old Testament and in the teachings of Jesus and the Johannine literature of the New. Prophets like Isaiah, Hosea, and Micah saw God as an almighty power who could judge the world harshly but who was also kind, loving, and deeply concerned for his human creation. Jesus presented the Supreme Being as a gracious parent ever near to those who would seek a relationship to the divine. The author of 1 John achieved an even more essential vision: to him, God *is* love.

In general, it appears that people have seen in a divine being those qualities that they have themselves most needed or valued at any particular time. Because the biblical authors wrote from a patriarchal viewpoint, they tended to picture their deity as a masculine force—a judge, lawgiver, king, and warrior. Thus when the early Hebrews were a poor, oppressed minority in Egypt, they looked to Yahweh to show his power to deliver them from their enemies. The ten plagues that Yahweh inflicts upon pharaoh and the Egyptians are a demonstration of his irresistible might, proof that he is stronger than other gods. In the Exodus narrative there is little concern for Yahweh's objective justice or mercy, for such qualities would have been seen as irrelevant to those who needed a god with a strong arm.

From the earliest poems and songs that have survived from Israel's oral traditions, we note that Yahweh typically was viewed as a fighter, a supernatural general who could crush enemy armies. As Moses exulted when pharaoh's cavalry was drowned in the Sea of Reeds:

> Yahweh I sing: he has covered himself in glory,
>   horse and rider he has thrown into the sea.
> Yah is my strength, my song,
> he is my salvation. . . .
> Yahweh is a warrior;
> Yahweh is his name.

Exodus 15:1–3

The warrior Yahweh also led Israel's armies to victory over the Canaanites. Joshua's conquest of the Promised Land occurred because his god was invisibly fighting against Israel's enemies (Josh. 5:13–15).

To the priestly writers of Leviticus and similar material, their god was holy, set apart from ordinary life and approached only through elaborate rituals and sacrifices. As presented in the New Testament, the Pharisees tended to hold a similar view. The deuteronomic writers of Israel's historical books, such as 1 and 2 Kings, saw Yahweh as the lord of history, the manipulator of human events who causes the rise and fall of nations. In this role, Yahweh is also judge of the earth, the impartial administrator of rewards and punishments according to the recipient's moral behavior. The authors of Genesis 1, Psalm 104, and Job 38–42 saw their god as the mysterious power whose word alone was enough to create the world and whose incomparable wisdom directs the workings of nature.

In contrast, some Bible writers viewed their god as all too human, attributing to him both the virtues and defects of a human personality. At times their deity is represented as a typical Near Eastern king, powerful and fundamentally just but prone to jealousy, quick-tempered, and easily provoked to punish insubordination. This god is a destroyer as well as a creator, venting his wrath through flood, famine, plague, drought, earthquake, and fire from heaven. Since it was believed that the biblical god controlled everything that happened (Amos 3:3–8), natural disasters were typically interpreted as his express will, though occasionally a Bible writer injected a note of doubt about this. For the author of Ecclesiastes, for example, the deity is remote from and uninterested in daily life, and the element of chance typically controls human affars: "I see this too under the sun: the race does not go to the swift, nor the battle to the strong; there is no bread for the wise, wealth for the intelligent, nor favor for the learned; all are subject to time and mischance" (Eccles. 9:11).

Many of the Latter Prophets, who raised Israel's religion to its greatest heights, balanced the fear-inspiring aspects of their god's strength by also emphasizing his *hesed*, a term denoting steadfast love, loyal kindness, and a devotion beyond mere duty. Hosea presents Yahweh as severely punishing disobedience, but also as recoiling from his intention to destroy Israel because of his great love for it (Hosea 11:9). The Torah, with its demands that the Israelites are to love Yahweh with their whole being (Deut. 6:5–6) and to love their neighbors as themselves (Lev. 19:18) implies a similarly generous love in Yahweh.

Perhaps the single most sublime description of the Supreme Being in either Old or New Testament occurs in Isaiah 40, where the poet articulates a vision of Israel's god philosophically unmatched elsewhere in the Bible. All the basic tenets of ethical monotheism are made explicit: Yahweh is One—eternal, almighty, and omniscient. Like the author of Psalm 90, the poet contrasts Yahweh's transcendent majesty with humanity's fragility and impermanence. Men and women are mere blossoms that fade in a day, blades of grass quickly withered by the sun.

The great disparity between Yahweh's eternity and human mortality is similarly emphasized in the second creation account in Genesis. Adam, the "earth creature," is formed from "dust," which Yahweh animates with the "breath of life." Like fish, animals, and birds, Adam—representing humankind— is a *nephesh*, a term commonly translated "living soul" but denoting a sentient creature that is *entirely* mortal. In the Old Testament, human beings have no share in Yahweh's immortality. The Israelites saw men and women as a *unity* of body and breath; the notion of an imperishable spirit or soul inhabiting a mortal body was foreign to Hebrew thought. The Egyptian, Babylonian, and later Greek concept of humanity as a *duality*—the classic Platonic dichotomy between the immortal *psyche* and the corruptible flesh—appears in Judaism only in post–Old Testament times. The apocryphal Wisdom of Solomon, written about 50 B.C.E., accepts the Greek view of the soul's immortality, but this was not the prevailing Hebrew belief. When the possibility of an afterlife first suggested itself to Jewish writers, it characteristically took the form of *resurrection*— a recreation of the earthly body, not the entrance of the soul into an eternal home. Not until the book of Daniel (12:1–3), probably the last canonical work of the Hebrew Bible to be written, does the hope of resurrection to a future life find expression. In Jewish thought of the biblical period, both the Torah and the covenant relationship are designed for this present life alone.

In Genesis, men and women were to find their purpose in exercising dominion over the earth and its living creatures (Gen. 1:26–28). Created male and female "in the image of God," human beings imitated the deity in ruling over lesser creatures. A few Bible writers stressed this quasi-divine aspect of humanity, which alone among Yahweh's earthly work manifested qualities of creative wisdom, insight, justice, and benevolence. The author of Psalm 8 asks, "Ah, what is man that [Yahweh] should spare a thought for him?" (Ps. 8:3–8). The rather surprising answer to this rhetorical question is that, despite humanity's weakness when compared to Yahweh, human beings themselves exhibit divine attributes.

Humankind is created only "little less than a god," crowned "with glory and splendor," and installed as ruler of "all things." This passage might have originally applied to Israel's king, who reigned as Yahweh's *messiah* (anointed one), but it also suggests an ideal pattern for the relationship between God and humanity. As Yahweh rules Heaven, so he delegated to men and women the power to govern the earth. Both the story of Eden and the story of Yahweh's active *hesed* in initiating covenant bonds between himself and humankind illustrate a kind of cooperative partnership intended to carry out the divine will. In certain passages it seems as though Yahweh himself senses a unique tie to his earthling creatures. After Yahweh has virtually obliterated him, Job muses that his god would ultimately recognize again an unbreakable bond and long "for the work of his hands" (Job 14:15).

The New Testament, with its doctrines of a preexistent Logos (John 1) and a resurrection to heavenly life (1 Cor. 15), would seem to present an abrupt change in the divine-human relationship. Familiarity with Jewish literature of the intertestamental period, however, reveals that certain currents of post–Old Testament thought had developed notions of an afterlife and heavenly rewards before the first century B.C.E. (See the discussions of the books of Enoch, Baruch, 2 Esdras, etc. in Part 6.) Christianity parallels or borrows many of these then-popular Jewish concepts.

The human sense of alienation from the deity, which the author of Genesis 3 had dramatized in the fall of Adam and Eve, figures large in the thinking of Paul and other New Testament writers. Yet Paul argues that human beings can become reconciled to God through simple *acceptance* and *trust* in the deity's willingness to save them. Paul's doctrine of human redemption through faith in the saving power of Jesus' sacrificial death was crucial to Christianity's success among non-Jewish peoples. While some New Testament writers present Jesus as the model of a new humanity justified through faith, the author of the Fourth Gospel goes further and declares that the eternal Word (Logos), by whom God created the universe, "became flesh" in the person of Jesus. This Gospel strongly implies an identification between the Creator and the "word made flesh." John's Jesus, unlike the Synoptic's "Son of Man," boldly declares that "the Father and I are one" and "he who has seen me has seen the Father" (John 14:9; 17:21). According to all four Gospels, Jesus' crucifixion is the event that reconciles the Christian god to humankind and opens the way not only for Israel but for all people to discover the divine purpose (see also 2 Cor. 5:18–21).

In spite of the changing and developing picture of godhood projected by the various Bible writers, one viewpoint regards the deity as immutable. Second Isaiah describes this Being as "the first and the last" and unchangingly the only God (Isa. 44:6). A Christian writer adds: "With him there is no such thing as alteration, no shadow of a change" (James

1:17). By the beginning of the Common Era, the deity was Absolute—in truth, love, wisdom, and mercy; the harsher qualities once attributed to Yahweh were now seen as belonging to his cosmic enemy, "the devil."

22. *Who is the devil? What relationship has this figure to the biblical deity?*

Although "the devil" looms large in the popular imagination, the term occurs relatively infrequently in the New Testament and not at all in the Hebrew Bible. From the Greek word *diabolos, devil* means "accuser" or "slanderer." Revelation 12:9–12 identifies "the devil" with the Genesis serpent and the Hebrew "satan," but this correlation took place very late in biblical history, appearing first in pseudepigraphal works like the books of Adam and Eve.

Despite this late identification of the two figures, "the satan" of the Old Testament is not the same entity as "the devil" of the New. The concepts rendered by these two different terms developed independently of each other. The word *satan* derives from a Hebrew root meaning "obstacle"; personified (given human qualities), it means "opposer" or "adversary."

Viewed from a purely historical perspective, the satan figure evolved from the dark shadow of Yahweh himself. According to knowledgeable historians, the satan emerges from negative elements in Yahweh's morally ambiguous character and eventually becomes an embodiment of all the violent and destructive attributes once considered part of the divine nature. This historical development is evident if one traces the satan concept chronologically from earliest to latest biblical references. At the outset, some Bible writers saw all things, good and evil alike, as emanating from a single source—Yahweh. Israel's strict monotheistic credo decreed that Yahweh alone caused both joys and sorrows, prosperity and punishment (Deut. 28). In the oldest literary source of Genesis, Yahweh first creates a world of sentient creatures, then "regrets" this creative work, annihilating virtually all living things, both animal and human (Gen. 2:6–8). At this stage in Israel's religious thinking, Yahweh is not only creator and destroyer, he is also represented as tormentor and deceiver. Thus we read in 1 Samuel 16:14–23 that Yahweh personally sends an "evil spirit" to madden King Saul; in 1 Kings 22:18–28 he dispatches a "lying spirit" to mislead Ahab. Both of these incidents show "evil" (defined from a human viewpoint and applied exclusively to disobedient people) as one of the means Yahweh employs to effect his will. As late as the sixth century B.C.E., the anonymous prophet called "Second Isaiah" presents Yahweh as the originator of both light and darkness, good *and* evil (Isa. 45:7).

Israel's writers reach a second stage of development when they place the source of human trouble not in Yahweh himself but in one of the *bene ha Elohim* (literally, "sons of the gods"). These mysterious beings are depicted as members of Yahweh's heavenly court; among them is "the satan," who plays the role of "accusing" Yahweh's people and testing the loyalty of Yahweh's subjects (Job 1–2; Zechariah 3:1–9). Although the satan is by this time a henchman separate from Yahweh himself, he remains completely under the deity's control and thus functions as a manifestation of the deity's negative qualities, generating suspicion and demanding punishment for human frailty. In Job, Yahweh allows himself to be "tempted" by "Satan" (now a proper name) and permits the undeserved calamities that befall the faithful Job. By contrast, in Zechariah's vision of the celestial throne room, Yahweh resists the adversary's contempt for sinful humanity and wills his compassion and mercy to prevail.

It should be noted that, in each of the few Old Testament passages in which the satan is a personage, he is always the adversary of *humanity*, not of God. The satan figure acts as Yahweh's spy and prosecuting attorney whose job is to bring human misconduct to the deity's attention and, if possible, persuade Yahweh to punish it. Throughout the Old Testament the satan remains among the divine "sons," serves as God's administrative agent, and thus reveals a facet of the divine personality.

The clearest example of Satan's assumption of the darker aspects of Yahweh's nature occurs in the two accounts of King David's census. In the first version, which dates from the tenth century B.C.E., Yahweh puts it into David's head to sin by taking a census of Israel—always hated by the people since it was done for purposes of taxation and military conscription—for which act the god punishes not David but the people with a plague (2 Sam. 24:1–25). In the second version, written hundreds of years later, it is not Yahweh but "the satan" who inspires the census (1 Chron. 21:1–30); Yahweh only punishes. Evidently, with the passage of time and development of an expanded sense of justice, it was no longer possible to see Yahweh as both the cause and enemy of sin and as the vindictive avenger of sin as well. The negative qualities that earlier writers had assumed to be in their god were eventually transferred to his opposite.

Following the Babylonian exile (after 538 B.C.E.), when Judah was dominated by the Persian Empire, Persian and other foreign religious ideas apparently infiltrated Jewish thinking. Zoroastrianism, the official Persian religion, was dualistic, holding that the universe was ruled by two opposing supernatural forces. The powers of Good (Light) were led by Ahura Mazda, while those of evil were directed by Ahriman, the Zoroastrian devil. According to this belief, at the end of time a climactic battle between good and evil would result in evil's destruction and the triumph of Light. Until then the two powers struggled incessantly, resulting in alternating elements of happiness and misery in human existence.

With its hierarchies of angels and demons, systems of rewards and punishments in an afterlife, and concept of an all-good god waging war against a wicked opponent (the devil), Zoroastrianism strongly influenced later Hebrew ideas about the satan as not only humanity's but also Yahweh's enemy. Significantly, no Hebrew literature written before the Persian period pictures the satan as an individual. Only in postexilic books like Tobit and Daniel are individual angels, such as Michael, Gabriel, and Raphael, or demons, such as Asmodeus, given personal names. With the influx of Greek and other ideas following Alexander's conquest of the Near East in 330 B.C.E., views of an afterlife populated with angels and demons proliferated (see the Pseudepigrapha, Part 6). By New Testament times Persian, Greek, Syrian, and other foreign notions had been thoroughly Hebraized and subordinated to the religion of Yahweh. After the first century C.E., however, Judaism rejected many of these Persian or Hellenistic concepts. The canonical Hebrew Bible grants the satan scant space and little power.

Whereas the Old Testament satan can do nothing without Yahweh's express permission, in the New Testament he behaves as an independent force who competes with the Creator for human souls. According to the temptation scenes in the Synoptic Gospels (Matthew, Mark, and Luke, which adopt a "single view" of Jesus' life), he even attempts to win the allegiance of the Messiah. Interestingly, Jesus does not dispute Satan's claim to control the world or to offer it to whomever he wishes (Mark 1:12–13; Matt. 4:1–11; Luke 4:1–13; 2 Cor. 4:4). According to Mark's Gospel, one of Jesus' major goals is to break up Satan's kingdom and the hold that he and lesser evil spirits exercise on the people. Hence Mark stresses Jesus' works of exorcising devils and dispossessing the victims of demonic control. The New Testament, then—in sharp contrast to the Old—shows Satan and "the devil" as one, a focus of cosmic evil totally opposed to the Creator God. This "evil one" is the origin of lies, sin, suffering, sickness, and death. But his power is limited only to the present age; he is doomed to annihilation in Revelation's symbolic "lake of fire" (Rev. 20:1–5).

RECOMMENDED READING

Russell, Jeffrey Burton. "Hebrew Personifications of Evil" and "The Devil in the New Testament." In *The Devil: Perceptions of Evil from Antiquity to Primitive Christianity,* pp. 174–220 and 221–49. Ithaca, N. Y.: Cornell University Press, 1978.

THE OLD TESTAMENT

❦

THE HEBREW BIBLE

PART 2

HISTORY AND GEOGRAPHY
OF THE NEAR EAST

THE ANCIENT NEAR EAST

Long before the Bible was written, ideas and stories that eventually found their way into its pages circulated among the civilizations of the ancient Near East. The oldest of these civilizations, the Sumerian, developed about 3200–3100 B.C.E. in the delta area of the Euphrates River at the head of the Persian Gulf, an area the Greeks later named Mesopotamia. The first people to establish a highly complex urban society, the Sumerians not only invented cuneiform writing but also recorded a wealth of information about their culture, including its mythology, science, and religion. As the eminent scholar Samuel Noah Kramer has observed, history begins at Sumer, which produced the first written accounts of creation, the flood, and the gods' concern for humankind. Although the Gilgamesh cycle was completed in later times, the earliest forms of the epic originated among the Sumerians.

About 2350 B.C.E. Sumeria was invaded by a Semitic people known as the Akkadians. Assimilating the earlier Sumerian culture, the Akkadians established the world's first empire under Sargon I, whose early history interestingly parallels that of Moses. According to Akkadian legend, Sargon's mother cast him adrift on the Euphrates in a pitch-covered basket, but instead of a king's daughter finding him as in the Moses story, a farmer, drawing water to irrigate his field, pulled the infant to safety and raised him as his own. From such humble origins Sargon rose to displace the Sumerian monarch Ur-Zababa as the ruler of Kish and to found the Mesopotamian Empire.

The empire did not last long, however. During the two centuries following 2000 B.C.E. a new Semitic group known as the Amorites or "Westerners" invaded many parts of the Fertile Crescent, a roughly semicircular area extending from Mesopotamia southwestward through Syria and Palestine to Egypt. Merely raiding and looting some areas, the Amorites settled in others, building new towns in northern and western Palestine and founding two important city-states in Mesopotamia—Mari in the north and Babylon in the south-central region. At Mari archaeologists have found clay tablets that record customs resembling those described in the patriarchal stories of Genesis. Babylonia's most famous king of this period, Hammurabi, codified ancient Sumerian and later Semitic laws that were forerunners of ordinances found in the Pentateuch.

The Amorite invasions coincided with the age of the patriarchs Abraham, Isaac, and Jacob, who traveled freely between Mesopotamia, Palestine, and Egypt at about this time. Although the relation of the patriarchs to the larger migratory movements of Semitic peoples between about 2000 and 1500 B.C.E. is not precisely known, the picture of them given in Genesis, which depicts their wanderings and intermittent conflicts with settled peoples and other nomads, is remarkably like the Amorite style of life.

While numerous complexly organized but independent city-states sprang up in Mesopotamia, Egypt developed a united, stable nation. By 2400 B.C.E. Egypt had built the Great Pyramids and other monuments that have endured to the present, and its fertile Nile Delta had become the goal of many nomadic groups, some of whom settled there at least temporarily. But Egypt's native control of her territory was broken from 1720 to 1570 B.C.E. when the Hyksos ("sea people" or "foreigners"), some of whom were Semitic, occupied the country. As will be seen later, the Hebrew settlement in Egypt may have coincided with the Hyksos rule. In time, however, Egypt expelled the foreigners to establish the native Egyptian Eighteenth Dynasty, and this may have led to an enslavement of remaining Semitic outsiders, including the Hebrews.

Important urban centers also existed in Syria, Phoenicia, and Palestine, the last of which was frequently under Egyptian control. The Canaanites, whose fertility religion so regularly corrupted the Hebrews, had settled not only in Palestine but along Syria's southwestern coast, known in biblical times as Phoenicia and Lebanon. The seagoing Phoenicians built the trade-rich ports of Tyre, Sidon, and Byblos, with which Israel's later kings made profitable business arrangements. To the north stood Ugarit, a Canaanite stronghold that seems to have had ties to the Mycenaen (pre-Greek) world farther west; the famous Ugaritic or Ras Shamra texts, dating from about 1600–1400 B.C.E., were found here. Damascus, a commercial center on the caravan routes that connected Egypt with Asia Minor and Mesopotamia, is the oldest of Syria's presently inhabited cities. It was on his way to Damascus 1,900 years ago that Saul, persecutor of Christians, became Paul the missionary for Christ.

The Bible story begins, then, when Mesopotamian city-states in the northeast and Egypt in the southwest ruled most of the known world. The biblical narratives cover a succession of nations and empires; some of these are outlined in Table 2-1.

RECOMMENDED READING

Beek, Martin A. *Atlas of Mesopotamia*. London: Thomas Nelson & Sons, 1962.

The Cambridge Ancient History, Fasicles Nos. 1–59, rev. ed. Cambridge, England: Cambridge University Press.

Gordon, Cyrus. *The Ancient Near East*, 3rd ed. New York: W. W. Norton, 1965.

Hallo, W. W., and Simpson, W. K. *The Ancient Near East: A History*. New York: Harcourt Brace Jovanovich, 1971.

Jacobsen, Thorkild. *The Treasures of Darkness: A History of Mesopotamian Religion*. New Haven, Conn.: Yale University Press, 1976.

Kramer, Samuel N. *Cradle of Civilization*. New York: Time-Life Books, 1967.

_____. *History Begins at Sumer*. New York: Doubleday Anchor Books, 1959.

_____. *The Sumerians*. Chicago: University of Chicago Press, 1963.

Mallowan, M. E. L. *Early Mesopotamia and Iran*. New York: McGraw-Hill, 1965.

Moscati, Sabatino. *The Face of the Ancient Orient: A Panorama of Near Eastern Civilization in Pre-Classical Times*. New York: Doubleday Anchor Books, 1962.

Saggs, H. W. F. *The Greatness That Was Babylon*. New York: New American Library, 1962.

Wilson, John A. *The Culture of Ancient Egypt*. Chicago: University of Chicago Press, 1963.

REPRESENTATIVE ARCHAEOLOGICAL DISCOVERIES IN THE FERTILE CRESCENT RELATING TO THE BIBLE

During the past century, archaeology—the science of excavating, identifying, and interpreting the material remains of ancient cultures—has done much to illuminate the biblical record. Thanks to the archaeologist's spade, the ruins of many long-lost cities in Egypt, Mesopotamia, Syria, and Canaan have been unearthed, sometimes with astonishingly rewarding results. Among hundreds of major discoveries relating to the Bible, the following few are representative. (See Table 2-2 for a contextual overview.)

EBLA TABLETS

Excavations in Northern Syria at Tell Mardikh, a mound covering the site of Ebla—an ancient trading city destroyed by the Assyrians about 2250 B.C.E.—have yielded thousands of clay tablets inscribed in cuneiform script. Unfortunately, only a small portion of the tablets thus far have been translated and published, but preliminary studies indicate that the Ebla discoveries have great potential relevance for biblical research. If early evaluations are correct, the Eblaite language is akin to both Canaanite and biblical Hebrew. Some Assyriologists, experts in Sumero-Akkadian linguistics, have found remarkable parallels between some

TABLE 2-1 Events in the Ancient Near East Related to Biblical History

Approximate Date B.C.E.*	Egypt	Palestine (Canaan)	Mesopotamia
3000 B.C.E.			Sumerian city-states—first high urban civilization
	Establishment of the Old Kingdom with capital at Memphis; pyramids built		Akkadian invasion and settlements (c. 2360–2180)
2000	Middle Kingdom (c. 2030–1720)	Middle Bronze Age (2100–1550)	Sumerian revival; Third Dynasty at Ur (2060–1950)
			Growing influence of Amorites
		Nomadic patriarchs	
1800			First Babylonian Dynasty (Amorite) (1830–1530)
			Mari Age (1750–1697)
			Hammurabi (1728–1686)
	Invasion of the Hyksos (c. 1720–1560)		
1600		Ugaritic mythological texts (c. 1600–c. 1400)	

Date	Egypt	Israel / Hebrews	Assyria
	New Kingdom (Empire) with capital at Thebes (1560–c. 1100)	Late Bronze Age (1550–1200)	
	Eighteenth Dynasty (1552–1306)		
1400			
	Akhenaton (1364–1347)	Amarna Period	
	Brief monotheistic revolution		
	Nineteenth Dynasty (1306–1200); Rameses II (1290–1224)	Hebrews in Egypt	
		Exodus	
1200			Assyrian domination and decline
		Iron Age I (1200–1000)	
		Israelite Confederacy	
		Philistine Settlement	
		Iron Age II (1000–600)	
1000	Twenty-first Dynasty (1085–934)	David's capture of Jerusalem; Israelite Empire (c. 1000–922)	
	Twenty-second Dynasty (c. 935–725)	Secession of northern ten tribes: formation of separate kingdoms: Judah and Israel	
	Sheshonk I (Shishak) (935–914); Invasion of Palestine (Karnak List)		
800	Egypt's decline		Revival of Assyria: Assurnasirpal II (883–859)
		Prophets Amos and Hosea	Tiglath-Pileser III (745–727)
			Expansion of Assyrian Empire

*Dates are approximate. Authorities commonly do not agree on dates before 721 B.C.E.

TABLE 2-2   Representative Archaeological Discoveries in the Fertile Crescent Relating to the Bible

Biblical Book	Historical Period
Genesis	The World of the Patriarchs (Ancient Mesopotamia, Syria, and Palestine)
	Ebla Tablets
	Mari Tablets
	Nuzi Tablets
Exodus, Deuteronomy	Ancient Law, the Mosaic Torah, and Egypt
	Code of Hammurabi
	Amarna Letters
	Rosetta Stone
Joshua, Judges, Psalms	Israel's Conquest of Canaan
	Jericho Excavations
	Ugaritic Texts
2 Kings	Israel's Divided Monarchy and Canaanite Neighbors
	Moabite Stone
2 Kings, Isaiah 40–45, Daniel	Release from the Babylonian Captivity
	Cyrus Cylinder
Post–Old Testament	The Second Jewish Revolt Against Rome (132–135 C.E.)
	Bar Kochba Letters

Eblaite terms and terms later used in the Old Testament. The striking correspondence between personal and place names occurring in the Ebla tablets and those appearing in the Genesis account of the patriarchs seems particularly promising to many scholars. It may be years before the experts' conclusions appear in print, but the Ebla material is almost certain to enhance our understanding of Near Eastern ideas and customs prevailing in the last few centuries before Abraham and the other patriarchs.

MARI TABLETS

Mari was an ancient Sumero-Babylonian city on the Euphrates River's west bank (in modern Syria near the Iraqi border). Here archaeologists discovered a royal library containing more than 20,000 clay tablets approximately 4,000 years old. Although Mari is not mentioned in the Bible, its literature provides important background to the Old Testament, particularly material relating to the patriarchal age of Abraham, Isaac, and Jacob.

NUZI TABLETS

These clay tablets, discovered in the ruins of ancient Nuzi on the upper Tigris River, provide information concerning Hurrian customs and law current during the patriarchal age, the mid-second millennium B.C.E.

CODE OF HAMMURABI

This law code of 282 sections inscribed on a block of black diorite nearly eight feet tall was originally erected for public reading in the Babylonian city of Sippar; but raiding Elamites carried it to Susa, where archaeologists found it more than 3,000 years later. The find is significant to Bible students because Hammurabi's laws are expressed in the same form and, in some cases, have the same content as Old Testament laws. Certain resemblances to the Mosaic Covenant, particularly as presented in Exodus, Leviticus, and Deuteronomy, are striking:

1. A carved picture at the top of Hammurabi's stele shows the Babylonian king receiving the laws from the sun god Shamash much as Moses received the law from Yahweh.

2. The Babylonian laws are not only codified like the later Hebrew legislation (Exod. 20:22–23:33; 24:7) but seem to reflect the same Semitic concept of justice, such as the *lex talionis* ("eye for eye" and "life for life") as given in Leviticus 24:19–21 and Deuteronomy 19:21, corresponding to the Hammurabi Code, section 196 ff.

3. Laws are framed in the same way, using the casuistic form: *If* such and such happens, *then* such and such will be the punishment—a form that is especially prevalent in Deuteronomy (e.g., Deut. 19:5–6, 11–13; 21:15–17; 22:6–7).

4. In addition, both Old Testament and the much older Babylonian laws impose virtually the same penalty for the same offense, as in the parallel treatment of incest in Leviticus 20:11 ff. and Hammurabi 154–158. The Hammurabi Code, which incorporates even older Sumerian laws, reveals that in many important respects Old Testament law was based on, and derived from, previously existing Semitic legal practices.

AMARNA LETTERS

A collection of cuneiform tablets found at Amarna, Egypt, including correspondence between Amenhotep III and Amenhotep IV (the monotheist

Akhenaton) and Canaanite and Phoenician rulers, the Amarna tablets describe the political disorder in these areas during the early fourteenth century B.C.E.

ROSETTA STONE

Discovered in 1799 during Napoleon's invasion of Egypt, this black basalt slab preserved an identical message in Greek and in two forms of hitherto unknown Egyptian writing, the hieroglyphic and demotic scripts. This provided a Grenoble schoolmaster, Jean-François Champollion, with the key to translating Egyptian hieroglyphics, the ancient form of picture writing, thus enabling subsequent linguists and archaeologists to read the thousands of inscriptions on the tombs, temples, and monuments of ancient Egypt.

JERICHO EXCAVATIONS

In the Book of Joshua, which records the Israelite conquest of Canaan, Jericho is the first stronghold to fall to the invading Hebrews. While tending to confirm that a less civilized nomadic group infiltrated Palestine between about 1250 and 1200 B.C.E., archaeological investigations present a different picture of Jericho's fate. Although the settlement had existed from about 7800 B.C.E. and was perhaps the oldest city in the world, it was apparently an uninhabited ruin by the time the Israelites arrived in Canaan. Thus the story of Jericho's spectacular collapse either applies to another city captured by the Israelites or to an earlier period when kinsmen of the later biblical group invaded the area and destroyed the city.

UGARITIC TEXTS

Uncovered between 1929 and 1939, the site of Ugarit (modern Ras Shamra, on the Mediterranean coast about twenty-five miles southwest of Antioch) has yielded a treasury of ancient mythological and religious literature, including several Canaanite epics featuring Baal, El, and Danel, whom some scholars regard as the prototype of the righteous Danel mentioned by Ezekiel and later the hero of the Book of Daniel.

Of primary importance are the numerous parallels these texts offer to Old Testament diction and poetic style. Yahweh's mythical battle with the dragon and with Leviathan appears to be derived from Ugaritic literature (Job 41:1; Ps. 74:13–14; Isa. 27:1; 51:9), as are many of the epithets common to both the Canaanite El and Yahweh (Deut. 33:26; Pss. 68:4, 33; 104:3; Isa. 19:1). Although most of the Ugaritic texts date from about 1400 B.C.E, they represent an oral tradition several centuries older. Apparently the Israelites who later settled Canaan borrowed much of their religious vocabulary and many forms of expression from Ugaritic and Canaanite models.

MOABITE STONE

This flat basalt slab found in 1868 is important in demonstrating that a theological concept expressed in the historical books of the Old Testament was not unique to Israel. In Joshua through 2 Kings, Israel's historians typically ascribed their national defeats to the anger of Yahweh, who they believed used pagan armies to punish them for their sins. As the Moabite Stone reveals, the same theological interpretation of events prevailed in Moab, Israel's near neighbor and traditional enemy. According to the stone's inscription, Mesha, king of Moab (middle to late ninth century B.C.E), attributed his country's invasion and occupation by Israelite troops to the wrath of Chemosh, the Moabite national god. The inscription also celebrates the restoration of Moab, thanks to Chemosh's blessing, after the Israelite usurper Jehu had irreparably weakened Israel by slaughtering all his countrymen associated with King Ahab's dynasty, thus permitting formerly subject nations like Moab to revolt successfully against Israel (2 Kings 3:9–10).

CYRUS CYLINDER

This is a clay cylinder upon which Cyrus the Great recorded his capture of Babylon, attributing his success to Babylon's chief deity, Marduk, who accepted him as a righteous prince and appointed him ruler of the known world.

BAR KOCHBA LETTERS

Discovered near the Dead Sea, these documents do not bear directly on the Old Testament period but are contemporaneous with some of the later books of the New Testament, such as Jude, the Pastoral Epistles, and 2 Peter. The letters—dispatches to his officers—were written by Simon Bar Kochba, leader of the second Jewish revolt against Rome (132–135 C.E.) and one whom some regarded as the promised Messiah. Interestingly, no New Testament writer refers directly or explicitly to the devastation of Jerusalem by the Romans in either 70 C.E. or 135 C.E.

RECOMMENDED READING

Albright, William Foxwell. *Archaeology and the Religion of Israel.* New York: Doubleday Anchor Books, 1969. A scholarly introduction to biblical archaeology first published in 1942 and repeatedly updated and revised.

_____. *Yahweh and the Gods of Canaan.* New York: Doubleday Anchor Books, 1969. Historical analysis of the contrasting religions of Canaan and Israel.

Burrows, Millar. *What Mean These Stones?* New York: Meridian, 1957.

Cornfield, Gaalyah, and Freedman, David Noel, eds. *Archaeology of the Bible: Book by Book.* New York: Harper & Row, 1976. Organizes archaeological discoveries and their relation to specific biblical books.

Freedman, David N., and Greenfield, J. C., eds. *New Directions in Biblical Archaeology.* Garden City, N. Y.: Doubleday, 1969.

Kenyon, Kathleen. *Archaeology in the Holy Land,* 3rd ed. New York: Praeger Publishers, 1970.

Pritchard, James B., ed. *Ancient Near Eastern Texts Relating to the Old Testament,* 3rd ed., with Supplement. Princeton, N. J.: Princeton University Press, 1969. Scholarly translations of ancient documents and inscriptions providing background to the Old Testament.

Wright, George Ernest, ed. *The Bible and the Ancient Near East.* New York: Doubleday Anchor Books, 1965. A collection of critical essays honoring William F. Albright, a leading figure in biblical archaeology.

———. *Biblical Archaeology,* rev. ed. Philadelphia: Westminster Press, 1962. Demonstrates how archaeology has illuminated aspects of both Old and New Testament history.

THE PROMISED LAND

The land of Canaan (Palestine) probably has more religious associations for more people than any other part of the earth's surface, for it is the Holy Land to Catholic, Eastern Orthodox, Protestant, Jew, and Muslim alike. During the past 4,000 years more wars have been fought for its possession than for almost any other geographical area. From Egyptian, Amorite, and Israelite in the ancient world to Turk, Arab, Palestinian, and Israeli in modern times, millions have died attempting to gain or hold this small territory, which is roughly the size of Maryland. The generalized map of Palestine on the facing page shows the location of some major sites mentioned in the Old Testament.

Much of the area's importance arises from its location. A relatively narrow strip (roughly 150 miles long and 70 miles wide) between the eastern end of the Mediterranean Sea and the inland deserts, Palestine was a land bridge between the three great civilized centers of the ancient world. Egypt lay to the southwest, Asia minor to the northwest, and Mesopotamia to the northeast. Except for brief periods when these areas were militarily weak, armies repeatedly marched through the Palestinian corridor, generally devastating the regions they occupied. During peaceful times, however, Palestine flourished, as traders and caravans bearing grain, spices, gold, hide, and textiles traveled along the three main trade routes that crossed the country. Control of these international commercial highways provided considerable wealth for which many nations contended.

One thinks of modern Palestine as dry and rather barren, but in biblical times it was at least partly forested and relatively well watered. Then as now, however, the climate varied considerably in the country's four major regions. The western region is a low coastal plain, twenty to thirty miles wide at most. This narrow strip, which provided the chief highway to Egypt, was under Egyptian rule when the Israelites first

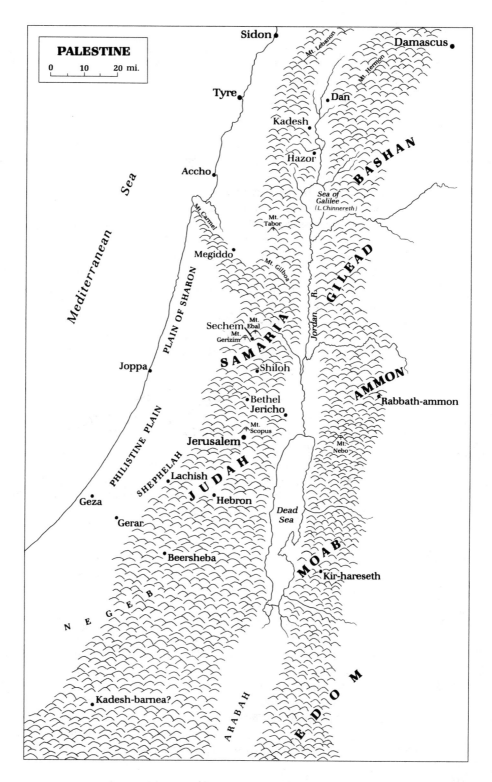

PALESTINE

0   10   20 mi.

Sidon

Damascus

Mt. Lebanon

Tyre

Mt. Hermon

Kadesh

Dan

Mediterranean Sea

Hazor

BASHAN

Accho

Sea of Galilee
(L. Chinnereth)

Mt. Carmel

Mt. Tabor

Megiddo

Mt. Gilboa

PLAIN OF SHARON

GILEAD

Jordan R.

Sechem

Mt. Ebal
Mt. Gerizim

SAMARIA

Joppa

Shiloh

AMMON

Bethel

Rabbath-ammon

Jericho

PHILISTINE PLAIN

Mt. Scopus

Jerusalem

Mt. Nebo

SHEPHELAH

Lachish

JUDAH

Geza

Hebron

Dead Sea

Gerar

Beersheba

MOAB

Kir-hareseth

N E G E B

E D O M

Kadesh-barnea?

ARABAH

41

invaded Canaan following 1250 B.C.E, although the Philistines occupied it during most of Israel's history. (Ironically, the whole country came to be known as Palestine, a name derived from Philistia, the hated scourge of the Israelites.)

Inland, running roughly north-south, is the second major region, a limestone ridge of low mountains and small valleys. This central hill country, much less fertile than the coastal plain, extends from the Valley of Beersheba in the south to the mountains of Lebanon in the north. The hilly range is broken in the north by the broad Plain of Megiddo, formed by the Kishon River, which flows northwestward to the Mediterranean Sea just north of Mount Carmel, a precipitous rocky massif that juts into the sea and forms the northern boundary of the coastal plain.

Megiddo's level fields join the Valley of Jezreel to the east, near Mount Gilboa, forming an east-west–trending greenbelt, the most fertile part of the country. The site of several bloody and decisive battles in Israel's history, the Megiddo area is cited in Revelation 16:16 as the location of Armageddon, the final cosmic war between God and the Devil. Not far to the north, where the limestone hills rise steeply to merge with the Lebanon Range, was the small village of Nazareth, where Jesus grew to manhood. A poor, rather bleak area, it afforded few attractions other than its southward view of Megiddo's gentle plains.

Between Palestine's mountainous backbone and the Transjordan hills to the east is the Great Rift Valley, which runs from north to south the full length of the country. This geological fault zone provides the channel for the Jordan River, which rises in the Sea of Galilee and flows sixty-five miles south to the Dead Sea, a great salt lake 1,290 feet below sea level, the lowest point in the earth's land surface. Paralleling the Jordan on both sides is a lush band of vegetation; around the Dead Sea, however, nothing grows, making it a striking image of utter desolation. According to local folktales, the sea now covers the remains of Sodom and Gomorrah, which had lain near its shores before the area was decimated by a natural catastrophe.

Located east of the Jordan River, the fourth general region, Transjordan, is a rugged mountainous terrain cut by deep canyons that flood during heavy rains. Extending from the plains of southern Syria east of Galilee to the Brook Zered at the southern end of the Dead Sea, Transjordan averages about 1,500 feet above sea level, although many of its peaks rise to twice that height. Legend has it that Jesus' family fled to Transjordan when the Romans temporarily lifted their siege of Jerusalem, and it is probable that some Palestinian Christians found refuge in this sparsely populated area during the Roman wars (66–70 C.E.).

But Palestine's division into four distinct regions is more meaningful than ordinary geographic sectioning might suggest. In terms of Israel's history, radically different areas meant that their inhabitants were relatively self-contained and somewhat culturally isolated from fellow citizens who inhabited topographically dissimilar areas. Farmers cultivated the fertile plains, small valleys, and terraced hillsides, growing wheat, barley, olives, and grapes. On nearby stony ridges shepherds pastured sheep or goats that subsisted on occasional tufts of grass. By contrast, Israel's chief cities, located in the central hill country, were trade centers open to considerable cultural exchange with itinerant traders from Egypt, Mesopotamia, Syria, Phoenicia, and other affluent urban civilizations.

Palestine's regional and economic diversity sometimes led to suspicion and distrust among the three main occupational groups—farmers, shepherds, and commercial city dwellers. Shepherds, living a seminomadic outdoor life, regarded the cities as sources of financial exploitation and corruption, and eighth-century prophets, such as Amos and Hosea, typically sided with the country people in this regard. City people in turn regarded farmers and villagers as backward and given to compromising their faith by the worship of agricultural and fertility deities. To a degree, then, Israel's class and religious conflicts emanated from the economic and cultural divergences caused by Palestine's unusually diverse geography.

Even more decisive than its diverse internal geography was Palestine's position between the great powers of the ancient world. Except for a few decades during the reigns of David and Solomon, this strategic land bridge joining Asia to Africa was continually trampled on by other nations. Israel's successive military domination by Assyria, Babylon, Medo-Persia, Macedonian Greece, and Rome gave its thinkers a distinctive philosophy of history and of their god's will. The Bible writers saw in their nation's relentless sufferings not an accident of geography but the inevitable consequences of their national sins, a belief that will be discussed further in the summaries of Deuteronomy and Kings.

RECOMMENDED READING

Aharoni, U. *The Land of the Bible.* Translated by A. F. Rainey. Philadelphia: Westminster Press, 1976.

Baly, Denis. *The Geography of the Bible*, 2nd ed. New York: Harper & Row, 1974.

May, Herbert G., ed. *Oxford Bible Atlas*, 2nd ed. London: Oxford University Press, 1974.

Wright, G. E., and Filson, F. V., eds. *The Westminster Historical Atlas to the Bible.* Philadelphia: Westminster Press, 1956.

Before beginning a discussion of individual Old Testament books, it is helpful to review some of the major events of Bible history. In studying Table 2–3, however, the reader is cautioned to remember that the dates are only roughly approximate and that scholars differ in their attempts to correlate events in Egypt, Mesopotamia, and Palestine with the biblical record. The ancient world had no common method of reckoning time; dating of events before the seventh or sixth centuries B.C.E is especially conjectural.

TABLE 2-3 Major Events in Old Testament History

Approximate Date B.C.E.	Event	Biblical Source
About 1850	Abraham leaves northern Mesopotamia and journeys to Canaan	Gen. 12
About 1700 (?)	Jacob (Israel) and his twelve sons settle in Egypt	Gen. 46
About 1280–1250	Moses leads the Israelites out of Egypt to Mount Sinai	Exod. 13–15
Following 1250	Joshua leads the conquest of Canaan	Josh. 1–24
About 1200–1030	Israel is a loosely knit twelve-tribe confederacy; period of the Judges	Judg. 1–21
About 1020	Samuel anoints Saul king of Israel over a united twelve-tribe kingdom	1 Sam. 10
About 1000–961	David creates an Israelite empire; makes Jerusalem the national capital	2 Sam. 2–21; 1 Kings 2
About 961–922	King Solomon rules; builds the temple at Jerusalem	1 Kings 3–11
922	Kingdom split into ten-tribe northern state (Israel) and two-tribe southern state (Judah)	1 Kings 12
721	Assyria conquers Israel, destroys its capital, Samaria; deports the population	2 Kings 17
701	Sennacherib besieges Jerusalem; Assyrian withdrawal (?)	Isa. 36–37; 2 Kings 18–19
621	Book of Deuteronomy "discovered"; Josiah reforms Judah's religion	2 Kings 22–23; 2 Chron. 34–35
598–597	Nebuchadnezzar sacks Jerusalem; first deportation of Jewish captives	
587	Nebuchadnezzar destroys Jerusalem, burns Solomon's temple; takes Jews captive to Babylon	2 Kings 24

It should further be noted that no attempt has been made in the following brief essays to discuss every aspect of the contents of the thirty-nine books of the Old Testament. The summaries provide introductory material necessary or helpful to understanding individual books but do not substitute for reading the Bible itself. In general, only those themes

TABLE 2-3 (continued)

Approximate Date B.C.E.	Event	Biblical Source
539	Cyrus the Great of Persia captures Babylon	
538	Jewish remnant returns to Jerusalem	Ezra 1
520–515	The second temple is built and dedicated	Ezra 6
	(Judah a province of the Persian Empire)	Hag. 2
445 ff.	Ezra and Nehemiah: religious reforms; the Torah promulgated	Neh. 8
About 332	Alexander the Great of Macedonia includes Palestine in his empire	1 Macc. 1
323–197	The Ptolemys of Egypt rule Palestine (Hellenistic period)	
197–142	Seleucid dynasty of Syria rules Palestine	2 Macc. 4
167–164	Antiochus IV attempts to force Hellenistic religion on the Jews; pollutes the temple	1 Macc.; Dan. 11:30
164	The Maccabean revolt is successful; the temple is cleaned and rededicated	Dan. 7:25; 12:7; 8:14, 9:27
142–63	The Jews expel the Seleucids; Judea becomes an independent kingdom under the Hasmonean dynasty	1 Macc.
63	General Pompey makes Palestine part of Roman Empire; partitions Judea	
66–70 C.E.	Jewish revolt against Rome	
70 C.E.	The Romans destroy Jerusalem and the temple	
90–91 C.E.	Jewish rabbis assemble at Jamnia to formulate biblical canon	

or events that the author thought most significant are included, and these are signaled by headnotes with corresponding scriptural readings. At the end of each major section, recommended readings will direct the student to authoritative works that offer more thorough coverage of particular biblical topics.

PART 3

THE LAW (TORAH)

To a citizen of ancient Israel and to modern Jew alike, the Pentateuch (the first five books of the Old Testament) forms the core of Judaism. Those books—Genesis, Exodus, Leviticus, Numbers, and Deuteronomy—comprise the Torah, the law or instruction that, according to tradition, Yahweh gave to Israel through Moses. The Torah contains not only the Ten Commandments but hundreds of statutes, ordinances, and detailed directions for sacrifice and worship that regulated every phase of Israel's daily and religious life. It is, in fact, Israel's constitution, for obedience to its commandments, including its dietary and ceremonial aspects, is what distinguished Israel from other nations.

The heart of the Torah is Exodus, the second book of the Old Testament, which records Yahweh's redemptive act in delivering Israel from slavery in Egypt and leading her to Sinai where he revealed his law and concluded the Mosaic Covenant forever binding Israel to him as his chosen people. In turn, Israel promised to recognize him alone as God and to do all that he commanded. The first of the Ten Commandments makes this covenant relationship clear.

> I am Yahweh your God who brought you out of the land of Egypt, out of the house of slavery.
> You shall have no gods except me . . .
> For I Yahweh your God am a jealous God and I punish the father's fault in the sons . . . but I show kindness to thousands of those who love me and keep my commandments.
>
> Exodus 20:1–6

Although the covenant has been named after Moses, the real hero of Exodus and of the rest of the Pentateuch is Yahweh himself; for all that the human characters do, all they achieve by war, conquest, or wealth, is explicitly ascribed to Yahweh's actions. Moses, his brother Aaron, even pharaoh are merely instruments moved into their places as part of Yahweh's grand historical design. As Yahweh tells pharaoh, his purpose in forcing Egypt to release the Israelites is to make a name, as well as a nation, for himself: "Had I stretched out my hand to strike you and your subjects with pestilence, you would have been swept from the earth. But

I have let you live for this: to make you see my *power* and to have my *name* published throughout the world" (Exod. 9:15–16; italics added).

The Pentateuch, which illustrates Yahweh's disciplining and educating his people through forty years in the Sinai wilderness, ends on a strangely inconclusive note, however; for before he dies, according to Deuteronomy, Moses is allowed only a glimpse of the Promised Land beyond the River Jordan. The Pentateuch anticipates Israel's conquest and possession of Canaan, but it does not include the fulfillment of Yahweh's promise that Abraham's descendants would inherit a Palestinian homeland. Breaking off before the people's hopes are fully answered, it points to the future, looking confidently ahead to the happy conclusion of Israel's arduous journey toward a god-ruled world.

Tradition unanimously credits Moses with the composition of Genesis through Deuteronomy. Most of the ancient rabbis believed this, and conclusively to some Christians, the New Testament refers repeatedly to Moses' authorship (Matt. 8:4; 19:7–8; Mark 1:44; 7:10; 10:3–5; 12:19, 26; Luke 5:14; 16:29; 24:27, 44; John 1:17; 5:45–47; 7:19; 8:5; Acts 3:22; 13:39; 15:5, 21; Rom. 10:19; 1 Cor. 9:9). But this does not necessarily mean that Moses wrote the Pentateuch as we now have it; rather, these statements probably mean no more than that associating the law with Moses was a convenient means of referring to it in ordinary speech. Most modern scholars regard the laws ascribed to Moses as a natural but later outgrowth of a nuclear Mosaic tradition.

During the past two centuries scholarly analysis has produced a variety of theories to explain the repetitions, inconsistencies, stylistic differences, and abrupt shifts in emphasis and theological viewpoint that characterize Genesis through Deuteronomy. The most generally accepted theory, known as the Documentary Hypothesis—also called the Graf-Wellhausen Hypothesis after the nineteenth-century German scholars who most cogently presented evidence for it—holds that the Pentateuch is a composite work containing at least four major documentary sources (See Table 3-1).

The earliest source is called J because its author typically uses the name Yahweh (in German, *Jahweh*) for God. According to documentary critics, the Yahwist wrote during Israel's early monarchy, around 950 B.C.E., when national pride in the people's ancestral origins swept the country. Using a vivid, imagistic, earthy style, the J historian took Israel's story all the way back to the creation (Gen. 2), told the stories of Adam and Eve, the flood, Abraham and the other patriarchs, the exodus from Egypt, and the conquest of Canaan.

The J document is thought to have originated in southern Israel (Judah). About a century later, a second, northern source for the Pentateuch was compiled. Like J, the northern writer (called E or the Elohist because he typically uses the generic term *Elohim* for God) incorporates into his story much older material that had previously been transmitted orally. While judged to exhibit a more refined sensibility than J, his style

TABLE 3-1 Four Principal Sources of the Pentateuch

Source	Characteristics	Approximate Date B.C.E.
J (Yahwist)	Uses the personal name *Yahweh* for God; vivid, concrete style; anthropomorphic view of deity; begins with Creation (Gen. 2:4b); uses term "Mount Sinai" for place where Mosaic Covenant was concluded; composed in the southern kingdom (Judah).	About 950
E (Elohist)	Uses *Elohim* (plural form of "divine powers") for God; style more abstract, less picturesque than J's; view of God less anthropomorphic than earlier source; uses term "Horeb" for covenant mountain; begins with story of Abraham; composed in northern Israel (Ephraim).	About 850
D (Deuteronomist)	Reflects literary style and religious attitudes of Josiah's reform (621 B.C.E.); insists that only one central sanctuary acceptable to Yahweh; best represented in Deuteronomy; composed in the north (?); (Later D school also edits histories of Joshua through 2 Kings).	About 650–621
P (Priestly)	Emphasizes priestly concerns, legalistic and cultic aspects of religion; dry, precise style; lists censuses and genealogies; derived from priestly preservation of Mosaic traditions during and after Babylonian exile (following 587 B.C.E.).	About 550–400

is less concrete and colorful. His version of Israel's history, presumably told from the viewpoint of one who lived in Ephraim in the north, reputedly begins with Abraham and continues through the settlement of Canaan. At some point in this document's history, the Decalogue (Ten Commandments) and Covenant Code (Exod. 20–23) were set within its narrative.

The next important step was the combining of J and E to produce JE, perhaps around 750 B.C.E. Whatever anonymous historian or scribe joined these two formerly independent narratives apparently did not care to eliminate contradictory or redundant material. Typical examples appear in the two versions of Abraham's wife's being captured by a foreign king, a tale that is found again in the story of Abimelech and Isaac's wife Rebekah (Gen. 12:10–20; 20:1–18; 26:6–11). The JE redactor merely dovetailed these repetitious or conflicting accounts, retaining both traditions as equally venerable.

Some scholars have argued persuasively that JE may at one time have formed a Hexateuch (six books) that originally contained narratives of the conquest of Canaan, extending into material now included in Joshua, Judges, and possibly into 1 and 2 Samuel as well. According to this hypothesis, the priestly writers who edited the Torah during and after the Babylonian exile removed the history of settlement and nation building that brought Israel's story to a natural culmination. If the entire JE epic had been inspired by the success of the Israelite Empire under David and Solomon, it is easy to see why captive priests in Babylon, who had seen the Israelites driven from their land and their once glorious monarchy destroyed, wished to purge the Torah of its originally political ending. It was better to return to the promise of a kingdom than to record its failure.

The fifth book of the Pentateuch, Deuteronomy (meaning "second law" in Greek and known as D), is usually dated about 650 B.C.E., although like J and E it contains material much older than the time of its written composition. Scholars believe that it was produced by Yahwist scribes and priests reacting to King Manasseh's political cooperation with Assyria and his consequent toleration of foreign religions. Purporting to be three speeches that Moses delivered shortly before his death, Deuteronomy shows great familiarity with a settled agrarian existence in Canaan (though it may, of course, include genuine Mosaic traditions not preserved in J or E). In any case, it is believed to be the Book of the Covenant accidentally found while the Jerusalem temple was being repaired in 621 B.C.E. Public readings from this book significantly strengthened King Josiah's attempts to purify and reform Israel's worship of Yahweh (2 Kings 22–23; 2 Chron. 34–35).

Giving all this heterogeneous material a coherent framework was to be the contribution of priests who lived during and after the Babylonian exile (from 587 B.C.E. to about the end of the fifth century). This priestly reworking of JE and D culminated about 400 B.C.E. after the mission of Ezra, who presented a revised and canonized Torah to the restored Jewish community. The P (for "priestly") document includes not only the regulations preserved in Leviticus and similar legalistic passages but also the beautiful hymn of creation found in Genesis 1. Working over a long period, the priests thoroughly assimilated JED sources, adding what seemed to them necessary modifications and commentary and possibly excising JE's account of the conquest and early monarchy. The rather dry priestly style is characterized by a concern for dates, numbers, genealogies, liturgical rites, temple ceremonies, and such matters as clean and unclean sacrificial animals.

Thus P became the Pentateuch's unifying structure, incorporating JED and perhaps other sources as well. Once the completed Torah had been promulgated and circulated throughout postexilic Israel, it is doubtful that any other major changes took place. Indeed, so careful were later scribes in copying the law that they counted every word and letter in a manuscript line, starting afresh if they discovered any transcriptional errors. Finally accepted by the Jewish community as sacred and complete, the Pentateuch became the immovable foundation of Israel's faith.

In reviewing these conventional scholarly divisions of the Pentateuch, however, the reader must not assume that biblical criticism is altogether quite so clear-cut or simple. Although most contemporary Bible experts accept some form of the Documentary Hypothesis, they do not agree about which particular passages belong to which of the four principal sources or even about whether the four sources were originally written documents at all. One popular modification of the Graf-Wellhausen theory argues that the various strands of tradition woven into the Pentateuch derive largely from oral traditions about the cult and religious life of Israel. (A term frequently used by biblical scholars, *cult* refers to a formal system of religious veneration, commonly worship of a national god, and to ritual involving a sacred object or holy place.)

Public recitation of the laws, ceremonies, and historical memories associated with Moses were performed at numerous shrines and religious centers in ancient Israel, such as Shechem, Kadesh, Shiloh, and Jerusalem, where the Israelites periodically assembled to celebrate and renew their covenant pledges to Yahweh. Evolving differences between the national traditions proclaimed at these various shrines may have contributed to the different strata of thought or theological viewpoints found in the Pentateuch. Regardless of the relative proportion of oral or written sources, however, it is virtually certain that the Pentateuch as we now have it is the product not of one man but of generations of Israelites' deepest religious experience.

RECOMMENDED READING

Alonso-Schokel, Luis, S. J. *Understanding Biblical Research.* New York: Herder and Herder, 1963.

Bailey, Lloyd R. *The Pentateuch.* Nashville: Abingdon Press, 1981.

Cassuto, U. *The Documentary Hypothesis and the Composition of the Pentateuch.* Translated by Israel Abrahams. Jerusalem: Magnes, 1961. A critical evaluation of the documentary thesis by a Jewish scholar.

Eissfeldt, Otto. *The Old Testament: An Introduction.* New York: Harper & Row, 1965.

Ellis, Peter. *The Yahwist: The Bible's First Theologian.* Notre Dame, Ind.: Fides, 1968.

Fohrer, Georg. *Introduction to the Old Testament.* Nashville: Abingdon Press, 1968.

Grant, Robert M. *A Short History of the Interpretation of the Bible.* New York: Macmillan, 1966.

Habel, Norman. *Literary Criticism of the Old Testament.* Philadelphia: Fortress Press, 1971.

Hahn, H. H. *The Old Testament in Modern Research.* London: SCM Press, 1956.

Hayes, John H., ed. *Old Testament Form Criticism.* San Antonio: Trinity University Press, 1974. Essays covering various Old Testament genres.

Koch, Klaus. *The Growth of the Biblical Tradition: The Form-Critical Method.* Translated by S. M. Cupitt. New York: Charles Scribner's Sons, 1969.

Noth, Martin. *A History of Pentateuchal Traditions.* Englewood Cliffs, N. J.: Prentice-Hall, 1972.

Thompson, J. A. "Textual Criticism, O.T." In *The Interpreter's Dictionary of the Bible: Supplementary Volume,* pp. 886–91. Nashville: Abingdon Press, 1976.

❦ Genesis

The Creation and Fall	*Chapters 1–4*
Noah and the Flood	*6–9*
Abraham	*12–24*
Isaac and Jacob	*27–35*
Joseph and His Brothers	*37–50*

In the beginning . . .

Genesis 1:1

From the creation of heaven and earth in chapter 1 to the descent of Israel's tribes into Egypt in the concluding chapters, Genesis is a record of historical origins seen through the eyes of faith. In general content the book can be divided into four main sections. The first part (chapters 1–11) concerns universal history—creation, the flood, and the origin of various national and linguistic groups. After this prologue, Genesis narrows its focus to the lives of four great ancestors of the Hebrew people—Abraham, Isaac, Jacob, and Joseph. The second section (chapters 12–24) tells the story of Abraham, to whom all Jews trace their ancestry. Conclusion of the Abrahamic Covenant is the most important part of this narrative.

The third section (chapters 25–36) combines the story of Isaac with that of his brilliant son Jacob, whose own twelve sons are founders of the traditional twelve tribes of Israel. The final section (chapters 37–50) presents the story of Joseph and his brothers, primarily to explain how the twelve tribes came to dwell in Egypt. The book concludes with Joseph's prophetic hope that Israel will eventually return to Canaan, the Promised Land.

The Creation and Fall Genesis opens with a sublime hymn to God's creative majesty, recounting the six days of creation that culminate in the appearance of humankind made "in the image of God [*Elohim,* a plural form of deity used to denote Israel's god as well as foreign deities]" (Gen. 1:27). Comparing the priestly account (Gen. 1:1–2:4), which may have been composed during Israel's exile in Babylon, with the older Babylonian creation myth, the *Enuma Elish*, is instructive. According to both versions, creation begins with a watery chaos out of which an ordered cosmos develops in distinct stages. Tiamat, the primal dragon of chaos in the *Enuma Elish*, is echoed in Genesis' use of *tehom* (Hebrew, "the deep," the original watery abyss):

> When God began to create the heaven and the earth—the earth
> being unformed and void, with darkness over the deep [*tehom*]
> and a wind from God sweeping over the water . . .*
>
> Genesis 1:1

The ancient theme of conflict, war between different generations of gods, that characterizes most Near Eastern creation myths has been banished from the Genesis account. However, brief allusions to the old stories appear in other parts of the Bible. Praising the Creator, a psalmist revives the old myth of Yahweh's primeval battle with Rahab (perhaps a Canaanite name for the chaotic water monster):

> You [Yahweh] control the pride of the ocean,
> when its waves ride high, you calm them;
> you split Rahab in two like a carcass
> and scattered your enemies with your mighty arm.
>
> Psalms 89:9–10

In the *Enuma Elish*, Marduk, Babylon's chief deity, forms earth and firmament (the sky or physical heavens) out of the two halves of Tiamat's corpse, exactly as Yahweh is described splitting Rahab (see also Job 26:1–14; Ps. 74:13–17; Isa. 51:9). In Genesis God similarly forms "an expanse in the midst of the water, that it may separate water from water"* and calls the expanse (firmament) between the lower and upper waters "sky" (Gen. 1:6–8).

The differences between the biblical and Babylonian creation narratives are also important. Whereas Genesis presents an omnipotent Creator who exercises absolute and undisputed control of the universe, the *Enuma Elish* pictures the numerous Sumero-Babylonian gods quarreling savagely among themselves and fighting a cosmic battle for supremacy. Further, the *Enuma Elish* shows Marduk "with his own hands" constructing the world out of parts of Tiamat's body. By contrast, Elohim brings order out of chaos and light out of darkness through the power of his

---

The Torah: The Five Books of Moses. Philadelphia: The Jewish Publication Society of America, 1967. Note that the editors of this version translate Genesis 1:1 to show that creation does not begin from nothing, but is a process of shaping chaotic matter into an orderly system.

word alone (Gen. 1:3). Finally, whereas Marduk assembles man from the blood of Kingu, Tiamat's defeated consort, merely to perform menial work for the Babylonian gods, Elohim creates man and woman to reflect his own divine qualities and to enjoy dominion over the earth and all the life it contains. In Genesis human beings are the rulers of earthly creation, and the whole arrangement is pronounced "very good" (Gen. 1:28–31).

Genesis' style and viewpoint change abruptly, however, in the second chapter. The second creation account (Gen. 2:4b–25), which scholars attribute to the J source, is somewhat less exalted than the first and presents a more anthropomorphic or "human" view of the Creator. Referring to the deity as Yahweh or "Yahweh Elohim," this account paints him as a just but stern ruler similar to "the lord of the covenant" in Exodus 19–20. This deity is a "jealous god" who regards disobedience as intolerable rebellion.

There are other significant differences between Genesis' two versions of creation. In the priestly hymn, man and woman are created simultaneously and appear only after all lower forms of life have already been created. In the second account, Adam is formed early in the creative process, after which Yahweh fashions animals and brings them to the man to be named (Gen. 2:18–20). When no animal proves suitable as Adam's counterpart, Yahweh designs a woman (Eve) out of Adam's rib. The J writer stresses the bond and likeness between the two new beings: man (*ish*) and woman (*ishshah*) are of the same "bone" and "flesh," united metaphorically as "one body" (Gen. 2:21–24). Since '*adam* is not a proper name but the Hebrew term for "earth creature" or humankind, the writer makes it clear that the human creation is complete only when both male and female are formed.

Human enjoyment of Eden, the paradise garden that Yahweh made for the first couple, does not last long. Tempted by one of Yahweh's animal creations, the serpent—described not as evil but "shrewd" or "subtle"—Eve eats from "the tree of the knowledge of good and evil," which Yahweh had planted in the midst of Eden. When Adam joins Eve in tasting the prohibited fruit (not specifically an apple), the two suddenly become aware of their nakedness, an awakening that dispels their original innocence. When Yahweh next strolls through the garden to enjoy "the cool of the day," he notes that the human pair are now afraid and conscious of their nakedness.

The "curses" or judgments and pronouncements that follow express the writer's sense of what was lost through human disobedience—humanity's willful breaking of a divine command. For its part in the revolt against divine sovereignty, the serpent is condemned to crawl on its belly and "eat dust" (Gen. 3:14–15). The woman is told that her pain in childbirth will increase and that her husband will "lord it over her" (Gen. 3:16). Male dominance of women characterized the patriarchal society of which the writer was a part; the author apparently viewed female subjugation as a social arrangement resulting from the first couple's mutual disruption of the divine purpose. For the man's sake, the earth itself is cursed, whereas he is doomed to unremitting toil and death. While explaining how the unity of partnership between the sexes and between human beings and the earth was thus broken, the narrator also answers several age-old questions about the human condition: Why is life so difficult? Why must we work so hard to live? Why is giving birth so painful? Why must we die?

The threat of immediate death connected with eating from the tree of knowledge (Gen. 2:16–17; 3:3–4) is not carried out, which may be seen as Yahweh's first act of mercy, but Adam and Eve are expelled from Eden to the harsh world outside. J's explanation of the banishment attributes a curious motive to Yahweh. "The man," Yahweh observes, "has become like one of us, with his knowledge of good and evil" (possibly a synonym for knowing "everything"). Lest the man also eat from the "tree of life" and "live forever," Yahweh posts angels with a flaming sword to keep humanity from the crucial life-giving tree (Gen. 3:22–24). In the ancient world, the two chief qualities distinguishing the gods from mortals were the former's superior knowledge and immortality. Because humans had already acquired knowledge reserved for the gods, Yahweh prevents their becoming fully like the other divine beings in his heavenly court by denying them everlasting life.

The theme of competition between Yahweh and his intelligent creatures occurs again in the Tower of Babel episode (Gen. 11:1–9) when Yahweh recognizes that a humanity united in a common language and culture will find "nothing too hard for them to do." To weaken the human potential, he overthrows their united efforts (represented by the temple tower or ziggurat), confuses their languages, and scatters them over "the whole face of the earth." By including this incident, the narrator can express his view of Yahweh's contempt for human ambition.

After Adam and Eve's disobedience has alienated them from their Creator, the human condition rapidly deteriorates. Cain, their firstborn son whose grain sacrifices Yahweh rejects, jealously murders his brother Abel whose blood-producing animal sacrifices please the deity. After Yahweh marks Cain's brow to protect him from his enemies, Cain flees eastward, the archetypal fugitive and outsider. Thus concisely does the writer explain the origins of human guilt, pain, futile labor, envy, fraternal rivalry, and murder.

Chapter 5 is a genealogical list of Adam's descendants, all remarkable for their extreme longevity, particularly Methuselah, who lived to be 969 years old. Another antediluvian patriarch who has aroused much speculation is Enoch, who at the comparatively youthful age of 365 (perhaps representing a solar year), "vanished because God took him" (Gen. 5:24). Like the prophet Elijah, who was taken heavenward many years later in a fiery chariot, Enoch has become a mysterious figure. The pseudepigraphal books of Enoch purport to have been composed by the Genesis patriarch (see pp. 232–235).

Noah and the Flood   Traditionally the flood has been ascribed to humankind's rampant wickedness augmented by the Nephilim, a race of giants born to mortal women who had mated with "the sons of God" (Gen. 6:1–4), though Genesis makes no explicit connection between the Nephilim and the general corruption and violence that then overwhelmed the earth. Regretting that he has created humankind, Yahweh determines to exterminate all flesh except for Noah and his immediate family. Like his prototype in the Babylonian *Epic of Gilgamesh*, Noah obeys his god's instructions to build a great wooden ship and to house in it two (or seven) of every kind of animal, bird, and reptile. After Yahweh closes the ark door behind Noah, it rains for forty days and nights, the resultant flood destroying all life outside the ark.

When the flood subsides, Noah emerges from the ark and offers an acceptable sacrifice to Yahweh, who issues a mandate to "be fruitful" and repopulate the earth. Yahweh now promulgates the first of four important Old Testament covenants between himself and individuals or nations. The Noachan Covenant differs from the others not only in emphasizing the sacredness of all life but also because it is made with "every living creature of every kind" (Gen. 9:16).

Promising Noah never again to destroy the world by water (though he implicitly reserves to himself other means of annihilation), Yahweh creates the rainbow as a visible symbol of his reconciliation with humankind. The story thus closes with still another parallel to the Gilgamesh flood account. In the Babylonian epic, after the gods feast on Utnapishtim's sacrifice, the goddess Ishtar flings her jeweled necklace into the sky. Ishtar's jewels remain as a sparkling pledge that the gods will refrain from returning the world to its original state of watery chaos.

Chapters 10 and 11 trace the genealogies of Noah's three sons, Shem, Ham, and Japheth, who represent the three principal branches of the human family known to the ancient Hebrews. From Shem come the Semitic peoples, among them the Babylonians, Assyrians, Arabs, and Israelites. Ham was the eponymous (name-giving) ancestor of the Egyptians and their (then) dependents, including the Canaanites, and Japheth was the supposed progenitor of the Aegean Sea peoples including the Greeks and Philistines. This "table of nations" concludes Genesis' survey of the prehistorical period.

Abraham   As several New Testament writers perceived, Genesis presents Abraham as preeminently a man of faith (Heb. 11:8–10) who hears the voice of God and obeys instantly. It is this total willingness to submit every part of his life to Yahweh's will that sets him apart from other people. Abraham's devotion to Yahweh is surpassed only by Yahweh's wish to honor him as he had honored no other person.

Calling Abraham to abandon his former life in Haran (northwestern Mesopotamia), Yahweh announces his purpose to make Abraham a "great nation" and to make his name "so famous it will be used as a blessing."

> I will bless those who bless you:
> I will curse those who slight you.
> All the tribes of the earth
> shall bless themselves by you.

Genesis 12:2–3

Thus Abraham, his wife Sarah, his nephew Lot, and all their flocks and retinue journey to Canaan, which land Yahweh promises to Abraham's descendants—all the territory from "the wadi of Egypt to the Great River" Euphrates (Gen. 15:18). Only during the reigns of David and Solomon during the tenth century B.C.E. did Israel's boundaries extend to these limits.

Although Genesis includes many anecdotes about Abraham's life, two events stand out as of paramount importance: the concluding of the Abrahamic Covenant and Abraham's consenting to sacrifice his beloved son Isaac. The Abrahamic Covenant is a solemn contractual agreement by which Yahweh reiterates his pledge to make Abraham "the father of a multitude of nations" (particularly the future Israel), to give Abraham's "countless" descendants "the whole land of Canaan," and to be their god in a special covenant relationship forever. Circumcision of Abraham and all his descendants was to be a required physical sign of the covenant (Gen. 17:1–4). Miraculously, within a year of the covenant's establishment, the first "child of the promise," Isaac, was born to the aged patriarch and his hitherto barren wife (Gen. 18:9–15; 21:1–7).

Abraham's devotion to Yahweh is equal to the severest demands placed upon it. When he believes that God requires it, Abraham prepares to give Isaac as a burnt offering. After an angel prevents completion of the sacrifice and substitutes a ram in the boy's place (regarded as the origin of Jewish animal sacrifices), Yahweh repeats his covenant promises and adds that as a reward for Abraham's obedience, "*all* nations of the earth" would someday bless themselves because of him (Gen. 22:15–18; italics added).

An incident that follows the concluding of the Abrahamic Covenant well illustrates the Genesis writers' view of Abraham's ethical character and moral courage. Learning that Yahweh plans to investigate reports of nearby Sodom's wickedness (chiefly its violence and inhospitality to strangers) and then to destroy it, Abraham is appalled. "Will the judge of the whole earth not administer justice?" he asks, begging Yahweh to spare all for the sake of the few good who may live there. Apparently cornered by Abraham's repeated questioning, Yahweh finally declares that he will not destroy the city for the sake of even ten righteous souls.

Although Yahweh does decide to incinerate Sodom and its four sister cities of the plain, out of regard for Abraham he rescues Lot and his two daughters (Lot's wife was changed into a pillar of salt when she looked back toward the doomed cities). Abraham's boldness in arguing with Yahweh on behalf of human rights is not unique in the Old Testament

❦ The Covenants with Noah and Abraham

An extremely important biblical concept, a covenant (Hebrew, *berit*) is a vow, promise, contract, agreement, or pact. The Bible writers commonly use the term to express Yahweh's purposeful relationship with an individual or a nation. In the ancient Near Eastern culture out of which the Bible grew, there were two principal forms of covenant: (1) the *suzeraintly covenant*, a political treaty between a superior party who dictated the terms of the arrangement and an inferior party who obeyed them; and (2) the *parity covenant*, an agreement between equals who were both obligated to observe its provisions.

In the Hebrew Bible, Yahweh, the great king or suzerain, initiates four major covenants—all an expression of divine graciousness in the god's voluntarily binding himself to a person or a people. Genesis contains the texts of two covenants. The first (Gen. 9:1–17) is universal in scope, encompassing all living creatures, both animal and human. Promulgated through Noah, this covenant emphasizes the sacredness of life, commands humanity to multiply (echoing the directive in Eden), and presents Yahweh's promise never again to drown the world in a flood. As a reminder of the divine promise, Yahweh sets a rainbow in the sky.

The second covenant Yahweh makes in Genesis is with a single person, Abraham (and his descendants). Since ancient compilers apparently used a variety of sources, Genesis contains several versions or aspects of the Abrahamic Covenant. In Genesis 15 Yahweh, like a powerful king making a land grant to a favored subject, promises the land of Canaan (Palestine) to Abraham's progeny (the Israelites). The oath is ratified by an ancient ritual in which Yahweh passes between the two halves of a dismembered sacrificial animal. (A parallel covenant rite is described in Jer. 34:18–21.) A later priestly account of the covenant (Gen. 17) repeats Yahweh's pledge about Canaan, states that Abraham will father a "multitude of nations," including a line of kings, and stresses circumcision of all Jewish males as a sign "in perpetuity" of the god's self-imposed bond with Israel. Yahweh also promises that "all the nations of the earth" will "bless themselves" because of Abraham (Gen. 12:3; 22:18). The Noachan and Abrahamic covenants differ strikingly in degree, if not entirely in kind, from the Mosaic Covenant enunciated in Exodus (see pages 66–67). Although both Noah and Abraham display a trusting obedience to Yahweh's call, which is presumably the reason for their being selected as covenant-bearers, the Genesis covenants place much less stress on reciprocal obligation from the human parties involved. According to the priestly rendition of the Abrahamic vow, the patriarch is to "bear himself blameless," implying a continuing moral relation between him and Yahweh (Gen. 17:1–2), but the deity does not require an oath of obedience or a long list of legal stipulations comparable to that demanded in the Mosaic pact. (But see the priestly reference to Abraham's keeping statutes and laws in Gen. 26:4–6.)

(both Moses and Job stage similar debates), but it is the first example of the Almighty acknowledging humanitarian arguments (Gen. 18:16–33). "Overwhelmed . . . with blessings," Abraham dies at age 175 and is buried near Sarah's grave in Canaan (Gen. 25:7–11).

Isaac, Rebekah, and Jacob   After devoting a dozen chapters to Abraham, Genesis passes briefly over the career of Isaac, who seems to have been a colorless personality in tribal memory. A much stronger character is that of Isaac's wife Rebekah, who behaves with telling decisiveness. In Genesis 24 when Abraham's servant returns to the patriarch's relatives in Upper Mesopotamia to find a wife for Isaac, Rebekah first manifests the hospitality that marks an admirable person and then, recognizing a divinely presented opportunity, volunteers to accept an unknown bridegroom and cast her lot in a strange land. Later it is she who manipulates Isaac, child of the promise, to bless his (potentially) more worthy son, Jacob. Depicted as having received Yahweh's prenatal revelation of intent concerning her younger child, Rebekah plays a key role in Israel's destiny, ensuring that the covenant promises are transmitted through Yahweh's chosen agent (Gen. 27:5–28:5). By placing a woman at the center of his account of the second-generation ancestors, the narrator achieves a meaningful balance between male and female participation in fulfilling the divine plan.

A spiritual cousin of the quick-witted Greek hero Odysseus (Ulysses), Jacob begins his career by persuading his older twin brother, Esau, to give him the birthright (inheritance) that traditionally belonged to the eldest son (Gen. 25:29–34). Under Rebekah's influence, Jacob tricks the blind and dying Isaac into bestowing the paternal blessing upon him rather than upon Esau, earning his brother's understandable enmity. Later Jacob outwits his father-in-law, Laban (for whom he had labored fourteen years to earn his favorite wife, Rachel), escapes with Laban's status-conferring household idols (the teraphim), and eventually becomes a rich man (Gen. 25:19–34; 27:1–32:2).

While traveling toward Haran, still inhabited by his Mesopotamian kinfolk, Jacob has his first significant experience of the divine. Sleeping outdoors with a stone for his pillow, he dreams of a "ladder" reaching from earth to heaven upon which angels are ascending and descending (resembling the Mesopotamian concept of deities using the ceremonial stairway of a Babylonian ziggurat). Yahweh appears in the dream and restates the Abrahamic Covenant, adding a promise to ensure Jacob's personal safety on his journey. On awakening, Jacob is awed by the sanctity of the place, which he renames Bethel, "House of God" (Gen. 28:10–22). Unwilling to commit himself to Yahweh on the basis of a mere dream, however, he vows to make Yahweh his god only on certain conditions: "*If* God goes with me and keeps me safe . . . *if* he gives me bread to eat and clothes to wear, and *if* I return home safely . . . *then* Yahweh shall be my God" (Gen. 28:20–22; italics added).

A more direct encounter occurs at Peniel, where Jacob literally wrestles with God, from whom he coerces a blessing and who consequently changes Jacob's name to Israel, interpreted here as "he who has been strong against God" (Gen. 32:23–32). This mysterious incident, in which he feels that he has "seen God face to face," indicates that even the wily Jacob has inherited some of his grandfather Abraham's spirituality. Jacob is further blessed through the birth of twelve sons, progenitors of the future twelve tribes of Israel.

Joseph and His Brothers   With the exception of a brief interpolated tale involving Judah and Tamar (Gen. 38), the remainder of Genesis tells the success story of Jacob's favored son, Joseph. Although a self-contained literary unit, the Joseph saga significantly advances the general historical plan of Genesis, for here we see Yahweh's will operating in the lives of unsuspecting individuals for the accomplishment of his predestined purpose. Interestingly, it is only a petty family squabble among brothers that sets the elaborate story in motion and, in the Hebrew view, ultimately changes the course of world history.

Jealous of their father's partiality to Joseph, his ten older brothers conspire to sell him into slavery. An Ishmaelite caravan takes him to Egypt, where after several misadventures, he correctly interprets pharaoh's dreams about an impending famine and is appointed governor of the country. The next stage of Yahweh's plan is now manifest: the famine brings Joseph's brothers to Egypt for grain. Although they do not recognize him, Joseph—after putting his family through years of anguish—eventually reveals his identity and, with impressive self-dramatization, forgives them. At pharaoh's invitation the aged Jacob also comes to Egypt along with his sons' families and livestock. Grateful to Joseph for making Egypt secure and powerful during an international famine, pharaoh grants land to the previously nomadic Hebrews, who according to one version of the story, settle in Goshen, an area of the Nile Delta.

A historical note: If the Israelite tribes remained in Egypt for 430 years as the Pentateuch states, and if the exodus occurred during the thirteenth century B.C.E. as many scholars suppose, Joseph would have arrived in Egypt during the seventeenth century B.C.E., after the Hyksos had conquered Egypt and established a new Citadel and dynasty in the Goshen area. Since many of the Hyksos were Semitic, it is possible that the pharaoh of the Joseph saga was a Semite who favored people of his own ethnic background. This would explain why Joseph, a Semite, rather than a native Egyptian was selected for the important post of governor. It would also help to clarify the statement in Exodus 1:18 that a new king who "knew nothing of Joseph" began to oppress the Hebrews; for after the Egyptians drove out the Hyksos during the sixteenth century B.C.E., it seems likely that everyone associated with the hated occupation would be treated badly by the new native dynasty.

There are difficulties to this theory. That the Israelites actually spent 430 years in Egypt, for example, is by no means certain; Exodus 6:16–20 indicates that only four generations—Levi to Moses—lived there. Genesis may have simplified a complex political situation, for there is no solid evidence that the Hyksos period coincided with the patriarchal migration to Egypt. It remains an attractive hypothesis, however, that accords well with the biblical narrative.

RECOMMENDED READING

Beltz, Walter. *God and the Gods, Myths of the Bible.* Translated by Peter Heinegg. New York: Penguin Books, 1983. An insightful examination of the biblical narratives, tracing their origins and parallels in earlier religions and myths.

Eissfeldt, Otto. "Genesis." In *The Interpreter's Dictionary of the Bible,* vol. 2, pp. 366–80. New York and Nashville: Abingdon Press, 1962.

Fromm, Erich. *You Shall Be as Gods: A Radical Reinterpretation of the Old Testament and Its Tradition.* New York: Fawcett World Library, 1969. A humanistic view of Yahweh and humankind.

Heidel, Alexander. *The Babylonian Genesis,* 2nd ed. Chicago: University of Chicago Press, 1963.

Hunt Ignatius, O.S.B. *The World of the Patriarchs.* Englewood Cliffs, N. J.: Prentice-Hall, 1967.

Sarna, Nahum M. *Understanding Genesis.* New York: Schocken Books, 1970.

Speiser, E. A., ed. *Genesis* (Anchor Bible). Garden City, N. Y.: Doubleday, 1964. Scholarly translation with extensive notes.

Trible, Phyllis. *God and the Rhetoric of Sexuality.* Philadelphia: Fortress Press, 1978. A close explication of Genesis 2–3 and other relevant biblical texts.

Vawter, Bruce. *On Genesis.* Garden City, N. Y.: Doubleday, 1977.

von Rad, Gerhard. *Genesis.* Philadelphia: Westminster Press, 1972.

Westerman, Claus. *The Promises to the Fathers: Studies on the Patriarchal Narratives.* Translated by David E. Green. Philadelphia: Fortress Press, 1980.

❦ Exodus

Moses	*Chapters 2–6*
The Ten Plagues and Passover	*7–12*
Crossing the Reed Sea	*14–15*
The Route of the Exodus	*16–18*
Mosaic Covenant	*19–24, 32–34*

I am Yahweh your God. . . . You shall have no gods but me.

Exodus 20:1–3

Exodus expresses the core of Israel's faith more than any other book in the Old Testament. An elaborate expansion of ancient creeds orally recited at Israelite sanctuaries (Deut. 26:6–10; Josh. 24:2–13), Exodus celebrates the origins of Israel's special relationship to Yahweh. Rather than an objective history in the modern sense, this second volume of the Torah is a composite record concerned with theologically interpreting national memories of the great events that bound Israel to Yahweh forever. Dominating the narrative are Yahweh's two saving acts that brought the nation into existence: the escape from slavery in Egypt and the revelation of the Law at Mount Sinai. Combining narrative, legal codes, poetry, and theology, the book presents a vivid characterization of Yahweh and his loyal servant Moses.

As in Genesis, the disparate strands of J, E, and P are intricately interwoven. According to most scholarly analyses of the text, the Yahwist writer (J) supplies the main narrative, supplemented by excerpts from the E (Elohist) document. The final priestly editors apparently thoroughly reworked the JE story, adding considerable genealogical, legal, and ritual material (such as that describing the tabernacle in chapters 35 through 40). They also seem to have added numerous details to J's account, heightening the miraculous elements in the Reed (not Red) Sea episode, and providing a second version of Moses' reception of the divine name (Exod. 6:3–13).

To date, historians and archaeologists have been unable to verify any of the events described in Exodus. No known Egyptian records refer to the escape of Hebrew slaves or the drowning of pharaoh's army. Nor do Egypt's surviving archives mention the biblical Moses or the devastating plagues that his god Yahweh reputedly inflicted on the country. This lack of historical evidence supporting the Exodus narrative, however, is less important than the Israelites' conviction that Yahweh had acted on their behalf. Gratitude for Yahweh's rescue of his people from bondage remains to this day an enduring part of Israel's religious heritage and forms the basis of the covenant bond between the people and their god.

Moses   The opening verses skip briefly over the several-hundred-year gap between the close of Genesis and the birth of Moses, stating that Egypt was now ruled by "a new king" or dynasty that "knew nothing of Joseph" or of Egypt's cause to be grateful to him and his fellow Hebrews (Exod. 1:8). Alarmed by the rapidly increasing Hebrew population, the new administration, probably the native Eighteenth Dynasty, has enslaved the Israelites, forcing them to labor at building urban projects in the Nile Delta. In a further effort to eliminate the supposed Hebrew threat, pharaoh has ordered that all newborn Hebrew males be killed.

The next several chapters concentrate on the biography of Moses, the man destined to deliver the Hebrews from slavery. Born under pharaoh's command that all boys of his race be drowned, Moses is saved when his mother secretly sets him adrift on the Nile in a watertight cradle. A childless daughter of pharaoh finds the boy and raises him as her own. Moses, a Levite, thus becomes familiar with the royal court and, according to a later tradition, is educated in "all the wisdom of the Egyptians" (Acts 7:22).

After killing an Egyptian overseer who has been abusing two Hebrew slaves, Moses flees the country and settles in Midian, a desert area south of Edom, where he marries and lives as a shepherd for forty years. At this point occurs one of those mysterious and overwhelming religious experiences that change people's lives irreversibly. Climbing Mount Horeb (or Mount Sinai, in J's version) to investigate a bush that burns without being consumed, he hears a voice announce that he is in the divine presence, on holy ground: "I am the god of your fathers," the voice says, "the God of Abraham, the God of Isaac, and the God of Jacob." Revealing that he intends to free his people from Egyptian bondage and settle them in Canaan, he commands Moses to return to Egypt and confront pharaoh with the demand to "let my people go."

When Moses, reluctant to undertake so formidable a task, demurs, suggesting that the Hebrews will not know which god is sending him, the voice replies: "I Am who I Am. . . . You are to say to the sons of Israel: Yahweh, the God of your fathers . . . has sent me to you. This is my name for all time; by this name I shall be invoked for all generations to come" (Exod. 3:14–15; for a second version of Moses' commission, see Exod. 6:2–13). The revelation of the divine name Yahweh is significant. Derived from the Hebrew verb "to be" ("I Am," first person singular), the name implies a god of action, one who brings new things into being. In Exodus he is about to transform a group of slaves into a new nation and guide them to a higher way of life. Unlike the generic terms *Elohom* or *Adonai*, Yahweh is a personal name denoting the creative and eternal nature of its owner.

The Ten Plagues and Passover The Hebrews in Egypt at first openly doubt Moses' authority to lead them. Also, as Yahweh had predicted, pharaoh (who is not named but may have been Egypt's last great ruler, Rameses II) adamantly refuses to part with his forced laborers. Angered, Yahweh displays his power through ten plagues calculated to break pharaoh's pride. Beginning with a bloody pollution of the Nile and other Egyptian waters, the plagues gradually increase in severity. Swarms of frogs, then mosquitoes, then gadflies afflict the Egyptians. Pharaoh begs Moses to end the plagues but treacherously goes back on his word when the pests disappear.

The Exodus writers characteristically attribute pharaoh's stubbornness to Yahweh, who is depicted as deliberately hardening pharaoh's heart (Exod. 7:3; 10:1, 20, 27; 14:8), thus forcing him to "sin" in refusing to let Israel go. The god's apparent interference with the Egyptian ruler's free will may distress modern readers, but in the Exodus tradition pharaoh's resistance was necessary to the deity's purpose. He *had* to be uncooperative in order for Yahweh's power to be revealed (Exod. 9:15–16; 10:1–2). If Egypt had meekly submitted to Moses' demands, there would have been no awesome plagues, no "signs and wonders" demonstrating the supremacy of Israel's god.

As pharaoh's stubbornness persists, the plagues increase in horror. The fifth brings sickness and death to Egyptian livestock, although the Hebrew flocks remain untouched. In the sixth, boils and sores break out on human and beast, though the Hebrews are again unaffected. In the seventh, a tremendous storm of lightning and hail destroys Egyptian crops. The eighth brings an invasion of locusts that devour what is left of Egypt's vegetation. In the ninth, total darkness covers the entire land except where the Hebrews live. Pharaoh then orders Moses out of his presence, refusing to see in these calamities the hand of the god of slaves.

Theologically, the tenth and last plague is the most important. In a final demonstration of divine power, Yahweh, or his Angel of Death, passes over Egypt at midnight and takes the life of every Egyptian first-born male, from pharaoh's crown prince to the son of the slave woman who grinds the corn. This time the Hebrews do not sit passively by; Moses orders each family to sacrifice a lamb, smear its blood on their doorposts, and stay in their homes to eat a ceremonial meal—the solemn feast of unleavened bread and bitter herbs. Thus, according to Exodus, the Passover ritual was established during Israel's last night of slavery while the divine executioner "passed over" their dwellings, made secure by the symbolic "blood of the lamb." This feast remains one of the most important of Jewish observances and is the forerunner of Jesus' Last Supper and the Christian Communion.

Crossing the Reed Sea For a final demonstration of Yahweh's might, pharaoh is motivated to lead his army in pursuit of the fleeing Israelites. Trapped between Egyptian charioteers and the Reed Sea (not the huge Red Sea as is sometimes mistakenly supposed), the Hebrews are spectacularly rescued: "Yahweh drove back the sea with a strong easterly wind all night, and he made dry land of the sea" (Exod. 14:22). The Hebrews cross dryshod, but the Egyptians giving chase are drowned when "the sea returned to its bed."

Whatever the natural causes of this might be—the effects of a volcanic eruption or tsunami wave striking the marshlands of the Egyptian coast—its timing for Israel was miraculous. To the Hebrews who witnessed it, the deliverance was proof that Yahweh can and does save his people. One of the oldest parts of Exodus is the victory song that Moses' sister Miriam sings over the fallen Egyptians:

> Sing of Yahweh: he has covered himself in glory,
> horse and rider he has thrown into the sea.
>
> Exodus 15:21

As the expanded version of Moses' battle hymn states, Yahweh had now publicly established himself among the recognized powers:

> Who among the gods is your like, Yahweh?
> Who is your like, majestic in holiness,
> terrible in deeds of prowess, worker of wonders?
>
> Exodus 15:11

Throughout Old Testament history, Yahweh's saving act at the Reed Sea is referred to as the decisive moment in Israel's past, the moment at which Yahweh made Israel his own.

The Route of the Exodus More than 3,000 years after the event, scholars remain divided on the question of Israel's route from Egypt to Canaan. The problem is compounded by the fact that few of the sites mentioned in the Exodus narrative have been positively identified. Even the point at which the Israelites crossed the Reed Sea is unknown. Various lakes and swampy areas north of the Gulf of Suez have been suggested, but neither Lake Sirbonis (Lake Bardawil) nor a southern extension of the present Lake Menzaleh has received general scholarly acceptance as the location of Israel's deliverance. Because the Egyptians then maintained a line of heavy fortifications along the Mediterranean coast, the most direct approach to Canaan (Exod. 13:17–19), the Israelites were forced to follow an inland route through an arid wilderness. A plausible reconstruction of Israel's path across the Sinai Peninsula appears in the map on the facing page.

Mosaic Covenant The climactic act in the national epic is consummated at Mount Sinai, the holy mountain where Moses had experienced his epiphany (manifestation of God) and back to which Yahweh had commanded him to lead the Israelites. At Sinai (whose exact location has never been positively identified), Yahweh calls Moses and the symbolic seventy elders of Israel for special communion (Exod. 24). Out of the Mount Sinai theophany (revelation of God) Moses brings the Ten Commandments and Book of the Covenant, the nucleus of Israel's Torah (Exod. 19–24). (The Mosaic law in its entirety eventually included all the hundreds of rules and regulations found in the Pentateuch, although many of these derive from a time later than that of Moses.) See "The Mosaic Covenant at Mount Sinai," p. 66–67.

Although the Hebrew people have heard the law read to them and have willingly accepted its terms, a reaction soon occurs. While Moses remains on Mount Sinai communing with Yahweh, the people become restive and rebellious. In order not to forfeit his leadership over them, Moses' brother Aaron makes them golden calves as physical objects of worship (Exod. 32). On returning from the mountain, however, such is

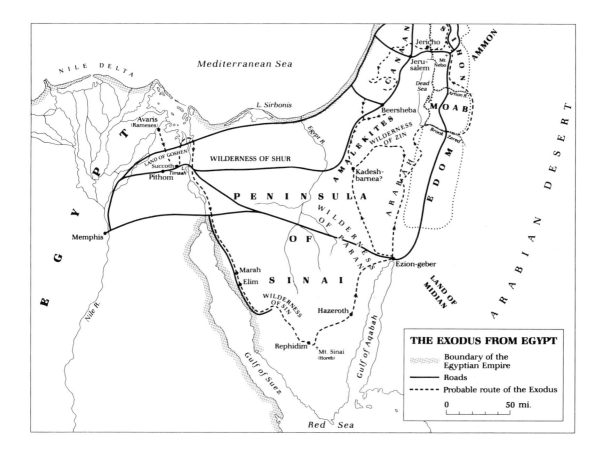

The Exodus from Egypt

Moses' fury at the Israelites' apostasy that he shatters the stone tablets upon which the Decalogue had been inscribed (though Yahweh later makes new tablets, which are traditionally kept in the portable Ark [chest] of the Covenant, described in minute detail in chapters 35–40 of Exodus).

The Israelites' thoughtless abandonment of Yahweh sparks a debate between Moses, the people's advocate, and Yahweh, whose anger at Israel is so great that he proposes to destroy them and make a nation derived from Moses instead. As Abraham had argued with God not to destroy Sodom, so Moses now pleads for his fellow Hebrews: Why give the Egyptians an opportunity to mock Yahweh, saying that he cannot finish what he has begun, not preserve alive the people he has led out of Egypt? God, suggests Moses, must also remember his promise to Abraham.

"So Yahweh relented and did not bring on his people the disaster he had threatened" (Exod. 32:11–14). Elsewhere in the Pentateuch (notably Num. 14:10–19) we find Moses again reminding Yahweh that his reputation depends on Israel's continued existence and future success as a

❧ The Mosaic Covenant at Mount Sinai

This agreement was called the Mosaic Covenant because Moses acts as mediator between Yahweh and the Israelites; it differs radically from the compacts with Noah and Abraham described in Genesis. In the Exodus version of the covenant, Yahweh makes no promises, except the implied one of being the patron and protector of Israel, and instead demands strict obedience to a vast body of laws, statutes, commandments, and regulations. (By contrast, Deuteronomy's later restatement of the covenant pictures Yahweh's making promises that are conditional upon Israel's continued obedience.) Scholars believe that Israel's law developed gradually over a long period of time, although tradition attributes to Moses *all* legal material in the Torah. It is probably impossible to determine precisely the terms of the original Mosaic pact between Yahweh and the Israelites. But numerous references scattered throughout Exodus, Leviticus, and Deuteronomy indicate that in legal form the covenant may have resembled a Hittite treaty. A study of ancient Near Eastern treaties shows that they typically included the following provisions: (1) the preamble; (2) an account of historical circumstances leading to the treaty; (3) the stipulations and requirements; (4) arrangements for public reading of the text and its safekeeping at a shrine; (5) a list of divine witnesses to the treaty; (6) a vivid catalogue of blessings for abiding by its terms and curses for violating them. All of these elements occur in the Torah, although they are

presently scattered throughout the biblical text.

Exodus 19 describes the awe-inspiring presence of Yahweh on the sacred mountain, shrouded in clouds rent by lightning. In Exodus 20 the traditional preamble and historical recapitulation are reduced to a brief statement identifying the suzerain—"I am Yahweh"—and the people's cause to be grateful to the deity, for Yahweh brought them "out of the land of Egypt, out of the house of slavery." Terms of the treaty between God and the people are then enumerated. The Israelites' vow to obey does not immediately follow the Decalogue, because later editors have inserted a block of additional legal material between chapters 20 and 24, where the oath of ratification now appears. The Israelites swear "with one voice" to abide by all of Yahweh's commandments (Exod. 24:3). Moses slaughters sacrificial animals, casting part of the blood on the altar (representing Yahweh), to seal the covenant bond. After Moses publicly reads from the Book of the Covenant and the people again vow to observe all that is written therein, he sprinkles the assembled Israelites with the rest of their blood, symbolizing the people's commitment to recognize only one suzerain.

No witnesses to Israel's solemn pledge to worship Yahweh exclusively are mentioned in Exodus. But Deuteronomy 30:19 calls "heaven and earth" to witness against the Israelites, an invocation many scholars have noted as a possible reference to Near Eastern earth and sky deities. Joshua 24, which describes a covenant renewal ceremony at the ancient Canaanite sanctuary of Shechem, contains several parallels to ancient treaty conventions. In one passage the people themselves are witnesses to their obligation to serve Yahweh alone (Josh. 24:22). In another it is a memorial stone that "has heard all the words" of Yahweh that acts as witness against the people if they break their oath. Consistent with Near Eastern custom, Joshua reads the covenant's provisions and then places the text in the shrine at Shechem. Promised blessings for keeping the covenant and curses for violating it are detailed in Leviticus 26 and Deuteronomy 28. Scholars believe that both of these passages are much later than the earliest accounts preserved in Exodus, but the later texts accurately reflect ancient conventions in treaty making. They also echo the then-current mode of formal cursing typical of international treaties. Yahweh's threat to trap future covenant breakers in a harsh world,

with the heavens like "brass" and the earth beneath like "iron" (Deut. 28:23; Lev. 26:19), is almost identical to the metallic imagery of curses listed in a treaty which Esarhaddon, king of Assyria, concluded about 677 B.C.E.

The legal *form* in which Israelite covenant laws are expressed, as well as some of the content, is also paralleled in other Near Eastern texts. *Apodictic* law, such as the Ten Commandments, with their imperative absolutes ordering the people not to steal, kill, or bear false witness, is apparently unique to Israel's religion. Hittite treaties record an overlord's direct orders to his vassals, but nothing resembling Israel's ethical injunctions. By contrast, *case law*, with its typical formula "If such and such is the case, then . . . must be done," characterizes many ancient Near Eastern cultures. The if, then pattern appears throughout the famous law code of Hammurabi (about 1690 B.C.E.) and also characterizes much legal material in the Torah (Exod. 20:22–23:5; Lev. 1–7; 12–15, etc.).

---

nation. In Numbers 14 he even quotes the deity's own earlier recital of Yahweh's beneficent qualities (stated in Exod. 34:6–8) and appeals to his sense of fairness and consistency. Such passages illustrate Israel's slowly growing awareness of Yahweh as an ethical and responsible god.

RECOMMENDED READING

Buber, Martin. *Moses: The Revelation and the Covenant.* New York: Harper & Row, 1958.

Childs, Brevard S. *The Book of Exodus.* Philadelphia: Westminster Press, 1974.

de Vaux, Roland. *The Early History of Israel.* Translated by D. Smith. Philadelphia: Westminster Press, 1978. Analyzes the Exodus and Sinai traditions.

Hillers, Delbert R. *Covenant: The History of a Biblical Idea.* Baltimore: Johns Hopkins Press, 1969.

McCarthy, D. J. *Old Testament Covenant: A Survey of Current Opinions.* Richmond, Va.: John Knox Press, 1972.

Mendenhall, George E. *Law and Covenant in Israel and the Ancient Near East.* Pittsburgh: The Biblical Colloquium, 1955. An influential study of correspondences between ancient treaty documents and the growth of Israel's covenant tradition.

———. "Covenant." In *The Interpreter's Dictionary of the Bible,* vol. 2, pp. 714–723. New York and Nashville: Abingdon Press, 1962. A concise, insightful summary of the biblical concept of covenant relationships.

Noth, Martin. *Exodus.* Philadelphia: Westminster Press, 1962.

Stamm, J. J., and Andrew, M. E. *The Ten Commandments in Recent Research.* Studies in Biblical Theology, 2nd ser, no. 2. Naperville, Ill.: Alec R. Allenson, 1967. Covers apodictic law.

❧ Leviticus

Day of Atonement	*Chapters 16*
Holiness Code	*17–26*

You therefore must be holy because I am holy.

Leviticus 11:44

Now one of the least read parts of the Bible, Leviticus nevertheless represents an important stage in the development of Israel's religion. Scholars believe that Israelite priests assembled the book during and shortly after the Babylonian exile (587–538 B.C.E.), when the entire Jewish nation lay in ruins and its upper classes were held captive in Babylon. Responding to a threatened loss of national and religious identity, the priests attempted to preserve and standardize Israel's forms of worship. The result is the enormous body of cult material catalogued in the Torah.

Although most of Leviticus' laws and regulations presuppose a return to the homeland and temple, it also contains rules on circumcision and diet that could be observed even in exile. These rituals and legal stipulations, which begin in Exodus 25–31 and 35–40 and carry over into Numbers 1–10, belong almost exclusively to the priestly document (P). Their purpose is to demonstrate that by conscientiously observing all the legal and liturgical requirements set forth by the priests, the Israelite people will remain distinct and different from the Gentile nations that endeavor to overwhelm or absorb them, thereby helping to ensure continuance of Israel's unique legacy.

In spite of the Septuagint title, Leviticus has little to do with the Levites or their law; it concentrates almost exclusively on the descendants of Aaron and their priestly functions. The book falls into two broad sections—chapters 1–16 and 17–26—both of which embody distinct legal codes. The first section presents a variety of guidelines for the worshiping community, including instructions to lay people on how to make proper sacrifices of animals or grain, such as those rendered for the sins of the high priest (Lev. 4:3–12), the community (Lev. 4:13–26), and the individual (Lev. 4:27–35; 5:1–13).

Chapters 8–10 of this section outline procedures for installing the Aaronite priests. Chapters 11–15 deal with various kinds of ritual and physical uncleanness (including prohibited foods), with diseases such as leprosy (Lev. 13:1–17, 47–59; 14:1–57), as well as with sexual taboos concerning both men and women (Lev. 15:1–33). The second part of Leviticus, known as the Holiness Code, is distinguished by the frequent refrain "I am Yahweh," which occurs only once in the first section (Lev. 11:45).

Day of Atonement   Chapter 16 describes one of Israel's most significant ceremonies, the scapegoat offering. Annually, on the Day of Atonement (Yom Kippur), the high priest is instructed to prepare two goats for sacrifice. At the Tent of Meeting, the priest draws lots for the goats, slaughtering one as a sacrifice to Yahweh and keeping the other alive as a symbolic bearer of the people's collective sins. Ritually laying hands on the live goat, the priest transfers the nation's sins to the animal, which metaphorically laden with Israel's misdeeds, is then led out into the desert "to Azazel." The scapegoat thus removes the punishable object of Yahweh's wrath from the community and transfers it to the uninhabited wilderness. (Scholars have long debated whether Azazel is a place or a desert demon that destroys the "sinful" goat.)

The term *scapegoat* has come to mean any innocent person who suffers for the crimes of others; its fullest Old Testament expression is found in Isaiah's Song of the Suffering Servant, in which a guiltless man bears the sins of his people and by so doing wins forgiveness for them:

> On him lies a punishment that brings us peace,
> and through his wounds we are healed.
>
> Isaiah 53:5

The atonement (reconciliation) ceremony was effected to bring harmony between the Israelites and their god. It was a means of approaching and becoming at one with Yahweh.

Holiness Code   The reiterated refrain "I am Yahweh" in chapters 17–26 of the Holiness Code emphasizes Yahweh as the source of holiness and also of the laws whose observance makes Israel's holiness manifest. It would be a mistake, however, to conclude that the priestly writers believed Yahweh to be pleased only by ritual and sacrifice. Like other books of the Pentateuch, Leviticus demands Yahweh's worshipers to be not only ceremonially clean but to meet high social and moral standards of behavior as well.

Amid rather dry priestly regulations for making burnt offerings, the reader will find passages of great ethical and psychological insight. On the matter of social justice, for example, we are told: "You must neither be partial to the little man, nor overawed by the great; you must pass judgment on your neighbor according to justice. . . . You must not bear hatred for your brother in your heart. . . . You must love your neighbor as yourself. I am Yahweh" (Lev. 19:15–18). In addition to containing the only command in the Pentateuch to love one's neighbor as a religious duty, Leviticus also enjoins the Israelites to treat strangers and foreign residents with compassion, remembering that they themselves were once outsiders in a strange land (Lev. 19:34).

The Holiness Code concludes by placing Israel's laws and ceremonies in the general context of her covenant with Yahweh. In a passage reminiscent of the deuteronomic school of thought, chapter 26 enumerates the respective blessings or curses that will follow obedience or disobedience to the laws contained in this book. Security, divine protection, military victory, and material prosperity are guaranteed if Israel keeps all her god's commandments; drought, famine, disease, poverty, military defeat, and total ruin are predicted if the nation fails to honor these edicts (Lev. 26:3–43). Promising to remember his covenant with Abraham, the deity also promises to rescue his people from their enemies' power and restore them to Canaan. Although there was probably an ancient tradition that national disaster would befall a disobedient Israel, this description of the Babylonian exile and return indicates a relatively late date for this particular passage.

Noting certain similarities between the Holiness Code and the legal code of Ezekiel, some critics believe that Leviticus 17–26 dates from the time that Ezekiel was written (the sixth and possibly fifth centuries B.C.E.). It seems more likely, however, that Ezekiel was simply dependent upon Leviticus, which, though it assumed its final shape after the exile, undoubtedly contains much older material and may reflect procedures and rites used at the temple services in Jerusalem long before the captivity. Like other parts of the Pentateuch edited by postexilic priests, Leviticus was not the product of a single historical period but represents ideas, practices, and customs that developed over several centuries.

RECOMMENDED READING

Brueggemann, Walter. "The Kerygma of the Priestly Writer." In *The Vitality of Old Testament Traditions*, edited by Walter Brueggemann and Hans Walter Wolff, pp. 101–13. Atlanta: John Knox Press, 1975.

Cross, Frank Moore. "The Priestly Houses of Early Israel." In *Canaanite Myth and Hebrew Epic: Essays in the History and the Religion of Israel*, pp. 293–325. Cambridge, Mass.: Harvard University Press, 1973. Indispensable for understanding how the priests edited the Pentateuch.

de Vaux, Roland. *Studies in Old Testament Sacrifice.* Cardiff, Wales: University of Wales Press, 1964.

Eissfeldt, Otto. "The Holiness Code." In *The Old Testament: An Introduction,* pp. 233–39. New York: Harper & Row, 1965.

Levine, B. A. "Priestly Writers." In *The Interpreter's Dictionary of the Bible: Supplementary Volume,* pp. 683–87. Nashville: Abingdon Press, 1976.

Noth, Martin. *Leviticus.* Philadelphia: Westminster Press, 1975. Provides information about the priestly tradition and Israel's cultic worship.

❦ Numbers

Yahweh's Anger at Israel	*Chapters 13–14*
Israel Rebels Against Moses	*11–14; 16*
Balaam's Blessing	*22–24*

It is you, Yahweh, . . . you go before them in a pillar of cloud by day and a pillar of fire by night.

Numbers 14:14

Although Numbers begins with a census or numbering of the people (hence its Septuagint title), it is mainly a patchwork of Israel's forty-year wandering in the Sinai wilderness, interspersed with collections of legal material resembling those in Leviticus. Because of its apparent haphazard editing, however, Numbers is not an easy work to read, and its literary history remains a puzzle to source critics. Somewhat to oversimplify the problem, most of the legal sections can be assigned to P and the narrative portions to JE combined. Like other parts of the Torah, it includes some material of great antiquity, though its final editing took place in postexilic times.

Since the sections recording Israel's journey from Mount Sinai to the plains of Moab east of the River Jordan do not present a continuous history, it is extremely difficult to piece together a clear sequence of events. Certain incidents, such as the several rebellions against Moses' leadership, are recounted in detail, while whole decades of travel are passed by in silence. Indeed, there is no sense of forty years' elapsing between the peoples' fearful refusal to enter Canaan reported in chapter 14 and the preparations to attack the Canaanites mentioned at the book's end.

Yahweh's Anger at Israel   Numbers is specific, however, about the traditional cause of Israel's forty-year delay in reaching the Promised Land.

According to chapters 13:25–14:38, ten of the twelve spies sent to reconnoiter Canaan return with discouraging reports of impregnably fortified cities and savage giants, which so terrify the Israelites that they are prepared to stone even Joshua and Caleb, the only two spies to give a favorable view of their prospects. Ready to destroy his people for their lack of confidence in him, Yahweh is dissuaded when Moses reminds him that the Gentile nations are watching his experiment with Israel and that he stands to lose face if he allows his people to perish in the desert. Yahweh must also recall his promise to Abraham as well as his words to Moses on Mount Sinai:

> Yahweh is slow to anger and rich in graciousness,
> forgiving faults and transgressions . . .
>
> Numbers 14:18, 19

In the "abundance of his graciousness," then, Yahweh must not exterminate the people.

Yahweh's forgiveness is limited, however. He does not obliterate them but decrees that no Israelite over the age of twenty will live to enter Canaan; for every day that the spies reconnoiter the area, Israel must wander a year, until their "dead bodies . . . fall" in the desert. Practically speaking, the forty-year gap between leaving Egypt and settling in Canaan had its cultural and religious advantages. The older generation, imperfectly versed in the Yahwist faith and contaminated by their association with Egyptian idolatry, would be eliminated. Only those younger Israelites thoroughly indoctrinated in the Mosaic religion would be allowed to form the new nation. The two exceptions were Joshua and Caleb who, alone among the elder group, had faith in Yahweh's ability to defeat the Canaanite militia.

Israel Rebels Against Moses Although Moses has repeatedly deflected Yahweh's wrath from smiting Israel, his protective role is unappreciated by the people he defends. Early in the wilderness trek the Israelites complain bitterly about their restricted diet. Yahweh supplements the daily supply of manna—a powdery food that falls from heaven each night—by sending them quail to eat but also sends a plague to punish them for wanting more than he had volunteered to provide. Moses' authority is more seriously undermined in his own household when his brother Aaron and sister Miriam declare that their communication with God is as good as his. For her presumptuousness, Miriam (but not her equally presumptuous brother) is struck with leprosy (Num. 12). Moses, kindhearted as always, intervenes with Yahweh, and after a seven-day excommunication from the camp, Miriam is cured.

The principal challenge to Moses' position, however, comes from a respectable group of Israel's leaders, including Korah, who is a Levite, and Dathan, Abiram, and On of the tribe of Reuben, along with 250 other "men of repute," who argue that because all Israel is consecrated to Yahweh's service, Moses and Aaron have no right to assume so much authority. During a confrontation between the rebels and Moses at the Tent of Meeting, the earth opens to swallow Korah and the others, including their wives, children, and possessions. The 250 men associated with the revolt are consumed when Yahweh sends fire from heaven (Num. 16:28–35).

Balaam's Blessing   Preserved in chapters 22–24 is an old folktale that illustrates how a Near Eastern soothsayer of the Bronze Age performed his job. This is the humorous story of Balaam, a Canaanite prophet hired by King Balak of Moab to curse Israel, whose presence in the area he regards as a threat. Although Balaam conscientiously invokes the customary curses, Yahweh turns them into blessings. Even Balaam's donkey, who reprimands her master, plays a part in thwarting Balak's designs. Neither pagan king nor hired prophet can resist Yahweh's plans for Israel.

Ironically, while Balaam involuntarily obeys Yahweh, the Israelites indulge in fertility rites with Moabite women and the orgiastic worship of Baal of Peor. Although the usually pacific Moses retaliates by impaling the guilty leaders, Yahweh is not satisfied; he sends a plague that kills 24,000 people and is ended only when Phineas, son of the high priest, executes an Israelite who has taken a Midianite concubine. This act dissipates Yahweh's anger temporarily, though he later orders a holy war of annihilation on the Midianites, all of whom are to be slaughtered except young virgins to populate Israelite harems (Num. 31).

To most contemporary readers the picture that Numbers paints of Yahweh is not altogether sympathetic. The deity seems little more than arbitrary power, impatient, violent, and destructive—a god easy to fear but difficult to love. Yahweh is still represented as the national god of Israel, one who shows little concern for other peoples except to destroy them when they impede Israel's progress. As in Exodus, however, it is his supernatural strength that wholly absorbs the writers' attention.

From the JE narratives there is no conclusive evidence that Moses and his people were monotheists, that they saw Yahweh as the sole and universal god. In the Mosaic tradition the Israelites were unquestionably committed to serving Yahweh alone, an exclusive allegiance affirmed in the covenant relationship. But while they are to have "no other gods" before him, the narrators never state that other gods do not exist. The old question of whether the Mosaic religion was monotheistic, long debated among scholars and theologians, is still unresolved.

RECOMMENDED READING

Noth, Martin. *Numbers.* Philadelphia: Westminster Press, 1968.

🍎 Deuteronomy

Moses' Second Speech	*Chapters 5–28*
Moses' Third Speech	*29–30*
Moses' Last Days and Death	*31–32; 34*

Listen, Israel: Yahweh our God is the one Yahweh.

Deuteronomy 6:4

The Greek-speaking Jews from the second century B.C.E. onward called the Pentateuch's fifth book Deuteronomy (literally, "second law"). But the Hebrew title *Eleh Hádevarim* ("These are the words [of Moses]") is more accurate, for, unlike the other books of the Torah in which Yahweh directs his words to Moses who then transmits them to Israel, Deuteronomy shows Moses speaking directly to the people. The book takes the form of three farewell sermons that Moses delivers shortly before his death. The scene is the plains of Moab east of Jordan, along which the Israelites are massed just prior to their invasion of Canaan. Deuteronomy is thus the final recapitulation of Israel's covenant faith before Yahweh leads them into the land he had promised their ancestors.

The alert reader will notice, even in English translation, striking differences in style, phrasing, outlook, and theological assumptions between Deuteronomy and other parts of the Pentateuch. Because it purports to be a cycle of public addresses, the book is highly rhetorical, even artificial, in style, and the hortatory tone prevails throughout in such phrases as "with all your heart and soul," "in order that it may go well with you," "be thankful," "in a place he himself will choose," "a land where milk and honey flow," and "if only you obey the voice of Yahweh your God."

Compared with earlier sections of the Torah, too, Deuteronomy offers a more humane, sophisticated teaching, stressing both Yahweh's "steadfast love" for Israel and the people's moral obligation to "remember" his heroic acts on their behalf by loving him with their entire being. More than most other parts of the Pentateuch, Deuteronomy emphasizes social justice, personal ethics, and neighborly responsibilities, and it is therefore not surprising that later Jewish writers cite it frequently. In the New Testament, Jesus is shown employing Deuteronomy to refute the Devil himself (Matt. 4; Luke 4).

Most biblical historians agree that the Book of the Law found in 621 B.C.E. when King Josiah was conducting temple repairs (2 Kings 22:8–10) was Deuteronomy or at least its nucleus (Deut. 12–26). According to 2 Kings 22–23, this discovery inspired Josiah to promote radical changes in Judah's religion. Since Deuteronomy 12 demanded that Israel sacrifice only at a single central sanctuary, which both king and priests took to be the temple at Jerusalem, Josiah ordered the wholesale destruction of outlying altars, shrines, and cult sites at which the country people had worshiped for centuries.

Although it was discovered in Josiah's time, Deuteronomy was probably compiled a generation or two earlier during King Manasseh's reign, a period of foreign religious influence when fanatical Yahwists were not encouraged to insist on Israel's strict allegiance to the Mosaic law (see 2 Kings 21). Many scholars also believe that the deuteronomic material originated not among the Jerusalem priests but among those of the northern tribes. Such traditions may have stemmed from a covenant-renewal ceremony that Joshua had instituted at Shechem (Josh. 24); transferred to the old sanctuary at Shiloh during the period of the judges, they were preserved among the northern Israelites. According to this theory, the protodeuteronomic material was probably brought south to Jerusalem by refugees from the Assyrian destruction of Samaria in 721 B.C.E. Ironically, a tradition intended to enhance a cult center in the northern kingdom was ultimately used to support the preeminence of Solomon's temple.

It seems probable that Deuteronomy was added to and reedited even after Josiah's time. The book has two introductions, one of which may have been appended after the seventh century B.C.E. The Song of Moses (Deut. 32) seems to be a late addition, though it may be a genuinely antique document. The Blessing of Moses (Deut. 33) probably embodied another ancient tradition that it seemed fitting to an editor to include in the Torah. Moses' three sermons and their supplements can be outlined by chapters as follows:

1. First Speech (1–4)

2. Second Speech (5–26, 28)

3. Third Speech (29–30)

4. Shechem Covenant Ceremony (27)

5. Ancient Poetry: Song of Moses (32) and Blessing of Moses (33)

6. Story of Moses' Death (34)

Moses' Second Speech   In his first speech Moses reviews all that has happened since the departure from Mount Sinai, pointing out that Yahweh has faithfully kept his covenant promises and urging the Israelites to keep theirs by obeying Yahweh's laws. His second speech, however, comprises the bulk of Deuteronomy; and here we find a somewhat expanded version of the Ten Commandments (Deut. 5:6–21) and other ordinances, known as the Covenant Code (Deut. 12–26), that resemble the legal material found in Exodus 20–23. There are also echoes of Leviticus and Numbers in this section.

In general, it appears that the compiler of Deuteronomy is attempting to update and revise Israel's ancient legal and sacrificial practices in the light of seventh-century understanding of the Mosaic heritage. As mentioned above, the emphasis on a single central shrine meant a revolution in Israel's way of worship. The abolishing of sacrifices at all rural altars threw many Levites out of work; reduction of the number of yearly festivals, which all Israelites were expected to attend at the designated sanctuary, further disrupted old customs.

Perhaps in response to the influence of Israel's eighth-century prophets (led by Isaiah, Micah, Amos, and Hosea), Deuteronomy 18 predicts that God will send Israel a prophet "like Moses" into whose mouth he will place his commandments. This passage also gives a means of distinguishing the false from the true prophet: one who lures Israel into worshiping other gods is false; one whose words come true is authentic. These criteria are not very helpful to a prophet's contemporaries, for they will have to wait for events to confirm or invalidate a seer's predictions before deciding whether to heed or ignore him. In retrospect, however, after the prophet's words have been preserved in writing, a later generation can determine whether his message had been authentic and his teachings valid.

Much of the second speech is devoted to laws regarding civil organization, marriage and divorce regulations, social welfare, and criminal justice. Since the Torah made no provisions for building prisons, convicted criminals either paid fines or were summarily executed; physical mutilation of the guilty party was occasionally permitted. For those committing involuntary manslaughter, cities of refuge were established, but Deuteronomy also recognized the right of relatives of the person slain to avenge their kinsman's death. If the "blood avengers" caught and killed the accidental slayer before that person reached a place of asylum, they were entitled to do so.

Premeditated murder, however, was a capital offense, as were adultery, idolatry, blasphemy, heresy, homosexuality, and many other acts. Deuteronomy repeats the *lex talionis* (law of retaliation) given in Exodus:

> Life for life, eye for eye, tooth for tooth, hand for hand,
> foot for foot.

> Deuteronomy 19:21

However harsh to modern eyes, this principle was a humanitarian improvement over previously existing practices. One could no longer demand a life for an eye but only the exact equivalent of one's own injury.

After describing a covenant-renewal ceremony to be held at Mount Ebal in northern Israel after the people cross the Jordan River (Deut. 27), the book provides a list of material rewards (blessings) if Israel keeps the law and a much longer list of punishments (curses) if it disobeys the law

(Deut. 28). This passage expresses the essence of what is known as the Deuteronomist Hypothesis of history. Briefly, it states that Israel's future is totally conditional on her collective religious behavior. Obedience to the Torah will bring national prosperity; disobedience will result in national disaster, including military defeat and exile. This bleak vision closes Moses' second sermon.

Moses' Third Speech   The third and final speech (Deut. 29–30) seems more like a rhetorical conclusion to the second address than a separate discourse. Here Moses enumerates additional sufferings destined to befall Israel if she sins. "In anger, in fury, in fierce wrath," Yahweh will devastate their land and inflict so much misery that even survivors will wish they had died. In common with the prophets, however, there is a promise that when the people repent their sins and return to Yahweh, he will forgive them and restore a small remnant of them to their homeland. The people are repeatedly reminded that the responsibility for their future rests squarely on their own shoulders.

In truly "winged words," Yahweh emphasizes the people's freedom of choice. Setting before them "life and prosperity" or "death and disaster," he urges them to choose a life in which they and their descendants can live to enjoy the love of their god. The ancient song ascribed to Moses (Deut. 32) is actually a hymn glorifying Yahweh and denouncing the people's misuse of their free will:

> He [Yahweh] is the rock, his work is perfect,
> for all his ways are Equity.
> A God faithful, without unfairness,
> Uprightness itself and Justice.
> They [the people] have acted perversely,
> those he begot without blemish,
> a deceitful and underhand brood.
> Is this the return you make to Yahweh?
> O foolish, unwise people!
>
> Deuteronomy 32:4–6

Evil fortune, then, is directly the community's responsibility, for both Yahweh and his creation are perfect.

Moses' Last Days and Death   After the Blessing of Moses (Deut. 33), which strongly resembles Jacob's blessing (Gen. 49), Deuteronomy records Moses' death. Prohibited from entering the Promised Land for an unspecified reason [perhaps his taking credit for bringing water from the rocks at Meribah (Num. 20:2–13)], the 120-year-old Moses glimpses Canaan from a high mountain and dies alone, hidden from the people he has guided for forty years. His unfulfilled career provides an effective symbol for his nation's future experience. As an awed commentator penned in conclusion, "Never has there been such a prophet in Israel as Moses, the man Yahweh knew face to face" (Deut. 34:10).

In its literary excellence and generally humanitarian spirit, Deuteronomy is a fitting capstone to the Pentateuch, the five-act epic of Israel's birth. But it is also the first part of a much longer literary work; for the same religious school or group that compiled and edited Deuteronomy also produced the sequence of historical books—Joshua through 2 Kings (omitting Ruth)—that follows. When viewed as an introduction to Israel's subsequent history, Deuteronomy is not a mere repetition of the Mosaic law and covenant but a necessary statement of the principles on which that history is to be judged. The deuteronomist historians were unswerving in their conviction that Israel was to be evaluated by one test alone—its collective obedience to Yahweh's covenant.

RECOMMENDED READING

Clements, R. E. *God's Chosen People: A Theological Interpretation of the Book of Deuteronomy*. London: SCM Press, 1968.

Lohfink, N. "Deuteronomy." In *The Interpreter's Dictionary of the Bible: Supplementary Volume*, pp. 229–32. Nashville: Abingdon Press, 1976.

Nicholson, E. W. *Deuteronomy and Tradition*. Philadelphia: Fortress Press, 1967.

von Rad, Gerhard. *Deuteronomy*. Philadelphia: Westminster Press, 1966.

_____. "Deuteronomy." In *The Interpreter's Dictionary of the Bible*, vol. 1, pp. 831–38. New York and Nashville: Abingdon Press, 1962.

_____. *Studies in Deuteronomy*. Studies in Biblical Theology, no. 9. London: SCM Press, 1953. A form-critical approach.

Weinfeld, Moshe. *Deuteronomy and the Deuteronomic School*. Oxford: Clarendon Press, 1972.

Wright, G. Ernest. "Introduction and Exegesis to Deuteronomy." In *The Interpreter's Bible*, vol. 2, pp. 311–537. New York and Nashville: Abingdon Press, 1953. A good introduction.

PART 4

THE PROPHETS

The second major division of the canonical Old Testament is called The Prophets, although the first part of this section—Joshua through 2 Kings—primarily consists of historical narrative. Known to the Hebrews as the Former Prophets, those books present a theologically oriented account of Israel's religious and political history from the conquest of Canaan in the thirteenth century B.C.E. to the destruction of the Jewish state by the Babylonians in the sixth century B.C.E. The Former Prophets thus provide necessary background for the collection of books known as the Latter Prophets, works bearing the names of individual prophets like Isaiah, Amos, and Micah, which form the second section of this two-part division of the Hebrew Bible.

Since the order of the prophetic books in the Hebrew Bible helpfully separates the Prophets from the third great division of the biblical canon—the Writings—this textbook will follow the traditional Jewish arrangement. Thus Ruth (which comes after judges in most Protestant and Roman Catholic Bibles), as well as other nominally historical books like Ezra and Chronicles, will be considered among the Writings, where ancient Jewish editors originally placed them.

The anonymous writers of the 700-year-long period covered in the books of the Former Prophets stress a religious interpretation of the military and political events they record, but they tell us little about the lives and teachings of the great prophets who appeared during this time, with the notable exceptions of Elijah and Elisha. To enable the reader to study the nature, function, and historical development of Israelite prophecy as a coherent unit, our discussion of the prophetic tradition is placed as an introduction to the Latter Prophets, a category designating the prophets whose messages were written down under their own names (see pp. 106–151).

FORMER PROPHETS

The narratives in Joshua through Kings include seven crucial periods or events: (1) the conquest of Canaan under Joshua's leadership; (2) the twelve-tribe confederacy described in Judges; (3) the origin and development of the united monarchy, which reached its apex under David and Solomon in the tenth century B.C.E.; (4) the rebellion of the northern ten tribes after Solomon's death in 922 B.C.E.; (5) the parallel dynastic histories of the divided kingdom, culminating in Assyria's destruction of Israel and its capital, Samaria, in 721 B.C.E.; (6) King Josiah's religious reforms in Judah following 621 B.C.E.; and (7) Babylon's obliteration of Judah and the Jerusalem temple in 587 B.C.E..

These seven developments in the course of seven centuries span the rise and fall of the Israelite state. After the Babylonian captivity, Israel (Judah) was never again an independent power but merely a politically unimportant, though commonly troublesome, province in a larger pagan empire, whether that of Persia, Macedonian Greece, or Rome. Some modern historians think it significant that the long line of Israelite prophets began with Israel's emergence as an autonomous nation and ended with the state's political decline. The Israelites regarded prophecy as having ceased soon after their return from the Babylonian exile (538 B.C.E.). After a new sanctuary was built on the site of Solomon's temple (about 515 B.C.E.) and the priest Ezra brought a reedited version of the Mosaic Torah back from Babylon in the fifth century B.C.E., priestly ritual and authoritative teaching of the Law gradually replaced the prophetic tradition. New prophets comparable to Isaiah or Elijah no longer appeared in Israel. With the demise of prophecy, traditions associated with the ancient prophets became increasingly revered. By about 200 B.C.E. the whole section of the Prophets, including both the historical and the prophetic books, was accepted as part of the Hebrew Bible.

Although the books of the Former Prophets offer an important historical framework for the prophets' activities, today's reader may be disappointed by their many omissions. The unknown authors of Joshua, Judges, Samuel, and Kings were not interested in compiling a complete record of the political, social, economic, cultural, or even religious movements in ancient Israel. They wrote from a deliberately limited viewpoint. Profoundly imbued with the deuteronomic theory of retribution, the writers emphasized that breaking the Mosaic law was inevitably the cause of Israel's political and military misfortunes. The spirit of these narratives is prophetic in its rigorous attribution of Israel's early national achievements to strict observance of the Mosaic Covenant and the nation's ultimate collapse to punishment for disobeying Yahweh. Events that a modern historian would see as resulting from specific economic or military conditions these writers ascribe to Israel's success or failure in pleasing Yahweh.

The anonymous compilers of the Former Prophets are called Deuteronomists because they adopted their religious and historical assumptions from the Book of Deuteronomy (discovered during Josiah's reign in 621 B.C.E.). These writer-editors apparently reworked older material, including oral traditions and records from royal archives, to bring them into conformity with the deuteronomist perspective. Although much material in the books of Samuel—which may date from the tenth century B.C.E.—seems to have been revised only slightly, the deuteronomist hand is heavily felt throughout the rest of the narratives composing the Former Prophets.

The deuteronomist writers are characterized by the following traits: (1) They regard the Yahwist prophets as heroes and present figures such as Elijah and Elisha as champions of religious purity. (2) They treat Jerusalem as preeminent, the only site at which Yahweh accepts the sacrifices mandated by the Mosaic law. Because the northern kingdom (after 721 B.C.E.) maintained various rival sanctuaries, all its kings are uniformly blacklisted. (3) They regard David as the ideal king, the prototype of the godly ruler, against whom his successors are measured and—with the outstanding exceptions of Hezekiah and Josiah—found wanting. The Deuteronomists apparently reedited their material, particularly Joshua, Judges, and Kings, during the Babylonian exile (587–538 B.C.E.). The last event they record is deposed King Jehoiachin's release from a Babylonian prison (2 Kings 25:27–30).

The books of the Former Prophets, then, not only give the historical-theological milieu of the prophetic movement, they also remind the reader that the word of Yahweh was heard in the actions and events that shaped Israel's history. The deuteronomist school firmly believed that Yahweh's intentions were evident not merely through what was truly spoken but through what visibly happened as well, though one had to be spiritually alert to see the significance of events and to recognize the divine hand in them.

RECOMMENDED READING

Fretheim, Terence E. *Deuteronomic History.* Nashville: Abingdon Press, 1983.

Joshua

Invasion and Conquest	*Chapters 2–22*
Farewell Speech and Covenant Renewal	*23–24*

As for me and my house, we will serve Yahweh.

Joshua 24:15

Joshua, the sixth book of the Bible, tells the story of Israel's invasion and occupation of Canaan not as objective history but as seen through the eyes of faith—a divinely supported blitzkrieg, lightning fast and totally successful. While tending to confirm the invasion of Canaan by a culturally inferior people during the thirteenth century B.C.E., archaeological excavations do not present so simple a picture. Diggings at Lachish, Debir, and Hazor prove that these cities were attacked and burned during this period, for over the ruins of a relatively advanced Canaanite civilization have been found the remains of invading tribes, possibly those of the Israelites. According to archaeological dating, however, Jericho was laid waste some two centuries before Joshua's day, as was the nearby city of Ai, whose name means "ruin."

It may be that the embellished attack stories preserved in Joshua belong to an earlier epoch when these cities were sacked by tribes related to the biblical Hebrews. More influential than historical fact, however, is the meaning attached to the conquest narrative. This idealized account could have been the Deuteronomists' way of showing that a nation faithful to its covenant vows would be inevitably victorious, thereby encouraging the seventh- or sixth-century audience to render full allegiance to Yahweh. Jericho's walls fell not by human hand but by Yahweh's might, an unmistakable sign that an obedient Israel was invincible.

Various repetitions, inconsistencies, and contradictions in the text indicate that Joshua, like the Pentateuch, is based on multiple sources. Whereas the J and E traditions in Genesis through Numbers were bound together by P, it is D (the Deuteronomist) who gives Joshua its framework. The book does contain some later P material, primarily in the second half, but it is mainly a product of the deuteronomist schools. Its first edition could therefore not be earlier than the time of Josiah, although the JE elements may belong to the early monarchial period. (As suggested earlier, the J and E narratives may originally have included accounts of the conquest that the P school later deleted. Fragments of the lost JE version may now be embedded in the present books of Joshua-Judges.)

Joshua also contains quotations from poems collected in the now-lost Book of Jashar, some of which may have been contemporaneous with the victories they celebrate. Joshua thus seems to include material spanning a lengthy time period—poetry that was first composed orally during the conquest as well as priestly commentary from the postexilic age.

Invasion and Conquest   In spite of its sometimes confusing story line, Joshua's version of the conquest is exciting. Leader of the united tribes of Israel, Joshua is intentionally presented as a second Moses. Like Moses, he leads the people through parted waters—this time those of the Jordan River, which is held back at floodtide to permit Israel's crossing. Instead of Moses' staff, however, it is the Ark of the Covenant carried by the priests that effects the miracle (Josh. 3–4). Like Moses, too, Joshua experiences a theophany, this time not of Yahweh but of the captain of

Yahweh's invisible armies, which are prepared to annihilate the Canaanite enemy (Josh. 5:13–15). He further resembles the great lawgiver in adding to the Book of the covenant, in proclaiming Yahweh's commandments, and in presiding over a covenant-renewal ceremony at Shechem (Josh. 4:1–9; 23–24).

After entering Canaan, the Israelites do not at once begin their military campaign. Instead, all the males born during the forty-year wandering assemble at Gilgal to be circumcised, an operation that incapacitates them for several days, though the threatened residents of nearby Jericho make no attempt to take advantage of their vulnerability (Josh. 5:1–12). Now ritually acceptable, the warriors still do not immediately attack the Canaanite stronghold but follow Joshua's instructions to march silently around the city seven times until a signal is given, when they are to raise a loud shout, blow their trumpets, and charge Jericho's ramparts (Josh. 6). That is the earlier of two accounts of Jericho's fall that have been woven imperfectly into a single narrative. The second version emphasizes the priests' role in carrying the Ark of the Covenant and sounding ram's-horn trumpets during some thirteen circuits of the town (Josh. 6:4, 8–9, 11–13).

On the final day the city walls collapse except for that part supporting the house of Rahab the harlot (possibly the priestess of a Canaanite fertility cult), who had hidden Israelite spies when they had reconnoitered the city. The entire population is placed under the "sacred ban," which means that the people are massacred as an offering to Yahweh. The Israelites' belief that Yahweh required the deaths of all non-Hebrews in Canaan may shock modern sensibilities, but the concept of holy war plays an important part in the history of many Near Eastern religions.

After the spectacular victory at Jericho, the Israelites suffer a setback at Ai (Josh. 7). Inquiring of Yahweh why his people have been ignominiously routed, Joshua is told that Yahweh was not with them because an Israelite soldier has violated the ban on Jericho by stealing and hiding some booty. Casting lots, Joshua eliminates all citizens except a man named Achan, who admits having taken some of Jericho's valuables for himself. Achan, his wife, children, and flocks are then stoned to death. After they have purged the sinner from their midst, the Israelites easily succeed in capturing Ai (Josh. 8).

The campaign is thereafter an uninterrupted series of Israelite triumphs. All enemies are defeated, including the giant race of Anakim who had intimidated the Israelite spies forty years earlier (Num. 13:33). Thirty-one kings and their armies are vanquished, although large areas, such as the Philistine territory to the southwest, remain unconquered. Joshua divides the conquered country among the twelve tribes (Josh. 13–22), thus bringing to a satisfactory conclusion the first part of Yahweh's plan for the region.

Farewell Speech and Covenant Renewal   Joshua's final speech to the people (Josh. 23–24) is modeled on Moses' farewell address in Deuteronomy, which it resembles in diction, style, and sense of urgency. Like his predecessor, Joshua reminds Israel of her debt to Yahweh and of the people's obligation to obey the law faithfully. Asking them to choose today between Yahweh and the gods their fathers had worshiped beyond the River Euphrates in Mesopotamia, he sets the proper example: "As for me and my house, we will serve Yahweh" (Josh. 24:15).

After reciting the covenant laws before the assembled community at Shechem, Joshua erects a stone pillar to act as witness that the people have heard Yahweh's commandments and have agreed to abide by them. This covenant ceremony (Josh. 24) is regarded as one of the most important passages in the Old Testament, for it embodies an authentic tradition of Israel's earliest reaffirmation in Canaan of the Sinai covenant. It has been suggested that the Israelites held the ceremony at Shechem, which they did not have to fight to possess, because the area—an ancient cult center of Baal Berith ("Lord of the Covenant")—was already occupied by related tribes or at least by a people friendly to the Israelites.

Did these people who worshiped the Canaanite El (to whom Jacob had built an altar nearby) also embrace the Yahwist religion of the new arrivals? Did they agree to accept Yahweh, his mighty acts in Egypt, and the desert experience as part of their own heritage? Some prominent scholars see in the Shechem covenant ceremony an extension of the covenant provisions to kindred tribesmen who had not participated in the exodus experience. If true, this would explain why there is no record of the Israelites' having to struggle for control of the highly desirable Shechem region.

A sixth act to the Pentateuch, Joshua marks the beginning of a historical transition for Israel from a rootless nomadic way of life to a settled agrarian existence. Israel's isolated desert honeymoon with Yahweh is over; now it must attempt to worship him amid the snares and temptations of Canaanite culture. Seen in the context of what was to follow, Joshua's warnings against religious compromise sound with new force.

RECOMMENDED READING

Gottwald, Norman K. *The Tribes of Yahweh: A Sociology of the Religion of Liberated Israel, 1250–1050 B.C.E.* Maryknoll, N. Y.: Orbis Books, 1979.

Kaufmann, Yehezkel. *The Biblical Account of the Conquest of Palestine.* Translated by M. Dagut. Jerusalem: Magnes, 1955.

Kenyon, Kathleen M. *Archaeology in the Holy Land,* 3rd ed. New York: Praeger, 1970. By an authority on the excavations at Jericho.

Soggin, J. Alberto. *Joshua.* Philadelphia: Westminster Press, 1972.

Wright, G. Ernest. *Biblical Archaeology,* 2nd ed. Philadelphia: Westminster Press, 1962. An expert introduction to archaeological discoveries in Palestine, including those relating to the conquest.

🎙 Judges

In those days there was no king in Israel, and every man did as he pleased.

Judges 21:25

Judges is a transitional book covering the period between Joshua's death and the establishment of the monarchy (about 1200–1020 B.C.E.). It contains a double introduction (Judg. 1:1–2:5 and 2:6–3:6, the second a later Judean preface), a central section recounting the exploits of a series of judges who fought Israel's many enemies (Judg. 3–16), and an appendix including miscellaneous anecdotes that could not be fitted into the story of any particular judge (Judg. 17–21). Like Joshua, Judges is a composite work fusing perhaps J and E or other related sources into a deuteronomist framework.

Era of the Judges   Here again Israel's national fortunes are linked to its religious loyalty. When the people worship Yahweh exclusively, they win their battles; when they "prostitute themselves to Baal," they suffer defeat. Those who destroy Baal's altars and sacred poles are praised; those who tolerate Canaanite religion are condemned. Historical movement in Judges is cyclical. When a judge faithful to Yahweh presides, the people overwhelm their enemies and prosper. After the Yahwist judge dies, the people revert to Baal worship, causing Yahweh to desert them and deliver them into their enemies' power. In their anguish, the people cry out to Yahweh, who "feels pity" and raises up a new judge to overthrow the oppressors. After a generation of revived Yahwism, the people again backslide and the whole cycle begins again. (The deuteronomist editors' theology of history is explicitly set forth in Judges 2:11–23.)

The dozen judges who rescue Israel from foreign domination are not judicial figures in the legal sense; they do not preside over a court or usually render verdicts among disputing parties. They are charismatic ("spirit-filled") military leaders who drive off local tribes that repeatedly raid Israel's territory in the Palestinian hill country. In general, the judges did not rule over all twelve Israelite tribes as Joshua, the first judge, is reported to have done. At most, an individual judge can muster support from two or three tribes, sometimes only a clan or two. Thus, the judges did not reign successively over a united Israel, and individual leaders were able to influence only a small portion of the Israelite confederacy, a term some scholars use to describe the extremely loose political structure of Israel in the days before monarchy (kingship) was established. Because some of the judges' administrations may have overlapped, it is difficult to calculate precisely how long this period of Israelite history lasted.

Deborah and Barak   The Bible writers did not regard this, in retrospect, as an admirable era. Not only was Israel repeatedly devastated by enemy attacks and humiliated by the Philistines, but the whole tenor of life was both precarious and savage. Judges 4 records the activities of a celebrated female judge, the prophetess Deborah, and her associate Barak, who commanded 10,000 men against a Canaanite coalition. The completeness of their victory is epitomized by the act of a "mere" woman, Jael, who single-handedly strikes down the fleeing Canaanite general Sisera (Judg. 4:4–22).

Jael's patriotic murder of her foreign guest is commemorated in a long poem (Judg. 5:1–31) that scholars believe to be one of the oldest parts of the Bible. An individual death on behalf of the nation also climaxes the episode involving Jephthah, another military leader who, to repay Yahweh for his victory over the Ammonites, sacrifices his only child, an unnamed daughter (Judg. 11:29–40).

Gideon and Abimelech   Even a basically inspirational story like that of Gideon, who with his band of only 300 men routed the Midianites, is marred by episodes of cruelty (Judg. 6–8). Still worse, however, is the account of Gideon's son Abimelech, who after murdering his seventy brothers, manages to have himself crowned at Shechem, the old sanctuary of the tribal confederacy. Abimelech rules only a few northern clans living near Shechem and his reign lasts only three years, but before he is killed he has tortured, maimed, and slaughtered thousands of his compatriots. The brief reign of Gideon's son vividly illustrates the evils of a despotic kingship and helps to support the antimonarchial view encountered in subsequent books of the Former Prophets.

Samson and Delilah   One of the most vividly remembered of Israel's folk heroes, Samson—famous for his brawn and his riddles—is strangely unlike any of the other judges whose exploits have been recorded. An angel twice foretells his birth to a childless couple who, as divinely instructed, dedicate the child as a Nazirite. As visible signs of their con-

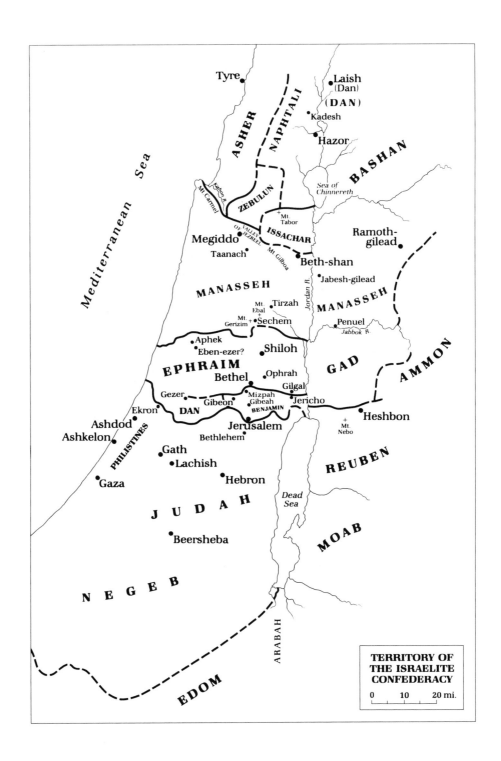

Tyre

Laish
(Dan)
(DAN)

Kadesh

ASHER

NAPHTALI

Hazor

BASHAN

Sea of
Chinnereth

ZEBULUN

Mt.
Tabor

ISSACHAR

Ramoth-
gilead

Megiddo

Mt Carmel

VALLEY
OF
JEZREEL

Mt Gilboa

Beth-shan

Taanach

Jabesh-gilead

Jordan R.

MANASSEH

MANASSEH

Mt.
Ebal

Tirzah

Mt.
Gerizim

Sechem

Penuel

Jabbok R.

Aphek

Eben-ezer?

Shiloh

EPHRAIM

Ophrah

GAD

AMMON

Bethel

Gilgal

Gezer

Mizpah

Gibeah

Jericho

Gibeon

BENJAMIN

DAN

Ekron

Jerusalem

Heshbon

Ashdod

Mt.
Nebo

Ashkelon

PHILISTINES

Bethlehem

Gath

REUBEN

Lachish

Gaza

Hebron

Dead
Sea

JUDAH

Beersheba

MOAB

NEGEB

ARABAH

EDOM

Mediterranean Sea

Kishon R.

**TERRITORY OF
THE ISRAELITE
CONFEDERACY**

0   10   20 mi.

secration to Yahweh, Nazirites were to abstain from wine and other alcoholic drinks, eat only ritually "clean" foods, and leave their hair uncut. A man of strong passions as well as superhuman physical strength, Samson is Yahweh's very human instrument chosen to humiliate the Philistines. The Philistines, a seafaring people who then occupied the southwest coast of Palestine, had already mastered the techniques of manufacturing iron weapons and horse-drawn war chariots—skills the Israelites apparently lacked—and they threatened to overwhelm Yahweh's people.

Unlike Gideon or Jephthah, Samson does not lead an army against the enemy but fights the Philistines single-handedly, typically for personal reasons involving his relationships with women. Samson's sexual affairs, whether with wife or harlot, repeatedly involve him in dangerous confrontations with the enemy (Judg. 14:1–15:8; 16:1–3). The hero's most celebrated entanglement is with Delilah, whom the Philistines bribe to betray her hitherto invulnerable lover. Breaking his Nazirite vow by revealing the secret of his strength, Samson, shorn of his hair, is abandoned by Yahweh to be captured, blinded, and enslaved. Only when his hair begins to grow again does Yahweh's spirit return, allowing Samson a final revenge on his tormentors by pulling down the temple of Dagon upon 3,000 Philistine idolators, so that "those he killed at his death outnumbered those he had killed in his life" (Judg. 16:30).

Some critics regard Samson, whose name means "sun" or "solar," as a mythological figure whom a Hebrew writer transformed into an Israelite champion. This view, however, overlooks Samson's thematic significance. Despite his flaws, Samson reveals a profound concern for his Nazirite vows and devotion to Yahweh. His rejection by his fellow Israelites, who fail to perceive him as Yahweh's chosen one (Judg. 15:9–20), and his sacrificial death while toppling the house of a false god, link him with other heroes of faith such as the suffering servant of Isaiah 53.

The War Against Benjamin   The deuteronomist editors reserved the most barbarous narrative in Judges for the conclusion. Chapters 19–21 describe the rape-murder by the Benjaminites of a Levite priest's concubine, whose body the Levite cuts into eleven pieces and sends to eleven Israelite tribes, asking them to avenge the atrocity by declaring holy war on the Benjaminites. The tribe of Benjamin is thereafter almost totally exterminated. Having sworn never to marry their own daughters to any Benjaminite, the other tribes conspire to get around their vow by encouraging the few surviving men of Benjamin to kidnap the women of Shiloh. In this way the nearly extinct Benjaminites can recruit mates from fellow Israelites without the other tribes' breaking their oaths. Like the sorry tale of Abimelech, this episode may at one time have served an antimonarchial purpose, for Israel's first king, Saul, was both a failure and a Benjaminite, the scion of a tainted group.

Apparently shocked at the social and moral disorders he transcribed, Judges' editor could not resist penning a final disapproving comment: "In those days there was no king in Israel, and every man did as he pleased." Compared with this anarchy, the monarchy with its centralized government seemed a decided improvement.

RECOMMENDED READING

Albright, William F. *Yahweh and the Gods of Canaan: A Historical Analysis of Two Contrasting Faiths.* Garden City, N. Y.: Doubleday Anchor Books, 1969.

Boling, Robert G. *Judges.* Garden City, N. Y.: Doubleday, 1975.

Cross, Frank Moore. *Canaanite Myth and Hebrew Epic, Essays in the History of the Religion of Israel.* Cambridge, Mass.: Harvard University Press, 1973.

de Vaux, Roland. *The Early History of Israel.* Translated by D. Smith. Philadelphia: Westminster Press, 1978.

Fretheim, Terrence E. *Deuteronomic History.* Nashville: Abingdon Press, 1983.

❦ 1 Samuel

Israel's Last Judge	*Chapters 1–7*
Samuel and Saul	*8–15*
Saul and David	*16–31*

It is not you they have rejected; they have rejected me [Yahweh] from ruling over them.

1 Samuel 8:8

In Hebrew, which was originally written without vowels, the Book of Samuel was contained on a single scroll. In Greek, however, the book required two scrolls, and the Septuagint translators therefore divided the work into 1 and 2 Samuel. Although combining diverse sources, the books are masterpieces of historical narration. Long before Herodotus and Thucydides "invented" historical analysis, the Hebrew writer(s) of Samuel produced a history in which vivid characterization, grasp of events, psychological insight, and uncompromising honesty far surpassed the achievements of any contemporary historian.

Source critics have speculated that the several documents or oral traditions woven into Samuel include (1) a recounting of Samuel's infancy, (2) a history of the Ark of the Covenant, (3) a history of the monarchy favoring its establishment, (4) a deuteronomic history unfavorable to the monarchy, and (5) a hypothetical court history of David's reign on which 2 Samuel 9–20 and 1 Kings 1–2 were based.

Other experts have argued that much of Samuel was derived from circles that produced the J and E sources for the Pentateuch and that the resultant book was later slightly revised by the deuteronomist school. Still others believe that, though incorporating a variety of sources, Samuel was essentially complete before the deuteronomic reform. Certainly the book includes poems of great antiquity, such as the Song of Hannah (1 Sam. 2:1–10), David's lament over Saul and Jonathan (2 Sam. 1:19–27), David's lament over Abner (2 Sam. 3:33 ff.), and the Hymn of David (2 Sam. 22).

Although named after Samuel, the first major character to appear in the book, 1 Samuel is really David's story and that of the monarchy he founded. But there is no servile flattery such as is found in other Eastern dynastic histories. The court history is justly admired for its clear-sighted candor in recording the human weaknesses and flaws of one who was already a national hero. On comparing Samuel's portrait of David, with his admixture of courage, ambition, calculation, and religious fervor, with the idealized version in 1 Chronicles, Samuel's accuracy and reliability are immediately obvious.

Israel's Last Judge   Chapters 1–7 of 1 Samuel concern the career of Samuel, who is not only the last of Israel's judges but a prophet as well and whose moral stature and influence are so great that he can make and unmake Israel's first kings. The account of Samuel's early life is skillfully interwoven with a concise survey of Israel's political and religious situation, which is now even worse than that described in Judges.

The high priesthood, represented by the aged Eli, is impotent. The Philistines not only defeat the Hebrew armies but capture the Ark of the Covenant, the portable shrine on which Yahweh is invisibly enthroned. The loss of this most sacred possession is a terrible blow to Israel's prestige. Its capture does not long benefit the superstitious Philistines, however, who attribute both the toppling of Dagon's statue and a plague of tumors to the Ark's malignant presence among them. Although a twenty-year peace ensues following the Ark's return to Israel, continued Philistine hostility denies the Hebrews any real security.

Samuel and Saul   Israel is thus precariously situated when the people demand that Samuel, now old and without a worthy successor, appoint them a king. Although no higher motive is assigned their request than a desire to "be like the other nations" (1 Sam. 8:19), it must have been evident to realistic tribal leaders that national survival demanded the national unity that only an able king could give. A loose tribal confederacy and uncooperative individualism were neither organized nor efficient enough to meet the current military crisis.

Samuel, however, represents the conservative viewpoint, which argued that establishing a monarchy was tantamount to rejecting Yahweh's theocratic rule. He warns the people that a king will burden them with taxes, forced labor, military conscription, and outright confiscation of their best property (1 Sam. 8:10–22). But when the people insist, he privately anoints Saul (about 1020–1000 B.C.E.), an obscure member of the tribe of Benjamin (1 Sam. 9:14–10:8). (Note the second account of Saul's being chosen king in 1 Sam. 10:17–27.)

The choice is logical, for Saul, tall and handsome, looks like a leader, and his tribe is so small and politically insignificant that it does not arouse the jealousy of others. Nonetheless, Samuel proves a severe critic of his king. After Saul offends him by officiating at a sacrifice (1 Sam. 13:8–15) and by sparing the life of Agag, an Amalekite king (whom Samuel proceeds to butcher himself), the judge withdraws his support, in effect excommunicating Saul (1 Sam. 15:10–35). His support eroding, suffering from epilepsy and extreme depression, Saul declines into paranoia. His prestige wanes further when the Philistines again take the initiative.

Saul and David   At this point David, the charismatic youth destined to replace Saul as king, not only makes his appearance but is introduced twice. In the first version (1 Sam. 16), he comes to Saul's court as a musician to charm away the evil spirits with which Yahweh is afflicting the king. In the second (1 Sam. 17), he reenters the picture to accept the challenge of Goliath, the Philistine champion, to single combat. Otherwise unarmed, David fells Goliath with a stone from his slingshot. He also immediately attracts the devotion of Saul's heir, Jonathan, and arouses the king's envy (1 Sam. 17:1–18:5). After the Israelite women indiscreetly sing, "Saul has killed his thousands, and David his tens of thousands," Saul jealously plans to eliminate his rival by having him lead attacks against the Philistines.

Blessed with the ability to command loyalty, David uses Jonathan's friendship as well as the love of Saul's daughter Mical, whom he marries, to elude the king's several attempts to murder him. Finally, however, David is forced to flee Israel and take refuge among the Philistines, upon whose king he also lavishes his abundant powers of deception (1 Sam. 18:6–19:16). Secretly anointed king of the tribe of Judah by Samuel (1 Sam. 16:2), David survives by his wits, eluding capture and twice refusing to kill Saul when he has the opportunity to do so. His restraint is well repaid, for when the Philistines eliminate Saul and Jonathan at the Battle of Gilboa the way is open for David (about 1000–961 B.C.E.) to ascend the throne (1 Sam. 31).

🌢 2 Samuel

Your House [the Davidic dynasty] and your sovereignty will . . . be established forever.

2 Samuel 7:16

Reign over Judah and Israel Since 1 and 2 Samuel were originally one book, there is no true break in the narrative between the two histories. 2 Samuel begins with David's exquisite lament over Saul and Jonathan, whose love for him had been "more wonderful than the love of a woman" (2 Sam. 1:26). He is then anointed king over his own tribe of Judah; but Saul's surviving son, Ishbaal, retains the loyalty of the northern tribes, and not until he is murdered is David proclaimed king over all Israel.

One of David's early exploits is to capture the Jebusite city of Jerusalem. On the border between the territories of Judah and Benjamin, this neutral settlement, which has long been a Canaanite religious sanctuary (Gen. 14:18–24), was an ideal administrative center. But by bringing the Ark of the Covenant to Jerusalem, David makes his capital the religious as well as the political center of the twelve-tribe nation.

An able executive and military strategist, David rapidly expands Israel's boundaries so that they include the farthest reaches of the land promised to Abraham nearly a millennium before. At its greatest extent, David's empire stretched from the Euphrates River in the northeast to the frontiers of Egypt in the south. The Philistines are totally routed and the other Canaanites either driven out or permanently subdued. Seldom does a single person so quickly transform the fortunes of a country, and it is not surprising that in ages to come, when Israel had fallen far short of Davidic splendor, popular memories concerning this "lion of Judah" would shape the people's messianic hopes. The Lord's Anointed or Messiah—a term applied to *all* Davidic rulers—was to be one like David, beloved of Yahweh, a conquering hero, a savior of the people.

Davidic Covenant The fourth and last Old Testament covenant, promulgated in 2 Samuel 7:12–16 by the prophet Nathan, emphasizes Yahweh's special relationship with David, for Yahweh promises unconditionally to maintain a direct descendant of David on Israel's throne forever. (See "The Davidic Covenant," pp. 94–95.)

Yahweh's oath to preserve the Davidic dynasty, and by implication Jerusalem as well, eventually led to a popular belief in the invincibility of the holy city, an assumption later championed by Isaiah of Jerusalem (Isa. 28:16; 29:5–8; 30:15; 36–37) and still later violently denounced by Jeremiah (Jer. 7 and 26). After the Babylonians deposed Zedekiah, the last Davidic king, in 587 B.C.E., the David-Zion Covenant was interpreted as applying to a future "son of David," the Messiah, who would restore his predecessor's kingdom.

David and Bathsheba   The Succession Narrative, which was perhaps based on eyewitness reports and written during Solomon's reign, is contained in 2 Samuel 9–20 and 1 Kings 1–2. This contemporary account portrays the king realistically, faithfully recording his sins as well as his military and political accomplishments. An episode that reveals much about David's complex psychology concerns his adultery with Bathsheba, the wife of Uriah the Hittite, one of David's hired soldiers.

On learning that Bathsheba is carrying his child, David cunningly orders Uriah into the front lines of battle, where he is betrayed and killed (2 Sam. 11:2–27). In any kingdom other than theocratic Israel, the matter would have ended there; the monarch would have satisfied his lust, and no one would have dared to protest. To the prophet Nathan, however, not even the king is above Yahweh's law. Appearing one day in court, he tells David of a rich man with many flocks who took the one lamb of a poor man and killed it. Indignant, David denounces the rich man for his greed and lack of compassion. "You," Nathan answers, "are the man" (2 Sam. 12:1–15).

Perhaps in no other Near Eastern country would Nathan have escaped death after such an accusation. David, however, humbly acknowledges his guilt and repents. As the prophet observes, he cannot escape Yahweh's judgment, which decrees the death of Bathsheba's child and augurs a future of strife and treachery in David's own household. In his old age, David's reign is marred by several revolts, including one led by his son Absalom, who attempts to usurp his throne. David is forced to flee from his palace and does not return until after Absalom's death (2 Sam. 13–18). Thus are Nathan's prophetic words fulfilled.

Appendices   The appendices attached to 2 Samuel preserve six incidents that have not been chronologically integrated into the main story, of which the most interesting for their theological views are the first and last additions. In the first (2 Sam. 21), a three-year famine, conveniently interpreted as a sign of divine wrath against Saul's family, gives David an

❦ The Davidic Covenant

In biblical order, the fourth and last major covenant is Yahweh's promise to David to keep David's heirs on the throne of Israel "forever." In the earliest form of the covenant (2 Sam. 7:8–17), Yahweh states that he may punish Israel's disobedient kings but that he will not withdraw his favor from the Davidic rulers as he had from Saul, David's predecessor. Through the prophet Samuel, David is told unequivocally, "Your house [royal dynasty] and your sovereignty will always stand secure before me [Yahweh] and your throne be established forever."

Confidence that Yahweh would honor the pledge to maintain the Davidic dynasty in perpetuity helps to explain the uninterrupted succession of Davidic rulers who reigned in Jerusalem for more than four centuries. Whereas the northern kingdom of Israel (formed about 922 B.C.E.) was repeatedly wracked by violent changes of ruling dynasties, the southern kingdom of Judah remained loyal to David's "house." This remarkable political stability was due largely to the dynastic covenant theology.

Each Davidic king was Yahweh's *messiah* (Hebrew, *mashiach* or "anointed one"), consecrated with holy oil at his coronation and regarded as the "chosen one" of Israel (Pss. 2; 18; 20; 110; 132). After the last reigning Davidic ruler, Zedekiah, was deposed and killed in 587 B.C.E., some Bible writers, particularly the deuteronomist school, reinterpreted the original agreement in terms of the *Moses-Sinai concept* of a covenant,

which made divine favor dependent upon strict obedience to Yahweh's law (1 Kings 2:4; 3:14–15; 6:12–14; 11:30–39, etc.). Thus the fall of David's house to the superior might of Babylon's King Nebuchadnezzar was seen as the justifiable consequence of disobedient Davidic kings like Manasseh (2 Kings 23:26–27).

Other Bible writers rejected the deuteronomist view expressed in Kings and insisted that the promise to David's dynasty was *unconditional* as stated in 2 Samuel (7:13–16 and 23:1–5). The author of Psalm 89 bitterly laments that the Davidic Covenant had been abrogated, not by faithless kings but by Yahweh's incomprehensible actions in allowing Israel's humiliating defeat (Ps. 89:19–51). By contrast, the prophet Jeremiah used the form of a covenant lawsuit to stress his perception that Israel deserved her fate for having broken the Sinai agreement (Jer. 2:2–37; 5:1–25; 11:1–17, etc.).

After the restoration from the Babylonian captivity (587–538 B.C.E.), the author of Chronicles rewrote the history of the Davidic monarchy, emphasizing David's role in establishing the priestly Ark of the Covenant in Zion, the holy mountain in Jerusalem. The close association of the priestly temple cult and royal family in Jerusalem (2 Sam. 6–7; 1 Kings 5–9; Ps. 132) had undoubtedly helped to strengthen the Davidic dynasty during its days of power. When the monarchy ceased to exist, king and court were replaced by priestly leaders. Although the postexilic temple was no longer a royal shrine, it remained the center of the national religion and provided a link with the monarchial past (Haggai 1–2; Zech. 3–4; 1 Chron. 13; 15–17; 21–29; 2 Chron. 1–8; 24–28; 34–38; 36:22–23).

The Chronicler and other late writers, accepting Yahweh's will in thus extinguishing the Davidic kingship, were consoled with the rule of a priestly theocracy. Others began to apply the old prophetic promises made to David and his house (Isa. 7; 9; 11; Pss. 2; 110, etc.) to a future royal prince who would restore the Davidic sovereignty as a political reality. Conceived as a conquering warrior like David before him, this future hero would be Yahweh's ultimate Anointed One. Hope for the restoration of David's royal line in Judah eventually led to keen expectations of a messiah who would revitalize Yahweh's people and lead them to triumph over their enemies.

---

excuse to eliminate Saul's seven surviving sons, obvious rallying points for future revolts, whom he delivers to their old enemies the Gibeonites for impalement.

The last supplement (2 Sam. 24) presents Yahweh inciting David to take a census of the people, which act the god then punishes by sending a pestilence that ravages 70,000 Israelites. (Apparently noting the illogic of such divine capriciousness, the Chronicler later revised the story to make "Satan" give David the idea of conducting a census, a move highly unpopular among the people because the population was numbered mainly for purposes of taxation and military conscription [1 Chron. 21]). On the advice of the prophet Gad, David buys a threshing floor and erects upon it an altar to Yahweh. Perhaps because it is built on the site of the future temple, his offerings stop the epidemic. Thus consistent with his general character, David is both the cause of his people's trouble and the instrument of its cure. On this note 2 Samuel rather inconclusively ends.

RECOMMENDED READING

Clements, Roland. *Abraham and David, Studies in Biblical Theology,* 2nd ser., no. 5. Naperville, Ill.: Alec R. Allenson, 1967.

Cross, Frank M. "The Ideologies of Kingship in the Era of the Empire: Conditional Covenant and Eternal Decree." In *Canaanite Myth and Hebrew Epic: Essays in the History of the Religion of Israel.* Cambridge, Mass.: Harvard University Press, 1973.

Hertzberg, H. W. *The Books of Samuel.* Translated by J. S. Bowden. Philadelphia: Westminster Press, 1964.

Hillers, Delbert R. *Covenant: The History of a Biblical Idea.* Baltimore: Johns Hopkins University Press, 1969.

Landay, Jerry M. *The House of David.* New York: Saturday Review Press/E. P. Dutton, 1973.

Maly, Eugene H. *The World of David and Solomon.* Englewood Cliffs, N. J.: Prentice-Hall, 1976.

von Rad, Gerhard. *Old Testament Theology.* Vol. I, *The Theology of Israel's Historical Traditions.* Translated by D. M. G. Stalker. New York: Harper & Brothers, 1962.

Whybray, R. N. *The Succession Narrative: A Study of II Samuel 9–20; I Kings 1 and 2, Studies in Biblical Theology,* 2nd ser., no. 9, 1968.

ꙮ 1 Kings

Solomon's Succession and Reign	*Chapters 1–11*
The Great Schism	*12–13*
Elijah and King Ahab	*17–19; 21–22*

I consecrate this house you [Solomon] have built;
I place my name there forever.

1 Kings 9:3

Like the books of Samuel, 1 and 2 Kings were originally a single work that the Septuagint translators later divided into two parts. Together these volumes carry the history of Israel from the death of King David to the fall of Jerusalem and the Babylonian captivity (587 B.C.E.). As might be expected, the books are based on a number of older sources, including court records and traditional material concerning the prophets Elijah and Elisha. They also refer frequently to the Book of the Annals of Israel and the Book of the Annals of Judah, two dynastic histories that have since been lost. These sources were rigorously edited and reshaped to conform to the theological viewpoint of the deuteronomist historians, who produced the first version of Kings after Josiah's religious reforms late in the seventh century B.C.E. It may be that the first edition of the D history was issued to help justify and support Josiah's policies and that a second edition was prepared during or after the exile to explain why Yahweh had permitted Jerusalem's destruction.

Here, even more than in Judges and Samuel, the deuteronomic standard of obedience to the law is rigidly applied. A king who permits sacrifice only at Solomon's temple is praised; one who allows sacrifice at any of the shrines outside the holy city is condemned. No other accomplishments, no matter how politically or economically beneficial, can wring a word of approbation from the Deuteronomists. Modern historians lament that 1 and 2 Kings omit so much vital information about the various reigns. But the deuteronomist writers were not concerned about presenting a complete view of their subject; they were interested exclusively in determining why Yahweh permitted Babylon, a pagan empire, to overthrow David's royal line and destroy the temple.

Solomon's Succession and Reign (about 961–922 B.C.E.)   1 Kings opens with an account of King David's last days and Bathsheba's behind-the-scenes plotting to have her son, Solomon, rather than David's older son, Adonijah, succeed to the throne. (The story of Solomon's succession is probably based on the same court history that underlies 2 Sam. 9–20.) On his deathbed David reminds Solomon that although he has promised to spare those of his enemies who are still alive, his successor is bound by no such vow. Solomon accordingly consolidates his power by murdering Adonijah and numerous others who might threaten the security of his crown. In a special blessing, Yahweh then grants him "a discerning judgment" and a heart "wise and shrewd" (1 Kings 3:4–15), so that he soon earns international fame for the astuteness of his policies (1 Kings 3–11).

Solomon's extensive building program includes erecting a magnificent royal palace with a special mansion for his most important wife, the daughter of pharaoh, with whom he has concluded a political alliance. In erecting a temple in Jerusalem to house the Ark of the Covenant, thus further centralizing the national religion in his capital city (1 Kings 5–7), he also allies Israel with Phoenicia by importing numerous planners, architects, and craftspeople capable of executing his ambitious designs. Public dedication ceremonies at the new temple, which is built on the model of a Phoenician sanctuary, are the highlight of Solomon's reign (1 Kings 8).

In a cloud reminiscent of that which led Israel through the wilderness, Yahweh accepts the temple as his earthly dwelling place, although Solomon acknowledges that heaven itself cannot contain the god's true majesty, much less the house he has built. (Interestingly, it is the king rather than the Levitical priests or sons of Aaron who officiates at the temple inaugural.) Yahweh then reaffirms the covenant by which he had promised to keep David's heirs reigning in Jerusalem forever (1 Kings 9:1–9), though, unlike the original covenant terms in 2 Samuel 7:12–26, these are conditional upon the royal line's unfailing obedience to Yahweh. This loophole is given to clear the way for Yahweh's permitting the Davidic dynasty to end.

After an admiring survey of Solomon's unparalleled wealth, fame, military and diplomatic prowess (1 Kings 10), the Deuteronomist concludes his evaluation of the reign by criticizing Solomon's numerous marriages to foreign women, whom he blames for seducing the king into idolatry. Out of respect for David, Solomon is allowed to die peacefully (922 B.C.E.), but the kingdom is to be stripped from his heirs (1 Kings 11).

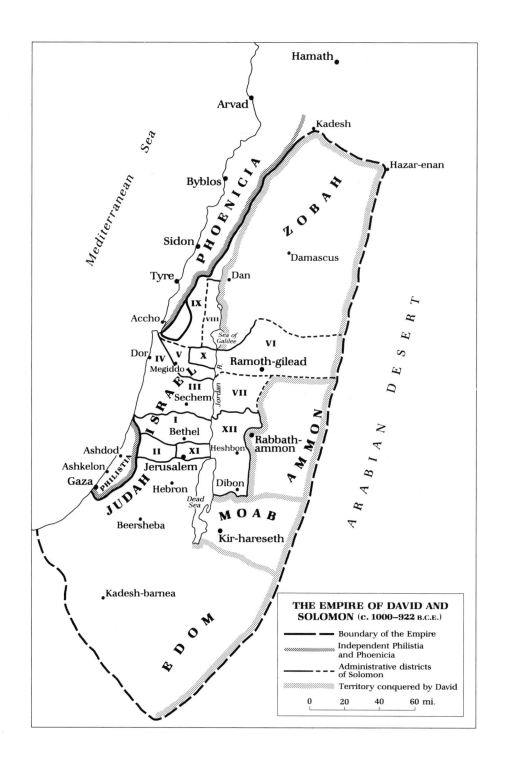

THE EMPIRE OF DAVID AND
SOLOMON (c. 1000–922 B.C.E.)

— — — Boundary of the Empire

Independent Philistia
and Phoenicia

– – – Administrative districts
of Solomon

Territory conquered by David

0   20   40   60 mi.

The Great Schism   Rehoboam (922–915 B.C.E.), Solomon's successor, foolishly refuses to lighten the heavy burden of taxes and forced labor which Solomon's building projects have placed on the people (1 Kings 12), and his rejection of the northern tribes' plea for a more humane administration sparks a widespread revolt against the House of David. The ten northern tribes withdraw from the monarchy and form their own kingdom, to be called Israel:

> What share have we in David?
> We have no inheritance in the son of Jesse!
>
> 1 Kings 12:16

Remaining faithful to the Davidic rulers, the southern tribes of Judah and Benjamin form the smaller and poorer Kingdom of Judah with its capital at Jerusalem.

Hereafter Kings will record the history of a divided kingdom, alternately describing reigns in the northern kingdom and then events in Judah. (See Table 4-1.) This jumping back and forth, coupled with a monotonous emphasis on obedience to the law, makes some of Kings rather turgid reading, although royal conflicts with certain prophets considerably enliven parts of the narrative.

The rebel leader Jeroboam, the first king of northern Israel (about 922–901 B.C.E.), sets up rival sanctuaries at Bethel and Dan, where he erects two golden calves, probably as pedestals for the invisibly enthroned Yahweh (1 Kings 12–13); indeed, most of the northern monarchs make some effort to follow the Mosaic faith. While the southern nation of Judah, ruled by an unbroken succession of Davidic kings, maintains relative stability, however, the northern kingdom suffers repeated overthrows of its kings, none of whom is able to establish a dynasty as enduring as David's. Since the history is told from a disapproving southern (Judean) viewpoint, even Omri (876–869 B.C.E.), one of Israel's most effective rulers, is accorded only a few lines (1 Kings 16:23–24), although long after his dynasty had fallen the emperors of Assyria still referred to Israel as "the land of Omri."

Elijah and King Ahab (869–850 B.C.E.)   Considerably more space is allotted to the misdeeds of Omri's successor, King Ahab (1 Kings 17–22), who is married to the notorious Jezebel, daughter of the king of Tyre. Ahab's endorsement of Baal worship brings him into confrontation with the most formidable prophet that Israel has yet produced, Elijah the Tishbite, who stages a contest between Yahweh and Baal on Mount Carmel near the Mediterranean coast (1 Kings 18). In spite of their ritual antics, the Canaanite priests fail to arouse Baal to action, but Elijah's god sends fire from heaven, consuming the offered sacrifice. Triumphant, Elijah slaughters the priests of Baal and announces that Yahweh is ending the long drought that has afflicted Israel.

TABLE 4-1 Events and Rulers in the Divided Kingdom

Approximate Date B.C.E.	Mesopotamia and Egypt	Israel	Judah	Hebrew Prophets
900	Twenty-second Dynasty of Egypt (935–725) Pharaoh Shishak invades Palestine (c. 918)	Jeroboam I (922–901) Nadab (901–900) Baasha (900–877) Elah (877–876) Zimri (876) Omri (876–869)	Rehoboam (922–915) Abijah (915–913) Asa (913–873) Jehoshaphat (873–849)	Elijah (Israel)
850	Shalmaneser III (859–825) of Assyria Battle of Qarqar (853) Hazael of Syria (842–806)	Ahab (869–850) Ahaziah (850–849) Jehoram (849–842) Jehu's Revolt (842) Jehu (842–815)	Jehoram (849–842) Ahaziah (842) Athaliah (842–837) Joash (837–800)	Elisha (Israel)
800		Jehoahaz (815–801) Jehoash (801–786) Jeroboam II (786–746)	Amaziah (800–783) Uzziah (783–742)	
750	Tiglath-pileser of Assyria (745–727) Shalmaneser V (726–722)	Zechariah (746–745) Shallum (745) Menahem (745–738) Pekahiah (738–737) Pekah (737–732) Hoshea (732–724)	Jotham (742–735) Ahaz (735–715)	Amos (Israel) Hosea (Israel) Isaiah (Judah) Micah (Judah)

Date	Egypt / Assyria / Babylon	Israel & Judah	Kings of Judah	Prophets
725	Twenty-fourth Egyptian Dynasty (725–709)	Fall of Israel (722/721)	Hezekiah (715–667)	
	Sargon II of Assyria (721–705)			
	Twenty-fifth Egyptian Dynasty (716–663)			
700	Sennacherib (704–681)			
	Assyrian invasion of Judah (701)			
	Esarhaddon of Assyria (681–669)		Manasseh (687–642)	
	Ashurbanipal (668–627)			
650	Twenty-sixth Egyptian Dynasty (664–525)		Amon (642–640)	Jeremiah
			Josiah (640–609)	
			Deuteronomic reforms (621 and following)	Zephaniah
				Nahum
600	Fall of Nineveh (612)		Jehoahaz (609)	
	Pharaoh Necho (610–594)		Jehoiakim (609–598/97)	
	Battle of Carchemish (605)		Jehoiachin (598/97)	Habakkuk
	Growth of Neo-Babylonian Empire under Nebuchadnezzar (605–562)		First Babylonian sack of Jerusalem (598/597)	
			Zedekiah (597–587)	Ezekiel
			Fall of Jerusalem (587)	Jeremiah taken to Egypt
			Babylonian captivity (587–538)	

SOURCE: In general, this table follows the dates derived from W. F. Albright, *Bulletin of the American School of Oriental Research*, no. 100 (December 1945); and adopted by John Bright, *A History of Israel* (Philadelphia: Westminster Press, 1972), pp. 480–81.

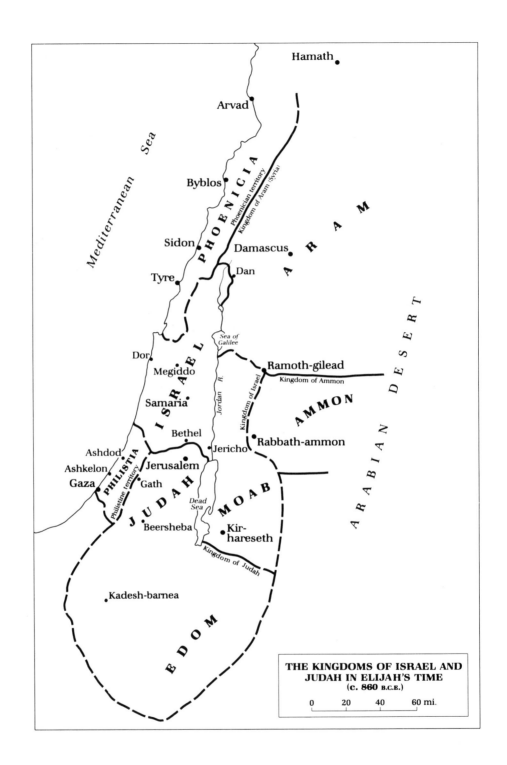

THE KINGDOMS OF ISRAEL AND
JUDAH IN ELIJAH'S TIME
(c. 860 B.C.E.)

0   20   40   60 mi.

Driven from his homeland under Jezebel's threat of execution, the solitary prophet—who believes himself to be the only one alive still faithful to Yahweh—retreats to the desert origin of his faith, Horeb (Mount Sinai). Hidden in the same rocky cleft that had once sheltered Moses, Elijah, too, encounters Yahweh—not in wind, earthquake, fire, or other spectacular phenomena but in "a gentle breeze," or in more familiar translation "a still small voice" (1 Kings 19:9–18).

The narrative then shifts to Ahab's unlawful coveting of Naboth's vineyard, which Jezebel obtains for him by falsely accusing Naboth of blasphemy (1 Kings 21).

After the unfortunate Naboth has been stoned in accordance with Mosaic law, Elijah appears and pronounces doom upon Ahab and his descendants, who are to be exterminated. Like King David before him, Ahab admits his sin and repents, thus causing Yahweh to delay his punishment, though shortly afterward he is killed at the Battle of Ramoth-gilead (1 Kings 22). The book closes with brief summaries of the reigns of Ahab's ally, Jehoshaphat, king of Judah (873–849 B.C.E.), and Ahab's son, Ahaziah of Israel, who ruled only two years (850–849 B.C.E.).

☙ 2 Kings

No king before him [Josiah] had turned to Yahweh as he did, with all his heart . . . in perfect loyalty to the Law of Moses; nor was any king like him seen again. Yet Yahweh did not renounce the heat of his great anger which blazed out against Judah.

2 Kings 23:25–26

Elisha and Jehu   The history of Israelite and Judean rulers continues uninterrupted in 2 Kings. After reporting Ahaziah's death in chapter 1, the historian returns in chapters 2–8 to the Elijah-Elisha prophetic cycle. When Elijah, the archetypal man of God, is carried to heaven in a fiery chariot and whirlwind, he leaves his prophetic cloak behind for his disciple Elisha, whose reported miracles are even more numerous and spectacular than those of his predecessor. In the course of his career Elisha causes an iron axhead to float on water, a child to rise from the dead, jars of oil to fill magically, poisoned soup to become edible, twenty barley loaves to feed a hundred men, and lepers to be cleansed, in addition to foretelling droughts, famines, victories, and deaths.

The prophet's political influence is equally impressive. Through a messenger, Elisha secretly anoints Jehu, a former captain of Ahab's guard, king of Israel, and Jehu, supported by the army, plunges the nation into a bloodbath (2 Kings 9–10). Citing Elijah's curse on Ahab's house, Jehu massacres all of Ahab's surviving sons, grandsons, friends, priests, administrators, and political supporters, totally annihilating his dynasty. With Jehonadab, a Yahwist fanatic, Jehu then assembles all Baal worshipers in the great temple that Ahab had built in Samaria, the capital city, and after offering sacrifice to Baal, orders eighty trusted executioners to butcher everyone inside. The temple is demolished and its site turned into a public latrine.

For all his savage intolerance, however, even Jehu does not entirely win the Deuteronomists' approval. In neglecting to remove Jeroboam's golden calves from Bethel and Dan, he did not serve Yahweh wholeheartedly. Nor was Jehu an effective king: his purges and massacres may have pleased some Yahwists, but he so depleted the nation's supply of trained and competent leaders that Israel rapidly lost territory on every side. When Jehu (842–815 B.C.E.) died after a reign of twenty-eight years (of which only the violent first year is described in Kings), he left Israel politically weak, without allies, and considerably smaller in size than it had been under Omri and Ahab (2 Kings 10:32–35).

Assyria and Judah   Although the northern kingdom enjoyed renewed prosperity under such kings as Jeroboam II (786–746 B.C.E.), revolution and violent changes of rulership continued to undermine Israelite strength; while after centuries of relative stasis, Assyria was now once again on the march, swallowing up kingdoms and peoples as it expanded. Assyria's territorial encroachments and increasing demands for tribute culminated in the siege of Samaria, which fell to Sargon II in 721 B.C.E. Since it was Assyria's policy to deport defeated populations to discourage future rebellions, the ten northern tribes were forcibly relocated elsewhere in the Assyrian Empire and new people were moved into Israelite territory.

Chapter 17 describes a plague of lions that afflicted the resettled foreigners until a priest of Yahweh was brought back from exile to teach them the proper ritual to pacify the god of the land. This passage is intended to explain how the northern Israelites came to be "lost tribes"; its biased account of the origin of the Samaritans, an ethnically mixed group that practiced a form of the Jewish religion, is of doubtful historical value. Despised by the "true" Jews of Judah, the Samaritans were uncharitably regarded as foreign corrupters of the faith—a hostility still current in New Testament times, when Jesus probably shocked his Jewish audience by making a Samaritan the moral hero of one of his parables.

The remainder of 2 Kings concerns the last years of the Kingdom of Judah (2 Kings 18–24). Sennacherib (704–681 B.C.E.), the Assyrian emperor, lays waste the Judean countryside and surrounds Jerusalem, though he unexpectedly does not capture the holy city. According to 2 Kings and a parallel account in Isaiah 36–37, Yahweh's Angel of Death strikes down 185,000 Assyrian soldiers, forcing Sennacherib to lift his siege and return to Nineveh, the Assyrian capital. This account has some confirmation from nonbiblical sources, including the Greek historian Herodotus, but the exact nature of Jerusalem's deliverance is not clear. At all events, the surprising escape contributed to the popular idea that Jerusalem, site of Yahweh's temple, could not fall, an idea that the prophet Jeremiah would later attack vigorously.

Following the religiously satisfactory reign of Hezekiah (715–686 B.C.E.) comes that of Manasseh (687–642 B.C.E.), whom the Deuteronomists judge to be the worst king in Judah's history (2 Kings 21) and whose sins they regard as so heinous that they attribute Jerusalem's final destruction to them (2 Kings 23:26–27). In spite of his pro-Assyrian policies, his idolatries, his dabbling in witchcraft and black magic, however, Manasseh rules for forty-two years, longer than any other Davidic monarch, and dies peacefully in his bed.

Josiah's Reforms   In the course of making temple repairs, which probably included removing Manasseh's heathen idols, a Book of the Law is found whose effect is to reform Judah's religion. Josiah (640–609 B.C.E.), the last politically effective king of Judah, not only has the newly received Deuteronomic Law publicly proclaimed but conducts a nationwide demolition of all shrines and altars (whether dedicated to Yahweh or Baal) that compete with the central sanctuary in Jerusalem. His zealous reforms extend into the former land of Israel as well (2 Kings 22:1–23:25).

Like Moses and Joshua, he holds a covenant-renewal ceremony and orders the celebration of Passover, which had apparently been allowed to lapse under Manasseh's influence. But neither he nor his people receive the rewards that Deuteronomy has promised for faithfulness. In 609 B.C.E. Josiah is cut down in a battle at Megiddo, where he had gone to intercept an invasion by Pharaoh Necho of Egypt. After his premature death, the nation sinks again into chaos and misfortune (2 Kings 23–24).

Babylonian Conquest   In 612 B.C.E., Nineveh, Assyria's hated capital, had fallen to the combined forces of the Medes and Babylonians. Although Pharaoh Necho had rushed into the power vacuum that Assyria's collapse had created in the Near East, the Egyptians were soon defeated by Nebuchadnezzar, king of Babylon, at the Battle of Carchemish (605 B.C.E.). The tiny state of Judah must next submit to the Babylonian yoke; its last kings are merely tribute-paying vassals of Nebuchadnezzar, who is now master of the Near East.

Josiah's son Jehoiakim (609–598 B.C.E.), whom Nebuchadnezzar has placed on Judah's throne, unwisely rebels but dies before the Babylonians can capture Jerusalem, leaving his son and successor, Jehoiachin, to suffer the consequences of the revolt. In 598/597 B.C.E. Jehoiachin and his family are taken as prisoners to Babylon, the temple is stripped of its treasures, and 10,000 members of Judah's upper classes are deported to Mesopotamia (2 Kings 24). Nebuchadnezzar then appoints Jehoiachin's uncle Zedekiah (597–587 B.C.E.) king in his place.

When Zedekiah, too, rebels against Babylon, Nebuchadnezzar captures and destroys the holy city and its temple. The Babylonians demolish the city walls, loot and burn surrounding villages, and carry off most of the remaining population, leaving only the poorest citizens behind. Nebuchadnezzar appoints Gedaliah governor of the ruined city, but even this token of survival is lost when Gedaliah is assassinated by fanatical Jewish nationalists. Fearing Babylonian retaliation, many of the peasant survivors flee to Egypt.

The fall of Jerusalem meant the annihilation of the Davidic monarchy and all the national and religious hopes associated with it as well. When the deuteronomist historians exiled in Babylon wrote this portion of 2 Kings, they appear to have viewed the catastrophe as so total that it could be expressed only in the tersest, most unemotional style. The nation had reached its nadir, not to be matched until the Romans again destroyed Jerusalem some six and a half centuries later. The single glimmer of hope lay in deposed King Jehoiachin's release from prison (2 Kings 24:27–30). Fortunately, however, the work of Israel's great "writing prophets" continued, revitalizing the people's hopes and reminding them that Yahweh had punished his people but not abandoned them altogether. (For a list of the Babylonian kings and the Persian emperors who succeeded them, see Table 4-2.)

RECOMMENDED READING

Cross, Frank M. "The Themes of the Book of Kings and the Structure of the Deuteronomic History." In *Canaanite Myth and Hebrew Epic: Essays in the History and the Religion of Israel*, chap. 10. Cambridge, Mass.: Harvard University Press, 1973.

Gray, John. *1 and 2 Kings*. 2nd ed. Old Testament Library. Philadelphia: Westminster Press, 1970.

Montgomery, James A., and Gehman, Henry S. *The Books of Kings*. International Critical Commentary. New York: Charles Scribner's Sons, 1951. A thorough critical examination of the texts.

LATTER PROPHETS: MAJOR AND MINOR

In the historical books of Samuel and Kings, prophetic figures such as Nathan, Gad, Ahijah, Micaiah, Elijah, and Elisha appear as leading actors

TABLE 4-2 Neo-Babylonian and Persian Empires

Date B.C.E.	Events in Babylon or Persia	Events in Judah
625	Nabopolassar of Babylon (626–605)	
600	Nebuchadnezzar creates New Babylonian Empire (605–562) Nebuchadnezzar conquers Judah (587) Amel-Marduk (562–560) Neriglissar (560–556)	First captivity of Jerusalem (598/97) Ezekiel prophesies in Babylon Fall of Jerusalem and deportation of Jews (587) Exile
550	Nabonidus (556–539) Cyrus (550–530) captures Babylon (539); founding of Persian Empire Cambyses (530–522) extends Persian Empire to include Egypt Darius I (522–486)	Second Isaiah in Babylon Cyrus' edict freeing Jews (538) Jewish remnant returns to Judah Zerubbabel, governor of Judah Haggai and Zechariah Temple rebuilt (520–515)
500	Persia invades Greece; defeated at Marathon (490) Xerxes I (486–465); second Persian invasion of Greece (480–479) Artaxerxes I (465–424)	Joel Malachi
450		
425	Xerxes II (423) Darius II (423–404)	Nehemiah comes to Jerusalem (445)
400	Artaxerxes II (404–358)	Ezra's reforms; final (?) edition of Torah promulgated
350	Artaxerxes III (358–338) Arses (338–336) Darius III (336–331) Alexander the Great of Macedonia (336–323); conquers Persia, Egypt, Mesopotamia, western India, etc.; begins Hellenistic period	

in Israel's national drama. During the tenth and ninth centuries B.C.E. these and other prophets are associated with religious shrines like Shiloh and the royal courts of kings like David, Solomon, or Ahab. Not until the mid-eighth century B.C.E. did Israel produce *nevi'im* (prophets) whose words would eventually be recorded and collected in separate volumes carrying the prophets' own names. The Hebrew word *navi* (singular) means "one who is called" or "one who announces"; its Greek equivalent, *prophetes*, from which our English word is derived, means "a spokesman for God," one chosen to proclaim Yahweh's will.

To understand the nature and purpose of Israel's prophets it is helpful to review what little is known about their historical development. In Deuteronomy 18 (which scholars believe was compiled in the seventh century B.C.E. when the *nevi'im* had already arisen in Israel), Moses is shown describing the prophetic office. The prophet is to function as a link between the people and Yahweh, who employs the prophet to convey Yahweh's "words" (oracles). The *navi* is specifically said to be Israel's means of ascertaining the divine will—in direct contrast to the Canaanite practices of seeking supernatural help by consulting sorcerers, soothsayers, or spirit mediums who "call up the dead," religious figures to whom some Israelites apparently were attracted (Deut. 18:9–12). Yahweh sends Israel the *nevi'im*, whose messages have the force of divine commands. Anyone ignoring the prophetic word and attempting to communicate directly with the unseen world—a practice the Torah labels a Canaanite "abomination"—risked death by stoning or fire (Lev. 20:27; Exod. 22:18).

Among the earliest Hebrew prophets were those called "ecstatic"— people who, seemingly possessed by Yahweh's spirit, worked themselves into a religious frenzy, throwing themselves writhing upon the ground and uttering unintelligible sounds. As with the later Orphic and Dionysic cults in ancient Greece, such emotional seizures were induced through orgiastic music or dance (1 Sam. 10:5–6; 2 Kings 3:15). According to 1 Samuel 10, Saul was seized by Yahweh's spirit shortly after the prophet Samuel had anointed him king. Joining a prophetic band that played "harp, tambourine, flute, and lyre," Saul is thrown "into an ecstasy" and "changed into another man," temporarily losing his individual identity. A later account of the incident adds details associated with the primitive ecstatic experience: Saul stripped off his clothes, fell into a trance, and "lay there naked all that day and night" (1 Sam. 19:18–24).

Even in later Israel, prophets were noted for their bizarre, even grotesque, behavior. Isaiah, naked except for a loincloth, paraded through Jerusalem's streets to illustrate the city's imminent humiliation and ruin. Jeremiah wore a yoke first of wood then of iron, symbolic of bearing the Babylonian oppression (Jer. 27). Ezekiel carried the prophets' symbolic acts to an even greater extreme, cooking his food over a fire of human excrement (Ezek. 4:12–15), refusing to mourn for his dead wife (Ezek. 24:15–27), and lying bound like a prisoner for 190 days on one side, then

40 days on the other (Ezek. 4:4–8). In these and other ways the great prophets dramatized their messages through strangely expressive conduct.

According to 1 Samuel 9, Israel's early prophets were called seers. The old term is appropriate, for Yahweh was believed to grant seers special insight into a given situation, permitting them to apprehend spiritual realities not accessible to others. Seers and prophets (the terms are *almost* interchangeable) traditionally received Yahweh's oracles through dreams and visions (Num. 12:6). Some of the early prophets belonged to schools or brotherhoods called "sons of the prophets." Elijah and Elisha were apparently leaders of such guilds at Bethel, Jericho, and Gilgal (2 Kings 2:3–4; 4:38), though they were not permanently attached to a particular cultic center.

A careful reading of prophetic literature distinguishes Israel's classical prophets from certain modern concepts of the role. The *nevi'im* were not primarily fortunetellers or prognosticators of future history. Their function was to perceive and then announce Yahweh's will in an immediate circumstance—in terms comprehensible or at least relevant to their original audience. Rather than predicting events in a far-distant future, the *nevi'im* endeavored to illuminate Yahweh's intentions in the present. They strove to bring Yahweh's people back into harmony with the Mosaic Torah or, failing that, to specify the punishments for disobedience.

The prophetic calling included women, the first of whom was Moses' sister Miriam (Exod. 15:20–21; Num. 12:2). In the period of the Judges, Deborah was both a tribal leader and a prophet (Judg. 4:4). When priests discovered the lost manuscript of Deuteronomy during Josiah's reign, they brought the matter to Huldah, "a prophetess," for interpretation and advice (2 Kings 22:14). The prophetess Noadiah was one of Nehemiah's noted opponents in postexilic Jerusalem (Neh. 6:14; see also Isa. 8:2). Women participated in the prophetic dispensation well into New Testament times (Luke 2:36; Rev. 2:20).

As an Israelite institution, prophecy began with the creation of the united monarchy and ended shortly after its demise. Officially recognized prophets were familiar figures at the courts of David, Solomon, Jeroboam, Ahab, and other kings of both Israel and Judah. After the Babylonians deposed the last Davidic monarch in 587 B.C.E., however, prophecy declined as a major force in the covenant community. In the years following the Babylonian exile, priestly teachers of the Mosaic Torah replaced both king and prophet as leaders and religious guides of Jewish society.

The Hebrew Bible places the three major prophets—Isaiah, Jeremiah, and Ezekiel—first among the Latter ("writing") Prophets, a ranking that probably derives as much from their great length as from their enormous theological influence. The books of the twelve minor prophets—Hosea through Malachi—are minor only in length, not in religious significance. From the earliest, Amos, who prophesied during the eighth century B.C.E., to Jonah, a book written in the late sixth or early fifth century B.C.E., the twelve present a 300-year continuum of Yahweh's oracles to Israel. These minor prophets are arranged in roughly chronological order, although other factors, such as a book's size, also figured in their positioning. Following is an introductory survey of the Latter Prophets and a statement of the order in which the individual prophets appeared, if not that in which the books bearing their names were written.

HISTORICAL AND SOCIAL BACKGROUND
TO THE MESSAGES OF THE LATTER PROPHETS

The Latter Prophets of Israel and Judah, like other contributors to biblical literature, appeared largely in response to urgent political or ethnical crises that troubled their people. Most of the Latter Prophets belong to one of three critical periods: (1) the Assyrian era, (2) the Babylonian crisis, or (3) the postexilic adjustment. The earliest of the "writing" prophets (those whose works were recorded in their names) were active during the second half of the eighth century B.C.E. A time of swift change and political upheaval, a revitalized Assyrian Empire then threatened the very existence of the two kingdoms of Israel and Judah. Amos and Hosea preached in the northern kingdom, warning of a terrible retribution for the people's faithlessness to the Mosaic Covenant ideals of social justice and loyalty to Yahweh. Within two decades after northern Israel's collapse before the Assyrian military juggernaut (722/21 B.C.E.), Judah seemed doomed to a similar fate. Like their two predecessors in the north, the Judeans Isaiah and Micah interpreted the historical situation as Yahweh's punishment for Judah's religious and social sins. (The two prophets, however, manifest strikingly different attitudes toward the Davidic monarchy and royal sanctuary in Jerusalem.)

Another cluster of late seventh- and sixth-century prophets responded to a second period of international turmoil. In rapid succession Assyria fell (612 B.C.E.), inspiring Nahum's rejoicing, and Egypt's Pharaoh Necho attempted to fill the Near Eastern power vacuum (defeating and killing Judah's "good" King Josiah along the way), only to be defeated by Babylon's Nebuchadnezzar at the decisive Battle of Carchemish (605 B.C.E.). Judah, which had begun a profound religious reform and political expansion under Josiah (about 621 B.C.E.)—developments made possible to Assyria's growing weakness—quickly found itself subject to a new imperial master, the Neo-Babylonian Empire. Reduced again to a tribute-paying vassal state, as it had been under Assyria, Judah plotted revolts against Nebuchadnezzar and looked to Egypt (a "frail reed") for military help.

During the Babylonian crisis the prophets Habakkuk and Jeremiah interpreted political events as signs of Yahweh's will working through human activity. Using the form of a legal prosecution or "covenant lawsuit" against law-breaking Judah, Jeremiah urged political submission to Babylon, which unwittingly acted as Yahweh's punishing agent.

Deported to Babylonia (597 B.C.E.), Ezekiel similarly proclaimed that Yahweh had abandoned his dwelling-place in Jerusalem's temple because of the people's promoting injustice and religious corruption. Ezekiel also produced visions of a new Jerusalem and splendidly rebuilt temple where a restored "remnant" would one day properly worship their god. These glowing visions of a happier future helped to encourage the Judean captives and provided a rallying point of hope that Yahweh had not utterly forgotten the covenant community. Toward the close of the Babylonian period, the unknown prophet called Second Isaiah announced not only that the captives' return to the Judean homeland was near but that Yahweh planned a glorious triumph for his "servant," Israel.

Second Isaiah's promises were not matched by the grim and impoverished realities of life in postexilic Jerusalem; the returned exiles nonetheless experienced prophetic encouragement. About 520 B.C.E. the prophets Haggai and Zechariah renewed promises of a brighter future and incited the apathetic Judeans to finish rebuilding Yahweh's temple. Still later, Joel, Malachi, and the anonymous poet known as Third Isaiah added their eschatological hopes to the prophetic writings. After the time of Ezra—priest, scribe, and transmitter of the Mosaic law (about 400 B.C.E.)—it was believed that traditional prophecy ceased. Late "prophetic" books like Daniel, for example, were not included among the canonical Prophets but were assigned to a later collection, the Writings.

ORDER OF THE PROPHETS' APPEARANCES

Eighth Century

Amos (about 750 B.C.E.) A Judean called to prophesy in the northern kingdom, Amos announces the "Day of Yahweh," vigorously denouncing the upper classes' luxurious living based on an unjust exploitation of the poor. Claiming that Israel had perverted religion into an empty ritual, Amos predicts political disaster and exile.

Hosea (about 746–735? B.C.E.) Comparing Israel's disloyalty to Yahweh in its worship of Baal to the breaking of a marriage bond, Hosea renews Amos' theme of economic and social corruption and deserved national disaster but also stresses Yahweh's *hesed* (loving devotion) and likens Yahweh's concern for Israel to a spouse's distress over a beloved but faithless mate.

Isaiah of Jerusalem (about 742–700 B.C.E.) A prophet intimately associated with the Jerusalem sanctuary and Davidic royal family, Isaiah resembles the northern prophets in denouncing the ruling classes' acquisitive greed and callous disregard for the poor. Active during the Assyrian invasion of Judah, he counsels "isolationism," a total reliance on Yahweh's power to save and predicts that a Davidic heir will establish universal peace and justice.

Micah   Unlike his contemporary Isaiah, Micah is a country villager who unequivocally condemns the rich urban landowners who "skin" and "devour" the peasant farmer. Criticizing the Jerusalem kings who permit such practices, Micah declares that the city and temple will be destroyed (Mic. 3:9–12).

Seventh Century
Zephaniah   Compiled during Josiah's reign (640–609), the book of Zephaniah opens with Yahweh's declared intention to sweep all life from the earth, continues with denunciations of Israel's neighbors, Moab and Ammon, and the oppressor, Assyria, but abruptly switches course and asserts that Yahweh has changed his mind and "repealed his sentence" against Judah (Zeph. 3:14–18). The prophet's abrupt change in attitude may have been a reaction to Josiah's religious reforms.

Nahum   Shortly before Nineveh's fall (612 B.C.E.), Nahum gloats over Assyria's destruction.

Habakkuk   Faced with Babylon's imminent conquest of Judah, Habakkuk ponders Yahweh's fairness, concluding that the righteous person must live having faith in God's ultimate justice.

Sixth Century
Jeremiah   During the reigns of Judah's last kings (Josiah to Zedekiah, about 626 until after 587 B.C.E.), Jeremiah stresses that Yahweh employs Babylon as the divinely appointed instrument of punishment against covenant-breaking Judah. Declaring that only those submitting to Babylon (and Yahweh) can escape destruction, Jeremiah envisions the future enactment of a covenant that will not be broken (Jer. 31:31). Unlike his predecessor Isaiah, who also advised Jerusalem's kings during foreign invasions, Jeremiah sees little merit in the temple cult or the Davidic ruling family.

Obadiah   Obadiah condemns Edom for helping the Babylonians sack Jerusalem (587 B.C.E.).

Ezekiel   A priest and mystic exiled in Babylonia during Judah's last years (after 597 B.C.E.), Ezekiel declares that Yahweh is too holy to continue dwelling among an unjust and violent people. Envisioning Yahweh's "glory" abandoning Jerusalem to Babylon's power, Ezekiel also foresees a glorious rebuilt sanctuary and divinely protected new Jerusalem.

Second Isaiah   Living in Babylonia during Cyrus the Persian's rise to power (between about 550 and 539 B.C.E.), this anonymous poet views Yahweh as the *only* God, the eternal foreordainer of human history who was then acting to restore Judah's faithful remnant to its homeland in Palestine. The four "servant songs" depict the redemptive role of Yahweh's chosen agent, Israel.

Haggai   Under Zerubbabel, a Davidic descendant whom the Persians appointed governor of the tiny restored community of Judah, Haggai argues that Yahweh will cause the wealth of nations to flow into Jerusalem if the Judeans will obediently rebuild the temple.

Zechariah   A contemporary of Haggai (about 520 B.C.E.), Zechariah produces a series of mystic visions involving the rebuilt temple, the high priest Joshua, the Davidic governor Zarubbabel, and Yahweh's messianic intentions for Israel. A later hand added chapters 9–12.

Late Sixth or Fifth Century

Third Isaiah   The third section of Isaiah (chs. 55–66) includes oracles from almost the whole period of Israelite prophecy, including the work of a postexilic prophet sharply critical of the restored community's religious failures.

Joel   Of uncertain date, Joel's book contains a series of apocalyptic visions picturing plagues and judgments signaling the Day of Yahweh. Calling for repentance, Joel foresees a climactic outpouring of holy spirit upon all humankind.

Malachi   This anonymous prophet also predicts a coming judgment on the frightening day of Yahweh's visitation. Promising a "messenger" to purify the temple cult, the prophet ends by announcing the future reappearance of Elijah.

Jonah   A moral fable contrasting Jonah's literalness with Yahweh's universality and compassion, this humorous tale provides insight into the ethical value of an unfulfilled prophecy.

RECOMMENDED READING

Buber, Martin. *The Prophetic Faith.* Translated by C. Witton-Davies. New York: Macmillan, 1949; Harper Torchbooks, 1960.

Clements, R. E. *Prophecy and Covenant.* Studies in Biblical Theology, no. 43. Naperville, Ill.: Alec R. Allenson, 1965.

Heschel, Abraham J. *The Prophets.* New York: Harper & Row, 1963. A major work by a great Jewish scholar.

Koch, Klaus. *The Prophets.* Vol. 1, *The Assyrian Age.* Translated by Margaret Kohl. Philadelphia: Fortress Press, 1982. A new study of the eighth-century prophets.

Lindblom, Johannes. *Prophecy in Ancient Israel*. Philadelphia: Fortress Press, 1962. A major study by a Swedish scholar.

Scott, R. B. Y. *The Relevance of the Prophets*, rev. ed. New York: Macmillan, 1968.

Vawter, Bruce. *The Conscience of Israel*. New York: Sheed & Ward, 1961. Discusses preexilic prophecy.

von Rad, Gerhard. *Old Testament Theology*. Vol. 2, *The Theology of Israel's Prophetic Traditions*. Translated by D. M. G. Stalker. New York: Harper & Row, 1965.

Ward, James. *The Prophets*. Nashville: Abingdon Press, 1982.

Westerman, Claus. *Basic Forms of Prophetic Speech*. Translated by H. K. White. Philadelphia: Westminster Press, 1967.

Wolf, Hans Walter. *Confrontations with Prophets*. Philadelphia: Fortress Press, 1983.

❦ Isaiah

Isaiah and the Syro-Ephraimite Crisis	*Chapters 1–11, 20*
Assyrian Crisis	*22, 28–31, 36–39*
Second Isaiah and the Servant Songs	*40–55*
Third Isaiah	*56–66*

**They shall beat their swords into plowshares,
and their spears into pruning hooks:
nation shall not lift up sword against nation,
neither shall they learn war any more.**

Isaiah 2:4; King James Version

Preeminent among the prophetic books is that of Isaiah, which preserves some of the loftiest thoughts and most memorable poetry in world literature. It is not a single, unified work, however, but an anthology of many prophetic oracles produced over many years. Scholars who have analyzed Isaiah's sixty-six chapters have generally agreed that the book can be divided into at least three distinct parts, each portion representing a different time period and a different author.

The first thirty-nine chapters (except for 24–27, 33–35, and 36–39) are thought to be largely the work of Isaiah of Jerusalem, who prophesied between about 742 and 700 B.C.E., when the Assyrian Empire engulfed Israel and threatened Judah as well. Chapters 40–55 present a historical situation in which Babylon, not Assyria, dominates. The figure of Isaiah does not appear after chapter 39. Striking differences in style, vocabulary, and theological perspective also indicate a new author at work. Chapters

56–66 seem to represent oracles from the eighth to the early fifth centuries B.C.E.—almost the whole age of prophecy. Scholars customarily treat each of Isaiah's three main divisions as a separate literary unit. Based on scholarly analyses of their style, literary form, theological content, and allusions to historical themes or events, the first and third sections are in turn divided into numerous smaller units. Isaiah 24–27 (the "little apocalypse") appears to belong to a period later than that of the historical Isaiah. Because of its elaborately developed eschatological concern, this passage is generally assigned a postexilic date. Chapters 36–39 have been lifted almost verbatim from 2 Kings 18:13 through 2 Kings 20:19, which summarize events from late in Isaiah's ministry. The book's last ten chapters (Isa. 56–66) stem partly from the late sixth century and are addressed to members of the restored Jerusalem community, though they also include fragments from earlier centuries. As noted below, some of the book's most powerful utterances are directed to an audience eagerly awaiting release from captivity. This section (Isa. 40–55) speaks cogently to the needs of Judean exiles living in Babylon between about 550 and 539 B.C.E.

Isaiah and the Syro-Ephraimite Crisis   According to Isaiah 1:1, the prophet was active during the reigns of four Judean kings: Uzziah (Azariah), Jotham, Ahaz, and Hezekiah. If Isaiah received his call to prophecy around 742–740 B.C.E. as chapter 6 suggests, he could have devoted more than forty years to his ministry. Although the individual oracles represented in the Isaiah scroll are arranged neither chronologically nor topically, scholars have tentatively assigned various portions of the book to three principal crises of Isaiah's lifetime: the Syro-Ephraimite War (735–734 B.C.E), Hezekiah's temptation to ally Judah with Egypt (about 711 B.C.E), and the Assyrian invasion of 701 B.C.E.

Oracles from the first phase of his career are contained in chapters 2–11 (the first chapter is a general preface to the whole of Isa. 1–39 and includes oracles from the prophet's entire career). Chapter 6 records what is generally regarded as Isaiah's call to prophesy. While worshiping at the temple Isaiah experiences a vision of Yahweh enthroned in heaven and encompassed by his angelic court. Overcome by a consciousness of his human imperfections, he feels his lips symbolically cleansed when touched by a burning coal, and he volunteers to carry Yahweh's word to Judah (Isa. 6:1–9). Having dedicated his life to the deity, he demands comparable allegiance from his people.

Many of Isaiah's early messages are concerned with social justice. Like his contemporaries Amos and Hosea who prophesied in the northern kingdom of Israel, Isaiah argues that Yahweh places greater importance on dealing mercifully and generously with widows, orphans, and strangers than he does on cultic observances. The nation will be judged harshly for its economic exploitation of the poor (Isa. 1:10–20; 3:13–15;

5:8–20; 10:1–4). For their sins, Israel and Judah will go into exile, though Yahweh will eventually restore a remnant (Isa. 11:10–16).

Unlike Amos and Hosea, however, Isaiah never attributes the coming punishment to a breaking of the Mosaic Covenant; instead he emphasizes Yahweh's special relationship to the Davidic dynasty in Jerusalem (see 2 Sam. 7). This reliance on the Davidic royal line and the sanctity of the Davidic capital may explain why Isaiah regarded every threat to Jerusalem and its anointed kings as an opportunity for the nation to demonstrate its absolute trust in Yahweh's promise to David's heirs. The prophet consistently urged Judah's rulers to rely exclusively on Yahweh rather than on diplomatic and military assistance.

Isaiah's policy is well illustrated by his prophetic advice during the Syro-Ephraimite War of the mid-730s B.C.E. As scholars reconstruct events, it appears that various Palestinian states, led by Syria and Israel (Ephraim), formed a coalition to resist Assyrian expansion into the area. When the kings of Damascus and Samaria besieged Jerusalem to force King Ahaz of Judah to join their alliance, Isaiah counseled a passive reliance on Yahweh to keep his vow to David and deliver the holy city (Isa. 7).

Ignoring Isaiah's counsel, Ahaz negotiated with Assyria, and thanks to Assyrian influence, the Syro-Ephraimite siege of Jerusalem was lifted. In saving his capital from the kings of Damascus and Syria, however, Ahaz had made it subservient to Assyria, so that Judah was now reduced to the status of a vassal state in the Assyrian Empire. Inevitably, Isaiah regarded Ahaz's compromise as a betrayal of Yahweh. He predicted that Assyria would soon become the "rod" of Yahweh's anger to punish those who had failed to show faith in their god (Isa. 7:18–25; 10:5–6, 28–32). But if Assyria exceeded its mandate to chastise his people, Yahweh would in turn destroy it (Isa. 10:7–19).

As a sign that Yahweh would rescue his people from the Syro-Ephraimite crisis, Isaiah had prophesied that a young woman would conceive and bear a son whose name, Immanuel ("God [El] is with us"), signified that Yahweh would protect those who trusted in him (Isa. 7:13–17). Although the author of Matthew's Gospel, relying on the Greek translation of Isaiah's "young woman" (virgin), interpreted this as a messianic prophecy (Matt. 1:22–24), it contains no direct reference to the Messiah but seems to imply the birth of a child in the prophet's own day.

Judging Ahaz as having failed to meet Yahweh's challenge of faith, Isaiah nonetheless foresaw a future Judean king who by fully depending on Yahweh would reap the promised blessings, a king whose sovereignty would be worldwide and under whose glorious reign the earth would be transformed into another Eden (Isa. 9:2–7 and 11:1–6). Since the term *messiah* simply means "anointed one," as Judah's kings were anointed with holy oil at their coronations, it is difficult to tell whether he envisioned Hezekiah, Ahaz's son and heir, or another more distant descendant of David fulfilling this role. While these passages associate a Davidic king with a renewed creation (Isa. 9:2–7; 11:6–9), other oracles present a new world order of universal peace (of which Jerusalem is to be the center) without mentioning a messiah (Isa. 2:2–4; 29:17–21; 19:19–25).

Assyrian Crisis The prophet's attention was brought back to more immediate problems when around 711 B.C.E the Assyrians attacked the city of Ashdod, which bordered on Judah's southwest frontier. This time Egypt attempted to form a Palestinian coalition to protect its own boundaries. To dissuade King Hezekiah from involving Judah in this alliance, Isaiah paraded naked through the streets of Jerusalem, vividly illustrating the certainty of exile and slavery that would result from relying on Egypt instead of on Yahweh for deliverance (Isa. 20). Although Hezekiah did not then commit himself to Egypt, a decade later he did join Egypt in an anti-Assyrian alliance, and Isaiah castigated king, courtiers, and other national leaders for abandoning Yahweh to join forces with an unreliable ally (Isa. 28–31).

In 701 B.C.E. the Assyrians retaliated: King Sennacherib swept down from the north, cut off communication with Egypt, and laid siege to Jerusalem as Isaiah had predicted (Isa. 29:1–4). In a celebrated inscription, Sennacherib describes sealing up Hezekiah in Jerusalem "like a bird in a cage" and extorting enormous sums of gold and silver, as well as skilled artisans and royal children, as payment for ending the siege. Although Hezekiah thus succeeded in buying off Sennacherib and Jerusalem escaped destruction, the surrounding countryside was devastated, and Judah, humbled and impoverished, was relegated to a political dependence from which it would only briefly revive.

Chapters 36 and 37, however, present a strikingly different account (repeated almost verbatim in 2 Kings 18:13–19:37, but with the conspicuous addition that Hezekiah stripped the temple and royal palace of their treasures to buy off Sennacherib, a pragmatic factor on which Isaiah is entirely silent). In the Isaiah-Kings version, Hezekiah is pictured as showing absolute faith in Yahweh's power to rescue Judah from the pagan hordes, a confidence that is rewarded by a miracle—a total Assyrian withdrawal.

Whether the Isaiah-Kings version represents a second Assyrian siege (later than that described in Sennacherib's inscription) or whether both the Assyrian and biblical accounts are exaggerated versions of the same event is not known. In any case, Jerusalem did not suffer the same destruction visited upon other rebellious Palestinian states, and its unexpected escape contributed dramatically to the belief that David's holy city was specially protected by the hand of Israel's god (see Jer. 7 and 26).

Some of the material in chapters 1–39 is thought to have been added later by Isaiah's disciples, who apparently formed a prophetic school that preserved, edited, and eventually compiled their master's words. The

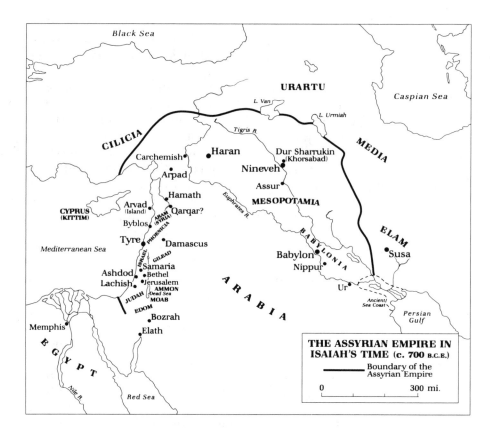

Black Sea

URARTU

Caspian Sea

L. Van

L. Urmiah

CILICIA

Tigris R.

MEDIA

Carchemish

Haran

Dur Sharrukin
(Khorsaphad)

Arpad

Nineveh

Assur

MESOPOTAMIA

Hamath

CYPRUS
(KITTIM)

Arvad
(Island)

Qarqar?

Euphrates R.

ELAM

Byblos

ARAM
(SYRIA)

PHOENICIA

Tyre

Damascus

BABYLONIA

Mediterranean Sea

ISRAEL

GILEAD

Babylon

Susa

Samaria

Nippur

Ashdod

Bethel

Lachish

Jerusalem

AMMON

JUDAH

Dead Sea

MOAB

Ur

EDOM

Ancient
Sea Coast

Persian
Gulf

Bozrah

Memphis

Elath

E G Y P T

A R A B I A

Nile R.

Red Sea

THE ASSYRIAN EMPIRE IN
ISAIAH'S TIME (c. 700 B.C.E.)

——— Boundary of the
Assyrian Empire

0   300 mi.

apocalyptic passages (Isa. 24–27), certain references to Babylon's fall, and the prose appendix that closes this section of the book (Isa. 36–39) are probably the work of followers or lesser prophets writing under Isaiah's influence.

Second Isaiah and the Servant Songs   Even the casual reader is likely to notice the sudden shift in tone, style, and theological viewpoint between chapters 39 and 40. Whereas Isaiah of Jerusalem, working during the eighth century B.C.E., had foretold a coming punishment, the author of this portion of the book states that the time of punishment is past. The geographical background of these passages is not Jerusalem but Babylon during the sixth century B.C.E., and the unknown poet whom we call the "Second Isaiah" addresses a group already chastened for its sins and about to be rewarded with freedom from fear, imprisonment, and despair.

In the victories of Cyrus, the Persian commander who was conquering country after country in the Near East of the 540s B.C.E., Second Isaiah saw the hand of Yahweh. He correctly predicts that Cyrus—whom he calls Yahweh's "Messiah" (Isa. 45:1)—will conquer Babylon (as he does in 539 B.C.E.), and release the captive Jews, and that a saving remnant will return to Jerusalem (Isa. 44:28–45; 45:1–6; 48:12–16, 20–22). Consoling and encouraging Israel, he reminds it in joyous poetry unsurpassed in world literature that Yahweh, all-powerful and all-loving, intends imminently to save and restore his people.

As a theologian, however, Second Isaiah is an uncompromising monotheist who makes explicit what had only been implied in earlier prophets: Yahweh alone exists, creates life, and directs human history, that of the pagan nations as well as of Israel. His god declares:

> I am the first and the last;
> there is no God besides me.

> Isaiah 44:6

Isaiah 40:12–31 contains monotheism's greatest hymn—a sweeping denial that other gods have any reality and an incomparable description of Yahweh's magnificence.

To the poet, Yahweh is both *transcendant* (above and beyond the world he creates) and *immanent* (personally involved in human affairs), for he not only manipulates historical events for his purpose but announces through the prophets what he intends to occur:

> Who from the very beginning foretold the future?
> Let them tell us what is yet to come.
> Have no fear, do not be afraid;
> have I not told you and revealed it long ago?

> Isaiah 44:7–8

In Second Isaiah's emphasis on Yahweh's wisdom, foreknowledge, and redeeming love we reach the high point of Old Testament prophecy.

One of the most compelling as well as puzzling features of Second Isaiah's message occurs in passages that scholars call the Servant Songs (Isa. 42:1–4; 49:1–6; 50:4–9; 52:13–53:12). These beautiful poems describe the ministry of a righteous Servant of Yahweh who even before birth realizes that he is chosen to receive God's spirit and bring justice to the world. Despite his noble work, however, he is misunderstood, classified with sinners, and condemned to an agonizing, humiliating death.

The most celebrated of these songs, the Suffering Servant, paints him as "despised and rejected of men: a man of sorrows, and acquainted with grief" (Isa. 53:3; King James Version); yet the Servant transforms Israel's awareness of what suffering means. Traditionally, as in the deuteronomist histories of Joshua through Kings, misery was regarded as God's punishment for sin. In Second Isaiah, however, the sufferer, though guiltless himself, takes the punishment for others' sins and suffers on behalf of the community:

Surely he hath borne our griefs,
and carried our sorrows: . . .
But he was wounded for our transgressions,
he was bruised for our iniquities:
the chastisement of our peace was upon him;
and with his stripes we are healed.

Isaiah 53:4–5; King James Version

The identity of the Servant has provoked considerable scholarly debate. In certain passages Second Isaiah seems to view him as Israel itself (Isa. 43:10); in others he seems to be an individual (Isa. 52:13–53:12). Perhaps the prophet saw him as both a person and a people, an individual who represented the community of Israel and God's chosen group as a collective whole, suffering by and for the nations. It is certain that Second Isaiah's view of the redemptive value of suffering greatly influenced the early Christian church, which saw Jesus at his crucifixion vicariously taking upon himself the punishment that justly belonged to all humankind.

Third Isaiah Parts of the third section of the Book of Isaiah appear to depict conditions in postexilic Judah when the restored exiles confronted an unsatisfying reality of poverty and political helplessness that was a far cry from the brilliant prospects Second Isaiah had envisioned. At this point a new member of the prophetic school descended from Isaiah of Jerusalem—known for want of a better title as "Third Isaiah"—added his own message to the prophetic collection, denouncing the returned exiles' idolatry, religious apathy, and failure to keep the Sabbath properly.

Third Isaiah also injected an apocalyptic element, looking beyond the bleak present to "new heavens and a new earth" in which Judah's sins are forgotten and the land becomes an earthly paradise with peace, plenty, and longevity for all (Isa. 65:17–25). This promise of a renewed creation (repeated in Isa. 66:22) would become an important eschatological (referring to a doctrine of "last things") hope of Christianity (2 Pet. 3:13; Rev. 21:1). The penultimate chapter of the last book of the Bible describes the still-future fulfillment of Third Isaiah's vision (see Rev. 21).

RECOMMENDED READING

Blank, Sheldon H. *Prophetic Faith in Isaiah.* New York: Harper & Row, 1958.

Childs, Brevard S. *Isaiah and the Assyrian Crisis.* Studies in Biblical Theology, no. 3. London: SCM Press, 1967.

Kaiser, Otto. *Isaiah 1–12.* Philadelphia: Westminster Press, 1972.

_____. *Isaiah 13–39.* Philadelphia: Westminster Press, 1974.

McKenzie, John L. *Second Isaiah.* Garden City, N. Y.: Doubleday, 1968.

Muilenburg, James. "Introduction and Exegesis to Isaiah 40–66." In *The Interpreter's Bible*, vol. 5, pp. 151–773. New York and Nashville: Abingdon Press, 1956. Excellent commentary.

North, Christopher R. *Isaiah 40–55.* New York: Macmillan, 1964.

_____. *The Suffering Servant in Deutero-Isaiah.* 2nd ed. New York: Oxford University Press, 1956. A helpful review of different interpretations of the Servant passages.

Smart, James D. *History and Theology in Second Isaiah: A Commentary on Isaiah 35, 40–66.* Philadelphia: Westminster Press, 1965.

Westermann, Claus. *Isaiah 40–66.* Philadelphia: Westminster Press, 1969.

❦ Jeremiah

Oracles Against Judah	*Chapters 1–25*
Biographical Narratives	*26–45*
Promised New Covenant	*31–33*

**See the days are coming—it is Yahweh who speaks—
when I will make a new covenant
with the House of Israel (and the House of Judah).**

Jeremiah 31:31

In its present form, the Book of Jeremiah is a bewildering collection of prophecies, anecdotes, warnings, short poems, and prose narratives that defies any principle of organization. Although one of the most chaotically assembled of the prophetic books, it is at least by and about one man rather than two or three. The book can be divided into four parts: (1) poetic oracles uttered at various times during Jeremiah's long career (Jer. 1–25); (2) biographical narratives interspersed with prophetic material (Jer. 26–45); (3) a collection of diatribes against the pagan nations (Jer. 46–51); and (4) a brief historical appendix closely resembling 2 Kings 24–25 (Jer. 52).

Chapter 36 gives a valuable insight into how at least part of the book took form. During the winter of 605–604 B.C.E., Jeremiah dictated to his secretary, Baruch, a scroll summarizing all the prophecies about Judah and Jerusalem that he had delivered since he had begun his career during the thirteenth year of Josiah's reign. After Baruch read the scroll to an assembly in the temple, word of it reached King Jehoiakim, who ordered it read again in his presence.

As a royal secretary intoned sections of the scroll, Jehoiakim cut them from the manuscript and contemptuously burned them in an open brazier, then ordered the arrest of Jeremiah and Baruch, who had already gone into hiding. Undeterred by the king's response, Jeremiah dictated a whole new scroll to Baruch, adding many similar prophecies. This second scroll may have formed the nucleus of our present Book of Jeremiah, for it probably contained large portions of what are now chapters 1–6 and 10–23, which are written mostly in the first person.

Oracles Against Judah   Because Jeremiah, who lived from about 640 to shortly after 587 B.C.E., acted under the conviction that Yahweh was about to punish Judah for its accumulated sins and that the new Babylonian Empire (established 605 B.C.E.) was the divinely chosen instrument of destruction, his message is one of almost unrelieved gloom and doom. Not only does he see certainty of suffering for his people, he believes that Judah deserves this fate, for it has broken the covenant, oppressed the poor, exploited widows and orphans, and literally as well as metaphorically "filled the streets of Jerusalem with innocent blood."

For approximately forty-one years the prophet preached this message, which caused him to be hated, shunned, and persecuted by his fellow Judeans, many of whom regarded him as a traitor to his country (Jer. 26:7–11; 32:1–5; 37:11–15; 38:14–28). Using exactly the classic form of indictment and punishment, Jeremiah proclaimed Yahweh's judgment fearlessly: in failing to keep the Mosaic Covenant, Judah's ruling classes had broken the law, and unless they repented instantly they would pay the penalty of death (Jer. 7–8; 11; 21–22; 26–28).

He urged Judah's various kings, particularly Jehoiakim and Zedekiah, to see that Babylon's supremacy was not merely a political reality against which it would be disastrous to struggle but to realize that the newly reborn Babylonian Empire was Yahweh's judgment on his people for their faithlessness, idolatry, and social injustice (Jer. 21; 22:1–9; 36; 37:16–21; 38:14–28). After Nebuchadnezzar had had thousands of Judah's religious and political leaders deported to Babylon in 598/597 B.C.E., Jeremiah wrote to the exiles telling them not to expect an early return but to build houses, plant gardens, and settle down as comfortably as possible for a long captivity (Jer. 29).

Jeremiah seems to have regretted the nature of his prophetic calling and to have suffered greatly at having to proclaim such a harsh view of Yahweh's intentions.

> Woe is me, my mother, for you have borne me to be
> a man of strife and of dissension for all the land.
> I neither lend nor borrow,
> yet all of them curse me.

* * *

> Yahweh, remember me, take care of me,
> and avenge me on my persecutors.

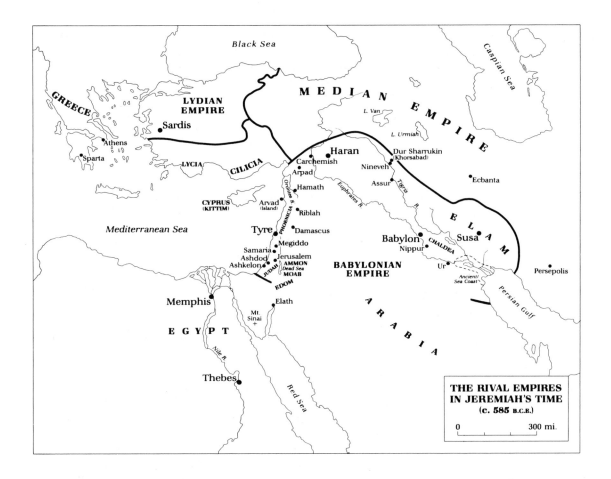

**THE RIVAL EMPIRES
IN JEREMIAH'S TIME
(c. 585 B.C.E.)**

0   300 mi.

Your anger is very slow; do not let me be snatched away.
Realize that I suffer insult for your sake.

Jeremiah 15:10, 15

Weary of rejection, he even tried to stop preaching to those who had no wish to hear it but found that the undelivered word burned "like a fire in [his] bones" and that he had to continue his work.

Biographical Narratives We know Jeremiah's inner life, his love for his people, and his unhappiness at being ostracized from them not only from several "confessions" (Jer. 11:18–23; 12:1–5; 15:10–11, 15–20; 17:14–18; 18:18–23; 20:7–11) but from the memoirs of Baruch, which are contained in chapters 26–45. From these biographical sections we learn that the prophet was born of a priestly family of Anathoth, a village three to four miles north of Jerusalem, that he was called to prophesy while still a boy, and that he witnessed rapid historical changes during his youth.

Assyria's power was broken with Nineveh's fall in 612 B.C.E.; King Josiah's religious reforms and the accompanying territorial expansion were halted by the king's untimely death in 609 B.C.E. At the Battle of Carchemish in 605 B.C.E. the Babylonians, who there defeated Pharaoh Necho, became the dominant world power.

Although at one time Jeremiah probably supported Josiah's reforms, he seems to have become disillusioned when the people observed the correct sacrificial forms prescribed by Deuteronomy but did not otherwise change their behavior (Jer. 3:6–10). Under King Jehoiakim, who tried to escape Babylon's control by allying Judah with Egypt, Jeremiah's bitter denunciation of such resistance as contrary to Yahweh's will was greeted with ridicule and charges of treason. After Nebuchadnezzar had captured Jerusalem and deported many of its leading citizens, Jeremiah intensified his warnings. When the prophet Hananiah falsely promised deliverance from Babylon, Jeremiah contradicted him by going about Jerusalem wearing a wooden yoke, the symbol of coming slavery. When Hananiah angrily smashed the wooden yoke, Jeremiah returned wearing one of iron (Jer. 27–28).

During the Babylonians' final siege of Jerusalem, the prophet was accused of attempting desertion (Jer. 37) and thrown into a muddy well to die (Jer. 38). This persecution was the Judaean government's response to Jeremiah's "treason." The prophet advocated a radical—and "unpatriotic" solution to the Babylonian threat: Jerusalem was to open its gates and surrender to the enemy. If the city capitulated, Jeremiah argued, it would not be burned and its citizens would escape with their lives. In a secret interview with King Zedekiah, last of the Davidic monarchs, Jeremiah urged the king to act boldly, ignore his counselors' mistaken will to resist, and submit to Nebuchadnezzar, thereby sparing his people the horrors of slaughter and destruction when Jerusalem inevitably fell. The prophet's recommendations were not based on political expedience, a policy of survival at all costs. Instead, he offered Zedekiah and the nation a religious challenge—to place their *trust* entirely in Yahweh's power to save. But Zedekiah, who was as weak and vacillating as his father, Josiah, had been zealous and resolute, fails to accept Yahweh's offer of safety (Jer. 38:14–28). As a result of the king's timid decision to heed his official advisers and not the prophet, Zedekiah sees his sons killed before his eyes and the holy city in flames. He is then blinded, chained, and led into captivity (Jer. 39:1–8).

To the Jerusalem leadership, Jeremiah's attitude toward Solomon's temple was as offensive as his "defeatist" pacifism. Throughout the siege he declared that those who believed that the sanctuary, center of sacrificial worship, could protect them were relying on an illusion (Jer. 7 and 26). Rather than depending upon a mere building, which the corrupt had profaned, Judah must cleanse itself of crime and idolatry to regain Yahweh's favor and protection.

Shortly before Jerusalem fell, Jeremiah made a rare gesture of faith in the future. As his world was disintegrating around him, he bought a field in Anathoth to demonstrate his belief that land ownership in Judah would someday again be profitable (Jer. 32). In 587 B.C.E., however, after a harrowing siege, Nebuchadnezzar took Jerusalem, demolishing its walls, palaces, and temple.

Having learned of Jeremiah's policy of submission, the Babylonians offered to take him to Babylon along with other prominent Jews, but the prophet preferred to remain among the poor in the ruined city. After Gedaliah, Nebuchadnezzar's governor, was murdered, Jeremiah was forcibly carried into Egypt, where we last see him, aged but unmellowed, violently attacking the refugees in Egypt for worshiping the Queen of Heaven (Jer. 43–45). Though he was paid no more attention in exile than during his forty-year preaching in Jerusalem, legend suggests that the prophet was silenced only by martyrdom.

Promised New Covenant Perhaps Jeremiah's greatest contribution to the survival of the Jewish religion was his perception that Judah's faith did not depend upon outward signs of Yahweh's presence or protection. David's throne, the holy city, Solomon's temple, even the nation itself could vanish; but when all the national religious symbols were destroyed, Yahweh would nonetheless maintain his relationship with those who believed in him. As the prophet's own communication with his god was not broken in the idolatrous land of Egypt, neither would the faithful in Babylon lose contact with Yahweh, who could be worshiped without a temple anywhere in the world.

Jeremiah's most famous prophecy foretold a time when the old covenant that Yahweh had made through Moses would be replaced by a new and better covenant.

> See, the days are coming—it is Yahweh who speaks—when I will make a new covenant with the House of Israel (and the House of Judah), but not a covenant like the one I made with their ancestors on the day I took them by the hand to bring them out of the land of Egypt. . . . No, this is the covenant I will make. . . . Deep within them I will plant my Law, writing it on their hearts. Then I will be their God and they shall be my people.
>
> Jeremiah 31:31–33

This new covenant inscribed on human hearts would not be a superficial or short-lived reform but an everlasting bond between Yahweh and his people because it would spring from the worshiper's deepest emotion, an inborn love for the covenant god.

RECOMMENDED READING

Blank, Sheldon H. *Jeremiah: Man and Prophet*. Cincinnati: Hebrew Union College Press, 1961.

Bright, John. *Jeremiah*. Anchor Bible, vol. 21. Garden City, N. Y.: Doubleday, 1965. Fine commentary.

Hyatt, J. Philip. "Introduction and Exegesis to Jeremiah." In *The Interpreter's Bible*, vol. 6, pp. 777–1142. New York and Nashville: Abingdon Press, 1956. Good introduction.

Muilenburg, James. "Jeremiah the Prophet." In *The Interpreter's Dictionary of the Bible*, vol. 2, pp. 823–25. New York and Nashville: Abingdon Press, 1962.

Skinner, John. *Prophecy and Religion*. New York: Cambridge University Press, 1922. A standard work.

❦ Ezekiel

Visions and Symbols	*Chapters 1–3*
Departure of Yahweh's Glory	*8–11*
Individual Responsibility	*18*
Oracle Against the King of Tyre	*28*
Promises of Restoration and Defense	*37–39*
Future Israel	*40–48*

When I bring them [Israel] back from the countries of their enemies, when I reveal my holiness in them for many nations to see, they will know that I am Yahweh their God. . . . I shall never hide my face from them again.

Ezekiel 39:27–29

Some of the symbols that Ezekiel evokes to describe his visions are so bizarre that among untrained readers increasingly fantastic interpretations abound. One best-selling author, for example, maintains that in his image of Yahweh's blazing chariot (Ezek. 1:4–28; 11:22–23) the prophet is describing flying saucers and visitors from outer space. Even without this peculiarly twentieth-century slant, however, readers are sure to be bewildered by Ezekiel's imagery. No other prophetic book in the Old Testament, with the possible exception of Zechariah, contains such strange hallucinatory material. Even Daniel's animal symbolism is less perplexing.

The book is well organized, however, with its prophecies arranged in generally chronological order. It records a series of visions that Ezekiel, who was also a priest, received while he was a captive in Babylon during the first deportation (597 B.C.E. and after). Ezekiel can be divided into six sections of unequal length: (1) Chapters 1–3 describe the prophet's initial visions and Yahweh's appointing him to prophetic office (593 B.C.E.). (2) Chapters 4–24 emphasize prophecies concerning the imminent destruction of Jerusalem. (3) In chapters 25–32 the prophet directs his words of doom to foreign nations. (4) Chapter 33, the book's turning point, concerns Jerusalem's fall. (5) Since the people have now been punished, chapters 34–39 promise their future restoration. (6) Chapters 40–48, which strongly resemble the book of Leviticus, describe the priestly reorganization of the restored community and its temple.

Visions and Symbols   The narrative begins in 593 B.C.E., during the fifth year of deposed King Jehoiachin's exile, when Ezekiel is living in a Jewish community on "the River Chebar," a large irrigation canal near the Euphrates River in Babylonia. In a trance, Ezekiel sees four winged animals "of human form" that closely resemble the colossal stone cherubs that guarded the gates of many Mesopotamian cities and would have been familiar sights to the prophet and other exiles.

The accompanying image of wheels within wheels having eyes along their rims probably represents Ezekiel's attempt to picture Yahweh among his heavenly servants in other than strictly anthropomorphic terms. The prophet characteristically speaks of Yahweh's "glory" in the Jerusalem temple rather than of the god himself. Certainly, images of fiery beings, a sapphire throne, and spiritual voices vividly express the awe and sense of mystery that Ezekiel feels during his communions with the divine (Ezek. 1–2).

After eating a scroll (representing Yahweh's message to Judah) that tastes like honey, Ezekiel is appointed watchman over the House of Israel, earning his own salvation by warning others of the impending judgment (Ezek. 2:8–3:21). Those who heed the warning will be spared the holocaust; those who ignore it will suffer destruction. Ezekiel here sounds the note of free will and individual responsibility that will recur throughout the book.

In the first of many strange actions Ezekiel performs to dramatize parts of his message, the prophet begins his ministry by being struck dumb and hence unable to communicate his warning (Ezek. 3:22–27). He cooks his food over human excrement to foreshadow how people trapped during Nebuchadnezzar's siege will be forced to eat "unclean food." When his wife dies, he neither weeps nor mourns in order to illustrate that Yahweh will not mourn the loss of his polluted temple (Ezek. 4:9–17; 24:15–27).

Ezekiel's public displays sometimes border on the abnormal. Tightly bound in ropes, he lies down on one side for 190 days to symbolize the duration—each day for a year—of the northern kingdom's exile, then lies on his other side for another 40 days to designate the length of Judah's captivity (Ezek. 4:1–8). Finally, he shaves off his beard and the hair on his head, burning a third of the hair, striking another third with a sword, and scattering the last third to the winds, retaining only a few stray hairs that he binds up in his robe. This demonstration is to inform the people that a third of them will die of pestilence and famine, a third by violence, and the remaining third will become captives in Babylon. The few hairs that he keeps represent those whom God will allow to escape (Ezek. 5).

Departure of Yahweh's Glory   Chapters 8–11 form a unit concerning the profanation of the temple and the departure of Yahweh's "glory" from Jerusalem. Stationed in Babylon, Ezekiel feels himself lifted by the hair and carried to Jerusalem where he envisions the idolatry that pollutes the sanctuary. Women there weep for Tammuz, a young fertility deity similar to the Greek Adonis, while Judah's corrupt elders secretly burn incense to hideous reptilian deities. Yahweh sends an angelic scribe who strides through the city marking the foreheads of those who deplore the religious abominations committed in the temple. Those unmarked, who have compromised their Yahwist faith with pagan rites, are to be slain by six divine executioners.

Ezekiel then sees the "glory of Yahweh" rise from its traditional seat between the gold cherubim in the temple's innermost sanctuary and pass through the city gates to the east. This strange event is probably meant to show that Yahweh's *kavod* (a Hebrew term that can be translated as "glory" or "influence") has permanently abandoned the temple and now roams the world, operating in new and unpredictable ways. Like Jeremiah, Ezekiel realized that Yahweh did not need a material shrine in which to house his presence, nor would he protect a sanctuary that had been contaminated. With Yahweh's departure from the temple, he could be with his people anywhere, including idolatrous Babylon.

Individual Responsibility   Chapters 12–17 deal with a variety of themes, most of which depict the sins that have alienated God from Judah. Chapter 18, however, minutely examines the moral consequences of the national disaster for the individual Jews who have survived it. Here Ezekiel declares that God will no longer judge and punish the people collectively; now that the nation is gone, each individual has responsibility for his or her own fate. The sinner will still be punished but not for the wrongdoing of others.

Ezekiel thus assumes the authority of a lawgiver, a latter-day Moses who corrects the old misconception of the second commandment in which Yahweh is represented as vowing to punish the father's sins in the sons even to the fourth generation (Exod. 20:5). Why, Ezekiel asks, cling mindlessly to the inherent injustice of the old system or persist in repeating the old proverb that when fathers eat sour grapes the sons' teeth are set on edge? "As I live—it is the Lord Yahweh who speaks—there will no longer be any reason to repeat this proverb in Israel. See now: all life belongs to me; the father's life and the son's life, both alike belong to me. The man who has sinned, he is the one who shall die" (Ezek. 18:3–4).

Like Joshua, Ezekiel emphasizes the individual's freedom of choice— Yahweh and life or disobedience and death: "House of Israel, in future I mean to judge each of you by what he does—it is the Lord Yahweh who speaks. Repent, renounce all your sins . . . and make yourselves a new heart and a new spirit! Why are you so anxious to die, House of Israel? I take no pleasure in the death of any one. . . . Repent and live!" (Ezek. 18:31–32).

Oracle Against the King of Tyre   Chapters 25–32 are devoted to denunciations and judgments against various foreign nations. Of particular interest is the oracle attacking the king of Tyre, a powerful Phoenician port city (Ezek. 28). This passage, like Isaiah 14, uses brilliant imagery to describe the downfall of a pagan king who opposes Yahweh's rule.

> You were once an exemplar of perfection,
> full of wisdom,
> perfect in beauty;
> you were in Eden, in the garden of God.
>
> * * *
>
> Your heart has grown swollen with pride
> on account of your beauty.
> You have corrupted your wisdom
> owing to your splendor.
> I have thrown you to the ground.
>
> Ezekiel 28:13, 17

It is possible that the prophet, a political prisoner who knew the value of symbolism, discreetly aimed his barbs at the Tyrian monarch rather than at Nebuchadnezzar, the real object of his attack.

Promises of Restoration and Defense   Chapter 33, which is pivotal, briefly describes Jerusalem's fall and the miserable fate of those remaining amid the ruins. After this event, the prophet abandons his visions of judgment and concentrates on Israel's future restoration (Ezek. 33–39), foreseeing that Yahweh will send a shepherd, a descendant of David, to guide Israel, with whom the god will conclude a covenant of peace so that they will live in perfect security (Ezek. 34). The prophet, however, does not foresee a restoration of the Davidic monarchy. Yahweh declares that he will take vengeance on the nations who desolated Israel and Judah, not because he pities his people but to vindicate his name, to convince them that he is supreme among gods. The phrase "then they will know that I am Yahweh" resounds throughout this section (Ezek. 36).

Perhaps the most influential of Ezekiel's visions occurs in chapter 37. Beholding a long valley littered with human bones, he hears a voice ask, "Son of man, can these bones live?" Miraculously, the fragmented skeletons reassemble themselves and are again clothed in flesh. Yahweh directs the winds to breathe life into them, and their resurrection is complete. Here Ezekiel predicts the rebirth of Israel, which was symbolically dead, and this image was eventually to become part of Israel's religious hope. It was not until the Book of Daniel was written in the second century B.C.E. that a belief in the individual's resurrection was explicitly stated (Dan. 12:1–3).

Once the nation was restored to its homeland, however, what was to prevent its again being devastated by Gentile armies? To assure the people that Yahweh would protect Israel's future security, the prophet introduces the strange allegory of Gog and Magog (Ezek. 38–39). In a kind of end-of-time vision that scholars call "eschatological," Ezekiel sees Jerusalem's would-be attackers destroyed by Yahweh's direct intervention, and Israel's slain enemies are so numerous that it takes seven months to bury their corpses.

This spectacular rescue is performed not only for the nation's sake but for the additional vindication of Yahweh, whose stature in the eyes of other nations had been seriously reduced by the humiliating defeat of his people and destruction of his temple. To restore his international prestige and reputation, Yahweh resolves to act resolutely in the future. Chapter 39 closes with his reaffirmation to return to Jerusalem all who are currently scattered among foreign countries so that the heathen will be forced to "know that I am Yahweh their God."

Future Israel   The final section (Ezek. 40–48), a kind of blueprint for the future Israelite theocracy, offered a concrete hope to the Jewish exiles in Babylon. Room by room and court by court, giving exact measurements and dimensions, Ezekiel describes the rebuilt temple, then envisions Yahweh's return to his restored sanctuary: "I saw the glory of the God of Israel approaching from the east. A sound came with it, like the sound of the ocean, and the earth shone with his glory. . . . The glory of Yahweh arrived at the Temple by the east gate. . . . I saw the glory of Yahweh fill the Temple" (Ezek. 43:1–6). The prophet's visions have thus come full cycle, from beholding Yahweh deserting the doomed sanctuary to beholding Yahweh's "glory" returning to a greater temple.

The idealized new temple was to be administered not by the Levites but by descendants of the priest Zadok, whose name means "righteous." Levites may serve as attendants, but only the Zadokites are to enjoy full priestly authority. After listing regulations and liturgical details of temple worship, Ezekiel (or the disciples who compiled and edited his work) has a final vision of a life-giving stream of water issuing from beneath the sanctuary, a fitting symbol of the spiritual cleansing that Yahweh intends to have emanate from his restored shrine.

In several ways Ezekiel's message resembles that of Jeremiah. Both attribute the nation's political troubles to its many sins, especially social injustice and idolatry. Both predict that Yahweh will assuage his anger with a national catastrophe culminating in the destruction of Jerusalem and exile in Babylon. Both emphasize individual responsibility for one's life and foretell a return from the Babylonian captivity. A priest as well as a prophet, however, Ezekiel emphasizes the necessity of practicing Jewish rites, customs, holidays, dietary observances, and communal worship even in exile, realizing that the exiles' moral behavior *and* strict adherence to ceremonial requirements would ensure their national and religious survival. With this emphasis, Ezekiel became the spiritual progenitor of later Judaism.

RECOMMENDED READING

Ackroyd, Peter R. *Exile and Restoration: A Study of Hebrew Thought in the Sixth Century* B.C.E. Westminster Press, 1968.

Eichrodt, Walther. *Ezekiel.* Philadelphia: Westminster Press, 1970.

Howie, C. G. "Ezekiel." In *The Interpreter's Dictionary of the Bible,* vol. 2, pp. 203–13. New York and Nashville: Abingdon Press, 1962.

Raitt, Thomas M. *A Theology of Exile.* Philadelphia: Fortress Press, 1977.

Zimmerli, Walther. "Ezekiel." In *The Interpreter's Dictionary of the Bible: Supplementary Volume,* pp. 314–17. Nashville: Abingdon Press, 1976.

Hosea

Hosea's Marriage	*Chapters 1–3*
Crimes and Punishments	*4–6*
Future Reconciliation	*11–14*

My people perish for want of knowledge.

Hosea 4:6

Hosea, unlike Amos, the Judean shepherd who preceded him as a prophet in the northern kingdom, was a native son of Israel. Also unlike his predecessor, Hosea tempered his announcements of Yahweh's punishment with expressions of grief at Israel's imminent sufferings and hope for his nation's future. Hosea began delivering Yahweh's oracles of judgment during the reign of Jeroboam II (about 747 B.C.E.) and continued into the reign of Israel's last king, Hosea (732–724 B.C.E.). After the fall of the northern kingdom, his words were probably carried south to Judah, where they were collected, written down, and interspersed with later references to David-Zion themes (Hos. 1:7; 3:5). An editor added a postscript advising the reader to take the prophet's message to heart.

Hosea's Marriage   The social, religious, and moral decay that marked the last days of the northern kingdom are reflected not only in the prophet's message but in his private life as well. The book's first section (Hos. 1–3) is intended to show that Hosea's domestic situation exactly paralleled his prophetic view of Yahweh's relationship to Israel: both he and his god were loving husbands who had suffered betrayal by their wives. Israel, Yahweh's bride (whom he had redeemed from slavery in Egypt), had betrayed her divine protector by worshiping Baal, the Canaanite fertility god. To illustrate the nation's faithlessness, Hosea had been commanded: "Go, and marry a whore, and get children with a whore, for the country has become nothing but a whore by abandoning Yahweh" (Hos. 1:2).

Hosea had obediently married Gomer, who may have been a priestess of fertility in a Baalistic cult, and fathered children by her, naming each one symbolically to reflect Yahweh's anger with Israel's religious infidelity. The prophet saw in Gomer's repeated adulteries a mirror image of Israel's "whoring" after Canaan's agricultural deities. It was to Baal the people looked to provide rain, bless their crops, and ensure general prosperity, having forgotten Yahweh's "marriage" covenant with them in the Sinai wilderness. Although for its sins Israel stands condemned to national death, the deity will not permanently abandon his disloyal consort (Hos. 2). Yahweh's steadfast love will eventually reconcile him to his errant people, as Hosea is reunited with his faithless wife (Hos. 3).

Crimes and Punishments   Part 2 (Hos. 4–14) forms a somewhat random collection of poetic declarations against Israel's idolatries, foreign alliances, and exploitation of the poor. Hosea charges the corrupt priesthood with rejecting proper knowledge of their god (Hos. 4:4–11). Priests, nobles, and king are the nation's ruin (Hos. 5:1–7); even the people's repentance is insincere and short-lived (Hos. 6:1–6).

Hosea particularly laments the popularity of cultic rituals and sacrifices, which keep the people from recognizing how empty their religion is (Hos. 8:11–13). What Yahweh desires is "love, not sacrifice; knowledge of God, not holocausts" (Hos. 6:6). The prophet foresees that the Israelites will be scattered, some returning to Egypt, others carried to Assyria, where they will "eat food that is unclean" (Hos. 9:3–6). Although he does not refer to these events, Hosea may have lived to experience the fulfillment of his oracles when Assyria devastated Samaria in 721 B.C.E. and deported many of the survivors.

Future Reconciliation   In spite of their certain punishment, Hosea argues, Yahweh will remember his people. Chapter 11 contains one of the Bible's most moving expressions of divine love, which Hosea perceives as stronger than divine vengeance. While the remaining chapters remind Israel of the reasons for its god's present wrath, they also assert that Yahweh waits to effect a reconciliation (Hos. 12:9–11). Indeed, Israel's exile may lead to a "second honeymoon" with Yahweh, like the Mosaic sojourn in the Sinai Desert (Hos. 2:3, 16–17). The book concludes with a final call for Israel's return and a promise of future happiness (Hos. 14).

RECOMMENDED READING

Mays, James L. *Hosea*. Philadelphia: Westminster Press, 1969.

Smart, James D. "Hosea, Man and Book." In *The Interpreter's Dictionary of the Bible*, vol. 3, pp. 648–53. New York and Nashville: Abingdon Press, 1962.

Ward, James M. *Hosea: A Theological Commentary*. New York: Harper & Row, 1966.

Wolff, Hans Walter. *Hosea*. Philadelphia: Fortress Press, 1974.

Wolff, Hans Walter. *Confrontations with Prophets*. Philadelphia: Fortress Press, 1983.

 Joel

Plague of Locusts	*Chapters 1–3*
Day of Yahweh	
Glorious Future	

I will pour out my spirit on all [humanity].
Your sons and daughters shall prophesy,
your old men shall dream dreams,
and your young men see visions.

Joel 2:28

The Book of Joel presents some of the most striking imagery found in the Old Testament. Although it gives no conclusive evidence of the time it was written, the conditions it describes—locust invasions, drought, and crop failure—suggest that the prophet was active during the fifth century B.C.E., a period of severe economic hardship for the restored community of Judah.

Plague of Locusts The book consists of two parts. The first (Joel 1:1–2:27) vividly relates the devastation wrought by a plague of locusts, which Joel, following the prophetic-deuteronomic tradition, interprets as a sign that Yahweh is angry with his people. He urges the Judeans to repent (Joel 2:12–17), promising that Yahweh will then graciously end the plague (Joel 2:18–27). Chapter 2 describes either an invading army or likens the locusts to a foreign invasion. Which of the two is meant is unknown, but the crisis inspires Joel to declare that the Day of Yahweh, a gloomy time of judgment that Amos had previously announced (Amos 5:18–20), is at hand.

Day of Yahweh The second part of Joel (Joel 2:28–3:21) presents some difficulties because the manuscript text appears to have many passages out of order. For this reason, some modern editors, such as those of the Jerusalem Bible, have reconstructed the sequence of several verses to make better sense of Joel's message. The main theme, however, is clear enough: the locust or military invasion heralds Yahweh's imminent visitation of both Judah and the nations, an event of cosmic terror:

> The sun will be turned to darkness, and the moon to blood, before the great and terrible day of the Lord comes.
>
> Joel 2:31; Revised Standard Version

Although the day of Yahweh will involve "portents in the heavens and on earth, blood and fire and columns of smoke" (Joel 2:30), it will also provide an opportunity to obtain individual salvation, for at that time "all who call on the name of Yahweh will be saved" (Joel 2:32). After repentance, Joel foresees the dawn of a new age. Not only will the land recover from its present desolation and prosper, but Yahweh will pour out his spirit upon all humankind so that dreams, visions, and prophecies will reopen channels of communication between the deity and his creation (Joel 2:28–29).

Glorious Future In his climactic vision of the "end time," Joel predicts that godless nations will be summoned to the Valley of Decision (Joel 3:14), where the ultimate war between good and evil (called Armageddon in Rev. 16:12–16) will take place. In a reversal of Isaiah's prophecy (Isa. 2:4), Joel sardonically urges the pagan warriors to

Hammer your plowshares into swords,
your sickles into spears.

Joel 4:10

After the Gentile hosts suffer final defeat, Yahweh will send his people unprecedented blessings:

When that day comes,
the mountains will run with new wine,
and the hills flow with milk,
and all the river beds of Judah run with water.

Joel 3:18

Joel specifically promises that Yahweh will never again make Judah a public shame, as he had done when it was conquered by Babylon (Joel 2:20), and foresees that Yahweh will always protect his holy city:

But Judah will be inhabited for ever,
Jerusalem from age to age . . .
and Yahweh will make his home in Zion.

Joel 3:19–21

Joel contains in miniature the pattern for Judgment Day and the New Age upon which later Bible writers elaborated in such books as Daniel, 2 Esdras, and Revelation. The eschatological features that Joel foresees as occurring at the consummation of history include: (1) a series of natural, political, and supernatural disasters—"signs" in heaven and earth—that portend the wrath to come; (2) a cosmic battle fought in both the material and spiritual realms, in which Yahweh and his people triumph over their enemies; (3) an outpouring of Holy Spirit upon Yahweh's people; and (4) the divine presence among the faithful.

Understandably, Joel is frequently quoted by later Jewish and Christian writers. The pseudepigraphal Book of Enoch reflects Joel's ideas and imagery, as does the New Testament Book of Acts, which interprets the Pentacostal miracle as the fulfillment of Joel 2:28–29 (see Acts 2:1–4, 7–21). The Synoptic Gospels cite Joel's references to astronomical phenomena as events heralding Jesus' Second Coming (see Mark 13:24–25; Luke 21:11, 25; Matt. 24:29).

RECOMMENDED READING

Kapelrud, Arvid S. *Joel Studies*. Uppsala: Almquist & Wiksells, 1948.

Wolff, Hans Walter. *Joel and Amos*. Philadelphia: Fortress Press, 1977.

❧ Amos

Oracles of Doom	*Chapters 1–2*
Three Sermons	*3–6*
Visions of Judgment	*7:1–9:8a*
Epilogue	*9:8b–15*

The Lord Yahweh do[es nothing] without revealing his plans to his servants the prophets.

Amos 3:7

Although placed third among the Minor Prophets, Amos was the first biblical prophet to have his words recorded in book form and to introduce major themes that would thereafter become the staple of prophecy. Active about 750 B.C.E. during the reign of Jeroboam II, Amos was an older contemporary of Hosea and Isaiah of Jerusalem. A native of Judah from the small town of Tekoa located about twelve miles south of Jerusalem, a shepherd and pruner of sycamore (fig) trees, Amos—as he insists—was not a professional prophet (Amos 7:14). Nonetheless, he answered Yahweh's call to proclaim a stern message of doom in the northern kingdom. His book shows considerable familiarity with northern customs, economic conditions, and religious practices, many of which he condemns astringently.

Oracles of Doom   The book is divided into four main sections: (1) brief oracles of doom (Amos 1–2); (2) three sermons (Amos 3–6); (3) five visions of judgment (Amos 7:1–9:8a); and (4) an epilogue (Amos 9:8b–15). The first portion, related in an abrupt, austere style, is a series of oracles against Israel's various neighbors—Syria, Philistia, Tyre, Edom, Ammon, and Moab—that the prophet excoriates for their inhuman treatment of conquered peoples. But his Israelite audience was soon shaken from complacency when the prophet turned his attack against Israel itself. Amos perceived that Yahweh not only refused to tolerate cruelty among his chosen people but required higher behavior from Israel than from nations that did not have the Mosaic law.

Foremost among Israel's crimes was its exploitation of the poor. Although under Jeroboam the nation had grown rich and comfortable, the wealth had accumulated into too few hands, leaving many landless and in want. This unequal distribution of the nation's goods Amos condemned as abhorrent to Yahweh, who will punish them

> Because they have sold the virtuous man for silver
> and the poor man for a pair of sandals,
> because they trample on the heads of ordinary people
> and push the poor out of their path.
>
> Amos 2:6–7

Amos saw that behind the national prosperity and private luxury was a callous indifference to human rights, which was no less a sin than sacrificing to idols. He was the first prophet to argue that social justice is as vital to religion as worshiping one god alone (Amos 8:4–8).

Three Sermons   In the three sermons that follow (Amos 3–6), the prophet reminds Israel that Yahweh causes everything that happens, whether it be the fall of a city or the message of his prophets (Amos 3:3–8). He then predicts the destruction of Bethel's popular sanctuary and the ruin of the magnificent palaces and "houses of ivory" that the wealthy had built (Amos 3:13–15). Similarly, in chapter 5 he foretells that the houses, fields, and vineyards that rich landowners have accumulated will never yield their benefits to those who cheat the poor and defenseless (Amos 5:7–12).

Nor is the ceremonial religion practiced by "respectable" citizens acceptable.

> I hate and despise your feasts,
> I take no pleasure in your solemn festivals.
> When you offer me holocausts,
> I reject your oblations. . . .
> Let me have no more of the din of your chanting,
> no more of your strumming on harps.
> But let justice flow like water,
> and integrity like an unfailing stream.
>
> Amos 5:21–24

Amos' insistence that ethical behavior is more important than ritual observances is typical of Israel's prophets, but he was the first to emphasize this important concept.

Visions of Judgment   Amos fostered another significant reversal in Israel's religious outlook. Until his time the Day of Yahweh was thought to be a time of rejoicing, a future era when Yahweh would vanquish all

Israel's enemies and cover his people with glory. Blasting such complacent expectations, Amos proclaimed the Day of Yahweh to be a day of judgment, a period of darkness and grief for sinful Israel (Amos 5:18–20). This so distressed his hearers that Amaziah, the priest of Bethel, forbade the prophet to speak and expelled him from the sanctuary (Amos 7:10–17), which did not, however, prevent Amos from continuing his pronouncements of doom.

Israel, he said, was like a basket of summer fruit, ripe for destruction (Amos 8:1–4), and none will escape the day of wrath:

> Should they burrow their way down to Sheol,
> my hand will haul them out;
> should they scale the heavens,
> I will drag them down.

Amos 9:2

Amos saw Yahweh as directing the fate of all nations, not of Israel alone. He had brought the Philistines from Crete just as he had brought Israel from Egypt; they and the Ethiopians were all the same to him (Amos 9:7–8). Assyria, then just beginning its imperial expansion, was also under Yahweh's jurisdiction and would be the chosen instrument to punish Israel. Amos thus foresaw the northern kingdom's fall to Assyria in 721 B.C.E., though he expressed this insight in terms of hyperbole and metaphor rather than by foretelling specific events and dates.

Epilogue   So unrelieved was Amos' pessimism that a later hand added a brief epilogue predicting Israel's future restoration and prosperity (Amos 9:11–15). But his dire warnings and harsh judgments nevertheless set the tone for many later prophets, among them Jeremiah, who resembles the shepherd from Tekoa in delivering an unrelievedly gloomy message.

RECOMMENDED READING

Coote, Robert B. *Amos Among the Prophets: Composition and Theology.* Philadelphia: Fortress Press, 1981.

Koch, Klaus. *The Prophets.* Vol. I, *The Assyrian Age.* Translated by Margaret Kohl. Philadelphia: Fortress Press, 1982.

Mays, James L. *Amos.* Philadelphia: Westminster Press, 1969.

Smart, James D. "Amos." In *The Interpreter's Dictionary of the Bible*, vol. 1, pp. 116–21. New York and Nashville: Abingdon Press, 1962.

Ward, James M. *Amos and Isaiah: Prophets of the Word of God.* Nashville: Abingdon Press, 1969.

Wolff, Hans Walter. *Confrontations with Prophets.* Philadelphia: Fortress Press, 1983.

❧ Obadiah

Oracles Against Edom   *Verses 1–21*

As you have done, so will it be done to you.

Obadiah 15

Oracles Against Edom   Shortest of the Old Testament prophetic books, Obadiah is a single chapter of oracles against Israel's near neighbor Edom, probably delivered shortly after the Babylonians had destroyed Jerusalem in 587 B.C.E. Apparently Edom had joined in the plundering of Judah, for which the writer bitterly condemns Edom and predicts its imminent desolation. The Edomites' gloating over fallen Judah is seen as particularly heinous because, according to ancient traditions, they were descended from Esau, Jacob's (Israel's) twin brother (see Gen. 25:19–27:45; 36:1–19). Their unbrotherly conduct will be repaid in kind (Obad. 15), but Judah's exiles will return to occupy Mount Zion (Obad. 19–21). Other Bible writers also cite Edom's ungenerous actions (Jer. 29:7–22; Ezek. 25:12–14; Ps. 137:7).

RECOMMENDED READING

Muilenburg, James. "Obadiah, Book of." In *The Interpreter's Dictionary of the Bible*, vol. 3, pp. 578–79. New York and Nashville: Abingdon Press, 1962.

❧ Jonah

A Reluctant Prophet   *Chapters 1–4*

Am I [Yahweh] not to feel sorry for Nineveh, the great city . . . ?

Jonah 4:11

Unique among the prophetic writings, the book of Jonah is not a collection of oracles but a brief prose tale about a narrow-minded man whose god is much greater than he had anticipated. The style of the book is terse, its intent broadly humorous, and the joke is on those who think that Yahweh condemns all people except those belonging to a particular religious or racial group. Although the time of writing is unknown, it is probably postexilic, its theme of toleration perhaps a reaction to Ezra's severe and rigid view of Judaism (see pages 188–192).

A Reluctant Prophet   Jonah's story occupies but four brief chapters. In the first, Yahweh calls Jonah to preach at Nineveh, capital of the hated Assyrian Empire, but the reluctant prophet decides instead to leave Palestine and take ship for Spain at the opposite end of the Mediterranean. Yahweh stops the ship with a great storm that terrifies the Gentile sailors. Casting lots, they learn that Jonah is the cause of their danger but are too humane to cast the Hebrew jinx overboard. Only after begging Yahweh's forgiveness do they hurl Jonah into the sea, where the god has arranged for a large fish to swallow him.

The second chapter consists largely of Jonah's prayer from the belly of the sea creature. It is the only poetic passage in the book and may have been inserted by a later writer. Although Jonah's lament reveals little religious insight—he still seems to think that Yahweh hears prayers only at the Jerusalem temple—Yahweh has the fish spew Jonah out near shore.

The humor of the totally improbable dominates chapter 3. After his "resurrection" from the fishy grave, Jonah finally goes to Nineveh. Tersely announcing that the city will be destroyed in forty days, he is unpleasantly surprised when the entire Assyrian population, from the king downward, immediately repents; even the animals wear sackcloth in the hope that Yahweh will relent and spare their city. Noting their improved behavior, Yahweh changes his mind and does not obliterate the Assyrians, which infuriates Jonah. Though in chapter 4 he pretends to have known all along that Yahweh is compassionate, he is privately indignant that Yahweh did not act on his original plan. Feeling betrayed, he asks to die.

While the prophet sulks outside Nineveh's gates, Yahweh causes a leafy plant to grow and shade him from the sun. When a worm kills the plant, Jonah again complains and wishes for death. The book ends with Yahweh questioning Jonah about his (Yahweh's) right to pardon whom he pleases, especially religiously blind people like the Ninevites "who cannot tell their right hand from their left." There is no record that Jonah ever understands the meaning of Yahweh's catechism.

It is difficult to assess the purpose of this curious tale because the author does not spell out his message. The work seems to be an amusing parable teaching that Yahweh is universal and considers the lives of pagan nations to be as valuable as those of his chosen people. If so, is the book a tract against the Jewish exclusiveness that prevailed after the time of Ezra? Certainly its details were not meant to be taken seriously. For who would believe that Nineveh was so gigantic that it took a man three days to walk across it? Or that Jonah literally stayed three days in the stomach of a fish? Or that the Ninevites' domestic animals walked about in mourning garb? Such touches are surely aspects of the author's slyly humorous design.

RECOMMENDED READING

Fretheim, T. E. *The Message of Jonah*. Minneapolis: Augsburg Publishing House, 1977.

Neil, W. "Jonah, Book of." In *The Interpreter's Dictionary of the Bible*, vol. 2, pp. 964–67. New York and Nashville: Abingdon Press, 1962.

❦ Micah

Interpolations—Zion's Future Glory   *Chapters 1–6*

This is what Yahweh asks of you:
only this, to act justly,
to love tenderly,
and to walk humbly with your God.

Micah 6:8

Micah, fourth and last of the eighth-century prophets, was a younger contemporary of Isaiah of Jerusalem. Active between 740 and 700 B.C.E., he directed his earliest prophecies against Israel's idolatries, predicting the fall of the northern kingdom (Mic. 1:2–7). A native of Moresheth, a small town west of Jerusalem, Micah took a country dweller's dim view of urban life and what he regarded as its inevitable corruption. He perceives the city as a source of sin that doomed both Samaria and Jerusalem (Mic. 1:5). He denounces the tyranny of dishonest merchants and greedy landowners (Mic. 2:1–5, 6–11; 3:1–4; 6:9–14), equating their guilt with that of Judah's corrupt princes, judges, priests, and false prophets (Mic. 3:9–12; 7:1–4).

Unlike Isaiah, Micah espouses the cause of the village peasant and is sharply critical of the Davidic dynasty and temple cult. He scornfully denies that the sanctuary's presence in Jerusalem will protect the holy city from harm and predicts that both city and temple will be reduced to rubble (Mic. 3:1–3, 9–12). Condemning the Jerusalem aristocracy and priesthood (Mic. 6:1–2, 9–16), he also rebukes hired seers who speak false comfort and fear to tell the people unwelcome truths (Mic. 3:5–8). Micah even rejects the belief that animal or any other sacrifice is required by Israel's deity. In the book's most famous passage, he argues that Yahweh asks only for acts of justice and love and for humble communion with one's god (Mic. 6:6–8). Here the insight of the rural prophet wars with the prerogative of the city priest, for if Micah's words were to be taken literally, would Judah need either Levite or sanctuary?

Interpolations—Zion's Future Glory   Some scholars believe that Micah may have been one of Isaiah's disciples, which would account for a prediction of universal peace in almost exactly the same words as a passage in Isaiah (compare Mic. 4:1–4 and Isa. 2:2–4). Other scholars suggest that the optimistic promises and visions of Judah's future glory (Mic. 4:1–5:15; 7:8–20) were added by a later hand. According to the latter view, Micah originally condemned Judah for its violation of the Mosaic Covenant, and an editor subsequently inserted references to Yahweh's unconditional promise to preserve the Davidic kingdom. The references to a faithful remnant returning to Judah from exile, after which every citizen will sit under his or her vine and fig tree in peace and prosperity (Mic. 2:12; 4:4–8) may have been interpolated into the text after Micah's time. The famous prophecy of Bethlehem's one day being the birthplace of a ruler whose "origin goes back to the distant past, to the days of old" (Mic. 5:2) is viewed similarly as a later addition. Despite scholars' suspicion that Micah's original message underwent editorial modification, in its present form the book represents the typical prophetic paradox in which Yahweh is presented simultaneously as the stern judge and merciful savior of his people.

Although his words must have been unpopular with the authorities, Micah's oracles were preserved on a scroll housed in the temple, an institution whose destruction he had foretold (Jer. 26:16–18).

RECOMMENDED READING

Leslie, E. A. "Micah." In *The Interpreter's Dictionary of the Bible*, vol. 3, pp. 369–72. New York and Nashville: Abingdon Press, 1962.

Mays, James L. *Micah*. Philadelphia: Westminster Press, 1976.

Wolff, Hans Walter. *Micah the Prophet*. Translated by R. D. Gehrke. Philadelphia: Fortress Press, 1981.

 Nahum

Fall of Nineveh   *Chapters 1–3*

Yahweh is a jealous and vengeful God,
Yahweh avenges, he is full of wrath.

                              Nahum 1:2

Of Nahum's personal life or theological beliefs we know nothing except that his message was unlike that of any other known Hebrew prophet. He neither decried his people's sins nor prophesied their retribution; instead, his entire book is composed of three poems rejoicing over the ruin of Nineveh, capital of the Assyrian Empire. His gloating, unmitigated by compassion, contrasts markedly with the merciful attitude found in Jonah.

Fall of Nineveh Nahum probably wrote about 612 B.C.E., either while the combined Medes and Babylonians were besieging Nineveh or shortly after the city's capture. In any case, the Medo-Babylonian coalition brought an end to Assyrian hegemony in the Near East, and the Jews were undoubtedly not alone in celebrating their enemy's downfall. A notoriously cruel taskmaster, Assyria had not only deported whole populations from their homelands but had routinely performed atrocities that included physically mutilating and disfiguring captured persons, butchering women and children, and leading away chained prisoners with metal hooks in their jaws.

Nahum sees Nineveh's collapse as evidence of Yahweh's vengeance upon Assyrian inhumanity (Nah. 1:2–3), for Yahweh is here perceived as the universal sovereign. Although he had used Assyria as his "rod of correction" to punish Israel and Judah for their sins, Assyrian savagery had determined that it, too, must be humbled. Chapters 2 and 3 provide excellent examples of Hebrew poetry at its most vivid. Nahum's description of armed legions marching against Nineveh and plundering its treasures is harrowingly realistic (Nah. 2); his enumeration of Assyria's crimes is equally eloquent (Nah. 3).

Nahum interprets Nineveh's fate as part of Yahweh's long-range plan to improve the condition of his people. Released from Assyrian bondage, perhaps Israel but certainly Judah will enjoy a happy era of freedom (Nah. 1:15; 2:2), "for never again shall the wicked come against you" (Nah. 2:15; Revised Standard Version). This optimism was unjustified, however, for only three years later King Josiah was killed by Pharaoh Necho as Egyptian troops passed through the Plain of Megiddo on their way to support remnants of the Assyrian army (2 Kings 23:29–35). Egypt then controlled Judah's affairs until about 605 B.C.E., when the Babylonians defeated Egyptian forces at the Battle of Carchemish and assumed jurisdiction over Palestine, reducing Judah once again to a vassal state.

RECOMMENDED READING

Leslie, E. A. "Nahum, Book of." In *The Interpreter's Dictionary of the Bible*, vol. 3, pp. 498–99. New York and Nashville: Abingdon Press, 1962.

❦ Habakkuk

The upright man will live by his faithfulness.

         Habakkuk 2:4

Yahweh's Justice Habakkuk is less a book of prophecy than a collection of philosophical meditations and a psalm describing Yahweh as a world conqueror. The first section (Hab. 1–2) is cast as a poetic dialogue between Yahweh and Habakkuk, who bitterly complains of his god's inaction in world affairs. Apparently written between about 600 and 587 B.C.E. when the Babylonian (Chaldean) armies threatened Judah, the first chapter asks why Yahweh remains silent while this "fierce and fiery" nation plunders and murders innocent people, including people much better than they.

The answer is that such Gentile oppressors are Yahweh's "instruments of justice" (Hab. 1:12), chosen to carry out his will even though they do not recognize him as God. The implication is that Babylon's task is to punish Judah, but unlike Jeremiah or Ezekiel, Habakkuk does not argue that Judah's sins deserve so catastrophic a punishment. Indeed, he differs strikingly from the deuteronomic historians of the period in *not* asserting that the people's suffering is a result of their collective guilt.

In chapter 2 Habakkuk declares that he will "stand on [his] watchtower" and await Yahweh's response, which is simply this: "The upright man will live by his faithfulness." That is, people must have faith that their god will eventually see justice done; this confidence in divine control of the outcome will sustain the righteous soul in its trials.

The balance of Habakkuk 2:5–20 is a veiled threat of vengeance upon Babylon (or some other oppressor of the chosen people), whose punishment for abusing Yahweh's heritage is certain though it may not be swift. This section closes with a satire against idolatry, juxtaposed with the statement that "Yahweh is in his Holy Temple" and the nations should keep silent before him. Although this passage indicates that the temple was still standing at the time of writing, it may come from a later hand than Habakkuk's and thus refer to the postexilic sanctuary.

Judge of the Earth The third chapter pictures Yahweh as angrily striding from the east amid storm clouds and lightning—a mighty warrior flashing his arrows, hurling his spear, and riding in horse-drawn chariots. This manifestation of divine strength is probably a response by a later writer to Habakkuk's original skepticism that Yahweh would bring justice to world affairs, for the god of chapter 3 is clearly willing and able to execute immediate vengeance upon Israel's oppressors, and this vision decisively answers Habakkuk's plaintive cry about "how long" (Hab. 1:2) Yahweh will tolerate wrongdoing. The militant psalm, which was probably sung in the second temple, concludes with a quiet affirmation of trust in the deity.

RECOMMENDED READING

Leslie, E. A. "Habakkuk." In *The Interpreter's Dictionary of the Bible*, vol. 2, pp. 503–5. New York and Nashville: Abingdon Press, 1962.

🍂 Zephaniah

Day of Yahweh	*Chapters 1:1–2:3*
Curses and Promises	*3*

Seek Yahweh, all you, the humble of the earth, . . . seek integrity, seek humility.

Zephaniah 2:3

Day of Yahweh With Zephaniah we return to the typical concerns of Israel's prophets: the condemnation of sin and declaration of Yahweh's impending wrath. Indeed, Zephaniah foresees a universal destruction in which all life forms—humans, beasts, birds, and fish—are to be exterminated (Zeph. 1:2–3). Yahweh will slaughter foreign kings, Judean royalty, greedy merchants, and skeptics alike who believe that "Yahweh has no power for good or for evil" (Zeph. 1:4–13). Like Amos, the prophet regards the Day of Yahweh as frighteningly near:

> A day of wrath, that day,
> a day of distress and agony,
> a day of ruin and devastation,
> a day of darkness and gloom,
> a day of clouds and blackness,
> a day of trumpet blast and battle cry. . . .
> I am going to bring such distress on men

> that they will grope like the blind . . .
> their blood will be scattered like dust,
> their corpses like dung.

Zephaniah 1:15–17

On the day of Yahweh's "jealousy" the earth will be consumed and all its inhabitants destroyed (Zeph. 1:18).

Although we do not know what specific conditions fostered the prophet's pessimism, he wrote during the reign of King Josiah (640–609 B.C.E.) but before the discovery of the Book of Deuteronomy (621 B.C.E.) had stimulated Josiah's sweeping religious reforms. The Jerusalem whose sins Zephaniah denounces was thus a prereform city that may have been contaminated by the pro-Assyrian idolatries of Manasseh's administration. It seems, then, that Zephaniah was the first prophet to speak out after the long silence that Manasseh and his immediate successor, Amon, had imposed on the Yahwist religion.

After categorically asserting that Yahweh will spare no living thing, Zephaniah concedes that a few humble people who keep the commandments "may perhaps find shelter" on the day of wrath (Zeph. 2:3). In fact, chapter 2 implies the survival of a faithful remnant, for after Philistia, Moab, and Ammon have been destroyed, Jewish survivors will confiscate their land (Zeph. 2:6–7; 9–10).

Curses and Promises   Chapter 3 attacks the "rebellious," "defiled," and "tyrannical" leaders of Jerusalem who have failed to learn justice from the object lessons to be found in the destruction of other cities. As a result, Yahweh will gather the nations to pour out his fury on Judah (Zeph. 3:8). After painting a bleak future for humanity, however, Zephaniah concludes by offering some rays of hope. In a series of terse oracles he asserts that the Gentile states will come to worship Yahweh (Zeph. 3:9–10), that a humble remnant of Israel will seek refuge in Yahweh (Zeph. 3:11–13), and that Jewish exiles will be delivered from their oppressors (Zeph. 3:19–20).

It is tempting to suppose that the following uncharacteristically joyous passage was Zephaniah's response to King Josiah's reform movement:

> Shout for joy, daughter of Zion. . . .
> Yahweh has repealed your sentence;
> he has driven your enemies away.
> Yahweh, the king of Israel, is in your midst;
> you have no more evil to fear.

Zephaniah 3:14–15

If this surmise is true, perhaps Zephaniah believed that Josiah's cleansing of the temple, his reinstituting the Passover and other Mosaic observances, had restored Yahweh's presence to the Judean community. Josiah's military successes may also have indicated to the prophet that Yahweh had changed his mind about obliterating a nation stained with Manasseh's sins. In any case, the prophet's image of Yahweh dancing invisibly at Judah's festivals (Zeph. 3:18) represents a striking shift in his vision.

RECOMMENDED READING

Leslie, E. A. "Zephaniah, Book of." In *The Interpreter's Dictionary of the Bible*, vol. 4, pp. 951–53. New York and Nashville: Abingdon Press, 1962.

❦ Haggai

Yahweh's Temple   *Chapters 1–2*
Zerubbabel   *2:22–23*

**I will shake all the nations and the treasures of
all the nations shall flow in,
and I will fill this Temple with glory. . . .**

Haggai 2:7–8

Yahweh's Temple Although a remnant of devout Jews had returned from Babylon around 538 B.C.E and laid the foundations of a new sanctuary on the site of Solomon's temple, they had since become discouraged and allowed the work to lapse. Economic conditions were bad, and the tiny postexilic community struggled merely to survive. Interpreting the repeated crop failures and subsequent famine as signs that Yahweh is angry because his shrine has not been completed (Hag. 1:4–11), Haggai, who prophesied in the year 520 B.C.E., urges the governor and the high priest to persuade the people to return to the project, which they do enthusiastically. Older Jews who remember the glories of Solomon's temple are disappointed in the modest dimensions of the new sanctuary, but Haggai promises that it will soon be filled with treasures flowing into Jerusalem from all nations (Hag. 2:7).

Zerubbabel The prophet also conveys Yahweh's plan to "shake the heavens and the earth," to "overturn the thrones of kingdoms" (Hag. 2:22), and to establish Zerubbabel, Jerusalem's governor and a descendant of one of the last Davidic kings, as "a signet ring." The implication seems to be that the Persian Empire, of which Judah was then a small part, would be overthrown and Judah's independence restored with Zerubbabel as its reigning monarch. Haggai thus seems to regard the governor as a political "messiah" or anointed king (Hag. 2:23). Zechariah, an exact contemporary of Haggai, apparently had the same hope (Zech. 4:6–10); but Zerubbabel soon afterward disappears from history, and we hear no more of him.

RECOMMENDED READING

Ackroyd, Peter R. *Exile and Restoration: A Study of Hebrew Thought in the Sixth Century B.C.E.* Philadelphia: Westminster Press, 1968.

Neil, W. "Haggai." In *The Interpreter's Dictionary of the Bible*, vol. 2, pp. 509–21. New York and Nashville: Abingdon Press, 1962.

🦋 Zechariah

Historical Zechariah	Chapters 1–8
Second Zechariah	9–14

**Many peoples and great nations will come
to seek Yahweh . . . in Jerusalem
and to entreat the favor of Yahweh.**

Zechariah 8:22

Whereas Haggai's message was direct and straightforward, that of Zechariah, his fellow prophet of the postexilic period, is often ambiguous and obscure. The Book of Zechariah makes clear that Yahweh wishes to have the temple rebuilt and that Zerubbabel is a likely candidate to restore Judah's political fortunes, but beyond that all certainty vanishes. Scholars divide the book into two parts. The first eight chapters are mostly by the "Historical Zechariah," who began prophesying in 520 B.C.E. Chapters 9–14, called the "Second Zechariah," seem to have been written by other seers, perhaps a Zecharian school of prophets, at various later dates.

Historical Zechariah Zechariah, who appears to have come from a priestly family, lived in a restored community in which want and insecurity had taken the place of the glorious future predicted by Second Isaiah. Although Zechariah stressed the necessity of rebuilding the temple to attain Yahweh's favor and material blessings, he also addressed himself to the community's underlying disillusionment in eight visions (Zech. 1–6) which, interpreted by an angelic figure, are generally aimed at calming the people's apprehensions about what Yahweh intends to do with them. Hopes that Zerubbabel would mount the throne of David are dashed when Darius, emperor of Persia, quells an incipient revolt and consolidates his power. After Zerubbabel disappears from history,

Zechariah concentrates on the prospects of Joshua, the high priest, whom he refers to as the "branch" or shoot from David's stock (Zech. 3:8–10).

Particularly interesting is Zechariah's vision in chapter 3 of Joshua standing before Yahweh's celestial throne. When Satan (the Adversary) appears to accuse the high priest (who represents the Judean remnant), Yahweh's angel removes Joshua's dirty garments—symbolic of the community's sins—and reclothes him in splendid robes. This change of attire shows that Yahweh has forgiven his people's sins and that the period of national mourning is over; if the community henceforth keeps Yahweh's commandments, it will prosper. Zechariah's mystical experience thus provides hope that Yahweh is at last acting to improve the condition of his restored nation.

Similarly, the vision in 6:9–15 emphasizes Joshua's messianic role as "the branch," the person destined to rebuild the sanctuary, wear the royal insignia, and "sit on his throne as ruler" (Zech. 6:13). Because this passage also refers to cooperation between a restored king and priest, scholars have suggested that the prophecy originally applied to the Davidic Zerubbabel who, with Joshua, was joint leader of the community. After Zerubbabel's aspirations came to nothing, however, scribes substituted Joshua's name for that of the former governor. Although plans for a renewed Davidic monarchy had become both futile and dangerous, it was still possible to envisage the high priest as Yahweh's Anointed and spiritual leader of the Jewish state.

Chapters 7 and 8 respectively survey the moral meaning of Israel's rise and fall as a nation and promise the people ultimate redemption through a Messiah who will create a new dispensation in which the whole earth will become a paradise. This section concludes with the prediction that not only will powerful nations come to Jerusalem to worship Yahweh but that ten foreigners will cling to a single Jew, begging him to teach them Yahweh's law. With its emphasis on Zion (or Jerusalem) as the religious center of the universe, this section echoes ideas first expressed in Isaiah 2, 9, and 11.

Second Zechariah The second half of Zechariah contains diverse oracles, some from as late as the Greek period in the fourth century B.C.E. These strange visions and predictions appear to be the work of several apocalyptic writers whose intended meanings are now nearly impossible to grasp, although the section (which resembles the apocalyptic passages in Isa. 24–27) was a favorite with early Christians, who found numerous messianic references in it

Zechariah 9:9 declares that Jerusalem's king will come to the city "humble and riding on a donkey, on a colt, the foal of a donkey." The author of Matthew's Gospel, perhaps misunderstanding the poet's use of parallelism here, depicts Jesus as riding on two different animals at once (Matt. 21:1–7). Zechariah also mentions "thirty shekels of silver" (Zech. 11:13–14), the sum for which Judas betrays his master. A particularly obscure oracle pictures Jerusalem as mourning "one whom they have pierced" (Zech. 12:10), in a passage where Yahweh also promises to make "the House of David like God" leading victorious armies. Equally cryptic is the allusion to striking a shepherd and scattering his sheep (Zech. 13:7), which follows an apparent declaration that the gift of prophecy has been removed from Israel (Zech. 13:2–6).

Chapter 14 is a full-fledged eschatological vision describing the final consummation of history. In a climactic battle, Yahweh will gather all nations to Jerusalem. The enemy will plunder the city and slaughter nearly all its inhabitants; but at the last desperate moment Yahweh will intervene, striding from the Mount of Olives—which will be sundered by titanic earthquakes—to fight for Israel.

After annihilating his enemies, Yahweh will transform the earth and its climate. Cold and frost will cease, streams will issue from Jerusalem, mountains will disappear, and all Palestine will become a plain (a highly desirable change for farmers and shepherds). Meanwhile, the non-Jewish nations will suffer a plague that rots their eyes in their sockets and causes them to attack one another irrationally. The nations that survive this catastrophe will henceforth make pilgrimages to Jerusalem, then elevated above all other cities, to worship at Yahweh's temple, and Yahweh "will be king of the whole world."

RECOMMENDED READING

Ackroyd, Peter R. *Exile and Restoration: A Study of Hebrew Thought in the Sixth Century B.C.E.* Philadelphia: Westminster Press, 1968.

Neil, W. "Zechariah, Book of." In *The Interpreter's Dictionary of the Bible*, vol. 4, pp. 943–47. New York and Nashville: Abingdon Press, 1962.

❦ Malachi

Pleasing Yahweh	Chapters 1–2
The Coming Messenger	3

Look, I am going to send my messenger
to prepare a way before me. . . .
Who will be able to resist the day of his coming?

Malachi 3:1–2

In Protestant and Catholic Bibles, Malachi appears as the last Old Testament book, an appropriate placement because the book concludes with a prediction that Yahweh will send a "messenger" who will prepare his people for the climactic event of history, the Day of Yahweh. The title means "my messenger" and may have been taken from the reference at 3:1 and not be the name of a historical prophet. Although the text gives no information about the writer or time of composition, the book is customarily dated in the fifth century B.C.E., shortly before the time when traditional prophecy in Israel is thought to have ceased.

Pleasing Yahweh   The first two chapters contribute little to Israel's prophetic legacy. Casting his message in question-and-answer form, the writer presents Yahweh's complaints that the people offend him by sacrificing defective animals at the temple. The author's concern is exclusively with the physical aspects of worship; he has nothing to say about the moral implications. Even so, one can assume that he views the offering of an unblemished animal, as Mosaic law required, as the outward symbol of a worshiper's wholehearted wish to please his or her god; to do less betrayed an imperfect commitment to Yahweh. Chapter 2 ends with a vigorous attack on divorce, which the prophet also regards as breaking faith with Yahweh.

The Coming Messenger   Malachi's prediction that the temple will be inspected and cleansed by Yahweh's messenger, "the angel of the Covenant" (Mal. 3:1), is thematically connected with the earlier denunciations of inferior sacrifices, but in chapter 3 the prophet broadens his charge to include responsibilities to widows, orphans, strangers, and the poor. The author briefly returns to mundane functions, like tithing (Mal. 3:6–12), but then asserts that Yahweh's justice will prevail only when the god himself intervenes to champion the righteous and punish the wicked. Although in this life the arrogant and ruthless often exploit the humble and faithful, justice will triumph when the Day of Yahweh arrives. It consequently behooves one to keep the commandments, even though one may temporarily suffer for it.

Finally, Malachi promises that, before "that great and terrible day" arrives, Yahweh will send Elijah the prophet—who in 2 Kings 2:11–12 had been carried off alive to heaven—to reconcile the generations, fathers and children, lest Yahweh "strike the land with a curse" (Mal. 3:24). The belief that Elijah would return to prepare the way for the Messiah or the Kingdom of God and Day of Judgment played a significant part in later Jewish expectations. Even today a place is set for Elijah, the long-awaited guest, at Passover observances.

RECOMMENDED READING

Dentan, Robert C. "Introduction and Exegesis to Malachi." In *The Interpreter's Bible*, vol. 6, pp. 1115–44. New York and Nashville: Abingdon Press, 1956.

Neil, W. "Malachi." In *The Interpreter's Dictionary of the Bible*, vol. 3, pp. 228–32. New York and Nashville: Abingdon Press, 1962.

PART 5

THE WRITINGS

The third major division of the Hebrew Bible, the Writings (*Kethuvim*), was the last to be accepted as canonical. In theme and literary form it is also the least unified part of the Bible. The diverse material in the Torah is bound together by Yahweh's series of promises or covenants with the patriarchs and with Israel at Sinai. The historical narratives of Joshua through Kings (the Former Prophets) are unified by the writers' controlling intent to show Yahweh as Lord of History, expressing his will through Israel's political rise and fall. Even the fifteen books of the Latter Prophets, for all their diverse responses to changing political and religious circumstances over a period of four centuries, form a coherent tradition. By contrast, the Writings present a wide variety of viewpoints expressing the multifaceted religious experiences of postexilic Israel.

The long line of prophets began during the early monarchy and ended soon after Judah's return from exile when the monarchy no longer existed, whereas the Writings belong primarily to the postexilic period (approximately the fifth to the second centuries B.C.E.). This miscellaneous collection includes poetry (Psalms, Song of Solomon, Lamentations), wise sayings (Proverbs), short stories (Ruth and Esther), priestly history (Ezra-Nehemiah and Chronicles), magnificent wisdom literature (Job and Ecclesiastes), and apocalyptic visions of the end of time (Daniel).

WISDOM LITERATURE

In ancient Israel, people belonging to three callings or professions could speak with authority—the priest, the prophet, and the sage. According to Jeremiah (18:18), the priest's business was to instruct in covenant law (the Torah), the prophet's to convey Yahweh's "word," and the sage's to provide wise advice (see also Ezek. 7:26). The "wise," including both men and women, held positions of public respect and commonly served as counselors to kings (2 Sam. 14:21; 16:23; 20:14–22). Prophets were sometimes critical of the professional class of sages—as they were of priests—but the wisdom movement ultimately outlasted the prophetic line and produced some of the greatest books in the Bible.

The origins of Israel's wisdom tradition are unknown, but archaeological discoveries have revealed that long before Israel came into existence, thinkers in Egypt, Mesopotamia, Edom, and Phoenicia had produced astute guides to the "good life." Among Hebrew writers, however, wisdom material acquired a new tone and emphasis: "The fear of Yahweh is the beginning of knowledge" (Prov. 1:7). Although the writers of many proverbs—short, memorable sayings summarizing insights about life—stressed observation and experience as a source of knowledge, they regarded wisdom as much a divine gift as the prophetic word (Prov. 2:6). Wisdom, rather than the Torah, was envisioned as Yahweh's first creation and, personified as a gracious divine woman, acted as a liaison between the deity and humanity (Prov. 8). This theme of Wisdom as a creative spirit linking humankind with a primary attribute of the Creator is most fully developed in a late apocryphal work, the Wisdom of Solomon (7:22–9:18).

Renowned for his shrewd judgments, King Solomon—the reputed author of 3,000 proverbs—stood at the head of Israel's wisdom tradition (1 Kings 3:1–28; 4:29–34). Later ages, honoring Solomon's role in establishing a national institution of wise government counselors and other sages, attributed a large body of wisdom writings to him. These include the canonical books of Proverbs, Ecclesiastes, and Song of Solomon, the apocryphal Wisdom, and the pseudepigraphal poetry collections known as the Psalms and Odes of Solomon.

In Hebrew literature, wisdom was expressed in many different literary forms. Early types included riddles, fables, and proverbs (Judg. 9:18–15; 14:14; 1 Kings 4:32). In later times, anonymous sages produced far more complex and sophisticated works, such as the book of Job, where subtle theological arguments are sustained through lengthy debates about divine justice and the meaning of human suffering. Works like Ecclesiastes contain an amalgam of the sage's personal reflections on life's futility and meditations on death, as well as paradoxical maxims, proverbs, and expressions of proverbial wisdom.

The author of only one wisdom book is known—Jesus Ben Sirach, who compiled the observations, teachings, and experiences of a lifetime in Ecclesiasticus. This weighty volume, the longest of its kind in the Bible, reveals the existence of "wisdom schools" at which young people were educated by a recognized wisdom authority. One of the last-written books of the Apocrypha, the work entitled Wisdom of Solomon (about the first century B.C.E.) is the only Old Testament work that specifically links the righteousness born of wisdom to hopes of personal immortality (Wisdom 1:12–3:9; 5:4–24; etc.).

Besides these works, certain psalms also contain wisdom motifs (Pss. 1, 8, 16, 17, 19, 34, 37, 49, 73, 92, 104, 112, 119, and 139) as do the prose tales of Joseph and Daniel, wise men loyal to their Jewish heritage who rose to power in foreign nations (Gen. 39–41; Dan. 1–6). Both of these figures are depicted as recipients of a divine gift, the wisdom to interpret dreams foreshadowing the future. The greatest wisdom literature, however, is based on the authors' profound reflections upon the significance of ordinary life, with its unequal distribution of good and evil fortune, unexpected calamities, and the ambiguity of its ethical "message."

Because of its diversity in outlook, thought, and form, wisdom material defies easy classification. Its characteristic themes are strikingly different from those in the Torah and the Prophets. Wisdom books typically make no references to the covenant relationship that bound Israel to Yahweh. Neither Job nor Ecclesiastes even mentions the Mosaic Torah; but both agree that many religious assumptions, such as a divinely favored "right side's" winning in life's battles, are unjustified by human experience. The deuteronomists' thesis that Yahweh directs human history, of which individual lives are a part, is also conspicuously absent.

Evaluating the ethical quality of human life from a variety of perspectives, the wisdom authors typically come to rather seditious conclusions. Their observations and analyses of experience tend to subvert some other Bible writers' interpretation of Israel's history. The prophetic tradition held that Yahweh observed all people's actions, inevitably punishing the bad and rewarding the good, an assumption shared by the deuteronomic historians, who interpreted Israel's growth and destruction as the consequence of keeping or breaking covenant laws. Among the Hebrew thinkers who vigorously disputed this simplistic view of life was the anonymous poet who wrote Job.

RECOMMENDED READING

Brueggemann, Walter A. *In Man We Trust: The Neglected Side of Biblical Faith.* Richmond, Va.: John Knox Press, 1972.

Bryce, Glendon E. *Israel and the Wisdom of Egypt.* Lewisburg, Pa.: Bucknell University Press, 1975. Analyzes the influence of Egyptian wisdom on the book of Proverbs.

Crenshaw, James. *Studies in Ancient Israelite Wisdom.* New York: KTAV Publishing House, 1976.

Lambert, W. G. *Babylonian Wisdom Literature.* Oxford: Clarendon Press, 1960.

Murphy, Roland E. *Seven Books of Wisdom.* Milwaukee: Bruce, 1960.

_____. *Wisdom Literature and Psalms.* Nashville: Abingdon Press, 1983.

Rankin, O. S. *Israel's Wisdom Literature.* Edinburgh: T. & T. Clark, 1936.

Scott, R. B. Y. *The Way of Wisdom in the Old Testament.* New York: Macmillan, 1971.

von Rad, Gerhard. *Wisdom in Israel.* Translated by J. D. Martin. Nashville: Abingdon Press, 1973.

Wood, James. *Wisdom Literature.* London: G. Duckworth, 1967.

Job

Yes, I am a man, and he [Yahweh] is not; and so no argument, no suit between the two of us is possible. There is no arbiter between us.

Job 9:32–33

The Bible's prime example of *speculative wisdom*—the kind of intellectual activity that questions the principles and assumptions commonly accepted by society—the Book of Job is a profound exploration of the issue of God's responsibility for evil and the extent to which he is morally bound, by the intrinsic goodness of his own nature, to protect sentient creatures from unmerited pain. It is also concerned with the psychological relationship between humanity and God, as well as with the intellectual honesty of a righteous person whose integrity does not allow him to evade the dilemma by falsely confessing to sin in order to justify his god's harsh treatment of him. The author's rejection of conventional explanations and his unorthodox demand that Yahweh meet Job on equal terms to explain His questionable morality undoubtedly shocked pious readers when the book was new, as it may still shock some readers today. Because the questions it raises have never been satisfactorily resolved, the book is as provocative now as it was 2,500 years ago.

Scholars do not agree on when Job was written. Although Hebrew tradition ascribed the book to Moses, both its language and theological outlook are later than the Mosaic period. The book seems to be the product of a troubled age when the moral assumptions of the Mosaic law had lost much of their former authority. Mosaic books had argued that the good person, obedient to Yahweh's regulations, would automatically enjoy security, prosperity, and long life, but the history of Israel did not support this comfortable belief. After the Babylonians under Nebuchadnezzar had demolished both Yahweh's sanctuary and the Israelite state—acts involving the suffering and deaths of hundreds of thousands of people—it was necessary to rethink Israel's traditional philosophy of history.

During the Babylonian exile, then, Israel's wisdom writers had to grapple with troubling questions. How could Yahweh allow such a disaster to afflict his chosen people? How could he permit his holy temple to fall into pagan hands? The prophets had answered that Israel suffered defeat because the Israelites had, by sinful disobedience to the Mosaic Covenant, forfeited their privilege of divine protection. Since it is unthinkable that Yahweh does wrong, individuals must deserve whatever evils befall them.

The anonymous author of Job, writing sometime after the exile, probably in the fifth century B.C.E., could not agree that Israel's oppression was justified either by Deuteronomy's simplistic system of rewards and punishments or by the prophets' insistence that the people had earned their miseries. Combining the traditional reverence for Yahweh with an acutely critical intelligence and demand for moral logic, he uses an old folktale of the legendary patriarch Job to illustrate his conviction that neither the God-fearing person nor the blasphemer receives what he or she deserves in this life. But if God is in control of the universe, why is this so? The writer's attempt to probe this mystery leads him to reexamine the basic concept of divinity.

While most of Job is in poetry, the prologue and epilogue are in prose, and most scholars believe that the prose sections represent an old fable that the author used as a framework for his central poetic drama. The book can be outlined as follows.

1. Prose prologue (1–2)

2. Poetic dialogues (3–31)

3. Elihu's speech (32–37), in which Elihu, repeating much of what has already been said, defends Yahweh's actions by accusing Job of self-righteousness (This section was probably interpolated by a later writer.)

4. Yahweh's two speeches from the whirlwind (38–42:26)

5. Job's repentance (42:1–6)

6. Prose epilogue (42:7–17), in which Job is asked to sacrifice for the three orthodox friends who had not "spoken truly" of Yahweh, as Job had done

Prologue The prologue presents Job as a thoroughly upright and godly man who in no way deserves the evils inflicted upon him. Described as "sound and honest," one "who feared God and shunned evil" (Job 1:1 and 2:3), he is meant to represent a universal type, the person of good will found everywhere throughout history. For this reason the writer does not make him a Jew but a native of Uz (perhaps the south of Edom) who lived long before Israel's birth. So scrupulous is Job about not offending

God, however, that he offers sacrifices for his children in case they, even in thought, have sinned. No wonder Yahweh declares that "there is no one like [Job] on the earth" (Job 1:8).

Ironically, Job's outstanding righteousness attracts the interest of "the satan," a heavenly being who acts as Yahweh's prosecuting attorney. Appearing among "the sons of God" before Yahweh's throne, he suggests that Job will not remain loyal if deprived of family, property, and reputation. For reasons known only to himself, Yahweh accepts this challenge and allows Satan to strip Job of all he holds dear, including his sons and daughters. When Job still blesses Yahweh's name, Satan next persuades Yahweh—who admits that this persecution of his devoted worshiper is "without cause" (Job 2:4)—to infect him with a painful disease. Again, however, Job resists the temptation to "curse God and die."

Sufferings and Complaints   In chapter 3 the action shifts from the heavenly court to Job's dungheap, where, in a long and despairing monologue, he curses the day he was born. He is joined by three friends, Eliphaz, Bildad, and Zophar, who, following the comfortable assumptions of conventional wisdom, insist that Job's present misery must be the result of some vile but unknown sin. Each friend gives a speech, and Job in turn replies, refuting his contention. As the debates become more heated, Job's early patience gives way to a realization of two unorthodox truths: (1) that his humanity entitles him to certain moral rights, which Yahweh seems to ignore in permitting him to suffer undeservedly; (2) that if he is guiltless, who is responsible for the evil that he and all other people endure?

In chapters 9 and 10 Job challenges Yahweh to appear before him as a human being so that their conflict may be settled in terms of human justice. Anticipating Yahweh's appearance in the whirlwind, however, he realizes that he has no chance to present the justice of his cause before so formidable an opponent. A human being is no match for the strength of God. Furthermore, the power that afflicts him is the same that will judge him.

> Suppose I am in the right, what use is my defense?
>> For he whom I must sue is judge as well.
> If he deigned to answer my citation,
>> could I be sure that he would listen to my voice?
> He, who for one hair crushes me,
>> who, for no reason, wounds and wounds again,
> leaving me not a moment to draw breath,
>> with so much bitterness he fills me.
> Shall I try force? Look how strong he is!
>> Or go to court? But who will summon *him*?
>
> Job 9:15–19; italics added

With courage born of his honest recognition that good people can be more compassionate and moral than their gods seem to be, Job suggests that Yahweh must learn what it is like to be human, to bear the sorrows of mortality.

> I shall say to God, "Do not condemn me,
>> but tell me the reason for your assault.
> *Is it right* for you to injure me,
>> cheapening the work of your own hands
>> and abetting the schemes of the wicked?
> Have *you* got *human eyes,*
>> do *you see as mankind sees?*
> Is *your* life *mortal* like man's,
>> do your years pass as men's days pass?
> You, who inquire into my faults
>> and investigate my sins,
> *you know very well that I am innocent,*
>> and that no one can rescue me from your hand."

Job 10:2–7; italics added

Reversing the traditional wisdom that asks us to look at things from the deity's perspective, Job boldly demands that God try to see the world from the vantage point of pain-ridden, mortal humanity.

Yahweh Speaks As Job foresaw, however, Yahweh does not appear in human form to debate rationally the cause of injured innocence. Ignoring the mental anguish and disillusionment in divine goodness that are the principal sources of Job's suffering, Yahweh manifests himself as untamed natural force—the whirlwind. Almost sardonically, he challenges Job to match him in wisdom, power, and dignity.

> Do you really want to reverse my judgment,
>> and put me in the wrong to put yourself in the right?
> Has your arm the strength of God's,
>> can your voice thunder as loud?

Job 40:8–9

Faced with Yahweh's irresistible might, Job can only cower before the terror of omnipotence revealed.

> I know that you are all-powerful;
>> what you conceive you can perform. . . .
> I retract all I have said,
>> and in dust and ashes I repent.

Job 42:2, 6

Is the poet's message here simply that human mortality cannot challenge God's eternity or that human logic and ethics are futile, if not irrelevant, when confronted with infinitude? Is Yahweh telling Job that because Yahweh controls the cosmos, he makes his own definitions of what is just? Or, as a strict monotheist, is the author suggesting that a single universal deity must combine in himself all things, including what humans call good and evil? As Second Isaiah observed, Yahweh is the source of both natural and moral opposites:

> I am Yahweh, unrivaled,
> I form the light and create the dark.
> I make good fortune and calamity,
> it is I, Yahweh, who do all this.

Isaiah 45:7

However unsatisifying these responses are, there is some suggestion that Job's god is more than an unknowable, uncontrollable force. The voice from the whirlwind is aware that his creation suffers, and this fact offers some grain of comfort to the afflicted. Job, who had previously formed his concept of God only "by hearsay" (religious tradition?), has now come to "see" him through direct experience. But what does Job at last perceive? Unfortunately, the curtain now drops on the protagonist's inner life; in the ensuing prose epilogue he is given no further opportunity to speak. Has Job been intimidated into silence by the onslaught of divine power? Or come to accept a universe in which human righteousness bears no relation to personal happiness or misery? Or perhaps his are now "thoughts too deep for tears."

The fairy-tale ending in which Job becomes wealthier than before and begets more sons and daughters to replace those Yahweh had allowed to be killed, should not obscure the major insights that Job's experience has given him. Job's revelation is strikingly different from that for which Eliphaz, Bildad, and Zophar had so earnestly argued. Job has learned that the deity is both savior and destroyer, the inexplicable bringer of both joy and calamity, and which aspect of himself he will manifest to any individual or nation is unpredictable. If the book is taken as a reflection (not necessarily an allegory) of Yahweh's dealings with Israel during the exile and restoration, it does not presume to interpret the meaning of the people's historical experience but only deepens the mystery.

RECOMMENDED READING

Crenshaw, James L., ed. *Theodicy in the Old Testament*. Philadelphia: Fortress Press, 1983.

Dhorme, Edouard Paul. *A Commentary on the Book of Job*. Translated by Harold Knight. London: Thomas Nelson & Sons, 1967. Reprint of a major study of Job, first published in 1926.

Gordis, Robert. *The Book of God and Man: A Study of Job.* Chicago: University of Chicago Press, 1965.

Hone, Ralph E., ed. *The Voice out of the Whirlwind: The Book of Job.* San Francisco: Chandler Publishing Co., 1960. Includes King James Version of text of Job and a collection of interpretive essays.

Kallen, H. M. *The Book of Job as a Greek Tragedy.* New York: Moffat, Yard & Co., 1918. A stimulating comparison of Job to the tragedies of Aeschylus and Euripides.

Pope, Marvin H. *Job.* Anchor Bible, 5th ed. Garden City, N. Y.: Doubleday, 1978. An up-to-date translation with many useful notes.

_____. "Job, Book of." In *The Interpreter's Dictionary of the Bible*, vol. 2, pp. 911–25. New York and Nashville: Abingdon Press, 1962.

Sanders, Paul S., ed. *Twentieth-Century Interpretations of the Book of Job: A Collection of Critical Essays.* Englewood Cliffs, N. J.: Prentice-Hall, 1968. A variety of viewpoints.

Terrien, Samuel L. "Introduction and Exegesis to Job." In *The Interpreter's Bible*, vol. 4, pp. 877–1198. New York and Nashville: Abingdon Press, 1954. A valuable introduction to the study of Job.

_____. *Job: Poet of Existence.* Indianapolis: Bobbs-Merrill, 1958.

von Rad, Gerhard. *Wisdom in Israel.* Translated by James D. Martin. Nashville: Abingdon Press, 1973. An excellent theological study.

HEBREW POETRY

Like most ancient poetry, that of the Hebrews grew out of dance and song, pleasing the ear not through rhyme but through its musical rhythms. Israel's poets balanced ideas so that the first line of a poem was typically paralleled in the second line by a similar thought expressed in slightly different words. This structure and balance of two poetic lines is called *parallelism*, of which there are three basic types.

In *synonymous parallelism*, the idea in the first part of a line is duplicated in the second part but with a few changes in phrasing.

> Who else is God but Yahweh,
> who else a rock save our God?

> Psalm 18:31

> The heavens declare the glory of God,
> the vault of heaven proclaims his handiwork.

> Psalm 19:1

In *antithetical parallelism*, the first part of a line expresses one thought and the second part its opposite. Proverbs includes many examples of this.

> A wise son is his father's joy,
> a foolish son his mother's grief.

Proverbs 10:1

> The slack hand brings poverty,
> but the diligent hand brings wealth.

Proverbs 10:4

Synthetic or formal parallelism is not, strictly speaking, parallelism at all. In this poetic form, the first line states a thought, the second adds a new idea, and the third completes the statement. David's lament over the fallen Saul and Jonathan illustrates this pattern.

> O Jonathan, in your death I am stricken,
> I am desolate for you, Jonathan my brother.
> Very dear to me you were,
> your love to me more wonderful
> than the love of a woman.

2 Samuel 1:26

This repetition, variation, and expansion of a central theme or idea is characteristic of Hebrew poetry from its earliest war chants to its most sophisticated lyrics. Even in English translation, Hebrew poetry's repetitiveness, concreteness, and imagistic vividness stir the feelings as do few other works of world literature.

❧ Psalms

Hymns of Praise, Trust, or Thanksgiving	*Psalms 8, 19, 23, 24, 46, 103, 104, 114, 115, 118, 131, 136, 139, 150*
Enthronement, Royal, or Messianic Psalms	*93, 96, 97, 98, 99; 2, 21, 45, 72, 110*
Psalms of Lament, Petition, and Indebtedness	*22, 44, 55, 74, 78, 79, 80, 105, 106*
Psalms of Blessing and Cursing	*1, 109, 137*
Psalms of Wisdom, Meditation, and Instruction	*32, 37, 49, 52, 73, 90, 112, 119, 128*

Let everything that breathes praise Yahweh.

Psalm 150:6

The Book of Psalms is a collection of 150 sacred poems that in their totality express virtually the full range of Israel's religious faith. The title derives from the Greek *psalmoi*, which denotes religious songs performed to musical accompaniment. The Septuagint uses *psalmoi* to translate the Hebrew title *Tehillim*, "Praises," an appropriate name for an anthology in which many psalms are hymns praising Yahweh.

Although the Psalms as a group have been described as the hymnal of the second temple, this designation is only partially accurate. While the psalms were not collected into a book for use in worship until the postexilic period, some of them belong to a much earlier age. Several seem to have been composed specifically for performance at royal coronations, which means that they were written when Davidic kings still reigned in Jerusalem. One, Psalm 45, was used to celebrate the marriage of an Israelite monarch with a foreign bride.

The tradition that David wrote the Psalms is probably owing to David's popular reputation as a musician and poet. In fact, however, the Psalms are Davidic mainly in the sense that they belong to a literary development that may have stemmed from a royal patronage of poetry. The biblical text, while attributing many psalms to David, also ascribes number 72 to Solomon, number 90 to Moses, and various others to Asaph and the sons of Korah. Most scholars believe that few, if any, can be ascribed to David himself. Number 137 unmistakably dates from the Babylonian captivity, as does number 74, which laments the destruction of Solomon's temple. Few others can be precisely dated. In its final form, the Book of Psalms represents many generations of devotional poetry.

Structurally, Psalms is divided into five different books representing collections of varying ages: (1) Psalms 1–41, which may be the oldest edition of the work; (2) Psalms 42–72; (3) Psalms 73–89; (4) Psalms 90–106; and (5) Psalms 107–150. Psalm 1 acts as a general introduction to the collection; Psalm 150 is a concluding doxology (expression of praise) to the whole. In an effort to organize the poems thematically, scholars have created various categories and classifications, grouping them according to their principal topics or functions. No matter how one classifies them, however, it should be remembered that nearly all psalms were composed for public performance at the temple as communal expressions of Israel's faith.

In ancient Israel there seems to have been little distinction between private prayer and public worship. The Israelite attending temple services communed with God as a member of the covenant community, not as an isolated individual. The Psalms, then, can be said to be cultic songs, performed at the nation's religious festivals, which centered at the temple. Psalm 24, for example, appears to have been sung at a holy procession during which the Ark of the Covenant was brought to Zion, "the mountain of Yahweh," on which the temple stood.

Hymns of Praise, Trust, or Thanksgiving   Hymns of praise, trust, or thanksgiving make up by far the most numerous group. Many of these, such as numbers 8, 24, 113–118, 136, and 150, celebrate Yahweh's majesty, wisdom, and power. Others, such as 19, extol the Hebrew god as creator of the universe and author of the law. Psalm 104, which is apparently dependent on an Egyptian hymn to the sun god credited to Pharaoh Ahkenaton, similarly pays tribute to the deity's creative might. Undoubtedly the most famous of all psalms, number 23 ("Yahweh is my shepherd") so beautifully expresses the believer's trust in God's loving care that in the Judeo-Christian world it has become an inspirational companion at life's major crises.

Enthronement, Royal, or Messianic Psalms   Sometimes classed as "enthronement" psalms, Psalms such as numbers 93 and 97 typically celebrate Yahweh as sovereign ruler of the heavens or over foreign nations. Similarly, "royal" psalms emphasize Yahweh's anointed king and may have been sung at coronations during the monarchy, though some scholars, who believe that Israel observed a seasonal New Year similar to that of the Babylonians, interpret them as reenactments of the national leader's receiving his divine appointment to serve as his god's representative on earth (good examples are Pss. 2, 20, 21, and 110). After the end of the Davidic dynasty, many of these were reinterpreted as prophetic of a future descendant of David, the Messiah.

Psalms of Lament, Petition, and Indebtedness   "Lament" or "petition" psalms include both individual and communal supplications. In the individual prayers, the petitioner commonly praises God, then asks for rescue from his enemies and vengeance upon them (Ps. 55). Although many laments are concerned with forgiveness of personal sins (Pss. 38, 510), some imply that God himself has been slow to rectify injustice (Pss. 10, 58, 59). Communal laments such as Psalm 74 stress Israel's misfortunes and beg Yahweh to retaliate against the nation's oppressors. Psalm 44 is particularly interesting in rejecting the traditional deuteronomist view and stating flatly that the people had done nothing wrong but had suffered simply because Yahweh was their god (Ps. 44:17–22). By contrast, psalms that recapitulate Yahweh's past historical acts on Israel's behalf— the exodus and conquest of Canaan—were edifying reviews of the people's indebtedness to the national deity (Pss. 78, 105, 106).

Psalms of Blessing and Cursing   Somewhat shocking to modern sensibilities attuned to the concept that religion teaches the return of good for evil are the psalms of blessing and cursing. Psalm 1, for example, arbitrarily divides all people into two classes—the righteous and the wicked—and promises doom for the latter; no shades of gray are acknowledged. In Psalm 109 the poet enthusiastically lists disasters with which the writer asks God to afflict persons who have offended him or her. These include the wish that one's enemies be condemned by a corrupt judge, punished for the sins of their ancestors, and tormented by the certainty that their orphaned children will be driven in poverty from their homes. Psalm 137, which begins in lyrical beauty ("By the streams of Babylon"), concludes in vindictive fury, promising a blessing on the person who will seize Babylonian infants and dash out their brains against a rock. From these and other examples it is obvious that the orthodox worshiper regarded retaliatory justice as more religiously fitting than mercy.

Psalms of Wisdom, Meditation, and Instruction   There are, to be sure, other possible ways of classifying the various psalms, many of which are mixed types, combining praises with petitions for mercy and curses with requests for divine aid. Psalm 22, for example, begins as a lament ("My God, my God, why have you deserted me?"), changes in verse 22 to a hymn of praise, and ends on a note of confident triumph. Other psalms are mixtures of thanksgiving and instruction, royal and lament, or praise and supplication. In general, however, Psalms constitutes a microcosm of Israel's deepest religious insights and convictions. Although some were composed nearly 3,000 years ago, the emotions they inspire are as relevant to the contemporary reader as they were to the "sweet singers of Israel" who brought them into being.

RECOMMENDED READING

Anderson, Bernard W. *Out of the Depths: The Psalms Speak for Us Today*. Philadelphia: Westminster Press, 1974.

Barth, Christoph. *Introduction to the Psalms*. Translated by R. A. Wilson. New York: Charles Scribner's Sons, 1966. An illuminating introduction.

Gunkel, Hermann. *The Psalms: A Form-Critical Introduction*. Translated by Thomas M. Horner. Introduction by James Muilenburg. Philadelphia: Fortress Press, 1967. By a pioneer of the form-critical method.

Mowinckel, Sigmund. *The Psalms in Israel's Worship*. 2 vols. Translated by D. R. Ap-Thomas. Nashville: Abingdon Press, 1962.

Terrien, Samuel L. *The Psalms and Their Meaning for Today*. Indianapolis: Bobbs-Merrill, 1952. A nontechnical study.

Weister, Artur. *The Psalms*. Old Testament Library. Translated by Herbert Hatwell. Philadelphia: Westminster Press, 1962.

🌳 Proverbs

The fear of Yahweh is the beginning of knowledge.

Proverbs 1:7

Job deals with such abstract speculative questions as the meaning of human suffering, but the Book of Proverbs is almost entirely concerned with *practical wisdom* and with finding one's proper place in the social and religious order. "Proverb" translates the Hebrew term *mashal*, which means a statement of truth or standard of proper behavior. The biblical proverbs are typically based on observation and experience rather than on divine revelation and are commonly nonreligious in tone. Thus

> The rich man's wealth is his stronghold,
> poverty is the poor man's undoing.
>
> Proverbs 10:15

is simply an observed fact of life: riches give security and poverty the opposite.

Like much wisdom literature, Proverbs is not peculiarly Jewish; most of its admonitions could apply equally well in a pagan society totally different from Israel's theocracy:

> The generous man is his own benefactor,
> a cruel man injures his own flesh.
>
> Proverbs 11:17

It is not surprising, then, that archaeologists have found almost word-for-word parallels of biblical proverbs in Mesopotamia and Egypt; indeed, a whole passage from the wisdom book of the Egyptian sage Amenemope has been taken over almost verbatim in Proverbs 22:17–23:11. Now, however, scholars realize that proverbs and other wisdom writings were produced in many Near Eastern cultures and that Israel's sages in some cases borrowed from older literary collections.

Proverbs Attributed to Solomon   Since King Solomon, who was credited with more than 3,000 proverbs (1 Kings 4:29–33), has been traditionally associated with the production of adages or wise sayings, the superscription ascribing Proverbs to Solomon (Prov. 1:1) may mean no more than that these proverbs are written in the "manner" of Solomon. Other writers, in fact, are specifically cited. Agur, son of Jakeb, is the author of chapter 30; Lemuel, king of Massa, of chapter 31; and various unnamed sages of 24:23–24. Like the Psalms, Proverbs grew from many different sources over a span of centuries.

Value of Wisdom   What principally distinguishes some of Israel's proverbs from those of Edom, Babylonia, or Egypt is the theme that true wisdom promotes loyalty to Yahweh and sensitivity to the divine will. The wise person makes his or her behavior accord with divine law (Prov. 3; 19:16); the wise person is the righteous person who harmonizes his or her conduct with Yahweh's will (Prov. 16:1, 9; 19:21, 23). Proverbs also affirms the orthodox theme that in this world the righteous are rewarded and the wicked punished (Prov. 11:17–21; 21:21). Fearing Yahweh, observing the commandments and behaving discreetly will ensure a long and prosperous life. Only the fool rejects admonition and suffers accordingly.

Proverbs' emphasis on the pragmatic "getting ahead" in life endeared it to Israel's middle and upper classes. The directive to "study the ant, thou sluggard" (Prov. 6:6–11) is one of several that attribute poverty to laziness (see also Prov. 24:30–34). Considerable proverbial wisdom is aimed at young people who wish to establish themselves at court and become the counselors of kings. Others offer advice on table manners and how to behave in the company of rich and powerful persons whom one wishes to impress favorably. The sages point out that achieving these ambitious goals requires self-discipline, reverence for Yahweh, and the special combination of humility and penetrating insight that enables the wise to perceive the cosmic order and attain one's place in it.

Wisdom and Folly   The writer of Proverbs characteristically assumes the role of a father advising his son against bad company in general and seductive women in particular (Prov. 1–2). Folly (lack of wisdom) is likened to a harlot who corrupts youth, while Wisdom is personified as a noble woman who seeks to save young men from their own inexperience and bad judgment. In chapter 1, Wisdom is pictured as calling from the streets and housetops, promising rich treasure to those not too ignorant to appreciate her. The theme of "Lady Wisdom's" supreme value climaxes in chapter 8, in which she is presented as nothing less than Yahweh's associate in creation:

> Yahweh created me when his purpose first unfolded,
>   before the oldest of his works.
> From everlasting I was firmly set,
>   from the beginning, before earth came into being.

* * *

I was by his side, a master craftsman [alternatively, "darling child"],
    delighting him day after day,
    ever at play in his presence,
at play everywhere in his world,
    delighting to be with the sons of men.

Proverbs 8:22, 23, 30, 31

This passage, which shows Yahweh creating the world with Wisdom, a joyous feminine companion at his side, seems to have influenced such later Jewish thinkers as Philo Judaeus, who lived in Alexandria, Egypt, during the first century C.E. Philo's attempt to reconcile Greek philosophy with Hebrew revelation included his doctrine of the Logos ("Word") by which God created the universe. (*Logos*, a masculine term in Greek, became more acceptable to Hebrew patriarchal thinking than *Sophia*, "Wisdom," which is feminine.) The Hymn to Logos with which John opens his Gospel is derived from Philo's (and ultimately Proverbs') assumption that a divine mediator stands between God and the world.

The Perfect Wife   The book closes with a famous alphabetic poem on the perfect wife. Although promiscuous women and domineering wives receive considerable censure throughout Proverbs, the wife who works hard and selflessly to manage her husband's estate and increase his wealth is praised as beyond price (Prov. 31).

RECOMMENDED READING

Bryce, Glendon E. *Israel and the Wisdom of Egypt.* Lewisburg, Pa.: Bucknell University Press, 1975.

McKane, William. *Proverbs.* Philadelphia: Westminster Press, 1970.

Scott, R. B. Y. *Proverbs. Ecclesiastes.* Anchor Bible, vol. 18. Garden City, N. Y.: Doubleday, 1965.

Whybray, R. N. *Wisdom in Proverbs: The Concept of Wisdom in Proverbs 1–9.* Studies in Biblical Theology, no. 45. London: SCM Press, 1965.

FESTIVAL SCROLLS

The five books of the Festival Scrolls (Megillot)—Ruth, Song of Songs, Ecclesiastes, Lamentations, and Esther—were used respectively at the five principal festivals of the Jewish liturgical year (see Table 5-1). Placed together as a unit in the Hebrew Bible canon, they are scattered among the Prophets and Writings in most English translations, a practice that derives from the Septuagint but obscures the books' original relationship.

Although they differ greatly in style, tone, and theological content, the five scrolls collectively present a multifaceted view of human nature

TABLE 5-1 The Megillot and Associated Festivals

Book	Festival
Ruth	*Pentecost:* the harvest festival
Song of Songs	*Passover:* read on the eighth day
Ecclesiastes	*Tabernacles or Feast of Booths:* autumn agricultural feast of thanksgiving
Lamentations	*Fast of the Ninth of Ab* (July–August): mourning for the destruction of the Jerusalem temple by the Babylonians in 587 B.C.E. and the Romans in 70 C.E.
Esther	*Purim or Festival of Lots* (February–March): celebration of Jewish deliverance from Persian attack

ranging from the elegant cynicism of Ecclesiastes to the tender love story of Ruth. Except for Lamentations, the deity is seldom mentioned in these books; in Esther he is not referred to at all. There are no legalistic absolutes here such as we find in the Law or certainties about Yahweh's will such as we hear in the Prophets. Each book offers a different suggestion for handling life's problems; and each, in spite of the various crises and sorrows it depicts, affirms that life is good.

❦ Ruth

Ruth, Naomi, and Boaz   *Chapters 1–4*

You left your own father and mother . . .
to come among a people whom you knew nothing about. . . .
May Yahweh reward you for what you have done!

Ruth 2:11–12

Ruth is placed first in the Megillot probably because it is set "in the days of the Judges" (Ruth 1:1), the earliest time period attributed to any of the five books. Following the Septuagint, English Bibles usually print it immediately after the Book of Judges, although scholars almost unanimously agree that it was written during postexilic times as a gentle plea for tolerance of foreigners in Judah at a time when the Jews were forbidden to marry non-Jewish women; if this is so, the book may have appeared between 400 and 350 B.C.E. In a narrative of artful simplicity, the author reminds his countrymen that David, their greatest king, had a foreign great-grandmother, a Moabitess whose name was Ruth.

Ruth, Naomi, and Boaz   Because of a famine in Judah, the Israelite Elimelech, his wife Naomi, and their two sons settle in Moab, a country on Israel's southeastern border. After Elimelech dies, his two sons marry Moabite women. Ten years later the sons also die, leaving Naomi alone in a strange nation. Deciding to return to Israel, where she hears that bread has become plentiful, Naomi advises her two daughters-in-law to return to their families and find new husbands. A conventional figure, Orpha goes back to her people, but Ruth, Naomi's other daughter-in-law, refuses to part from the Israelite woman she has come to love. In words that the King James translation has made a classic expression of devotion, Ruth declares: "Entreat me not to leave thee, or to return from following after thee: for whither thou goest, I will go: and where thou lodgest, I will lodge: thy people shall be my people, and thy God my God" (Ruth 1:16).

Naomi and Ruth travel together to Bethlehem, where, according to the Mosaic provision for the poor, Ruth gleans the fields of Boaz, a relative of Elimelech. Thanks to Naomi's shrewd advice, Ruth makes a nocturnal visit to Boaz, who falls in love with her. In one of the fine psychological touches of this brief story, the middle-aged Boaz urges her to look for a younger man, but Ruth wisely indicates her preference for the kindly landowner. After making sure that one of Elimelech's nearer kinsmen does not care to exercise his right to marry widowed Ruth, Boaz takes her as his wife. (The Levirate Law of Deut. 25:5–6 decreed that if a man died childless, his nearest male relative was obligated to marry the widow in order to perpetuate the decedent's line.)

The author skillfully saves his most important point for the end. The son born to Boaz and Ruth is Obed, who became the father of Jesse, the father of David (Ruth 4:17–22). As the book makes clear, a foreign woman from an idol-worshiping country not only became a dedicated Yahwist in Israel but was an ancestress of Israel's divinely appointed monarch. By implication, the total exclusion of foreigners from the covenant community, mandated by Ezra and Nehemiah, was not necessarily the will of Israel's god.

RECOMMENDED READING

Campbell, Edward F. *Ruth*. Garden City, N. Y.: Doubleday, 1975.

Harvey, D. "Ruth, Book of." In *The Interpreter's Dictionary of the Bible*, vol. 4, pp. 131–34. New York and Nashville: Abingdon Press, 1962.

🐦 Song of Songs

Love Lyrics   *Chapters 1–9*

I am sick with love.

Song of Songs 5:8

The only erotic poetry in the Bible, the Song of Songs, has long been a puzzle to many. Its frank celebration of physical passion seems to have caused such embarrassment that it was deemed necessary to label it an allegory—a fictional narrative whose characters and actions are symbolic of some higher truth. To Jews it became an allegory of Yahweh's love for his chosen people; to Christians it became an expression of Christ's love for his "bride," the spiritual Church. To modern scholars it appears to be what it probably was—a collection of love lyrics that affirmed the enjoyment of human sexuality. Some historians believe that these verses were sung at country weddings in ancient Israel, although references to marriage are completely absent from the text.

Love Lyrics If the poems were originally intended as part of rustic marriage rites, it is possible to reconstruct their function as follows: In a custom that dates back to primitive times (and is reportedly still practiced in parts of the Near East), during a week-long nuptial festival the rural bride and groom are treated as "king" and "queen" with the local peasantry serving as their "royal attendants." Since the participants are usually rural folk, the groom may be both a "shepherd lad" (as he is called in the Song) and a "king."

This explains the shepherd's role as King Solomon (3:11), famous for his 1,000 wives and mistresses; the presence of a chorus that serenades the couple; and the pastoral setting that emphasizes the beauties of nature amid which the outdoor people labor and make love. Attribution of the work to Solomon probably derives from that monarch's prominence in the marriage tradition and his fictional role as "king" of the wedding celebration.

The essentially dramatic character of the work is apparent in the Jerusalem Bible version, which has edited the poems as individual lyrics sung alternately by the bride and bridegroom with choral responses interspersed throughout. Thus arranged, it is easy to imagine the poems performed as music dramas or chorales at bucolic weddings.

RECOMMENDED READING

Gordis, Robert. *The Song of Songs and Lamentations.* rev. ed. New York: KTAV Publishing House, 1974.

Meek, T. J. "Introduction and Exegesis to the Song of Solomon." In *The Interpreter's Bible*, vol. 5, pp. 91–148. New York and Nashville: Abingdon Press, 1956. Meek interprets the poems as cultic festival songs.

Pope, Marvin H. *The Song of Songs.* Anchor Bible. Garden City, N. Y.: Doubleday, 1977.

🍇 Ecclesiastes

Futility of Human Aspiration	*Chapters 1–2*
Sheol	*3; 10*
Paradoxes	*7–11*
Postscripts	*12:1–14*

The race does not go to the swift, nor the battle to the strong; . . . all are subject to time and mischance.

Ecclesiastes 9:11–12

Ecclesiastes, the third book of the Megillot, more properly belongs to the wisdom literature. Like Job, it is a speculative attempt to discover a pattern of meaning amid the world's disorder, in which good may go unrewarded and evil flourish. Unlike the agonizing poet of Job, however, the author of Ecclesiastes remains coolly detached from the injustice and misery he sees around him. An aloof observer of human folly, he derives a certain dry amusement from his ivory-tower perspective on the world.

An element of Proverbs' practical wisdom also permeates the work. Having experienced much, the writer has found that there is "nothing new under the sun" that has not been seen, said, or felt a thousand times before. He therefore advises his readers not to be taken in by the world's sham innovations. True wisdom lies in observing everything, knowing how little has genuine value, and refusing to become committed to the hopeless pursuits to which most people blindly devote their lives.

Although the superscription to the book attributes its authorship to *Qoheleth* or *Koheleth*, "son of David, king in Jerusalem"—presumably Solomon—most scholars regard this as merely a literary device that offers the writer an elevated position from which imaginatively to experience everything enjoyed by Israel's wealthiest and wisest monarch (Eccles. 1:12–2:12). The Solomon persona is soon dropped and not referred to after the second chapter.

Koheleth means "one who presides over a congregation," a term the Septuagint translators rendered as "Ecclesiastes," from the Greek *ekklesia* ("assembly"). But Koheleth was not a preacher as some English translations call him; he was a professional sage living in Jerusalem who may have assembled a circle of student-disciples about him. Because the author seems familiar with various strands of Greek philosophy, including that of Heraclitus, Zeno the Stoic, and Epicurus, experts tend to place the book's composition sometime during the Hellenistic era, after the campaigns of Alexander of Macedonia had brought Greek culture to Palestine. In its present form, the book resembles a somewhat rambling essay studded with aphorisms, short poems, and meditations on the futility of existence. An epilogue (Eccles. 12:9–14) preserves some student and later editorial reactions to Koheleth's unorthodox teaching.

Futility of Human Aspiration   Most of Ecclesiastes' principal ideas are stated in the first two chapters. The remaining ten mainly illustrate and elaborate the basic perception that the rewards of humanity's customary activities are either short-lived or nonexistent. The book opens with a description of the eternal cycle of nature, in which all things—sun, rivers, seas—are seen as moving in endless circles and eventually returning to their place of origin to begin the same cycle again. It is merely society's bad memory that causes people to imagine that anything new ever occurs. Individual observers simply are not around long enough to recognize that, in the long view, all that is repeats itself without essential change.

Aware that knowledge is a burden because wisdom makes the illusion of happiness impossible, Koheleth nonetheless determines to sample the various pursuits that are commonly believed to provide fulfillment in life. He first tries pleasure, a deliberate savoring of "folly." Although he enjoys being able to "deny his eyes nothing they desired" and "refuse his heart no pleasure" (Eccles. 2:10), he finds the experiment in hedonism empty. He next tries "great" enterprises, such as elaborate building programs, but finds these endeavors equally unsatisfying. He then concentrates on amassing wealth but concludes that this, too, is meaningless. Koheleth acknowledges some valid pleasure in hard work but cautions that all effort is ultimately "vanity" and a "chasing of the wind" (Eccles. 2:1–11).

The author offers several reasons for his negative view of human activity: (1) No matter what he achieves in life, he must ultimately die and leave everything to someone else, perhaps an unworthy heir who will waste it all. (2) Regardless of his successor's conduct, time itself will destroy whatever he builds or creates. (3) No matter how hard he labors or how wisely he plans, life can never compensate him for the toil and sacrifice expended to achieve his goals. (4) Death will inevitably frustrate all his intentions and hopes.

Sheol   Lurking behind the author's pessimism is a conviction that death is the absolute end to life, that there is no conscious existence beyond the grave (Sheol) to which all will descend without reaping either rewards or punishments that the present world does not offer. He has no hope that the deity will distinguish between human and animal lives, let alone between virtue and sin.

> Indeed, the fate of man and beast is identical; one dies, the other too, and both have the selfsame breath; man has no advantage over the beast, for all is vanity. Both go to the same place [Sheol]; both originate from the dust; and to the dust both return. Who knows if the spirit of man mounts upward or if the spirit of the beast goes down to the earth?
>
> Ecclesiastes 3:19–21

In view of the traditional Old Testament belief that *all* the dead are indiscriminately housed in the grim underworld of Sheol, the author's question here should be understood as purely rhetorical, emphasizing the inequitable fact that the righteous worshiper fares no better after death than an animal. Indeed, it is better, the writer ironically continues, to be a "live dog" (living Gentile) than a "dead lion" (deceased king of Judah), for: "The living know at least that they will die, the dead know nothing; no more reward for them, their memory has passed out of mind. Their loves, their hates, their jealousies, these all have perished, nor will they ever again take part in whatever is done under the sun" (Eccles. 9:5–6).

The dead in Sheol are eternally oblivious, without hope of future resurrection. Hence Koheleth advises the living to live fully now (Eccles. 9:7–9), for "there is neither achievement, nor planning, nor knowledge, nor wisdom in Sheol where you are going" (Eccles. 9:10). Such counsel resembles that of the Epicurean philosophy, which held that human beings are a chance collection of atoms that disintegrates at death. The consciousness or "soul" is as physical as the body and, like the body, perishes utterly. Like the Roman poet Horace, Koheleth advised the wise person to seize the day and wring from it whatever pleasures are possible.

The writer also entertains some typically Stoic ideas. Chapter 3, which begins with "There is a season for everything, a time for every occupation under heaven," seems to imply that a providence directs all things. Because the author is a Hebrew, he probably regarded Israel's god as the enforcer of the cosmic timetable. But Koheleth's god is apparently interested only in enforcing natural laws, not in giving meaning or order to human lives. Even the Stoic idea of a providentially managed universe is modified by Epicurean warnings that chance typically determines one's fate: "The race [of life] does not go to the swift, nor the battle to the strong; there is no bread for the wise, wealth for the intelligent, nor favor for the learned; all are subject to time and mischance" (Eccles. 9:11). It would be almost impossible to make a declaration more at variance with the Deuteronomist or the Prophets.

Paradoxes The author's love of paradox is a characteristic of the book that troubles some readers; he seldom makes a statement that he does not somewhere else contradict. Advising one to savor life and to drink wine with a joyful heart (Eccles. 9:7), he also states that it is better to frequent the house of mourning than the house of feasting (Eccles. 7:3). The day of death is better than the day of birth (Eccles. 7:1), but he would rather be a "living dog" than a "dead lion" (Eccles. 9:4). All people are "in the hand of God" (Eccles. 9:1) and should live righteously. (Eccles. 8:10–13); but it is as much a mistake to behave too virtuously (Eccles. 7:16) as it is to be excessively wicked (Eccles. 7:17).

These paradoxical views are among the book's chief strengths, however, for the writer is not contradicting himself but asserting that life is too complex for absolute certainties. Just as there is a time to live and a time to die, there are occasions when radically different attitudes and behaviors are appropriate. Koheleth refuses to be confined to any single philosophical position. Whereas many Greek thinkers made logical consistency the test of truth, Ecclesiastes' author perceives the irrational elements in life and refuses to omit observable variety in the interests of theoretical coherence. In a world where the deity does not seem to act (and it is significant that Yahweh, the lord of history, is mentioned by name nowhere in the work), illogic and absurdity must be acknowledged. Koheleth's admonition is to be aware and take no chances.

Postscripts The book closes with a poignant allegory of old age and death (Eccles. 12:1–8), but later writers added a series of brief postscripts. In the first, a disciple praises Koheleth for his wisdom and "attractive style" and adds a proverb extolling the value of wise teachers (Eccles. 12:9–11). A later editor, perhaps scandalized by the author's human-centered philosophy, warns the reader that writing and studying books is exhausting (Eccles. 12:12). It was perhaps a still later redactor who appended the final admonition to "fear God" and keep the commandments (Eccles. 12:14). The presence of this orthodox advice—inserted elsewhere into Koheleth's text as well (Eccles. 5:6b, for example)—could have been partly responsible for the eventual admission into the biblical canon of this deeply skeptical, religiously uncommitted book.

RECOMMENDED READING

Blank, Sheldon H. "Ecclesiastes." In *The Interpreter's Dictionary of the Bible*, vol. 2, pp. 7–13. New York and Nashville: Abingdon Press, 1962.

Gordis, Robert. *Koheleth: The Man and His World*. New York: Jewish Theological Seminary of America Press, 1951. A translation with interpretative notes.

Rankin, O. S. "Introduction and Exegesis to Ecclesiastes." In *The Interpreter's Bible*, vol. 5, pp. 3–88. New York and Nashville: Abingdon Press, 1956.

Scott, R. B. Y. *Proverbs and Ecclesiastes*. Anchor Bible, vol. 18. Garden City, N. Y.: Doubleday, 1965.

Wright, Addison G. "The Riddle of the Sphinx: The Structure of the Book of Qoheleth." In *Studies in Ancient Israelite Wisdom*, edited by James L. Crenshaw, pp. 245–66. New York: KTAV Publishing House, 1976.

❦ Lamentations

Dirges and Laments   *Chapters 1–5*

**Yahweh has accomplished his intention . . .
he has destroyed without pity.**

Lamentations 2:17

Dirges and Laments   Lamentations is the work that is chanted in sorrow when Jews gather each year to mourn the destruction of Jerusalem. According to tradition, the city fell to the Babylonians on 9 August 587 B.C.E. and again on the same day and month to the Romans in 70 C.E. The five poetic dirges and laments composing this brief book express the people's collective grief for the loss of their holy city. While the prophetic books record public pronouncements of doom against the Judean capital, Lamentations embodies the private anguish of individuals who witnessed the fulfillment of Yahweh's harsh judgment.

Although a relatively late tradition assigns Lamentations to the prophet Jeremiah, its authorship is unknown. The book itself does not mention the writer, and many scholars believe that it is the work of two or three different poets. The oldest parts are thought to be chapters 2 and 4, which were written shortly after Jerusalem's capture by Nebuchadnezzar. Chapters 1 and 3 appeared somewhat later in the sixth century B.C.E., and chapter 5 at some point between about 540 and 325 B.C.E. The first four poems are acrostics: each has twenty-two verses in which the first word of each verse begins with a different letter of the alphabet in sequential order. The last chapter also has twenty-two verses, but they are not arranged alphabetically.

From such artifice it is apparent that Lamentations is not a spontaneous outpouring of emotion, although the poets' feelings run deep and many passages are extremely moving. Chapters 2 and 4 seem to be the work of an eyewitness to the horror of the holy city's devastation.

> My eyes wasted away with weeping,
>   my entrails shuddered,
> my liver spilled on the ground
>   at the ruin of the daughters of my people,
> as children, mere infants, fainted
>   in the squares of the citadel.
>
> They kept saying to their mothers,
>   "Where is the bread?"
> as they fainted like wounded men
>   in the squares of the city,
> as they poured out their souls
>   on their mothers' breasts.
>
> Lamentations 2:11–12

The poet reports that some mothers ate the flesh of their infants during the famine caused by Nebuchadnezzar's siege. Formerly vigorous young men, wasted "thin as a stick," collapsed from hunger and died in the streets (Lam. 4:7–10). Corpses became too numerous to bury.

The writers of chapters 1, 2, and 4 agree that Jerusalem's fall was the direct result of its sins, particularly those of the priests and prophets who had falsely promised deliverance (Lam. 4:13). The question now is, Has Yahweh forsaken his people permanently? Since they have suffered so greatly for their mistakes, will Yahweh at last show pity? Perhaps because he lived to see Jerusalem's restoration, the poet of chapter 3 is confident that Yahweh takes no pleasure in continuing to abuse his human creation (Lam. 3:31–33). But the writer of chapter 5, to whom Yahweh's future intentions remain a mystery, simply asks:

> You cannot mean to forget us for ever?
> You cannot mean to abandon us for good?
>
> Lamentations 5:20

RECOMMENDED READING

Gordis, Robert. *The Song of Songs and Lamentations.* rev. ed. New York: KTAV Publishing House, 1974.

Gottwald, Norman K. "Lamentations, Book of." In *The Interpreter's Dictionary of the Bible*, vol. 3, pp. 61–62. New York and Nashville: Abingdon Press, 1962.

Hillers, Delbert R. *Lamentations.* Garden City, N. Y.: Doubleday, 1972.

❦ Esther

King Ahasuerus' Edict	*Chapters 1–10*
Haman Outwitted	
Feast of Purim	

The king granted the Jews, in whatever city they lived, the right to . . . slaughter and annihilate any armed force of any people . . . that might attack them.

Esther 8:11

Although the apocryphal Greek version of the tale of Esther reverts to the traditional view that Israel's god controls history and manipulates events to save his people, the Hebrew version of the story offers virtually no religious teaching. Though the Jews are here threatened with genocide, the writer does not mention the deity but implies that if Jews are to survive in a hostile world, it will not be through divine intervention but by their own efforts. Set in the days when Ahasuerus (Xerxes I) ruled the Persian Empire (486–465 B.C.E.), the tale purposes to explain how the joyous nationalistic feast of Purim came to be established. A long short story or novella, Esther lacks the sensitive characterization of Ruth but offers instead an exciting melodrama.

King Ahasuerus' Edict   When Ahasuerus divorces Queen Vashti for her refusal to exhibit herself before his male courtiers, Mordecai, who is both a supremely devout Jew and a loyal subject of the Persian emperor, maneuvers events so that his beautiful cousin Esther, whom he has adopted (Esther 2:7), becomes queen. In the meantime, Mordecai has discovered a conspiracy against the emperor's life but is able to send a warning in time so that the conspirators are discovered and executed. Although Mordecai's deed is recorded in the Persian court annals, Ahasuerus does not know that he owes his life to a Jewish subject.

Haman, whom the emperor has promoted to chief administrator at the court, becomes furious when Mordecai refuses to bow down before him and resolves not only to murder the Jew but to liquidate his entire race. Telling Ahasuerus that an "unassimilated" people who obey their own customs rather than the emperor's laws are settled throughout the empire, Haman persuades Ahasuerus to issue an edict permitting their mass execution and confiscation of their property. Haman casts lots (*purim*, hence the name of the festival) to determine the date of the massacre, which is to be the thirteenth day of the month of Adar (February–March).

Haman Outwitted Having previously been commanded by Mordecai to keep her Jewishness a secret, Esther is now persuaded to appear unbidden before the emperor—even though to intrude upon the royal presence uninvited carries a penalty of death—and beg him to rescind his decree. As Haman erects a lofty gallows on which to hang Mordecai for disobeying the chief vizier, Ahasuerus learns from the court annals that Mordecai has saved his life, and Haman is duped into suggesting high honors for the emperor's rescuer. Esther then reveals Haman's evil machinations, which were intended to destroy her, a Jewess, and Mordecai, to whom Ahasuerus owes his life. Dramatic justice is served when Haman is hanged on the gallows he had built for Mordecai.

Feast of Purim Unfortunately, the Jews living in the Persian Empire are still in danger, for the law of the Medes and Persians does not permit the theoretically infallible monarch to retract his orders. Ahasuerus does, however, issue a second edict instructing all Jews to fortify and defend themselves, which they do with spectacular success (Esther 8). Chapter 9 recounts how the Jews slew all who would have murdered them, after which they hold a victory celebration, the feast of Purim. The irony is that their triumph falls on the very day that Haman had selected for their extermination.

Most scholars, Jewish as well as Christian, regard Esther as patriotic fiction rather than historical fact, for despite its authentic picture of Persian court life and political intrigue during the fifth century B.C.E., the book contains several historical errors. Although we know much of Xerxes I, for example, there is no record that he was married to Vashti or that he had a Jewish queen named Esther. The Persian Empire was never (as the book insists) divided into 127 different provinces, nor did Xerxes order Jews in his territories to attack his Persian subjects. Mordecai, moreover, is said to have been deported to Persia from Babylon, which would make him at least 100 years old during Xerxes' reign, and the alluring Esther could not have been much younger.

There are, then, decidedly more mythical than historical elements in the story. The name Esther itself is a variation of "Ishtar," the Babylonian goddess of love and fertility. The name Mordecai derives from "Marduk," the leading Babylonian deity. Indeed, some interpreters have suggested that the book's Jewish author deliberately fictionalized an old Babylonian myth in which Marduk defeats his demonic enemies (Haman and his cohorts in this narrative). Certainly, the present book is a clear-cut example of the forces of good triumphing over evil as they did in the ancient myth.

At all events, Esther has found a vital place in the Jewish consciousness; to many pious Jews it is the most significant book in the Megillot. The annual reading of the book at Purim does not merely commemorate the Jews' turning the tables on their enemies in ancient Persia; it is also a profound statement about the heroic resistance necessary, in the face of overwhelming anti-Semitic aggression, to ensure Jewish survival at any place and any time in the modern world.

RECOMMENDED READING

Humphreys, W. Lee. "Esther, Book of." In *The Interpreter's Dictionary of the Bible: Supplementary Volume*, pp. 279–81. Nashville: Abingdon press, 1976.

Moore, Carey A. *Esther.* Garden City, N. Y.: Doubleday, 1971.

APOCALYPTIC LITERATURE

No form of biblical literature is more bewildering to the average reader than the apocalyptic, a term derived from the Greek *apocalypsis*, which means "a revealing." An apocalypse is a revelation or unveiling of things to come, typically a preview of the end of an age and the beginning of a new world order. In the Old Testament, only Daniel is a fully apocalyptic work, although there are apocalyptic elements in Isaiah 24–27, Ezekiel 37, Zechariah 9–14, and Joel 3. The New Testament closes with the most famous apocalypse, Revelation, but includes many other apocalyptic passages, such as Mark 13, Matthew 24–25, Luke 21, 1 Corinthians 15, 1 and 2 Thessalonians, Jude, and 2 Peter. In the Apocrypha, 2 Esdras is a true apocalypse, and Baruch also contains some apocalyptic features.

Apocalptic literature is concerned with *eschatology*— a doctrine of "last things," such as judgment (the prophetic Day of Yahweh), a climactic battle against Yahweh's enemies, the establishment of his universal rule, and the return of the dead to life for rewards or penalties. When Israel accepted the belief that prophetic oracles had ceased after the time of Ezra (about 400 B.C.E.), apocalyptic visions of the future, typically written in the name of a famous figure of the past, met a need for the people's continued communication with their god. From about 200 B.C.E. to the second century C.E., then, Yahweh's reputed intentions for the future were vividly illustrated in such works as Daniel, 2 and 3 Baruch, 1 and 2 Enoch, and many similar books, most of which have since been lost.

Apocalypses are at once a literature of despair and of hope: of despair, because apocalyptic writers can see no tolerable future for their national or religious group in the natural order of things; of hope, because they fervently place their confidence in God to intervene in human history, to appear himself or through his agent to stage a spectacular rescue of the righteous and a humiliation or destruction of their enemies. Thus the apocalyptic is a literature of man's extremity, a mode that sees the human condition as hopeless and that concentrates all its trust in God's willingness to suspend natural law and consume the world as we know it for the sake of a uniquely favored national or religious group.

It cannot be overemphasized that apocalypses such as Daniel and Revelation were produced during times of crisis and persecution to encourage the faithful to continue practicing their religion when they were being threatened with or subjected to arrest, torture, and death. Their writers saw the present misery as so bad that God simply *had* to act to save his people. The evils befalling them were proof that the end had come and the Kingdom was about to be established.

In other words, apocalyptic literature is concerned with what was then the immediate future; its predictions were not written for people living hundreds or thousands of years in the future. Using the cryptic time references in Daniel and Revelation to calculate the date of Christ's Second Coming or the end of the world, some nineteenth- and twentieth-century religious groups have been misled into proposing certain years, such as 1843, 1844, 1874, 1914, 1975, or 1984, as the times when God would incinerate the earth, slaughter the wicked, or establish a new world. But such predictions have not been accurate because their proponents have misunderstood the nature of apocalyptic writing and misapplied its message.

Although related to classical prophecy, which emphasized obedience to Yahweh's will in situations of contemporary life, apocalyptic literature is distinguished from purely prophetic works on the basis of six characteristics.

1. Most apocalypses are pseudonymous—that is, they are attributed to an outstanding figure of the past who lived long before the actual writer, thereby enabling the latter to present past history as if he were predicting it, to review the current crisis, and then to state his expectations about the immediate future.

2. All apocalyptic books are written in highly symbolic language, using sometimes bizarre images of beasts, birds, idols, dragons or other monsters, usually to depict pagan kings or nations. This secret code, understood by the believer but not by his or her oppressors, protected the writer from charges of treason or sedition. Thus when Daniel describes the humbling of Nebuchadnezzar, a Babylonian monarch who lived centuries before the author's time, he uses open, direct

language; when he predicts the fall of Antiochus IV, the contemporary tyrant persecuting the Jews, he employs obscure, veiled terms. Reading such passages today is less perplexing if we realize that the writer did not intend to be understood by the uninitiated.

3. Apocalypses foretell a series of dire calamities that are signs that the end is near. The author of Revelation, for example, presents seven series of plagues, pestilences, and other afflictions poured out on the unbelievers before they are finally destroyed. Many of these horrors hark back to the ten plagues visited upon Egypt, which are the archetypal examples of divine wrath.

4. Apocalyptic writers divide the global population into two mutually exclusive groups: the righteous (a tiny minority) and the wicked (all the rest of the world). They make no psychological distinctions between, and allow no moral shades of gray within, these two classes. The salvation of the few is always achieved at the expense of the many.

5. The picture of God in the apocalyptic vision is consequently a morally limited one. He is almost invariably depicted as an enthroned king, a formidably powerful being who brings all history to a violent consummation to demonstrate his sovereignty, confound his enemies, and preserve his few worshipers. That such goals could be achieved by less catastrophic means did not appeal to the apocalyptic mentality or satisfy the apocalyptic yearning.

6. Apocalypses typically present hopes for a life beyond the grave, promising either personal immortality or a general resurrection of the dead. Considering their universally negative view of this world and the impossibility of obtaining justice here, it is logical that such writers would look to an afterlife in which appropriate rewards and punishments would be made. In this, however, they diverged from the traditional Hebrew view in which Sheol, the underworld, is the common and eternal resting place for all humankind, good and bad alike. The apocalyptists' rejection of the soul's everlasting oblivion and their insistence that God does make moral distinctions between virtuous and wicked lives marked a theological advance over the older orthodox belief and was adopted by several later Jewish groups, including the Pharisees, Essenes, and early Christians.

🌱 Daniel

**In the time of these kings the God of heaven will
set up a kingdom which shall never be destroyed,
and this kingdom will not pass into the hands of
another race; it will shatter and absorb
all the previous kingdoms, and itself last forever.**

Daniel 2:44

Although the Book of Daniel purports to have been written during the Babylonian captivity in the sixth century B.C.E. when its author was successively a member of the Babylonian, Median and Persian courts, scrupulous examination of the text reveals that it was composed between about 167 and 164 B.C.E. when the Jews were suffering intense persecution by the Macedonian-Syrian ruler Antiochus IV Epiphanes. It is chronologically the latest written book in the canonical Hebrew Bible. This fact, together with its striking differences in form and style from the prophetic books, may explain why it was not included among the Prophets and instead placed among the Writings, for Daniel is not a typically prophetic work but seems a deliberately literary creation whose main character embodies and reflects the long tradition of Israel's sacred literature.

Daniel himself is, like Joseph (see Gen. 39–41), a devout Jew transported to a foreign nation of idol worshipers. Like Joseph, he remains faithful to his god under severe testing and is elevated by pagan rulers to positions of high honor. Like Joseph, too, he is basically a solitary figure, although an unusually shrewd one. Educated in the "wisdom of the Chaldeans [Babylonians]," empowered to reveal the meaning of divinely inspired dreams and thereby predict the future, supernaturally aided in his escapes from danger, Daniel is not an ordinary person, and it is difficult to regard him as merely a role model for Jews struggling to maintain their religious integrity under adverse circumstances.

If, however, Daniel were as outstanding a figure during the sixth century B.C.E. as the present book represents him, it is strange that he is never mentioned by his contemporaries or by later historians. Ezekiel, a prophet who lived in Babylon during the exile, thrice refers to an ancient sage named "Danel" who is associated with the patriarchs Noah and Job as a prototype of righteousness (Ezek. 14:4, 20; 20:3), but the Old Testament nowhere speaks of a "Daniel" who lived with Ezekiel in captivity. Since archaeological discoveries at Ugarit have also revealed the existence of a legendary King Danel who was a model of wisdom and rectitude, it is possible that over the centuries the Israelites adopted this originally foreign character and reclothed him in typically Jewish virtues until he eventually became the exemplar cited by Ezekiel. Later, a writer of the second century B.C.E., wishing to create a representative figure whose name and reputation for godliness would be well known but whose life and career were shrouded in mystery, chose "Daniel" as his hero.

Daniel divides naturally into two main sections. The first six chapters—which may have been written well before Antiochus' persecutions—recount Daniel's adventures under the successive reigns of Nebuchadnezzar, Belshazzar, "Darius the Mede," and Cyrus the Persian. The apocalyptic elements are subdued in this part, which concentrates on Daniel's strict allegiance to his god and the conflict into which it brings him with various pagan authorities.

Like Esther and Mordecai, Daniel is a victim of court intrigue. Unlike the Jews in the Book of Esther, however, he scrupulously observes Hebrew dietary laws (which makes him stronger than those who dine on the "king's food") and publicly manifests his Jewishness by refusing to participate in the religious ceremonies of his Babylonian or Persian overlords. A thematically important event in the biographical portion of the book is Daniel's interpretation of Nebuchadnezzar's dreams, the contents of which prepare the reader for the apocalyptic visions in chapters 7–12, which compose the second main section of the book.

Nebuchadnezzar's Dreams   According to chapter 2, Nebuchadnezzar has dreamed of a huge statue with a head of gold, chest and arms of silver, belly and thighs of bronze, legs of iron, and feet of mixed iron and clay. Suddenly a great stone uncut by human hands hurtles from heaven to smash the idol's clay feet; the colossus disintegrates, and the stone grows into a mountain that fills the entire earth. Daniel interprets the various metals composing this statue as symbolizing a series of kingdoms that rule his part of the world.

Nebuchadnezzar (Babylon) is the head of gold; and the nations that follow him—though Daniel does not specify them—are probably Media (silver), Persia (bronze), Macedonian Greece (iron), and the lesser Hellenistic kingdoms of Egypt and Syria (iron combined with clay to signify the weaker successors of Alexander's ironlike empire). The gigantic meteorite represents the Kingdom of God that is destined to obliterate and replace all pagan governments and last forever (Dan. 2:44).

Chapter 3 tells of three faithful Hebrew youths—known by their Babylonian names as Shadrach, Meshach, and Abednego—who are thrown into a hot furnace for declining to worship Nebuchadnezzar's golden image. After they emerge unsinged, the Babylonian king is represented as enthusiastically praising the Jews' "Most High God" who so miraculously delivers his servants (Dan. 3:24–30). Despite this reputed lip service, however, Nebuchadnezzar is given another lesson in that deity's omnipotence.

In another dream the king beholds an enormous tree sheltering all forms of bird and animal life but hears a heavenly authority order the tree cut down and given a "beast's heart" until all around acknowledge the sovereignty of the "Most High" (Dan. 4:11–14). Called to explain the dream, Daniel, the "chief of magicians" (Dan. 4:6), says that Nebuchadnezzar is the tree and that he is to be struck down—to lose his reason and kingship—"seven times" until he fully realizes that all power, political as well as celestial, comes from Daniel's god.

A short time later, while Nebuchadnezzar is touring his capital and boasting that he had built it by his own power, he is afflicted with a form of insanity that drives him to flee society and live like a beast. When he finally extols the "Most High" as the universal king, his sanity is restored (Dan. 4:25–34). This first-person narrative concludes with Nebuchadnezzar's prayerful recognition that Daniels' god humbles "those who walk in pride" (Dan. 4:34).

There is no record, however, that Nebuchadnezzar, a successful conqueror and able administrator, ever suffered a seven-year fit of insanity or that he temporarily adopted the monotheistic beliefs of the Jews he held as prisoners and slaves. The modern reader's credulity may be strained by the notion that a polytheistic ruler in Babylon repeatedly and publicly praised the god whose temple he had destroyed and whose nation he had defeated; but at the time these tales were first circulated, they may have provided a hope that whatever ungodly monarch then oppressed the Jews might still be taught humility before Yahweh.

Fall of Babylon   In Chapter 5 Belshazzar is ostensibly Babylon's ruler, though historically he was merely acting governor or prince regent for his father, King Nabonidus. At the height of a riotous celebration—possibly the Babylonian New Year festival—handwriting mysteriously appears on the palace walls. Summoned to interpret the cryptic signs, Daniel declares that Belshazzar is doomed to have his kingdom stripped from him and given to "the Medes and the Persians" (Dan. 5:25–31). That night, one "Darius the Mede" (unknown to history) takes the city. The author's blunder is puzzling because other biblical works, including Second Isaiah, Ezra, and Chronicles, make it clear that Cyrus of Persia captured Babylon (539 B.C.E.).

Chapter 6 states that Daniel underwent yet another test of his faith under the new "Median" administration. Like Ahasuerus in the Book of Esther, Darius is tricked by Daniel's rival courtiers into issuing an edict that for thirty days forbids anyone to pray except to the monarch. Loyal to his Jewish rites, Daniel is caught disobeying and confined in a den of lions. When he leaves the den unharmed, the "Median ruler's" reaction to the miracle exceeds even that of Nebuchadnezzar. Darius not only confesses the supremacy of Daniel's god but orders that everyone in his far-flung empire learn to fear the Jewish deity (Dan. 6:26–28).

Apocalyptic Visions   The strange visions and predictions of the second portion of Daniel, which is fully apocalyptic, make it the most controversial part of the Old Testament, particularly among certain fundamentalist groups. During the past few centuries hundreds of sects have been founded on differing interpretations of Daniel's eschatology. Most experts agree, however, that the understanding and application of Daniel's visions were intended primarily for the author's fellow Jews during the terrible days of Antiochus IV's attempt to eradicate the Jewish religion, perhaps just before the Maccabean revolt.

Chapters 7–12 contain four main visions that survey Near Eastern history from the sixth to the second centuries B.C.E. from the perspective of a Babylonian or Persian captive. Chapter 7 disguises the Babylonian, Median, Persian, and Macedonian empires as beasts: a lion with eagle's wings (Babylon); a bear with ribs in its mouth (Media); a winged leopard with four heads (Persia); and a ferocious ogre with iron teeth and ten horns (the Macedonian Greeks and their successors, the Ptolemies of Egypt and the Seleucids of Syria). The boastful "little horn" that also turns up is probably Antiochus, who intended to coerce the Jews into abandoning their traditional worship.

Daniel's parade of monsters is interrupted by a more traditional prophetic vision of the "Ancient of Days" who confers "glory and kingship" on "one like a Son of Man," presumably a Messiah figure, although Daniel nowhere mentions the Messiah by title (Dan. 7:10–14). The passage implies, however, that the writer expects a supernaturally appointed, everlasting Kingdom to replace the bestial pagan nations that rule in his own day. This section closes with more veiled remarks about the "little horn" (Antiochus IV) who makes war on the "saints" (devout Jews), tries to change the "law" (temple observances), and attempts to abolish the Mosaic religion altogether. Again, it is certain that the persecutor will be overwhelmed by the coming Kingdom.

The vision of chapter 8—supposedly given when Daniel was living at Susa, the Persian capital—depicts a ram with two horns (the dual power of Medes and Persians) being gored by a he-goat sporting a great horn (Alexander of Macedonia), which in turn is broken and replaced by four smaller horns (the four divisions of Alexander's empire made after his death). From one of these lesser horns (the Seleucid dynasty of Syria) springs a prodigious horn (again Antiochus) who tramples the "Land of Splendor" (Palestine), challenges the "armies of heaven," takes away the "perpetual sacrifice" (Antiochus forbade offerings at the Jerusalem temple), and institutes an "abomination of desolation" (the Syrian king slaughtered a pig on the temple altar and erected a statue of Zeus in the inner

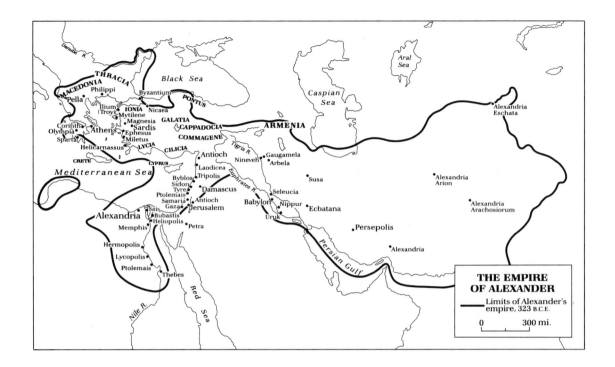

THE EMPIRE
OF ALEXANDER

Limits of Alexander's
empire, 323 B.C.E.

0   300 mi.

court as part of his policy to force the Jews into accepting a Hellenistic way of life). The angel Gabriel makes most of this vision explicit to Daniel, except for the part concerning Antiochus, which for reasons of safety had to be kept vague. Following this angelic exegesis, Daniel collapses and is ill for several days.

Chapter 9 features Daniel's most moving prayer, in which he confesses his people's sins and asks his god to deliver them from their enemies, for the first time in the book using the personal name Yahweh, god of the covenant and lord of history (Dan. 9:5–19). This prayer leads to the angel Gabriel's revisionist explanation of Jeremiah's prophecy that Jerusalem would lie desolate for "seventy years" after the Babylonian conquest and then be restored. Why has the city been so consistently enslaved by foreign powers since then? Jeremiah, explains Gabriel, meant that "seventy weeks of years" (490 years?) were to pass before the consummation of all things, which in the second century B.C.E., when this interpretation was written, was then imminent.

Chapters 10–11 are a tangled thicket of prophecies about battles between "the King of the South" (Ptolemies) and the "King of the North" (Seleucids) and the further machinations and fall of Antiochus. There seem to be allusions to the Maccabean wars here; although at the time these passages were written it appears that the Maccabees had not yet recaptured the temple and rededicated its altar, the author correctly foresees that the temple will be cleansed and priestly services resumed in the near future. He is less accurate in predicting Antiochus' punishment, however, for that fanatical king dies a natural death abroad, not in Palestine (Dan. 11:21–45).

Resurrection Undoubtedly regarding Antiochus' depredations as inaugurating the "end time," the author of Daniel postulated a resurrection to compensate contemporary Jews who had died defending their faith against the Syrian persecutor, and this explicit affirmation of a life after death (Dan. 12:2–3) was to be the most enduring part of his message.

In chapter 12 Gabriel tells Daniel that when history draws to its *predetermined* climax in the pagan nations' assault on the righteous, Michael (described as the prince or guardian spirit of Israel) will "stand up" for his people and decisively defeat their enemies. At that point a resurrection of "many" just and unjust persons who had been "sleeping in the dust" will occur. Daniel—who as a literary character is placed during the Persian era—is told to sleep among his ancestors until he is raised for his "share" at the end of time (Dan. 12:1–13).

Although a familiarity with the apocalyptic mode makes it evident that Daniel was not composed for people living the last quarter of the twentieth century, the book's fundamental themes remain universally relevant. Its picture of the deity firmly in control of earthly history, aiding the devout to survive adversity, and promising the ultimate triumph of life and faith over death and evil make Daniel an integral part of the biblical heritage.

RECOMMENDED READING

Charles, R. H. *Eschatology: The Doctrine of a Future Life in Israel.* New York: Schocken Books, 1963 (reprint).

Collins, J. J. *The Apocalyptic Vision of the Book of Daniel.* Harvard Semitic Monographs 16. Missoula, Mont.: Scholars Press, 1977.

Hanson, Paul D. *The Dawn of Apocalyptic.* Philadelphia: Fortress Press, 1975.

Hartman, Louis F., and De Lella, Alexander A. *The Book of Daniel.* Garden City, N. Y.: Doubleday, 1978.

Koch, K. *The Rediscovery of Apocalyptic.* London: SCM Press, 1972.

Lacocque, Andre. *The Book of Daniel.* Atlanta: John Knox Press, 1978.

Mowinckel, Sigmund. *He That Cometh.* Nashville: Abingdon Press, 1956.

Nickelsburg, George W. E. *Jewish Literature Between the Bible and the Mishnah.* Philadelphia: Fortress Press, 1981.

Porteous, Norman W. *Daniel.* Philadelphia: Westminster Press, 1965.

Russell, D. S. *Apocalyptic, Ancient and Modern.* Philadelphia: Fortress Press, 1978.

_____. *The Method and Message of Jewish Apocalyptic: 200 B.C.–A.D. 100.* Philadelphia: Westminster Press, 1964.

Stone, Michael. *Scriptures, Sects and Visions: A Profile of Judaism from Ezra to the Jewish Revolts.* Philadelphia: Fortress Press, 1980.

WORK OF THE CHRONICLER

If the Bible's historical narratives were placed in strict chronological order according to content, the books of Kings would be followed by 1 and 2 Chronicles, which largely duplicate their material. Chronicles would in turn be followed by Ezra and Nehemiah, which record postexilic history of the fifth century B.C.E., after which would come 1 and 2 Maccabees (from the Apocrypha), which bring Israel's history into the mid-second century B.C.E. The original Hebrew Bible, however (whose order this text observes), places Ezra-Nehemiah before Chronicles, the last book in the Jewish canon. Chronicles may have been given this prominent end-position because its history concludes with the decree of Cyrus, the conqueror of Babylon and founder of the Persian Empire, that the captive Jews are free to return to their homeland and rebuild its temple.

Scholars are virtually unanimous in seeing Ezra and Chronicles as the work of a single author called "the Chronicler" (Nehemiah's memoirs were apparently incorporated by a later editor). Although he utilized many different documentary sources for his account, the Chronicler manifests a consistent style, attitude, and interest in priestly concerns throughout his work. The four books were compiled during the fifth century B.C.E., when Judah was a small unit in the Persian Empire, probably around 400 B.C.E. Together they provide our main source of information about Israel's postexilic experience.

❦ Ezra

Return from Exile	*Chapters 1–6*
Ezra's Mission	*7*
Foreign Wives	*9–10:17*

Artaxerxes, king of kings, to the priest Ezra, scribe of the Law . . . you are to appoint scribes and judges to administer justice for . . . all who know the law of your God. You must teach those who do not know it.

Ezra 7:12, 25

Although Ezra and Nehemiah probably formed a single book originally, the two histories present conflicting information about the sequence of events they record. Part of the confusion arises from the fact that we do not know who first returned to help rebuild Jerusalem—the priest-scribe Ezra or the Persian-appointed governor of Judah, Nehemiah. The Chronicler precisely dates his history by citing particular years of the Persian Emperor Artaxerxes; but since there were two monarchs of this name during the fifth century B.C.E., scholars are uncertain which one the writer meant. Although even experts do not agree on the basic order of events, it seems likely that Nehemiah came to Jerusalem first (around 445 B.C.E.) and that Ezra appeared during the governor's second twelve-year term.

Return from Exile   Ezra opens with Cyrus' proclamation endorsing the return of the Jews from Babylon to Jerusalem to rebuild Yahweh's temple (around 538 B.C.E.), an edict consistent with the Persian ruler's policy of tolerating and even encouraging local religious cults throughout his empire. A long list of repatriated exiles follows in chapter 2, while chapter 3 describes the first sacrifices on a rebuilt altar "set up on its old site" and the laying of foundations for a second temple. Poignantly, the tears of those old enough to remember the much larger dimensions of Solomon's temple mingle with the joyous shouts of the younger generation as the priests lead the people in singing praises.

Chapters 4–6 record the Jewish leader Zerubbabel's rejection of Samaritan aid in reconstructing the sanctuary, following which Judah's slighted neighbors conspire to persuade the Persian emperor (then Xerxes I) that Jerusalem is a potentially rebellious city whose rebuilding should be stopped. The emperor agrees, and the temple remains unfinished until two postexilic prophets, Haggai and Zechariah, convince Zerubbabel and Joshua, the high priest, to start work again.

When a Persian official questions the legality of this project, the Jewish elders appeal to the new Persian emperor, Darius, to investigate the court records for Cyrus' original authorization to erect a new temple. Cyrus' edict is not only found and enforced, but it obligates the Persians to supply money for rebuilding and procuring sacrifices. The second temple is completed and dedicated in about 515 B.C.E., permitting a Passover celebration at Yahweh's sanctuary for the first time in more than seventy years.

Ezra's Mission   Chapter 7 introduces Ezra, a Babylonian Jew who had devoted himself to intense study and teaching of the Mosaic law and who is represented as the first in a long line of distinguished rabbis who were decisive in forming and preserving Judaism. Emperor Artaxerxes commissions Ezra to travel to Jerusalem to supervise the temple, to evaluate conditions in the Judean province according to Mosaic standards,

The Persian Empire at its greatest extent (c. 500 B.C.E.)

and to appoint scribes and judges to administer civil and moral order for the whole Jewish population (Ezra 7:11–26). Chapter 8 lists the new returnees and the treasures of silver and gold that Ezra had been appointed to bring to the temple.

Foreign Wives Chapters 9–10 record Ezra's distress at the returned exiles' intermarrying with foreign women. He was raised in exclusively Jewish circles in Babylon where strict adherence to the law and racial purity were observed, so he determines to enforce his concept of the nation's duty. After begging his god to forgive the people for marrying those who follow pagan religions, Ezra calls upon the people to reject these mixed alliances at a great assembly before the temple. Weeping, the men agree to divorce their non-Jewish wives, and Ezra arranges to see that the resolution is enforced. The book ends with a list of those guilty of unsanctified marriages.

The Book of Ezra gives a positive view of the Persian government's remarkable cooperation with and consideration for Jews in its empire, a view that accords with the picture of Jews dispersed amid the Persian state presented in the books of Esther and Tobit. Ezra himself, the priest and learned scribe who brings a copy of the Mosaic law with him from Babylon to regulate and unify Jewish life in the restored community, is a key figure in the further development of Judaism. Both the Pharisees and later rabbis could trace their roots to this zealous promoter of Mosaic traditions, as could the writers of several apocryphal books, such as 1 and 2 Esdras (the Greek form of Ezra).

RECOMMENDED READING

Meyers, Jacob M. *Ezra. Nehemiah*. Garden City, N. Y.: Doubleday, 1965.

Pfeiffer, Robert H. "Ezra and Nehemiah, Books of." In *The Interpreter's Dictionary of the Bible*, vol. 2, pp. 214–19. New York and Nashville: Abingdon Press, 1962.

Talmon, S. "Ezra and Nehemiah: Books and Men." In *The Interpreter's Dictionary of the Bible: Supplementary Volume*, pp. 317–28. Nashville: Abingdon Press, 1976.

🌱 Nehemiah

Return to Jerusalem	*Chapters 1–2, 4–6*
Promulgation of the Mosaic Law	*8–9*
Nehemiah's Zeal	*10–13*

And Ezra read from the Law of God, translating and giving the sense, so that the people understood what was read.

Nehemiah 8:8

Return to Jerusalem   Originally combined with Ezra, the book of Nehemiah enlarges our picture of conditions in postexilic Judah and Jerusalem. The book opens with an account of Nehemiah's grief when, as an official cupbearer to the emperor at Susa, the Persian capital, he learns of the miserable conditions in Jerusalem. Weeping over reports of the city's poverty and ruin, he asks, and wins the consent of, Emperor Artaxerxes to allow him to go to Jerusalem and rebuild the city.

Nehemiah travels with an armed guard to Jerusalem, where he encounters local opposition to the refortification of the city. (Reconstructing the city's defensive walls would naturally increase its apparent independence, which the Jews' enemies could interpret as subversive to Persian rule.) When Sanballat (the governor in Samaria), Tobia the Ammonite, and Geshem the Arab first deride and then threaten to attack Nehemiah's workmen, the latter arms his builders, who thereafter complete the city walls in record time. After Artaxerxes officially appoints Nehemiah governor, Nehemiah is able to maintain order and to institute significant economic and social reforms, such as cancelling debts and freeing slaves.

Promulgation of the Mosaic Law Perhaps the most significant incident recorded in Nehemiah is Ezra's extended public reading of the Mosaic law (Neh. 8). Apparently the resettled Judeans no longer understood the classical Hebrew in which the Torah was written, for Ezra, after declaiming aloud from the sacred scrolls, translated and "gave the sense"—that is, interpreted the law's meaning—"so that the people understood what was read" (Neh. 8:8). Scholars have debated exactly which form of the Torah Ezra presented to the people, but it may well have been the Pentateuch that we have now, for during the Babylonian captivity, schools of priests and scribes labored to compile, preserve, and interpret Israel's Mosaic legacy for their own day.

Whether the Torah that Ezra brought back to Jerusalem was the entire Pentateuch or a form of the priestly document (P), his work thereafter became the basis and standard for the Jewish community. The religious reforms that Ezra and Nehemiah inculcated in the national consciousness included revivals of such age-old festivals as the Feast of Tabernacles and a covenant-renewal ceremony (Neh. 9), the latter featuring additional public teaching of the law and a long poetic recital of Israel's history emphasizing its covenant obligations to Yahweh.

Nehemiah's Zeal Chapters 10–13 record the people's vow to abide by the covenant to support the temple service, which involved numerous financial and other responsibilities. Marriages to foreign women are again forbidden, and strict observance of the Sabbath is enjoined. Chapters 11–12 report the repopulating of Jerusalem, Levitical genealogies, and the formal dedication of the new city wall. The final chapter concludes Nehemiah's memoir, recounting how he bustled about the city personally enforcing Sabbath keeping, persuading individuals to give up their foreign wives, and asking his god to remember his good works "for [his] happiness."

Like Ezra, Nehemiah was a conscientious proponent of Jewish exclusivism, tolerating neither heathen customs nor pagan women in the holy city. While his rigid insistence on ceremonial and racial particularism may strike the modern reader as unsympathetic, these requirements were necessary at a time when the Jews were few in number and surrounded by enemies. Without such separatism, both national and religious identity might have been lost.

RECOMMENDED READING

Meyers, Jacob M. *Ezra. Nehemiah.* Garden City, N. Y.: Doubleday, 1965.

Pfeiffer, Robert H. "Ezra and Nehemiah, Books of." In *The Interpreter's Dictionary of the Bible*, vol. 2, pp. 214–19. New York and Nashville: Abingdon Press, 1962.

Talmon, S. "Ezra and Nehemiah: Books and Men." In *The Interpreter's Dictionary of the Bible: Supplementary Volume*, pp. 317–28. Nashville: Abingdon Press, 1976.

❦ 1 Chronicles

Times of David   *Chapters 10–29*

David grew greater and greater, and Yahweh Sabaoth [of armies] was with him.

1 Chronicles 11:9

The concern with dates, genealogies, temple liturgy, and priestly traditions that characterizes Ezra-Nehemiah is likewise manifest in 1 and 2 Chronicles, which are by the same author. The two books were originally one until the Septuagint editors divided the work into two scrolls entitled *Paralipomena*, meaning "things omitted"—that is, historical incidents not included in the books of Samuel and Kings. It was Saint Jerome who called the work *Chronicon*, the Latin name from which the English title is derived, a close approximation of the Hebrew title, *Dibhre Hayamim*, which means "annals."

In fact, however, Chronicles is largely a derivative history that retells the story of Israel from the time of Adam to Cyrus' decree ending the Babylonian exile. For his account the author relies almost exclusively on Samuel and Kings, adding little to these sources except his own strongly cultic and Levitical bias. It has been suggested that during the early Hellenistic period when the Chronicler wrote (sometime in the late fifth or early fourth century B.C.E.), Judah's national religion had degenerated into complacency. Not only had the country lost its political autonomy, but perhaps even the priests and temple functionaries had grown lax in their duties.

If so, this might explain why the Chronicler transforms much of the material from Samuel and Kings to conform to his Levitical bias. One may assume that he intended to remind the people of their more religiously vital past, to recall them to their present cultic obligations, to emphasize the preeminence of temple worship, and to focus on the monarchy's relation to this. Although the first nine chapters of 1 Chronicles comprise a history of the world from Adam to King Saul, given in the form of a genealogy that emphasizes Levitical ancestry, the remaining twenty chapters are devoted to David's administration.

In these chapters (1 Chron. 10–29), David is depicted not as a military and administrative genius but as a devout religionist who establishes the elaborate temple cult, contributes heavily to its support, and recruits whole retinues of artisans and musicians for its services. In the Chronicler's story, preparation for building the sanctuary becomes the main goal of David's kingship, as constructing, dedicating, and maintaining the sanctuary became the chief objective of Solomon's administration.

Times of David With regard to the times of King David, the author's major alterations of his source material include the following:

1. Making Saul's death a judgment caused by his visit to the witch of Endor (1 Chron. 10:13–14), an obvious betrayal of the Yahwist cult

2. Having David proclaimed king of all Israel at Hebron (1 Chron. 12:23–40), when historically only Judah first acknowledged him there

3. Interpolating a long prayer by David when he brings the Ark of the Covenant to Jerusalem (1 Chron. 16:7–36), thus clothing the monarch in priestly garb

4. Insisting that David contributed enormous sums of gold toward building the temple as a good example to later Israelites (1 Chron. 22:14–16; 28:14–19)

5. Stating that David was responsible for assigning the Levites—cantors, gate keepers, and bakers—their temple duties (1 Chron. 23:2–27:34)

6. Asserting that David determined the plans, furnishings, and functions of the temple and that Solomon merely carried them out (1 Chron. 28:1–31)

7. Deleting all references to David's misdeeds, including his adultery with Bathsheba

8. Attributing to David a final speech in which he urges generous financial support for the construction and upkeep of the temple (1 Chron. 29:1–20)

9. Implying that David transferred the reins of power to Solomon while he was still alive and that Solomon ascended the throne without opposition (1 Chron. 29:22–28)

The Chronicler's primary intent here is not to provide fresh insights into David and Solomon (whose faults, recorded in 2 Samuel and 1 Kings, he omits) but to insist that the nation's principal mission is to worship Yahweh wholeheartedly and to demonstrate that the failure of later kings to honor the Jerusalem sanctuary led to the monarchy's collapse. By showing how royal apostasy and lack of zeal for temple worship caused the nation's downfall, he hopes to rouse his audience from its apathy and revive participation in the Levitical services. And while his distortions of historical fact to make this point may be debatable, his thesis is nevertheless consistent with the rest of Israel's sacred history.

RECOMMENDED READING

Elmslie, W. A. L. "Introduction and Exegesis to 1 and 2 Chronicles." In *The Interpreter's Bible*, vol. 3, pp. 341–548. New York and Nashville: Abingdon Press, 1954.

Meyers, Jacob M. *1 Chronicles.* Garden City, N. Y.: Doubleday, 1965.

Pfeiffer, Robert H. "Chronicles 1 and 2." In *The Interpreter's Dictionary of the Bible*, vol. 1, pp. 572–80. New York and Nashville: Abingdon Press, 1962.

---

2 Chronicles

Solomon to Josiah	*Chapters 1–35*
Manasseh's Sins and Repentance	*33*

I [Yahweh] chose Jerusalem for my name to make its home there, and I chose David to rule over Israel my people.

2 Chronicles 6:6–7

---

2 Chronicles opens with the glories of Solomon's reign and then surveys Judah's history from the time of his successor, Rehoboam, to the issuing of Cyrus' edict permitting the return of the Jews to Jerusalem. Unlike the author of Kings, the Chronicler does not attempt to give a parallel history of the divided kingdom but concentrates almost entirely on Judah, referring to the northern kingdom only when it concerns Judah's affairs. As in the first book, the writer's interest revolves around the temple.

Solomon to Josiah The first nine chapters recount the splendors of Solomon's legendary wealth and his building program, emphasizing the construction, dedication, and divine consecration of the temple; nothing is said about Solomon's weaknesses or eventual corruption by his many foreign wives. He repeats the dramatic confrontation between Rehoboam and the rebellious northern tribes who withdraw from the monarch when the new king refuses to modify his harsh policies (2 Chron. 10–11).

Thereafter the Chronicler rapidly scans the line of Judean rulers, pausing to elaborate on the reigns of four "good" kings—Asa, Jehoshaphat,

Hezekiah, and Josiah—and to expand passages dealing with the prophets. He devotes much more space than the author of Kings to enumerating the reforms of Hezekiah, who is miraculously delivered from the Assyrian menace, and Josiah, whose reinstitution of the Passover feast became a standard for later observances (2 Chron. 28–32 and 34–35).

Manasseh's Sins and Repentance   Between these two approved monarchs came Manasseh, whose fifty-five-year reign exceeded that of any other Judean king (2 Chron. 33). 2 Kings lists Manasseh's crimes, which include burning his son as a pagan sacrifice, but it is silent on his alleged repentance. The Chronicler, however, states that while a captive of the Assyrians in Babylon, Manasseh sought Yahweh, who relented and restored him to his throne (though the Chronicler does not explain how this astonishing reversal occurred). Manassah then personally conducted a religious reform, cleansing the temple of the pagan cults he had established there and rebuilding Yahweh's altar. The writer notes that the prayer that moved Yahweh to rescue the former "black magician" was preserved in the Annals of Hozai (2 Chron. 33:20), which is not the same as the Prayer of Manasseh included in the Apocrypha.

Unexpectedly, portions of 2 Chronicles make somewhat more interesting reading than does the rather dry version of David's reign in the first book, where the author's ecclesiastical apparatus overwhelms the narrative. Although 2 Chronicles repeats much of 2 Kings, it adds some colorful details and ends with a hopeful promise of the people's liberation. As the last book in the Hebrew Bible canon, it apparently anticipates a future for Judaism in which the priest rather than the king will play the dominant role.

RECOMMENDED READING

Elmslie, W. A. L. "Introduction and Exegesis to 1 and 2 Chronicles." In *The Interpreter's Bible*, vol. 3, pp. 341–548. New York and Nashville: Abingdon Press, 1954.

Meyers, Jacob M. *2 Chronicles*. Garden City, N. Y.: Doubleday, 1965.

Pfeiffer, Robert H. "Chronicles 1 and 2." In *The Interpreter's Dictionary of the Bible*, vol. 1, pp. 572–80. New York and Nashville: Abingdon Press, 1962.

PART 6

EXTRACANONICAL WORKS

OLD TESTAMENT APOCRYPHA

The Apocrypha (or "hidden" books) are part of the Septuagint Bible, the Greek translation of the Old Testament made for Jews living in Alexandria, Egypt, during the last three centuries before Jesus. The Roman Catholic church accepted these books, most of which were written between about 200 B.C.E. and 100 C.E., as "deuterocanonical" (belonging to a second or later canon). St. Jerome, whose Latin Vulgate is the official Bible of the Roman Church, followed the Septuagint lead and included the apocryphal books in his translation. Most Protestant churches, however, observe the Jewish decision to include only those books of the Hebrew Bible apparently endorsed by the Palestinian rabbis at Jamnia about 90 C.E.

In Roman Catholic versions, the Apocrypha are interspersed among the Old Testament books, while Protestant Bibles, if they include the Apocrypha at all, place them as a separate group between the Old and New Testaments. Regardless of one's view of their doctrinal authority, the Apocrypha are important because they reflect the religious and intellectual climate and theological developments of later Judaism, thus forming an invaluable link between the Old and New Testament periods. Traditionally, the apocryphal books are listed with those attributed to Ezra first and the Maccabean histories last.

RECOMMENDED READING

Eissfeldt, Otto. *The Old Testament: An Introduction.* New York: Harper & Row, 1965.

Goodspeed, Edgar J., ed. and trans. *The Apocrypha: An American Translation.* New York: Random House, 1959.

Humphreys, W. Lee. *Crisis and Story: Introduction to the Old Testament.* Palo Alto, Calif.: Mayfield Publishing Co., 1979.

Rost, Leonhard. *Judaism Outside the Hebrew Canon: An Introduction to the Documents.* Nashville: Abingdon Press, 1976.

Soggin, J. Alberto. *Introduction to the Old Testament.* Philadelphia: Westminster Press, 1976.

🍎 1 Esdras (or 3 Ezra)

Contest at the Persian Court　　　*Chapters 3:1–5:6*

Truth is great and supremely strong.

1 Esdras 4:41*

This book, which probably dates from about 150 B.C.E., is known as 1 Esdras to Protestants and 3 Ezra to Catholics (in Catholic Bibles, Ezra and Nehemiah are called 1 and 2 Esdras, respectively). 1 Esdras (the Greek form of Ezra) reproduces the material found in 2 Chronicles 35–36, the whole of Ezra, and Nehemiah 7:38–8:12. Only one section, that dealing with Jewish wisdom at the Persian court (1 Esd. 3:1–5:6), has no parallel in the canonical texts.

1 Esdras may represent a fragment of a Greek translation of the Chronicler's works that is older than the canonical version preserved in the Septuagint. The exact relationship of its original Hebrew-Aramaic form to the analogous material in the Hebrew Bible is unknown. The narrative begins with the reign of Josiah, an elaboration of 2 Chronicles 35, and ends with Ezra's proclamation of the Mosaic law to the exiles returned from Babylon. Like the works of the Chronicler, the book reflects a priestly viewpoint, with heavy emphasis on temple rituals, festivals, the duties of Levites and their ecclesiastical prerogatives. It may have been written during the Maccabean period, when the temple was cleansed and rededicated.

Contest at the Persian Court　Although 1 Esdras adds little to the historical record, it introduces a memorable anecdote about Zerubbabel, a descendant of King David whom the Persians appointed governor of Judah. In a contest between three guardsmen of the Emperor Darius, each young man is to nominate what he regards as the strongest force in the world; the emperor and his noblemen are to judge the merits of their respective nominations and reward the winner. The guardsmen suggest in turn that wine, kings, women, and truth are supreme powers.

---

* Quotations from 1 and 2 Esdras are from Edgar J. Goodspeed, ed. and trans., *The Apocrypha: An American Translation* (New York: Random House, 1959).

Zerubbabel, champion of truth, wins Darius' favor and is granted his request to go to Palestine and rebuild Jerusalem.

RECOMMENDED READING

Meyers, Jacob M. *1 and 2 Esdras.* Garden City, N. Y.: Doubleday, 1974.

❦ 2 Esdras (or 4 Ezra)

To what end has the capacity for understanding been given me? For I did not mean to ask about ways above, but about those things which pass by us every day; why Israel . . . whom you loved [is] given up to godless tribes.

2 Esdras 4:22–23

---

2 Esdras is a composite work of Jewish and Christian origin and one of the latest books to find its way into the Apocrypha. Although chapters 3–14, the central portion of the book, purport to have been written by the historical priest Ezra while he was a captive in Babylon about 557 B.C.E., scholarly analysis of the text indicates that this section was probably composed in either Hebrew or Aramaic late in the first century C.E., after the Romans had destroyed Jerusalem and the temple. Like the New Testament Book of Revelation, which it greatly resembles in theme and outlook, 2 Esdras may have been produced during the persecutions of the Emperor Domitian.

After 2 Esdras had been translated into Greek, an anonymous Christian writer added chapters 1 and 2 around 150 C.E. Perhaps a century later, another Christian, also writing in Greek, appended chapters 15 and 16. But 2 Esdras did not appear in the Septuagint; it entered Christian Scripture via Old Latin translations and Jerome's Vulgate, although conflicting Ethiopic, Syriac, Greek, Arabic, Armenian, and other versions exist as well.

Ezra's Theodicy   The first two chapters are mainly Christian apologetics implying that God has repudiated "natural" Israel as his chosen people and adopted instead a "spiritual" Israel, the Christian Church, as his own. Chapters 3–14 consist of seven apocalyptic visions, of which the first three are cast in the form of philosophical dialogues between Ezra and various angels. These angelic mentors counter Ezra's repeated questioning of his god's justice with attempts to defend the deity's ways to humans. In general, Ezra's questions are more penetrating than the answers he receives.

If Babylon (read "Rome") was God's chosen instrument to punish Israel, Ezra asks, why are Babylon's citizens so much worse behaved than the Jewish people Babylon oppresses? Why has God allowed an enemy nation that mocks him to destroy those who have at least tried to worship him (2 Esd. 3:25–32)? Would not God's lesson to both Jewish and pagan nations be less equivocal if he punished directly, "with his own hands," rather than through an ungodly intermediary like Babylon (Rome) (2 Esd. 5:28–30)? Is it not better to remain unborn than to live and suffer without knowing why (2 Esd. 4:12)? The angels' reply is that God will act to dispense justice in good time. The flourishing of wickedness is only temporary; it will be terminated according to a foreordained timetable (2 Esd. 4:27–32), and it is not humankind's business to worry about the divine schedule.

Ezra is concerned not only about the earthly plight of his people but about the fate of their souls after death. Reluctantly agreeing that many act wrongly while only a few are righteous, he nonetheless disputes the justice of condemning sinners to everlasting torment without any further chance of repentance. Chapter 7, vividly picturing the blessings of salvation and the agonies of the damned, is the most complete picture of afterlife and judgment in the Old Testament Apocrypha.

2 Esdras gives us, in addition, the Old Testament's first statements of original sin—the belief that all humankind has inherited Adam's sin and is therefore born deserving of death (2 Esd. 5:21–26; 7:46–48, 70–72). This doctrine of humanity's inherent propensity toward vice is also expounded by the Apostle Paul in Romans 5 and has since become dogma in many Christian denominations. Finally, the author also seems to express a belief in the existence of the human soul before birth (2 Esd. 4:42).

Apocalyptic Visions   In chapter 9 the book changes from a Jobian theodicy to a more purely apocalyptic preview of the "last days." The fourth vision depicts a woman mourning her dead son who is suddenly transformed into a thriving city. Uriel explains that the woman is Jerusalem, her lost son the destroyed temple, and the splendid city a future glorified Zion (2 Esd. 9–10). Chapters 11–12, with their portrait of a mighty eagle, are reminiscent of John's visions in Revelation. This proud eagle (Rome) that now dominates the earth is destined to disappear when a lion (the Messiah) appears to judge it for its persecution of the righteous (2 Esd. 11:38–12:34). The sixth vision emphasizes the certainty of the Messiah's imminent appearance and his just destruction of the pagans who oppress Jerusalem (2 Esd. 13).

The Bible and Apocrypha   Ezra's preeminent importance to Jewish religion is emphasized in chapter 14, where the "Most High" inspires him to write ninety-four sacred books. Twenty-four of these books are canonical Scripture—the published Old Testament—while the remaining seventy are reserved for the "wise" who alone can understand them. This passage indicates that the author credited Ezra with replacing the Hebrew Bible that the Babylonians had allegedly destroyed. The extrabiblical books are presumably the Apocrypha and other apocalyptic works, such as 2 Esdras itself.

Following his literary efforts, Ezra is transported to heaven to dwell with other holy men. In light of the Jewish traditions upon which the author draws, Ezra is clearly seen as a heroic figure who embodies the virtues of priest, prophet, and lawgiver. A second Moses, he also incorporates the honors of Elijah and the antediluvian patriarch Enoch, both of whom had been similarly caught up to heaven.

The two final chapters, a Christian addition of the second century C.E., emphasize the deity's coming vengeance on the wicked. Predicting a series of terrors and calamities (again reminiscent of Revelation), the book assures the reader that the ungodly nation (Rome), as well as all other empires that afflict the righteous, will fall and that the guilty will be consumed by fire (2 Esd. 15–16).

RECOMMENDED READING

de Lange, Nicholas. *Apocrypha: Jewish Literature of the Hellenistic Age.* New York: Viking Press, 1978.

Dentan, Robert C. *The Apocrypha: Bridge of the Testaments.* Greenwich, Conn.: Seabury Press, 1954.

Goodspeed, Edgar J., ed. and trans. "The Second Book of Esdras." In *The Apocrypha: An American Translation,* pp. 39–106. New York.: Random House, 1959.

Meyers, Jacob M. *1 and 2 Esdras.* Anchor Bible. Garden City, N. Y.: Doubleday, 1974.

Nickelsburg, George W. E. *Jewish Literature Between the Bible and the Mishnah.* Philadelphia: Fortress Press, 1981.

 Tobit

Tobit, Tobias, and Sarah   *Chapters 1–14*

The prayer of each of them [Tobit and Sarah] found favor before the glory of God, and Raphael was sent to bring remedy to them both.

Tobit 3:16

Although the Septuagint editors placed Tobit among the historical books, it is really a work of imaginative fiction. The action is set during the seventh century B.C.E. when many Jews from the northern kingdom were scattered throughout the Assyrian Empire. The central figure, Tobit, an aged and pious Jew of the Naphtali tribe, is an exile living in Nineveh, the Assyrian capital. Though remarkably true in its psychology of character and artistic handling of plot and theme, the book contains several historical and geographical errors. While the customs, attitudes, and theological beliefs presented in the story suggest that it was written during the Hellenistic period, perhaps about 185–175 B.C.E., the author is unknown.

Tobit, Tobias, and Sarah   The book's purpose is to encourage Jewish exiles to maintain their religious integrity, the author insisting that Israel's god hears their prayers and will eventually reward the faithful. This message is dramatized in a well-constructed plot consisting of three closely related narrative strands. The main plot concerns Tobit, an exemplary Jew who strictly observes all aspects of the law but who suffers the illnesses and privations of a latter-day Job. A subplot involves his kinswoman Sarah, a beautiful virgin whose seven husbands have all been killed on their wedding night by the jealous demon Asmodeus. A second subplot concerning Tobit's son Tobias, who travels to Media, exorcises the demon and marries Sarah, effectively ties all the narratives together.

Tobit's story is joined to Sarah's by the deity's hearing their simultaneous prayers for death (Tob. 3:16–17). Tobit prays to die because, for piously burying slaughtered Israelites, he has not only been stripped of all his possessions but has been blinded by bird droppings (Tob. 2:9–3:6). Sarah, unhappy that a maid has accused her of murdering her seven husbands, similarly longs to end her life (Tob. 3:7–15). The earthly connection is provided when Tobias journeys to Ecbatana in Media to claim money that Tobit had entrusted to his kinsman Raguel, who is also Sarah's father.

The Archangel Raphael, disguised as a man named Azariah, guides young Tobias to Ecbatana, provides the necessary instructions to exorcise Asmodeus (who flees to Egypt, where an angel binds him), and permits the union of Tobias and Sarah. Raguel, who had spent the wedding night digging a grave for his new son-in-law, is astounded by Tobias' survival. Upon Tobias' triumphant return to Nineveh with the money and a new wife, Raphael also cures Tobit's blindness with fish gall (Tob. 11:10–15).

A treasure house of second-century Jewish social customs and beliefs, this delightful tale deals with such matters as guardian angels (Tob. 5:21; 12:12–13), priestly distinctions (Tob. 1:6–7), dietary restrictions (Tob. 1:10–12), personal prayers (Tob. 3:2–15; 8:5–8), the importance of a decent burial (Tob. 1:17–19; 2:3–8; 14:12), the power of demons and the use of fish entrails in exorcising them (Tob. 3:8; 6:6–8; 8:1–3), seven angels of the heavenly court (Tob. 12:15), and the value of wise parental advice (Tob. 4:3–19). Tobit's popular view of angels, guardian spirits who act as intercessors (Tob. 12:12), and demons seems to reflect the influence of Persian dualism (Zoroastrianism) with its doctrine of warring spirits of good and evil.

The last chapters—Tobit's thanksgiving psalm (Tob. 13) and an epilogue recounting his advice that Tobias and Sarah leave Nineveh to escape the city's impending destruction (Tob. 14)—may be later additions. The final section, in which Tobit prophesies Nineveh's fall and Jerusalem's restoration, contains the remarkable prediction that "all the nations of the world will be converted to the true worship of God" (Tob. 14:6).

RECOMMENDED READING

Wikgren, A. "Tobit, Book of." In *The Interpreter's Dictionary of the Bible*, vol. 4, pp. 658–62. New York and Nashville: Abingdon Press, 1962.

❦ Judith

Assyrians Threaten Judah	Chapters 1–7
Judith Slays Holofernes	8–16

The Lord our God is with us still, displaying his strength in Israel and his might against our enemies.

Judith 13:11

Like Tobit, Judith is a historical romance written by an unknown author during the Hellenistic period and set in the distant past. The book begins with a glaring historical error—that Nebuchadnezzar (605–562 B.C.E.) reigned in Nineveh over the Assyrians, when in reality his father, the king of Babylon, had destroyed Nineveh in 612—which may have been intentional, to show at the outset that the narrative was not meant to be factual history. The true political situation is probably that of the Syrian oppression of the Jews under Antiochus IV (175–164/63 B.C.E.). Nebuchadnezzar, then, represents Antiochus, the despot who tried to eradicate Israel's religion (1 Macc. 1:14–50; Dan. 3:3–15), and the writer advises armed revolt, asserting that Israel's god will defend his people if they remain faithful to him (Jth. 13:11; 16:17).

Judith was probably written around 150 B.C.E., about a decade after the Maccabees had successfully repulsed the Syrians. The heroine's name, the feminine form of "Judah," literally means "Jewess" and may be intended to symbolize the nation or to remind the reader of Judas, its Maccabean leader. Judith embodies the traditional biblical heroism of the solitary Israelite struggling against a pagan superpower, as David fought Goliath or as Jael felled Sisera (1 Sam. 17:20–54; Judg. 4:17–24; 5:25–30). Judith's triumph over Holofernes, the Assyrian commander, is her nation's victory over their collective enemies.

Assyrians Threaten Judah   The book is divided into two parts. The first (Jth. 1–7) states that after conquering Media, Nebuchadnezzar sent Holofernes to punish countries that had not supported his campaign. After overrunning various other nations, the Assyrians laid siege to Bethulia, a fortified city that may represent Jerusalem, which Antiochus had sacked. When Bethulia is ready to submit, the ruler Uzziah decrees that Israel's deity be given another five days to rescue the people.

Judith Slays Holofernes   In the second part (Jth. 8–15), Judith, a beautiful widow, berates the leaders who put their god to the test and volunteers to save the city herself. After offering a prayer, she perfumes herself, dresses in her gayest clothes and jewelry, and enters the Assyrian camp, pretending to defect because of her admiration of Holofernes. Flattered, the Assyrian commander invites the seductive Jewess into his tent, where, after plying him with wine, she takes his sword and decapitates him.

Stowing the head in her travel bag, Judith and her maid convey it to Jerusalem, where it is displayed on the city wall. Dispirited by their leader's death, the Assyrians withdraw, allowing the Jews to loot their camp. Judith dedicates her share of the booty to the Jerusalem temple. In an epilogue, Judith hails her god for protecting his people (Jth. 16:17). After her death at an advanced age, she is honored by her compatriots as a national heroine.

Although Judith was written at a time when slaughtering an enemy could be regarded as an act of religious piety, it is more than a nationalistic war story. Its emphasis on the power of Israel's god to rescue an obedient people echoes a theme recurrent in biblical history: it is not "by sword or spear" that Israel carries the day but only through the will of its god, who can save by the frail hand of a lone woman (see also 1 Sam. 17:46–47).

RECOMMENDED READING

de Lange, Nicholas. *Apocrypha: Jewish Literature of the Hellenistic Age.* New York: Viking Press, 1978, pp. 114–28.

Winter, P. "Judith, Book of." In *The Interpreter's Dictionary of the Bible*, vol. 2, pp. 1023–26. New York and Nashville: Abingdon Press, 1962.

❦ The Additions to Esther

Religious Interpolations   Chapters 10:3a–16:24*

And Mordecai said, "All this is God's doing."

Additions to Esther 10:3a

The Septuagint version of the Book of Esther contains six parts not found in the Hebrew original. Although a few scholars hold that the Additions existed first in Hebrew, most believe they were not composed and interpolated into the biblical text until about 114 B.C.E. when Esther was translated into Greek. The Septuagint editors interspersed the Addition at various points in the story, weaving the Hebrew original and Greek expansions into a single whole; but when Jerome prepared the Latin Vulgate, he removed the Additions from the main body of the work and placed them at the end (Add. to Esther 10:3a–16:24).

Modern translations that include the apocryphal excerpts handle the textual problem in various ways. The Jerusalem Bible restores the Additions to the canonical Hebrew narrative but prints them in italics to distinguish them from the Hebrew text. The New English Bible places them among the Apocrypha and, for coherence, translates the entire Greek version of Esther with the supplements fitted into their proper sequence.

Religious Interpolations The Additions were apparently intended to heighten the religious implications of Esther's story. While the Hebrew version contains neither prayers nor references to Israel's god, the Additions emphasize the efficacy of prayer and the deity's saving power (Add. to Esther 13:8–18; 14:3–19; 15:8; 10:9); they even preface the account with an apocalyptic dream of Mardochaeus (Mordecai) that places the Jews' deliverance from Persian attack in the context of Yahweh's ultimate victory over all worldly powers (Add. to Esther 11:2–12).

A devout practitioner of Torah Judaism and Kosher dietary laws, the Esther of the Greek version refuses to eat Gentile food (Add. to Esther 14:17) and finds her marriage to a non-Jewish husband, Emperor Ahasuerus (Xerxes I), repellent (Add. to Esther 14:15). These added touches stress the strict observance of Jewish law and abhorrence of having to comply with the requirements of a pagan environment by a heroine who implores the deity:

> As for ourselves, save us by your hand,
> and come to my help, for I am alone

---

* Chapter and verse numbers in the Additions follow Jerome's ordering of the Vulgate text.

and have no one but you, Lord.
You have knowledge of all things,
and you know that I hate honors from the godless,
that I loathe the bed of the uncircumcised,
of any foreigner whatever.
You know I am under constraint,
that I loathe the symbol of my high position
bound round my brow when I appear at court;
I loathe it as if it were a filthy rag
and do not wear it on my days of leisure.
Your handmaid has not eaten at Haman's table,
nor taken pleasure in the royal banquets,
nor drunk the wine of libations.

Additions to Esther 14:14–17

The Additions increase the suspense of Esther's unsolicited interview with the emperor by dramatizing the emotions it arouses (Add. to Esther 15:6–19). They also attempt to lend authenticity by reproducing the text of Artaxerxes' letter condemning Haman (who turns out to be a Macedonian spy), praising the king's Jewish subjects and commanding them to defend themselves when attacked (Add. to Esther 16:1–24). Like the Hebrew original, the Additions present the Jewish characters operating in an atmosphere of intrigue and competition instigated by jealous pagans. But unlike the canonical tale, the Additions transform the violent episode of Jewish self-defense into a declaration of their god's omnipotence; for here even Artaxerxes testifies to this deity's control of events (Add. to Esther 16:4, 21).

RECOMMENDED READING

Moore, Carey A. *Daniel, Esther, and Jeremiah: The Additions.* Garden City, N. Y.: Doubleday, 1977.

❦ The Wisdom of Solomon (or Wisdom)

Wisdom is a spirit, a friend to man.

Wisdom of Solomon 1:6

Although the Wisdom of Solomon presents itself as King Solomon's address to the world's rulers (Wisd. of Sol. 1:1), it is really the work of an anonymous writer aimed at Jews living in exile, some of whom were apparently tempted to compromise or relinquish their religion under the allurements of Greek culture and philosophy or the pressure of Gentile discrimination. The author's familiarity with Greek terms and philosophic ideas (Wisd. of Sol. 8:7, 19–20; 12:1) indicates that he lived during the Hellenistic period, perhaps about 100 B.C.E. He appears to have been a well-educated member of the Jewish community in Alexandria, Egypt, a populous cosmopolitan city that then rivaled Athens as the world's leading intellectual center.

By demonstrating that Judaism's ethical and religious wisdom is superior to that of the Gentiles, the author hopes to encourage Jews to maintain their traditional allegiances. He endeavors also to show that his religion offers a view of world history and divine justice that will appeal to the moral and rational Gentile as well. A creative synthesis of Hebrew and Greek thought, the Wisdom of Solomon is theologically one of the most important books in the Apocrypha and a major contribution to biblical wisdom literature. The book may be divided into three parts: (1) the rewards of Wisdom (personified as God's Spirit) and the promise of immortality (Wisd. of Sol. 1–5); (2) the origin, character, and value of Wisdom (Wisd. of Sol. 6–9); and (3) the Wisdom of Israel's deity operating in human history (Wisd. of Sol. 10–19).

Rewards of Wisdom   The first section contrasts the fate of the wicked— whose twisted reasoning is vividly rendered in 2:1–20—with that of the righteous. Although the ungodly may prosper on earth and oppress the good, the soul's survival after death (different from the bodily resurrection depicted in Dan. 12:2) guarantees that the deity's justice will ultimately prevail. Asserting that "God created man for immortality" and "made him the image of his own eternal self" (Wisd. of Sol. 2:23), the author assures his readers that "the souls of the just are in God's hand and torment shall not touch them" (Wisd. of Sol. 3:1).

Foolish skeptics might believe that the just perish utterly, but their sufferings are merely a test to refine their worth and their deaths are a disguised blessing; they are destined to judge nations and rule over the world (Wisd. of Sol. 3:2–8; see also Rev. 2:26–27; 20:4). The ungodly, meanwhile, are not punished arbitrarily but according to their own evil designs (Wisd. of Sol. 3:10). This concept of an afterlife in which immortal souls are rewarded for their good deeds on earth is the author's response to the problem of undeserved suffering that had troubled writers of such other wisdom books as Job. Here the deity's justice toward his human creation is vindicated because he provides an eternity of bliss to compensate for temporary earthly pain.

Origin, Character, and Value of Wisdom Comparable Greek ideas appear in the second section, which features "Solomon's" praise of Lady Wisdom, the bringer of immortality (Wisd. of Sol. 6:1; 8:13). The speaker, who takes Wisdom as his "bride," implies that the soul exists in heaven prior to its incarnation or imprisonment in a physical body (Wisd. of Sol. 8:19–20; 9:15). This belief in an immaterial, preexistent soul that escapes to the spirit realm at the body's dissolution is typical of Platonic and Neo-Platonic thought.

Similarly representative of Greek ethical philosophy is the author's exposition of the four classical virtues, which became the four cardinal virtues of Christian morality:

> Or if it be virtue you love,
> why, virtues are the fruit of her labors,
> since it is she who teaches temperance and prudence,
> justice and fortitude;
> nothing in life is more serviceable to men than these.
>
> Wisdom of Solomon 8:7

Wisdom in Sacred History In the lengthy third part, the author presents an idealized survey of early humankind (Wisd. of Sol. 10) and of Israel's history, contrasting the deity's judgments on the heathen with his saving care of the chosen people, to whom Wisdom lent strength and understanding. The moralistic discussion of Israel and Egypt (Wisd. of Sol. 11–19) is interrupted by a diatribe against idolatry (Wisd. of Sol. 13:1–15:17) that is reminiscent of Second Isaiah's castigation of the Babylonian gods (Isa. 40; 46). The imaginative reinterpretation of Israel's past in the final chapters may have been intended to inspire hope among the exiled Jews that their god still intervened in human affairs on their behalf (Wisd. of Sol. 16:7–8; 19:22).

The author attributes the presence of evil and death to "the Devil's spite" (Wisd. of Sol. 2:23–24), an interpretation of the serpent's role in Genesis 3 that would culminate in the doctrine of original sin expounded by Paul (Rom. 5) and the writer of 2 Esdras 3:7. (For other passages that influenced New Testament writers, compare Wisd. of Sol. 1:7 with Col. 1:17; Wisd. of Sol. 3:7 and Matt. 13:42; Wisd. of Sol. 3:14 and Matt. 19:12; Wisd. of Sol. 5:16 and Rev. 2:10; Wisd. of Sol. 5:16–19 and Eph. 611–17; Wisd. of Sol. 6:3–4 and Rom. 13:1–12; Wisd. of Sol. 14:22–31 and Rom. 1:18–32.)

Finally, the reference to divine Wisdom manifesting itself as God's "all-powerful Word" leaping "down from the heavens, from the royal throne" into "the heart of a doomed land" where "he touched the sky, yet trod the earth" (Wisd. of Sol. 18:15, 16) anticipates the doctrine of the Word (Logos) developed by Philo Judaeus, a later Alexandrine Jewish scholar. Philo's Logos concept was then adopted and modified by the author of

John's Gospel to explain the incarnation of the prehuman Jesus (John 1:1, 14). Such foreshadowing of ideas popular in Christianity may explain why the Wisdom of Solomon was recommended reading in many early churches and was included with New Testament writings in the Muratorian Canon.

RECOMMENDED READING

Hadas, Moses. "Wisdom of Solomon." In *The Interpreter's Dictionary of the Bible*, vol. 4, pp. 861–63. New York and Nashville: Abingdon Press, 1962.

Reese, James M. *Hellenistic Influence on the Book of Wisdom and Its Consequences.* Rome: Biblical Institute Press, 1970.

❦ Ecclesiasticus (or Wisdom of Jesus Ben Sirach)

Sayings and Reflections   Chapters 1–42
Hymns and a Eulogy   42–51

Thoughts are rooted in the heart,
  and this sends out four branches,
good and evil, life and death.

        Ecclesiasticus 37:17–18

The longest wisdom book in the Bible, Ecclesiasticus is also the only apocryphal writing whose author, original translator, and date are known. The writer identifies himself as Jesus Ben (son of) Sirach (Ecclus. 50:27), a professional teacher of wisdom who conducted a school or house of learning in Jerusalem (Ecclus. 51:24). In a preface to the main work, Ben Sirach's grandson reveals that he brought the book to Egypt, where he translated it from Hebrew into Greek at a date equivalent to 132 B.C.E.; his grandfather had composed it in Jerusalem about 180 B.C.E. The title, which means "church book," may reflect either its extensive use in church worship or the fact that though the Jews eventually denied it a place in the Hebrew Bible, the Christian Church received it into the canon.

Sayings and Reflections Written in the tradition of Proverbs, Ecclesiasticus is largely a collection of wise sayings, moral essays, hymns to wisdom, practical advice to the young and inexperienced, instructions in proper social and religious conduct, private meditations, and extended reflections on the human condition. Like other postexilic sages, Ben Sirach perceives an ordered design in the universe and counsels others to conform their lives to it. A learned, respected, influential representative of upper-class Judaism, his tone is genial, pragmatic, and urbane. Writing more than a decade before the persecutions of Antiochus IV, he believes that life can be a positive experience if one only learns to conduct oneself with prudence, insight, and the right degree of shrewdness.

Completely a man of the present, Ben Sirach rejects any belief in angels, demons, or life after death. Not for him are apocalyptic enthusiasms. "The son of man," he asserts, "is not immortal" (Ecclus. 17:30). With his emphasis on the law, temple service, good works, and denial of a resurrection or afterlife, Ben Sirach seems to be a forerunner of the Sadducees. Like that intensely conservative, aristocratic party that largely controlled the priesthood and temple in the first century C.E., he appears to regard the law as final and unchanging, an essentially static guidebook to both the moral and material good life.

Ecclesiasticus also resembles Proverbs and the Wisdom of Solomon in consisting mostly of poetry, chiefly couplets of parallel lines. The first forty-two chapters, containing many brief aphorisms interspersed with longer discourses, offer advice and admonition on many diverse topics: the fear of God as the basis of wisdom (Ecclus. 1:20; 32:14–33:3); humility (Ecclus. 3:17–26); generosity to the poor (Ecclus. 4:1–11; 7:32–40); choosing prudent friendships (Ecclus. 6:5–17; 12:8–19; 22:19–32); trusting in God (Ecclus. 2:1–23; 11:12–30); humanity's moral responsibilities (Ecclus. 16:24–17:13); female spite (Ecclus. 25:13–36); a good wife (Ecclus. 26:1–23); proper manners and control of drinking at banquets (Ecclus. 31:12–32:17); honoring doctors and respecting scholars (Ecclus. 38:1–15; 31:1–15); the human predicament and fate of the wicked (Ecclus. 40:1–11; 41:5–16).

Chapter 24:1–30 contains a splendid oration by Lady Wisdom, whom Ben Sirach explicitly identifies with the Mosaic law (Ecclus. 19:20, 24:23):

> I came forth from the mouth of the Most High,
>   and I covered the earth like a mist . . .
> From eternity, in the beginning, he created me,
>   and for eternity I shall remain.
> I ministered before him in the holy tabernacle,
>   and thus was I established on Zion.
> In the beloved city he has given me rest,
>   and in Jerusalem I wield my authority.
>
> Ecclesiasticus 24:3, 9–11

Hymns and a Eulogy Chapters 42:15–43:33 comprise a hymn praising the deity's glory as revealed in physical nature, a poem that rivals Psalm 19 in beauty. This is followed by the best-known passage in the book—"let us now praise famous men"—a eulogy of twenty-nine Old Testament heroes from Enoch to Nehemiah, including Abraham, Joseph, Aaron (Is-

rael's first high priest, who is given more space than the lawgiver Moses),
David, Hezekiah, and Elijah. Ezra's name is conspicuously absent, presumably because this great interpreter of the law was regarded as the
progenitor of a religious movement that culminated in Pharisaism, a
development of which Ben Sirach strongly disapproved.

The tribute to Israel's ancestors climaxes in the praise of Simon the
high priest (about 225–200 B.C.E.), whom Ben Sirach lauds as personifying
the best of his nation's traditions (Ecclus. 50:1–24). As intercessor between
the people and their god, Simon was privileged to enter the temple's Holy
of Holies annually on the Day of Atonement (see Lev. 16) and there pronounce the divine name Yahweh, which by Hellenistic times was considered too sacred to utter publicly. The book concludes with an epilogue
containing Ben Sirach's hymn of personal thanksgiving (Ecclus. 51:1–12)
and an autobiographical résumé of the rewards of pursuing wisdom
(Ecclus. 51:13–30).

The emphasis that Ben Sirach places on the practical advantages of
strict moral conduct, wealth, and worldly success and his view that temple services are the most important part of Israel's worship well represent
attitudes characteristic of latter Sadduceeism. His assumption that his
god's intentions for humankind were completely and unchangingly revealed in the Mosaic code and temple liturgy helps to explain why the
Sadducees as a party did not long survive the Roman destruction of
Jerusalem and its sanctuary in 70 C.E.

RECOMMENDED READING

Hengel, Martin. *Judaism and Hellenism.* London and Philadelphia: SCM Press,
1979.

Snaith, John G. *Ecclesiasticus: or The Wisdom of Jesus Son of Sirach.* Cambridge
Bible Commentary on the New English Bible. London: Cambridge University
Press, 1974.

❧ Baruch

Exiles' Prayer	*Chapters 1–3:8*
Hymn and Poems	*3:9–5:9*
Letter of Jeremiah	*6:1–72*

[Wisdom is revealed in] the book of the commandments of God,
the Law that stands for ever;
those who keep her live,
those who desert her die.

Baruch 4:1

Baruch is the only book of the Apocrypha whose mode resembles the prophetic. Although it purports to have been written about 582 B.C.E. (Bar. 1:2) by the secretary and companion of the prophet Jeremiah (Jer. 36:4–10), scholars agree that it is a composite work to which at least three different writers anonymously contributed. The book's four parts have been dated from about 200 B.C.E. for the earliest additions to after 70 C.E. for the latest additions. Although set during the Babylonian exile, it more accurately reflects the problems of non-Palestinian Jews dispersed throughout the Hellenistic world.

Exiles' Prayer   The first part (Bar. 1:1–3:8) contains several confusing contradictions. It states, for example, that the "book of Baruch" was written in Babylon five years after the Babylonians had burned Solomon's temple (Bar. 1:2), yet it pictures the exiles asking the high priest and his assistants in Jerusalem to offer prayers in "the house of the Lord" (Bar. 1:14). Equally confusing is the statement that Baruch read "this book" to an assembly of Jewish exiles living in Babylon (Bar. 1:1–4), when it is clear that the book relates events that occurred long after the public reading.

The rest of this prose section (Bar. 1:15–3:8), which resembles parts of Daniel (see Dan. 9:4–19), depicts the exiled Jews confessing the sins that caused their nation's downfall (Bar. 1:15–2:10; 2:20–26) and beseeching divine mercy (Bar. 2:11–19; 3:1–8). It also contains a prophecy that the scattered people will be restored to their homeland (Bar. 2:27–35).

Hymn and Poems   The second part (Bar. 3:9–4:4), apparently by a different author, is a didactic hymn praising Israel's god for revealing his wisdom in the Mosaic law. The third section (Bar. 4:5–5:9), echoing motifs in Second Isaiah and Lamentations, contains poems of hope and comfort as well as of sorrow for Jerusalem's fall. The poet realizes that Israel's exile is a punishment for its violations of the law but foresees a joyous return to Palestine (Bar. 5:1–9).

Letter of Jeremiah   Although the ancient manuscripts place this document after Lamentations, the Latin Vulgate and most English Bibles that include the Apocrypha attach it to Baruch, where it appears as chapter 6 (the New English Bible prints it as a separate book following Baruch). Purporting to be a letter from Jeremiah to Jews about to be deported to Babylon, the document is in fact a much later work, apparently modeled on the prophet's authentic sixth-century letter to Babylonian exiles (see Jer. 29). Estimates on the date of composition vary from 317 to about 100 B.C.E.

The writer's theme is the evil of idolatry, to which he devotes the most virulent and extensive attack in the Bible. Although the only heathen god specifically mentioned is Bel (Marduk) (Bar. 6:4), scholars believe that he is really denouncing Hellenistic deities that Jews scattered abroad might for social and political reasons be tempted to worship. "Babylon" would then be a symbol for areas outside Palestine where Jews had been dispersed.

The author extends Jeremiah's prediction that the exile would last seventy years (Jer. 25:12) to "seven generations" (Bar. 6:3), which, taking a biblical generation as forty years (Num. 32:13), would mean that the Jews would remain exiled until the end of the fourth century B.C.E. The letter thus updates earlier biblical themes and applies them to contemporary situations in the Hellenistic diaspora.

RECOMMENDED READING

Moore, Carey A. *Daniel, Esther, and Jeremiah: The Additions.* Garden City, N. Y.: Doubleday, 1977.

❧ Additions to Daniel

The Song of the Three Holy Children	*Chapters 3:24–90*
Susanna	*13*
Bel and the Dragon	*14*

"You are great, O Lord, God of Daniel,"
Cyrus exclaimed, "there is no god but you."

Bel and the Dragon 14:42

The Song of the Three Holy Children   The Greek version of Daniel includes, among many briefer additions, three relatively long poetic and narrative units not found in the Hebrew canon. The first of these consists of psalms or hymns reputedly sung by Shadrach, Meshach, and Abednego while confined in a Babylonian furnace. Their songs are inserted into the Hebrew-Aramaic text of Daniel between verses 23 and 24 of chapter 3 (forming verses 3:24–90 in Catholic Bible editions).

The opening poem, the Prayer of Azariah (the Hebrew name of Abednego), is a lament confessing Israel's collective sins and beseeching its god for mercy, though the psalm strangely never alludes to Azariah's fiery ordeal. The references to Jewish suffering under "an unjust king, the worst in the whole world" (Song of Three Children 3:32) and to the suppression of temple services (Song of Three Children 3:38–40) indicate that the poem may have been composed during the persecutions of Antiochus IV, perhaps about the same time the apocalyptic portions of Daniel 7–12 were written.

The choral psalm that the three young men sing in unison (Song of Three Children 3:52–90) is a vigorous hymn of praise extolling the "God of [their] ancestors" and inciting the natural elements—earth, air, sea, and sentient life—to praise the deity. Some critics have suggested that this poem, which resembles the canonical Psalm 148 in thought and Psalm 136 in form, may be a popular hymn of thanksgiving for Maccabean victories. Experts are not agreed, however, on either the exact time of composition or the original language of these poems. Like other additions to Daniel, they may have been written in Hebrew, Aramaic, or Greek during the late second or early first century B.C.E.

Susanna Because Daniel is still a "young boy" (Sus. 13:46) when its action takes place, this cleverly plotted short story is sometimes placed at the beginning of the book, although some modern Catholic translations such as the Jerusalem Bible include it as chapter 13.

In Babylon during the captivity (587–539 B.C.E.), Susanna, a beautiful and virtuous young wife, rejects the lustful advances of two Jewish elders who are also judges. When they spitefully accuse her of adultery and she is condemned to death by their testimony, the "holy spirit" inspires Daniel to demand a more thorough investigation. Separating the elders, who then give contradictory evidence, he convicts them of bearing false witness, so that they suffer the fate they had planned for Susanna. Although commonly regarded as a suspenseful "detective story," Susanna's experience was probably recorded to criticize corrupt judges of the Jewish diaspora who abused their legal authority.

Bel and the Dragon This third apocryphal addition, usually appended to Daniel as chapter 14, is a prose account of three incidents in which Daniel demonstrates either his superior powers of deduction or the deceitful machinations of heathen priests who attempt to ruin him. In the first incident, Daniel proves to "King Astyages" (Cyrus of Persia, who now rules at Babylon) that the great statue of Bel (the Babylonian god Marduk) does not eat the food left before it but that the offerings are consumed by lying priests and their families (Bel and Dragon 14:1–22). Disabused of his superstition, Cyrus orders the priests and their relatives slain and commissions Daniel to destroy Bel's idol and temple.

In the next episode, Daniel poisons a dragon, or large serpent, to show his credulous ruler that it is not a god but a mortal reptile (Bel and Dragon 14:23–27). When Babylonians who had revered the serpent learn that Daniel has killed it, they accuse the king of "turning Jewish" and persuade him to throw the iconoclastic foreigner into a lions' pit, where he remains for six days. During this period an angel carries the prophet Habakkuk from Judah to Babylon so that he can feed Daniel, then immediately returns the prophet to Judah. When the king discovers on the seventh day that Daniel is still uneaten, he releases him, praises his god, and hurls his rivals into the pit, where they are promptly devoured (Bel and Dragon 14:28–42).

As in the story of Susanna, the author here emphasizes that the Hebrew god will "not desert those who love him" (Bel and Dragon 14:39). Indeed, like the canonical Daniel, the Additions consistently dramatize that the Jewish deity watches over those who faithfully keep his commandments and reject the snares of idol-worshiping pagans.

RECOMMENDED READING

Moore, Carey A. *Daniel, Esther, and Jeremiah: The Additions.* Garden City, N. Y.: Doubleday, 1977.

ꙮ Prayer of Manasseh

Plea for Mercy   *Verses 1–15*

Bowed down with a heavy chain of iron,
I grieve over my sins.

Prayer of Manasseh 10*

Plea for Mercy   The shortest independent book in the Old Testament, this devotional poem of fifteen verses is supposedly the work of King Manasseh, whom 1 Kings 21 condemned as the most evil monarch in Judah's history. Although the incident is not mentioned in Kings' account of his long reign, 2 Chronicles 33:5–10 alleges that the Assyrians took Manasseh captive to Babylon, where by repenting his sins—which included idolatry, sorcery, and human sacrifice—he appeased Yahweh, who restored him to his throne. Back in Jerusalem, Manasseh reportedly purged the city of "alien gods," removed an idol from Yahweh's temple, and rebuilt the altar there.

Although the Chronicler notes that Manasseh's prayer was recorded "in the Annals of Hozai" (2 Chron. 33:19), it is doubtful that this apocryphal poem, which most scholars assign to the second or first century B.C.E., is based on that earlier work. Echoing the psalms of individual lament, such as numbers 69–71, the poem is a courageous acceptance of the writer's responsibility for his sins and a declaration of faith that his god is good and merciful:

---

* Quotations from Prayer of Manasseh are from *The New English Bible*, Oxford Study Edition (New York: Oxford University Press, 1976).

For thou art Lord Most High,

compassionate, patient, and of great mercy,

relenting when men suffer for their sins,

for out of thy great goodness thou, O God,

has promised repentance and remission to those who sin
against thee,

and in thy boundless mercy thou hast appointed
repentance for sinners as the way to salvation.

Prayer of Manasseh 7

In spite of the poem's intensity and lyric beauty, the sixteenth-century Council of Trent rejected it, along with 1 and 2 Esdras, from the Catholic Bible. Until then, it had been considered deuterocanonical and part of the Old Testament Apocrypha.

❦ 1 Maccabees

The Great Persecution	*Chapters 1*
Revolt of the Maccabees	*2*
Judas Maccabeus	*3–9:22*
Jonathan	*9:23–12*
Simon	*13–16*
John Hyrcanus	*16*

A terrible oppression began in Israel; there was nothing like it since the disappearance of prophecy among them.

1 Maccabees 9:27

The most accurate and valuable historical work in the Apocrypha, 1 Maccabees covers the tumultuous period from about 168 to 134 B.C.E., during which the Jews overthrew their Greek-Syrian overlords and established an independent state. Without this and the less trustworthy account in 2 Maccabees, we would have virtually nothing of Israel's history between Ezra's reforms (about 400 B.C.E.) and the birth of Christ.

Probably written about 100 B.C.E., 1 Maccabees gives an apparent eyewitness description and remarkably unprejudiced account of the fight for religious freedom by Judas Maccabeus (for whom the book is named) and his brothers during the persecutions of the Syrian tyrant Antiochus IV. In addition to its objectivity, 1 Maccabees is notable for its plain, swiftly moving style and for the complete absence of miracles, supernatural elements, and divine interventions from the narrative. Like the canonical

Book of Esther, it presents historical events as the result of purely human activity.

While his protagonists offer prayers and strictly observe the Mosaic law, the author never attributes their military or political victories to God's direct help, though he does seem to indicate that faithful Jews who are willing to sacrifice their lives opposing the heathen will achieve success. Since he never refers to divine providence or to the hope of immortality for the faithful dead, many scholars believe the unknown writer belonged to the Sadducee party, a religiously conservative group that developed during this period.

The Great Persecution   A brief preface recounts Alexander's conquest of Persia and his successor's division of the Macedonian Greek Empire (Palestine was first awarded to the Ptolemies of Egypt and then conquered by the Syrian Antiochus III; see Table 6-1). The book then focuses on Antiochus IV's misguided effort to impose religious unity on all his subjects by outlawing the Jewish religion. Antiochus burns copies of the Mosaic law and forbids the offering of sacrifices to any but Hellenistic gods, the circumcision of infants, and the keeping of Sabbath or other holy days. To enforce his prohibitions, he erects a fortress citadel in Jerusalem and fills it with Syrian soldiers. Finally, he builds an altar to Zeus in Yahweh's temple and sacrifices pigs and other ceremonially unclean animals at the sanctuary.

Revolt of the Maccabees   Fearful of the Syrians' power, many Jews reluctantly compromised their faith and sacrificed to the state-imposed gods. Others, attracted by Greek culture and philosophy, more willingly supported Antiochus' policies. A large number, however, refused to abandon their ancestral faith; among these was the priest Mattathias, who with his five sons—John, Simon, Judas, Eleazar, and Jonathan—moved from Jerusalem to their native village of Modein. When one of Antiochus' commissioners tried to bribe Mattathias into publicly obeying the royal edict, the old man killed both the commissioner and a fellow Jew who had sacrificed, then fled to the hill country with his sons (1 Macc. 2).

After Syrian soldiers massacre a thousand Jews who piously refuse to defend themselves on the Sabbath, Mattathias and his followers prudently decide that self-defense does not violate Sabbath rules. Fighting a guerrilla war against the occupation troops, Mattathias' group destroys many pagan altars and forcibly circumcises many Jewish boys. Near death, Mattathias appoints the most capable of his sons, Judas Maccabeus (in Greek, the "Hammerer"), as his successor.

Judas Maccabeus   Chapters 3–9 recount the incomparable service of Judas Maccabeus to the Hebrew nation. Against tremendous odds he defeats the Syrian armies in several decisive battles, then marches into

Date B.C.E.	Rulers over Palestine		Events in Judah
	Egypt (Ptolemys)	Syria (Seleucids)	
323	Ptolemy I Lagi (323–285)	Seleucis I (312–280)	
300	Ptolemy II Philadelphus (285–246); Alexandrine Jews begin translation of Torah and Prophets (Septuagint Bible)	Antiochus I (280–261)	
		Antiochus II (261–246)	Judah under Ptolemaic control
250	Ptolemy III Euergetes (246–221)	Seleucis II (246–226)	
		Seleucis III (226–223)	
	Ptolemy IV Philopator (221–203)	Antiochus III (223–187)	
200	Ptolemy V Epiphanes (203–181)	Seleucids capture Palestine (200–198/197)	Judah under Seleucid control
		Seleucus IV (187–175)	Persecution of Jews; desecration of the temple (168 or 167)
	Ptolemy VI Philometor (181–146)	Antiochus IV Epiphanes (175–163)	Maccabean revolt under Mattathias (d. 166) and Judas Maccabeus (d. 160); rededication of the temple (165 or 164)
		Antiochus V (163–162)	
150		Demetrius I (162–150)	
			Judah independent under Hasmoneans (142–63)

Jerusalem where he cleanses the ransacked temple and rebuilds its altar. He then institutes the joyous festival of rededication (Hanukkah)—according to tradition, three years after the day on which Antiochus had polluted the sanctuary. When Antiochus unexpectedly dies in 163 B.C.E, Judas concludes an armistice with the Syrians, assuring his people religious freedom. After war is resumed three years later, Judas defeats the Syrian general Nicanor, who had rashly threatened to burn the temple.

Among the most significant of Judas' deeds is his treaty of friendship

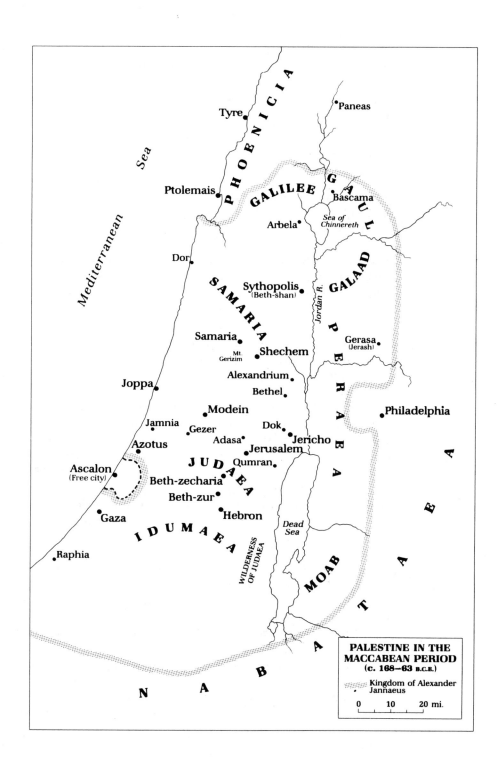

Mediterranean Sea

Tyre

Paneas

PHOENICIA

Ptolemais

GALILEE

GAULA

Bascama

Arbela

Sea of Chinnereth

Dor

SAMARIA

Sythopolis
(Beth-shan)

Jordan R.

GALAAD

Samaria

Mt. Gerizim

Shechem

PERAEA

Gerasa
(Jerash)

Alexandrium

Bethel

Joppa

Modein

Philadelphia

Jamnia

Gezer

Dok

Adasa

Jericho

Azotus

Jerusalem

JUDAEA

Qumran

Ascalon
(Free city)

Beth-zecharia

Beth-zur

Gaza

Hebron

Dead Sea

IDUMAEA

WILDERNESS OF JUDAEA

Raphia

MOAB

NABATAEA

**PALESTINE IN THE
MACCABEAN PERIOD**
(C. **168–63** B.C.E.)

Kingdom of Alexander
Jannaeus

0   10   20 mi.

219

with Rome, the mighty new empire then rising in the West. The author of 1 Maccabees (who must have written before Rome took over Palestine in 63 B.C.E.) ironically regards Rome as the champion of peace and political integrity, the protector of smaller states who willingly place themselves within its sphere of influence.

Jonathan   After Judas falls in battle, his brother Jonathan becomes leader of the Jews (160–142 B.C.E.). Sharing his predecessor's charismatic gifts, Jonathan rallies the people against further Syrian aggression, which is repelled. Alexander, the new claimant to the Syrian throne, shrewdly concludes a peace settlement with Jonathan and in 152 B.C.E. appoints him high priest—by this time a political as well as religious office—thus establishing a line of Hasmonean (an ancestral name of the Maccabees) priest-kings that lasts until 40 B.C.E. when the Romans appoint Herod king of the Jews. During later political turmoil, however, Jonathan is led into the Syrian camp and treacherously slain (1 Macc. 9:23–12:53).

Simon   The last of the Maccabean brothers, Simon now assumes military leadership and eventually the high priesthood as well. Although he marshals an army, he fights fewer battles than did his brothers; his forte seems to have been diplomacy, for he bribes Syrian troops to withdraw and thus ensures peace for about seven years. Taking advantage of this lull and of Syria's internal strife, Simon builds numerous fortresses around the country and forms an alliance with the Syrian ruler, who confirms his appointment as high priest and simultaneously releases the Israelites from taxation and tribute. This act effectively assures Jewish autonomy (142 B.C.E.) and marks a new independence for the Jewish state.

John Hyrcanus   In 134 B.C.E., however, the Syrians again attack, and many Jews are imprisoned or killed. The aged Simon commissions two of his sons, Judas and John, who lead the Jewish army victoriously against the invaders. After Simon and his other sons, Mattathias and Judas, are murdered by Simon's traitorous son-in-law, John (surnamed "Hyrcanus") becomes Judah's priest-king (1 Macc. 16). This event is the last recorded in Old Testament history. (For a summary of Palestinian history leading to the emergence of Christianity, see Part 7, "Between the Testaments.")
Although the author of 1 Maccabees ignores the possibility of supernatural aid in the Jewish struggle for independence from Syria, his theme that faithfulness and courage under persecution can result in freedom is undeniably inspirational. The hectic period he describes, with its excesses on both sides, also provides the historical background for such canonical books as Esther, which similarly depicts the Jews fighting for their lives against pagan oppressors, and Daniel, which recounts the struggles between the Seleucids and Jews in eschatological terms (Dan. 11:21–12:13).

RECOMMENDED READING

Bickerman, Elias. *From Ezra to the Last of the Maccabees.* New York: Schocken Books, 1962. A brief introduction to the period.

de Lange, Nicholas. *Apocrypha: Jewish Literature of the Hellenistic Age.* New York: Viking Press, 1978.

Goldstein, Jonathan A. *I Maccabees.* Garden City, N. Y.: Doubleday, 1976. Covers the Maccabean period thoroughly and includes a translation and interpretation of 1 Maccabees.

Hengel, Martin. *Judaism and Hellenism,* 2 vols. London: SCM Press, 1974.
———. *Jews, Greeks, and Barbarians: Aspects of the Hellenization of Judaism in the Pre-Christian Period.* Philadelphia: Fortress Press, 1980.

Nickelsburg, George W. E. *Jewish Literature Between the Bible and the Mishnah.* Philadelphia: Fortress Press, 1981. A survey of both apocryphal and pseudepigraphal works in their historical context.

Stone, Michael. *Scriptures, Sects and Visions: A Profile of Judaism from Ezra to the Jewish Revolts.* Philadelphia: Fortress Press, 1980. A concise, clearly written discussion of ideas during the pre-Christian period.

❦ 2 Maccabees

Corruption, Persecution, and Integrity	Chapters 1–15
Religious Beliefs	6, 7, 10, 12, 15

The Hebrews were invincible because the mighty God fought for them.

2 Maccabees 11:13

A Greek work, probably written in Alexandria, Egypt, about 124 B.C.E., 2 Maccabees is not a continuation of the history of 1 Maccabees but a revised version of events related in the first seven chapters of the earlier book. According to the compiler's preface (2 Macc. 2:19–32), it is an edited abridgement of a five-volume historical work (since lost) by "Jason of Cyrene," who is otherwise unknown. The period covered is approximately 176 to 161 B.C.E.

While 1 Maccabees is a relatively straightforward, reliable, and human (perhaps Sadduceean) account of the Jewish revolt against Antiochus IV's enforced Hellenization of Judah, the second book's credibility is undermined by its emphasis on exaggerated numbers, miracles, and supernatural apparitions. The writer of 2 Maccabees, who seems to have been a Pharisee, not only presents the successful rebellion as an act of God

(2 Macc. 11:13; 15:27) but injects considerable religious commentary into his narrative (2 Macc. 5:17–20; 6:12–17; 8:36; 12:40), along with such typical Pharisaic doctrines as belief in a bodily resurrection (2 Macc. 7:9; 14:46).

Corruption, Persecution, and Integrity   The book opens with two letters from Palestinian Jews to their fellows in Egypt, urging the latter to observe Hanukkah, the festival of the temple's rededication (2 Macc. 1:1–2:18). After outlining his sources in a preface (2 Macc. 2:19–32), the "abbreviator" traces the increasing corruption of the high priesthood in the persons of Jason and Menelaus (2 Macc. 3–4); Antiochus IV's campaign to unify his ethnically diverse subjects by imposing Hellenistic culture and religion on them; the Jews' consequent sufferings (2 Macc. 5–7); Judas Maccabeus' unexpectedly effective guerrilla resistance, which culminates in the purification of the temple (2 Macc. 8–10); and Judas' further battles against such foes as Nicanor, chief general of Demetrius I, one of Antiochus' successors (2 Macc. 10–15).

Although some of its material is of doubtful authenticity, 2 Maccabees offers vivid descriptions of the greed, intrigue, and treachery of Jason and Menelaus (2 Macc. 4–5), who betray their people for personal gain. Equally memorable are the author's depictions of the tortures endured by Jews who refuse to compromise their faith. The nobility of the ninety-year-old Eleazar, a distinguished teacher who is bludgeoned to death, and the courage of seven brothers and their mother, all of whom are mutilated and burned alive by Antiochus, are classic examples of Jewish integrity (2 Macc. 6–7).

Religious Beliefs   Also noteworthy is the author's theological philosophy of history, which attributes the Jewish people's martyrdom under Antiochus to their god's wish to discipline them. Intense suffering is here seen, paradoxically, as a sign of divine benevolence, for while the deity allows the pagan nations to multiply their crimes and guilt—with the implication that the coming retribution will be all the more severe—Israel is punished *before* its "sins come to a head." That numerous disasters befall the Jews, in short, is evidence that their god has *not* deserted them (2 Macc. 6:12–17).

The writer's other religious beliefs apparently include a future resurrection of the dead (2 Macc. 7:9; 14:46); belief in the efficacy of a prayer to release the dead from sin (2 Macc. 12:43–45); the doctrine that the righteous dead can intervene on behalf of the living (2 Macc. 15:12–16); and the concept that God created the world out of nothing (2 Macc. 7:28). Such Pharisaic beliefs appear to have been increasingly prevalent in the time of Hellenistic Judaism. Certainly, such notions as prayers for souls in Purgatory and the intercessory prayers of saints later became important in Roman Catholicism. Perhaps because it supported these doctrines, 2 Maccabees was condemned in Protestant circles.

RECOMMENDED READING

Goldstein, Jonathan A. *2 Maccabees*. Garden City, N. Y.: Doubleday, 1979.

PSEUDEPIGRAPHA

In addition to the canonical and apocryphal books of the Old Testament, early Jewish writers produced a body of religious literature known collectively as the Pseudepigrapha, although this label is somewhat misleading because not all the works so designated are pseudonymous—ascribed by anonymous writers to famous figures of the past such as Enoch, Noah, Moses, or Isaiah; some books, like 3 and 4 Maccabees, make no claims of illustrious authorship.

Dating from about 200 B.C.E. to 200 C.E., these writings include a variety of literary types, ranging from apocalypses and sacred legends to interpretative retellings of canonical narratives. Like the Apocrypha, pseudepigraphal books appeared in Hebrew, Aramaic, and Greek. Because of limited space, only brief summaries of the major works are given here.

RECOMMENDED READING

Charles, R. H. *Apocrypha and Pseudepigrapha of the Old Testament*, vol. 2. Oxford: Clarendon Press, 1913. Charles provides translations, with critical introductions and numerous annotations of the texts, of most of the pseudepigraphal books. Since this volume appeared long before discovery of the Dead Sea Scrolls, however, the reader must approach some of the author's conclusions with caution.

Charlesworth, James H., ed. *The Old Testament Pseudepigrapha*. Vol. 1, *Apocalyptic Literature and Testaments*. Garden city, N. Y.: Doubleday, 1983. A scholarly new edition of the Pseudepigrapha (including several documents not in Charles' collection), with new translations and historical-critical annotations on the text. A major work of scholarship.

de Lange, Nicholas. *Apocrypha: Jewish Literature of the Hellenistic Age*. New York: Viking Press, 1978. Discusses several pseudepigraphal works.

Eissfeldt, Otto. *The Old Testament: An Introduction*. New York: Harper & Row, 1965. In this English version of a standard German work, the author includes précis of the background and content of fourteen pseudepigraphal books.

Nickelsburg, George W. E. *Jewish Literature Between the Bible and the Mishnah*. Philadelphia: Fortress Press, 1981.

Rost, Leonhard. *Judaism outside the Hebrew Canon: An Introduction to the Documents*. Nashville: Abingdon Press, 1976.

Stone, Michael. *Scriptures, Sects and Visions: A Profile of Judaism from Ezra to the Jewish Revolts*. Philadelphia: Fortress Press, 1980. A readable and concise survey of ideas and practices developing in Judaism from late Old Testament to New Testament times.

❧ Letter of Aristeas

The good life consists in the keeping of the enactments of the law.

Letter of Aristeas, verse 127

This document is ostensibly a letter from Aristeas—a courtier of the Egyptian monarch Ptolemy II (285–246 B.C.E.)—to his brother Philocrates, containing an eyewitness account of the origin of the Septuagint Bible. A treatise rather than a letter, it relates how Ptolemy, when informed by the head of the Alexandria library that his collection lacked a copy of the Jewish Torah, sent Aristeas and Andreas to Jerusalem to obtain the original text.

The book describes negotiations with the high priest Eleazar, the selection of six leading scholars from each tribe of Israel, the reception of the seventy-two Jewish experts at the Ptolemaic court, their labors in translating the Hebrew text into Greek, and their production in seventy-two days of seventy-two identical translations, the reliability of which is affirmed by leaders of Alexandria's Jewish constituency. In popular usage, however, the number of translators was rounded off to seventy, a figure that gave the Septuagint its name.

Despite its wealth of concrete detail, scholars regard this story as more legend than historical fact. It is possible that in the mid-third century B.C.E. a librarian added a Greek transcription or translation of the Pentateuch to his official collection and that the reigning king may have sponsored the acquisition; but the royal honors that the author claims were showered on the Jewish translators are surely fictional.

Moreover, the Letter of Aristeas was not written by a contemporary of Ptolemy II but about 150 years later. The author was probably an Alexandrine Jew familiar with the Egyptian court, who wrote to demonstrate the authority of the Septuagint and the superiority of Hebrew wisdom (manifested in the law) to Greek learning. Hence the writer features extended dialogues between Torah-trained Jews and Greek philosophers, with the former triumphing in every dispute.

In this regard, the book well illustrates the tension between the Hebraic and Hellenic cultures that prevailed in the cosmopolitan setting of Hellenistic Alexandria. The fact that well-educated Jews found Greek ideas attractive made a Greek version of the Torah all the more necessary. Although an eventual fusion of Greek and Hebrew thought fertilized the growth of Hellenistic Judaism, later Palestinian rabbis rejected most of the synthesis.

RECOMMENDED READING

Charles, R. H. "The Letter of Aristeas, with an Introduction." In *Apocrypha and Pseudepigrapha of the Old Testament*, vol. 2, pp. 83–122. Oxford: Clarendon Press, 1913.

Charlesworth, James H., ed. *The Old Testament Pseudepigrapha*. vol. 2, *Expansions of the Old Testament and Other Legends, Wisdom, and Philosophical Literature*. Garden City, N. Y.: Doubleday, 1984.

Zuntz, G. "Aristeas." In *The Interpreter's Dictionary of the Bible*, vol. 1, pp. 219–21. New York and Nashville: Abingdon Press, 1962.

❦ Book of Jubilees

> **And the Jubilees shall pass by, until Israel is cleansed**
> **from all guilt . . . and error,**
> **and dwells with confidence in all the land,**
> **and there shall be no more a Satan or evil one,**
> **and the land shall be clean from that time forevermore.**
>
> **Book of Jubilees 50:5**

The Book of Jubilees takes its name from the fact that the author divides world history into "Jubilees" or periods of forty-nine years, based on the Jubilee concept given in Leviticus 25. He further partitions each forty-nine-year epoch into seven weeks of years, all of which contain seven solar years of 364 days. This rigid compartmentalizing of the world's chronology is typical of the writer's priestly and legalistic approach.

Jubilees is also known as "Little Genesis" because it reproduces almost the entire narrative of the first Bible book, adding interpretative commentary and details from Jewish oral tradition along the way. In this expansion and elaboration of the canonical text, the author provides a virtual Midrash characteristic of the late second century B.C.E. when Jubilees was written. (*Midrash* is a Hebrew term meaning an explanation or scholarly interpretation of Scripture, typically that produced by scribes and rabbinical Pharisees.)

As the Chronicler imbued Israel's monarchial history with a priestly slant, so the author of Jubilees retells Genesis (and the first twelve chapters of Exodus) from a Pharisaic viewpoint, emphasizing the absolute supremacy of the law, both canonical as preserved in the written Torah and oral as retained in the Pharisees' traditions. He thus makes the patriarchs Abraham, Isaac, and Jacob fervent practitioners not only of the Mosaic legal system but of the Pharisaic additions to that law as well. His purpose is to show that the law existed from the beginning, that it is thus the supreme moral value in the universe, and that its delivery to Moses on Mount Sinai was a complete and final manifestation of divine wisdom.

Jubilees presents an angel relating the whole story (Gen. 1 through Exod. 12) so that Moses can preserve it in the Pentateuch. As noted, however, Jubilees' version of Israel's prehistory includes many anachronistic elements. At age fourteen Abraham is said to have rejected his father's idols and embraced a perfect monotheism (Bk. Jub. 11:16–18). After describing Abraham's death (Bk. Jub. 23:1–8), the author interjects a long apocalyptic prophecy in which the angel tells Moses of the disasters to follow humankind's disobedience and Israel's future forsaking of the covenant; but after the chastened Israelites return to studying the law and heeding its commands, their god will again restore them to long life and prosperity (Bk. Jub. 23:13–32).

Such eschatological predictions give the author's theology a more flexible quality than his rather pedantic legalism might indicate (see also Bk. Jub. 1:4–29 for a parallel eschatological prophecy). At the same time, however, Jubilees strictly enjoins the reader to observe all distinctions between things clean and unclean, to avoid idolatry and other heathen contaminations, and to honor the Sabbath fully. The author insists, in addition, upon circumcision (Bk. Jub. 15), upon keeping all the ritual feast days, upon obligatory fruit, grain, and animal offerings, and upon regulations concerning women's sexual impurities (Bk. Jub. 21: 15:31–32; 22:16–20; 30:7–17; 3:8; 50:6–13).

Some scholars have detected a resemblance between Jubilees' theology and that expressed in several documents recovered from the Qumran community; the presence of fragments from nine manuscripts of the original Hebrew version of the book found among the Dead Sea Scrolls confirms the link. Although written first in Hebrew, Jubilees survives most completely in an Ethiopic translation. Both it and Latin translations are taken from a Greek edition of the Hebrew original, which may be dated at about 100 B.C.E.

RECOMMENDED READING

Charles, R. H. "The Book of Jubilees, with an Introduction." In *Apocrypha and Pseudepigrapha of the Old Testament*, vol. 2, pp. 1–82. Oxford: Clarendon Press, 1913. Complete text in English with critical introduction and copious notes.

Charlesworth, James H., ed. *The Old Testament Pseudepigrapha.* vol. 2, *Expansions of the Old Testament.* Garden City, N. Y.: Doubleday, 1984.

Davenport, Gene L. *The Eschatology of the Book of Jubilees.* Leiden: E. J. Brill, 1971.

Eissfeldt, Otto. *The Old Testament: An Introduction.* New York: Harper & Row, 1965.

Tedsche, S. "Jubilees, Book of." In *The Interpreter's Dictionary of the Bible,* vol. 2, pp. 1002–3. New York and Nashville: Abingdon Press, 1962.

🐛 Martyrdom and Ascension of Isaiah

[Isaiah] spake with the Holy Spirit until he was sawn in twain.

Martyrdom of Isaiah 5:14

Originally three separate documents—the first Jewish and the second two Christian—that were put together by a Christian editor in the third or fourth century C.E., the Martyrdom and Ascension of Isaiah has survived in an Ethiopic translation and in fragments of Greek, Latin, Coptic, and Old Slavonic copies. The section dealing with the martyrdom was probably composed in Hebrew and was perhaps based on martyr legends arising from the persecutions of Antiochus IV (note the martyrdoms of Eleazar and the seven brothers in 2 Macc. 6:18–7:42). It may have appeared in the Qumran community during the first century B.C.E.

The Martyrdom of Isaiah is apparently based on a reference in 2 Kings 21:1–18 to Manasseh's idolatries and shedding of innocent blood. The narrative states that Isaiah, who had foretold Manasseh's religious corruption and his own martyrdom, fled to the desert with a small group of followers. But the aged prophet was betrayed by Bechira, a jealous rival, and brought to Manasseh, who had him sawed in two. This may also be the legend to which the author of Hebrew alludes (Heb. 11:37).

The second document, which exists only as a fragment, purports to be Isaiah's prophecy of Jesus' ministry, the establishment of the Church, the appearance of a Satanic figure (Belial), and the last judgment. A Christian work, it may have appeared about 100 C.E.

The Ascension of Isaiah, the third part of this collection spuriously attributed to the eighth-century prophet, is also a Christian work, perhaps dating from the second century C.E. It tells of Isaiah's journey through the seven heavens of Hebrew folklore to the presence of the "Most High," who orders the Messiah (Christ) to descend to earth. Isaiah then sees visions of Jesus' birth, crucifixion, and resurrection.

RECOMMENDED READING

Charles, R. H. "The Martyrdom of Isaiah, with an Introduction." In *Apocrypha and Pseudepigrapha of the Old Testament*, vol. 2, pp. 155–62. Oxford: Clarendon Press, 1913. Includes only the martyrdom section.

Eissfeldt, Otto. *The Old Testament: An Introduction.* New York: Harper & Row, 1965. Offers brief summaries of the martyrdom, prophecy, and ascension legends.

Rist, M. "Isaiah, Ascension of." In *The Interpreter's Dictionary of the Bible*, vol. 2, pp. 744–46. New York and Nashville: Abingdon Press, 1962.

❦ Psalms of Solomon

Long enough, O Lord, has thine hand been heavy on Israel.

Psalms of Solomon 2:22

Popular among early Christians, this collection of eighteen psalms fell from use and was not rediscovered until the 1600s. Although originally composed in Hebrew, the Psalms of Solomon survives only in Greek copies in a Syriac version translated from the Greek. The text does not attribute these psalms to King Solomon, however. Since the canonical Psalms ("of David") was already closed, the later poems may have been ascribed to his heir because he was known as Israel's second most celebrated poet (1 Kings 5:12).

References to General Pompey's ending of the Hasmonean dynasty, to his conquest of Judah (Ps. Sol. 8:15–21), and to his death later in Egypt (Ps. Sol. 2:26–35) indicate that some of the psalms were written between about 63 and 48 B.C.E., when these events occurred. Psalms of Solomon 17:7, which speaks of one "alien to our race," may allude either to Pompey or to Herod, the unpopular half-Jew who ruled as Roman-appointed king of Judea from 40 to 4 B.C.E.

It seems likely that all eighteen psalms were composed between about 63 and 30 B.C.E. Whether they are the work of one or several Hebrew poets is not known, though references to belief in the resurrection (Ps. Sol. 3:12; 13:11; 14:9–10) and free will (Ps. Sol. 9:4) seem to indicate that the writer(s) may have been connected with the Pharisees. Some scholars suggest that the poet may have had links with the Qumran community or Essene sect, as the last two psalms (17 and 18) evince strong messianic expectations.

Like the canonical Psalms, this collection includes hymns (Ps. Sol. 2:30, 33–37; 3:1–2), songs of lamentation (Ps. Sol. 2:19–25; 7; 8:22–34;

16:6–15), and songs of thanksgiving (Ps. Sol. 13:1–4; 15:1–6; 16:1–5), although here several literary genres are typically mixed within a single poem. Thus Psalms of Solomon 2:1–14 opens as a national lament, becomes a meditation in verses 15–18, switches to historical review in verses 19–21, changes to a prayerlike lament in verses 22–25, reverts to meditation on a historical event in verses 26–27, and finally combines further reflection, a hymn, a confession of faith, and a general invocation of all people to fear God and praise him in verses 28–37. As in the canonical book, the Psalms of Solomon makes a rigid distinction between sinners and saints.

RECOMMENDED READING

Charles, R. H. "Psalms of Solomon, with an Introduction." In *Apocrypha and Pseudepigrapha of the Old Testament*, vol. 2, pp. 625–52. Oxford: Clarendon Press, 1913.

Eissfeldt, Otto. *The Old Testament: An Introduction.* New York: Harper & Row, 1965.

Winter, P. "Psalms of Solomon." In *The Interpreter's Dictionary of the Bible*, vol. 2, pp. 958–60. New York and Nashville: Abingdon Press, 1962.

🐱 3 Maccabees

**The God of heaven surely protects the Jews,
fighting on their side continually as a father for his children.**

3 Maccabees 7:6

Misnamed, this book has nothing to do with the Maccabees but is a legendary account of how the Jews living in Egyptian exile came to celebrate a joyous festival of deliverance. Its theme—the narrow escape of exiled Jews from mass slaughter by their pagan enemies—strongly resembles that of Esther. A Greek composition, it probably originated in Alexandria, Egypt, late in the first century B.C.E.

Its seven chapters contain two major episodes. In the first, Ptolemy IV Philopator, after defeating Antiochus III at Raphia in 217 B.C.E., attempts to enter the Jerusalem temple but is stopped by a miraculous judgment (3 Macc. 1:1–2:24). In the second part, Ptolemy tries to force the Egyptian Jews into idolatry. When they refuse, he orders them trampled to death by elephants as a public spectacle. After the Jews are miraculously saved three times, Ptolemy, now respectful of their god, not only subsidizes an annual celebration but issues a decree permitting them to execute Jews who have compromised their faith (3 Macc. 6:22–7:23). The parallel to Ahasuerus' edict allowing the endangered Jews to defend themselves is obvious, as is the resemblance of the Egyptian festival to Purim.

RECOMMENDED READING

Brownlee, W. H. "Maccabees, Books of." In *The Interpreter's Dictionary of the Bible*, vol. 3, pp. 201–15. New York and Nashville: Abingdon Press, 1962.

Eissfeldt, Otto. *The Old Testament: An Introduction.* New York: Harper & Row, 1965.

❦ 4 Maccabees

Reason is supreme master over the passions.

4 Maccabees 1:14

Unlike the first three books named after the Maccabees, 4 Maccabees is not a historical narrative but a philosophical discourse on the proposition that reason reigns supreme over the passions. Thoroughly Greek in form, style, language, and philosophic vocabulary, it is also fully Jewish in the anonymous author's attempt to illustrate that true wisdom and virtue lie in knowledge of the Jewish law and absolute fidelity to its principles (4 Macc. 1:15–17).

The salient example upon which the author draws to illustrate his thesis that reason controls the emotions is the martyrdom of Jews rationally faithful to their law during the persecutions of Antiochus IV. His retelling of the sufferings and death of the priest Eleazar and the seven brothers and their mother (recounted in 2 Macc. 6–7) is probably why this book received its title.

Of particular interest is the author's selective fusion of Greek and Hebrew thought, a theological synthesis in which foreign ideas are used to reinforce and illustrate Jewish religious convictions. Although he asserts, for example, that wisdom is manifested in the four cardinal virtues of classical philosophy—self-control, justice, courage, and temperance (4 Macc. 1:18–35)—he demonstrates the value of these Stoic qualities through their application in the lives of such faithful Jews as Joseph (4 Macc. 2:2–3), Moses (4 Macc. 2:17), Jacob (4 Macc. 2:19), David (4 Macc. 3:6–18), and the martyrs of the Maccabbean period (4 Macc. 5–17).

It becomes evident in these passages, and especially in the author's eulogy of the martyrs (4 Macc. 17:9–18:24), that integrity to the Hebrew god is the real source of wisdom and that the pagan virtues are mere labels for higher attributes known to Jews alone. Like Second Isaiah (Isa. 53), he declares that the righteous suffer vicariously for the sins of their compatriots (4 Macc. 1:11; 6:29; 17:21–22). Employing another Greek concept, the writer asserts that Jews who died for their allegiance to the law have found everlasting life. He makes it clear, however, that the immortality of their souls is not necessarily inherent but "received" or bestowed by their god (4 Macc. 14:6; 18:23).

Scholars do not agree in dating the book. Estimated times of composition range from the mid-first century B.C.E. to as late as 117/118 C.E. Like the apocryphal Wisdom of Solomon, with which it has many doctrinal affinities, 4 Maccabees was probably written by an Alexandrine Jew.

RECOMMENDED READING

Charles, R. H. "The Fourth Book of Maccabees, with an Introduction." In *Apocrypha and Pseudepigrapha of the Old Testament*, vol. 2, pp. 653–85. Oxford: Clarendon Press, 1913.

😈 Sibylline Oracles

> **But when Rome shall rule over Egypt as well, which she still hesitates to do, then the mightiest kingdom of the immortal king over men shall appear.**
>
> **Sibylline Oracles 3:46–48**

The sibyl, after whom this collection of prophecies is named, was a prophetess or series of prophetesses famous in classical Greece and Rome. Inspired by Apollo, the sibyl foretold the fate of individuals and nations, although most such predictions were written down long after the events foretold had already occurred. During the second century B.C.E. this time-honored method of ascribing prophecies of more recent historical events to a figure of the remote past was taken up by Jewish writers who by this means could review past occurrences as if foretelling them and then go on to predict the immediate future. Such was the mode of apocalyptic writing that replaced Israel's classical prophecy, which was thought to have ended after Ezra's day.

Adopted by Jewish apocalyptists, the sibyl became a daughter-in-law of Noah and thus associated with the very beginning of the present world system (Sib. Or. 3:826). In this new guise she was moved to prophesy Israelite as well as Greek history and to denounce both idolatry and the

Jews' political enemies. In all, fifteen books of oracles were collected in which pagan, Jewish, and Christian elements are combined, edited, and revised. Of the twelve books that survive (Books 1–8 and 11–14), the largest block of mainly Jewish writings occurs in Books 3, 4, and 5; Books 6, 7, 8, and 13 are of Christian origin. These diverse materials were collected by a Christian editor in the sixth century C.E.

Especially noteworthy in Book 3, which contains a Jewish revision and expansion of earlier pagan material, is an eschatological passage foretelling the coming of a Messiah at a time "when Rome shall rule over Egypt" (Sib. Or. 3:46–61) and predictions of disaster for heathen nations when the messianic kingdom arrives (Sib. Or. 3:573–812). Throughout Book 3 the author somewhat incongruously blends Gentile history with exhortations to unbelieving pagans and descriptions of eschatological catastrophes. References to the Egyptian monarch Ptolemy VII lead scholars to believe that the book was mostly written during his reign (145–116 B.C.E.). Allusions to later events—such as the second triumvirate (43 B.C.E.) and Cleopatra (about 30 B.C.E.)—were probably added by a later editor.

Book 4, a series of cryptic utterances in which certain historical events are cited as signs of imminent calamity, was written after the great eruption of Vesuvius in 79 C.E. (Sib. Or. 4:130–136). The veiled reference to Nero's return from the dead at the head of an invading army (Sib. Or. 4:137–139) expressed a belief popular in the late first century C.E. (see also the use of this legend in Rev. 17:8–9).

Book 3 was written in Egypt; Book 4's place of origin is not known. Book 5, which includes a lament over the fall of Jerusalem (Sib. Or. 5:397–413), probably appeared in Egypt toward the close of the second century C.E. Some of the Christian books were probably written even later.

RECOMMENDED READING

Charles, R. H. "The Sibylline Books [3, 4, and 5 only], with an Introduction." In *Apocrypha and Pseudepigrapha of the Old Testament*, vol. 2, pp. 377–406. Oxford: Clarendon Press, 1913.

❧ Ethiopic Book of Enoch (1 Enoch)

And the first heaven shall depart and pass away,
And a new heaven shall appear . . .
And all shall be in goodness and righteousness,
And sin shall no more be mentioned forever.

1 Enoch 91:16, 17

Ascribed to Enoch, the antediluvian patriarch who was reputedly transported alive to heaven (Gen. 5:24), the Book of Enoch is a heterogeneous collection of the work of many unknown authors. Composed and compiled during the Hellenistic period, it is designated as Ethiopic because its text has been transmitted in that language.

The oldest materials in the compilation (found in 1 En. 6–11; 54–55:2; 60; 65–69; and 106–107) are believed to be fragments of a Book of Noah or Book of Lamech (mentioned in Bk. Jub. 10:13 and 21:10), which may date from the first half of the second century B.C.E. The Ten Weeks Apocalypse (1 En. 93 and 91:12–17), which apparently antedates the Book of Daniel, may have appeared about 170 B.C.E. Most of Enoch's other components may be assigned to the late second and first centuries B.C.E., with the "Similitudes" (1 En. 37–71)—with their messianic references to the "Son of Man"—probably dating from the first century C.E. or slightly earlier.

Emulating the Pentateuch, Psalms, Proverbs, and Ecclesiasticus, an editor-compiler arranged the Enoch collection into five distinct parts—its division into 108 chapters did not become standard until the nineteenth century. After a prefatory speech in which Enoch is depicted proclaiming the ultimate destinies of the wicked and righteous (1 En. 1–5), section 1 describes the fall of the Watchers (angels who mated with the daughters of humans to produce the giants; see Gen. 6:1–4), their punishment, and Enoch's metaphysical journeys through the earth and Underworld (1 En. 6–36).

Section 2 contains a series of parables concerning a variety of topics, including the Messiah, the rewards of the righteous, judgment by the Son of Man, the torments of the fallen angels, and similar eschatological matters (1 En. 37–71). Section 3 includes a primitive scientific treatise on astronomy, a discussion of the sun, moon, and planets, and of human calendars based on them (1 En. 72–82). Section 4 presents a sequence of dream visions, notably of the (then) coming flood, and an allegorical panorama of world history that designates Jews as tame animals and pagans as wild beasts. It begins with Adam as a white bull and culminates in the appearance of the Messiah as a lamb who becomes a "great animal" with black horns (1 En. 83–90).

Section 5 is a book of exhortation that includes Enoch's admonition for his children, an apocalypse in which world history is divided into periods of ten weeks of varying length, and pictures of blessings for the righteous and woes for the godless (1 En. 91–105). The book concludes with a fragment from the Book of Noah describing miracles occurring at the patriarch's birth and Enoch's last words of encouragement for the pious who await their god's day of reckoning (1 En. 106–198).

From even this cursory survey of its contents, it is apparent that the Book of Enoch—an anthology of history, astronomy, law, poetry, eschatological doctrines, and apocalyptic visions—provided a wealth of theological ideas, some of which were extremely influential on Hellenistic Judaism. After the disastrous wars with Rome (66–70 and 132–135 C.E.), however, which were apparently inspired in part by apocalypse-fed expectations, the Jews largely repudiated this kind of writing. By then, Christians had taken up many of these speculations and eschatological hopes and adapted them to their own doctrinal needs.

Among the early Christians, then, Enoch was understandably popular, although after the fourth century C.E. its influence declined. In time, all complete manuscripts of this Hebrew-Aramaic work vanished. It was not until the end of the eighteenth century that an Ethiopic translation was found in Abyssinia. The first English version of the entire book appeared in 1821. In 1952 a number of Aramaic fragments of Enoch were found among the Dead Sea Scrolls, and some scholars believe that the book probably originated in the Qumran community.

RECOMMENDED READING

Charles, R. H. "Book of Enoch, with an Introduction." In *Apocrypha and Pseudepigrapha of the Old Testament*, vol. 2, pp. 163–281. Oxford: Clarendon Press, 1913.

Charlesworth, James H., ed. *The Old Testament Pseudepigrapha.* Vol. 1, *Apocalyptic Literature and Testaments.* Garden City, N. Y.: Doubleday, 1983, pp. 5–100.

Knibb, Michael A., trans. *The Ethiopic Book of Enoch: A New Edition in the Light of the Aramaic Dead Sea Fragments.* Oxford: Clarendon Press, 1978.

Milik, Jozef T. *The Books of Enoch: Aramaic Fragments of Qumran Cave 4.* Oxford: Clarendon Press, 1976.

Nickelsburg, George W. E. *Jewish Literature Between the Bible and the Mishnah.* Philadelphia: Fortress Press, 1981, pp. 43–55, 145–160.

❦ Slavonic Book of Enoch (2 Enoch)

**[Enoch's] books are many, and in
them you will learn all the Lord's works,
all that has been from the beginning of
creation, and will be till the end of time.**

2 Enoch 47:2

The Slavonic Book of Enoch (so called because it has survived only in a Slavonic translation) was originally written in Greek. Although the book's present form may represent a Christian edition from as late as the seventh century C.E., it undoubtedly arose from a Jewish original dating from perhaps the first century C.E. Injunctions to visit the Jerusalem temple three times a year (2 En. 51:4) and references to ongoing sacrificial procedures (2 En. 59:1–2; 61:4; 62:1) indicate that at least these portions were written before 70 C.E. Charles suggested Alexandria, Egypt, as the likely place of composition. A first-person narrative of sixty-eight chapters, it describes Enoch's ascension to the tenth heaven, where he beholds the face of God and is taught all knowledge; his thirty-day return to earth to transmit this wisdom to his sons; and his permanent return to heaven.

The first section of the book (2 En. 1–21) offers a fascinating survey of the ten levels of the spirit world through which Enoch ascends. While the concept may seem strange to modern theology, the author makes several of the levels places of darkness and torment. The "second heaven," for example, is a gloomy prison for rebellious angels (2 En. 7); the "third heaven" is divided into a sensuous Eden for the righteous and a flaming darkness for sinners (2 En. 8–10); the fifth level contains the giant angels who had provoked a revolt against God and whom Enoch persuades to beseech the deity's pity (2 En. 18). Enthroned in the "tenth heaven" is God himself, a formidable image with a face burning "like iron made to glow in fire" (2 En. 22:1). This section is an outstanding example of Hebrew mysticism and occult beliefs of the late Hellenistic period.

In the second part (2 En. 22–38), the deity instructs Enoch in the mysteries of creation and interprets human history from the time of Adam to the flood. The third section (2 En. 39–66) shows Enoch imparting to his sons what he has learned and admonishing them to study his 366 books containing the divine wisdom. Typical of apocalyptic mentality is the author's insistence that all history, including that of individual lives, is predetermined (2 En. 53:2–3). The last two chapters record Enoch's final ascension and a summary of his extraordinary accomplishments (2 En. 67–68).

2 Enoch may have appeared too late to influence Christian thought directly, but its views of heaven and of the rewards and punishments of the afterlife remarkably parallel some New Testament beliefs. Certainly, its picture of the ten celestial stages strongly affected Dante's presentation of heaven in the *Divine Comedy*.

RECOMMENDED READING

Charles, R. H. "The Book of the Secrets of Enoch, with an Introduction." In *Apocrypha and Pseudepigrapha of the Old Testament*, vol. 2, pp. 425–69. Oxford: Clarendon Press, 1913.

Charlesworth, James H., ed. *The Old Testament Pseudepigrapha*. vol 1, *Apocalyptic Literature and Testaments*. Garden City, N. Y.: Doubleday, 1983, pp. 91–221.

☙ Assumption of Moses

He prepared me [Moses] from the foundation
of the world, that I should be the
mediator of His covenant.

Assumption of Moses 1:14

The original portion of this two-part work, which contained an account of Moses' ascension to heaven and a dispute between Archangel Michael and the Devil over the patriarch's body (alluded to in Jude 9), has been lost. The surviving first portion of the book, then, is not an "assumption" but a "testament" in which Moses bequeaths his role as mediator of the covenant and leader of Israel to Joshua. His exhortations to Joshua (Asmp. M. 1; 11–12) frame a central section in which the lawgiver foretells the future history of his people (Asmp. M. 2–10).

After describing Israel's history from the conquest of Canaan to the reign of Herod the Great (40–4 B.C.E.), the anonymous writer makes several apocalyptic predictions. Stating that "when this is done the times shall be ended" (Asmp. M. 7:1), he prophesies the appearance of treacherous men (Asmp. M. 7), horrible sufferings for the Jews inflicted by an earthly "king of kings and one that ruleth with great power" (Asmp. M. 8), the martyrdom of the Levite Taxo (otherwise unknown) and his seven sons (Asmp. M. 9), and the overthrow of Satan and establishment of God's kingdom (Asmp. M. 10). This last event is accomplished by eschatological signs reminiscent of Old Testament apocalyptists and echoed in the apocalyptic passages of the New Testament (Matt. 24; Mark 13; Luke 21; 1 and 2 Thess.).

From the specific references to Herod and his heirs and the nebulous vision of events to follow, it appears that the Assumption of Moses was written about 4 B.C.E. or shortly thereafter. Although the work now exists only in a Latin translation, it was composed in Hebrew or Aramaic and may have originated in the Qumran community or other Essene circles.

RECOMMENDED READING

Charles, R. H. "The Assumption of Moses, with an Introduction." In *Apocrypha and Pseudepigrapha of the Old Testament*, vol. 2, pp. 407–24. Oxford: Clarendon Press, 1913.

Eissfeldt, Otto. *The Old Testament: An Introduction.* New York: Harper & Row, 1965.

🐚 Syriac Apocalypse of Baruch (2 Baruch)

And the Most High . . .
revealed unto me the word, that I might
receive consolation,
And He showed me visions that I should not
again endure anguish,
And He made known to me the mystery of the times.

2 Baruch 81:4

This composite work, apparently produced by several unknown Hebrew writers about 100–110 C.E., has come down to us only in a Syriac version based on a Greek translation of the Hebrew or Aramaic original. The event that occasioned its composition seems to have been the destruction of Jerusalem in 70 C.E., which had raised the question of the Hebrew god's intentions toward his people, a question that encompassed the broader issues of sin, unmerited suffering, and the meaning of human life. The visions recorded in this apocalypse were supposedly revealed to Baruch, secretary to the prophet Jeremiah, in 591 B.C.E. (2 Bar. 1:1).

Like 2 Esdras, a roughly contemporaneous work that it strongly resembles, 2 Baruch may be divided into seven parts of unequal length. In the first part (2 Bar. 1–12), the "word of the Lord" informs Baruch that Jerusalem is to be destroyed not by human agency but by angels. While Jeremiah accompanies the exiles to Babylon, Baruch remains amid Jerusalem's ruins to sing a dirge over the fallen capital.

To his complaints in the second part (2 Bar. 13–20) that God allows the righteous to suffer while the worldly prosper, Baruch receives "the Lord's" answer. Knowing the divine judgment, humankind sins willingly. Although the righteous endure hardship in this world, such adversity strengthens their characters, and they will be rewarded in the world to come (2 Bar. 15–17). When the swiftly approaching New Age arrives, all will be made equitable.

In the third section (2 Bar. 21–34), the deity reveals that the end can come only when the appointed time period has elapsed. That consummation is near, however, and Baruch will be preserved until certain signs take place. The deity further reveals that twelve "woes" will afflict the earth and that the Messiah will appear to rule a temporary messianic kingdom. After he returns to heaven, the dead will be resurrected (2 Bar. 30).

In the fourth part (2 Bar. 35–46), Baruch sees in a night vision a great forest, a vine, and a spring that respectively symbolize four worldly empires, the Messiah, and his kingship. The fifth division (2 Bar. 47–52) contains Baruch's long petition to save his people, an announcement about the supreme horror of the final woe, and a description of the bodily forms of the resurrected dead.

The sixth part (2 Bar. 53–76) features a complex vision involving a cloud and a series of thirteen (or fourteen) black and white waters. The cloud signifies the world's predestined course; the alternating dark and bright waters stand for human acts of sin and righteousness, such as Adam's fall and Abraham's integrity; the fourteenth light water is the Messiah, who inaugurates the New Age. The last section (2 Bar. 77–87) records Baruch's instruction to a tiny band of faithful Jews remaining in Jerusalem. It also records two letters—one to the two and one-half tribes exiled in Babylon, the other to the nine and one-half tribes dispersed throughout Assyria.

RECOMMENDED READING

Charles, R. H. "2 Baruch, the Syriac Apocalypse of Baruch, with an Introduction." In *Apocrypha and Pseudepigrapha of the Old Testament*, vol. 2, pp. 470–526. Oxford: Clarendon Press, 1913.

Charlesworth, James H., ed. *The Old Testament Pseudepigrapha*. vol. 1, *Apocalyptic Literature and Testaments*. Garden City, N. Y.: Doubleday, 1983.

❦ Greek Apocalypse of Baruch (3 Baruch)

Lord, why didst thou set on fire thy vineyard, and lay it waste?

3 Baruch 1:2

---

3 Baruch resembles 2 Baruch in attempting to resolve the problem of evil and undeserved pain by means of apocalyptic visions that assure the ultimate triumph of good. Although written by a Jew, the work was probably reedited by a Christian redactor. Since its present form echoes the Syriac Apocalypse of Baruch, it must have appeared after 130 C.E. and perhaps as late as the first part of the third century.

The work begins with Baruch's lament over Nebuchadnezzar's destruction of Jerusalem, which is answered by an angel who undertakes to unveil to him "the mysteries of God" (3 Bar. 1). Instead of explaining why God permits evil to flourish, however, the angel conducts Baruch on a tour of five heavens (perhaps seven in a now lost original version) (3 Bar. 2–16). Thus, while the book opens as a theodicy, it quickly becomes a cosmological tour of the spirit realm. Like the metaphysical experiences described in the books of Enoch, these passages strikingly resemble modern accounts of astral projection, or travels of the soul when out of the body.

Particularly vivid is the description of the third heaven, in which a man "wearing a crown of fire" drives a chariot drawn by forty angels (a mythical symbol for the sun god Apollo), while the Phoenix follows the sun, catching solar rays on its wings. Also noteworthy is the author's fusion of Hellenistic religious and mythological symbols with a Hebraic revelation (3 Bar. 6–8).

In the fifth heaven Baruch holds a conversation with Archangel Michael, whose duty it is to present "the merits [prayers] of men to God" (3 Bar. 14:2). Though Michael carries to the deity Baruch's question of why he allows his people to suffer at the hands of unjust men, no reply is vouchsafed except a conventional repetition of the deuteronomic axiom that breaking the commandments brings all kinds of calamity (3 Bar. 13–16). The apocalypse ends with Baruch's return to earth and his glorification of God (3 Bar. 17).

While 3 Baruch does not directly confront the problem of evil, it does imply that the existence of a spirit world in which sinners and the righteous will ultimately receive their just rewards gives meaning to human activity. It may be that a lost Hebrew or Aramaic version of the book more fully emphasizes the deity's compensation of his people for their earthly miseries in an afterlife. Thus, in a sense, Baruch's survey of the five heavens, with its promise of immortality, answers his questions about God's justice more satisfactorily than does Job's voice from the whirlwind.

RECOMMENDED READING

Charles, R. H. "The Greek Apocalypse of Baruch, or 3 Baruch." In *Apocrypha and Pseudepigrapha of the Old Testament*, vol. 2, pp. 527–41. Oxford: Clarendon Press, 1913.

❦ Testaments of the Twelve Patriarchs

As the heaven is higher than the earth,
so is the priesthood of God higher than the earthly kingdom.

Testaments of the Twelve Patriarchs 21:4

This apocalyptic work purports to be the last words or testaments of the twelve sons of Jacob to their descendants. Although modeled on the Blessing of Jacob to his twelve sons (Gen. 49), the Testaments of the Twelve Patriarchs does not for the most part contain prophesies about the individual tribes' future destiny; it consists mainly of exhortations by each patriarch, using his own particular character and moral behavior as a model either to shun or to emulate. With its many ethical precepts and wise sayings, the Testaments would seem a part of Israel's wisdom literature were it not that many passages embody visions or revelations of divine secrets, such as the nature of angels and the heavenly world.

The deathbed advice given by Jacob's twelve sons is summarized below.

1. Reuben, citing his own case (see Gen. 35:22; 49:4), warns against "the seven spirits of deceit," which inspire lust and foster immorality.

2. Simon, referring to his murderous jealousy of Joseph, cautions against envy.

3. Levi, who has been privileged to visit the seventh heaven and receive direct divine appointment to the priesthood, urges respect for the Torah and for wisdom and states that he learned from the Book of Enoch that his progeny would corrupt the office until a messianic high priest appeared to establish the New Age.

4. Judah instructs his sons to avoid wine, women, and greed and to subordinate themselves to Levi's descendants. (The exaltation of the Levitical priesthood suggests that the Testaments have a priestly source.) He also notes that his tribe will produce a messianic king but that he will be secondary to the priestly Anointed One.

5. Issachar promotes the values of a pious countrydweller.

6. Zebulun asks his sons to behave charitably.

7. Dan exhorts against wrath and lying.

8. Naphtali advises his progeny to conduct themselves with piety, purity, and kindliness, thus reflecting the harmony of the cosmos, though he also prophesies that Israel will rival Sodom in wickedness until, through Levi and Judah, their god ushers in the New Age.

9. Gad warns against hatred and urges brotherly love.

10. Asher exhorts his heirs to candor and honest dealings with their fellows.

11. Joseph delivers an elaborate oration on chastity.

12. Benjamin, who refuses any longer to be called "ravenous wolf" (Gen. 49:27), recommends uprightness in all things and cites Joseph as a model of godly conduct.

There is much scholarly debate about the origin of this work. Some experts believe that it is fundamentally a Jewish work with Christian interpolations; others believe that it is a Christian work incorporating an older Jewish text; still others maintain that it was composed by the Essenes or the Essenelike community of Qumran, which had many doctrinal similarities to Christianity. Estimated dates for its various parts range from the second century B.C.E. to the second century C.E.

Biblical critics agree, however, that pseudepigraphal works like the Testaments contain many *haggadic* elements, an adjective referring to the Hebrew Haggadah—stories, legends, or explanatory narrations of the first centuries C.E. that supplement or expand the nonlegal sections of the Pentateuch. Typically, haggadic narratives are imaginative developments of a thought suggested by the Pentateuch, as are the sometimes fanciful additions to Genesis found in the Book of Jubilees and the Testaments. Such commentaries preserve a rich tradition of oral legends that have otherwise been lost.

RECOMMENDED READING

Charles, R. H. "The Testaments of the Twelve Patriarchs, with an Introduction." In *Apocrypha and Pseudepigrapha of the Old Testament*, vol. 2, pp. 296–367. Oxford: Clarendon Press, 1913.

Charlesworth, James H., ed. *The Old Testament Pseudepigrapha*. vol. 1, *Apocalyptic Literature and Testaments*. Garden City, N. Y.: Doubleday, 1983, pp. 775–828.

Eissfeldt, Otto. *The Old Testament: An Introduction*. New York: Harper & Row, 1965. Pages 631–36 provide a good review of problems in determining the Jewish or Christian origin and date of the Testaments of the Twelve Patriarchs.

Nickelsburg, Geroge W. E. *Jewish Literature between the Bible and the Mishnah*. Philadelphia: Fortress Press, 1981, pp. 231–241.

❧ Books of Adam and Eve

**The Devil spake: "O Adam! all my hostility,
envy, and sorrow is for thee,
since it is for thee that I have been
expelled from my glory, which I
possessed in the heavens. . . ."**

Life of Adam and Eve 12:1

Jewish and early Christian writers delighted in producing fictional accounts of the first human pair. The haggadic narratives under consideration here, which derive from Hebrew sources but are in their present form Christian works, consist of two supplementary and sometimes contradictory tales: (1) the Life of Adam and Eve (*Vita Adae et Evae*), which survives in a Latin version translated from the Greek, and (2) a parallel Greek narrative that is misnamed the Apocalypse of Moses.

As the following summary will indicate, some elements of the Adam and Eve story are found only in the Life, others only in the Apocalypse, and still others in both. In R. H. Charles's standard edition of the Pseudepigrapha, however, passages from the Life and Apocalypse are interspersed to present a coherent narration. Analogous selections from a Slavonic translation of the Life are also included.

The Life opens with Adam and Eve already expelled from paradise. Unable to find nourishment, they attempt to assuage the deity's wrath through prayer and penitence. But Eve, who punishes herself by standing immersed in the icy Tigris River, is again deceived by Satan into relinquishing her ascetic task, for which lapse Adam reproaches her (Life 1–11).

When Adam complains that Satan persecutes them without reason, the latter replies that Adam was the cause of his expulsion from heaven. For after man was created "in God's image," the deity commanded all the heavenly host to worship this human replica of the divine. Refusing to adore a younger and inferior creature, the Devil and those who sided with him were permanently cast out of the celestial abode. By thus observing the Old Testament prohibition against idolatry and further pursuing the Mosaic law of retaliation, the Devil instigated Adam's deprivation of "joy and luxury" as he himself had been deprived for the man's sake (Life 12–17). Unmoved, Adam endures forty days' penance in the Jordan River.

The Life continues with the birth of Cain and Abel, Abel's murder, the birth of Seth and of sixty additional children (Life 18–24). Adam then tells Seth of an earlier vision in which the deity had described Adam's coming death (Life 25–29). When Adam is dying, Seth and Eve try to obtain the healing oil from the "tree of mercy," but the Archangel Michael orders them back from the gates of paradise and claims the finality of Adam's death (Life 30–44; Apocalypse 5–14). Eve then gives her version of the fall (Apocalypse 15–34), and Adam dies at age 930 (Life 45–48).

After Adam's soul is conveyed to paradise in the third heaven, angels accompany the deity to earth, where he entombs Adam's body and the hitherto unburied corpse of Abel. Adam and all his progeny are promised a resurrection (Apocalypse 35–42). Six days later Eve also dies praying to be buried in her husband's unknown tomb, after which Michael instructs Seth never to mourn on the Sabbath, which is a holy day symbolic of future life and the New Age (Life 49–51; Apocalypse 52–53).

Although fanciful, the narrative is a sensitive recreation by unknown Hellenistic Jews of what the original human couple's life was conceived to be like after the fall. The Hebrew versions on which the later Christian edition is based may have been composed during the first century C.E., before the Roman destruction of Jerusalem.

RECOMMENDED READING

Charles, R. H. "The Books of Adam and Eve, with an Introduction." In *Apocrypha and Pseudepigrapha of the Old Testament*, vol. 2, pp. 123–54. Oxford: Clarendon Press, 1913.

Charlesworth, James H., ed. *The Old Testament Pseudepigrapha.* vol. 2, *Expansions of the "Old Testament" and Other Legends, Wisdom and Philosophical Literature, Prayers, Psalms, and Odes, Fragments of Lost Judao-Hellenistic Works.* Garden City, N. Y.: Doubleday, 1984.

DEAD SEA SCROLLS

In 1947 and after, Bible scholars received a wealth of new material when the library of an ancient monastic community, now called Khirbet Qumran, was discovered in caves near the northwest corner of the Dead Sea. These Dead Sea Scrolls are thought to have been produced by the Essenes, an ascetic Jewish sect that flourished in Palestine from the second century B.C.E. to 68 C.E., when it was destroyed or dispersed by the Romans.

The manuscripts found in the Qumran caves include works representing several categories: (1) copies of canonical Old Testament books, including a complete scroll of Isaiah and fragments of every book of the Hebrew Bible except Esther; (2) copies and fragments of apocryphal and pseudepigraphal works, such as Tobit, Enoch, and the Book of Jubilees; (3) fragments of commentaries on canonical works, such as Habakkuk, Isaiah, Hosea, and Micah; and (4) entirely new compositions whose existence had not been known before. The fourth group includes the following:

- A Manual of Discipline giving requirements and regulations for life in the Qumran community

- The Zadokite Document (a version of which had been discovered in a Cairo synagogue in the 1890s), which outlines the "New Covenant" made in the "land of Damascus" (possibly a symbol for the Qumran settlement) under which the Essene group lived

- An extensive collection of Essene hymns that were probably sung during Qumran worship services (the Essenes rejected the temple liturgy and what they viewed as its corrupt priesthood)

- A scroll entitled the War of the Sons of Light Against the Sons of Darkness, a surprisingly mundane battle plan for the cosmic war that would culminate in the establishment of God's kingdom

- A compendium of Messianic rules designating qualities of age, physical condition, and doctrinal orthodoxy for members of the community—especially relevant to Christians for its description of a communal meal of bread and wine that strikingly resembles Jesus' Last Supper

- Liturgical fragments containing blessings for the obedient and cursings for the ungodly
- Passages of biblical interpretation on such topics as the Blessing of Jacob, the Admonition of Moses, a prayer attributed to Nabonidus, an exposition of signs marking the last days, and an anthology of messianic predictions

The Dead Sea literature is extremely important to biblical research. The copies of canonical books from the Hebrew Bible, some fragments of which date back to the second century B.C.E., are by far the oldest known biblical manuscripts extant. The complete scroll of Isaiah, which is perhaps 900 years older than any other previously known Isaiah manuscript, shows few variations from the Masoretic Hebrew text from which most translations of the Old Testament are made. Other Qumran copies of Scripture differ significantly from the "standard" Masoretic edition. The variations between some of the Qumran biblical texts and later copies of the Hebrew Bible suggest that by the first century B.C.E. Judaism had not yet adopted an officially recognized version of the Old Testament.

The presence in the Qumran library of apocryphal and pseudepigraphal works interspersed among canonical books indicates that the Essenes may have accepted a larger canon than that eventually promulgated by later Judaism. Whether the Essenes regarded works like Enoch or the Book of Jubilees as part of the Bible is open to question, but numerous copies of these and similar compositions among the Dead Sea documents reveal that they were read and studied.

The New Testament is silent on the Essenes, their desert monastery, and their austere lives of pious scholarship. The absence of references to the Essenes may reflect the fact that by the time the Gospels were written the sect had ceased to exist as an identifiable group. Some historians, however, stress apparent similarities between Essene teachings and the teachings of first-century Christianity. Both Essenes and Christians emphasized eschatological concerns, living in intense expectation of divine intervention into human history. Both groups saw themselves living in "end time" and both minimized "worldly" matters to prepare themselves for an imminent day of judgment. Attempts to identify Jesus with figures in the Qumran sectarian literature, such as the Teacher of Righteousness, however, have been futile. Scholars do not believe that Jesus' so-called lost years were spent as a member of an Essene commune. By contrast, John the Baptist, whom the Gospels paint as a desert ascetic condemning the Jewish religious and political leadership (as did the Essene monks) and preaching a doctrine of repentance before an impending holocaust, seems to echo some of the Essenes' characteristic doctrines. What relationship John might have had to the Essene community, however, is entirely conjectural.

RECOMMENDED READING

Cross, Frank Moore. *The Ancient Library of Qumran and Modern Biblical Studies.* Garden City, N. Y.: Doubleday, 1961.

_____. *Qumran and the History of the Biblical Text.* Cambridge, Mass.: Harvard University Press, 1975.

Gaster, Theodor H. *The Dead Sea Scriptures in English Translation.* Garden City, N. Y.: Doubleday, 1976.

Ringgren, Helmer. *The Faith of Qumran.* Philadelphia: Fortress Press, 1961.

Simon, Marcel. *Jewish Sects at the Time of Jesus.* Philadelphia: Fortress Press, 1967. A concise, informative work.

Vermes, Geza. *The Dead Sea Scrolls in English.* Baltimore: Penguin Books, 1962.

_____. *The Dead Sea Scrolls: Qumran in Perspective.* London: Collins, 1977.

PART 7

BETWEEN THE TESTAMENTS

POLITICAL EVENTS

To understand Jesus, his disciples, and their times, it is necessary to know something about historical developments between the end of the Old and the beginning of the New Testament periods. Familiarity with the Old Testament Apocrypha helps. As 1 Maccabees tells us, Palestine had been dominated by Hellenistic forces from the close of the fourth century B.C.E. Following the sudden death of Alexander of Macedonia in 323 B.C.E., his empire was divided among his four generals. Palestine at first went to Ptolemy of Egypt but was controlled after 198/97 B.C.E. by the Seleucid dynasty of Syria. 1 Maccabees also records the Jewish revolt that drove the Syrians from Palestine in 142 B.C.E. This resulted in the establishment of the native Hasmonean (Maccabean) dynasty, which ruled an independent Jewish state until 63 B.C.E.

That year marked the end of Jewish political autonomy, however, for rival claimants to Judah's throne had fought bitterly from 67 to 63 B.C.E.— one of them, John Hyrcanus II, appealing to Rome for help in ousting his younger brother, Aristobulus II, who had made himself both high priest and king. In response, Rome dispatched General Pompey, a military rival of Julius Caesar, whose troops overthrew Aristobulus and installed John Hyrcanus as high priest and ethnarch (63–40 B.C.E.) over a Judean state much reduced in size and prestige. The change in title from "king" to "ethnarch" (provincial governor) is significant, for after 63 B.C.E. Jewish rulers were mere puppets of Rome, and the Holy Land just another province in the empire.

After the death of John Hyrcanus, the Roman Senate appointed Herod, son of a powerful Idumean governor, king of Judea (40–4 B.C.E.), a territory he eventually extended to include much of Palestine. But Herod's long reign, however politically successful, was unpopular with the Jews. Only half-Jewish himself, he tried to win their favor with an elaborate building program whose reconstruction of the temple in Jerusalem made it one of the most splendid edifices in the ancient world. But his unorthodox religion, many murders, and tyrannical behavior made him almost universally hated.

On Herod's death, his kingdom was divided among his three sons. Archelaus (4 B.C.E.–6 C.E.), who received Judea, Idumea, and Samaria, was a despot whom the Emperor Augustus banished to Gaul, following which his territory was administered by a Roman prefect or procurator who was directly responsible to the emperor. Herod Antipas (4 B.C.E.–39 C.E.), the second son, ruled Galilee and Perea; although he continued his father's building programs, he, too, was an inept and unpopular leader. Apparently the most able of Herod's heirs, Philip (4 B.C.E.–34 C.E.), reigned over the region northeast of Galilee and managed to escape notoriety.

A grandson of Herod the Great and a favorite of the Emperor Claudius, Herod Agrippa I (41–44 C.E.) briefly reunited Palestine, but after his premature death his kingdom reverted to direct Roman control. Between the Jews and their Roman overlords, suspicion and hatred mounted until in 66 C.E. open revolt broke out, the Judean countryside was devastated, and in 70 C.E. Jerusalem was besieged and captured. As Jesus, correctly assessing the political trends of his day, had predicted (Mark 13), the holy city was demolished and the temple destroyed. A last attempt to recover Jewish freedom in 132–135 C.E. was ruthlessly crushed by the Romans. Thereafter the Jews were forcibly dispersed throughout the Roman Empire, and almost 1,900 years would pass before they again established an independent state.

The difficult relations caused by overlapping political jurisdictions in first-century Palestine are well illustrated in the Gospel accounts of Jesus' trial, in which Jewish, Roman, and Herodian elements compete in handling a ticklish religiopolitical situation. The measure of religious liberty that the Romans accorded Jews was concentrated in the Sanhedrin, or Great Council, which was composed of Sadducees and other leaders. But this religious body, which condemned Jesus for blasphemy, apparently lacked the authority to execute him. Pilate, representative of Rome, quizzed Jesus on his claim to be king of the Jews—a treasonous act against the Emperor Tiberius—but finding the accused to be a Galilean, he sent him to Herod Antipas, the ruler of Galilee, who happened to be in Jerusalem at the time. It was Pilate, however, who finally condemned Jesus on the grounds of sedition against Rome (Luke 22:66–23:25).

RECOMMENDED READING

Angus, Samuel. *The Environment of Early Christianity.* New York: Charles Scribner's Sons, 1920. A thorough investigation of the historical background.

Bickermann, Elias. *From Ezra to the Last of the Maccabees.* New York: Schocken Books, 1962. Covers Israel's history from the Persian period (fifth century B.C.E.) to the Roman period (first century C.E.).

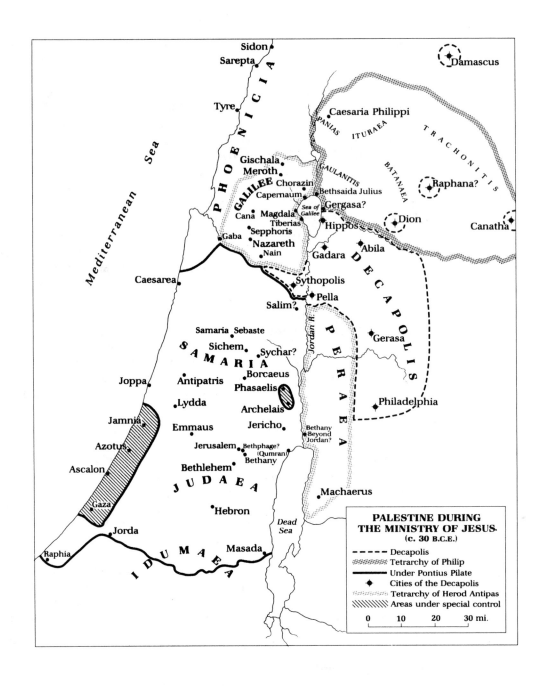

**PALESTINE DURING
THE MINISTRY OF JESUS.**
(c. 30 B.C.E.)

- - - - Decapolis
░░░░ Tetrarchy of Philip
──── Under Pontius Pilate
◆ Cities of the Decapolis
▒▒▒▒ Tetrarchy of Herod Antipas
▨▨▨▨ Areas under special control

```
0    10    20    30 mi.
```

Sidon

Sarepta

Damascus

Tyre

PHOENICIA

Caesaria Philippi

PANIAS

ITURAEA

TRACHONITIS

Gischala

Meroth

GALILEE

Chorazin

Capernaum

Bethsaida Julius

GAULANITIS

BATANAEA

Raphana?

Cana

Magdala

Sea of Galilee

Gergasa?

Tiberias

Sepphoris

Hippos

Dion

Canatha

Gaba

Nazareth

Nain

Gadara

Abila

DECAPOLIS

Mediterranean Sea

Caesarea

Sythopolis

Pella

Salim?

Samaria Sebaste

Sichem

Sychar?

SAMARIA

PEREA

Gerasa

Borcaeus

Joppa

Antipatris

Phasaelis

Lydda

Archelais

Philadelphia

Jamnia

Emmaus

Jericho

Bethany Beyond Jordan?

Azotus

Jerusalem

Bethphage?

(Qumran)

Bethany

Ascalon

Bethlehem

JUDAEA

Gaza

Hebron

Machaerus

Jorda

Dead Sea

Raphia

Masada

IDUMAEA

Jordan R.

Cook, S. A., Adcock, F. E., and Charlesworth, M. P., eds. *The Cambridge Ancient History.* New York: Macmillan Publishing Co., 1924–1939. 12 vols. Detailed coverage of the Greek and Roman periods, especially in vols. 7, 9, and 10.

Foerster, Werner. *From the Exile to Christ: A Historical Introduction to Palestinian Judaism.* Translated by G. E. Harris. Philadelphia: Fortress Press, 1964.

Freyne, Sean. *Galilee from Alexander the Great to Hadrian, 323 B.C.E. to 135 C.E.* Notre Dame, Ind.: University of Notre Dame Press, 1980.

Glover, T. R. *The World of the New Testament.* Cambridge, England: Cambridge University Press, 1931. A standard scholarly work.

Grant, Robert M. *Early Christianity and Society.* New York: Harper & Row, 1977.

Jeremias, Joachim. *Jerusalem in the Time of Jesus.* Translated by F. H. Cave and C. H. Cave. London: SCM Press, 1969. Discusses economic and social conditions in Palestine during Jesus' lifetime.

Josephus, Flavius. *The Jewish War,* rev. ed. Translated by G. A. Williamson. New York: Penguin Books, 1981. Includes background on Herod's reign and events preceding the Jewish revolt.

Peters, F. E. *The Harvest of Hellenism: A History of the Near East from Alexander the Great to the Triumph of Christianity.* New York: Simon & Shuster, 1970. A comprehensive presentation of Greek and Roman history affecting Palestine.

Pfeiffer, Robert H. *History of New Testament Times.* New York: Harper & Row, 1949. Covers Roman rule from Pompey's conquest (63 B.C.E.) to outbreak of Jewish revolt (66 C.E.).

Reicke, Bo. *The New Testament Era.* Philadelphia: Fortress Press, 1968.

Rhoads, David M. *Israel in Revolution, 6–74 C.E.* Philadelphia: Fortress Press, 1976.

Russell, D. S. *The Jews from Alexander to Herod.* London: Oxford University Press, 1967.

Safrai, S., and Stern, M., eds. *The Jewish People in the First Century.* Assen: Van Gorcum & Co., 1974, 1976, 2 vols. Essays on different historical and political topics.

Schurer, Emil. *The History of the Jewish People in the Time of Jesus Christ.* Translated and revised by Geza Vermes and Fergus Millar. Edinburgh: T & T Clark, 1973, 1979. 2 vols.

Tcherikover, Victor. *Hellenistic Civilization and the Jew.* Translated by S. Applebaum. Philadelphia: Jewish Publication Society, 1959.

Yadin, Yigael. *Bar-Kokhba: The Rediscovery of the Legendary Hero of the Last Jewish Revolt Against Imperial Rome.* London: Weidenfeld and Nicholson, 1971. Emphasizes archaeological discoveries relating to Bar Kokhba's revolt against Rome.

————. *Masada: Herod's Fortress and the Zealots' Last Stand.* London: Weidenfeld and Nicholson, 1966.

LANGUAGE AND LITERATURE

If political divisions made life difficult in first-century Palestine, Jewish literature flourished during the intertestamental period (roughly 150 B.C.E.–70 C.E.), as works preserved in the Apocrypha, Pseudepigrapha, and Dead Sea Scrolls demonstrate. In addition to copies of almost every canonical book of the Old Testament and extensive commentaries on them, the Qumran caves yielded numerous nonbiblical works, including a Manual of Discipline, the Zadokite Document, an apocalyptic tract on the War of the Sons of Light Against the Sons of Darkness, and many other religious documents featuring a coming Messiah, a teacher of righteousness, and a new covenant (see pp. 243–245).

The Jewish Christians who produced the New Testament wrote in Koine Greek, the international language of Hellenistic civilization brought to the Near East by Alexander's troops. This change from Hebrew to popular Greek reflected a movement away from the Old Testament view that the deity had revealed his will to one nation alone to a Christian belief that people of all nations were now part of a new covenant. (The Greek word *diatheke*, customarily translated as "testament," more properly means "covenant.") This cosmopolitan Hellenistic outlook was vigorously espoused by the Apostle Paul in his insistence that Jews and Gentiles were equal before God.

Use of Greek language and literature profoundly affected early Christian thought in other ways as well. As such apocryphal books as Wisdom of Solomon, 2 Maccabees, and 2 Esdras show, Greek and other foreign ideas concerning the soul's immortality and future life had become increasingly popular among Jews during late Hellenistic and Roman times. The apocalyptic tradition—with its perplexing mixture of Jewish, Persian, Greek, and other influences—flourished from the late Old Testament period well into the Christian period. The apocalyptic emphasized *eschatological* concerns—visions of "end time," divine judgment, heaven, hell, and resurrection. These concepts, along with a belief in hierarchies of angels and demons (apparently adopted from Persian and other sources), permeated much of Jewish thought in Jesus' day and figure prominently in the New Testament. In Christian circles, Hellenistic Jewish thinking about resurrection and the next world (vividly portrayed in pseudepigraphal books like 1 and 2 Enoch and the Testament of Abraham), coupled with Plato's doctrine of the imperishable soul (*psyche*), ultimately replaced the old Hebrew belief that the dead slept mindlessly and permanently in Sheol (the grave, or underworld; Eccles. 9:5, 10). Indeed, Sheol had already become identified with Hades, which included a place of punishment (the "lake of fire" or Gehenna) for the wicked dead. Greek philosophy and the Greek love of allegorizing religious stories were popular among educated Jews in Alexandria, Egypt, where the Septuagint Bible, the Greek version of the Old Testament used by Christians, was produced. The Greek doctrine of the Logos (God's creative Word), introduced by the Greek philosopher Heraclitus and promulgated by Philo Judaeus of Alexandria, became Christian doctrine in the prologue to John's Gospel.

RECOMMENDED READING

Barrett, C. K. *The New Testament Background: Selected Documents.* New York: Macmillan, 1957. Provides original material from Greco-Roman and Jewish texts.

Bultmann, Rudolf. *Primitive Christianity in Its Contemporary Setting.* Translated by R. H. Fuller. New York: Meridian Books, 1956. Analyzes the cultural and religious environment of early Christianity.

Enslin, Morton S. *Christian Beginnings.* New York: Oxford University Press, 1961.

Glover, T. R. *The Conflict of Religions in the Early Roman Empire.* 12th ed. London: Methuen Co., 1932.

Grant, F. C. *Roman Hellenism and the New Testament.* New York: Charles Scribner's Sons, 1962.

Hengel, Martin. *Jews, Greeks and Barbarians: Aspects of the Hellenization of Judaism in the Pre-Christian Period.* Philadelphia: Fortress Press, 1980.

———. *Judaism and Hellenism.* 2 vols. London: SCM Press, 1973.

Lohse, Eduard. *The New Testament Environment.* Translated by J. E. Steely. Nashville: Abingdon Press, 1976.

Sandmel, Samuel. *Judaism and Christian Beginnings.* New York: Oxford University Press, 1978.

Stone, Michael E. *Scriptures, Sects and Visions: A Profile of Judaism from Ezra to the Jewish Revolts.* Philadelphia: Fortress Press, 1980.

Theissen, Gerd. *Sociology of Early Palestinian Christianity.* Translated by J. Bowden. Philadelphia: Fortress Press, 1978.

Toombs, Lawrence E. *The Threshold of Christianity.* Philadelphia: Westminster Press, 1960. An accessible discussion of Jewish literature between the Testaments.

LEADING RELIGIOUS GROUPS

Probably during the Maccabean period, Judaism fragmented into a variety of religious parties or denominations. In *Wars of the Jews* 2.8, an account of the revolt against Rome, Flavius Josephus, the first-century Jewish historian, describes the four major groups, two of which—the Pharisees and Sadducees—the Gospel writers present as Jesus' leading opponents. In reviewing these four principal groups, however, it should be emphasized that most Jews of Jesus' day did not belong to such parties. Many of them probably admired the Pharisees' erudition and piety but followed no strict party line themselves. Classed as unteachable "sinners" by the orthodox, the people of the land worshiped as best they might (Mark 2:15), and it was to these generally poor and uneducated masses that Jesus directed his message.

PHARISEES

Although scholars have estimated that the Pharisees (which apparently means "separatists") never had more than about 6,000 members, their influence was nevertheless tremendous. According to Josephus (*Antiquities* 13.10), so great was their authority that they were able to dictate public opinion on kings, priests, and nearly all religious matters. In New Testament times they were Judaism's chief interpreters of Scripture, particularly of the Torah (Law).

The Pharisees accepted as binding not only the Pentateuch, the Prophets, and the Writings (the three major divisions of the Hebrew Bible) but the "oral law" as well. This "tradition of the elders" (Mark 7:3), an extensive and growing body of legalistic interpretation that the rabbis had compiled over many generations, was later codified in the Mishna (about 200 C.E.) and preserved in the Talmud, a vast written collection of Jewish religious interpretations. While this approach to Scripture allowed the Mosaic law to be explained and applied to changing conditions of daily life, the strict and sometimes ingenious interpretations imposed a heavy burden on Jews not well educated or wealthy enough to observe the oral law in all its multifarious detail.

The Pharisees were progressive in embracing many ideas, some apparently of Greek origin, that later became part of Christian doctrine. They believed in a coming judgment day, resurrection of the dead, a future life of the soul, rewards of the righteous and punishment of sinners, and the existence of angels, demons, and other spirits. Doctrinally, Jesus has more in common with the Pharisees than is generally supposed, and Paul remained proud of his Pharisaic education even after he had been converted to Christianity (Acts 23:6–9; Phil. 3:4–7).

Although Pharisaism has become synonymous with hypocrisy in the popular mind, this judgment, inspired by the Gospels' bitter criticism of some Pharisees (Matt. 23:1–36), is unfair. Devoted to keeping alive the faith of their ancestors and expert in applying the Mosaic law to every facet of life, the Pharisees largely controlled the synagogues, the Jewish meeting places for study, prayer, and explication of the Scriptures. Some may have been rigid or overly ingenious in their interpretation of the Torah's requirements (Matt. 23:6–23), but as a group they pursued a standard of religious dedication and personal righteousness that impressed even the Gentiles. We recall that it was Gamaliel, a Pharisee, who protected Peter and his fellow Christians from persecution when he recommended that they be allowed to continue in their new faith. Paul, Christianity's leading missionary to the non-Jewish world, apparently saw no contradiction in being both a follower of Jesus and a Pharisee, appealing for support from his fellow Pharisees when he stood trial before the Jerusalem religious council (Acts 23:6–9; Phil. 3:5–6).

Unfortunately, by the close of the first century C.E., a great gulf had opened between Pharisaic Judaism and Christianity, although both groups based their faith on promises in the Hebrew Bible. Early Christians had difficulty understanding why the Jewish people as a whole did not accept Jesus of Nazareth as their Messiah and blamed this refusal on their leaders, the Pharisees. In turn, the Jewish leadership regarded Christians as a heretical sect and, after about 90 C.E., expelled them from the synagogues.

SADDUCEES

An extremely conservative aristocratic group, the Sadducees followed a policy of cooperation with the Romans who then occupied Palestine. Since many of them were wealthy landowners, they had the most to lose from civil disorder—and rigorously opposed a Jewish nationalism that might attempt to overthrow the status quo. Although widely regarded as collaborationists with the hated Romans, the Sadducees enjoyed considerable prestige and influence in Jewish religious life. Their name (Greek *Saddoukaioi*, from the Hebrew *Zaddukim*) is thought to reflect their claim to be the spiritual heirs of Zadok, high priest in King Solomon's time. Because the prophet Ezekiel had stated that only the "sons of Zadok" could "approach Yahweh" in the temple service (Ezek. 40:46), the Sadducees, serving as officiating priests at the Jerusalem sanctuary, stressed their inherited right to this role. High priests like Caiaphas (who condemned Jesus) were always of their number, for the Sadducees dominated the Great Council (Sanhedrin) as well as the temple cult. Their adoption of Hellenistic customs and their friendship with Rome helped them successfully to manipulate political affairs. The Sadducees' determination to preserve the uneasy accommodation with Rome is reflected in their eagerness to get rid of Jesus, whom they apparently regarded as a potential revolutionary and a threat to Judea's political security. Their view that rebellion against Rome would lead to total annihilation of the Jewish nation was vindicated during the Jewish Revolt (66–70 C.E.), when Roman troops obliterated Judah.

As conservative religiously as they were politically, the Sadducees practiced a literal reading of the Torah, rejecting the Pharisees' "oral law" and other interpretations of the biblical text. It is uncertain how much of the Prophets or Writings they accepted, but they did not accept Pharisaic beliefs about a coming judgment, resurrection, afterlife, angels, or demons. As a group, the Sadducees did not survive the first Christian century. Their close association with Rome, their refusal to accept developing ideas based on the Prophets, the Writings, and the Apocrypha, and their narrow concentration on temple ritual spelled their doom. After the temple's destruction (70 C.E.), the Sadducees were reduced to insignificance. The Pharisees, emphasizing education and progressive reinterpretation of Scripture, became the founders of modern Judaism.

ESSENES

Scholars are tempted to identify the Qumran community that produced the Dead Sea Scrolls with the Essenes, the third group or philosophy that Josephus mentions. Rejecting mainstream Judaism and its temple worship as hopelessly corrupt, many Essenes withdrew into desert communities where they meditated, studied and copied Scripture, and disciplined themselves to await the coming Messiah. Dualists, they believed that the world, both material and spiritual, was divided into opposing camps of light and darkness, good and evil, God and "the Devil" and they trained for the holy war of Armageddon in which God would vanquish the forces of evil.

While some Essenes lived in towns and raised families, the Essene desert communities were monastic; their members practiced celibacy, held all things in common, avoided trade and symbols of wealth, and led an austere hard-working existence. Their emphasis on prayer, the imminent appearance of a Messiah, the end of the world, a new covenant, ceremonial meals of bread and wine, and ritual purification through bathing may have influenced John the Baptist, who led a similarly ascetic life in the desert and also performed water baptisms. Some scholars have speculated that Jesus himself may have been associated with the Essenes between the ages of twelve and thirty, a period on which the Gospels are silent.

ZEALOTS

Although neither Essenes nor Zealots are mentioned in the New Testament, the influence of their ideas is felt. An intensely patriotic group that advocated violent overthrow of Roman control, the Zealots sought a strong-armed Messiah who would restore Judah's kingdom to its former power and prestige. Certain of Jesus' disciples may have held such beliefs (Luke 6:15; Acts 1:13); indeed, Judas' betrayal may have been a misguided attempt to force Jesus to lead a revolt against Rome.

Although many Jews had followed revolutionary ideas since Maccabean times, the Zealots were not organized as a specific political party until 66 C.E., when they attempted to drive the Romans from Palestine. But their blind nationalism forced the Jews on a suicidal course. According to Josephus, it was the Zealots' refusal to surrender, even after Jerusalem had been captured, and their occupation of the temple stronghold that compelled the Romans to destroy the sanctuary, a desecration that the pagan armies had not originally intended. This catastrophe and the later rebellion of 132–135 C.E. discredited both the Zealot cause and the apocalyptic mode that had partly inflamed its expectations. Both armed revolution and end-of-the-world predictions were henceforth repudiated by orthodox Judaism.

RECOMMENDED READING

Baeck, Leo. "The Pharisees." In *The Pharisees and Other Essays*, pp. 1–50. New York: Schocken Books, 1966.

Bonsirven, J. *Palestinian Judaism in the Time of Jesus Christ.* Translated by William Wolf. New York: McGraw-Hill, 1965.

Burrows, Millar. *The Dead Sea Scrolls.* New York: Viking Press, 1955.

Davies, W. D. *Introduction to Pharisaism.* "Facet Books—Biblical Series," no. 16. Philadelphia: Fortress Press, 1967.

Finkelstein, Louis. *The Pharisees.* 2 vols. Philadelphia: Jewish Publication Society of America, 1962. Provides reliable information.

Foerster, Werner. *From the Exile to Christ: A Historical Introduction to Palestinian Judaism.* Translated by G. E. Harris. Philadelphia: Fortress Press, 1964.

Gaster, T. H. *The Dead Sea Scrolls in English Translation,* rev. ed. Garden City, N. Y.: Doubleday, 1964.

MacDonald, J. *The Theology of the Samaritans.* London: SCM Press, 1964.

Neusner, Jacob. *From Politics to Piety: The Emergence of Pharisaic Judaism.* Englewood Cliffs, N. J.: Prentice-Hall, 1973.

Ringgren, Helmer. *The Faith of Qumran.* Philadelphia: Fortress Press, 1961. An excellent work.

Rivkin, Ellis. "Defining the Pharisees." *Hebrew Union College Annual,* 1970, pp. 205–49.

Simon, Marcel. *Jewish Sects at the Time of Jesus.* Philadelphia: Fortress Press, 1967.

Vermes, Geza. *The Dead Sea Scrolls: Qumran in Perspective.* London: Collins, 1977.

THE HISTORICAL JESUS

After many decades of intense research, scholars have reluctantly conceded that it is virtually impossible to discover "the historical Jesus." The Jesus we know from the Gospels and other New Testament books—almost our only source of his biography—is a Jesus described and interpreted by the early Church, a community of believers who looked backward in time to clothe the historical personage in postresurrection glory. What Jesus actually said as opposed to what the Church thought or assumed he said is to the biblical scholar a matter of conjecture. The Gospels cannot tell us directly because, despite their similarities, they do not agree consistently on his words or their original intent. Attempts to distinguish the real Jesus, such as Albert Schweitzer's *Quest of the Historical Jesus,* have not been convincing.

Several Roman and Jewish writers, however, provide strong evidence that Jesus of Nazareth did exist and that his life and teachings inspired a new religion. Pliny the Younger, who governed the Roman province of Bithynia (north-central Turkey) from about 111 to 115 C.E., wrote to the Emperor Trajan about official government policy in handling Christians who refused to participate in "emperor worship," a public act popularly regarded as much an expression of patriotism as of religious commitment. Pliny reported that Christians gathered to "partake of a meal [the Eucharist or Holy Communion]" and to sing "a hymn to Christ, as if to a god" (*Letters* 97), adding that cities, villages, and country districts had already been "thoroughly infected" by the "seditious" cult.

Tacitus, the eminent Roman historian, noted that one "Christus" had been executed under Tiberius and Pontius Pilate and implied (mistakenly) that his followers had contributed to the Jewish rebellion against Rome in 66–70 C.E. (*Annals* 15.44). Suetonius recorded that Claudius (41–54 C.E.) had expelled the Jews from Rome because of trouble arising from "Chrestus" (probably a variant spelling of Tacitus' "Christus") (*Twelve Caesars* 25). Flavius Josephus, the first-century Jewish historian who interpreted his people's customs to the Romans, twice mentioned Jesus. The first reference contains later Christian interpolations, but the second is apparently authentic and testifies to the historicity of Jesus' life (*Antiquities* 18.3.3; 20.9.1). References in the Talmud, although pejorative, also confirm Jesus' existence.

The pagan authors' mere confirmation of Jesus' existence will satisfy neither believer nor historian. To the believer, Jesus is "the image of the invisible God" in whom "the complete being of the Godhead dwells embodied" (Col. 1:15–20; 2:9–10). He is the incarnation of the Logos, the divine Word, who so fully reveals the Creator that he is represented as saying that "anyone who has seen me has seen the Father" (John 14:9). These New Testament descriptions of Jesus' metaphysical nature are not capable of scientific verification but must remain an expression of faith. Supernatural events that by definition occur outside life's normal historical processes, such as Jesus' miraculous ability to control a storm, walk on water, or rise from the dead, cannot be studied *in themselves* but only in their conceptual development among the community of faith. The modern critic does not deal with Jesus conceived as divinity but must approach the living man as the object of historical inquiry, leaving to theologians the task of interpreting the paradox of Jesus as both divine and human.

A major challenge confronting modern scholarship is to discover the authentic "voice of Jesus" amid the many sayings attributed to him in the Gospels. To many New Testament scholars, it seems evident that the majority of Jesus' original sayings and parables have been modified, first in oral transmission and then by the Gospel writers who compiled and edited them for theological purposes. What scholars believe were originally brief, simple comparisons between sowing seed and preaching appear to have grown into full-blown allegories in their Gospel editions (Mark 4:3–20; Matt. 13:4–30; Luke 8:4–15). In addition, some of Jesus' teaching appears to reflect not the concerns of his own day but the interests of the Christian community at the time the Gospels were written (Matt. 10:5–42; 23:1–39; 24:9–27; Luke 19:11–27; 21:12–24, etc.). The situation is further complicated by the fact that the early Christians formed a "spirit-inspired" community in which visions and pronouncements from the risen Jesus were not uncommon (Acts 9:1–16; 22:1–21; 26:12–19; Rev. 1:9–3:22, etc.). This continuing communion with the risen Christ seems to have had the effect of ascribing teaching *about* Jesus *to* Jesus.

In reading the New Testament, the student must continually ask, "To what extent did the Christian faith shape the accounts of Jesus' life and words?" Only the most skeptical would deny altogether that Jesus' teachings determined much of Christian belief, but the precise relationship between Christian doctrine and the historical Jesus remains problematical.

In their search for material that can be assigned to the living Jesus, historians have developed various criteria for measuring the likelihood that a saying or action is "genuine." Certainly a number of Jesus' deeds and experiences are not likely to have been invented by the faithful who regarded him as the Jewish Messiah and Son of God. His crucifixion under Pontius Pilate, attested to by Tacitus and other non-Christian sources, was not the kind of death—public, shameful, and reserved for slaves and criminals—believers would fabricate for their divine leader. Paul candidly describes the awkward fact of Jesus "nailed to the cross" as a "stumbling block to Jews" and "sheer folly" to the Greeks (1 Cor. 1:23, 18). Jesus' baptism by John is another event the Church would not have invented. One whom later doctrine held "sinless" would not be presented as undergoing baptism "in token of repentance, for the forgiveness of sins" (Mark 1:4) unless there existed a firm report that Jesus had indeed submitted to John's ministrations. Jesus' associations with all kinds of disreputable people—tax collectors, prostitutes, and other "sinners"—as well as allegations that he was viewed as "a glutton and a drinker"—also pass the probability test on grounds that no believer would create such tales (Matt. 10:18–19; Luke 15:1–3; 7:33–8:3).

Norman Perrin, a leading New Testament scholar, has suggested four standards by which to ascertain the probable historicity of statements attributed to Jesus. The first criterion is *dissimilarity*, which holds that the earliest form of a saying may be viewed as authentic if it differs significantly from both the tenets of first-century Judaism and early Christianity. The reasoning behind this test assumes that if Jesus had taught only ideas characteristic of the Judaism of his day, he would not have attracted the following he did. Similarly, those sayings that differ from, or at least were not emphasized by, the early Church may be genuine. It should be noted, however, that much of Jesus' teaching in the Gospels— such as his placing supreme importance on love and mercy—also characterized other Jewish teachers of the time (Mark (12:28–34).

A second criterion is *coherence.* Simply stated, this means that sayings from the oldest oral traditions that preceded the Gospels may be regarded as authentic if they essentially resemble material accepted on the grounds of dissimilarity. The third means of determining reliable material is through *multiple attestation*. This criterion permits the acceptance of teachings found in several different places in the pre-Gospel and the Gospel traditions. Dr. Perrin later added a fourth standard involving linguistic and environmental evidence. This method assumes that if a Hebrew or Aramaic form underlies Jesus' words, they are probably authentic. Because Jesus spoke Aramaic, sayings that reflect only a Greek background are considered less likely to be genuine. It is important to remember, however, that not all experts agree on which sayings of Jesus can be attributed to him. While some critics would recognize no more than eight sayings and a dozen parables as representing Jesus' authentic voice, many other scholars would cautiously accept a larger number of teachings. Scholarly criteria have been helpful in identifying Jesus' authentic sayings, but all sayings that do not meet these criteria are not necessarily inauthentic, and scholars are divided on many of them. (On this complex issue, the student is referred to the references listed below.)

Several recent studies, including those by such eminent Jewish scholars as Geza Vermes and Samuel Sandmel, have helped to illuminate our picture of Jesus by placing him in his Jewish Palestinian background. Rather than attempting to screen Jesus' historic pronouncements, these scholars try to explain Jesus as a part of his own time and place, a country prophet proclaiming his message amid the turbulent religious and political currents of first-century Judaism. Galilee, Jesus' homeland, was then an area torn by nationalism and political rebellion, rife with revolutionary intrigue and violence against Roman domination. As some historians point out, a charismatic leader from this district, attracting large unruly crowds, would automatically be regarded with suspicion by both the Sadducees and Roman authorities. Even if, as the Gospel writers believed, Jesus publicly stressed the peaceful nature of his kingdom and did not advocate armed revolt against Rome, in contrast to other Galilean patriots both before and after him—Pontius Pilate would not have been unduly reluctant to eliminate one whom his followers hailed as king. The Gospels make it clear that Jesus was tried as a potential troublemaker and executed on a *political* charge somehow linked to messianic claims of Jewish kingship. Thus an increased understanding of Galilee's reputation in the eyes of both Jewish high priest and Roman governor brings us closer to Jesus' historical situation.

From the letters of Paul and other pre-Gospel traditions, however, it is clear that the earliest Christians did not regard their leader as a political figure. Although his Galilean disciples had expected Jesus to restore "the sovereignty of Israel" (Acts 1:6; Luke 19:11), the earliest surviving Christian documents stress that believers were to live "at peace" awaiting the *Parousia* (Jesus' return in glory) (1 Thess. 4:9–12; 5:14).

RECOMMENDED READING

Barclay, William. *The Mind of Jesus.* New York: Harper & Row, 1960.

Beare, F. W. *The Earliest Records of Jesus.* New York: Abingdon Press, 1962.

Bornkamm, Gunther. *Jesus of Nazareth.* Translated by I. McLuskey and F. McLuskey with J. M. Robinson. New York: Harper & Row, 1960.

Breech, James. *The Silence of Jesus: The Authentic Voice of the Historical Man.* Philadelphia: Fortress Press, 1983. Examines the "core material"—eight sayings and twelve parables—that a scholarly consensus attributes to the historical Jesus.

Connick, C. Milo. *Jesus: The Man, the Mission, and the Message*, 2nd ed. Englewood Cliffs, N. J.: Prentice-Hall, 1974.

Enslin, Morton S. *The Prophet from Nazareth.* New York: McGraw-Hill, 1961.

Farmer, William R. *Jesus and the Gospel.* Philadelphia: Fortress Press, 1982. Argues for the primacy of Matthew over Mark.

Gogue, Maurice. *The Life of Jesus.* Translated by O. Wyon. London: Allen & Unwin, 1933.

Jeremias, Joachim. *New Testament Theology: The Proclamation of Jesus.* New York: Charles Scribner's Sons, 1971.

Klausner, Joseph. *Jesus of Nazareth.* Translated by H. Danby. New York: Macmillan, 1925.

McArthus, Charles, ed. *In Search of the Historical Jesus.* New York: Charles Scribner's Sons, 1969.

Montefiore, C. G. *The Synoptic Gospels*, 2nd ed., rev. New York: KTAV Publishing House, 1968.

Reuman, John. *Jesus in the Church's Gospels: Modern Scholarship and the Earliest Sources.* Philadelphia: Fortress Press, 1968.

Sandmel, Samuel. *Judaism and Christian Beginnings.* New York: Oxford University Press, 1978. Connects Jesus and early Christianity with first-century Judaism and Palestinian customs.

Schillebeeckx, Edward. *Jesus: An Experiment in Christology.* Translated by H. Hoskins. New York: Seabury Press, 1979. An eminent Roman Catholic scholar examines the historical and theological questions of Jesus' life.

———. *Christ: The Experience of Jesus as Lord.* New York: Seabury Press, 1980.

Schweizer, Eduard. *Jesus.* Translated by D. E. Green. Richmond, Va.: John Knox Press, 1971.

Stauffer, Etherbert. *Jesus and His Story.* Translated by R. Winston and C. Winston. New York: Alfred A. Knopf, 1960.

Taylor, Vincent. *The Life and Ministry of Jesus.* Nashville: Abingdon Press, 1955. A good introduction.

Vermes, Geza. *Jesus the Jew: A Historian's Reading of the Gospels.* New York: Macmillan, 1973. Places Jesus in the religious and sociopolitical setting of his first-century Galilean homeland.

THE NEW TESTAMENT

PART 8

THE BOOKS OF THE
NEW TESTAMENT

The first four books of the Christian Greek Scriptures are Gospels, a term derived from the Greek *evangelion* meaning "good news." As a literary form, however, the Gospels are difficult to define, for they are not historical biographies in the modern sense. The Gospel writers do not attempt to provide a complete life of Jesus; they are silent about his youthful development, education, and the forces that shaped his intellectual and religious outlook. Except for the birth narratives in Matthew and Luke and the brief episode about the twelve-year-old Jesus in the temple (Luke 2:41–51), they concentrate exclusively on Jesus' public ministry, emphasizing his miraculous healings, exorcisms, and teachings about the kingdom of God.

The evangelists believed that Jesus of Nazareth was both the long-awaited Jewish Messiah and the universal Savior, the divine man through whom the deity had chosen to reveal the fullness of the divine nature. Hence the Gospel authors' purpose in writing was to convey their understanding of Jesus' *theological* significance—and to convince their audience of its truth. This theological orientation, along with the supernatural events associated with Jesus' death and resurrection, provides scholars with a formidable challenge as they attempt to evaluate the Gospels in terms of ordinary historical analysis.

Acts, the fifth book of the New Testament, can perhaps be classed as a history of the early Church. Again, however, the author—the same person who wrote the Gospel of Luke—was not a disinterested historian, and Acts is as much Christian interpretation as it is objective history. Except for Revelation, an apocalyptic work, the remainder of the New Testament consists of twenty-one epistles or letters written by Paul and other first- and second-century Christians. New Testament literature, then, consists wholly of four Gospels, a religious history, twenty-one letters, and an apocalypse similar to Daniel or 2 Esdras. Table 8–1 lists major events in New Testament history.

TABLE 8-1 Major Events in New Testament History

Approximate Date	Event	Biblical Source
About 332 B.C.E.	Alexander the Great of Macedonia includes Palestine in his empire	1 Macc. 1:1–5
323–197	The Ptolemys of Egypt rule Palestine (Hellenistic period)	1 Macc. 1:6–10
197–142	Seleucid dynasty of Syria rules Palestine	2 Macc. 4
167–164	Antiochus IV attempts to force Hellenistic religion on the Jews; pollutes the temple	1 Macc. 1:10–67
164	The Maccabean revolt is successful; the temple is cleansed and rededicated	1 Macc. 2–6; 2 Macc. 8–10; Dan. 7:25; 12:7; 8:14; 9:27
142–63	The Jews expel the Seleucids; Judea becomes an independent kingdom under the Hasmonean dynasty	1 Macc.
63	General Pompey makes Palestine part of Roman Empire; partitions Judea	
40–4	Herod the Great rules as Roman-appointed king of Judea; rebuilds the temple	
30 B.C.E.–14 C.E.	Augustus Caesar rules as emperor of Rome	
About 6–4 B.C.E.	Birth of Jesus	Matt. 2; Luke 2
4 B.C.E.–39 C.E.	Herod Antipas rules as tetrarch of Galilee	Luke 13:31–32; Mark 6:14–29
5–10 C.E.	Birth of Saul at Tarsus (the Apostle Paul)	
14–37	Tiberius Caesar rules as emperor of Rome	Luke 3:1
26–36	Pontius Pilate serves as procurator of Judea	
27–29 (?)	Ministry of John the Baptist	Mark 1:2–11; 6:17–29; John 1:19–36; 3:22–36
27–30 or 29–33 (?)	Ministry of Jesus	Matt., Mark, Luke, John
30–33 (?)	Crucifixion and resurrection of Jesus	Matt., Mark, Luke, John
33–35 (?)	Conversion of the Apostle Paul	Acts 9:1–19; 22:1–21; 26:1–23; Gal. 1:11–16
41–54	Claudius is emperor of Rome; banishes the Jews from Rome (49 C.E.?)	Acts 18:2
41–44 (?)	Herod Agrippa I is king of Judea; imprisons Peter; beheads James and possibly John as well (44 C.E.?)	Acts 12
About 47–56	Paul makes three missionary tours among the Gentiles	
About 49	Paul attends first Church council held in Jerusalem	Acts 15; Gal. 2
50	Paul writes 1 and 2 Thessalonians; the "Sayings" of Jesus compiled (?)	

TABLE 8-1 (continued)

Approximate Date	Event	Biblical Source
54–68	Nero is emperor of Rome	
54–62	Paul writes a series of letters to various churches he had founded or visited	1 Cor. (54–55 C.E.); 2 Cor. (55–56 C.E.); Gal. (56 C.E.); Rom. (56–57 C.E.); Col. (61 C.E.?); Philem. (61 C.E.); Phil. (62 C.E.)
60–62 or 63 (?)	Paul under house arrest in Rome	
62	Martyrdom of James, brother of Jesus	
64	Burning of Rome and persecutions of Christians	
65–70 (?)	Gospel of Mark is written	
66–70	Jewish revolt against Rome; destruction of Jerusalem (70 C.E.)	
66–67	Flight of Jewish Christians from Judea to Pella, east of Jordan	
69–79	Vespasian is emperor of Rome	
79–81	Titus, conqueror of Jerusalem, is emperor	
80–85	Gospel of Matthew is written	
80–90	Gospel of Luke and Acts are written	
80–100	Letter of James is written	
81–96	Domitian is emperor; persecutes Christians late in reign	
85–90	Book of Hebrews is written	
90 (?)	Letter to the Ephesians is written; Paul's letters are collected (?)	
90–100	1 Clement is written; Gospel of John is composed	
90–91 (?)	Rabbis hold council at Jamnia; third part of the Hebrew Bible—the Writings—is canonized	
95–100	Various Jewish and Christian apocalypses are composed: 2 Esdras, Revelation, and 3 Baruch	
98–117	Trajan is emperor; persecutes Christians	
100–110	Letters of 1, 2, and 3 John are written	
100–140	The Didache, Shepherd of Hermas, Epistle of Ignatius are written; canonical New Testament books of 1 and 2 Timothy, Titus, 1 Peter, and Jude also appear	
117–138	Hadrian is emperor	
132–135	Final Jewish revolt against Rome	
150 (?)	2 Peter is written	

The New Testament includes many fewer literary genres or types, has less variety, and is often stylistically less memorable than the Hebrew Scriptures. It should be remembered, however, that while the Old Testament took from 1,000 to 1,200 years to create, the compositional time span of the New was relative brief, perhaps only 100 years (approximately 50 C.E.–150 C.E.). Moreover, instead of dramatizing the history of an entire nation as the Hebrew Bible does, the New Testament focuses on the lives and thought of a relatively few people—Jesus, his disciples, and a handful of other early Christians. Though the New Testament basically adds only one story to world literature, that story—the ministry and Passion of Jesus—has been described by some as the greatest story ever told.

The following discussion of the twenty-seven canonical New Testament books is intended to familiarize the reader with some of the basic events and themes contained in the Christian Greek Scriptures. No attempt has been made to cover every aspect of Christian teaching. For additional information on specific topics, consult the list of recommended readings at the end of the essay. Unless otherwise stated, all quotations are from the New English Bible.

THE GOSPELS

Although remarkably similar, the Gospels of Matthew, Mark, and Luke—called the Synoptics because they regard events with "one eye," or take a common viewpoint—do reflect certain differences. The question of their chronological order of composition, their sources, authorship, dates, and general relationships is known as the Synoptic Problem. After decades of studying these matters, most leading New Testament scholars have agreed on the following propositions.

1. Mark was the first Gospel to be written; it is also the shortest and simplest, containing neither birth stories nor a resurrection account.

2. Matthew and Luke used Mark as a principal source for their individual Gospels, together incorporating at least 610 of Mark's 661 verses.

3. Both Matthew and Luke drew from a (now-lost) hypothetical Greek document called Q (from the German *Quelle*, meaning "source"), which presumably supplied many of Jesus' teachings included in Matthew and Luke but not found in Mark.

4. Matthew and Luke each had individual sources of information about Jesus that were apparently unknown to Mark. How many of these sources were written and how many were oral traditions is not known.

Scholars have inferred six hypothetical developments behind the writing of the Synoptic Gospels. First, for probably twenty years or more after Jesus' death, the Christian testimony about him was entirely oral.

Stories circulated independently of one another as individual eyewitnesses of Jesus' words and deeds preached or settled in different Christian centers—Jerusalem, Antioch, Caesarea, Ephesus—where their particular gospels took root and grew. These geographically separated Christian centers gradually developed different traditions that were modified to fit changing conditions and needs. In this way, separate oral accounts of Jesus' teachings and actions developed, although most probably observed a generally accepted pattern or content.

Second, the sufficiency of the oral witness was broken when people who had seen and known Jesus began to die off. Since the average life span was brief in the first century, it may have been only about 50 C.E. when the Q document was written to preserve some 250 verses of Jesus' teachings, most of which Matthew and Luke later incorporated into their Gospels.

Several factors urged committing the oral Gospel to writing. As death reduced the number of surviving eyewitnesses, the Church feared that reliable facts about Jesus might be permanently lost. The expected early return of Christ did not take place. Realizing that their length of time in the world was unknown, Christians took steps to preserve the Gospel in writing. Early Christian arguments about the nature of Christ and other theological doctrines necessitated the creation of authoritative documents from the apostolic period. As more Gentiles and Jews became Christians and the center of Church life shifted from Jerusalem and Antioch to Ephesus and Rome, definitive written records of Jesus' message became vital in reeducating formerly pagan converts.

Third, between about 65 and 70 C.E. the Gospel of Mark was written. Eusebius, author of a fourth-century history of the Church, states that Mark, a disciple of Peter in Rome, was induced by Roman Christians to write his memoirs based on Peter's oral testimony. Eusebius also quotes Papias, an earlier churchman (about 140 C.E.), who noted that Mark had not known Jesus himself but had merely recorded Peter's recollections, which were "not in [proper chronological] order" (*Ecclesiastical History* 3:39). Despite Eusebius' plausible claims, however, many scholars now conclude that Mark drew upon oral traditions about Jesus, rather than the memoirs of a single disciple. If Mark's second-hand account of Jesus' life did not observe the proper historical chronology, it was nonetheless followed closely by Matthew and Luke, who reproduced his sequence of events.

Fourth, to answer Jewish criticism of Christian claims about Jesus and to emphasize Jesus' adherence to the Jewish law, a second Gospel was composed. The Gospel of Matthew, written possibly in Antioch about 80–85 C.E., incorporated 90 percent of Mark's account but greatly expanded the teaching content, presumably drawn from the Q document. Matthew also added a birth story from hitherto unknown oral traditions and carefully scrutinized the Old Testament for prophecies that Jesus fulfilled.

Regarding Jesus as a greater Moses who introduced both a new law and covenant and as a Davidic king destined to rule the universe, Matthew quoted or paraphrased the Old Testament about 130 times. Generally adhering to Mark's chronology, he arranged Jesus' teachings in the form of five public sermons probably meant to parallel the five books of the Mosaic Torah. So successful was his integration of Jesus' teachings with Mark's older narrative that Matthew's Gospel—with its strong orientation toward the Church (ecclesia)—soon became the most popular, standing first in rank among the four.

Fifth, about 85–90 C.E., perhaps only five or ten years after the appearance of Matthew, the most precise, literate, and artistic of the Synoptics was composed. Probably the work of a Gentile Christian, Luke reproduced about half of Mark along with considerable Q material and added another major source (designated L by scholars), which comprises about a third of his Gospel. Written as the first part of a two-volume work, the other half being Acts, Luke is also the longest of the Gospels.

Finally, John—the fourth Gospel and apparently the last written—is so different from the Synoptics that scholars regard it as a special case. John covers the same period of Jesus' life as do the Synoptics, beginning with his baptism and ministry in Galilee and concluding with his trial and execution near Jerusalem. But this Gospel presents so different a picture of Jesus' character and teaching that most scholars are at a loss to determine its historical value. In the fourth Gospel, Jesus' manner of teaching is changed radically. Instead of speaking in earthy images and parables drawn from the experience of his peasant audience, John's Jesus delivers long philosophical monologues embodying strange metaphors and mystical symbols. The thrust of Jesus' instruction is also changed. Rather than focusing on the inbreaking kingdom of God and a reinterpretation of the Jewish law, in John Jesus dwells primarily on the nature of his own being and his significance to the believer. Whereas Mark, Matthew, and Luke present Jesus as teaching a modified form of traditional Judaism, John shows little interest in preserving the religion *of* Jesus in order to promulgate a religion *about* Jesus, in which the teacher, rather than the message, becomes the object of veneration. John's insistence upon Jesus as a divine being walking the earth in human form renders his biography of the Galilean highly problematical to scholars who attempt to evaluate Jesus' life in terms of literal historical truth.

With its acceptance of four different Gospels, the second-century Christian community adopted works that had originated in four geographically separated areas, had been written for specific audiences to meet particular historical needs, and had presented significantly distinct theological interpretations of the meaning of Jesus' life and death. Taken together, the Gospels create a composite portrait of one who remains as compelling and enigmatic today as he was to his original hearers.

RECOMMENDED READING

Beardslee, W. A. *Literary Criticism of the New Testament*. Philadelphia: Fortress Press, 1969. Good treatment of the literary approach to interpreting the New Testament.

Bultmann, Rudolf. *History of the Synoptic Tradition*. Translated by John Marsh. New York: Harper & Row, 1963. Major form-critical work.

Bultmann, R., and Kudsin, K. *Form-Criticism*. Translated by F. C. Grant. New York: Harper & Row, 1962.

Cameron, Ron, ed. *The Other Gospels: Non-Canonical Gospel Texts*. Philadelphia: Westminster Press, 1982. Contains the texts of late first- and second-century narratives about the life of Jesus.

Dibelius, Martin. *From Tradition to Gospel*. Translated by G. L. Woolf. New York: Charles Scribner's Sons, 1935. Another form-critical study.

Grant, Frederick C. *The Gospels; Their Origin and Their Growth*. New York: Harper & Row, 1957. A useful introduction.

Grant, R. M. *A Historical Introduction to the New Testament*. New York: Harper & Row, 1963.

Kummel, W. G. *Introduction to the New Testament*, rev. ed. Translated by H. C. Kee. Nashville: Abingdon Press, 1975. A thorough review of New Testament scholarship.

McKnight, F. V. *What Is Form Criticism?* Philadelphia: Fortress Press, 1969.

Patte, Daniel. *What Is Structural Exegesis?*. Philadelphia: Fortress Press, 1976. New trend in biblical studies.

Perrin, Norman. *What Is Redaction Criticism?* Philadelphia: Fortress Press, 1969,

Perry, A. M. "The Growth of the Gospels." In *The Interpreter's Bible*, vol. 7, pp. 60–74. New York and Nashville: Abingdon Press, 1951.

Reumann, John. *Jesus in the Church's Gospels: Modern Scholarship and the Earliest Sources*. Philadelphia: Fortress Press, 1968.

Robinson, A. T. *Redating the New Testament*. Philadelphia: Westminster Press, 1976. Argues that all New Testament books were completed before Jerusalem's destruction in 70 C.E.

Rohde, Joachim. *Rediscovering the Teachings of the Evangelists*. Translated by D. M. Barton. Philadelphia: Westminster Press, 1968.

Sandmel, Samuel. *Judaism and Christian Beginnings*. New York: Oxford University Press, 1978.

Streeter, B. H. *The Four Gospels: A Study of Origins*. rev. ed. London: Macmillan & Co., 1930. A standard work.

Taylor, Vincent. *The Gospels: A Short Introduction*. 7th ed. London: Epworth Press, 1952.

Throckmorton, Burton H., Jr., ed. *Gospel Parallels: A Synopsis of the First Three Gospels*. Nashville: Thomas Nelson Publishers, 1979.

Walker, W. O., Jr., ed. *The Relationship Among the Gospels*. San Antonio: Trinity University Press, 1978.

TABLE 8-2 Parallel Outlines of the Four Gospels

Mark (c. 65–70 C.E.)

· · ·
· · ·

1. Prologue: Jesus' initial appearance; baptism; temptation (1:1–13).
2. Jesus' ministry in Galilee (1:14–8:33).
   a. Jesus' unique authority: exorcisms, healings, call of disciples (1:14–3:6)

· · ·

· · ·

b. Jesus' bewildering parables; misunderstanding and rejection by neighbors and family (3:7–6:6).
c. Jesus' instruction of disciples; death of John the Baptist; feeding of the multitudes and other miracles (6:6–8:13).
d. Peter's recognition of Jesus as Messiah (8:27–33).

· · ·

3. Jesus' role as Son of Man, suffering servant, and "hidden Messiah" (8:31–10:52).
   a. First prediction of Jesus' suffering and death (Passion); transfiguration; the significance of Elijah; cure of a demoniac (8:31–9:29).
   b. Second passion prediction; rivalry between disciples; the problem of divorce; the dangers of riches and rewards of renunciation (9:30–10:31).
   c. Third passion prediction; journey to Jerusalem; emphasis on service and sacrifice; curing of a blind man (10:32–52).
4. Jesus' ministry, suffering, and death in Jerusalem (11:1–16:8).
   a. Prearranged entry into Jerusalem: followers' messianic praises of Jesus; assault on Temple moneychangers (11:1–33).
   b. Public teaching in the Temple; controversies with Pharisees, Sadducees, and others (12:1–44).

Matthew (c. 80–85 C.E.)

· · ·

1. Jesus' genealogy; birth story (1:1–2:23).
2. Jesus proclamation of the Kingdom of Heaven (3:1–7:29).
   a. Jesus' baptism by John; temptation by Satan (3:1–4:11).
   b. Beginning of Galilean ministry (4:12–25).
   c. Sermon on the Mount (first block of interpolated teaching material) (5:1–7:29).

· · ·

· · ·

3. Calling of disciples; healings and other miracles in Galilee (8:1–10:42).
   a. Call of the Twelve and miraculous cures (8:1–9:38).
   b. Instructions to the Apostles (second block of teaching material) (10:1–42).
4. Jesus, the unrecognized Messiah, and the Mystery of the Kingdom (11:1–13:52).
   a. The Baptist's doubts about Jesus' messiahship; the Galileans' lack of faith in Jesus' message (11:2–30).
   b. Seven parables on the secrets of the Kingdom (third block of teaching material) (13·1–52).

· · ·

5. Additional miracles in Galilee; rules for the community of faith (13:53–18:35).
   a. Return to Nazareth and the beheading of John (13:53–14:12).
   b. Two feedings of the multitudes; healings in Phoenicia and Galilee (14:13–15:39).
   c. Peter's recognition of Jesus as Messiah; Jesus' prediction of his suffering and death (16:13–28).
   d. Transfiguration; second passion prediction (17:1–23).
   e. Discourse on Church's care for Jesus' "sheep" (fourth block of teaching material) (18:1–35).
6. Final teachings, sufferings, and death (19:1–28:20).
   a. Further teachings on the Kingdom: renunciation, parable of the vineyard laborers, third passion prediction, leadership through service (19:1–20:28).
   b. Entry into Jerusalem; expulsion of moneychangers from the temple; doctrinal disputes with Jewish leaders (21:1–22:46).
   c. Denunciation of religious bigotry and intolerance, the "seven woes" (fifth block of teaching material) (23:1 through 25:46)

Note: Ellipses (. . .) indicate that no parallel accounts exist.

Luke (c. 85–90 C.E.)

. . .

1. Formal introduction; birth narratives of John and Jesus (1:1–2:52).
2. Prelude to Jesus' ministry (3:1–4:13).
   a. Mission of John the Baptist and Jesus' genealogy (3:1–38).
   b. Jesus' baptism and temptation (4:1–13).

. . .

. . .

3. Jesus' ministry in Galilee (4:14–9:50).
   a. Jesus' rejection by his fellow citizens of Nazareth (4:14–30).
   b. Jesus' miraculous works; call of disciples; proclamation of the Kingdom (4:31–6:16).
   c. Sermon on the Plain (6:17–49) (the "small interpolation," 6:17–8:3).
   d. Healings; communications with the Baptist; welcoming women disciples (7:1–8:3).
   e. Use of parables (8:4–21).
   f. Healing of the sick; exorcizing demons; raising the dead; commissioning the disciples (8:22–9:9).
   g. Feeding the multitudes; Peter's confession; two passion predictions; the transfiguration (9:18–50).

. . .

4. The extended journey to Jerusalem (Luke's "great interpolation" of material peculiar to him: 9:51–10:14).
   a. Encounters in Samaria; mission of the 72 disciples; the commandment of love; the good Samaritan (9:51–10:42).
   b. Advice on prayer; source of Jesus' power; confrontations with Pharisees (11:1–54).
   c. Counsel on discipleship; the delayed return (*Parousia*); necessity of understanding symbolic portents and events (12:1–13:10).
   d. Healings, teachings, parables on the road to Jericho and Jerusalem (13:11–19:27).
5. Jesus' challenge to Jerusalem (19:28–21:38).
   a. Jesus' messianic entry into Jerusalem; assault on the Temple (19:28–46).
   b. Doctrinal debates in the Temple (19:45–21:4).
   c. Prophecy of Jerusalem's siege by the Romans (21:5–38).

John (c. 90–100 C.E.)

1. Hymn to the Logos (Word) (1:1–18).

. . .

2. Early ministry in Galilee (1:19–2:12).
   a. Jesus' superiority to John the Baptist (1:19–34).
   b. Calling of first disciples (1:35–51).
   c. Miraculous transformation of water into wine at wedding in Cana (2:1–12).
3. Early ministry in Jerusalem (2:13–3:21).
   a. First Passover observance (2:13).
   b. Expulsion of moneychangers from the Temple (2:13–25).
   c. Conversation with Nicodemus (3:1–21).
4. Ministry in Samaria and Galilee (3:22–4:54).
   a. John's witness to Jesus' superiority (3:22–36).
   b. Conversation with Samaritan woman (4:1–42).
5. Second visit to Jerusalem: Speech on the Son's relationship to the Father (5:1–47).
6. Ministry resumed in Galilee; second Passover observance (6:1–71).
   a. Feeding of the multitudes (6:1–15).
   b. Speech on Jesus as Bread of Life (6:22–66).
   c. Peter's confession (6:67–71).

7. Jesus' return to Jerusalem; teaching in the Temple (7:1–10:21).
   a. Jesus' witness to his nature and purpose (7:1–8:59).
   b. Curing of a blind man; the Pharisees' blindness (10:1–21).
   c. The resurrection of Lazarus; conspiracy to kill Jesus (11:1–54).

8. Jesus' final visit to Jerusalem and farewell discourses (11:55–17:26).
   a. Anointing at Bethany (12:1–11).
   b. Messianic entry into Jerusalem (12:12–50).

. . .

continued

TABLE 8-2 (continued)

Mark (c. 65–70 c.e.)	**Matthew** (c. 80–85 c.e.)
c. Eschatological prophecy of the Temple's destruction and imminent appearance of the Son of Man (13:1–37).	d. Prophecy of Jerusalem's fall and Jesus' return (*Parousia*) (24:1–25:46).
d. Conspiracy against Jesus; Judas' betrayal; "Last Supper" with disciples; Jesus' agony and arrest in Gethsemane (14:1–52).	e. The Last Supper; the betrayal by Judas; Jesus' arrest and hearing before the Sanhedrin (26:1–75).
e. Examination before the Sanhedrin and Peter's denials (14:53–72).	f. Jesus' political trial before Pontius Pilate; crucifixion and burial (27:11–66).
f. The trial before Pontius Pilate (15:1–20).	g. The empty tomb and resurrection appearances in Galilee (28:1–20).
g. The crucifixion, burial, and empty tomb (15:21–16:8).	

❦ Matthew

Infancy Narrative	*Chapters 1–2*
Baptism and Temptation	*3–4*
Sermon on the Mount	*5–7*
Instructions to the Twelve Disciples	*10:1–11:1*
Parables on the Kingdom	*13:1–52*
Instructions for the Church	*18*
Fifth Discourse	*23*
Signs of the Times	*24–25*
Parables of the Second Coming	*25*
Final Days and Resurrection	*21; 26–28*

Do not suppose that I [Jesus] have come to abolish the Law and the prophets; I did not come to abolish but complete.

Matthew 5:17

Although an early tradition assigns the Gospel of Matthew to Jesus' apostle of that name, the book itself makes no such claim. The assumption may derive from Matthew 9:9, which states that the tax collector who became a disciple was named Matthew (though he is called Levi in Mark 2:14). The belief that this Gospel was first written in Hebrew (or Aramaic) is preserved by Eusebius, the fourth-century Church historian, who quotes Papias as stating that "'Matthew compiled the Sayings [*logia*] in the Aramaic language, and everyone translated them as well as he could'" (*Ecclesiastical History* 3.39).

Although what these Sayings were is unknown, modern scholars agree

6. Jesus' final sufferings, death and resurrection (22:1–24:53).
   a. The Last Supper; Judas' betrayal; agony in Gethsemane (22:1–46).
   b. Jesus' arrest; trials before the Sanhedrin, Herod Antipas, and Pontius Pilate (22:47–23:25).
   c. Crucifixion and burial (23:26–56).
   d. The empty tomb; resurrection appearances near Jerusalem (24:1–53).

    c. Last Supper; washing of disciples' feet (13:1–38).
    d. Extended farewell speeches (14:1–17:26).
9. Jesus' arrest, trials, death, and resurrection (18:1–20:31).
    a. Hearings before Annas, Caiphas, and Pontius Pilate (18:1–19:16).
    b. The crucifixion and burial (19:17–42).
    c. The empty tomb; resurrection appearances near Jerusalem (20:1–31).
10. Epilogue: added resurrection appearances (21:1–25).

that they were not a primitive form of our present Gospel. Some critics have speculated that they were a collection of Jesus' teachings; others have argued that they were only a list of Old Testament prophecies about the Messiah used later by the author of Matthew. Current scholarly opinion is that the Gospel is anonymous and was written probably in Syria, perhaps in Antioch, possibly about 80–85 C.E.

One argument against Matthew's being the work of an apostle is that it draws so heavily on the earlier Gospel of Mark, itself a Greek work written by someone who was not an eyewitness of Jesus' career. The author (whom we call "Matthew" for convenience) follows Mark's order of events and utilizes about 90 percent of his text, something a writer who knew Jesus personally is not likely to have done.

Matthew, however, offers far more than a mere reproduction of Mark. Into the Markian framework the author places five extensive collections of Jesus' teachings (drawn from the Q document?) not found in the earlier Gospel. At the beginning of his account he adds a genealogy and birth narrative; at the end, a report of Jesus' resurrection appearances (absent from Mark). In addition to Mark, his sources apparently include written documents shared with Luke, as well as material unique to his Gospel (designated M), probably including oral traditions.

The writer's numerous quotations from the Hebrew Bible help to clarify his purpose in thus expanding Mark's Gospel. Perhaps writing for Greek-speaking Jewish Christians, Matthew wishes to present Jesus as the culmination of Jewish messianic expectations. At least a dozen times he emphasizes the fulfillment of Old Testament predictions by stating: "This was to fulfill the prophecy which says . . ." then quoting or paraphrasing an Old Testament text. To what extent this determination to prove that Jesus was the long-awaited Messiah colors Matthew's treatment of his life is unknown, though some critics have suggested that the author has invented incidents to which he can apply recognized messianic motifs.

MATTHEW   **273**

Structurally, the Gospel can be divided into thirteen narrative or didactic sequences:

1. Birth stories (1–2)

2. Jesus' baptism and early Galilean ministry (3–4)

3. Sermon on the Mount (5–7)

4. Jesus' miraculous cures and other mighty acts (8–9)

5. Directions on the disciples' missionary work (10:1–11:1)

6. Public and private responses to Jesus' activity (11–12)

7. Parables on the Kingdom (13:1–52)

8. Conflicts, rejections, and private conferences with the disciples (13:53–17:27)

9. Instructions on life in the Christian community (18)

10. Jesus' entrance into Jerusalem, cleansing of the temple, and debates with the Jewish hierarchy (19–22)

11. Jesus' confrontation with Jerusalem's leaders and his denunciation of the Pharisees (23)

12. Jesus' apocalyptic predictions and discourse on Judgment Day (24–25)

13. Jesus' trial, crucifixion, and resurrection (26–28).

Infancy Narrative Matthew begins his Gospel with a genealogy—three sets of fourteen generations each—linking Jesus with major figures in Old Testament history, culminating with Abraham, father of the Jews. Perhaps to answer contemporary Jewish slanders about Jesus' origins, Matthew then recounts the birth of Jesus to Mary, a virgin, and her husband, Joseph, a carpenter from Nazareth in Galilee. Characteristically, the writer inserts several Old Testament quotations into the birth narrative: Jesus is born in Bethlehem to fulfill Micah 5:2 and to a virgin (Greek, *parthenos*) to fulfill the Greek version of Isaiah 7:14. Foreshadowing that the child will be worshipped by many non-Jews, Matthew describes the nativity visit of foreign astrologers, "wise men" from Persia or Babylonia who apparently had concluded from a horoscope of Judah that its king was then due to appear. Roused by this news, King Herod—the Roman-appointed ruler of Judah—attempts to eliminate a potential rival by ordering the slaughter of all Bethlehem children under the age of two (Matt. 2:1–18). Herod's "massacre of the innocents" is intended to parallel a similar event in Egypt when Moses was born (Exod. 1); it is also cited as fulfillment of a prophecy in Jeremiah (see Table 8-3, p. 276).

Joseph and Mary's flight into Egypt to escape Herod's wrath is similarly accounted for, as a fulfillment of Hosea 11:1 ("out of Egypt I called my son"). Because this verse refers not to the Messiah but to Israel's exodus under Moses and is clearly cited out of context, many scholars express doubt about the entire Herod episode. Some critics have questioned whether Matthew, in his eagerness to find or create analogies between the major figure of the old covenant and the dominant figure of the new, has not invented some aspects of the infancy story. The only other New Testament account of Jesus' birth (Luke 2) does not mention either Herod's threat or the Egyptian sojourn, nor does Josephus or any contemporary pagan source refer to Herod's murder of Jewish children.

In fairness to Matthew's use of Old Testament proof texts to validate Jesus as the expected Messiah, it should be noted that biblical exegesis—analysis and interpretation of the text—was in first-century Palestine a very different discipline from what it is today. Modern scholars respect the integrity of a text, endeavoring to discover its original meaning by placing it in its literary and historical setting. In Matthew's time, however, every word, sometimes even every letter, of Scripture was regarded as having an inspired meaning. In this view, a passage's original context did not matter if a single word or line seemed applicable to the interpreter's theological purpose (see Table 8-3).

Baptism and Temptation   Jesus' baptism by John in the River Jordan has also long been a puzzle to the Church. If, as according to orthodox belief, Jesus was born sinless, why did he undergo a "baptism in token of repentance, for the forgiveness of sins," as Mark, the earliest Gospel and Matthew's chief source, makes it clear he did? (See Mark 1:4–5.)

Matthew avoids this question by omitting Mark's statement about the nature of John's baptism and by having the Baptizer emphasize his inferiority to Jesus (Matt. 3:14). Upon Jesus' rising from Jordan's waters, a voice from heaven announces, "This is my beloved Son, with whom I am well pleased" (Matt. 3:17). The public act of dedication, followed immediately by a descent of the Holy Spirit, informs the reader that Jesus of Nazareth, the carpenter's son, has become God's Anointed, the Messiah ("Christ" is the anglicized version of the Greek word for Messiah).

Following his baptism, Jesus retreats into the Judean wilderness for forty days of prayer and meditation, at the end of which the Devil appears to tempt him. Jesus rejects each of the three temptations—to turn stones into bread, to display his supernatural powers by hurling himself from the temple, and to rule "all the kingdoms of the world" through worship of Satan—by refuting the Devil's blandishments with quotations from Jewish law (Matt. 4:1–11; Deut. 8:3; 6:13; 6:16).

Sermon on the Mount   Matthew's principal addition to Mark is his insertion into the gospel narrative of five collections of teaching material. The first of these collections is the Sermon on the Mount, which is meant to parallel the Mosaic law revealed on Mount Sinai (Exod. 19–24). As a

(text continues on page 278)

TABLE 8-3   Representative Examples of Matthew's Use of the Old Testament to Identify Jesus as the Promised Messiah

Matthew: "All this happened in order to fulfil what the Lord declared through the prophet . . ." (Matt. 1:22)	Old Testament Source
1. "The Virgin will conceive and bear a son, and he shall be called Emmanuel." (Matt. 1:22)	1. A young woman is with child, and she will bear a son and will call him Immanuel. (Isaiah 7:14)
2. "Bethlehem in the land of Judah, you are far from least in the eyes of the rulers of Judah; for out of you shall come a leader to be the shepherd of my people Israel." (Matt. 2:5–6)	2. But you, Bethlehem in Ephrathah, small as you are to be among Judah's clans, out of you shall come forth a governor for Israel, one whose roots are far back in the past, in days gone by. (Micah 5:2)
3. So Joseph . . . went away . . . to Egypt, and there he stayed till Herod's death. This was to fulfil what the Lord had declared through the prophet: "I called my son out of Egypt." (Matt. 2:15)	3. When Israel was a boy, I loved him; I called my son out of Egypt. (Hosea 11:1)
4. Herod . . . gave orders for the massacre of all children in Bethlehem and its neighborhood, of the age of two years or less. . . . So the words spoken through Jeremiah the prophet were fulfilled: "A voice was heard in Rama, wailing and loud laments; it was Rachael weeping for her children, and refusing all consolation, because they were no more." (Matt. 2:16–18)	4. Hark, lamentation is heard in Ramah, and bitter weeping, Rachel weeping for her sons. She refuses to be comforted: they are no more. (Jeremiah 31:15)
5. "He shall be called a Nazarene." (Matt. 2:23)	5. Then a shoot shall grow from the stock of Jesse, and a branch (Hebrew, *nezer*) shall spring from his roots. (Isaiah 11:1)
6. When he heard that John had been arrested, Jesus withdrew to Galilee; and leaving Nazareth he went and settled at Capernaum on the Sea of Galilee, in the district of Zebulun and Naphtali. This was to fulfil the passage in the prophet Isaiah which tells of "the land of Zebulun, the land of Naphtali, the Way of the Sea, the land beyond Jordan, heathen Galilee," and says: "The people that lived in darkness saw a great light; light dawned on the dwellers in the land of death's dark shadow." (Matt. 4:12–16)	6. For, while the first invader has dealt lightly with the land of Zebulun and the land of Naphtali, the second has dealt heavily with Galilee of the Nations on the road beyond Jordan to the sea. The people who walked in darkness have seen a great light: light has dawned upon them, dwellers in a land as dark as death. (Isaiah 9:1–2)

TABLE 8-3 (continued)

Matthew: "All this happened in order to fulfil what the Lord declared through the prophet . . ." (Matt. 1:22)	Old Testament Source
7. . . . and he drove the spirits out with a word and healed all who were sick, to fulfill the prophecy of Isaiah: "He took away our illnesses and lifted our diseases from us." (Matt. 8:16–17)	7. Yet on himself he bore our sufferings, our torments he endured, while we counted him smitten by God, struck down by disease and misery . . . (Isaiah 53:4)
8. Jesus . . . gave strict injunctions that they were not to make him known. This was to fulfil Isaiah's prophecy: "Here is my servant, whom I have chosen, my beloved on whom my favour rests; I will put my spirit upon him, and he will proclaim judgement among the nations. He will not strive, he will not shout, nor will his voice be heard in the streets. He will not snap off the broken reed, nor snuff out the smouldering wick, until he leads justice on to victory. In him the nations shall place their hope." (Matt. 12:16–21)	8. Here is my servant, whom I uphold, my chosen one in whom I delight, I have bestowed my spirit upon him, and he will make justice shine on the nations. He will not call out or lift his voice high, Or make himself heard in the open street. He will not break a bruised reed, or snuff out a smouldering wick; he will make justice shine on every race, never faltering, never breaking down, he will plant justice on earth, while coasts and islands wait for his teaching. (Isaiah 42:1–4)
9. In all his teaching to the crowds Jesus spoke in parables; in fact he never spoke to them without a parable. This was to fulfil the prophecy of Isaiah: "I will open my mouth in parables; I will utter things kept secret since the world was made." (Matt. 13:34–35)	9. Mark my teaching, O my people, listen to the words I am to speak. I will tell you a story with a meaning, I will expound the riddle of things past, things that we have heard and know, and our fathers have repeated to us. (Psalms 78:2—*not* in Isaiah)
10. [Jesus instructs his disciples to bring him a donkey and her foal.] "If any speaks to you, say 'Our Master needs them'; and he will let you take them at once." This was to fulfil the prophecy which says, "Tell the daughter of Zion, 'Here is your king, who comes to you riding on an ass, riding on the foal of a beast of burden.'" (Matt. 21:2–5) [Matthew shows Jesus mounted on two beasts—the donkey *and* her foal. See Luke 19:29–36, where a single mount is mentioned.]	10. Rejoice, rejoice, daughter of Zion, shout aloud, daughter of Jerusalem; for see, your king is coming to you, his cause won, his victory gained, humble and mounted on an ass, on a foal, the young of a she-ass. (Zechariah 9:9)

continued

TABLE 8-3 (continued)

Matthew: "All this happened in order to fulfil what the Lord declared through the prophet . . ." (Matt. 1:22)	Old Testament Source
11. [Judas returns to the priests their bribe to betray Jesus; the money is used to buy a burial plot for the poor.] . . . and in this way fulfilment was given to the prophetic utterance of Jeremiah: "They took the thirty silver pieces, the price set on a man's head (for that was his price among the Israelites), and gave the money for the potter's field, as the Lord directed me." (Matt. 27:8–10) [In Exodus 21:32, thirty pieces of silver is the value of a slave.]	11. Jeremiah said, The word of the Lord came to me: Hanamel son of your uncle Shallum is coming to see you and will say, "Buy my field at Anathoth; you have the right of redemption, as next of kin, to buy it." As the Lord had foretold, my cousin Hanamel came to the court of the guard-house and said, "Buy my field at Anathoth in Benjamin. You have the right of redemption and possession as next of kin; buy it." I knew that this was the Lord's message; so I bought the field at Anathoth from my cousin Hanamel and weighed out the price, seventeen skekels of silver. I signed and sealed the deed and had it witnessed; then I weighed out the money on the scales. I took my copies of the deed of purchase, both the sealed and the unsealed, and gave them to Baruch. (Jeremiah 32:6–13) I said to them, "If it suits you, give me my wages; otherwise, keep them." Then they weighed out my wages, thirty pieces of silver. The Lord said to me, "throw it into the treasury." I took the thirty pieces of silver—that noble sum at which I was valued and rejected by them!—and threw them into the house of the Lord, the treasury. (Zechariah 11:12–13)

"greater Moses," Jesus introduces a new law for Christians that both completes and transcends the earlier Mosaic teaching.

The sermon begins with the Beatitudes ("blessings" or "happinesses"), which, though characteristic of first-century rabbinical morality in their praise of the peacemakers, the merciful, and the pure in heart, significantly modify assumptions typical of some Old Testament thought. Deuteronomy and Proverbs had argued, for example, that material prosperity and earthly success were signs of divine favor, while poverty and misfortune were evidence of divine punishment. But Jesus declares that the poor, the mourners, the meek, and those who hunger, thirst, and endure persecution "for his sake" are specially blessed, thus providing comfort and hope for those large masses of Palestinians shut out from the orthodox view of righteousness and from whom his following was largely drawn.

Of particular importance is Jesus' insistence that, though the Mosaic law is eternally valid, his new standard of righteousness surpasses (if not supersedes) that of the old law (hence Matthew's emphasis on Jesus' authority to give the law a new meaning). The contrast between old and new is stressed in six antitheses, in each of which Jesus opposes the supposedly traditional view with his authoritative reinterpretation: "You have learned that they were told 'Eye for eye, tooth for tooth.' But what I tell you is this: Do not set yourself against the man who wrongs you. If someone slaps you on the right cheek, turn and offer him your left" (Matt. 5:38–39). In refusing to return violence for violence, the cycle of retaliation is broken.

In the other five antitheses—"You have learned that they [your ancestors] were told . . . But what I tell you is this"—Jesus tends to internalize the law. That is, he prohibits not only the act of murder but the emotion, anger, that leads to it (Matt. 5:21–26), not only adultery but lust (Matt. 5:27–30), not only false witness but any empty vow (Matt. 5:33–37), not only hatred but any unloving motive (Matt. 5:43–48).

In chapter 6 Jesus discourages public displays of piety or lengthy formal prayers, offering instead a simple model of petitioning God—the "Lord's Prayer" (Matt. 6:9–13). He stresses forgiving others so that one's god may forgive oneself (Matt. 6:14–15) and urges his hearers to focus their minds "on God's kingdom and his justice before everything else" (Matt 6:33). The sermon ends with a parable (a brief narrative illustrating a spiritual truth or moral) about the man who builds his house on the rock of Jesus' teachings and is able to survive great trouble (Matt. 7:24–27). Again emphasizing Jesus' power to command, Matthew reports that the crowds "were astounded at his teaching; unlike their own teachers he taught with a note of authority" (Matt. 7:28).

Instructions to the Twelve Disciples   The second major collection of teaching material presents instructions to the twelve chief disciples (listed by name in Matthew 10:2–4), whom Jesus sends exclusively to "the lost sheep of the house of Israel" (Matt. 10:6), specifically forbidding missionary work among the Gentiles or Samaritans (Matt. 10:5–6). The Twelve are to preach the imminent coming of the Kingdom, heal the sick, raise the dead, cleanse lepers, and cast out demons and are told that they will not have completed their circuit of Israel's towns before the Son of Man appears (Matt. 10:23), an indication that the early Church believed that its missionary activity would continue until Jesus returned.

Of paramount importance in the disciples' work is their absolute loyalty to the Master. If allegiance to him demands forsaking father, mother, family, or friends, it must be done, for such loyalty transcends and abrogates all human commitments (Matt. 10:37). The person obeying Jesus must also expect to suffer, even to endure death (Matt 10:30–39), although the disciples are told not to fear those who kill the body but only the one who can destroy both soul and body in Gehenna, the place of punishment (Matt. 10:28).

Parables on the Kingdom   The third block of teaching material (Matt. 13:1–52) offers a series of parables on the Kingdom, including the parable

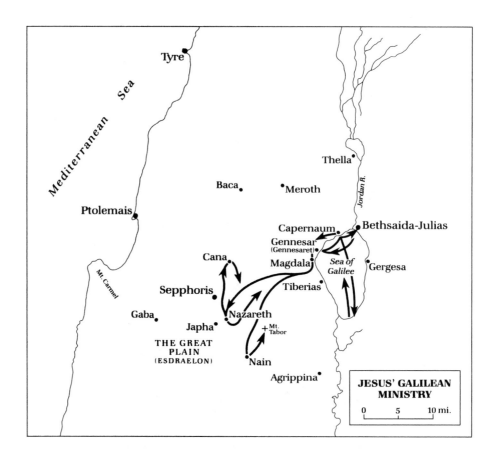

Map caption:
JESUS' GALILEAN
MINISTRY

0   5   10 mi.

of the sower (Matt. 13:3–23, 36–43), which parallels Mark 4:1–20. Here Matthew adopts Mark's notion that Jesus employed parables to confuse and discourage "outsiders" unworthy of receiving a message intended for an inner circle of disciples, typically citing an Old Testament passage to explain this (Matt. 13:10–17; Isa. 6:9–10). The assertion that Jesus deliberately phrased his message to prevent his audience from understanding it contravenes much of what we assume to be his character, however.

Other parables in this group include that of the wheat and tares (weeds) (Matt. 13:24–30), which emphasizes the separation and judgment of good and evil persons at the coming harvest (end of the world), and the parable of the net (Matt. 13:47–50), which indicates that final separation cannot occur until the end of time. Unique to Matthew, both parables stress an indefinitely delayed but sure punishment of the wicked, including those ostensibly belonging to the Kingdom.

Two other parables—the similes of the mustard seed (Matt. 13:31–32) and the leaven (Matt. 13:33)—point out the easily overlooked presence of the Kingdom and its phenomenal growth. Finally, the Kingdom is likened to a pearl "of very special value" and to buried treasure for which everything is wisely sacrificed (Matt. 13:44–45). Both the secret nature and incomparable worth of the Kingdom are here emphasized.

Instructions for the Church   More than any other Gospel, Matthew reflects the life of the Christian community two or three generations after Jesus' death. Indeed, the author is the only Gospel writer who speaks of the "Church" (from Greek *ecclesia,* "assembly") (Matt. 18:15–20; 16:18). Jesus' fourth discourse (Matt. 18) presents the role of the Church—defined as two or three believers gathered in Jesus' name—as primarily one of custodial and pastoral care. Themes of humility and ecclesiastical responsibility are emphasized throughout.

The parable of the "lost sheep" (Matt. 18:1–14), for example, stresses the Church's duty to each individual believer, while its awesome power over members is revealed in its commission to excommunicate the unrepentant (Matt. 18:15–17). In this passage the Church is also told that whatever it forbids or allows on earth is also forbidden or allowed in heaven (Matt. 18:18–19). Earlier (Matt. 16:19) this prerogative had been assigned to Peter, who was described as the "rock" upon which the Church will be founded. Clearly, Matthew's Gospel originated in a Christian milieu in which Peter was held in high esteem.

Jesus' admonition to his Church concludes with a behest to forgive offenses freely and indefinitely (Matt. 18:21). A long parable describing an unmerciful servant (Matt. 18:23–35) argues that Christians who have themselves been forgiven must also forgive others. Standing as it does at the climax of Jesus' discourse, this parable stresses the Christian community's obligation to treat its adherents graciously.

Fifth Discourse   This section contains a searing denunciation of the scribes and Pharisees—professional transmitters and interpreters of the law—upon whom Jesus is pictured as heaping "seven woes" (Matt. 23). By far the harshest anti-Jewish diatribe in the New Testament, itself profoundly unsympathetic to Judaism, it is thought to reflect the antipathy that existed between Christians and Jews in Matthew's day. If this view is correct, chapter 23 says more about the first-century Church, which apparently saw the Roman desolation of Judea as a divine visitation upon the Jews for having rejected Jesus, than it does about the historical Jesus' opinion of the Pharisees. The author also may have intended this section to parallel the list of curses in the fifth book of the Torah (Deut. 28).

Signs of the Times   In this prediction of the Parousia or Second Coming (Matt. 24), the author greatly expands Mark's account of Jesus' prophecy about the fall of Jerusalem. According to Mark 13:4, the disciples had merely asked when the temple was to be destroyed; but Matthew intensifies the eschatological sense of the question by linking the temple's ruin to the Parousia and "the end of the age" (Matt. 24:3). Jesus' reply is a good illustration of how contemporary Jewish eschatology was incorporated into the Christian tradition.

The many "signs" that will *precede* Jesus' return (mostly drawn from such Old Testament and later Jewish books as Joel, Daniel, Zechariah, and Enoch) include the appearance of false Messiahs; the occurrence of international wars, earthquakes, and famines; the persecution of Christians, many believers' loss of faith, and a worldwide preaching of Jesus' message about the Kingdom of God. Jesus' reference to an "abomination of desolation" (Matt. 24:15), echoing Daniel 9:27, 11:31, and 12:11, may be based on an earlier Jewish writing that had declared the Emperor Caligula's erecting an idol in the temple precincts to have fulfilled Daniel's prophecy and portended the temple's imminent destruction.

Matthew's caution—"let the reader understand" (Matt. 24:16)—suggests that the passage is not from Jesus' oral teaching but from a written source; in a parallel passage, Luke 21:20–24 does not allude to the "abomination" but to Roman armies besieging Jerusalem. At all events, Matthew interprets this sign as a warning to flee Judea for it introduces a time of distress so severe that if not "cut short, no living thing could survive" (Matt. 24:21–22)—unmistakable references to the Jewish revolt and fall of Jerusalem (66–70 C.E.), during which a group of Judean Christians left the holy city to seek refuge east of Jordan.

After the unendurable tribulation, moreover, the sun will be darkened, the moon will fail to give light, and stars will fall from their courses (Matt. 24:29–31)—cosmic anomalies that are likewise common in such apocalyptic literature as Joel 2:30–32 and Amos 8:9–10, apocryphal books like 2 Esdras, and pseudepigraphal works like Enoch. The narrator's flat declaration that his generation will not pass away before all the predictions are fulfilled (Matt. 24:34) indicates that he believed himself to be living in the last days.

Matthew emphasizes, however, that not even "the Son" knows the exact time of the Parousia, and such verses, stressing the unexpectedness of Jesus' return, do not fully harmonize with other passages giving explicit signs that will forewarn the alert. This discrepancy leads some scholars to conclude that Matthew employs at least two different traditions about the Parousia: one that is conventionally apocalyptic and contains a traditional list of spectacular portents; the other emphasizing the need to live a godly life at all times because the Master will appear without warning.

Parables of the Second Coming   Chapter 25 contains two parables and a prophetic vision of Jesus' *unannounced* reappearance. In the first (Matt. 25:1–13), five foolish virgins fail to provide their lamps with oil, so that when the bridegroom (Messiah) appears they are absent and therefore denied entrance to the marriage feast (messianic Kingdom). The parable of the talents (Matt. 25:14–30) also emphasizes constant preparedness and the unexpectedness of the Master's inspection of his servants.

Matthew's picture of Jesus' return to judge the world (Matt. 25:31–46) is more like a prophetic vision than a parable. According to this passage, the "Son of Man" appears to separate the godly (sheep) from the wicked (goats) and to assign them rewards or punishments. Significantly, it is humanitarian action rather than doctrinal belief that brings divine favor. The obedient are recognized by their good works, which earn them a place in the Kingdom; it is the failure of the "goats" to help those who need them that consigns them to eternal punishment.

Final Days and Resurrection   Matthew's account of Jesus' final days generally adheres to Mark's sequence of events. After describing Jesus' triumphal entry into Jerusalem on Palm Sunday (Matt. 21:1–11) and his driving the moneychangers from the temple (Matt. 21:23–24:1), he reports several private moments when Jesus is alone with his intimates. In the house of Simon the leper at Bethany, an anonymous woman anoints Jesus with an expensive oil, an act the disciples protest as too extravagant. Jesus' reply that her action will be retold wherever the Gospel is preached reflects Matthew's belief that Jesus is God's Anointed One who is now being prepared for death and burial (Matt. 26:1–2, 6–13).

Matthew's version of Judas' betrayal records that Judas received thirty pieces of silver from the chief priests (Matt. 26:14–16). He also reports that Jesus identified the traitor (Matt. 26:20–25), which Mark does not mention. After Jesus had been delivered to the Romans, Matthew adds, Judas, overcome with remorse, returned the blood money and hanged himself. The priests then used the silver to buy a burying ground for destitute strangers (Matt. 27:3–10), which investment Matthew sees as fulfillment of Jeremiah (32:6–13) and Zachariah (11:23–13).

Matthew closely follows Mark's version of the ceremonial Last Supper (Matt. 26:26–29; Mark 14:22–25), similarly emphasizing Jesus' introduction of a new covenant and the sacred symbolism of the Passover bread and wine. He also reproduces Jesus' assertion that he will not drink wine again with his disciples until he drinks it in the Kingdom. According to some commentators, this apocalyptic expectation suggests that Jesus believed his sacrifice would lead to the immmediate establishment of divine rule.

As in Mark, the disciples sleep while Jesus prays to be spared the coming agony; Judas identifies him to the mob; and Jesus is brought before the Sanhedrin, where he is charged with blasphemy (Matt. 26:36–66). To Mark's version of Jesus' trial, Matthew adds that Pilate's wife, tormented by a dream, urges him to have nothing to do with the accused (Matt. 27:19). Perhaps impressed by this portent, Pilate publicly washes his hands of responsibility for Jesus' death and reluctantly delivers him over for execution (Matt. 27:24–25).

Matthew increases the number of natural phenomena attending Jesus' death, stating that darkness fell at noon and that the earth shook violently, apparently opening the tombs of some unidentified "saints" who walked into Jerusalem and "appeared to many" (Matt. 27:52–53). He also provides two stories of a Jewish conspiracy to undermine belief in Jesus' resurrection. In the first, the chief priests and Pharisees are said to have persuaded Pilate to place a guard at Jesus' tomb to prevent his followers from stealing the corpse and proclaiming that their leader had risen from the dead (Matt. 27:62–66). In the second, after the resurrection, some Jewish elders are reported to have bribed the Roman soldiers to say that Jesus' body had been removed while the sentries slept (Matt. 28:11–15).

To Mark's record of the resurrection, Matthew contributes several additional details. After reporting a second severe earthquake (Matt. 28:2), he states that "an angel of the Lord" whose face "shone like lightning" dazzled the Roman guards and announced to the women who had come to anoint Jesus' body that the Master had risen from the dead (Matt. 28:3–6). This radiant being replaces the "young man" whom Mark reports the women as seeing (Mark 16:5).

Surprisingly, however, Matthew mentions neither Jesus' postresurrection appearance to the disciples in Judea (cited in Luke and the Appendix to Mark) nor the ascension. He merely states that Jesus appeared to the Eleven in Galilee and commissioned them to "make all nations my disciples," to baptize them "in the name of the Father, and the Son, and the Holy Spirit," and to teach them all that he had commanded (Matt. 28:19–20). The Gospel concludes with Jesus' promise that he will be with his followers "to the end of time" (Matt. 28:20).

RECOMMENDED READING

Bacon, B. W. *Studies in Matthew.* New York: Holt, 1930.

Bornkamm, Gunther; Barth, Gerhard; and Held, H. J. *Tradition and Interpretation in Matthew.* Philadelphia: Westminster Press, 1963.

Farmer, William R. *Jesus and the Gospel: Tradition, Scripture, and Canon.* Philadelphia: Fortress Press, 1982. Argues for primacy of Matthew's Gospel.

Fenton, J. C. *St. Matthew.* Pelican Gospel Commentaries. Baltimore: Penguin Books, 1963.

Fitzmyer, Joseph, S. J. *A Wandering Aramaean.* Missoula, Mont.: Scholars Press, 1979. Explores the Aramaic background of the New Testament, including Matthew's Gospel.

Filson, F. V. *The Gospel According to St. Matthew.* New York: Harper & Row, 1960.

Johnson, S. E. "The Gospel According to St. Matthew, Introduction and Exegesis." In *The Interpreter's Bible,* vol. 7, pp. 231–625. New York and Nashville: Abingdon Press, 1951.

Kee, Howard C. *Jesus in History,* 2nd ed. New York: Harcourt Brace Jovanovich, 1977.

Kilpatrick, G. D. *The Origin of the Gospel According to St. Matthew.* Oxford: Clarendon Press, 1946.

Kingsbury, Jack Dean. *Matthew: Structure, Christology and Kingdom*. Philadelphia: Fortress Press, 1975.

Lord, Albert. "The Gospel as Oral Tradition." In *The Relationship Among the Gospels*, edited by W. O. Walker, Jr. San Antonio: Trinity University Press, 1978.

Stendahl, Krister. "Exposition of Matthew." In *Peake's Commentary on the Bible*, edited by M. Black and H. H. Rowley, pp. 769–98. London and New York: Thomas Nelson & Sons, 1962.

_____. *The School of St. Matthew*. Philadelphia: Fortress Press, 1968.

Streeter, B. H. *The Four Gospels*. London: Macmillan & Co., 1924. Places each of the four Gospels in one of the major urban centers of early Christianity.

❦ Mark

Introduction and Baptism	*Chapters 1:1–13*
Ministry and Mighty Works	*1:14–9:41*
Parables of the Kingdom and Other Teachings	*4; 7; 8:27–10:31*
Conflict Stories	*2:5–3:30; 11:15–12:44*
Peter's Confession	*8:27–33*
Son of Man	*8:31; 9:9–13*
Transfiguration	*9:2–8*
Prophecies of Destruction	*13:1–37*
Last Supper	*14:12–31*
Passion	*14:32–16:8*

The Son of Man did not come to be served, but to serve, and to give up his life as a ransom for many.

Mark 10:45

At one time scholars believed that Mark, the first Gospel to be written, derived ultimately from the Apostle Peter. Eusebius, the fourth-century Church historian, reports—and also quotes Papias, bishop of Hierapolis (about 140 C.E.), as stating—that Mark's account of Jesus' life was based on Peter's Roman preaching. Like his mentor's oral teaching, however, which Papias described as "unsystematic," Mark's arrangement of events and of Jesus' sayings was "not in order." "I did not suppose," Papias observed, "that the things from the books would aid me so much as the things from the living and continuing voice" (*Ecclesiastical History* 3.39). Even though Papias reputedly learned the Christian *kerygma* ("proclamation") from former pupils of the "holy Apostles" themselves, dependence upon and reverence for the written records naturally increased when people who had known eyewitnesses of Jesus' ministry died out. In time the written records became Scripture, as authoritative and unchangeable as the Hebrew Bible.

Until recently, the testimony of Eusebius and Papias seemed a valid explanation of the apostolic sources underlying Mark's Gospel. Some scholars now believe, however, that a general oral tradition deriving from the Christian community provides its basis. *Form criticism* has been crucial in effecting this change in scholarly opinion. A method used to analyze and interpret ancient texts, form criticism attempts to isolate and define the characteristic structure and arrangement of a particular literary unit as well as to place it in a living context by discovering and delineating its social, cultural, political, or religious environment and the assumed purpose of its author(s).

Mark's Gospel is essentially anonymous. The author is not mentioned in the text; the superscription—"The Gospel According to Mark"—is a later Church embellishment, for second-century churchmen like Papias endeavored to associate extant writings about Jesus with apostles or their immediate disciples. Whether the author was the Mark or John Mark who was a companion of Paul (Philem. 24; Col. 4:10; Acts 12:12–25; 14:36–40) and Peter (1 Pet. 5:13) is not known. Irenaeus, another early churchman (about 130–200 C.E.), stated that the Gospel was composed in Rome after Peter and Paul had been martyred (about 64 C.E.).

Certainly Mark's Gospel seems well designed for Roman Christians. Emphasizing his mighty deeds, it presents Jesus as a heroic man of action, a charismatic leader who could cleanse lepers, heal the sick, exorcise demons, and raise the dead. Mark's unadorned narrative races swiftly—from his opening picture of John the Baptist, a wild desert ascetic proclaiming the imminent arrival of one "mightier" than he, to the awe-struck confession of the Roman soldier at the foot of the cross: "Truly this man was a son of God!" (Mark 15:39).

In form, Mark is probably an expansion of the early Christian confession of faith, bringing together the story of Jesus' suffering and death (the Passion) with recollections of his miracles, parables, and Galilean teaching. Although Mark seldom describes the situation from which Jesus' sayings emerged, his account is far more than a mere "string of pearls," a series of isolated deeds and pronouncements loosely strung together on a slim narrative thread. Despite the apparently fragmented chain of incidents he relates, Mark has carefully selected his material and artfully arranged it to illustrate his main concerns. The book can be divided into four parts: (1) a brief introduction promising "good news" (Mark 1:1–13); (2) an account of Jesus' ministry in and around Galilee (Mark 1:14–9:50); (3) a description of the journey south to Jerusalem (Mark 10); and (4) a report of Jesus' activities and martyrdom during Passover week in Jerusalem (Mark 11:1–16:8). The account of Jesus' last days is far more detailed than the reports about his earlier ministry.

Mark's Gospel places Jesus' mission in two distinct geographical settings. The first nine chapters present a relatively successful Galilean (or northern) ministry; the last six chapters focus on the southern experience in Jerusalem, where Jesus is rejected and killed. Both Matthew and Luke adopt Mark's north-south polarity, but John's Gospel ignores this geographical separation, showing Jesus active in or near Jerusalem for most of his public life.

Two themes dominate much of the narrative. The first, which scholars call the "Messianic Secret," is Mark's repeated insistence that Jesus forbade those who recognized his identity to speak of it. Again and again, both Jesus' intimate disciples and those whom he miraculously heals or cleanses or from whom he exorcises demons are charged not to reveal who he is (Mark 1:23–24, 34; 3:11–12; 8:30; 9:2–9). While some commentators have suggested that this "secret" was the writer's way of explaining why Jesus was not recognized as a divinely commissioned figure during his lifetime, others point out that Mark had a theological purpose in stressing the "hidden" quality of Jesus' messiahship. In Mark's Gospel Jesus does not disclose his true role because his understanding of the Messiah's function differs so radically from that of popular expectation. Instead of a Davidic warrior-king who would restore the Israelite nation, Mark's Jesus is a Messiah revealed only through suffering and death. To emphasize this view, the author links Peter's first recognition of Jesus' messiahship with the inevitability of Jesus' humiliating and painful execution (Mark 8:27–38; 9:30–32; 10:33–34). Jesus publicly acknowledges his identity only once—before the Sanhedrin, when his people's leaders contemptuously reject him (Mark 14:62). The only other occasion on which his divine nature is perceived is his death (Mark 15:39).

A second recurring motif is the strange obtuseness of Jesus' followers, who are represented as incapable of understanding almost anything their Master says or does. When Jesus stills a storm, the disciples are impressed but unaware of the act's significance (Mark 4:35–41). After his feeding of the multitudes, the disciples "had not understood the intent of the loaves" (Mark 6:52). After listening for months to Jesus' teaching, they are still ignorant of "what this 'rising from the dead' could mean" (Mark 9:9–10). They not only fail to comprehend the meaning of sharing in Jesus' glory (Mark 10:35–41), even the simplest, most obvious parables escape their understanding (Mark 4:10–13). As Jesus asks: "You do not understand this parable? How then will you understand any parable?" (Mark 4:13).

Even though Jesus has "explained everything" (Mark 4:33–34; see also Mark 8:31–32) and the disciples have presumably recognized him as the Messiah (Mark 8:27–32), they desert him after his arrest (Mark 14:50). Peter, who had earlier confessed Jesus to be the Messiah, three times denies knowing him (Mark 14:66–72). Almost the only character in Mark who perceives the meaning of Jesus' death is an unnamed

Roman centurion who affirms that "truly this man was a son of God!" (Mark 15:39).

Mark portrays Jesus' Palestinian followers as unaware and unappreciative and the Jewish religious establishment as composed of conniving hypocrites who scheme to murder the Son of God. Is this an attempt to minimize Christianity's dependence upon its Jewish antecedents? Is it an effort to disassociate international Christianity from Palestinian Christianity represented by Jesus' family and the Twelve? Some critics have argued that Mark was written in part to convince its Roman and Hellenistic audience that Christianity was not a troublesome or politically suspect Jewish sect and that its founder belonged to the greater world rather than to an exclusively Jewish milieu.

Introduction and Baptism   Like the writer of a classical epic, Mark plunges into the middle of the action. The opening line announces the epic theme—"the gospel of Jesus Christ the Son of God"—and he quotes from Isaiah 40:3 and Malachi 3:1 that a divinely appointed "herald" and a "voice crying aloud in the wilderness" are preparing a path for the Lord, thus linking what follows with familiar Old Testament expectations. He then abruptly introduces the fulfiller of these prophetic roles, John the Baptist, who opens the way for the Gospel's central character.

Without further reference to his hero's early life, except to state that he comes from the town of Nazareth in Galilee, Mark suddenly presents the adult Jesus at the River Jordan for baptism. Anointed with Holy Spirit, Jesus hears a heavenly voice pronounce him God's beloved son, after which he retreats to the desert to meditate and undergo Satanic temptation (unspecified in Mark but elucidated in Matthew and Luke) (Mark 1:1–13).

Ministry and Mighty Works   Jesus begins his campaign in Galilee after John's arrest by Herod Antipas, ruler of this district in northern Palestine, and his initial message is apocalyptic: "The time is fulfilled, and the kingdom of God is at hand" (Mark 1:15). Urging his hearers to repent and believe, he then begins to form an inner circle of disciples, calling Simon (Peter), his brother Andrew, and James and John (the "sons of Zebedee") to leave their fishing trade on the Sea of Galilee and become his followers (Mark 1:16–20).

Later he chooses another eight men to complete the Twelve, a number symbolic of the twelve tribes of Israel. These include Philip, Bartholomew, Matthew, Thomas, James (son of Alphaeus), Thaddeus, Simon the Canaanite, and Judas Iscariot (Mark 3:16–19). The fact that the names of the Twelve vary from Gospel to Gospel may reflect changes in the disciples' membership, though the significant number was retained, or it may be that some disciples were known by more than one name. Here, for example, Levi (Mark 2:14) may be the same as Matthew (see Matt. 9:9).

The first of twenty miracles that Mark attributes to Jesus occurs at the Capernaum synagogue. Expounding Scripture there, Jesus amazes his audience with the unexpected authority of his teaching and then astonishes them by performing his first exorcism, driving out the evil spirits that had possessed a man attending the synagogue. When the expelled demons acknowledge him as "Holy One of God," Jesus orders them to keep silent. Nonetheless, such incidents spread his fame throughout Galilee (Mark 1:21–28).

In the most famous of Mark's exorcism narratives, Jesus casts a "legion" of demons out of a Gadarene man, until then a social outcast who lived "among the tombs" and behaved so wildly that chains could not bind him. The homeless demons receive Jesus' permission to enter a herd of 2,000 swine, which promptly run berserk and plunge into the sea (Mark 5:1–20).

A more poignant tale of possession concerns a Syro-Pheonician woman who begs Jesus to cast a devil out of her daughter. At first Jesus refuses, observing that his duty is to his own countrymen, the Israelites; he cannot waste their "bread" on "dogs" (a common synonym for non-Jews). When the quick-witted woman points out that even dogs are allowed crumbs that fall from the table, Jesus grants her request and the devil departs from her child (Mark 7:24–30). To Mark, Jesus' ability to defeat demonic powers (Mark 1:32–34, 39; 3:11, 22; 9:14–29) is proof that the Messiah's victory over Satan's kingdom is assured.

Mark also emphasizes Jesus' spectacular success in mitigating the physical evils that afflict humankind. He cures Peter's mother-in-law of a fever (Mark 1:30–31), cleanses a leper (Mark 1:40–45), causes a paralytic to walk (Mark 2:1–12), heals a man's withered hand (Mark 3:1–5), restores sight to the blind (Mark 8:22–26; 10:46–52), causes the deaf to hear and the dumb to speak (Mark 7:31–37), and even raises a little girl from the dead (Mark 5:22–24, 35–43). The mere touch of his garment cures a woman who had been suffering a hemorrhage for twelve years (Mark 5:25–34).

In the last case Jesus specifically states that it is the woman's faith that made her well, a remark he repeats to the blind beggar whose sight he has restored (Mark 10:52). Mark recognizes that in order to be healed, recipients of Jesus' good works had to have faith. In Jesus' home territory, where family and neighbors—familiar with the carpenter's background— fail to see him as a worker of wonders, he is a prophet without honor. Marveling at their lack of faith, Jesus can "work no miracle there" except for healing a few sick people (Mark 6:4–6).

Jesus' command over nature, however, is unequivocal. When a storm threatens to capsize a boat in which he and his disciples are crossing the Sea of Galilee, he orders the wind and waves to cease (Mark 4:35–41); even more remarkable is the account of Jesus walking on water (Mark 6:45–52). Two other incidents—perhaps two versions of the same tradition—involve Jesus' multiplying a few loaves and fish to feed large crowds of people. In the first story, 5,000 are fed (Mark 6:30–44); in the second, 4,000 (Mark 8:1–10); in both cases the disciples gather numerous basketsful of leftover food. These accounts illustrate the "messianic banquet" theme—that of the chosen people enjoying feasts of abundance in the coming kingdom—as well as Jesus' compassion for those who go without food or drink in order to listen to his teachings.

Parables of the Kingdom and Other Teachings   Emphasizing Jesus' deeds rather than his teachings, Mark nevertheless includes eight parables. In the parable of sewing new patches on old garments or putting new wine in old wineskins, Jesus shows that his innovative new concepts cannot be fitted into the old traditions (Mark 2:21–22). In the parable of the sower, proclaiming Jesus' message is likened to planting seed; just as some seeds die, grow sparsely, or flourish according to the kind of soil on which they fall, so does Jesus' word find varying degrees of success according to the receptivity and goodwill of his hearers (Mark 4:3–20).

Both the parable of the growing seed (Mark 4:26–29), which is found in Mark alone, and the parable of the mustard seed (Mark 4:30–32) appear to stress the mysterious evolution of the Kingdom rather than to explain its nature or form. Because Jesus nowhere defines what he means by the Kingdom, experts have long debated whether it is a spiritual state that develops subjectively in the believer or an external rule imposed supernaturally from above.

The Synoptics repeatedly indicate that Jesus' followers regarded the Kingdom as an imminent apocalyptic event, and Mark asserts that Jesus himself held such an eschatological view. According to Mark 9:1, Jesus promises his hearers that "some of those standing here . . . will not taste death before they have seen the kingdom of God already come in power." In the apocalyptic prophecy of his return, he is also quoted as saying that "the present generation will live to see it all" (Mark 13:30). In short, Mark views Jesus as presenting a divinely appointed government that will forcibly manifest itself during the lifetime of his original followers.

Mark's last two parables similarly concern Jesus' return to earth (Parousia) to establish a theocratic rule. In the parable of the budding fig tree, the faithful are to look for signs heralding the Second Coming (Mark 13:28–29); in that of the watchful servants, the return is unexpected (Mark 13:34–37). In both, however, the Kingdom seems to be an external event.

Whereas the Old Testament Law had viewed material prosperity as Yahweh's blessing on an obedient Israel, Jesus seems to regard riches as an impediment to entering the Kingdom. To emphasize the difficulty of reconciling wealth with spiritual progress, he compares the rich young man who wants to gain eternal life with a camel getting through the eye of a needle (Mark 10:25), adding that those who forsake worldly goods for his sake will be amply rewarded "in this age" and "in the age to come [receive] eternal life" (Mark 10:26–31).

In contrast is the story in which a poor widow merits Jesus' approval by giving all she has to the temple treasury (Mark 12:41–44), unlike the wealthy who give larger sums out of their abundance. Jesus' respect for the weak and ineffectual is also well illustrated in his insistence that small children be allowed to approach him closely, "for the kingdom of God belongs to such as these" (Mark 10:14–15).

Consistently arguing that seeking the Kingdom entails persecution and loss, Jesus states paradoxically that whoever tries to remain safe is lost, while whoever gives his life for Jesus' message is safe (Mark 8:34–35): "What does a man gain by winning the whole world at the cost of his true self? What can he give to buy that self back?" (Mark 8:36–37). He repeats that the "first" among his followers must be their servant (Mark 10:42–45). Stressing his humility, Mark presents Jesus as setting an example of service and self-sacrifice that is the model for all believers.

Conflict Stories   Mark devotes considerable space to recounting Jesus' controversies with four hostile groups: (1) Pharisees, who object to his apparently cavalier attitude toward the Mosaic law; (2) scribes, the preservers and copyists of the law, who resent his "unauthorized" claims to reinterpret the Mosaic tradition; (3) Sadducees, the priestly aristocracy, who view him as disrupting their tenuous armistice with Rome; and (4) Herodians, who believe that he undermines the rulership of Herod Antipas. Although these groups normally oppose one another, here they unite to attack Jesus as a threat both to the purity of their religion and the security of the Jewish nation.

From the outset of his Galilean ministry Jesus is shown alienating the Pharisees and scribes, who variously accuse him of blasphemy in daring to forgive sins (Mark 2:5), associating with "tax collectors and sinners" (Mark 2:15–17), violating Sabbath laws (Mark 2:23–28; 3:1–6), using Satan's power to cast out devils (Mark 3:22–27), and profaning tradition by neglecting to wash ritually before a meal (Mark 7:1–8). Most of these narratives end with Jesus pronouncing a new teaching, such as those regarding clean and unclean foods or Sabbath observances or revising Mosaic divorce laws (Mark 10:2–12).

During a few brief days in Jerusalem, however, Jesus arouses the active hostility of almost every religious party and institution in official Judaism. His bold "cleansing of the Temple" (Mark 11:15–19)—overturning the moneychangers' tables and disrupting the sale of sacrificial animals—is seen as a dangerous attack on the priestly administration of the temple worship, and it is this act that probably seals his fate with the chief priests and Sadducees.

The next day he returns to the temple's precincts to confront a delegation of scribes, elders, and chief priests who demand to know by what authority he has behaved so violently. Jesus eludes their trap when, fearing the crowd's response, his opponents refuse to answer his question about John the Baptist (Mark 11:27–33). Pursuing this advantage, Jesus delivers a parable about some wicked tenants who murder their landlord's son—an allegory clearly aimed at his critics who are then conspiring to kill him (Mark 12:1–12).

Yet another group—some Pharisees and Herodians—approaches Jesus to trap him on the politically sensitive issue of paying taxes to Rome. Again, Jesus skillfully evades their trap by declaring that one pays Caesar money but gives God "what is due to God" (Mark 12:13–17). Although this pronouncement stresses one's primary allegiance to the deity, it permits Jesus' followers to be obedient tax-paying citizens of the empire.

When the Sadducees attempt to expose Jesus' position on a future life as logically absurd, Jesus points out that even a woman widowed seven times will have no problem in the afterworld because those resurrected are no longer confined to sexual identities but are "like angels in heaven" (Mark 12:18–25). Citing the Torah, the only part of the Hebrew Bible that the Sadducees accept, he quotes Yahweh's words to Moses at the burning bush—that he is the god of Abraham, Isaac, and Jacob (Exod. 3:6)—arguing that since Yahweh is "not God of the dead but of the living," the ancient patriarchs must still be alive from the deity's viewpoint (Mark 12:26–27).

Attracted by this clever refutation of the Sadducees, a "lawyer" asks Jesus to name the most important commandment. Told that love of God (Deut. 6:4) and love of neighbor (Lev. 19:19) are paramount, the lawyer commends Jesus' religious perception, and Jesus responds courteously that the lawyer is "not far from the kingdom of God" (Mark 12:28–34). This incident is revealing because it shows that Jesus dealt on equal terms with a professional interpreter of the law with whose insights he agreed and that not all his encounters with members of the Jerusalem hierarchy were antagonistic. Undoubtedly Jesus found many people who shared his approach to scriptural teaching, but the Gospel writers apparently neglected these friendly encounters to emphasize the controversies that led to his arrest and execution (Mark 14:1–2, 10–11).

Peter's Confession   Although Mark stresses the disciples' blindness in failing to perceive Jesus' real identity, he follows the tradition that Peter eventually recognized him as the Messiah. After charging the Twelve to reveal this secret to no one, Jesus teaches the disciples that he is destined to be rejected by official Judaism, killed, and after three days raised from the dead (Mark 8:27–33). Twice more, in Galilee and on the road to Jerusalem, Jesus predicts his imminent suffering and resurrection (Mark 9:31; 10:32–34), Mark thus emphasizing that Jesus foresaw what would happen to him and accepted it as the divine will.

Son of Man   Although Jesus does not publicly proclaim himself the Messiah—a heroic figure which both scriptural and popular tradition held to be a Davidic warrior-king who would restore Israel's political power and totally vanquish her enemies—he frequently speaks of himself as "the Son of Man." This phrase derives from the Old Testament, where it is given two general usages, neither of them messianic. In the Book of Ezekiel, where the prophet commonly pictures Yahweh addressing him as "son of man," the phrase seems to be no more than a pronoun substitute and without mystical significance. In other Old Testament books the phrase appears as a synonym for "mortal" or "human being" (see Ps. 8:4). The author of Daniel employs the term when he describes "one like a son of man" approaching the heavenly throne to receive universal dominion (Dan. 7:'13). This concept of the "Son of Man" as a divinely appointed ruler also occurs in the book of 1 Enoch (chs. 37–71), a work known to the early Christians and quoted in the Epistle of Jude.

In Mark's Gospel, "Son of Man" sometimes refers to Jesus as an earthly authority (Mark 2:10; 2:28). Jesus also applies the designation to himself when speaking of his predestined suffering (Mark 8:31; 9:9–13; 10:33–34, 45; 14:21, 41). In addition, Jesus seems sometimes to suggest that "Son of Man" is a person other than himself, a supernatural figure who will descend from heaven to establish the new world order (Mark 8:38; 13:26; 14:62). The phrase seldom appears outside the Gospels and always in a context in which Jesus is the speaker, but the exact significance of Jesus' usage is still widely debated.

Transfiguration Before departing for Jerusalem, three select disciples—Peter, James, and John—accompany Jesus to a secluded mountaintop where he amazes them by undergoing an awesome metamorphosis: "His clothes became dazzlingly white, with a whiteness no bleacher on earth could equal," and the figures of Moses and Elijah appear to talk with him. Characteristically obtuse, Peter breaks into Jesus' communion with these biblical archetypes, after which a cloud overshadows the group and a heavenly voice declares: "This is my Son, my Beloved, listen to Him." This incident emphasizes Jesus' fulfillment of, and superiority to, the Old Testament Law and Prophets. It also contrasts markedly with Jesus' injunction to the disciples not to speak of what they had seen until after the resurrection (Mark 9:2–9). His messiahship is not to be manifested except in his foreordained suffering and triumph over death.

Prophecies of Destruction In chapter 11 an unidentified crowd enthusiastically welcomes Jesus to Jerusalem (Palm Sunday). The public claim that he arrives "in the name of the Lord" to establish "the coming kingdom of our father David" (Mark 11:9–10) gives his entry a messianic significance, if not revolutionary overtones. Hence those who fear Jesus as a threat to the status quo have their suspicions confirmed (Mark 11:1–10).

After cleansing the temple, Jesus predicts that the sanctuary is doomed to destruction. When his disciples ask what signs will precede this calamity, Jesus foretells a series of false prophets, wars, earthquakes, famines, persecutions of the faithful, the appearance of an "abomination of desolation," celestial disorders, and an unendurable tribulation (Mark 13:1–23). The mysterious "Son of Man coming in the clouds with great power and glory" (Mark 13:24–27), who is not explicitly identified with the returned Messiah, will then dispatch angels to gather the faithful from all parts of the earth. Jesus warns that all these wonders will occur in the lifetime of his hearers, although no one knows the precise day or hour (Mark 13:28–32). The sense of urgency Mark imparts in these passages may have been stimulated by the Jewish revolt against Rome (66–70 C.E.), an event that might also have moved Mark to publish his Gospel.

Last Supper Jesus temporarily suspends his public ministry to observe the Passover and feast of unleavened bread with his twelve disciples, a celebration that solemnly recalls the Jews' last night in Egypt when the Angel of Death "passed over" their homes to slay the Egyptian firstborn (Exod. 11:1–13:16). While they dine together in an "upper room," Jesus announces that one of the Twelve will soon betray him (though in Mark he does not specify which, the reader has already been told in 14:10–11). Jesus then gives the customary bread and wine a new significance. The wine symbolizes his "blood of the [New] Covenant, shed for many" (Mark 14:24), a foreshadowing of the crucifixion. He thus introduces the "new dispensation" under which his followers are to live. Christians also interpret this occasion as the origin of the Eucharist, or Holy Communion.

Passion Following their ritual meal, Jesus and the Eleven retire to a garden or vineyard called Gethsemane. While Jesus prays to be spared the coming ordeal and his disciples sleep, an armed mob "sent by the chief priests, lawyers, and elders" appears to arrest him. Identified to the crowd by Judas' kiss, Jesus is conveyed to the high priest, around whom various religious leaders are assembled (Mark 14:28–15:1). In Mark it is not clear whether this impromptu hearing takes place at the high priest's house or at the Sanhedrin, but "false witnesses" are present to accuse Jesus of threatening to destroy the temple.

When Jesus refuses to answer the charges, the high priest asks him if he is "the Messiah, the Son of the Blessed One" (Mark 14:62). Jesus not only affirms that he is—the only occasion in Mark on which he specifically makes this claim—but proclaims that those present will witness "the Son of Man seated at the right hand of God and coming with the clouds of Heaven" (Mark 14:62). Although he does not identify himself as the "Son of Man," his reply outrages the council, which demands his death (Mark 14:63–64). As Jesus is being beaten and reviled, Peter fulfills his leader's prediction by denying him three times (Mark 14:66–72).

At daybreak Friday the "whole council held a consultation" (Mark 15:1; Revised Standard Version)—perhaps implying that the night meeting had been illegal and therefore lacked the authority to condemn Jesus—and sends the accused to Pontius Pilate, the Roman prefect or procurator who was in Jerusalem to maintain order during Passover week. Uninterested in Jesus' orthodoxy or in accusations of a religious nature, Pilate asks Jesus whether he claims to be king of the Jews—a threat to Roman rulership. Jesus replies that Pilate himself has indicated this and declines to respond to any other charges the chief priests level against him (Mark 15:1–5).

Consistent with his purpose of demonstrating that Jesus was innocent of plotting against Roman authority, Mark depicts Pilate as extremely reluctant to condemn him and places all blame on the Jewish hierarchy. To spare Jesus' life, Pilate attempts to observe the custom of releasing a condemned prisoner on Passover (a practice never mentioned in any secular history), but the mob demands that Barabbas, a convicted revolutionary, be freed instead. According to Mark, Pilate is forced to deliver Barabbas and send Jesus to be crucified (Mark 15:6–15).

Stripped, flogged, mocked, and crowned with thorns, Jesus is too weak to carry the crossbeam of his cross, so the Roman soldiers impress a bystander, Simon of Cyrene, to carry it for him (Mark 15:16–21). Taken to Golgotha ("Place of the Skull") outside Jerusalem, Jesus is crucified between two thieves. According to Pilate's order, his cross bears a statement of the political crime for which he is executed: aspiring to be king of the Jews (Mark 15:22–32).

Mark's narrative includes many details that must have belonged to the original oral form of the Passion story. The Roman soldiers cast lots for Jesus' clothes, passersby taunt him, an unnatural darkness covers the "whole land," Jesus begins to recite Psalm 22 (which opens with the lament "My God, my God, why hast thou forsaken me?"), someone offers him a sponge soaked "in sour wine" and speculates that Elijah "will come to take him down." At this point Jesus utters "a loud cry" and dies. The Roman centurion, impressed at Jesus' demeanor, calls him "a son of God," while the "curtain of the Temple" is rent in two (Mark 15:25–39).

According to Mark, no disciples attend Jesus' last hours. Only a group of women "watching from a distance" are present; these include Mary Magdalene; Mary, mother of James the younger; Salome, and other of Jesus' women followers from Galilee and Jerusalem (Mark 15:40–41). It is not one of the Twelve but Joseph of Arimathea, "a respected member of the Council," who asks Pilate for Jesus' body. Surprised that Jesus is already dead, Pilate grants the request. Joseph, who had "looked forward to the kingdom of God," removes the corpse, wraps it in "a linen sheet," and places it in a rock-hewn tomb, sealed by rolling a stone against the sepulcher door (Mark 15:42–47).

Mark reports that, after the Sabbath, the two Marys and Salome visit the tomb to prepare the body properly but find the stone rolled away and the crypt empty. An unidentified youth "wearing a white robe" informs them that Jesus has "been raised again" (Mark 16) and instructs them to tell the disciples that Jesus will appear to them in Galilee. Frightened by this turn of events, the women flee the tomb (Mark 16:1–8).

At this point Mark's Gospel ends as abruptly as it began. Some manuscripts dating from the fifth century and later include an additional twelve verses; other versions add only a few supplementary lines. Many scholars argue that Mark originally ended his account at the empty tomb. This thesis is supported by the fact that after this point in the narrative, Matthew and Luke—who follow Mark's order closely until now—present divergent traditions of Jesus' postresurrection appearances, which are entirely absent from Mark.

RECOMMENDED READING

Beach, Curtis. *The Gospel of Mark.* Harper & Row, 1959.

Best, Ernest. *The Temptation and the Passion in Mark.* Cambridge, England: Cambridge University Press, 1965.

Hartman, Lars. *Prophecy Reinterpreted: The Formation of Some Jewish Apocalyptic Texts and of the Eschatological Discourse, Mark 13 and Par.* Translated by N. Tomkinson. Lund, Sweden: CWK Gleerup, 1966. A detailed study of Jewish apocalyptic traditions embodied in Mark's prediction of the Parousia.

Kee, H. C. *Community of the New Age: Studies in Mark's Gospel.* Philadelphia: Westminster Press, 1976. A recommended historical-critical analysis of Mark's Gospel.

Kelber, Werner H. *Mark's Story of Jesus.* Philadelphia: Fortress Press, 1979.

Kingsbury, Jack Dean. *The Christology of Mark's Gospel.* Philadelphia: Fortress Press, 1983.

Lightfoot, R. M. *The Gospel Message of Mark.* Oxford: Clarendon Press, 1952.

Maloney, Elliott C. *Semitic Interference in Markan Syntax.* Chico, Calif.: Scholars Press, 1981. A scholarly examination of how Aramaic influences underlie the Greek of Mark's Gospel.

Marxsen, Willi. *Mark the Evangelist.* Translated by R. A. Harrisville. New York: Abingdon Press, 1969.

Nineham, D. E. *The Gospel of Mark.* Baltimore: Penguin, 1964.

Rhoads, David, and Michie, Donald. *Mark as Story: An Introduction to the Narrative of a Gospel.* Philadelphia: Fortress Press, 1982.

Robinson, J. M. *The Problem of History in Mark and Other Markan Studies.* Philadelphia: Fortress Press, 1982.

Slusser, D. M., and Slusser, G. H. *The Jesus of Mark's Gospel.* Philadelphia: Westminster Press, 1967.

Tuckett, Christopher, ed. *The Messianic Secret.* Philadelphia: Fortress Press, 1983.

Weeden: Theodore J. *Mark: Traditions in Conflict.* Philadelphia: Fortress Press, 1979.

❦ Luke

But [Jesus] said, "In the world kings lord it over their subjects; and those in authority are called 'Benefactors.' Not so with you: on the contrary, the highest among you must bear himself like the youngest, the chief of you like a servant. . . . Yet here I am among you like a servant."

Luke 22:25–27

The Gospel of Luke is the first part of Luke-Acts, a two-volume work that records the origin of Christianity and its expansion from Jerusalem to Rome. A second-century tradition that attributes both books to Paul's traveling companion, the "beloved physician" referred to in Colossians 4:14, plus the "we" passages in Acts, in which the writer seems to be an eyewitness of the events he describes, make a viable case for Luke's authorship. Although not all scholars are convinced of this, most commentators find it convenient to speak of him as Luke.

Five factors reveal something about the Gospel's approximate date of composition: (1) Luke uses about 50 percent of Mark's Gospel. (2) Certain passages imply that Jesus' prophecy of Jerusalem's destruction had already been fulfilled (Luke 19:41–44; 21:20–24). (3) Luke seems as unaware of Matthew's existence as Matthew was of his. (4) Acts, written sometime after the Gospel, was completed before the end of the first century. (5) Luke never refers to Paul's collected letters, which circulated among many churches by about 95 C.E. These factors suggest that Luke may have been written around 85–90 C.E. Although Alexandria, Rome, Ephesus, Caesarea, and Antioch have been proposed as its place of origin, no one theory has been widely accepted.

Besides drawing on Mark, whose chronology he generally follows, Luke includes many sayings and teachings of Jesus that appear in Matthew but are absent from Mark. Scholars believe that this shared material was taken from the Q document. In addition, Luke draws on private sources (L), both written and oral, and it is the L source, unique to Luke's Gospel, that gives the book its distinctive quality. Luke alone includes the parables of the good Samaritan, the prodigal son, the rich man and Lazarus, the rich fool, and the Pharisee and publican. Among the best-loved stories in the New Testament, these parables reflect Luke's characteristic preoccupation with human relations and social ethics. His suspicion of the rich, concern for the poor, sympathy for women and other oppressed groups give the L passages a particularly tender ambience.

After a formal introduction (Luke 1:1–4), the Gospel falls into five main divisions: (1) Jesus' birth and boyhood (Luke 1:5–2:52); (2) Jesus' baptism and temptation (Luke 3:1–4:13); (3) Jesus' ministry in Galilee (Luke 4:14–9:50); (4) Jesus' teachings during the prolonged journey to Jerusalem (Luke 9:51–19:27); and (5) Jesus' Jerusalem conflicts, arrest, trials, crucifixion, and resurrection (Luke 19:28–24:53).

Formal Introduction   The only Gospel writer to include a formal preface, Luke states that because "many" have already compiled Gospel accounts, he wishes to "write a connected narrative" so that his readers will receive "authentic knowledge" about what they have already been taught (Luke 1:1–4). Although both Luke and Acts are addressed to Theophilus, perhaps a Roman official, the two books are clearly directed at the entire Greco-Roman world, to which Christianity then appeared as a strange and unlawful religion.

Using a more polished literary style than earlier Gospel writers, the author strives to depict Christianity's universal appeal and indirectly to defend its founder and followers from charges of sedition. Hence he emphasizes aspects of the new faith that would attract Hellenistic converts and minimize peculiarly Jewish elements in Jesus' message. Although Luke cites some Old Testament prophecies, particularly in the birth narrative, from the outset he stresses that Jesus' life means "good news" to "all people" (Luke 2:10, Revised Standard Version; see also 3:5–9; 13:29; 24:47). In Luke's view, Christianity is destined from its inception to be an international faith.

Birth Narratives and Genealogy   The following summary is largely confined to what is unique in Luke's Gospel. Only Luke tells of the aged priest Zechariah and his barren wife Elisabeth, who become the parents of John the Baptist, forerunner of Jesus (Luke 1:5–25; 39–45; 57–80). It is also Luke who presents the Christmas story, beginning with the angel Gabriel's announcement to Mary that she will bear a son conceived by the Holy Spirit (Luke 1:26–38). In Latin translation, Gabriel's salutation to Mary becomes the Ave Maria, one of Christendom's most celebrated prayers. Mary's praise of the deity's graciousness—the Magnificat (Luke 1:46–55)—is typical of the formal set pieces, apparently drawn from primitive Christian liturgies, that Luke incorporates into his Gospel. This prayer is modeled on Hannah's song in 2 Samuel (2:1–10), in which a previously barren woman rejoices in conceiving a son.

Luke's depiction of Jesus' birth in a stable in the Davidic city of Bethlehem (Luke 2:1–40) differs from Matthew's account (Matt. 2:13–23) in several respects. Luke substitutes a visit from Judean shepherds for that of "wise men" from the East; he also omits any reference to Herod's attempt to kill the child. Jesus' presentation at the Jerusalem temple a month after his circumcision is the occasion for Simeon's prophecy that the babe will be "a revelation to the heathen" (the Nunc Dimittis hymn [Luke 2:29–32]), which stresses Luke's theme that Christianity is a religion for non-Jewish peoples.

Recounting the only incident of Jesus' boyhood preserved in the New Testament, the author concludes his version of Jesus' early life with an account of the twelve-year-old boy's visit to the temple, where he impresses some learned scribes with the acuteness of his questions and understanding (Luke 2:41–52). The statement that he "advanced in wisdom and in favor with God and men" (Luke 2:52) almost exactly reproduces the Old Testament description of young Samuel (1 Sam. 2:26) and is probably a conventional observation rather than a historically precise evaluation of Jesus' youthful character.

Miracles and Parables   Luke emphasizes both the activity of the Holy Spirit and Jesus' miraculous powers. Of the twenty miracles he relates, four appear in his Gospel alone: the cleansing of ten lepers (Luke 17:11–19), healing a man with dropsy (Luke 14:1–6), curing a crippled woman (Luke 13:10–17), and raising a widow's dead son (Luke 7:11–17).

In addition, more than a dozen of Jesus' most memorable parables are found in Luke alone. These include the good Samaritan (Luke 10:25–37), in which the moral hero is a man whose race and religion were despised by orthodox Jews; the rich fool (Luke 12:16–21), who devotes his life to acquiring material possessions only to die before he can enjoy them; the prodigal son (Luke 15:11–32), which emphasizes God's forgiveness of repentant wrongdoers; Lazarus and the rich man (Luke 16:19–31), which contains the only depiction in the Synoptics of rewards and punishments in the afterlife and which stresses the coming reversal of positions between the world's rich and poor; the persistent widow and the unjust judge (Luke 18:1–8), which concerns God's responsiveness to persistent prayer; and the Pharisee and the publican (tax collector) (Luke 18:9–14), which teaches that the humility of an honest sinner is more acceptable to God than the virtue of the self-righteous.

Role of Women   Luke's sympathy for women is manifest in the attention he devotes to them. He alone records the parables of the persistent widow and the woman's lost coin (Luke 18:1–8; 15:8–10), as well as conversations between Mary and her cousin Elisabeth (Luke 1:29–56); the words of the old prophetess Anna (Luke 2:36–38), the widow whose child Jesus resurrected (Luke 7:11–17), and the various women of Galilee with whom

Jesus associates. Jesus' forgiveness of a weeping prostitute who washes his feet with her tears and dries them with her hair shocks his male companions (Luke 7:36–50). On behalf of the repentant woman, he then recounts the parable of the two debtors, declaring that the more a sinner is absolved the more he or she can love.

Luke states that some of Jesus' most faithful disciples were women, several wealthy enough to help support his ministry (Luke 8:1–3). Mary Magdalene (from the suburb of Magdala), from whom Jesus drove seven devils, and Joanna, whose husband is a steward to Herod Antipas, are present at the crucifixion and are also among the women who find Jesus' tomb empty (Luke 23:55–24:12). The sisters Mary and Martha, whose attentions to him Jesus uses to teach a lesson in spiritual values (Luke 10:38–42), number among his close friends.

Trials and Crucifixion Although adhering closely to Mark's Passion narrative, Luke introduces one significant variation: when Pilate learns that Jesus is a Galilean and therefore under the jurisdiction of Herod Antipas, he sends his prisoner to Herod who is in Jerusalem for the Passover. At first pleased with the opportunity of persuading Jesus to perform a miracle, Herod loses interest when the accused refuses to cooperate. Contemptuously outfitting Jesus "in a gorgeous robe" (dress befitting a King), Herod returns him to Pilate's custody (Luke 23:6–12).

Luke's purpose here is to show that Herod finds Jesus guilty of nothing treasonous, which Pilate himself confirms (Luke 23:14–15). Pursuing the theme further, Luke contrasts Jesus, who has committed no crime, with Barabbas—a political rebel guilty of insurrection and murder—who is given freedom in Jesus' place (Luke 23:19, 25). Throughout his narration of the trials, Luke consistently emphasizes that Jesus has perpetrated no illegal act against Rome.

To the crucifixion account Luke makes two important contributions. The first is Jesus' request that his god forgive those who crucify him (Luke 23:34). This statement, which is not found in the earliest Lucan manuscripts, harmonizes with Jesus' known position on forgiving one's enemies, though it is not clear in the text whether he refers to the Jews who accuse him or the Romans who execute him. In the second addition, a thief crucified next to Jesus echoes Herod's and Pilate's judgment that Jesus "has done nothing wrong." When he asks Jesus to remember him in the Kingdom, Jesus answers, "Today you shall be with me in Paradise" (Luke 23:40–43).

Resurrection Appearances In writing of the resurrection, Luke departs from both Mark and Matthew, he alone telling of Jesus' appearance to two disciples walking on the road to Emmaus, a village near Jerusalem. Although the two men do not recognize him, they converse with him about the significance of the crucifixion. Only after Jesus has broken bread with them are their eyes opened to his true identity, at which point he vanishes (Luke 24:13–35).

In a variation on John's later account of Jesus' presenting his physical body to quell the doubts of Thomas, Luke reports Jesus suddenly appearing amid the Eleven, instructing them to touch him physically and partaking of food to prove that he is not a spirit (Luke 24:36–43). Luke also records Jesus' missionary command to carry his message from Jerusalem "to all nations," thus giving a final emphasis to his theme that Christianity is a universal religion. Some ancient manuscripts add that Jesus then departs "and was carried up into heaven," but most modern translations omit the phrase. The only explicit account of Jesus' ascension is given in Acts 1:9–10 by the same author.

RECOMMENDED READING

Barnett, C. K. *Luke the Historian in Recent Study.* London: Epworth Press, 1961. A survey of research on Luke-Acts.

Cadbury, H. J. *The Making of Luke-Acts.* New York: Macmillan, 1927. A major work on the literary and historical background.

Conzelmann, Hans. *Theology of St. Luke.* Translated by Geoffrey Buswell. New York: Harper & Row, 1960. An incisive treatment of Luke's theological purposes.

Ellis, E. E. *The Gospel of Luke.* London and Camden, N. J.: Thomas Nelson and Sons, 1966.

Fitzmyer, J. A., ed. *The Gospel According to Luke*, vol. I, Anchor Bible. Garden City, N. Y.: Doubleday, 1981.

Flender, H. St. Luke: *Theologian of Redemptive History.* Philadelphia: Fortress Press, 1961.

Gilmour, S. M. "The Gospel According to St. Luke, Introduction and Exegesis." In *The Interpreter's Bible*, vol. 8, pp. 3–434. New York and Nashville: Abingdon Press, 1951. A good introduction.

Leaney, A. R. C. *The Gospel According to St. Luke.* New York: Harper & Row, 1958.

Rivkin, Ellis. *What Crucified Jesus?* Nashville: Abingdon Press, 1984. Explores the political and social forces in Galilee and Judea that converged to execute Jesus.

Schmidt, D. "Luke's Innocent Jesus." In *Political Issues in Luke-Acts*, edited by Richard J. Cassidy and Philip J. Scharper. Maryknoll, N. Y.: Orbis, 1983.

Stuhlmueller, Carroll. "The Gospel According to Luke." In *The Jerome Biblical Commentary*, edited by J. A. Fitzmyer and R. W. Brown, vol. 2, pp. 115–64. Englewood Cliffs, N. J.: Prentice-Hall, 1968. An authoritative study.

Tiede, David L. *Prophecy and History in Luke-Acts.* Philadelphia: Fortress Press, 1980.

🌱 John

This is eternal life: to know thee who alone art truly God, and Jesus Christ whom thou has sent.

John 17:3

The Church early acknowledged the striking differences between the Gospel of John and the Synoptics. About 200 C.E. Clement of Alexandria noted that while the other Evangelists preserved the "facts of history," John wrote "a spiritual Gospel." The author of the Fourth Gospel is less interested in presenting mundane facts about the historical Jesus than he is in illuminating the theological significance of Jesus' biography. "These [signs] here written," he states, "have been recorded in order that you may hold the faith that Jesus is the Christ, the Son of God, and that through this faith you may possess life by his name" (John 20:31). Though the other Gospels were also written to inspire faith, here the emphasis on creating belief is paramount.

Before the end of the second century C.E. the Church had almost unanimously ascribed the Fourth Gospel to John, son of Zebedee, one of the twelve apostles. He was the disciple "whom [Jesus] loved" (John 13:23; 19:26), who had presumably escaped the early martyrdom of his brother James (executed by Herod Agrippa I between 41 and 44 C.E.) and attained a ripe old age in Ephesus, where he wrote the Gospel, three letters bearing his name, and the Book of Revelation.

Scholars dissatisfied by these traditions of authorship, however, believe it likely that John suffered the same fate as his brother at about the same time, as Jesus had foretold he would (Mark 10:39; Acts 12:1–2). If so, he could not have written the Fourth Gospel, which was composed at least two generations later. Some have suggested that the author was John the Elder, a prominent Church leader in Ephesus about 100 C.E. and mentioned by Papias. But there is no scholarly consensus on the matter; and since the Gospel text nowhere names its author, most commentators regard the work as anonymous.

During this century, papyrus fragments containing a few verses of John and dating from about 140–150 C.E. were found in Egypt. The oldest New Testament writing thus far discovered, the fragments indicate that the Gospel circulated abroad during the first half of the second century but was probably composed about 90–100 C.E. Ephesus remains the popular scholarly choice for place of origin.

After a prologue (John 1:1–18), the Gospel's central section can be divided into two parts. The first part (John 1:19–12:50) opens with an account of John the Baptist and closes with Jesus' revelation of himself as the light of the world. The second part (John 13:1–20:31) begins with John's version of the Last Supper and ends with Thomas' recognition of the resurrected Jesus as "Lord" and a summary of the author's intent. The epilogue (John 21) is thought to have been added by a later hand.

Relation to the Synoptics   Because of the book's thematic unity and the innovative way in which his creative imagination transforms the older Gospel traditions, it is difficult to ascertain John's sources. He was evidently familiar with Mark, whose distinctive style he occasionally echoes (cf. John 6:7 and Mark 6:37; John 12:3, 5 and Mark 14:3, 5). He may also have consulted Luke's Gospel; this is indicated by his stories of Mary and Martha, by his parallels to Luke's Passion narrative, and by his placing Jesus' first resurrection appearances to the disciples in Jerusalem instead of in Galilee.

Even so, John omits about 90 percent of the Synoptics' material and modifies the Synoptic order of events in several important respects.

1. Although the Synoptics agree that Jesus began his mission after the imprisonment of John the Baptist, John states that their ministries overlapped (John 3:23–4:3).

2. The Synoptics mention only one Passover and imply that Jesus' ministry lasted only a year; John refers to three Passovers (John 2:13; 6:4; 11:55), thus giving the ministry a duration of three to nearly four years.

3. Unlike the Synoptics, which present the Last Supper as a Passover meal, John states that it occurred the evening before Passover and that the crucifixion took place on Nisan 14, the day of preparation, when the paschal lambs were being sacrificed (John 13:1, 29; 18:28; 19:14). Many scholars believe John's chronology to be the more accurate, for it is improbable that the arrest, trial, and crucifixion occurred during Nisan 15, the most sacred time of the Passover celebration.

4. Whereas the Synoptics place the cleansing of the temple at the end of Jesus' ministry, John sets it at the beginning (John 2:13–21).

5. The Synoptics show Jesus working mainly in Galilee and coming to Judea only during his last days; John places much of his ministry in and around Jerusalem.

Besides modifying the chronology and geographical location of Jesus' ministry, John also radically changes the form and content of Jesus' teaching. Whereas the Synoptic Gospels assert that Jesus never spoke publicly "without a parable" (Matt. 13:34; Mark 4:34), the fourth Gospel omits all parables, replacing them with long philosophical discourses using highly symbolic language. Instead of the Synoptic use of brief similes and axiomatic statements rooted in the concrete experiences of daily life, John employs unexpectedly abstract, metaphysical speeches to convey Jesus' message. In addition, John shifts the focus of Jesus' teaching from a reinterpretation of Jewish law and the imminent kingdom to the cosmic truths revealed in Jesus' Incarnation. In John, the principal subject of Jesus' message is himself, a divine being who fully reveals the nature of God.

Viewing Jesus' earthly life as a brief manifestation of the eternal Word whose immortal spirit remains ever-present with the believing Christian, John includes no explicit reference to the Parousia. His Gospel contains no eschatological prophecies comparable to those in Mark 13, Matthew 24, and Luke 21. Citing John's doctrine of the Paraclete (Advocate or Comforter) that abides with the faithful (John 14:15–21, 26; 16:7–14; 20:22), some scholars suggest that John presents a "realized eschatology." According to this view, the Gospel writer does not stress a second coming because he believes that in spirit Jesus is already here.

Finally, John banishes the Synoptic theme of Jesus' growing awareness of his messiahship and the disciples' slowly dawning realization of his true identity. At the outset of his Gospel, John declares that Jesus' divine nature was immediately recognized and publicly proclaimed. Both John the Baptist and the disciple Nathanael are shown openly hailing Jesus as "the Son of God" and Israel's "Chosen One" (John 1:29–36, 49). Both Mark's concept of the "Messianic Secret" and the other Synoptics' motif of Jesus' gradually developing awareness of his identity and mission are absent. In John's account, from the beginning Jesus knows who he is; he expresses neither hesitancy nor doubt about his mission, experiences no spiritual agony in Gethsemane, and utters no cry of despair on the cross. Although John insists that Jesus was physically human (John 1:14), the author's chief interest clearly is to celebrate Jesus' divinity. Considering the many ways in which John diverges from the Synoptics, it seems possible that he drew upon an independent oral or written tradition that resembled the sources used by Mark, Matthew, and Luke but substantially differed from them.

Purpose and Themes Besides attempting to awaken faith in his readers, John's Gospel was designed as a powerful rebuke to false teachings that had arisen within the Christian community. His unfavorable references to the Jews in Jesus' Jerusalem speeches may represent a rebuttal to Judaism's criticism of the early Church. His decided subordination of John the Baptist to Jesus may be a reaction to a John the Baptist sect that denied Jesus' superiority to their leader. His identification of Jesus with the Word (Logos) that predates the world's creation was certainly intended to silence any claims by rival prophets, philosophers, or messiahs as to Jesus' absolute preeminence. John's declaration that "the Word became flesh" (John 1:14) refutes the incipient Docetic movement, which argued that matter was intrinsically evil and that Christ was therefore pure spirit.

John also counters the Gnostic heresy, a dualistic philosphy that divided the cosmos into light and darkness, good and evil, by insisting on Jesus' bridging the world of matter and spirit and triumphantly overcoming the forces of evil. The author's dualistic language—with its contrasts of light and darkness (John 1:15), flesh and spirit (John 3:6), the children of God and of the Devil (John 1:13; 8:44), and believers and the worldly (John 17:16) reflects not only Gnostic nomenclature but also that of the Dead Sea Scrolls. This literature, probably of Essene origin, anticipates John's dualistic oppositions and use of such terms as "son of light" and "the spirit of truth."

Despite the author's intention to criticize Gnosticism, many statements in the Gospel are classic expressions of Gnostic beliefs. Thus, to know (*gnosis*) the divine beings—Father and Son—is equated with acquiring "eternal life" (John 17:3). The assertion that "the spirit alone gives life; the flesh is of no avail" (John 6:63) and the emphasis on finding "true" life through rebirth in "spirit" (John 3:3–8) strikingly parallel Gnostic teachings.

Hymn to the Word   In the Prologue (John 1:1–18), John identifies the human Jesus with the Logos (Word). A philosophical term since the time of Heraclitus (born before 500 B.C.E.), in John's day *Logos* was used by the Stoic philosophers to express the principle of cosmic reason, the force that orders and sustains the universe, making it accessible and intelligible to the human mind. Greek philosophy also saw the Logos as a creative power that had formed *cosmos* (world order) out of the original *chaos* (dark void). In the Hebrew biblical tradition, a similar concept developed. According to Proverbs (8:22–31), Yahweh had Wisdom (personified as a gracious young woman) as his companion when he created the world. She was not only Yahweh's intimate helper in the creative process, she was also the god's channel of communication with humankind. In later manifestations of this biblical idea, Wisdom became both the agent or means of creation and the revealer of the divine mind (Eccles. 24; Wisdom of Solomon 6:12–9:18).

These parallel Greek and Hebrew ideas converge in the writings of Philo Judaeus, a Jewish scholar who lived in Alexandria during the first century C.E. A pious Jew profoundly influenced by Greek philosophy, Philo attempted to reconcile Hellenic logic with the revelation contained in the Hebrew Bible. Philo used the Hebrew concept of Wisdom as the creative intermediary between the transcendent Creator and the material creation, but he employed the Greek term *Logos* to designate its role and function. (Philo may have preferred *Logos* because it is masculine in Greek whereas Wisdom (*Sophia*) is feminine.) Philo's interpretation can be illustrated by an allegorical reading of Genesis 1, in which God's first act is to speak—create the Word (Logos)—by which power heaven and earth then come into being.

Echoing the Genesis creation account, John adapts Philo's doctrine to identify Jesus, in his prehuman existence, with the divine Logos that formed the universe (John 1:1–5; 9–14). The heavenly Logos then "became flesh" (John 1:14) to walk the earth as Jesus of Nazareth, the embodiment of God's creative force. With this statement of the Incarnation (the spiritual Logos becoming the man Jesus), John asserts Jesus' innate superiority to all other divine messengers, whether angels or prophets. He not only speaks the Word of God; he *is* that Word and reveals the godhead fully.

Seven Signs Having established Jesus' supernatural character and superiority to John the Baptist, John organizes his interpretation of the meaning of Jesus' mission around seven miracles or "signs," among which he inserts long discourses and dialogues, including several "I am" sayings.

The first sign is Jesus' changing water into wine at a wedding feast at Cana in Galilee (John 2:1–11). This miracle, found only in John, is followed by the cleansing of the temple in Jerusalem (John 2:13–22), after which Jesus cryptically compares his body (in which the Holy Spirit dwells) to the sanctuary itself, which after it is destroyed, he promises to raise up "in three days"—a foreshadowing of the resurrection (John 2:19).

Chapter 3 contains Jesus' conversation with Nicodemus on spiritual rebirth (John 3:1–31), which ends as a monologue in which Jesus declares that belief in the Son brings eternal life. For John, disbelief is the unpardonable sin. In chapter 4 Jesus visits Samaria, where his encounter with a woman drawing water at Jacob's well leads to the conversion of numerous Samaritans, who acknowledge him as "the Savior of the world" (John 4:42)—a statement stressing the universality of his role.

A similar theme pervades the second sign, in which Jesus, again in Cana, cures the dying son of a Roman centurion (John 4:46–54), the second non-Jew to whom he manifests his power. The third miraculous sign is Jesus' healing a chronic invalid (John 5:2–9) at the sheep-gate pool in Jerusalem, the significance of which appears in the long speech that follows (John 5:19–47). Here Jesus describes the Son's relationship to the Father, who has committed powers of judgment and forgiveness to him.

The fourth sign is Jesus' feeding of the 5,000 (John 6:1–14), probably a variant of the Synoptic incident (Matt. 14:13–21; Mark 6:30–44; Luke

9:10–17). In John, this event symbolizes Jesus' providing the world with spiritual nourishment (John 6:25–59), although as usual in John, Jesus' hearers misunderstand his intent. This time they forcibly attempt to make him king (John 6:15), not realizing that his kingdom "does not belong to this world" (John 18:36).

A fifth sign is Jesus' walking on water (John 6:16–21), which demonstrates the Son's power over nature. These passages contain the first of Jesus' "I am" pronouncements, which echo Yahweh's declaration of Being to Moses at the burning bush (Exod. 3:14). Beginning with Jesus' declaration "I am," they then equate the speaker with symbols of major significance, such as "the bread of life" (John 6:35), "the light of the world" (John 8:12), "the door of the sheep" (John 10:7), "the good shepherd" (John 10:11), "the resurrection and the life" (John 11:25), "the way," "the truth," "the life" (John 14:6), and "the real vine" (John 15:1).

Many scholars doubt that the historical Jesus actually made these sweeping claims and suggest that by attributing them to him, the author and the Christian community for which he speaks are simply expressing their post-resurrection faith in Jesus' divine authority. Some scholars have suggested that one rephrase the declarations as "He is" and regard them as a confession of the writer's faith.

Jesus performs the sixth sign at Jerusalem during the Feast of Tabernacles when he restores sight to a blind man (John 9:1–41), a cure meant to symbolize the giving of spiritual insight to those who believe in him; those like the Pharisees who deny his messiahship remain religiously blind. Jesus' discourse on the "good shepherd" and the controversies following this occupy chapter 10.

In chapter 11 occurs the seventh and most potent sign: the raising of Jesus' friend Lazarus, who had been in the grave four days. In John, it is this miracle rather than the riot in the temple that precipitates Jewish officialdom's conspiracy to eliminate Jesus (John 11:45–53). The remark attributed to Caiaphas, the high priest—that "it is more to your interest that one man should die for the people, than that the whole nation should be destroyed" (John 11:50)—is deeply ironic in unwittingly expressing the Christian belief that Jesus redeems the world through his death.

Almost immediately thereafter Jesus confirms this judgment, announcing that he must be "lifted from the earth" in order to "draw all men" to himself (John 12:31–33)—an allusion to the imminent crucifixion and the future conversion of the Gentiles. John concludes this section of his Gospel, marking the completion of Jesus' public ministry, with a reminder that Jesus' teaching has explicitly revealed the Father's will (John 12:49–50).

Last Teachings and Death The second part of John's Gospel opens with an account of the Last Supper that differs considerably from that related in the Synoptics; for John contains no references to a new cov-

❦ Gospel Parallels: The Empty Tomb

Mark (16:1–8)

When the Sabbath was over, Mary and Salome brought aromatic oils, intending to go and anoint him; and very early on the Sunday morning, just after sunrise, they came to the tomb. They were wondering among themselves who would roll away the stone for them from the entrance to the tomb, when they looked up and saw that the stone, huge as it was, had been rolled back already. They went into the tomb, where they saw a youth sitting on the right-hand side, wearing a white robe; and they were dumbfounded. But he said to them, "Fear nothing; you are looking for Jesus of Nazareth, who was crucified. He has been raised again; he is not here; look, there is the place where they laid him. But go and give this message to his disciples and Peter: 'He is going on before you into Galilee; there you will see him, as he told you.'" Then they went out and ran away from the tomb, beside themselves with terror. They said nothing to anybody, for they were afraid.

Matthew (28:1–9)

The Sabbath was over, and it was about daybreak on Sunday, when Mary of Magdala and the other Mary came to look at the grave. Suddenly there was a violent earthquake; an angel of the Lord descended from heaven; he came to the stone and rolled it away, and sat himself down on it. His face shone like lightning; his garments were white as snow. At the sight of him the guards shook with fear and lay like the dead.

The angel then addressed the women: "You," he said, "have nothing to fear. I know you are looking for Jesus who was crucified. He is not here; he has been raised again, as he said he would be. Come and see the place where he was laid, and then go quickly and tell his disciples: 'He has been raised from the dead and is going on before you into Galilee; there you will see him.' That is what I had to tell you."

They hurried away from the tomb in awe and great joy, and ran to tell the disciples.

---

enant or to the disciples' eating Jesus' body and drinking his blood. Instead, Jesus performs the menial task of washing his disciples' feet, after which Judas goes forth to betray him (John 13:1–30).

Almost five of the remaining eight chapters are devoted to a series of farewell discourses (John 13:31–17:26). Jesus declares his unity with the Father and promises to send his disciples the Paraclete (the "Counselor" or "Spirit of Truth") (John 14:16–17); he delivers an allegory presenting himself as the "real vine" whose followers must bear the fruits of love even when persecuted (John 15); he explains that his "leaving" (death) must precede the coming of the Holy Spirit (John 16:7–15); he prays that he and his followers may be one, as he and the Father are one, in the

Luke (23:55–24:11)

The women who had accompanied him from Galilee followed; they took note of the tomb and observed how his body was laid. Then they went home and prepared spices and perfumes; and on the Sabbath they rested in obedience to the commandment. But on the Sunday morning very early they came to the tomb bringing the spices they had prepared. Finding that the stone had been rolled away from the tomb, they went inside; but the body was not to be found. While they stood utterly at a loss, all of a sudden two men in dazzling garments were at their side. They were terrified, and stood with eyes cast down, but the men said, "Why search among the dead for one who lives? Remember what he told you while he was still in Galilee, about the Son of Man: how he must be given up into the power of sinful men and be crucified, and must rise again on the third day." Then they recalled his words and, returning from the tomb, they reported all this to the Eleven and all the others.

The women were Mary of Magdala, Joanna, and Mary the mother of James, and they, with the other women, told the apostles. But the story appeared to them to be nonsense, and they would not believe them.

John (20:1–9)

Early on the Sunday morning, while it was still dark, Mary of Magdala came to the tomb. She saw that the stones had been moved away from the entrance, and ran to Simon Peter and the other disciple, the one whom Jesus loved. "They have taken the Lord out of his tomb," she cried, "and we do not know where they have laid him." So Peter and the other set out and made their way to the tomb. They were running side by side, but the other disciple outran Peter and reached the tomb first. He peered in and saw the linen wrappings lying there, but did not enter. Then Simon Peter came up, following him, and he went into the tomb. He saw the linen wrappings lying, and the napkin which had been over his head, not lying with the wrappings, but rolled together in a place by itself. Then the disciple who had reached the tomb first went in too, and he saw and believed; until then then they had not understood the scriptures, which showed that he must rise from the dead.

So the disciples went home again; but Mary stood at the tomb outside, weeping. As she wept, she peered into the tomb; and she saw two angels in white sitting there, one at the head, and one at the feet, where the body of Jesus had lain. They said to her, "Why are you weeping?" She answered, "They have taken my Lord away, and I do not know where they have laid him."

work he has been sent to accomplish (John 17). This prayer contains a Gnosticlike statement that "to know" God and his Christ is "eternal life" (John 17:3).

Chapters 18–20 record Jesus' arrest (John 18:1–11), his trials before the high priest (John 18:15–27) and before Pilate (John 18:28–19:16), the crucifixion and burial (John 19:17–42), and resurrection appearances (John 20), including that before "doubting Thomas" (John 20:24–29). It is significant that although John proclaims Jesus' divinity from the beginning of his Gospel, he does not have him claim to be the Son of God or the Messiah to either the Sanhedrin or Pilate; he also omits mention of the natural phenomena—earthquakes, thunder, and midday darkness—that according to tradition accompanied Jesus' death. John's theophany is confined to revealing Jesus' triumph over death—the eighth and greatest sign (the sacred number seven plus one) to which all the others pointed.

RECOMMENDED READING

Brown, Raymond E. *The Gospel According to John*. Anchor Bible, vols. 29 and 29a. Garden City, N. Y.: Doubleday, 1966 and 1970. Provides the most complete historical and theological background and most thorough commentary on the text.

_____. *The Community of the Beloved Disciple*. New York: Paulist Press, 1979.

Bultmann, Rudolf. *The Gospel of John*. Translated by G. R. Beasley-Murray. Philadelphia: Westminster Press, 1971. Discusses John's sources with insightful interpretation.

Dodd, C. H. *The Interpretation of the Fourth Gospel*. Cambridge, England: Cambridge University Press, 1965.

Fortna, Robert T. *The Gospel of Signs: A Reconstruction of the Narrative Source Underlying the Fourth Gospel*. Cambridge, England: Cambridge University Press, 1970.

Howard, W. F. "Introduction and Exegesis to the Gospel of John." In *The Interpreter's Bible*, vol. 8, pp. 437–811. New York and Nashville: Abingdon Press, 1962.

Olson, Alan M., ed. *Myth, Symbol and Reality*. Notre Dame, Ind.: University of Notre Dame Press, 1981. Includes essays on the Logos.

Smith, Dwight Moody, Jr. *The Composition and Order of the Fourth Gospel: Bultmann's Literary Theory*. Yale Publications in Religion, no. 10. New Haven, Conn.: Yale University Press, 1964. Challenges Bultmann's hypotheses.

_____. "John, Gospel of." In *The Interpreter's Dictionary of the Bible: Supplementary Volume*, pp. 482–86. Nashville: Abingdon Press, 1976.

THE ACTS OF THE APOSTLES

A sequel to Luke's Gospel, the Acts of the Apostles is by the same author, addressed to the same recipient, Theophilus (Acts 1:1), and written for the same purpose: to present Christianity as a divinely inspired, socially respectable, politically law-abiding religion intended to be international in scope. Immediately before his ascension to heaven, which Acts alone describes, Jesus states the book's theme: the disciples are to carry the message from Jerusalem to Judea and Samaria and "away to the ends of the earth" (Acts 1:8).

Acts' organization is thus linear and (roughly) chronological. Its narrative traces the spread of Christianity from its Jewish birthplace through the eastern Mediterranean to the center of Gentile power, Rome itself. With Paul's preaching in Rome, however, the book ends. The writer records neither Peter nor Paul's martyrdom there under Nero (64–65 C.E.), possibly because he does not want to complicate his picture of Christians as responsible citizens but also because, with Paul's arrival at the world capital, his purpose is accomplished (Acts 28:14–30).

❦ Acts of the Apostles

The Jerusalem Church	*Chapters 1–12:23*
Paul's Mission	*12:24–28:31*
The Jerusalem Conference	*15*
Travels in Greece	*16–18*
Legal Skirmishes	*18–28*

If this idea of theirs [Jesus' followers] or its execution is of human origin, it will collapse; but if it is from God, you will never be able to put them down, and you risk finding yourselves at war with God.

**Rabbi Gamaliel to the Sandedrin;
Acts of the Apostles 5:38–39**

The Jerusalem Church Drawing on traditions concerning Peter and Paul to the near exclusion of other apostles and disciples, the author organizes his history around Christianity's step-by-step expansion into new geographical areas. Beginning in Jerusalem shortly after the resurrection, chapter 1 records Jesus' commission to witness throughout the earth (Acts 1:8), his ascension and promise to return from heaven (Acts 1:9–11), and the apostles' electing Matthias to replace Judas as one of the Twelve (Acts 1:15–26).

Chapters 2 through 8:3 focus on the numerical growth of the Jerusalem believers from a group of about 120 (Acts 1:15) to several thousand, including some priests (Acts 2:41; 4:4; 5:14–16; 6:1, 7). This section opens with the promised outpouring of Holy Spirit upon the disciples at Pentecost, inspiring them to speak in foreign tongues (symbolic of the multinational nature of Christianity)—an event Peter interprets as the fulfillment of Joel's prediction that in the last days "everyone" would prophesy (Acts 2:1–24; cf. Joel 2:28–32). The section culminates in Stephen's long "witness" to the Jews who stone him for blasphemy (Acts 6:8–7:60). The execution of this first Christian martyr and the persecution that follows have the effect of scattering Christians beyond Jerusalem into surrounding territories, where they continue to proclaim the Gospel.

Acts' next section (Acts 9:4–12:24) shows the fulfillment of Jesus' command to preach "all over Judea and Samaria" (Acts 1:8). In Samaria, Philip baptizes a number of converts, who receive the Holy Spirit after Peter and John are sent from Jerusalem to "lay hands" on them (Acts 8:4–25). Philip next goes south to Gaza where he brings an Ethiopian eunuch, an important government official, into the fold (Acts 8:26–38). But the most striking event to symbolize the transition of the Church from a Jewish to a Gentile orientation is the sudden conversion of Saul of Tarsus, a young Hellenistic Pharisee who had helped to persecute the Christians. After being temporarily blinded by a revelation of Jesus' postresurrection glory, Paul (his Greek name) becomes one of the most zealous promulgators of the faith and, more than any other person, is responsible for the universality of the early Church.

The author devotes chapters 10 and 11 to showing that Peter, who elsewhere represents the conservative Jewish position among early believers, is the chosen instrument to open Christianity's doors to non-Jews. Peter first receives a vision implying that all foods, as well as the non-Jewish peoples who eat them, are now "clean" and acceptable to God (Acts 10:9–16). Following the vision, a delegation brings Peter to the home of Cornelius—a Roman centurion who is also a "God-fearing" admirer of the Jewish religion—where Peter, directed by Holy Spirit, baptizes the entire household (Acts 10:1–8, 17–48).

Luke has Peter emphasize the landmark significance of this conversion: "I now see how true it is that God has no favorites, but that in every nation the man who is God-fearing and does what is right is acceptable to him" (Acts 10:34). Luke also represents Peter as persuading the "circumcision party" (Jewish Christians who strictly observe the Mosaic law) in Judea that "God has granted life-giving repentance to the Gentiles also" (Acts 11:18). When numerous Gentiles enter the Church at Antioch, the Jerusalem apostles dispatch Barnabas to report on the situation. Impressed by the converts' zeal, Barnabas imports Paul from Tarsus to help instruct them (Acts 11:19–30).

Acts concludes its review of witnessing activities "all over Judea and Samaria" with an account of Herod Agrippa's persecution of the Jerusalem community. After executing James, "the brother of John," he imprisons Peter, who is promptly delivered by "an angel" (Acts 12:1–19). Decisive evidence of divine displeasure at Herod's misdeeds is manifested when the king, after accepting divine honors, suddenly dies of a hideous disease, thus ending his reign (41–44 C.E.) over a briefly reunited Jewish kingdom (Acts 12:20–23).

Paul's Mission The remaining sixteen chapters (Acts 12:24–28:31) are devoted to the international missionary activities of Paul and his fellow workers. Barnabas and Paul successfully evangelize among the "God-fearing" Gentiles attending synagogues in various Hellenistic cities of Asia Minor (modern Turkey), though the Jewish leadership is typically represented as violently opposing their efforts (Acts 13:1–14:28). Their tour is interrupted, however, when dissension breaks out between Gentile and Jewish Christians over adherence to the Mosaic law. Among other things, the Judaizing party insists that Gentile converts be circumcised and observe Jewish dietary regulations.

The Jerusalem Conference According to Acts 15, the first recorded Church council takes place at Jerusalem, where the apostles and "elders" gather to consider whether a believer must first become a Jew in order to be a Christian. Christian Pharisees demand that the entire Mosaic law be kept, but Peter reportedly opposes this (Acts 15:10) and, citing his own key role in bringing Gentiles into the Church (Acts 15:7–11), thereby silences the Judaizers.

Quoting Old Testament prophecies indicating that their god would also make non-Jews his people, Jesus' "brother" James persuades "the whole Church" to adopt his resolution that no restrictions be imposed upon Gentile converts except the commands to abstain from eating meat sacrificed to pagan gods, consuming blood, or indulging in sexual immorality (Acts 15:12–29). The Jerusalem church sends Judas and Silas to accompany Paul and Barnabas back to Antioch to deliver the council's verdict.

This version of the Jerusalem conference, in which the issue is settled unanimously, contrasts markedly with Paul's account (Gal. 2:1–10) in which he declares that "not for one moment" did he compromise his position that Christians should live absolutely free of the law's "bondage." According to Galatians, Paul accepted no restrictions, whereas according to Acts 15 he willingly complied with four legal prohibitions. Further, although Acts represents Peter as arguing against required circumcision, Paul states that in Antioch, following the council, Peter weakly submitted to pressure from advocates of circumcision and withdrew from association with Gentiles (Gal. 2:11–14).

These differing accounts seem to be irreconcilable; but since Paul's is a contemporary witness and Acts was written many years after the event, scholars generally prefer Paul's version. It must be remembered that the author of Luke-Acts did not write to preserve an accurate record of the doctrinal disputes that divided the early Church but to idealize the Church as more united and internally cooperative than it actually was. Because his concerns were more theological than historical, he notes the existence, but minimizes the extent, of early Christian pluralism and dissension. Recent scholarship has helped illuminate the diversity of belief and practice to be found not only among early Christians but in the New Testament documents as well.

Travels in Greece   Shortly after the Jerusalem conference, Paul and Barnabas separate. Acts attributes the parting to a quarrel over John Mark's worthiness to accompany them on a tour of churches that they had founded earlier; but in Galatians Paul states that they differed over the question of Jewish law, Barnabas having been "carried away" by the "circumcision party" (Gal. 2:13). At all events, Paul and Silas alone visit the churches of Syria and Asia Minor until a vision directs Paul into Macedonia (Acts 15:40–16:10), where his activities follow the same pattern established earlier in Acts. He preaches first in the local synagogue and is typically well received by Gentile "God fearers" but persecuted by Jewish leaders, who flog, imprison, or accuse him of treason before the Roman magistrates (Acts 16:11–17:15).

Driven from Philippi, Thessalonica, and Beroea, Paul finds unusual tolerance in Athens, where he is invited to speak before an intellectually curious group at the Areopagus (highest council) (Acts 17:16–34). The fact that his speech differs little in tone, diction, or style from most of the other speeches in Acts, regardless of the speaker, suggests that the author did not reproduce the actual words of any historical personage but, following a literary tradition established by the Athenian historian Thucydides, simply allowed them to voice sentiments that were deemed appropriate to the occasion. For this reason, Paul's speeches in Acts do not always tally with the style and theology of his letters. In Acts, Paul never expresses the strong repudiation of the Law found in his letters, or his revolutionary "gospel" of salvation through faith.

Legal Skirmishes   The balance of Acts is largely devoted to recounting a series of legal skirmishes between Paul and various groups who oppose his work. Augmenting his theme that Christianity offers no threat to Roman security, the author takes pains to demonstrate that Paul is charged with sedition only because "envious" Jews stir up trouble against him. Roman officials repeatedly testify that he is guilty of no punishable action; indeed, when some Corinthian Jews charge him with defaming God, the Roman proconsul Gallio throws the case out of court (Acts 18:12–17). Similarly, when the Greek silversmiths of Ephesus, who fashion images of the goddess Arthemis (Diana) for sale to tourists, try to force Paul to stop his antiidolatry campaign, local authorities argue that they have no legal cause to do so (Acts 19:21–40).

On Paul's return to Jerusalem, Jewish resistance reaches a climax. Certain "Jews from the province of Asia" (Acts 21:27) accuse him of blasphemy and of profaning the temple; a mob attacks him; but Roman soldiers intervene and conduct him to the Sanhedrin. Disclosing that he is a Pharisee, Paul succeeds in dividing the council so that scribes of his party call for his release while the Sadducees and others denounce him (Acts 21:27–23:10). The divine plan behind allowing Paul to suffer persecution is now revealed: he must proclaim the Christian witness in Rome as he has in Jerusalem (Acts 23:11).

After being imprisoned at Caesarea for two years under the Roman governor Felix, Paul exercises his birthright as a Roman citizen and, under Festus (Felix's successor), "appeals to Caesar"—i.e., asks to be tried in the emperor's own court (Acts 25:1–21). The detailed narration of Paul's defense before Festus, King Herod Agrippa II, and his sister Bernice (Acts 25:8–26:32) is intended to demonstrate his innocence of any religious or political crimes. This intent is reiterated in a conclusion attributed to Festus and Agrippa: "This man . . . is doing nothing that deserves death or imprisonment"; he could, they say, have been set free "if he had not appealed to the emperor" (Acts 26:30–32).

Chapter 27, one of the "we" passages attributed to an eyewitness companion of Paul, vividly describes Paul's hazardous sea voyage toward Rome. Once in the imperial capital, he is kept under house arrest but is nevertheless free to evangelize "quite openly and without hindrance" (Acts 28:31). Having had Paul carry the Gospel deep within pagan territory, the author abruptly terminates the narrative, telling us nothing of Paul's subsequent fate.

RECOMMENDED READING

Cadbury, H. J. "Acts of the Apostles." In *The Interpreter's Dictionary of the Bible*, vol. 1, pp. 28–42. New York and Nashville: Abingdon Press, 1962. Good introduction.

Conzelmann, Hans. *Theology of St. Luke.* Translated by Geoffrey Buswell. New York: Harper & Row, 1960. An incisive critical study.

Davies, J. G. *The Early Christian Church.* Garden City, N. Y.: Doubleday Anchor Books, 1967. Discusses sources and historical background of the origins of Christianity.

Dibelius, Martin. *Studies in the Acts of the Apostles.* Edited by H. Greeven. Translated by M. Ling. New York: Charles Scribner's Sons, 1956.

Dunn, James D. G. *Unity and Diversity within the New Testament.* Philadelphia: Westminster Press, 1977. An insightful study of the several different forms of early Christianity, including the conflicts between the Palestinian Jewish Christians and the Hellenistic Gentile church.

Foakes-Jackson, F. J., and Lake, Kirsopp. *The Beginnings of Christianity.* 5 vols. London: Macmillan, 1920–33. A standard work.

Haenchen, Ernst. *The Acts of the Apostles.* Translated by Hugh Anderson and R. M. Wilson. Philadelphia: Westminster Press, 1971. An excellent commentary.

Hengel, Martin. *Acts and the History of Earliest Christianity.* Philadelphia: Fortress Press, 1980.

_____. *Between Jesus and Paul.* Translated by J. Bowden. Philadelphia: Fortress Press, 1983.

Keck, L. E. *Mandate to Witness: Studies in the Book of Acts.* Valley Forge, Pa.: Judson Press, 1964. A helpful work.

Keck, L. E., and Martyn, J. L., eds. *Studies in Luke-Acts.* New York and Nashville: Abingdon Press, 1966. An important collection of scholarly essays on current and probably future investigations of Luke's writings.

Lohse, Eduard. *The First Christians: Their Beginnings, Writings, and Beliefs.* Philadelphia: Fortress Press, 1983.

Macgregor, H. C. "Introduction and Exegesis of Acts." In *The Interpreter's Bible,* vol. 9, pp. 3–352. New York and Nashville: Abingdon Press, 1954.

Malherbe, Abraham J. *Social Aspects of Early Christianity,* 2nd. ed. Philadelphia: Fortress Press, 1983.

Markus, R. A. *Christianity in the Roman World.* New York: Charles Scribner's Sons, 1974. Traces the growth of Christianity from outlawed sect to its triumph as the state religion of imperial Rome.

Theissen, Gerd. *The Sociology of Early Palestinian Christianity.* Philadelphia: Fortress Press, 1978.

Wilken, Robert L. *The Christians as the Romans Saw Them.* New Haven and London: Yale University Press, 1984. A careful analysis of the social, religious, and political conflicts between early Christians and their Roman critics.

Williams, C. S. C. *A Commentary on the Acts of the Apostles.* New York: Harper & Row, 1957. Another helpful commentary.

PAUL AND THE LETTER FORM

It has been justly said that there is as much of Paul as of Jesus in official Christianity. Certainly it is true that among Paul's many contributions are at least two that decisively shaped the development of the Christian religion. (1) He was the first to produce a working theology—although usually incidental to pressing pastoral concerns—regarding such essentials as redemption through faith in the saving power of Jesus and the relation of the Mosaic law to Christianity. (2) As "Apostle to the Gentiles," he led the way in evangelizing non-Jews throughout the Roman Empire, thereby transforming Christianity from a Jewish sect into a universal religion.

Our knowledge of Paul's life and thought comes from two main sources: the Book of Acts, which gives an idealized account of his activities, and his letters, which contain scattered references to biographical matters and present occasional discussions of his theological beliefs. Since Acts gives a secondhand version of Paul's conduct and attitudes sometimes contradicting that expressed in his correspondence, however, most scholars advise against overreliance on Acts' chronology or its representation of his stand on the controversies that divided the early Christian community. Paul's own account is generally regarded as the more reliable.

The future apostle was born to a family of devout Pharisees in Tarsus, capital of Cilicia, a Roman province in southeastern Asia Minor. He was named Saul after Israel's first king and, like him, belonged to the tribe of Benjamin (Acts 23:6; 13:21; Phil. 3:5; Rom. 11:1). He inherited both Tarsian and Roman citizenship (Acts 21:39) and as a worker among the Gentiles became known by his Greco-Roman name, Paul (Paulus). Versed in rabbinical tradition, he is said to have studied in Jerusalem under the eminent Rabbi Gamaliel (Acts 23:3).

According to Acts, Paul was not only a fanatical persecutor of Christians but assisted at the stoning of Stephen (Acts 7:58; cf. Gal. 1:13–14). His sudden conversion to Christianity—of which Acts gives three versions (Acts 9:1–19; 22:1–21; 26:1–23)—did not diminish his natural ardor, however, for he became as zealous in promulgating the new faith as he had formerly been in opposing it. After Paul's dramatic change of attitude, which occurred about 33–35 C.E., he stayed for a time in "Arabia" and Damascus, then traveled to Jerusalem, where he met Cephas (Peter) and James, "the Lord's brother" (Gal. 1:18–19). But many years would pass before he again visited the Jewish Christians of the "mother church," from which he then claimed almost total independence (Gal. 1–2).

Acts organizes Paul's missionary activities into three separate journeys. On the first tour (Acts 13:1–14:28), Barnabas was the leader, and Paul accompanied him to Cyprus, southern Asia Minor, and back to Antioch, a leading Christian center that served as operational base for his evangelizing program. On the second journey (Acts 15:36–18:22), Paul, Silas (Silvanus), and Timothy revisited some churches in southern Asia Minor, then for the first time carried the Gospel to the European mainland, witnessing in Macedonia and Greek cities around the Aegean Sea—Philippi, Thessalonica, Beroea, Athens, and Corinth. Paul then traveled to Ephesus, whence he sailed to Caesarea, the Roman administrative capital of Judea.

On the third journey (Acts 18:23–21:16), Paul left Antioch to revisit churches in eastern Asia Minor and Europe, following which he returned to Jerusalem via Tyre and Caesarea. It was after this third journey that he was arrested at the Jerusalem temple, imprisoned for two years in Caesarea, and eventually sent to Rome for trial in Caesar's court. According to an unsubstantiated tradition, after he was tried and released he traveled to Spain, as he had intended before his arrest (Rom. 15:24). A more probable theory holds that Paul's Roman imprisonment culminated in his beheading during Nero's persecution (64 C.E.). Table 8-4 on page 320 lists the major events in Paul's life.

Of the twenty-seven books of the New Testament, twenty-one are cast in the form of letters, almost half of which consist of Paul's correspondence with various churches in Europe and Asia Minor. These writings resemble private Greek letters of the time, although Paul somewhat modifies the form to suit his distinctive message. A Greek correspondent typically began with a prescript stating his name, the name(s) of his

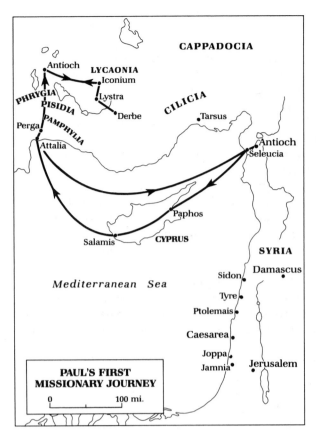

PAUL'S FIRST
MISSIONARY JOURNEY

0   100 mi.

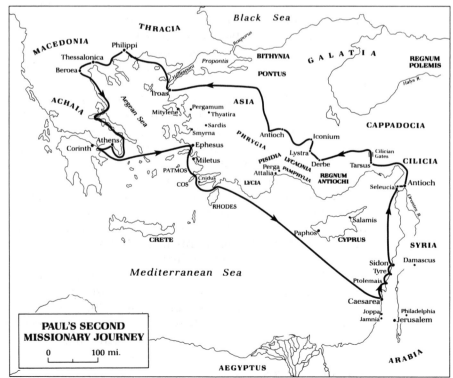

PAUL'S SECOND
MISSIONARY JOURNEY

0   100 mi.

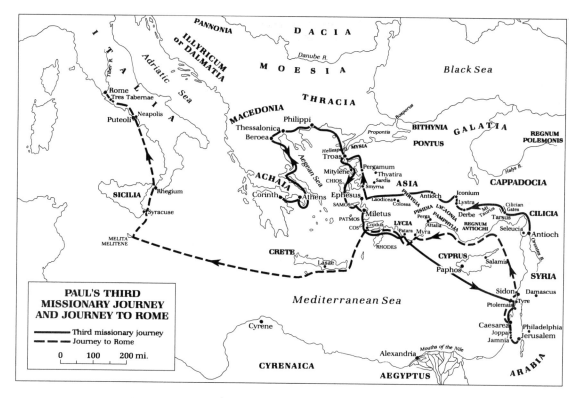

PAUL'S THIRD
MISSIONARY JOURNEY
AND JOURNEY TO ROME

——— Third missionary journey
- - - Journey to Rome

0   100   200 mi.

recipient(s), and a greeting. Paul varies this formula by mentioning the Christian allegiance of the writer and recipients, substituting "grace" and "peace" for the customary greetings, and frequently including an associate in the salutation. He also follows the Greek custom of prefacing his main theme with expressions of praise, thanks, or prayers for the welfare or spiritual well-being of his recipients.

Apparently all of Paul's letters were dictated to a secretary, who in the manner of first-century scribes, did not record the words precisely but merely paraphrased the gist of what was said (Rom. 16:21–22; Gal. 6:11; Col. 4:18; Philem. 19; 2 Thess. 3:17), a practice that explains their extemporaneous flavor. For although most of Paul's missives were composed under the pressure of meeting an emergency in a given church, some are carefully thought out and phrased with great deliberation (e.g., all of Rom.; 1 Cor. 13 and 15; Phil. 2).

Space does not permit recounting all the arguments for and against the authenticity of letters attributed to Paul, but the following classifications are generally accepted: (1) absolutely genuine: 1 Thessalonians, 1 and 2 Corinthians, Galatians, Romans, Philemon, and Philippians; (2) probably from Paul: 2 Thessalonians and Colossians; (3) probably not from Paul although developed from his doctrines: Ephesians; (4) decidedly not from Paul since they appear to derive from a later stage of Church development: 1 and 2 Timothy and Titus.

TABLE 8-4 Paul's Life and Correspondence: A Simplified Chronology

Approximate Date (C.E.)	Activity	Letters
5–10	Born in Tarsus, Asia Minor	
About 30–33	Studies at Jerusalem rabbinical school	
33–35	Assists at stoning of Stephen; converted on road to Damascus	
47–49	First missionary tour, including Galatia	
49	Attends Church council in Jerusalem	
49–52	Second missionary tour: opens Europe to Christianity	1 and 2 Thess. (50 C.E.)
52–56	Third missionary tour	1 Cor. (54–55); 2 Cor. (55–56); Gal. (56); Rom. (56–57)
About 60–62	Imprisonment in Rome	Col. (61?); Philem. (61); Phil. (62)
64 (?)	Execution in Rome	

RECOMMENDED READING

Beardslee, W. A. *Human Achievement and Divine Vocation in the Message of Paul.* Naperville, Ill.: Alex R. Allenson, 1961. A useful study.

Beare, F. W. *St. Paul and His Letters.* New York and Nashville: Abingdon Press, 1962.

Beker, J. Christiaan. *Paul the Apostle: The Triumph of God in Life and Thought.* Philadelphia: Fortress Press, 1981.

Bornkamm, Gunther. *Paul.* Translated by D. M. Stalker. New York: Harper & Row, 1971. A thorough study of Paul's life and work.

Davies, W. D. *Paul and Rabbinic Judaism,* rev. ed. London: SPCK, 1955. Relates Paul's ideas to first-century rabbinic Judaism.

————, ed. *Jewish and Pauline Studies.* Philadelphia: Fortress Press, 1983.

Dodd, C. H. *The Meaning of Paul for Today.* New York: Meridian Books, 1957.

Furnish, Victor P. *Theology and Ethics in Paul.* Nashville: Abingdon Press, 1968.

Goguel, Maurice. *The Birth of Christianity.* New York: Macmillan, 1954. Paul and Jewish Christianity.

Holmberg, Bengt. *Paul and Power: The Structure of Authority in the Primitive Church as Reflected in the Pauline Epistles.* Philadelphia: Fortress Press, 1980.

Hunter, A. M. *Paul and His Predecessors*, rev. ed. Philadelphia: Westminster Press, 1961. Reviews Paul's relation to earlier evangelists and primitive Christian doctrine.

Jewett, Robert. *A Chronology of Paul's Life*. Philadelphia: Fortress Press, 1979. Evaluates earlier systems of dating events in Paul's life and provides a new chronology.

Klausner, Joseph. *From Jesus to Paul*. Translated by W. F. Stinespring. Boston: Beacon Press, 1961.

Knox, John. *Chapters in the Life of Paul*. Nashville: Abingdon Press, 1950. Emphasizes the disparity between Paul's letters and the parallel accounts in Acts.

Knox, W. L. *St. Paul and the Church of Jerusalem*. Cambridge, England: Cambridge University Press, 1925. Paul's relation to the "mother church."

Meeks, Wayne A., ed. *The Writings of St. Paul*. New York: W. W. Norton, 1972. Contains text of Paul's letters and a collection of essays by leading scholars.

Sanders, E. P. *Paul, the Law, and the Jewish People*. Philadelphia: Fortress Press, 1983. Explores Paul's Jewish heritage.

Sandmel, Samuel. *The Genius of Paul: A Study in History*. Philadelphia: Fortress Press, 1979.

Schoeps, H. J. *The Theology of the Apostle in the Light of Jewish Religious History*. Translated by Harold Knight. Philadelphia: Westminster Press, 1961.

Stewart, James S. *A Man in Christ*. New York: Harper & Row, n.d. A comprehensive treatment of Paul's life and thought.

❧ Romans

Human Error	*Chapters 1:18–3:20*
Justification by Faith	*3:21–4:25*
Christian Freedom	*5:1–8:39*
Israel's Failure	*9:1–11:36*
Christian Ethics and Conduct	*12:1–15:13*

**Now that we have been justified through faith . . .
let us exult in the hope of divine splendor
that is to be ours.**

Romans 5:1, 2

The most carefully articulated and comprehensive account of his theology, Paul's letter to the congregation at Rome was probably written from Corinth about 56–57 C.E., when he had not yet visited the city or directly explained his version of the Gospel to the letter's recipients. His special care in delineating his thought to the Roman Christians may have arisen from several motives. First, he was dealing with an important church at the world's capital and wanted to present himself as an authoritative interpreter of the faith. Second, he wished to explain his views to a church presumably under the influence of Peter, a Jewish conservative who perhaps distrusted his internationalism. Third, he wished to ensure the Romans' welcome when he visited there and also to enlist their support for his planned mission to Spain.

While the book's controlling theme closely resembles that of Galatians—the superiority of faith in Jesus to "works" of Jewish law—its tone is calmer and more reasoned. His thesis is stated in chapter 1:16–17: the Gospel is God's power to save all who have faith—Jews first and then Greeks. As both precedent and prediction of his own understanding of faith's supremacy, he cites the prophet Habakkuk's perception that "he shall gain life who is justified through faith" (Rom. 1:17). God's graciousness is the source of salvation, which he offers to Jews and Gentiles alike. Faith is the only requirement, and faith produces righteousness (or justification in God's sight) and everlasting life.

Human Error   After his general greeting and introductory remarks (Rom. 1:1–15), Paul boldly surveys the human predicament (Rom. 1:18–3:20) from which only the power of the Gospel can save us. Although God has revealed himself to all people through the created world, people have deliberately turned away from him and fashioned idols that distort nature's message. While the Gentiles have "their own law" written in their hearts and consciences (Rom. 2:14–16)—which, he implies, theoretically might earn them life (Rom. 2:6–7)—most have fallen into error and await the wrath of God. Jews likewise need salvation through faith (Rom. 2:17–3:20); although they enjoy many spiritual advantages, they have failed to obey God's commandments fully and therefore also stand condemned.

Justification by Faith   In the next section (Rom. 3:31–4:24) Paul argues that since Jesus' death and resurrection no one can gain God's approval solely by trying to keep the Mosaic law. Jesus has introduced a new age in the history of salvation. God's declaring the believer righteous or "justified" through faith was foreshadowed by Abraham, the "father of the Jews," for Abraham received God's favor before he was circumcised and before the law came into being (Rom. 4:1–25). True children of Abraham, therefore, are not necessarily those descended from him "in the flesh" but those who show faith in God's Son—believing Gentiles as well as Jews.

Christian Freedom   In chapters 5:1–8:39 Paul further explores his doctrine of justification by faith and its consequences of freedom for the Christian. A believer's faith in the saving power of Christ's sacrificial death reconciles him to God. Paul contrasts Adam, whose disobedience introduced sin and death into the world, with Christ, whose perfect obedience brings life to all who believe (Rom. 5:12–21; see also 1 Cor. 15:45–50).

The Christian, then, is free from God's wrath and from sin (Rom. 6). But the freedom imparted by God's grace does not confer liberty to continue sinning; the faithful must meet the highest moral standards. While the Christian lives free from the Mosaic law, the law still serves to increase consciousness of sin and a need for grace. As Paul notes, sin's power is irresistible: "The good which I want to do, I fail to do, but what I do is the wrong which is against my will" (Rom. 7:19). Delivered by faith from sin and death (Rom. 5:29), the Christian lives by the Spirit, which makes him or her, like Jesus, a child of God (Rom. 8:14–17).

Even the physical universe, subject to futility and decay, receives hope of regeneration through Jesus' redemptive sacrifice (Rom. 8:18–25). Both the cosmos and the "children of God," rebegotten through the Spirit, are assured absolutely of saving communion with God and his Son:

> For I am convinced that there is nothing in death or life, in the realm of spirits or superhuman powers, in the world as it is or the world as it shall be, in the forces of the universe, in heights or depths—nothing in all creation that can separate us from the love of God in Christ Jesus our Lord.
>
> Romans 8:38–39

Israel's Failure   In Chapters 9–11 Paul suggests that the Jews have misunderstood God's purpose in Christ because they have sought salvation through works of the law but have not succeeded in fulfilling its purpose because they depended on their own efforts rather than faith to attain righteousness. Thus not all "children of the promise" to Abraham are true children of God; only those who exercise faith are. Gentiles benefit from the Jews' refusal to accept the new dispensation because God is now creating from all nations a new people for his name (Rom. 11:11–12).

But Paul absolutely dismisses the notion that God has abandoned the Jews: "God has not rejected his people" (Rom. 11:2). Already a "remnant" of Israel has accepted Christ, and Paul looks forward to the eventual conversion of the rest of the Israelites. He reminds his non-Jewish readers that they are only an artificial graft on the original olive tree (Israel) and that when "the Gentiles have been admitted in full strength . . . the whole of Israel will be saved" (Rom. 11:23–26). Then both the natural (Jewish) and grafted (Gentile) branches will grow together on a single tree (Rom. 11:1–32).

Christian Ethics and Conduct   Moving from theological to ethical considerations (Rom. 12–15), Paul observes that Christians should be motivated by love, not by a desire for vengeance (Rom. 12). They should obey all civil laws, for God has created governments to punish wrongdoers and ensure public order (Rom. 13). Those strong in the faith should respect a weaker person's scruples about dietary and ceremonial matters and avoid offending or "stumbling" him or her (Rom. 14).

Paul's concluding observations, personal greetings, and doxology are to be found in chapters 15:14–16; 27. (Most scholars believe that chapter 16, except for the doxology, represents a fragment of another Pauline letter, possibly to the Ephesians.) He closes with a personal message concerning his ministry and his intention to visit Rome on his way to Spain (Rom. 15:24). First, however, he must carry a collection from the Gentile churches to the "mother church" in Jerusalem. Ironically, Paul's determination to appease the Jewish Christians leads to his arrest, so that he first comes to Rome not as a free missionary but as a political prisoner.

RECOMMENDED READING

Barrett, C. K. *From the First Adam to the Last.* London: A. & C. Black, 1962.

Barth, Karl. *The Epistle to the Romans.* 6th ed. Translated by E. C. Hoskyns. London: Oxford University Press, 1933. A standard work.

Beare, F. W. "Romans, Letter to the." In *The Interpreter's Dictionary of the Bible,* vol. 4, pp. 112–22. New York and Nashville: Abingdon Press, 1962.

Bruce, F. F. *The Epistle of Paul to the Romans.* Grand Rapids, Mich.: Wm. B. Eerdsmans Publishing Co., 1963. A valuable work.

Bultmann, Rudolf. *Theology of the New Testament*, vol. 1. Translated by K. Grobel. New York: Charles Scriber's Sons, 1951. Discusses Paul's theological contribution to New Testament thought.

Fitzmyer, J. A. *Pauline Theology: A Brief Sketch.* Englewood Cliffs, N. J.: Prentice-Hall, 1967. Concise and helpful.

Furnish, V. P. *Theology and Ethics in Paul.* New York and Nashville: Abingdon Press, 1968. Includes a review of modern commentators on Paul's ethics.

Leenhardt, F. J. *The Epistle to the Romans: A Commentary.* Translated by H. Knight. London: Lutterworth Press, 1961.

Stendahl, K., ed. and trans. *Romans, Galatians, and Philippians.* Anchor Bible, vol. 33. Garden City, N. Y.: Doubleday, 1978.

Whiteley, D.E.H. *The Theology of St. Paul.* Philadelphia: Fortress Press, 1964

❦ 1 Corinthians

When I came to you, I declared the attested truth of God without display of fine words or wisdom. . . . And yet I do speak words of wisdom to those who are ripe for it, not a wisdom belonging to this passing age. . . . I speak God's hidden wisdom, his secret purpose framed from the very beginning to bring us to our full glory.

1 Corinthians 2:1, 6, 7

Paul's letters to the congregation in Corinth, a wealthy port city noted for its licentiousness, mirror the problems of an infant church divided by doctrinal disputes, rival leaderships, and sexual immorality. His most extensive correspondence to any one group, the Corinthian letters are particularly valuable for their references to Paul's personal life, their portrait of a first-century Christian community, their theological content, and their high literary quality (see 1 Cor. 13 and 15).

Although the reader might suppose that Paul wrote only two letters to Corinth (1 and 2 Corinthians), scholars find evidence that at least four different letters or fragments of letters are embedded in the Corinthian correspondence. The earliest letter, mentioned in 1 Corinthians 5:9–11, may be partly represented by 2 Corinthians 6:14–7:1. The second letter is our 1 Corinthians. A third, "severe" letter is thought to be preserved in 2 Corinthians 10–13. The fourth, "conciliatory" letter appears in 2 Corinthians 1:1–6:13 and 7:2–9:15. The first three were written from Ephesus; the last may have originated in Macedonia. All were composed between 54 and 56 C.E.

1 Corinthians may be outlined as follows: (1) greetings and introduction (1 Cor. 1:1–9); (2) Paul's recommendations for handling the various doctrinal and behavioral problems reported to him (1 Cor. 1:10–6:20); (3) Paul's detailed responses to theological and ethical questions posed in a letter to him from the Corinthians (1 Cor. 7:1–15:58); (4) instructions concerning the collection of money for Jerusalem (1 Cor. 16:1–4); and (5) final directions and farewell (1 Cor. 16:5–24).

Doctrinal and Behavioral Problems   Paul's immediate task in writing the Corinthians was to end the divisiveness that had split the church into cliques following such individual leaders as Paul, Cephas (Peter), or Apollos (an Alexandrine Jew whose eloquence had converted many to the faith). In passages that are sometimes misused to justify an anti-intellectual approach to Christianity (1 Cor. 1:17–3:4), he begins his appeal for unity by showing that human reason alone is not enough to understand the divine nature. Here it must be remembered that Paul had just experienced a largely unsuccessful confrontation with Greek intellectuals in Athens, as a result of which he had determined henceforth not to compete with worldly wisdom but to emphasize the essential fact of "Christ nailed to the cross" (1 Cor. 1:23; 2:2).

To the Greeks, who "look for wisdom" (rational explanations), Paul's message is a foolish myth about a crucified traitor. To the Jews, who demand miracles as proof of Jesus' claims to messiahship, Paul's Gospel is a "stumbling block" because the Messiah was foretold as a triumphant king, not a failed revolutionary (1 Cor. 1:21–24). Faced with Gentile and Jewish incredulity, Paul can only conclude that what appears as ignorance and weakness is really God's mysterious wisdom and power.

The Apostle implies that God intentionally chose people whom society regards as "low and contemptible, mere nothings" to accept the Gospel so that no believer could boast that he or she embraced Christianity because of his or her own intellect or superior perception. This arrangement eliminates all excuse for human pride (1 Cor. 1:26–31). Yet Paul does "speak God's hidden wisdom" to those mature enough to receive it (1 Cor. 1:6–10). This wisdom, involving the divine purpose revealed through Jesus, is imparted only by the Holy Spirit (1 Cor. 2:11–16) that enlightens and unites all believers in Christ so that no one need seek a human leader (1 Cor. 3:1–4:21).

Having dealt with factionalism, Paul turns to the problem of sexual misconduct, another source of disunity among the Corinthians, urging the excommunication of a man who had scandalized the community by living openly with his stepmother (1 Cor. 5:1–8). This consigning "to Satan" any Christian who is a slanderer, drunkard, idolator, or otherwise conspicuous sinner (1 Cor. 5:9–13) was later to prove a formidable weapon, for the excommunicated person, deprived of both religious and social rights, became a virtual outcast. Paul's theological justification for this practice is that the Christian's body is "a shrine of the indwelling Holy Spirit" (1 Cor. 6:19) that must not be profaned by sinful acts such as intercourse with prostitutes. Finally, in chapter 6, Paul orders the Corinthians to stop bringing lawsuits against fellow believers, stating that it is better to suffer a wrong than to expose other Christians to public criticism by airing their disputes in pagan courts (1 Cor. 6:1–8).

Questions Answered   In chapter 7 Paul begins answering questions addressed to him in a letter from the Corinthians. His dim view of marriage and unequivocal preference for a single life of sexual abstinence can be understood in the light of his eschatology. Expecting momentarily the return of Christ and the end of the world (1 Cor. 7:26, 29–31), he believed that it is best to devote oneself wholeheartedly to the Lord's work (1 Cor. 7:1–40). To the second problem—concerning whether a believer may lawfully eat food sold after it had been sacrificed to idols—Paul's solution is that the Christian, while technically free to act as he or she judges best, should do nothing that will trouble another believer's conscience (1 Cor. 8:1–11:1).

Proper Behavior in Worship To support his position on a third issue—the conduct of women during worship services—Paul invokes what he assumes to be a divinely ordained hierarchy: as God is the head of Christ and as Christ is the head of humankind, so man is the head of woman (1 Cor. 11:3). A woman attending church must veil her head "because of the angels" (1 Cor. 11:4–10), an obscure phrase perhaps referring to angels who fell from heaven when attracted by women's beauty (Gen. 6). Women are also prohibited from addressing the congregation (1 Cor. 14:34–35), although they enjoy the right to prophesy. Even so, "in Christ's comradeship woman is as essential to man as man to woman," for it is "through woman that man now comes to be" (1 Cor. 11:11–12).

A fourth problem concerned the Corinthians' behavior during the "Lord's Supper" (known variously as Communion, Mass, or the Eucharist). Apparently some worshipers at Corinth had transformed the commemoration into a near brawl; early comers overate, overdrank, and left nothing for "the poor" who arrived later. While Paul does not object to Christians enjoying a meal of fellowship together—a feast that foreshadows the coming Kingdom banquet—he insists that they emphasize the memorial character of the event. In the earliest recorded description of Jesus' last meal with his disciples, Paul stresses the sacred nature of the commemorative bread and wine offered on his followers' behalf (1 Cor. 11:17–34) and enjoins believers to observe the reenactment of this ceremony in orderly fashion.

Yet another source of disruption was the phenomenon of "speaking in tongues" (1 Cor. 12:1–31; 14:1–33), which Paul values least of all "spiritual gifts," such as prophesying, interpreting, and teaching. Reminding the Corinthians that he is more skilled than they at ecstatic speech, he nonetheless declares that he would rather "speak five intelligible words" than thousands in "the language of ecstasy" (1 Cor. 14:18–19), for it is comprehensible instruction and prophecy that strengthen the Church (1 Cor. 14:4–12).

Paul's emphasis on rational communication among believers is consistent with his theme of Christian unity. At the outset of his letter he had urged the Corinthians to "be firmly joined in unity of mind and thought" (1 Cor. 1:10). Although blessed with diverse spiritual gifts, they are all members of a single body, which he metaphorically compares to the human body with its many specialized parts. As the physical organs function cooperatively to achieve maximum benefits, so individual members of the Church must work together (1 Cor. 12:4–31), each person's ability contributing toward the success of the whole.

Excelling all other spiritual gifts is love, which provides the only valid motive for Christian action and teaching (1 Cor. 13). The Greek term *agapé* (also translated "charity," from the Latin *caritas*), which Paul uses in this famous passage, denotes neither sexual nor brotherly love but implies patient loving kindness, a principled giving of the self to others.

The Resurrection The most important theological concept with which Paul deals here is the nature of the afterlife. Apparently some Corinthians had rejected the Jewish-Christian doctrine of the resurrection; it is possible, too, that Greek believers denied the necessity of a bodily rising from the dead. Following the teaching of Egyptian wisdom and Greek philosophers like Pythagoras, Plato, and the Neo-Platonists, they may have believed that the body is unimportant and that the soul—an invisible, immaterial, immortal consciousness—survives the body's death and ascends to the external realm as pure spirit.

While Paul agrees that the physical self cannot inherit the Kingdom (1 Cor. 15:50), he seems to argue for the Hebraic view that the soul and body form a unity, a mortal state requiring complete transformation to achieve eternal life. The bodily resurrection of Christ, he insists, is absolutely central to Christian belief; without it, Christian faith is vain and the dead "are utterly lost" (1 Cor. 15:16–19). In what form, then, are the dead raised? While Paul does not answer directly, he implies that the resurrected being will be clothed in a "spiritual body" appropriate to a future life with Christ; what is perishable will receive imperishability, and what is mortal will acquire immortality. This triumph of life defeats the power of death (1 Cor. 15:3–57).

RECOMMENDED READING

Baird, W. *The Corinthian Church: A Biblical Approach to Urban Culture.* New York and Nashville: Abingdon Press, 1964.

Conzelmann, Hans. *1 Corinthians.* Translated by J. W. Leitch. In *Hermeneia,* edited by G. W. MacRae. Philadelphia: Fortress Press, 1975. Useful.

Gilmour, S. M. "Corinthians, First Letter to the." In *The Interpreter's Dictionary of the Bible,* vol. 1, pp. 684–92. New York and Nashville: Abingdon Press, 1962. Helpful introduction.

Hurd, J. C. *The Origins of 1 Corinthians.* New York: Seabury Press, 1965.

Orr, W. F., and Walther, J. A., eds. *1 and 2 Corinthians and 1 and 2 Thessalonians.* Anchor Bible, vol. 32. Garden City, N. Y.: Doubleday, 1976.

❦ 2 Corinthians

The Severe Letter	*Chapters 10–13*
The Final Letter	*1–9*

**Our eyes are fixed, not on the things that are seen,
but on the things that are unseen: for what is seen
passes away; what is unseen is eternal.**

2 Corinthians 4:18

The Severe Letter   Most scholars believe that 2 Corinthians represents at least two different letters to the church at Corinth. 1 Corinthians, which Paul's young companion Timothy had delivered, had not produced its desired effect. Instead of acknowledging Paul's moral leadership, the various factions had united against him. Jewish-Christian interlopers had challenged his authority and questioned his credentials as an apostle (2 Cor. 11:4). Even Paul's personal visit had failed to quell the rebellion (2 Cor. 2:1; 12:14). The result was the "severe letter" now largely preserved in 2 Corinthians 10–13.

In this missive, which differs strikingly from chapters 1–9, Paul bitterly reproaches the Corinthians for allowing "false apostles," probably representatives from the church at Jerusalem, to undermine their faith in him. Sarcastically, he quotes the Corinthians as saying that his letters are "weighty and powerful" but that Paul himself has "no presence" and as a speaker is "beneath contempt." He promises that when he arrives for a third visit his actions will reveal a man of the same mettle as his letters (2 Cor. 10:10–11). The present letter is only a foretaste of his disciplinary strength.

Wounded by the hostility of a church he had founded and nurtured, Paul ironically boasts of what he is, has accomplished, and has endured for the various churches' sake—hunger, thirst, beatings, shipwrecks, dangers of all kinds (2 Cor. 11:22–33). These passages are valuable both for the biographical information they supply and for the depth of anger and pain they reveal. It is not merely pique at the loss of his leadership that feeds Paul's passion, however, but his genuine concern and affection for the Corinthians. In spite of their betrayal, he still wants them to experience the "love and peace" for which they first became Christians (2 Cor. 13:11–14).

The Final Letter   Titus, another of Paul's missionary protégés, carries the disciplinary letter from Ephesus to Corinth, but Paul leaves for Macedonia before Titus returns. When Titus finally catches up with him, he brings the glad news that the Corinthians have disavowed their divisive leaders and now give their full support to Paul, recognizing him as an authentic apostle who had treated them honorably.

The first nine chapters of 2 Corinthians (2 Cor. 1:1–6:13 and 7:2–9:15) contain Paul's message of joyous reconciliation with the church at Corinth. He does not regret his former severity, which had cost him "many tears" (2 Cor. 2:4), because it had brought repentance and reaffirmation of the bond between him and his church. He no longer need parade his credentials because the Corinthians themselves are his living "letters of recommendation." Echoing Jeremiah 31:31, Paul contrasts the old covenant—tablets of stone—with the new covenant written on human hearts (2 Cor. 3:1–18).

Paul further develops the doctrine about the "spiritual body" that he had outlined in 1 Corinthians 15:42–57. In the earlier letter he had stated that the Christian's change to a superior bodily form will occur instantaneously at Christ's return. Now he seems to imply that the believer is already developing a spiritual body which will clothe him or her at the moment of death (2 Cor. 4:16–5:10). The Christian is therefore to cultivate one's spiritual nature lest like the unbeliever one be found "naked" at Judgment Day.

In the last two chapters of the reconciliation letter Paul reverts to practical matters. Collections for the Jerusalem poor, allowed to lapse during the rupture with Paul, are to be resumed at once. The Macedonian churches have given generously, an example that the Corinthians, grateful for God's gift of Christ, will liberally imitate. Paul reminds prospective donors that "God loves a cheerful giver" (2 Cor. 9:7).

RECOMMENDED READING

(*Note:* The bibliographic references to 1 Corinthians include material on 2 Corinthians.)

Holmberg, Bengt. *Paul and Power: The Structure of Authority in the Primitive Church as Reflected in the Pauline Epistles.* Philadelphia: Fortress Press, 1980.

Scheutz, John H., ed. *The Social Setting of Pauline Christianity.* Philadelphia: Fortress Press, 1982.

❦ Galatians

For through faith you are all sons of God in union with Christ Jesus. . . . There is no such thing as Jew and Greek, slave and free, male and female; for you are all one person in Christ Jesus.

Galatians 3:26, 28

Paul's letter to the churches in Galatia, a Roman province in southern Asia Minor, is a forthright exposition of two major themes: (1) Paul is an apostle by direct commission of the resurrected Jesus and does not derive his authority from any human agency, including the Jerusalem church; (2) Christians are free of the Mosaic law. However brief, Galatians is important because it succinctly records Christianity's declaration of independence from Judaism. Although there is much scholarly debate about when and where the letter was written, it probably originated in Corinth or Ephesus about 56 C.E. during Paul's third missionary journey.

Paul wrote Galatians because certain troublemakers—apparently Judaizers who insisted that Christians practice circumcision and observe the ceremonial requirements of the Mosaic law—were sowing discord in the Galatian churches. Paul's anxious, impassioned tone indicates the urgency of the problem, for if the legalists had their way, Christianity would never be more than a dissenting sect within Judaism.

Christianity's Independence   The letter begins abruptly, without Paul's usual greetings and thanksgivings (Gal. 1:1–5). After asserting his apostolic rights, conferred by God through Jesus, Paul plunges to the heart of the issue: Christianity is totally independent of Judaism (Ga. 1:6–2:21). Although Paul's message "owed nothing" to any of the other apostles at Jerusalem, Peter, James, and John had endorsed Paul's Gospel by shaking hands in agreement with it (Gal. 2:9). His Gospel thus recognized as legitimate, Paul was officially acknowledged as the Apostle to the Gentiles as Peter was the Apostle to the Jews (Gal. 2:6–8). In Antioch he had publicly rebuked Peter for treating Gentile converts as inferior to Jewish Christians when Peter knew that "faith in Jesus" was all that mattered (Gal. 2:11–14).

Faith over Law   In Galatians 3:1–5:12 Paul presents essentially the same argument—believers are justified by faith alone—that he later elaborated in Romans. Christians did not receive the Holy Spirit when keeping the law but only when they trusted the message of Christ. The law was not intended as a perfect and permanent guide in human affairs; faith has priority in both time and value, for long before the Mosaic law Abraham's faith had received God's blessing. Those who now strive to keep the law labor under a delusion, for human attainment of righteousness before God is a divine gift, not a reward for good works. By contrast, Christ brings freedom from the "curse of the Law" by bearing our punishment for failure to achieve its goals. The law, making us conscious of our moral inadequacy, acts as a tutor leading to Christ.

Paul concludes his argument by citing the Genesis story of Abraham's two sons, which he interprets as an allegory. Ishmael, son of the slave girl Hagar, represents the Judaism of Paul's day, in bondage to both the law and to Rome. Conversely, Isaac, son of the free woman Sarah, symbolizes the sons of Abraham by faith, the Christian community. They are citizens of the "heavenly Jerusalem," a free mother. Attempting to keep even one part of the law, such as circumcision, is to no avail, for those under law must observe it all. Paul emphasizes that "the only thing that counts is faith active in love" (Gal. 5:6).

Freedom Under the Spirit   In the third section of his letter (Gal. 5:13–6:10) Paul confronts the issue of the free Christian's moral responsibility. Does freedom from the law's restraints mean that one is authorized to indulge every desire of one's "lower nature"? Paul answers that the Spirit-led believer, motivated by love of neighbor, will control baser impulses and bear the "harvest of the Spirit"—love, kindness, goodness, and patience—qualities over which there is no law (Gal. 5:22–23). In a postscript written by his own hand, Paul reiterates his principal arguments, stressing the futility of circumcision, and reminds the Galatians of his sufferings for Jesus (Gal. 6:11–18).

RECOMMENDED READING

Dunn, James D. G. *Unity and Diversity Within the New Testament*. Philadelphia: Westminster Press, 1977.

Knox, J. "Galatians, Letter to the." In *The Interpreter's Dictionary of the Bible*, vol. 2, pp. 338–43. New York and Nashville: Abingdon Press, 1962.

Sanders, E. P. *Paul, the Law, and the Jewish People*. Philadelphia: Fortress Press, 1983.

Stendahl, K., ed. and trans. *Romans, Galatians, and Philippians*. Anchor Bible, vol. 33. Garden City, N. Y.: Doubleday, 1978.

❦ Ephesians

Unity Through Christ   *Chapters 1–6*

**For our fight is not against human foes, but against
the authorities and potentates of this dark world,
against the superhuman forces of evil in the heavens.
Therefore, take up God's armour.**

Ephesians 6:12

Although Ephesians purports to be by Paul (Eph. 1:1; 3:1) and bears
close resemblance to Colossians, many scholars doubt its Pauline origin.
Certainly the book's quiet devotional tone and smoothly organized sequence of thoughts differ from the Apostle's usual hectic welter of ideas
and impassioned language, but other factors also suggest that Ephesians
was written after Paul's time: (1) Along with typically Pauline concepts,
the book contains ideas about Christ's nature and universal role that
scholars consider more theologically advanced than those in Paul's genuine letters. (2) The letter implies that Gentile Christians dominated the
Church, whereas in Paul's day they were only a minority. (3) Judaizing
interlopers no longer pose a threat, indicating that the book was written
after Jerusalem's destruction in 70 C.E.

Although there remain solid arguments for Paul's authorship, the
present academic trend is to regard Ephesians as the work of an anonymous member of a Pauline school of thought who may have composed
it as a cover letter for Paul's collected writings. The book's generalized
nature is reflected in the lack of specific problems mentioned in the text
and in the absence of the words "in Ephesus" from any manuscript earlier
than the fourth century. More a religious meditation than a letter, it was
probably written between 90 and 100 C.E. But its promise of ultimate unity
for all believers and the full triumph of the Spirit over dissension and
hate makes it one of the most eternally relevant works of the New
Testament.

Unity Through Christ   The author's theme is that the unity of the universe through Christ (Eph. 1–3) must be reflected in the unity of the
Church, which is the earthly manifestation of the divine oneness (Eph.
4–6). God has now revealed his "hidden purpose": to bring "all in heaven
and on earth . . . into a unity with Christ" (Eph. 1:10). Although the human race had become alienated from God, God's redemptive act in Jesus'
death and resurrection had reunited the believing world to him. The
deity's age-old secret is now understood: "The Gentiles are joint heirs

with the Jews, part of the same body, sharers in the promise made in Christ Jesus" (Eph. 3:6).

In the second part of his letter (Eph. 4–6), the author explores four areas in which the Spirit imparts unity. The first area is the Church, where all believers "at last attain to the unity inherent in our faith" (Eph. 4:4–16), for there is "one body and one Spirit . . . one Lord, one faith, one baptism, one God" (Eph. 4:5–6). The second area is the pagan world (Eph. 4:17–5:20), whose ignorance and "foul desires" the Christian abandons to be "made new in mind and spirit," thus acquiring a "new nature of God's creating" (Eph. 4:21–24). In the third area, the Spirit permeates family life so that husbands, wives, children, and slaves show mutual love and forbearance (Eph. 5:21–6:9).

Finally, the Spirit offers protection against "cosmic powers" and "superhuman forces of evil in the heavens" (Eph. 6:10–20). Using the analogy of a well-equipped Roman soldier, the writer urges the Christian to arm himself against the dark powers with such spiritual defenses as "the belt of truth" and the "shield of faith," with which one can quench the Devil's "flaming arrows" (Eph. 6:13–17). Interestingly, the Devil's attack is not seen as part of a final apocalyptic conflict but as a present ongoing fight against evil forces represented by the vice and corruption of contemporary pagan society.

RECOMMENDED READING

Beare, F. W. "Introduction and Exegesis of Ephesians." In *The Interpreter's Bible*, vol. 11, pp. 597–749. New York and Nashville: Abingdon Press, 1953. Provides an illuminating introduction to problems of authorship and theology.

Best, E. *One Body in Christ.* London: SPCK, 1955. Insightful discussion of Church unity.

Garth, M., ed. and trans. *Ephesians.* Anchor Bible, vol. 34. Garden City, N. Y.: Doubleday, 1974.

Goodspeed, Edgar J. *The Meaning of Ephesians.* Chicago: University of Chicago Press, 1933. An important technical work arguing that Ephesians was written as a cover letter for Paul's collected works.

Johnston, G. "Ephesians, Letter to the." In *The Interpreter's Dictionary of the Bible*, vol. 2, pp. 108–14. New York and Nashville: Abingdon Press, 1962.

Mitton, C. L. *The Epistle to the Ephesians: Its Authorship, Origin, and Purpose.* Oxford: Clarendon Press, 1951.

🌿 Philippians

**He [Jesus] did not think to snatch at equality with God,
but made himself nothing, assuming the nature of a slave.**

Philippians 2:6–7

An authentic Pauline work, Philippians reflects Paul's special affection for the church at Philippi, the first in Europe, which he and his associate Timothy had founded (Acts 16:11–40). Paul's intimacy with the Philippians is reflected in the unusual warmth of his greetings and thanksgivings and by the fact that they were the only group from whom he would accept financial support (Phil. 4:15–16). Along with Colossians, Philemon, and possibly Ephesians, Philippians is known as one of the "captivity letters" presumably written in a Roman prison. If scholars are correct in assuming that it was sent from Rome about 62 C.E., it may be Paul's last surviving communication.

When the Philippians learned of Paul's imprisonment, they sent a representative, Epaphroditus, with a gift of money to help him. After Epaphroditus, who temporarily remained as Paul's assistant, became dangerously ill and wished to return home, Paul wrote the present letter to ensure that his companion would receive a proper welcome (Phil. 2:25–30). Judging by its admonitions, however, Paul also wished to deal with the divisions, Judaizing influences, and personal quarrels that afflicted the Philippian church. He does not mention the gifts he had received until nearly the close of his missive, possibly because he had already thanked the Philippians for their aid in an earlier letter.

Unity Through Humility　After hearty salutations and expressions of gratitude for the Philippians' concern, Paul assures them that his imprisonment has not hindered but advanced the spread of the Gospel by inspiring other Christians to "speak the word of God fearlessly" (Phil. 1:12–14). He is not worried about the future, for to him "life is Christ and death gain" (Phil. 1:21). If he wishes to survive, it is only "to add joy" to his friends' faith (Phil. 1:22–26).

Urging his recipients to conduct themselves worthily and to "think and feel alike" with "a common care for unity," Paul counsels them to avoid vanity or rivalry (Phil. 1:27–2:4) and to cultivate humility as Jesus had. Possibly quoting or paraphrasing a liturgical hymn about the Incarnation, he directs their attention to Jesus' lack of ambitious pride. For although the prehuman Jesus partook of the divine nature, "he did not think to snatch at equality with God" but instead lowered himself to become a human being. He then humbled himself further to die on the cross, for which act of obedience God had exalted him to a position above all others (Phil. 2:5–11). Christians should seek the same attitude, working out their salvation "in fear and trembling" (Phil. 2:12–13). Paul's subordination of Christ to the Father here echoes his view of the Son's submission to divine rule in 1 Corinthians (15:23–28).

Personal Expression of Faith   The shift to a sterner tone in Philippians 3:1–21 leads some critics to suggest that this passage represents an earlier memorandum reprimanding Judaizers who had infiltrated the church at Philippi, for Paul contemptuously dismisses them as "dogs" who ruin the Church's peace. In an important biographical discussion, Paul cites his ethnic qualifications to evaluate the advantages of being a Jew. He is, he writes, a person of exemplary Jewishness—a Benjaminite, a Pharisee, a former persecutor of Christians, and a "faultless" keeper of the law, but he regards his heritage as "so much garbage" compared with his spiritual gain as a Christian (Phil. 3:4–11).

This conclusion is typical of Paul's Gospel—that Jews with the law and Gentiles without it are equal "in Christ." Though he has not yet "reached perfection" in righteousness through faith, he continues to strive for "the prize," which is "God's call to the life above" (Phil. 3:12–14). The Philippians should imitate his endeavors and avoid "enemies" who are headed for destruction.

Faith and Love   In chapter 4 Paul moves from theological and ethical abstractions to concrete applications of his doctrine of faith and love. With sensitivity and tact, he pleads for a reconciliation between two estranged women, Euodia and Syntyche. He also thanks the Philippians for their gifts, which he happily accepts because such generosity reflects affirmatively on the giver (Phil. 4:15–20). It is not that he depends upon such aid, however, for he has acquired a spiritual independence of material circumstances and has learned to live with little or plenty. Paul well knows the uncertainty of the human lot and in his Christian maturity has been given "strength to bear anything" (Phil. 4:10–14). The letter, which closes with additional prayers and a benediction, reveals an appealing aspect of Paul's complex personality.

RECOMMENDED READING

Duncan, G. S. "Letter to the Philippians." In *The Interpreter's Dictionary of the Bible*, vol. 3, pp. 787–91. New York and Nashville: Abingdon Press, 1962.

Stendahl, K., ed. and trans. *Romans, Galatians, and Philippians*. Anchor Bible, vol. 33. Garden City, N. Y.: Doubleday, 1978.

🐦 Colossians

Source of Cosmic Unity   *Chapters 1–4*

The secret is this: Christ in you, the hope of a glory to come.

Colossians 1:27

Colossae, a small city in the Roman province of Asia, was located about 100 miles southeast of Ephesus, the provincial capital, and its church had apparently been founded by Epaphras, one of Paul's associates. Some New Testament scholars dispute Paul's authorship of this letter, which allegedly represents an "advanced" concept of Jesus' cosmic role, a Christology that some critics believe developed only after Paul's time. If it is a genuine Pauline work, it could have been composed in Rome in the early 60s C.E. Paul wrote to the Colossians to reaffirm the validity of what Epaphras had preached and to refute a false "philosophy" that threatened to distort the proper understanding of Christ's uniqueness.

Source of Cosmic Unity   Some members of the church at Colossae had apparently adopted a doctrine that blended pagan and marginal Jewish speculations about angels and "elemental spirits of the universe," to which they accorded some form of worship (Col. 2:8, 18). Paul denounced these "hollow and delusive" notions that failed to recognize Christ's preeminence. Asserting the absolute supremacy of Christ, he not only declared that Christ had existed in heaven before he came to earth as Jesus (the Incarnation) but argued that it was by, through, and for him that the entire universe, physical and spiritual, visible and invisible, had been created.

Christ, in "whom the complete being of God, by God's own choice, came to dwell," is the sole mediator between the deity and humankind and the only agent of cosmic reconciliation (Col. 1:13–20). The spirit beings or "cosmic powers" that the false philosophers revere are not legitimate intermediaries but were "discarded" and "led captive" at Jesus' death (Col. 2:9–15). Christ is master of all angelic forces as he is head of the Church.

Paul reminds the Colossians that they need not be intimidated by self-presuming authorities who mortify the body and piously forbid partaking of certain food and drink, for Christ's death put an end to such legal discriminations. No longer is there "Greek and Jew, circumcised and uncircumcised, barbarian, Scythians, slave and freeman; but Christ is all, and is in all" (Col. 2:20–3:11). Characteristically, Paul then moves from doctrinal matters to ethical exhortations: Christians are to live godly lives and to meet all domestic and social obligations (Col. 3:12–25). The book ends with his customary prayers, instructions, and greetings to and from various other believers (Col. 4).

RECOMMENDED READING

Barth, M., ed. and trans. *Colossians and Philomen.* Anchor Bible, vol. 34a. Garden City, N. Y.: Doubleday, 1974.

❦ 1 Thessalonians

The Parousia   *Chapters 1–5*

You have become a model for all believers . . . you turned from idols . . . to wait expectantly for the appearance from heaven of [God's] Son, Jesus, whom he resurrected from the dead, Jesus our deliverer from the terrors of judgment to come.

1 Thessalonians 1:7, 9, 10

Scholars generally agree that 1 Thessalonians is Paul's earliest surviving letter and thus the oldest Christian document in existence. Written about 50 C.E. to a church that Paul, with Timothy and Silas (Silvanus), had recently founded in Thessalonica (modern Salonica in northern Greece), it is remarkable chiefly for its eschatology, particularly the views expressed on Christ's Second Coming (1 Thess. 5:1–11) and the resurrection of the dead (1 Thess. 4:13–18).

The Parousia   In the first three chapters Paul praises the Thessalonians for their exemplary behavior while awaiting Christ's return (1 Thess. 1:9–10), reviews his labors among them, expresses his wish to visit them again, and exhorts them to cultivate their love for one another so that they will be perfect in holiness when Christ appears (1 Thess. 1–3). He then devotes the last two chapters to answering questions that troubled them.

First, like many Greek churches composed largely of pagan converts, the congregation at Thessalonica needed counseling on matters of sexual ethics. Paul reminds his correspondents that self-control and chastity are necessary to attain "holiness" (1 Thess. 4:1–8); he also advises them to keep busy and mind their own affairs (1 Thess. 4:11).

Second, Paul reassures them that their fellow believers who died before Christ's return assuredly will be raised to everlasting life "at the sound of the archangel's voice and God's trumpet call" (1 Thess. 4:13–16). When the Lord descends from heaven: "First the Christian dead will rise, then we who are left alive shall join them, caught up in clouds to meet the Lord in the air. Thus we shall always be with the Lord" (1 Thess. 4:17–18).

Paul has no patience with those who try to predict the exact date or time of the Parousia, which will come when least expected, "like a thief in the night" (1 Thess. 5:1–3). Christians should therefore keep awake, "armed with faith and love," and active in good works (1 Thess. 5:4–21). The book ends with Paul's usual prayers and a directive to have the letter publicly read "to the whole brotherhood" (1 Thess. 5:23–28).

RECOMMENDED READING

Baker, J. Christiaan. *Paul's Apocalyptic Gospel: The Coming Triumph of God.* Philadelphia: Fortress Press, 1982.

Orr, W. F., and Walther, J. A., eds. *1 and 2 Corinthians and 1 and 2 Thessalonians.* Anchor Bible, vol. 32. Garden City, N. Y.: Doubleday, 1976.

❦ 2 Thessalonians

Correcting Inaccuracies   *Chapters 1–3*

Stand firm . . . and hold fast to the traditions which you have learned from us by word or letter.

2 Thessalonians 2:15

Some experts dispute the authenticity of 2 Thessalonians; many others regard it as genuinely Pauline. If authentic, it may have been written at Corinth soon after (or, as some recent critics argue, possibly even before) 1 Thessalonians. Its purpose, at all events, is twofold: to correct a misconception that the "Day of the Lord" had already arrived (2 Thess. 2:2) and to insist that believers who lazily awaited the end must work to support themselves (2 Thess. 3:11–12).

Correcting Inaccuracies   The false idea that the Parousia had already occurred (2 Thess. 2:1–2) may have arisen partly from a misunderstanding of 1 Thessalonians, with its several references to the nearness of Christ's return (1 Thess. 1:10; 2:19; 4:15–5:11). Now advising his readers not to "lose their heads," Paul outlines certain events or "signs" that must occur before the day arrives (2 Thess. 2:3–12). Specifically, it cannot come "before the final rebellion against God, when wickedness will be revealed in human form, the [human] doomed to perdition" (2 Thess. 2:3). This unidentified "enemy" will attack all religion, claim to be a god himself, and even take "his seat in the Temple of God" (2 Thess. 2:4).

Although his original audience may have understood Paul's explanation, modern readers are puzzled by it. The "rebellion" probably echoes the apocalyptic concept prevalent in first-century Judaism that many would abandon their faith just before the Day of Judgment. But who is this proud human who will attempt to rival God? What is "the secret power of wickedness" at work? And who is the "Restrainer" whose disappearance will allow the wickedness to reveal itself? (2 Thess. 2:5–10). It is clear only that those who serve "the Lie" will be destroyed (2 Thess. 2:11–12).

Also connected with erroneous beliefs about the Parousia was the tendency of some people to give up working and live off the charity of other Christians (2 Thess. 3:6–16). For the idle, however, Paul has no sympathy: "The [person] who will not work shall not eat" (2 Thess. 3:11). He reminds the Thessalonians that when he and his associates lived among them, they "toiled and drudged . . . night and day, rather than be a burden" to them (2 Thess. 3:8) and that Christians are to follow this example of self-sufficiency. The letter closes with Paul's own signature, which, he says, "authenticates" all his correspondence, a procedure that may have been necessary because of forged letters circulating in his name (2 Thess. 2:2).

RECOMMENDED READING

Beare, F. W. "Thessalonians, Second Letter to the." In *The Interpreter's Dictionary of the Bible*, vol. 4, pp. 625–29. New York and Nashville: Abingdon Press, 1962.

(See references under 1 Thessalonians.)

THE PASTORAL EPISTLES

Called the Pastorals (from *pastor*, "shepherd" or "spiritual leader") because they stress pastoral (supervisory) and ecclesiastical (church-related) concerns, 1 and 2 Timothy and Titus were traditionally ascribed to Paul. Since the eighteenth century, however, scholars have increasingly doubted Pauline authorship, and most experts now attribute the three works to an unknown Christian schooled in Paul's doctrine who wrote between 90 and 140 C.E.

Differing from authentic Pauline writings in style, vocabulary, and tone, the Pastorals appear to reflect a second-century Church with an advanced organization in which "bishops," "elders," and "deacons" have precisely delineated functions, a situation that did not prevail in Paul's day. Although some commentators argue that the Pastorals incorporate fragments of genuine Pauline letters, most view them as entirely the work of a latter-day Paulinist who, for convenience, is referred to as "the Pastor." Scholars are not agreed about the order in which the three works were written.

RECOMMENDED READING

Barrett, C. K. *The Pastoral Epistles in the New English Bible.* Oxford: Clarendon Press, 1963. An informative commentary.

Becker, J. C. *The Church Faces the World: Late New Testament Writings.* Philadelphia: Westminster Press, 1960. A readable introductory study.

Dibelius, Martin, and Conzelmann, Hans. *The Pastoral Epistles.* Translated by P. Buttolph and A. Yarbro. In *Hermaneia,* edited by H. K. Koester. Philadephia: Fortress Press, 1972. An excellent study.

Easton, B. S. *The Pastoral Epistles.* New York: Charles Scribner's Sons, 1947.

Gealy, F. D. "Introduction and Exegesis to 1 and 2 Timothy and Titus." In *The Interpreter's Bible,* vol. 2, pp. 342–551. New York and Nashville: Abingdon Press, 1955. A helpful introduction to the Pastoral problem.

Harrison, P. N. *The Problem of the Pastoral Epistles.* Oxford: Humphrey Milford, 1921. Presents scholarly arguments against Pauline authorship.

Kelly, J. D. N. *The Pastoral Epistles.* New York: Harper & Row, 1963.

Quinn, J. D., ed. and trans. *1 and 2 Timothy and Titus.* Anchor Bible, vol. 35. Garden City, N. Y.: Doubleday, 1976.

✵ 1 Timothy

Erroneous Doctrines   *Chapters 1–6*
Ordering the Christian Congregation

I am writing these instructions to you so that . . . you may know how one ought to behave in the household of God, which is the church of the living God, the pillar and bulwark of the truth.

1 Timothy 3:14–15

The first two Pastorals are addressed to Timothy, the son of a Jewish mother and Greek father (Acts 16:1), who served as Paul's missionary companion and trusted friend (1 Cor. 16:10). However, if scholars are correct in concluding that the Pastorals are not by Paul but by an early to mid–second-century Christian writer deeply influenced by Pauline thought, it becomes clear that "Timothy" is not the historical evangelist but a literary character intended to symbolize orthodox leadership in the postapostolic Church. Such pastors struggled to keep alive Paul's "wholesome doctrine" at a time when "subversive teachings [heresies] inspired by devils" threatened to destroy Church unity (1 Tim. 4:2).

Erroneous Doctrines The writer's purpose here is, first, to combat "erroneous doctrines" (1 Tim. 1:3). Some commentators have suggested that the heresy attacked is Gnosticism, a cult of secret "knowledge" (1 Tim. 6:20), but too little is known of that diverse and complex heresy for claims to certainty. The author describes this unacceptable deviation from the true faith as involving "interminable myths," "genealogies," and fruitless "speculations" (1 Tim. 1:3–4). Its practitioners may have included Jewish legalists, self-appointed "teachers of the moral Law" (1 Tim. 1:7–11), and ascetics or "puritans" who forbade marriage and abstained from certain foods that God intended humans to eat (1 Tim. 4:1–3). Timothy (and the pastorship he represents) is the vehicle for transmitting Paul's original Gospels. He is to "pass on these orders and these teachings" (1 Tim. 4:11), thereby saving himself as well as those who listen to him (1 Tim. 4:16).

Ordering the Christian Congregation The author's second concern is to outline the qualifications for aspirants to Church offices (1 Tim. 3:1–13). Church officers must demonstrate all the virtues typical of Hellenistic ethical philosophy: they are to be "above reproach," sober, courteous, hospitable, in control of their families, and good teachers (1 Tim. 3:2–23). Such qualifications are vital for ecclesiastical leaders because the Church is "the pillar and bulwark of the truth" (1 Tim. 3:15), and only right-thinking, morally irreproachable people can successfully resist the false teachers who infiltrate it.

1 Timothy's review of the various human types who make up the Church—widows, elders, deacons, slaves, masters, heads of households (all of whom are instructed to submit to their respective superiors)—and of their characteristic duties and weaknesses gives a vivid picture of life in the second-century Christian community. As in authentic Pauline writings, the author seems to restrict the role of women, suggesting that their proper role is motherhood and their place the home (1 Tim. 2:11–15). His advice to people ambitious for wealth—"the love of money is the root of all evil things" (1 Tim. 6:10)—has become proverbial. In closing, Timothy, the prototype of the wise Church supervisor, is told to "keep safe" the doctrine entrusted to him and to avoid the "so-called knowledge" disseminated by heretics (1 Tim. 6:20–21).

🐦 2 Timothy

Correcting False Teachings   *Chapters 1–4*

Keep before you an outline of the sound teaching which you heard from me. . . . Guard the treasure put into our charge.

2 Timothy 1:13–14

2 Timothy more closely resembles Paul's genuine letters than either 1 Timothy or Titus. Although similarly concerned with refuting false teachings, its tone is more intimate and personal. Several passages in which the author depicts himself as abandoned by former associates and languishing alone in prison except for the companionship of "Luke" (2 Tim. 1:15; 4:9–11, 16) are especially poignant. Although these and other flashes of Paul's characteristic vigor and emotional fluctuations (see 2 Tim. 4:6–8, 17–18) have led some commentators to speculate that the work contains fragments of otherwise lost Pauline letters, such theories have not won general acceptance.

Correcting False Teachings   The writer, who feels an urgent need to preserve and promulgate the "sound teaching" originally received by Paul, instructs Timothy to guard Paul's Gospel like a "treasure" (2 Tim. 1:11, 14), particularly since others have strayed from following "wholesome doctrine." Repeatedly the Pastor interrupts his exhortations on correct moral conduct to rail against "foolish and ignorant speculations" (2 Tim. 2:23), which the Devil uses to breed quarrels and divisions within the Church (2 Tim. 2:26). Timothy must avoid "disputing about mere words," for such "empty and worldly chatter" infects the congregation "like a gangrene" (2 Tim. 2:16–18).

Orthodoxy of belief is particularly essential to keep Christians on the right path during "the final age of this world" (2 Tim. 3:1), for the last days will bring false teachers "who preserve an outward form of religion" while denying its reality (2 Tim. 3:5) (women are said to be especially susceptible to the insinuations of such heretics [2 Tim. 3:6–9]). The catalogue of vices that the author uses to describe humanity at the end time (2 Tim. 3:2–6) is typical of similar lists compiled in Hellenistic philosophy. Even believers will not adhere to "wholesome teachings" but will accumulate leaders who "tickle their ears" with "mythologies" (2 Tim. 4:3–4).

Timothy, representative of the apostolic tradition, must continue teaching patiently, enduring opposition, persecution, and deception (2 Tim. 3:14; 4:1–2, 5). But whereas the church was the bastion of truth in 1 Timothy, here it is the Hebrew Bible that upholds the truth, confounds error, and directs the believer to salvation. Scripture also provides "discipline in right living," causing the godly person to "be efficient and equipped for good work of every kind" (2 Tim. 3:15–17).

Although the author depicts Paul as deserted by friends and attacked by enemies, Paul's indomitable spirit is shown as unabated. Under a premonition of impending death he can still say: "I have run the great race, I have finished the course, I have kept the faith. And now the prize awaits me, the garland of righteousness which the Lord, the all-just Judge, will award me on that great Day; and it is not for me alone, but for all who have set their hearts on his coming appearance" (2 Tim. 4:6–8). At the epistle's close, the writer expresses confidence that he will be kept safe until the Parousia, when the Lord's "heavenly reign begins" (2 Tim. 4:18).

❧ Titus

Clerical Qualifications   *Chapters 1–3*

There are all too many . . . who talk wildly and lead men's minds astray. Such men must be curbed.

Titus 1:10, 11

The shortest of the Pastorals is addressed to "Titus," who had been a loyal friend and traveling companion of Paul (see Gal. 2:1, 3, 10; 2 Cor. 8:6, 16–23). Like the "Timothy" of the Pastorals, however, "Titus" represents the postapostolic Church leadership who preserved the Pauline traditions. Appropriately, "Titus'" commission is to establish an orthodox and qualified ministry. The letter's main purpose is to list the requirements and some of the duties of elders and bishops.

Clerical Qualifications The writer states that he left "Titus" in Crete to "institute elders in each town" (Titus 1:5). Such elders must be of "unimpeachable character, faithful to one's wife, and the father of children who are believers" with good reputations and under parental control (Titus 1:6). Bishops, in addition to possessing these qualifications, must be "hospitable, right-minded, temperate, just, devout, and self-controlled" (Titus 1:7–8).

Significantly, bishops must also "adhere to the true doctrine" and be able to teach others correctly and "confute objectors." Titus is the only book in the New Testament that uses the term "heretic" (Titus 3:10), which at this early date probably meant a person who held opinions of which the elders disapproved. Such dissenters from "wholesome doctrine" (Titus 2:1) are to be warned twice and then ignored (excluded from the Church?) if they fail to change their ways (Titus 3:10–11).

The author reminds his audience that because they are Christians in a nonbelieving world, they must live exemplary lives of obedience and submission to governmental authorities (Titus 3:1). Men and women, old and young, slaves and masters, are all to behave so that "the Gospel will not be brought into disrepute" (Titus 2:1–10). Christians are "a pure people marked out for God's own, eager to do good" and looking toward Christ's return (Titus 2:13–14). In a moving passage, the author contrasts the negative personality traits that many believers had had before their conversion with the grace and hope for eternal life that they now possess (Titus 3:3–8). In counsel similar to that in the letter of James, he urges believers to show their faith in "honorable" and "useful" works and to refrain from "foolish speculations, genealogies, quarrels, and controversies over the Law" (Titus 3:9–10).

Although lacking Paul's originality of thought and style, the unknown Pastor generally served his mentor's Gospel well. Not only did he impart valuable information about the second-century Church, he also contributed significantly to preserving Pauline orthodoxy and therefore the unity of the Church.

☙ Philemon

A Brother in Christ　　　　*Verses 1–25*

I am sending [Onesimus] back to you, and in doing so I am sending a part of myself.

Philemon 11

A Brother in Christ　A genuine Pauline document, Philemon is the sole personal letter of the Apostle to be included in the New Testament. It is addressed not to a congregation but to an individual Christian, Philemon, whose slave, Onesimus, had absconded with some money. While in Rome, however, the fugitive had met Paul and become converted to Christianity. Paul, urging Philemon to welcome the runaway mercifully, is now returning him to his master. Although Paul does not attack the institution of slavery, which the Romans would have condemned as subversive, he does suggest that Onesimus is no longer merely the property of his owner but a Christian brother whom Paul loves (Philem. 8–16).

In addition to soliciting Philemon's compassion, Paul hints broadly that returning Onesimus deprives him of a major comfort: "I should have liked to keep him with me, to look after me as you would wish, here in prison for the Gospel. But I would rather do nothing without your consent, so that your kindness may be a matter not of compulsion, but of your own free will" (Philem. 13–14).

Paul would like Philemon to free Onesimus so that the former slave can assist in the evangelizing work. With his personal signature, Paul undertakes to repay whatever Onesimus had stolen and asks that Philemon be equally generous toward him (Philem. 19–20). Expressing confidence that his recipient will do even more than he asks (Philem. 21), Paul ends with his customary salutations and benediction. One of the "captivity letters," Philemon was probably written in Rome about 61 C.E.

RECOMMENDED READING

Goodspeed, Edgar J. *The Meaning of Ephesians*. Chicago: University of Chicago Press, 1933. Argues that Ephesians was composed as a cover letter for Paul's collected letters and may have been the work of Onesimus.

Knox, John. *Philemon among the Letters of Paul*, rev. ed. New York: Abingdon Press, 1959. Knox develops Goodspeed's thesis that about 90 C.E., a Paulinist—perhaps Onesimus, who may then have been bishop at Ephesus—collected Paul's letters and circulated them among the entire Church.

HEBREWS AND THE CATHOLIC ("GENERAL") EPISTLES

Several relatively short writings that appear to have been composed for the Church as a whole rather than for any particular congregation or individual are known as the Catholic (meaning "universal" or "general") Epistles and traditionally include James; 1 and 2 Peter; 1, 2, and 3 John (actually a personal missive); Jude; and, in some compilations, Hebrews as well. Although 1 John, 1 Peter, and perhaps James were known in some Christian churches at a relatively early date, the others were not even mentioned until almost 200 C.E. Attributed to various well-known apostles, particularly those associated with the original Jerusalem church, the Catholic Epistles were not generally accepted until the close of the fourth century. The authenticity of 2 Peter was particularly open to question.

❧ Hebrews

**In this final age God has spoken to us in the Son
whom he has made heir to the whole universe,
and through whom he created all orders of existence:
the Son who is . . . the stamp of God's very being.**

Hebrews 1:2

An old tradition that Paul wrote Hebrews, which was disputed even in the early Church, is now generally discredited. In addition to differing in vocabulary and style, the book does not reflect Paul's characteristic thought on matters of faith, justification, reconciliation, or union with Christ. Although various attempts have been made to show that Barnabas, Priscilla (mentioned in Rom. 16:3; 1 Cor. 16:19; 2 Tim. 4:19), or the eloquent Apollos of Alexandria was the author, most scholars now conclude that the work is anonymous.

The last section (Heb. 13:18–25), with its salutations and first-person references to Timothy, seems likely to have been appended by a later hand. Moreover, although the closing paragraphs would seem to indicate that Hebrews is a letter, it reads more like an oratorical treatise or sermon, mixing theological analysis with exhortation. The work does not follow the rules prescribed by any particular literary form.

Because the text itself does not contain the phrase "to the Hebrews" or otherwise identify its recipients, scholars are also unsure of its intended destination. While the final "greetings to you from our Italian friends" (Heb. 13:24) suggests that the book originated in Italy, perhaps in Rome, some scholars have argued persuasively that it was written in Alexandria or Jerusalem. The date of composition is equally problematic, estimates ranging from 69 to 95 C.E.

Finally, although commentators at one time favored the idea that Hebrews was written to strengthen Christian integrity during a period of severe persecution, probably that of the Emperor Domitian (81–96 C.E.) more recent interpreters believe that the ordeal to which it refers had occurred during an earlier time, perhaps Nero's, in 64–65 C.E. (Heb. 10:32–34). It now appears that the author wrote to combat a falling away from the faith by emphasizing that God's ultimate revelation had come in Jesus Christ (Heb. 10:10–14) and that, since Christianity is the deity's final provision for salvation, believers must act accordingly.

Divine Revelation in Jesus Christ   Hebrews' main theme is the supremacy and absolute finality of the divine revelation through Jesus Christ. Specifically, the writer wishes to show that, as the perfect Son of God, Christ is superior to biblical prophets, angels, and the priesthood of the Mosaic law (Heb. 4:14–7:28). Hebrews is the only New Testament Book to argue that Jesus was not only a Davidic messiah-king but an eternal high priest as well.

To demonstrate that Jesus is greater than the Levitical priests who administer the Jerusalem temple, the author cites the story of Melchizedek and Abraham (Gen. 14:17–20) and a reference to Israel's kings as "like Melchizedek" (Ps. 110:4). According to Genesis, Abraham, returning from a successful war, paid Melchizedek, king of Salem and priest of "God Most High" (El Elyon), a tenth of his victor's spoils. Because the account mentions neither Melchizedek's ancestors nor descendants, the author concludes that his priesthood is without beginning or end. As king of righteousness and peace and an "eternal priest," Melchizedek is the prototype of Christ. Superior to Abraham, who paid him tithes, he is also superior to Abraham's Levitical descendants, the Jewish priests. Sinless, deathless, and confirmed by divine oath, Christ's priesthood endures forever.

Sanctuary, Covenant, and Sacrifice   In the author's view, Christ's high priesthood supercedes that of the Levites, as do his temple sanctuary, covenant, and sacrifice (Heb. 8:1–10:39). Apparently influenced by a form of Platonic dualism, the writer envisages two worlds: one is "real," the invisible realm of spirit in which Christ's heavenly sanctuary and sacrifice have their being; the other is inferior, a visible material world in which exist the earthly temple and Levitical priesthood. The realm above is eternal, that below is temporary.

In the visible Jerusalem temple, the high priest enters the innermost Holy of Holies once a year on the Day of Atonement to make a sin offering for the people (Lev. 16)—an imperfect offering that must be renewed annually. Christ, however, has entered the heavenly reality—the eternal temple—once and for all time with the sacrifice of his life, thus canceling out the need for any further sacrifices in the earthly temple at Jerusalem.

Christianity, then, is the only true religion, the fulfillment of Judaism, which was but a shadow of the final revelation. Christ's sacrifice is superior to Israel's temple offerings not only because it is sinless, perfect, and nonrepeatable, but also because it inaugurates a new covenant (Heb. 9:15). Like the Mosaic law, Christ's covenant is ratified by the blood poured out at his crucifixion, for without blood no forgiveness of sin takes place (Heb. 9:22). While the old law demands endlessly repeated animal sacrifices, the new law has but one—Christ's—which is permanently effective.

Those benefiting by Christ's everlasting sacrifice can hope, like him, to enter the heavenly sanctuary, their sins forgiven and their salvation assured (Heb. 10:5–19). Meanwhile, Christians should loyally adhere to the true religion because the Day of Judgment is near. If they willfully sin after having known the truth, they are condemned because Christ cannot die for them a second time (Heb. 10:20–31). This sentiment is expressed by no other New Testment author.

Faith in Unseen Realities   In chapter 11, one of the most famous passages in the Bible, the writer reaches the climax of his presentation. One takes advantage of God's unique revelation in the Son through faith, which "gives substance to our hopes, and makes us certain of realities we do not see" (Heb. 11:1). It is the unseen world—the heavenly realm where Christ sits at God's right hand—upon which the eyes of faith are fixed. After presenting a brilliant survey of Old Testament figures who lived by faith—from Abel, the first martyr, to the countless men and women who suffered death to attain the invisible Kingdom above—the author urges his readers to run a similar race for eternal life (Heb. 11:2–12:2). Like the faithful of old who had only a glimpse of what was to come, the Christian, who has the reality, must stand firm, enduring suffering as a necessary discipline (Heb. 12:3–13).

In a memorable image, the author reminds his readers that the ancient Israelites saw the old law introduced with awesome phenomena: fire, thunder, and earthquakes. Christians are witnesses to an even more holy covenant, which is promulgated not on earthly Mount Sinai but "before Mount Zion and the city of the living God, heavenly Jerusalem." If the Israelites who disobeyed that law were punished by death, how much more so will be those who fail to keep faith in the new dispensation? (Heb. 12:18–29).

RECOMMENDED READING

Buchanan, G. W., ed. and trans. *Hebrews.* Anchor Bible, vol. 36. Garden City, N. Y.: Doubleday, 1972.

Davies, W. D. "Ethics in the New Testament." In *The Interpreter's Dictionary of the Bible,* vol. 2, pp. 167–76. New York and Nashville: Abingdon Press, 1962. Includes discussion of Hebrews' ethical teachings.

Dinkler, E. "Hebrews, Letter to the." In *The Interpreter's Dictionary of the Bible,* vol. 2, pp. 571–75. New York and Nashville: Abingdon Press, 1962. A relatively brief but useful discussion.

Filson, F. V. *Yesterday: A Study of Hebrews in the Light of Chapter 13.* London: SCM Press, 1967.

Manson, W. *The Epistle to the Hebrews: An Historical and Theological Consideration.* London: Hodder & Stoughton, 1951. Offers some controversial views about the origin and purpose of Hebrews.

Neil, W. *The Epistle to the Hebrews.* London: SCM Press, 1955. A more popular treatment influenced by Manson's thesis.

Purdy, Alexander C. "The Epistle to the Hebrews, Introduction and Exegesis." In *The Interpreter's Bible*, vol. 11, pp. 577–763. New York and Nashville: Abingdon Press, 1955. Provides helpful historical background and theological commentary.

❦ James

Ethical Conduct and Pragmatic Morality   *Chapters 1–5*

If one . . . should stray from the truth . . . be sure of this: any man who brings a sinner back from his crooked ways will be rescuing his soul from death and canceling innumerable sins.

James 5:20

Although relatively late Church traditions ascribe this epistle to James, the "brother" or near kinsman of Jesus, most scholars now deny this claim because the work reveals no personal knowledge either of Nazareth or Jesus, to whose life or Gospel the author never refers. According to Josephus, James was martyred by command of the high priest Ananias II (*Antiquities* 20.9.1) about 60–62 C.E. Scholars now regard it as an anonymous work composed between about 80 and 100 C.E. Accepted only reluctantly by the Western and Syrian churches, it was one of the last New Testament books to attain canonical status.

James is addressed to "the Twelve Tribes dispersed throughout the world" (James 1:1), which probably refers not to the Israelites of the diaspora but to Christians scattered throughout the eastern Mediterranean region. Lacking salutations, greetings, or a complimentary close, the work resembles a sermon more than a letter. A collection of ethical precepts and proverbial advice, it strongly resembles Hebrew wisdom books. Its tone is impersonal and didactic, its advice extremely general. Without a discernible controlling theme, it presents practical exhortations on a series of miscellaneous topics.

Ethical Conduct and Pragmatic Morality   In chapter 1 the writer argues that Christians should rejoice in suffering because faith tested by trial builds fortitude (James 1:2–4). No one tempted to sin can say that God tests him or her, for temptation arises from a person's own desires, which give birth to sin and death (James 1:13–15). True religion is defined not as dogma or ritual but as humanitarian action—helping people in distress and remaining "untarnished by the world" (James 1:27).

Although James treats numerous practical and moral topics in somewhat haphazard fashion, four subjects are accorded relatively sustained coverage: (1) the evils of showing partiality to the rich and discriminating against the poor, which is failing to keep the law of neighborly love (James 2:1–12); (2) the necessity of showing faith through good works, for "faith divorced from deeds is lifeless as a corpse" (James 2:14–26); (3) the immorality of loose talk, for an unbridled tongue is "an intractable evil" (James 3:1–12); and (4) the sins of the rich who exploit the poor, thereby condemning themselves to destruction (James 4:13–5:6).

The author's insistence that faith without works is dead is not so much a contradiction of Paul's doctrine of justification through faith as it is a correction of those who use their faith as an excuse for inaction and selfishness (James 2:15–17). Similarly, the writer does not condemn the rich merely because they possess wealth but because they use it to oppress and defraud their economic inferiors (James 5:4–6). Efforts to accumulate riches are futile because "the age is near its close" (James 5:3). Those who love the world and its values are enemies of God (James 4:4) and will suffer his judgment.

Even James' instructions on prayer are eminently practical: prayer can heal the sick, effect forgiveness of sin, and even (in one case) affect the weather (James 5:13–18). In spite of the author's austere tone and emphasis on the pragmatic, his work powerfully expresses his central theme: to rescue "a sinner from his [or her] crooked ways" and thus save "his soul from death" (James 5:20).

RECOMMENDED READING

Barnett, A. E. "James, Letter of." In *The Interpreter's Dictionary of the Bible*, vol. 2, pp. 794–99. New York and Nashville: Abingdon Press, 1962.

Easton, B. S. "The Epistle of James, Introduction and Exegesis." In *The Interpreter's Bible*, vol. 12, pp. 3–74. New York and Nashville: Abingdon Press, 1957.

Dibelius, Martin. *James*. Revised by Heinrich Greeven. In *Hermeneia*, edited by Helmut Koester. Philadelphia: Fortress Press, 1976. An excellent study.

Mayor, Joseph B. *The Epistle of St. James*. 3rd ed. London: Macmillan & Co., 1910. An old but authoritative commentary, still relevant when supplemented by later studies.

Milton, C. L. *The Epistle of James*. Grand Rapids, Mich.: Wm. B. Eerdmans Publishing Co., 1966. A thorough analysis.

Reicke, Bo. *The Epistles of James, Peter, and Jude*. Anchor Bible, vol. 37. Garden City, N. Y.: Doubleday, 1964. First-rate annotations and commentary.

ꙮ 1 Peter

Exhortations Under Persecution   *Chapters 1–5*

**The end of all things is upon us, so you must lead
an ordered and sober life. . . . Above all, keep your love
for one another at full strength, because love cancels
innumerable sins.**

1 Peter 4:7, 8

Scholars are divided on the authorship of 1 Peter. Traditionalists maintain that it is the work of the Apostle Peter, who reputedly composed it in Rome during Nero's persecution of Christians (64–65 C.E.). If true, it is surprising that the epistle is addressed to churches in Asia minor (1 Pet. 1:1), since official persecution was then confined to the imperial capital. The epistle's closing remarks note that it was written "through Sylvanus" (1 Pet. 5:12), which among those who champion Peter's authorship, supposedly accounts for the work's excellent Greek.

Most scholars believe that 1 Peter is pseudonymous (written anonymously in the name of a well-known figure) and was produced during postapostolic times. Its references to "fiery ordeals" (1 Pet. 4:12–13) lead most experts to date it either during the persecutions of Domitian (about 95 C.E.) or of Trajan (about 112 C.E.). Since the situation it reflects closely parallels that described in the correspondence between Trajan and Pliny the Younger, governor of Bithynia, the latter date is commonly preferred.

The greetings from "her who dwells in Babylon" (1 Pet. 5:13) provide the key to the work's place of origin, for "her" refers to the Church, and "Babylon" (the old Testament archetype of the ungodly nation) was a Christian symbol for Rome (see Rev. 14:8; 18:2). The author's primary concerns are to encourage Christians to hold fast their integrity during persecution and to promote Christian ethics. He urges the faithful to live so blamelessly that outsiders can never accuse them of anything illegal or morally reprehensible. If one endures punishment, it should be only "as a Christian" (1 Pet. 4:14–16).

Exhortations Under Persecution Following the salutation (1 Pet. 1:1–2), the epistle, which resembles a baptism sermon, may be divided into three parts. In the first (1 Pet. 1:3–2:10), Christians are urged to regard their present trials as a test that will render their faith worthy of honor when Jesus reappears (1 Pet. 1:6–7). By remaining faithful they will attain the salvation of which the Hebrew prophets spoke (1 Pet. 1:10–11). Proper appreciation for Christ's sacrifice, which made him the "living stone" of the deity's spiritual temple, will also make the believer a living part of the heavenly sanctuary (1 Pet. 2:4–8). Christians, including Gentiles, are the new "chosen race"—"a royal priesthood, a dedicated nation, and a people claimed by God for his own" (1 Pet. 2:9–10).

The second part (1 Pet. 2:11–4:11) concentrates on the responsibilities and moral conduct of the people of God, "who should behave in a way that even pagans can recognize as good" (1 Pet. 2:12). Like Paul (Rom. 13:1), the author advises submission to governmental authorities (1 Pet. 2:13); servants likewise should be subject to their masters (1 Pet. 2:18) and women to their husbands (1 Pet. 3:1–2). Suffering inflicted by one's superiors should be borne as Christ bore his sufferings (1 Pet. 1:19–25; 3:13–18; 4:1–5). This section includes two fascinating passages about Jesus' descent into the Underworld (Hades), presumably during the interval between his death and resurrection (1 Pet. 3:18–20; 4:6), which inspired the tradition that Jesus entered Hell and rescued the souls of those who died before the way to Heaven was open.

The third section (1 Pet. 4:12–5:11) examines the ethical meaning of suffering "as a Christian." Believers should not be surprised by their "fiery ordeal" because as followers of Christ they must expect to share his sufferings (1 Pet. 4:12–16). Judgment has come, and it begins "with God's own household"—the Church. If the righteous are but narrowly saved, what will happen to the wicked? (1 Pet. 4:17–19). Elders must shepherd the flock with loving care; younger people must submit humbly to their rule (1 Pet. 5:1–7); and all must be alert, because the Devil prowls the earth "like a roaring lion" seeking to devour the unwary. The faithful who resist him will be strengthened (1 Pet. 5:8–10).

RECOMMENDED READING

Cullman, Oscar. *Peter: Disciple, Apostle, Martyr*, rev. ed. Philadelphia: Westminster Press, 1963.

Hunter, A. M. "Introduction and Exegesis of 1 Peter." In *The Interpreter's Bible*, vol. 12, pp. 77–159. New York and Nashville: Abingdon Press, 1957. Provides historical background and helpful interpretation.

O'Connor, Daniel W. *Peter in Rome: The Literary, Liturgical and Archaeological Evidence.* New York: Columbia University Press, 1969.

Reicke, Bo. *The Epistles of James, Peter, and Jude.* Anchor Bible, vol. 37. Garden City. N. Y.: Doubleday, 1964.

van Unnik, W. C. "Peter, First Letter of." In *The Interpreter's Dictionary of the Bible*, vol. 3, pp. 758–66. New York and Nashville: Abingdon Press, 1962. A useful introduction.

❦ 2 Peter

The Delayed Parousia   *Chapters 1–3*

Our Lord's patience with us is our salvation.

2 Peter 3:15

Virtually no authorities defend the Petrine authorship of 2 Peter, which is believed to have been written by an anonymous churchman in Rome about 150 C.E. The book's late date is confirmed by (1) the fact that it incorporates most of Jude (2 Pet. 2:2–17), itself a second-century work, and (2) its references to Paul's letters as "Scripture" (2 Pet. 3:16), a status they did not attain until the mid-second century C.E. Judged the last New Testament book to be composed, it was also one of the last to enter the canon.

The author assumes an apostolic identity for the purpose of representing the epistle's contents as embodying true apostolic doctrine. Before reaching his main theme, he repeatedly alludes to his apostolic status (2 Pet. 1:1), mentioning his presence at the transfiguration (2 Pet. 1:17–18), Jesus' prediction of his death (2 Pet. 1:14), his authorship of 1 Peter (2 Pet. 3:1), and his association with Paul (2 Pet. 3:15). Having thus established his credentials, he rails against the "false teachers" who pervert the apostolic traditions, upon whom judgment will fall as it did upon sinful angels whom God chained in Tartarus (2 Pet. 2:4), upon the corrupt world of Noah's time, and upon Sodom and Gomorrah (2 Pet. 2:5–6).

The Delayed Parousia   In chapter 3 the writer delivers his main arguments for the certainty of Christ's Second Coming (2 Pet. 3:3–15). Skeptics may point out that the "fathers" (apostles) who promised Christ's early return have all died and yet the world continues on exactly as before, but they forget that the world has already been destroyed once in Noah's flood (2 Pet. 3:3–6); similarly, the present world will be consumed by fire (2 Pet. 3:7). God does not unduly delay his judgment, because with him "one day is like a thousand years and a thousand years like one day." Only people trapped in earthly time think that the interval is long; for the deity, dwelling in eternity, the Parousia has already occurred. The Lord is not slow in answering his promise; he merely exercises patience so that as many people as possible will be saved (2 Pet. 3:8–9). This passage not only defends the primitive Christian belief that the Parousia was historically imminent but also deals with the question of divine justice. The author states that God permits evil to continue so that wrong-doers will benefit from an extended opportunity to reject evil and find salvation. The continuance of human history is thus a result of God's mercy.

Because the universe is destined to be consumed in flames, Christians must faithfully prepare for the Coming, "work to hasten it on" (2 Pet. 3:11–12), and look forward to entering "a new heavens and a new earth" foretold by Isaiah (Isa. 65:17). While patiently awaiting the fulfillment of the Lord's design, they must study the Scriptures (including Paul's letters), which the ignorant ruinously misinterpret (2 Pet. 3:14–16), taking care not to allow heretics to deceive them with their errors.

RECOMMENDED READING

Becker, J. C. "Peter, Second Letter of." In *The Interpreter's Dictionary of the Bible*, vol. 3, pp. 767–71. New York and Nashville: Abingdon Press, 1962.

(See references to 1 Peter.)

---

 1 John

Distinguishing Truth from Error   Chapters 1–5

The message you have heard from the beginning is this: that we should love one another.

                                        1 John 3:11

Although ancient traditions attributed to the Apostle John the Fourth Gospel, the Book of Revelation, and the three Epistles of John, modern scholars believe that he wrote none of them. While similarities of thought and style indicate that the same person may have written the Gospel and three epistles, the author is unknown. The writer of 2 and 3 John calls himself an "elder" but is otherwise unidentified, and scholars are virtually unanimous in agreeing that he is not the author of Revelation. The epistles probably originated in Ephesus about 100–110 C.E.

Distinguishing Truth from Error   A tract or sermon rather than a letter, 1 John was written to defend the doctrine that Christ came "in the flesh" (1 John 4:2) against certain heretics who denied the Incarnation. These the author denounces as "the Antichrist" (1 John 4:3), whose activity proves that "the last hour" has come (1 John 2:18). Scholars believe that the heretics referred to were the Docetists ("Seemists"), an offshoot of the Gnostics, who taught that Christ could not simultaneously be human and divine and argued that salvation lay in the knowledge (*gnosis*) of sacred mysteries. This form of Gnosticism tended to produce Antinomianism, the belief that those who were initiated into such knowledge could not sin and were therefore not bound by moral law. Such notions, which often led initiates to claim freedom *for* sin, also drew fire from other New Testament writers (see Rom. 6:1, 15; Jude 4; 2 Pet. 2:2).

Written before a strong central authority existed to enforce Christian orthodoxy, 1 John met an important need by setting forth three standards by which beliefs could be tested for their validity. When rival groups claimed to possess the true Spirit for their conflicting interpretations, they could be judged by the following:

1. Their ethical conduct: Those who really know the deity keep his commandments (1 John 2:3).

2. Their doctrine: Those who confess that Jesus Christ came in the flesh, as a physical human being, have God's Spirit (1 John 4:1–6).

3. Their exercise of Christian love: Those who show love for one another in service as well as word (1 John 3:18) are children of God (1 John 4:7). The unloving do not know God, "for God is love" (1 John 4:8–9).

The writer's formulation of criteria by which the Church could effectively "distinguish the spirit of truth from the spirit of error" (1 John 4:6) and thus reduce the subversive power of heresy contributed significantly toward the unity and harmony of the Christian community.

RECOMMENDED READING

Brown, Raymond E. *The Epistles of John*, Anchor Bible. Garden City, N. Y.: Doubleday, 1982.

Bultmann, Rudolf. *The Johannine Epistles*. Translated by R. P. O'Hara. Philadelphia: Fortress Press, 1973. An excellent scholarly analysis.

Caird, G. B. "John, Letters of." In *The Interpreter's Dictionary of the Bible*, vol. 2, pp. 946–52. New York and Nashville: Abingdon Press, 1962.

Smith, D. M. "John, Letters of." In *The Interpreter's Dictionary of the Bible: Supplementary Volume*, pp. 486–87. Nashville: Abingdon Press, 1976.

Wilder, Amos. "The First, Second, and Third Epistles of John, Introduction and Exegesis." In *The Interpreter's Bible*, vol. 12, pp. 207–313. New York and Nashville: Abingdon Press, 1957. An informative discussion.

 2 John

Warning Against Heretics　　　　*Verses 1–13*

Love means following the commands of God.

2 John 6

Warning Against Heretics   A letter of only thirteen verses, 2 John is from "the Elder" to "the Lady chosen by God and her children" (2 John 1), probably a reference to an unidentified church and its members. As in 1 John, the author warns his recipients against false teachers who deny that Christ appeared in physical form (2 John 7). Described again as "the Antichrist" and "archdeceiver," these heretics seem to be disseminating Docetic claims that the Word was not incarnated "in the flesh." The Elder recommends that they be denied fellowship and access to the Church (2 John 9–11).

🐛 3 John

An Appeal   *Verses 1–14*

The well-doer is a child of God.

3 John 11

An Appeal   In 3 John, a private letter to his friend Gaius, the Elder asks his recipient to extend hospitality to Demetrius, an itinerant missionary. By the time of writing, individual congregations have apparently become independent of such traveling evangelists, and some have refused them welcome or support. The Elder denounces Diotrephes, the leader of one congregation, for withholding help from both the writer and his emissaries, for excluding them from the church, and for spreading malicious gossip about them (3 John 9–10). Diotrephes' motives are not given, but he may have been one of the teachers of false doctrine mentioned in 2 John.

🐛 Jude

Warning Against False Teachers   *Verses 1–25*

I appeal to you to join the struggle in defense of the faith which God entrusted to his people once and for all.

Jude 3

Although the author identifies himself as Jude (Judas), "servant of Jesus Christ and brother of James"—and presumably also a kinsman of Jesus (see Matt. 13:55; Mark 6:3)—the text implies that the time of the apostles is long past and that their predictions are now coming true (Jude 17). Scholars generally agree that Jude is an anonymous work composed about 125 C.E., perhaps in Rome.

Warning Against False Teachers Like 2 Peter (which incorporates nearly all of this brief epistle) and the Johannine epistles, Jude was written to defend the faith against heretics who had "wormed their way" into the Church (Jude 3–4) and disrupted its "love-feasts" (Jude 12). Because the writer's descriptions of them are so general, it is difficult to identify these heretics, but their alleged immorality and insulting behavior (Jude 8–10) suggest that they may have been Gnostics and Antinomians similar to those whom "the Elder" attacked in 1, 2, and 3 John. The writer's blistering indictment of their "shameful deeds" (Jude 13)—which merit punishment comparable to that inflicted on Egypt (Jude 5), the fallen angels (Jude 6), and Sodom and Gomorrah (Jude 7)—make Jude vivid reading.

Besides its vituperation, Jude is notable for quoting several non-biblical sources along with well-known passages from the Old Testament. The author cites the pseudepigraphal Book of Enoch (Jude 14–15) and possibly the incompletely preserved Assumption of Moses (Jude 9). To balance its largely vindictive tone, the epistle closes with a particularly lyric doxology (Jude 24–25).

RECOMMENDED READING

Becker, J. C. "Jude, Letter of." In *The Interpreter's Dictionary of the Bible*, vol. 2, pp. 1009–11. New York and Nashville: Abingdon Press, 1962.

Reicke, Bo. *The Epistles of James, Peter, and Jude*. Anchor Bible, vol. 37. Garden City, N. Y.: Doubleday, 1964. Extremely helpful annotations.

THE CHRISTIAN APOCALYPSE

The least understood and most misinterpreted book in the Bible, Revelation belongs to that class of religious writings that is most calculated to bewilder the reader—the apocalyptic. Like other apocalypses (unveilings or previews of future events), Revelation is written in cryptic symbols, a literary code that only the initiated, presumably the author's original audience, would understand. It is also like other apocalypses, such as the Book of Daniel, in having been composed to meet an immediate crisis—in this case, the Emperor Domitian's persecution of Christians. Resembling contemporary Jewish apocalypses such as 2 Esdras and 2 Baruch, Revelation is a visionary response to Roman hostility that threatens to annihilate the author's community of faith.

🍃 Revelation

Visions and Symbols   *Chapters 1–22*

I saw a new heaven and a new earth.

Revelation 21:1

According to reputable scholars, the author of Revelation was neither the Apostle John nor the anonymous writer of the Fourth Gospel. The author identifies himself only as "John," God's "servant" (Rev. 1:1, 4, 9; 22:8), does not claim apostolic authority, never mentions having known the living Jesus, and presents a portrait of Jesus radically different from that of the gracious teacher-prophet of the Gospels. Some critics identify the apocalyptist with a John the Elder who lived in Ephesus about 100 C.E., but this hypothesis has not been widely accepted. Eusebius, who mentions John the Elder as a possible author, also notes that some churches did not include Revelation among the "recognized" books (*Ecclesiastical History* 3.39.6; 3.24.18; 3.25.4).

The book was probably written late in Domitian's reign, perhaps about 95 C.E., when Christians were persecuted for their "unpatriotic" refusal to worship the deified emperor, which John saw as the "Antichrist's" final attack on the Church and evidence of the end. He wrote to strengthen the faithful's resistance to engaging in public rituals that honored the emperor's divinity, an act regarded as idolatrous by Jews and Christians alike. To John, it is vital to avoid apostasy or compromise, especially since the Parousia is imminent and "the hour of fulfillment is near" (Rev. 1:3).

A consciously literary artist, John borrows many of his characteristic symbols, images, phrases, and theological assumptions from numerous Old Testament books, particularly Daniel, Ezekiel, Joel, Zechariah, and Jeremiah. Like Jewish apocalyptists of the Greco-Roman era, such as the author of 2 Esdras, he sees the Messiah appearing amid a series of catastrophic events, the near success of an Antichrist who oppresses the faithful, and the Messiah's counterattack that culminates in the establishment of a new cosmic order. Revelation thus presents the Roman persecutions (the Antichrist) as the beginning of a universal war between the forces of good and evil that will end in Christ's slaughter of all enemies and in the Kingdom's complete triumph.

Visions and Symbols While it is uncertain whether John intends his readers to see his visions as literal epiphanies that he himself experienced or as literary devices to convey his message, his presentation of visionary material is superbly well organized. After an introductory vision of

Christ (Rev. 1), he composes seven letters to the seven leading churches of Asia Minor, praising them for their integrity or blaming them for compromising with the world (Rev. 2–3). He prefaces his major revelation with visions of God (Rev. 4:1–11) and of Christ (Rev. 5:1–14), who are presently aloof from human affairs but who will soon intervene to destroy the wicked and redeem the faithful.

The author's emphasis on the number seven (which may symbolize divine completeness) is manifest in his arranging the central section of his book (Rev. 6:1–21:8) into a series of seven eschatological visions, each of which contains seven secondary visions, with a few interludes scattered amid the apocalyptic catastrophes described. The eschatological visions include the following:

1. Seven seals (Rev. 6:1–8:6)

2. Seven trumpets (Rev. 8:7–11:19)

3. Seven visions of the Dragon's (Devil's) worldly rule (Rev. 12:1–13:18)

4. Seven visions of those who worship the Lamb (Christ) and those who honor the Beast (Rev. 14:1–20)

5. Seven bowls of divine anger (Rev. 15:1–16:21)

6. Seven visions of Babylon's (Rome's) fall (Rev. 17:1–19:10)

7. Seven visions of the end of Satan's power and the creation of a "new heavens and a new earth" (Rev. 19:11–21:8)

In the final, atypically peaceful vision, John is shown the heavenly city (Rev. 21:9–22:5). The author records his survey of future history to demonstrate that the deity has a preordained plan for the world and a firm control of events both earthly and cosmic.

While it is impossible to give adequate coverage here to Revelation's vast complexities, a few of the more outstanding visions and symbols can be summarized. In the vision of the seven seals (Rev. 6:1–8:6), for example, Christ opens a seven-sealed scroll, and as each seal is broken, disasters occur on earth. Opening the first four seals releases four horsemen—probably representing war, revolution, famine, and death—that devastate humankind (Rev. 6:2–8). Breaking the fifth seal discloses Christian martyrs who cry out for vengeance (Rev. 6:9–11). Opening the sixth brings seismic and astronomical phenomena (Rev. 6:12–17), suggesting that all nature responds to the deity's punitive design. During a quiet interval, a symbolic 144,000 spiritual Israelites and a "vast throng" (probably of Gentiles) are sealed to worship at the heavenly throne (Rev. 7:1–17). The breaking of the seventh seal introduces the vision of seven trumpets, in which additional plagues beset the earth (Rev. 8:7–11:19).

Of particular interest is the seven-headed Dragon—a composite of apocalyptic beasts—who persecutes a pregnant woman dressed in sun, moon, and stars (Rev. 12:1–17). Identified as Satan, the "serpent of old" (Rev. 12:9; Gen. 3:1, 14–15), the red Dragon is a Judeo-Christian embodiment of the ancient Mesopotamian myth concerning Tiamat, the monster of chaos, whose story is told in the Babylonian creation epic, the *Enuma Elish*. As Marduk, the Mesopotamian creator-god, vanquishes Tiamat and brings order to the universe, so the Archangel Michael (the traditional spirit-prince of Israel) (Dan. 11:1) defeats the Dragon (Rev. 12:9), thus allowing a new cosmic order to appear. The victim of the Dragon's attack, a woman who gives birth to a male child destined to rule "all nations" (Rev. 12:5), apparently represents heavenly Israel as well as Jewish and Gentile Christians on earth—i.e., the Church that the Dragon attempts to destroy.

The beast with "ten horns and seven heads" probably symbolizes Rome, the earthly focus of Satan's power (Rev. 13:8). The two-horned beast may represent the Roman priesthood that helped to enforce emperor worship (Rev. 13:11–17). The mysterious "number of the beast" (666)— signifying a man's name—is now commonly thought to stand for Nero Caesar, whose name in Hebrew letters has the numerical value of 666 (Rev. 13:18). John may refer to a popular first-century legend that Nero was still alive and would return from the east heading a conquering army, a theme also presented in the Sibylline oracles (see p. 252).

After promising salvation to those who worship the Lamb and eternal torment to those worshiping the Beast (Rev. 14), John reviews the horrors destined to afflict the earth before the climactic Battle of Armageddon (Rev. 15:1–16:16). The next seven visions (Rev. 17:1–19:10) predict the fall of the Great Harlot and Babylon, both symbolizing Rome. The seventh and last series of visions (Rev. 19:11–21:8) describes the defeat of Gog and Magog (the Devil's forces), the abyssing of Satan, the thousand-year reign of Christ (the Millennium), the temporary loosening and final annihilation of Satan, the resurrection and judgment, and the creation of a "new heavens and a new earth" from which all pain and sorrow are to be excluded (Rev. 21:1). Following his vision of celestial Jerusalem, described metaphorically as a city of gold and jewels (Rev. 21:9–27), John hears Christ inviting all to drink "the waters of life" (Rev. 22:1–5).

Whereas the prophet Daniel had been instructed to seal up his vision until the time of the end (Dan. 12:4), John is told not to do so because "the hour of fulfillment is near" (Rev. 22:10). The writer apparently expected an immediate vindication of his eschatological hopes. He concludes his visionary record by cursing anyone who tampers with its predictions and by invoking the imminent appearance of Jesus (Rev. 22:18–20).

RECOMMENDED READING

Bowman, J. W. "Revelation, Book of." In *The Interpreter's Dictionary of the Bible*, vol. 4, pp. 58–71. New York and Nashville: Abingdon Press, 1962.

Charles, R. H. *The Revelation of St. John*. Vols. 1 and 2, International Critical Commentary. New York: Charles Scribner's Sons, 1920. A standard work providing a detailed analysis of John's apocalypse.

Connick, C. Milo. *The New Testament: An Introduction.* 2nd ed. Belmont, Calif.: Dickenson Publishing Co., 1978. A college-level textbook offering a clear and refreshingly commonsensical interpretation of Revelation's mysteries.

Fiorenza, E. Shussler. "Revelation, Book of." In *the Interpreter's Dictionary of the Bible: Supplementary Volume*, pp. 744–46. Nashville: Abingdon Press, 1976.

Lilje, Hans. *The Last Book of the Bible.* Philadelphia: Mullenberg Press, 1957. A readable and reliable interpretation.

Rissi, M. *Time and History.* Translated by G. C. Winsor. Richmond, Va.: John Knox Press, 1966.

Rist, Martin. "Introduction and Exegesis of the Revelation of St. John the Divine." In *The Interpreter's Bible*, vol. 12, pp. 345–613. New York and Nashville: Abingdon Press, 1957. A concise and informative analysis.

Russell, D. S. *The Method and Message of Jewish Apocalyptic: 200 B.C.–A.D. 100.* Philadelphia: Westminster Press, 1964. A useful review of apocalyptic literature of the Greco-Roman period.

AFTERWORD

The New Testment closes with the Apocalypse (Revelation), invoking the speedy return of Jesus to rescue and vindicate his Church. This placing of John's eschatological vision at the end of the Christian Bible is appropriate, for as scholars have noted Christianity began as "an apocalyptic sect within Judaism." Whether or not New Testament beliefs about the imminence of end time can be traced back to the historical Jesus, they are clearly an important hope of the early Church. The oldest surviving Christian document, 1 Thessalonians, shows that Paul expected to be alive when Christ returned (1 Thess. 1:9; 4:15). The Synoptic Gospels also stress the nearness of the final consummation, typically attributing this expectation to Jesus: "I [Jesus] tell you this: there are some of those standing here who will not taste death before they have seen the kingdom of God already come in power" (Mark 9:1). Both Mark and Matthew picture Jesus proclaiming that "The time has come: the kingdom of God is upon you" (Mark 1:15; Matt. 10:7), emphasizing that some of Jesus' original audience would "live to see it all" (Mark 13:30; 14:25; Matt. 10:23; 24:34).

Even after Jesus' death and resurrection, his followers continued to hope for the establishment of the divine kingdom promised by Daniel (Dan. 2:44). Two disciples walking to Emmaus on the first Easter morning fail to recognize the raised Jesus and tell him that they "had been hoping that he was the one to liberate Israel" (as the Davidic messiah was expected to do) (Luke 24:21). Only moments before Jesus' ascension to heaven, the disciples again are shown asking if he will *now* "establish once again the sovereignty of Israel" (Acts 1:6). Jesus' answer illustrates the author's view that before the kingdom arrives the "age of the Church"—a period of indefinite length—must intervene. The Christian community is assigned the task of witnessing about Jesus "to the ends of the earth" (Acts 1:8). Similarly, the apocalyptic predictions in Mark 13 and Matthew 24 state that a worldwide proclamation must precede Jesus' return (Mark 13:10; Matt. 24:14).

Before the end of the first century C.E. some Christians were keenly aware that early eschatological hopes had failed to materialize. Neither Christ nor the kingdom had appeared. In 1 Clement (an epistle that was included in some early editions of the New Testament), Clement, Bishop of Rome, states:

> Let that Scripture be far from us which says: "Wretched are the double-minded, those who doubt in their soul and say, 'We have heard these things even in our fathers' times, and see, we have grown old and none of this has happened.'"

> 1 Clem. 23:3–5, written about 96 C.E.

Two generations later, in a work attributed to the Apostle Peter, the problem of the "delayed Parousia" was again raised. Sceptics complained that Jesus' promised second coming had proved to be a nonevent; everything "continues exactly as it has always been since the world began" (2 Pet. 3:1–10). The writer responded to this criticism of an unconfirmed doctrine by asserting that a delayed world judgment allowed time and opportunity for sinners to repent and was thus an act of divine mercy.

Nonetheless, Jesus' nonreappearance undoubtedly provided a crisis of belief among many second-century Christians. Yet the believing community not only survived its initial disappointments but prospered. Despite dashed hopes that the Parousia would follow any number of seemingly "final" events—the Jewish revolt, the destruction of Jerusalem, the deaths of the last apostles, or the first- and second-century Roman persecutions of the Church—the new faith continued to grow in stature, wealth, and influence. By the fourth century it had become the state religion of the Roman Empire.

How was Christianity able to outlive the failure of its primitive eschatological expectations, so central to its early teachings? Historians, sociologists, and theologians have suggested many explanations to account for the Church's phenomenal persistence despite repeated disappointments. The proposed reasons for survival include the Church's strong sense of community, its providing a social and emotional haven for believers, its efficient organization, its ability to give its adherents a feeling of individual purpose, and the expertise of its leaders in accommodating to changing intellectual, political, and social realities. In addition, John's Gospel could be interpreted as teaching a "realized eschatology," a view that proclaimed Christ eternally present in spirit and precluded the necessity of his literal return. Perhaps as decisive as any of these factors was the Church's success in preserving eschatological principles by adapting and applying them to individual lives. Christianity originally borrowed most of its eschatological beliefs from Jewish sources, which had emphasized the external and material triumph of Yahweh's sovereignty over pagan nations. This *general* eschatology—the terrifying Day of Yahweh, cosmic battles between good and evil forces, divine judgment and the supernatural imposition of God's kingdom—was replaced by *personal* eschatology. Jewish eschatological literature, such as 2 Baruch, the Testament of Abraham, the books of Enoch, and 2 Esdras, had stressed Yahweh's (or the coming Messiah's) universal rule, violently imposed, but they had also provided graphic images of the consequences of apocalyptic events on individual human beings. In later Roman Christianity, eschatological teachings retained their emotional impact on a personal, individual level. All believers faced inevitable death, with the attendant dangers and terrors of the afterlife. Jewish and Christian apocalyptic writers painted memorable scenes of the respective fates awaiting the righteous and the wicked. Anticipation of the world's end might fade, but to the believer, postmortem judgment, heaven, hell, and resurrection were certainties. These eschatological concerns the Church defined and regulated. While normative Judaism rejected virtually all eschatological literature, with its highly speculative and ethically problematical views of divine justice, the Christian community effectively transferred its doctrine of "last things" to the human microcosm, postponing its hopes for the Parousia to an unknowable time in the indefinite future.

EXTRACANONICAL WORKS

The twenty-seven Greek books eventually included in the New Testament represent only a portion of Christian writings from the period. As noted earlier, several documents that are not now part of the official canon may at one time have been regarded as virtually on a par with such long-disputed works as James, 2 Peter, Jude, and Revelation.

The Codex Sinaiticus, an ancient New Testament manuscript discovered in 1859, contained the Shepherd of Hermas, a mystical apocalyptic composition, parts of which may have been written in the late first century C.E.; the Didache, a two-part volume that includes a manual of primitive Church discipline perhaps dating back to apostolic times; the the Epistle of Barnabas, a moralistic commentary on Scripture supposedly written by Paul's traveling companion.

Although these books were preserved in an appendix to the Codex, they apparently stood on the fringes of the Christian canon, several prominent early Church figures attributing considerable importance to them. Clement of Alexandria refers to the Didache as "Scripture," and Athanasius recommends its use for teaching Christian students. The Epistle of Barnabas (about 130 C.E.) and the First Epistle of Clement, bishop of Rome (about 90–100 C.E.), were also held in high esteem in many sectors of the Church. Indeed, they are closer in time to Christianity's origins than are many canonical New Testament books.

Among other primitive writings that remained influential for several centuries are the letters of Ignatius, bishop of Antioch in Syria, and those of Polycarp of Smyrna in Asia Minor, whose authority arose partly from the fact that he was said to have been taught by the Apostle John himself. In form and content, the letters of Ignatius and Polycarp to churches at Ephesus, Rome, Philadelphia, and Philippi often resemble Paul's New Testament correspondence.

CHRISTIAN APOCRYPHA

In addition to the works noted above, some of which may for a time have achieved quasi-canonical status, the early Christian community produced numerous other writings that, with one or two exceptions, were apparently never seriously considered part of Scripture. These books are known collectively as the Christian Apocrypha, and they encompass several literary genres modeled on New Testament forms, including gospels, epistles, apostolic "acts," and apocalypses. As Luke's preface testifies, biographies of Jesus were especially plentiful. Church leaders from the third and fourth centuries C.E. refer to a Gospel of the Hebrews, Gospel of the Egyptians, gospels attributed to all the twelve apostles individually and collectively and to Jesus himself. Some of these are known by name only; parts of others survive in manuscript fragments of brief quotations in commentaries by early Church scholars.

One major exception is the Gnostic Gospel ascribed to St. Thomas, found apparently complete in a Coptic translation in 1945 and containing 114 sayings of Jesus, some of which may be as authentic as those in the Synoptics. Other gospels are less historical, providing miraculous infancy narratives and doubtful information about Jesus' life not preserved in the canonical writings. These imitative and often fanciful works are attributed to a variety of New Testament figures, including the Virgin, Nicodemus, Gamaliel, and Pilate; one even purports to be by Eve.

Other Apocrypha include pseudepigraphal epistles by Peter and Paul and a correspondence between Paul and the Roman philosopher Seneca. Various histories or "acts" are ascribed to John, Peter, Paul, Andrew, and Thomas. Christian apocalypses, heavily influenced by Jewish eschatology, include books of Ezra (Esdras) and Sibylline Oracles. The most influential of these is the Apocalypse of Peter, famous for its horrific picture of souls tormented in hell. Dating from about 135 C.E. and thus older than 2 Peter, it survives in an Ethiopic translation. The student interested in reading the surviving documents from the Christian Apocrypha and other extracanonical literature is directed to the references below.

RECOMMENDED READING

Cameron, Ron, ed. *The Other Gospels: Non-Canonical Gospel Texts.* Philadelphia: Westminster Press, 1982. Scholarly translations of several early-Christian Gospels, including those attributed to Peter, James, and Mark.

Eusebius. *The History of the Church from Christ to Constantine.* Translated with an introduction by G. A. Williamson. Baltimore: Penguin Books, 1965. If the reader takes Eusebius' statements with caution, this history provides excellent atmospheric background for the early Church and fascinating anecdotes about the apostles and second-century Church leaders.

Fremantle, Anne, ed. *A Treasury of Early Christianity.* New York: New American Library, 1960. A paperback that includes selections from both the Christian Apocrypha and the writings of many first- through fifth-century Church figures, saints, and martyrs.

Hennecke, Edgar. *New Testament Apocrypha.* Vol. 1, *Gospels and Related Writings:* Vol. 2, *Writings Related to the Apostles, Apocalypses, and Related Subjects.* Edited by Wilhelm Schneemelcher. Translated by R. McL. Wilson. Philadelphia: Westminster Press, 1963. An authoritative work that provides translations of apocryphal texts.

Josephus, Flavius. *The Jewish War.* Translated by G. A. Williamson. Revised by E. Mary Smallwood. Baltimore: Penguin Books, 1981. An eyewitness account of political events in Palestine that provided the background for the birth and growth of Christianity, including the Jewish revolt against Rome (66–70 c.e.), its causes and aftermath, and a few references to Jesus and the martyrdom of his "brother" James.

Musurillo, Hebert A. *The Fathers of the Primitive Church.* New York: New American Library, 1966. A useful paperback collection of early Christian writings through the fourth century.

Pagels, Elaine. *The Gnostic Gospels.* New York: Random House, 1979. Argues that the Church suppressed Gnostic Christianity on political grounds.

Staniforth, Maxwell. *Early Christian Writings: The Apostolic Fathers.* Baltimore: Penguin Books, 1968. A paperback anthology of the more important Christian Apocrypha, with helpful prefaces and notes.

GLOSSARY OF MAJOR BIBLICAL CHARACTERS, TERMS, AND CONCEPTS

The following glossary identifies or defines a representative selection of major characters, concepts, places, and terms found in the canonical Old and New Testaments. For a more comprehensive treatment of individual terms, the reader is directed to George A. Buttrick, ed., *The Interpreter's Dictionary of the Bible*, 4 vols. (New York and Nashville: Abingdon Press, 1962) and its *Supplementary Volume* (1976). For useful one-volume references, see H. S. Gehman, ed., *The New Westminster Dictionary of the Bible* (Philadelphia: Westminster Press, 1970) and Madeleine S. Miller and J. Lane Miller, *Harper's Bible Dictionary*, 8th ed. (New York: Harper & Row, 1973).

Aaron The older brother of Moses and first head of the Israelite priesthood, Aaron was the son of Amram the Levite and his aunt Jochebed (Exod. 6:20). Because Moses reputedly had a speech defect, Aaron served as his spokesman before pharaoh (Exod. 4:14). According to the Priestly source in the Pentateuch, which stresses Aaron's special role, Moses anointed him and his four sons as founders of Israel's priesthood (Num. 3:1–3), consecrating them to administer the tabernacle (see Lev. 8 and Exod. 29). Although he led in the worship of the golden calf (Exod. 32:1–6), Aaron remained in divine favor. His son Eleazar succeeded him as high priest of Israel.

Aaronites Priestly descendants of Aaron's line (1 Chron. 12:27; Ps. 115:10). In the New Testament, Zecharias and Elisabeth, the parents of John the Baptist, were both Aaronites (Luke 1).

Abel The second son of Adam and Eve (Gen. 4:2) and brother of Cain, who murdered Abel when his animal sacrifice was accepted by Yahweh while Cain's grain offering was rejected. This story of the first murder (Gen. 4:3–10) occurs in the J portion of the Pentateuch and is referred to in the New Testament by Jesus (Matt. 23:35) and the author of Hebrews (Heb. 11:4). In Hebrew, the name Abel means "breath" or "vanity."

Abigail Wife of Nabal the fool, a wealthy shepherd who denied young David a share of his property. By wisely making a peace offering to David's guerrilla band, Abigail saved her husband's life. After Nabal's death, she married David (1 Sam. 25) and bore him a son, Chileab (2 Sam. 3:3).

Abimelech (1) In Genesis, a king of Gerar at whose court Abraham presented his wife Sarah as his sister (Gen. 20:1–18). The ruler and patriarch later made a covenant with each other (Gen. 21:22–34). (2) A Philistine king at Gerar to whom Isaac passed off his wife Rebekah as his sister and with whom he, too, later established a covenant (Gen.

26:1–33). (3) In Judges, the son of Gideon who slew his seventy brothers and made himself king at Shechem until he was killed during a siege (Judg. 9).

Abraham In Genesis 12–24, Abraham (at first called Abram, meaning "exalted father") is the supreme example of obedience to Yahweh and the founder of the Hebrew nation. By divine order, he leaves his adopted home in Haran, northern Mesopotamia, and travels to Canaan (Palestine), which land is promised to his descendants who are to become a mighty nation (Israel). Yahweh later demands that he sacrifice his only son by his wife Sarah. Because of Abraham's willingness to surrender Isaac, Yahweh reaffirms the Abrahamic Covenant, by which the patriarch's descendants are to become as numerous as "the sands of the sea" and a source of blessing to all nations. According to Genesis, the twelve tribes of Israel are descended from Abraham's grandson Jacob. The Age of Abraham, a period of mass nomadic movement in the ancient Near East, occurred during the nineteenth or eighteenth century B.C.E.

Absalom In 2 Samuel, the son of David and Maacah (2 Sam. 3:3). Noted for his physical beauty and fiery temperament, Absalom killed his half-brother Amnon to avenge his sister Tamar, fled to Geshur in Aram, but was reconciled with his father three years later. He later rebelled against David and drove him from Jerusalem but was defeated and killed by the loyalist Joab (2 Sam. 13–14).

Acrostic In Hebrew poetry, a series of lines or verses of which the first word begins with consecutive letters of the alphabet. Examples of this alphabetical sequence are found in Lamentations 1–4 and Psalm 199.

Adam In Genesis, the name Adam literally means "ruddy," from the Hebrew for "red"; it possibly derives from the Akkadian word meaning "creature." In the older creation account (Gen. 2:4–4:26) he is simply "the man [earthling]," which is not rendered as a proper name until the Septuagint version (about 250 B.C.E.). New Testament writers typically use Adam as a symbol of all humankind (as in 1 Cor. 15:21–49; Rom. 5:12–21). *See* Fall, The.

Adonai The Hebrew word for "Lord," a title of honor and majesty applied to the Old Testament deity, particularly during the late postexilic period, as a substitute for the personal name Yahweh, which was considered too sacred to pronounce.

Adonijah The son of David who tried unsuccessfully to succeed his father to Israel's throne and who was put death by Solomon (1 Kings 1:9–2:25).

Ahab Son of Omri and king of Israel about 869–850 B.C.E. Although Ahab practiced the Yahwist religion, he allowed his wife Jezebel, daughter of a Phoenician ruler, to encourage the Baal cult, which brought the condemnation of the prophet Elijah (1 Kings 17–22). A contemporary of Judah's King Jehoshaphat, Ahab was killed while defending Israel against Assyria's Shalmaneser III.

Ahasuerus (Xerxes) Son of Darius Hystaspes and Atossa, daughter of Cyrus the Great, the Ahasuerus of the Book of Esther is usually identified with Xerxes I (486–465 B.C.E.), who led the second Persian invasion of Greece and was defeated at the Battle of Salamis (480 B.C.E.). There is no record that he ever had a Jewish queen named Esther.

Ahaz King of Judah (about 735–716 B.C.E.) and father of Hezekiah, who succeeded him. Although Ahaz reigned during the ministries of Isaiah and Micah, he compromised the Yahwist religion to curry favor with Assyria, whose vassal Judah became (2 Kings 16).

Ai Meaning "the ruin" in Hebrew, Ai was a city reputedly destroyed by Joshua's conquest of Canaan (Josh. 7:2–5; 8:1–29) but which archaeology has demonstrated to have been already an abandoned site during the thirteenth century B.C.E when the Israelites entered Palestine.

Akkad (Accad) The narrow plain of Babylonia lying north of Sumer, locale of the Akkad dynasty, founders of the first real empire in world history (about 2360–2180 B.C.E.). In Akkad, named for its capital city, were many of the great cities of antiquity, some of which are mentioned in Genesis 10.

Akkadian (Accadian) (1) The period during which the early Semitic dynasty established by Sargon I dominated Mesopotamia (twenty-fourth–twenty-second centuries B.C.E.). (2) The Akkadian language, written in cuneiform script but sharing many features with Hebrew, Arabic, and Aramaic, was a Semitic tongue used in Mesopotamia from about the twenty-eighth to the first centuries B.C.E.

Alexander of Macedonia One of the most brilliant leaders and military conquerors of the classical world, son of King Philip of Macedonia, Alexander was born at Pella in Macedonia in 356 B.C.E. and died in Babylon in 323 B.C.E. During his relatively brief career he conquered most of the known world, created an empire that extended from Greece to India, propagated Greek culture throughout the Near East, and instituted a period of cosmopolitanism termed Hellenistic. His influence on Palestine is recounted in 1 Maccabees 1.

Alexandria A major port city and cultural center founded by Alexander the Great on the Egyptian coast. The home of a large Jewish colony during the Hellenistic period, Alexandria nourished a fusion of Hebraic and Hellenic (Greek) ideas, one result of which was the Greek Septuagint translation of the Hebrew Bible.

Allegory A literary narrative in which persons, places, and events are given a symbolic meaning. Some Hellenistic Jewish scholars of Alexandria tended to interpret the Hebrew Bible allegorically, as Paul does the story of Abraham, Sarah, and Hagar (Gal. 4:21–31).

Amalekites According to Genesis 36:12, these nomadic tribes were descendants of Esau who occupied the desert south and southeast of Canaan. Persistent enemies of ancient Israel, the Amalekites attacked Moses' group (Deut. 25:17–19), were defeated by Joshua at Rephidim (Exod. 17), and conquered by Gid-

eon (Judg. 6:33; 7:12) but were still troublesome in Saul and David's time (1 Sam. 15; 30:18).

Amarna Age A title assigned to the reign of Pharaoh Amenhotep IV (Akhenaton), whose new capital had been built at Amarna, Egypt.

Amen A term derived from a Hebrew word whose root suggests "so be it." Typically used as a confirmation (1 Kings 1:36), it implies agreement, as at the conclusion of a prayer (Matt. 6:13; 1 Cor. 14:16). In Revelation 3:14 "the Amen" is a synonym for Jesus Christ, who affirms the divine purpose.

Ammonites A Semitic group supposedly descended from Abraham's nephew Lot (Gen. 19:38). Chronic enemies of Israel (1 Sam. 11; 1 Kings 11), they occupied the eastern margin of the Transjordan plateau country but frequently crossed the Jordan to harass the Israelites.

Amorites A Semitic people (called "Westerners" or "highlanders") who moved into the ancient Near East about 2000 B.C.E. and founded the states of Mari and Babylon, of whom Hammurabi is the best-known Amorite ruler. The term was also applied to a tribe living in Canaan before the Israelite conquest (Num. 13:29; 21:26; Judg. 1).

Amos A shepherd and "dresser of sycamore [fig] trees" from the Judean village of Tekoa who denounced the religious and social practices of the northern kingdom (Israel) during the reign of Jeroboam II (about 786–746 B.C.E.), Amos was the first biblical prophet whose words were collected and preserved in a book.

Amphictyony A confederation of tribes or cities (typically of six or twelve members) organized around a particular deity's shrine. The term is commonly applied to the league of Israelite tribes during the period of the judges (about 1200–1000 B.C.E.).

Ananias (1) The high priest who presided over the full council (Sanhedrin) before which Paul was brought by Claudius Lycias for creating a "riot" in the Jerusalem temple (Acts

22:22–23:22). (2) An early Christian who with his wife Sapphira attempted to defraud the Pentecostal community at Jerusalem (Acts 5:1–10).

Anath A Canaanite agricultural goddess, sister-consort of the fertility god Baal.

Andrew A disciple of John the Baptist (John 1:35–40) who, according to John's Gospel, became the first of Jesus' followers and brought his brother Peter to Jesus (John 1:41–42). Mark gives another version of this calling (Mark 1:16–18; see also John 6:5; 12:22).

Angel From a Greek word meaning "messenger"; angels were commonly conceived in biblical times as emissaries from the deity who employed them to communicate his will to humankind. The oldest known rendition of angels in art occurs on the stele of Urnammu, a Sumerian king, but many scholars suggest that Israel's belief in angelology derives from Persian sources. Angels named in canonical Scripture include Michael and Gabriel, although apocryphal and pseudepigraphal literature lists others. Angels are particularly important in the birth stories of Jesus (Luke 1–2; Matt. 1).

Annas A former high priest before whom Jesus was brought for trial (John 18:13), Annas was father-in-law of Caiaphas, then the currently reigning high priest (see also Luke 3:2 and Acts 4:6).

Annunciation The name given to the Angel Gabriel's declaration to Mary of Nazareth that she was to bear a son, Jesus, who would inherit David's throne (Luke 1:28–32).

Anthropomorphism Attributing human characteristics to something not human; particularly, ascribing human emotions and motives to a deity.

Antichrist The ultimate enemy of Jesus Christ who, according to Christian apocalyptic traditions, will manifest himself at the end of time to corrupt many of the faithful, only to be vanquished when Christ appears. The term is used only in 2 and 3 John but is clearly referred to in Paul's second letter to the Thessalonians (2:1–12) and Revelation 13.

Antinomianism Literally meaning "opponents of law," the name applies to certain early Christian groups who argued that faith in Christ absolves the believer from obeying the moral law, a libertarian attitude attacked by Paul (Gal. 5:13–6:10) and the author of 1 and 2 John. *See* Heresy.

Antioch Two Hellenistic cities famous in Maccabean and New Testament times bore this name. (1) In Syria, Antioch was the capital of the Macedonian Seleucid kings and, under Roman rule, the capital of a province of the same name. According to Acts, the first Gentile Christian church was founded in Antioch (Acts 11:20, 21), where followers of "the way" were first called Christians (Acts 11:26). Paul began all three of his missionary journeys from here. (2) Pisidian Antioch, a major city in Galatia (in Asia Minor), was also the site of an important early church, this one founded by Paul and Barnabas (Acts 13:14–50).

Antiochus The name of several Syrian monarchs who inherited power from Seleucus I, a general and successor of Alexander the Great. The most famous were Antiochus III, who gained control of Palestine from Egypt in 198/197 B.C.E., and Antiochus IV (*Epiphanes*, or "God Manifest") (175–163 B.C.E.), whose persecution of the Jews led to the Maccabean revolt.

'Apiru Egyptian version of the term *Habiru*. *See* Habiru.

Apocalypse From the Greek *apokalypsis*, meaning to "uncover" or "reveal," the term refers to a special kind of prophetic literature that purports to foretell the future in terms of symbols and mystical visions and deals primarily with eschatological events.

Apocalyptic Literature A branch of prophetic writing that flourished in Judaism from about 200 B.C.E. to 140 C.E. and greatly influenced Christianity. Works such as Daniel, Enoch, 2 and 3 Baruch, 2 Esdras, and the Christian Book of Revelation are distinguished by cryptic language, symbolic imagery, and the expectation of an imminent cosmic catastrophe in which the forces of good ultimately defeat the powers of evil, resulting in the establishment of a messianic rule and consequent transformation of the universe. Jesus' prophecies of his return (Mark 13; Luke 21; Matt. 24) are a form of apocalyptic discourse.

Apocrypha From the Greek, meaning "hidden" books, Apocrypha refers to noncanonical or deuterocanonical literature, especially the fourteen books included in the Greek Septuagint and Latin Vulgate Bibles but not in the Masoretic Text of the Hebrew Bible. It also applies to a body of Christian works that typically parallel or spuriously "supplement" the New Testament canon.

Apodictic Law Law cast in the form of unconditional demands, such as the "thou shalt nots" in the Decalogue (Exod. 20).

Apollos A Hellenistic Jew of Alexandria, Egypt, noted for his eloquence, who was first a follower of John the Baptist, then embraced Christianity (Acts 18:24–28), and inadvertently became a rival of Paul at Corinth (1 Cor. 1:12; 3:4–6, 22–23; 4:6).

Apostasy From a Greek term meaning "to revolt," apostasy is the act of abandoning or rejecting a previously held religious faith. An apostate is one who has defected from or ceased to practice his or her religion.

Apostle One sent forth as a messenger, as one of an authorized New Testament group that assumed Church leadership after Christ's ascension. Lists of the original Twelve differ from account to account (Matt. 10:2–5; Mark 3:16–19; Luke 6:13–16; Acts 1:13–14).

Apothegm A term in biblical criticism referring to brief sayings or instructive proverbs found in the Gospels. *See also* Pericope.

Aqabah, Gulf of A northern arm of the Red Sea, part of the Jordan rift, which separates the Sinai Peninsula from Midian and Arabia.

Aquila A prominent early Christian expelled from Rome with his wife Priscilla by Claudius' edict (49 C.E.), Aquila is often associated with Paul (Acts 18; Rom. 16:3–5; 1 Cor. 16:19).

Aram According to Genesis 10:22, Aram was the son of Shem (a son of Noah) and progenitor of the Arameans, whom the Old Testament identifies with the Syrians (Gen. 24).

Aramaic The language of the Arameans (Syrians), Aramaic was a West-Semitic tongue used in parts of Mesopotamia from about 1000 B.C.E. The official language of the Persian Empire after about 500 B.C.E., it was spoken by the Jews after the Babylonian exile. Parts of the Old Testament were composed in Aramaic, and a Galilean dialect of Aramaic was probably the language spoken by Jesus.

Areopagus The civic court in Athens and the location of an important legal council of the Athenian democracy where, according to Acts 17, Paul introduced Christianity to some Athenian intellectuals.

Ark (1) The rectangular houseboat that Noah built to contain his family and pairs of all animals during the flood (Gen. 6:14–16). (2) The portable wooden chest—the Ark of the Covenant, supposedly dating from Mosaic times (Exod. 25:10–22)—that contained sacred artifacts of Israel's religion, such as Aaron's staff and the two stone tablets representing the Decalogue. Sometimes carried into battle (Josh. 6:4–11; 1 Sam. 4), the Ark of the Covenant was eventually brought to Jerusalem and kept in the innermost sanctuary of Solomon's temple. Its fate after the temple's destruction is unknown.

Armageddon A Greek transliteration of the Hebrew *Har Megiddon*, or "Mountain of Megiddo," a famous battlefield in the Plain of Jezreel in ancient Israel (Judg. 5:19; 2 Kings 9:27; 23:29). In Revelation 16:16, it is the symbolic site of the ultimate war between good and evil.

Artaxerxes King of Persia (465–423 B.C.E.), son of Xerxes I. According to Nehemiah 2, Artaxerxes commissioned Nehemiah, his Jewish cupbearer, to go to Jerusalem and rebuild the city's walls. Scholars are not agreed on whether Ezra returned to Jerusalem during the reign of Artaxerxes I or Artaxerxes II.

Asa Third king of Judah (about 913–873 B.C.E.) whose long reign was marked by various religious reforms. The authors of Kings and Chronicles judge him a "good" ruler (1 Kings 15:8–24; 2 Chron. 14:1–16:14).

Ascension, The The resurrected Jesus' ascent to heaven (Acts 1:6–11).

Ashdod One of the five major cities of the Philistines (Josh. 13:3), where the captured Ark of the Covenant was placed in Dagon's temple (1 Sam. 5:1–8).

Asher Reputed founder of an Israelite tribe that occupied a strip of Palestinian coast between Carmel and Phoenicia (Josh. 19:24–31; 17:10–11; Judg. 1:31–32; 5:17).

Asherah Hebrew name for the Canaanite goddess Asherat, "Lady of the Sea," a consort of El, Canaan's chief deity, whom the apostate Israelites worshiped at various times (see 1 Kings 11:5; 16:33; 18:19, etc.).

Ashkelon One of the five leading Philistine cities (Josh. 13:3; 2 Sam. 1:20).

Ashurbanipal Assyrian emperor (about 668–627 B.C.E.), grandson of Sennacherib, son and successor of Esarhaddon; called Asnapper in Ezra 4:10.

Assur (Asshur) (1) Chief deity of the Assyrians, king of their gods, and personification of war. (2) Assyria's first capital, located on the west bank of the Tigris River, site of an earlier Sumerian city. (3) The name of the country from which the Assyrians took their name.

Assyria (1) A large territory centered along the upper Tigris River in Mesopotamia, including the major cities of Assur, Calah, and Nineveh. (2) The empire that dominated the near East from the eleventh to the seventh centuries B.C.E. and whose leaders destroyed Israel in 721 B.C.E. and besieged Jerusalem in 701 B.C.E. It was destroyed by a coalition of Babylonians and Medes in 612 B.C.E.

Athens Greece's leading city-state and cultural capital in the fifth century B.C.E. and its leading intellectual center during Hellenistic and Roman times. According to Acts 17, the Apostle Paul introduced Christianity in Athens.

Atonement, Day of (*Yom Kippurim*) A solemn, annual Jewish observance in which Israel's high priest offered blood sacrifices ("sin offerings") to effect a reconciliation between the deity and his people (Lev. 16). The banishment of a "scapegoat" to which the priest had symbolically transferred the people's collective guilt climaxed the atonement rites (Lev. 16). The Day of Atonement marked the once-yearly entrance of the priest into the temple's Holy of Holies. The author of Hebrews argues that these ceremonies foreshadowed the sacrificial death of Jesus and his ascension to the heavenly sanctuary (Heb. 9).

Augustus The first emperor of Rome (27 B.C.E.–14 C.E.), Augustus Caesar brought peace to the Roman Empire after centuries of civil war. According to Luke 2:1, his decree ordering a census of "the whole world" brought Mary and Joseph to register in their ancestral hometown, Bethlehem, where Jesus was born.

Azazel The unidentified place or demon to which the scapegoat was sent on the Day of Atonement (Lev. 16:8, 10, 26).

Baal A Canaanite-Phoenician term meaning "lord" or "master," the name applied to Canaan's most popular fertility god. Worshiped as the power that caused germination and growth of farm crops, Baal was a serious rival to Yahweh after the Israelites settled in Palestine and became dependent upon agriculture (Judg. 2:11–14). He is pictured as a god of storm and rainfall in a contest with the Yahwist Elijah on Mount Carmel (1 Kings 18:20–46).

Babel A term meaning "the gate of God," Babel became synonymous with the confusion of languages that typified cosmopolitan Babylon (Gen. 11:4–9). The tower of Babel ("House of the Terrace-platform of Heaven and Earth") was a ziggurat. *See* Ziggurat.

Babylon An ancient city on the middle Euphrates that was capital of both the Old and Neo-Babylonian empires. Under Nebuchadnezzar II (605–562 B.C.E.), who joined forces with the Medes to defeat Egypt at the Battle of Carchemish (605 B.C.E.) and create the second Babylonian Empire, Babylon destroyed Jerusalem and its temple (587 B.C.E.). Babylon fell to the Persians in 539 B.C.E. Alexander the Great's plans to rebuild the old sanctuaries ended with his death in 323 B.C.E., and the city never regained its former glory. As the archetypal enemy of God's people, Babylon became the symbol of Satan's worldly power (Rev. 14:8; 18:2).

Balaam A Bedouin prophet or fortune-teller from Pethor on the Euphrates River whom Balak, king of Moab, hired to curse the Israelites when they attempted to cross Moab on their way to Canaan. Yahweh caused the hired soothsayer to turn his curse into a blessing on Israel (Num. 22–24), although another tradition blames Balaam for corrupting the Israelites (Num. 31:8, 15–17).

Baptism A religious ceremony first associated with John the Baptist (Mark 1:4; 11:30; Luke 7:29) and performed on converts in the infant Christian community (Acts 2:38–41; 19:3–5). Baptism may have derived from ritual cleansings with water practiced by the Essenes from some Pharisees' use of it as a conversion alternative to circumcision, or from initiation rites into Hellenistic mystery religions. In Christianity, it is the ceremony of initiation into the Church, performed either by total immersion in water or by pouring water on the head.

Barabbas A condemned murderer and possibly a revolutionary whom the Roman Procurator Pontius Pilate released instead of Jesus (Mark 15:6–15; Matt. 27:15–18; Luke 23:16–25; John 18:39–49).

Barnabas A prominent leader of the early Church in Jerusalem, associate and traveling companion of the Apostle Paul (Acts 9:26–30; 11:22–30; 13:1–3; 13:44–52; 14:1–15:4; 15:22–40; Col. 4:10; 1 Cor. 9:6; Gal. 2:1–13).

Barsabas The Christian leader of the Jerusalem church who was considered but not chosen to replace Judas among the Twelve (Acts 1:23–26).

Bartholomew One of the twelve apostles mentioned in all three Synoptics as well as in the list in Acts (Matt. 10:3; Mark 3:18; Luke 6:14; Acts 1:13), Bartholomew is sometimes identified with the Nathanael of John's Gospel (John 1:45–51 and 21:2).

Baruch Secretary and friend of Jeremiah, Baruch ("blessed") recorded the prophet's message, which probably became the nucleus of the Jeremiah scroll (Jer. 36; 32:9–14; 43:6). The apocryphal Book of Baruch was attributed to him, as were the apocalypses of 2 and 3 Baruch in the Pseudepigrapha.

Bathsheba Wife of Uriah, a Hittite soldier working in King David's service, Bathsheba's adultery with David and his murder of her husband evoked the denunciation of the prophet Nathan (2 Sam. 11:1–4; 12:1–23). Mother of Solomon, she conspired to place her son on Israel's throne (1 Kings 1:15–17).

Beatitudes The list of blessings or happinesses with which Jesus begins the Sermon on the Mount (Matt. 5:3–12). Luke gives a variation of these pronouncements (Luke 6:20–23).

Beersheba An ancient well in southern Palestine identified with the Genesis patriarchs (Gen. 21:22–34; 26:23–25, 32–33; 46:1); later a traditional location of the extreme southern border of the Israelite kingdom (Judg. 20:1; 2 Sam. 24:2; 1 Kings 4:25, etc.).

Behemoth A mysterious beast probably derived from Mesoptamian mythology but sometimes identified with the hippopotamus (Job 40:15–24). *See also* Leviathan.

Bel The Babylonian-Assyrian version of Baal, a common name for Marduk, chief god of Babylon (Isa. 46:1–4), sometimes called Merodach by the Jews (Jer. 50:2).

Belial An adjective meaning "not profitable" or "wicked" but used in the Old Testament as a proper name to denote an evil character, as "son of" or "daughter of" (Deut. 13: 13; Judg. 19:22; 1 Sam. 10:27). In 2 Corinthians 6:15, Paul uses the term as if it were synonymous with the Devil.

Belshazzar In Daniel, the last king of Babylon, son of Nebuchadnezzar (Dan. 5:1–31), though archaeological discoveries indicate that he was neither but merely prince regent for his father, Nabonidus.

Beltshazzar A name meaning "protect the king's life," given to Daniel by his Babylonian masters (Dan. 1:7; 2:26; 4:8, 9).

Benjamin The twelfth and last son of Jacob, second son of the patriarch's favorite wife, Rachel, and thus full brother of Joseph and half-brother of Jacob's other ten sons. Benjamin figures prominently in Joseph's saga (Gen. 42–44) and is regarded as the founder of the tribe of Benjamin, which, under the Israelite monarchy, occupied territory adjacent to that of Judah (Josh. 18:11–28; Judg. 1:8, 21). When the ten northern tribes seceded from the Davidic monarchy, Benjamin remained with the southern kingdom of Judah (1 Kings 12:21; Ezra 4:1).

Bethany An impoverished suburb of Jerusalem, home of Jesus' friends Mary, Martha, and Lazarus (John 11:1–44).

Bethel An ancient site, meaning "house of God," associated with the patriarchs Abraham (Gen. 12:8) and Jacob (Gen. 28:11–13, 22). Under the divided kingdom, Jeroboam I built a shrine at Bethel, near Judah's northern boundary (1 Kings 12:32). Amos denounced a prophet at the royal sanctuary there (Amos (7:10–17).

Bethlehem A village about five miles south of Jerusalem, birthplace of David (1 Sam. 17:12) and the place where Samuel secretly anointed him king of Israel (1 Sam. 16:1–2;

20:6). According to Micah 5:2, it was to be the Messiah's birthplace, an idea that influenced the Gospel writers' accounts of Jesus' nativity (Matt. 2:5–6; Luke 1; John 7:42).

Beth-peor An unidentified site east of the Jordan River in Moab, near which the Israelites camped before crossing Jordan and where Moses was buried (Deut. 3:29; 4:46; 34:6).

Bethsaida A village on the north shore of the Sea of Galilee, the home of Peter, Andrew, and Philip (John 1:44; 12:21). In New Testament times it consisted of an older Jewish section and a newer town, the capital of Philip the Tetrarch (see also Luke 10:13; Matt. 11:21).

Bildad One of Job's three friends who dispute with him the meaning of his afflictions (Job 2:11; 8; 18, etc.).

Bithynia In New Testament times, a Roman province in northern Asia Minor (modern Turkey) along the Black Sea coast and the location of several early Christian communities (Acts 16:7; 1 Peter 1:1).

Blasphemy Speech defaming the deity, a capital offense in Old Testament times (1 Kings 21:9–13) and the charge the Sanhedrin leveled against Jesus (Matt. 9:3; 26:65; John 10:36).

Boanerges "Sons of thunder," an epithet Jesus applies to James and John (Mark 3:17; Luke 9:52–56).

Boaz A wealthy landowner of Bethlehem (Ruth 2:1) who married the Moabite Ruth and became an ancestor of David (Ruth 4:22).

Booths, Feast of In ancient Israel, an autumn agricultural festival of thanksgiving during which the celebrants erected booths or shelters reminiscent of the wilderness encampments used during Israel's journey from Egypt to Canaan (Exod. 34:22); also known as the Feast of Tabernacles or Sukkoth (Lev. 23:39–44; Neh. 8:13–18).

Caesar A hereditary name by which the Roman emperors commemorated Gaius Julius

Caesar, great-uncle of Augustus (Octavian), the first emperor (Luke 2:1; 3:1; Mark 12:14; Acts 11:28; 25:11).

Caesarea An important Roman city that Herod the Great built on the Palestinian coast about sixty-four miles northwest of Jerusalem and named in honor of Caesar Augustus. Caesarea was Pontius Pilate's administrative capital and later a Christian center (Acts 8:40; 10:1, 24; 18:22; 21:8). Paul was imprisoned there for two years (Acts 23:23–35; 24–26).

Caesarea Philippi A inland city north of the Sea of Galilee built by Philip, son of Herod the Great (4 B.C.E.–34 C.E.), and named for the Emperor Tiberius; the site of Peter's "confession" that Jesus was the Messiah (Mark 8:27; Matt. 16:13).

Caiaphas Joseph Caiaphas, high priest of Jerusalem during the reign of the Emperor Tiberius (Matt. 26:3, 57–66; John 9:49; 18:13–28; Acts 4:6). Son-in-law to his immediate predecessor, Annas, he was appointed to the office by the Procurator Valerius Gratus and presided over Jesus' trial before the Sanhedrin.

Cain According to the J source of Genesis, the first son of Adam and Eve, who slew his brother Abel, thus becoming the archetypal murderer and fugitive (Gen. 4). The "mark of Cain" is not a curse but a sign that Yahweh protected him from his enemies.

Calah An ancient city on the Tigris, one of the early capitals of Assyria (Gen. 10:11–12).

Caleb Along with Joshua, one of the two spies sent to reconnoiter Canaan who brought back a favorable report of Israel's chances (Num. 13:14). For his trust in Yahweh, Caleb was allowed to enter Canaan, while all others of his generation died in the wilderness (Num. 13:30; 14:38).

Calf, Golden (1) An image that the apostate Israelites fashioned out of gold jewelry and other treasures taken from Egypt and which, under Aaron's direction, they worshiped as their deliverance from slavery (Exod. 32:1–6; Deut. 9:16). (2) Two calf images that Je-

roboam I set up at Bethel and Dan as rivals to the Jerusalem sanctuary were probably not revered as idols in themselves but as visible pedestals of the invisibly enthroned Yahweh (1 Kings 12:29).

Calvary The site outside Jerusalem's walls, exact location unknown, where Jesus was crucified (Luke 23:33). Calvary derives from the Latin word *calvaria*, a translation of the Greek *kranion*, meaning "skull"; Golgotha comes from the Aramaic for "skull" (Matt. 27:33; John 19:17).

Cana A town in Galilee where Jesus turned water into wine at a wedding feast (John 2:1–11) and healed a nobleman's son (John 4:46–54).

Canaan The Old Testament name for the land of Palestine west of the Jordan River, from Egypt in the south to Syria in the north (Gen. 10:19). According to Hebrew tradition, Canaan was the territory promised to Abraham's descendants (Gen. 15:7–21; 17:1–8) and infiltrated by the Israelite tribes during the thirteenth and twelfth centuries B.C.E. (Num. 21; Josh. 1–24; Judg. 1–2).

Canon A term derived from the Greek *kanon*, which may be related to the Semitic *qaneh*, a "reed," perhaps used as a measuring rod. In modern usage, a canon is a standard of measure by which a religious community judges certain writings to be authoritative, usually of divine origin. The Hebrew Bible is the canon of Judaism, while Christianity accepts both the Old Testament (sometimes including the Apocrypha) and the Greek New Testament. The canon is thus an official list of books considered genuine, worthy to be used in teaching and liturgy, and hence binding in doctrine and morals. The adjective *extracanonical* refers to books not included in the official canon or list.

Capernaum The "village of Nahum," a small port on the northwest shore of the Sea of Galilee that Jesus used as headquarters for his Galilean ministry and where he performed many "mighty works" (Matt. 9:1, 9–11; Mark 1:21–29; 2:3–11; Luke 7; John 4:46–54).

Carchemish An important Hittite site in northern Syria that overlooked the main crossing of the Euphrates on the trade route from Assyria to the Mediterranean. In 605 B.C.E. Nebuchadnezzar II defeated the Egyptian forces of Pharaoh Necho II here (2 Chron. 35:20; Jer. 46:2), thus ending Egypt's last significant attempt to reassert its hegemony in the Near East and establishing Babylon as the dominant power.

Carmel The name (meaning "garden" or "orchard") of a hilly range along the western border of Asher (Josh. 19:26), extending from the hill country of Samaria to the Mediterranean where Mount Carmel projects into the sea. Sacred to Baal because of its lush vegetation, Carmel was the site of Elijah's contest with the Canaanite priests (1 Kings 18).

Catholic Epistles A term referring to seven short New Testament epistles that were addressed to no specific person or church and were therefore intended for catholic ("universal") use.

Centurion A low-ranking officer in the Roman army in charge of a "century," or division of 100 men. A centurion named Cornelius became the first Gentile convert to Christianity (Acts 10).

Cephas A name meaning "stone" that Jesus bestowed upon Simon Peter (John 1:42).

Chaldea A Mesopotamian territory occupied by Semitic Arameans who founded the Neo-Babylonian Empire under Nabopolassar and his son Nebuchadnezzar, first in a brief line of Chaldean rulers (2 Kings 24:2; 25:4–13; Jer. 37:5–12). The Chaldeans were famous for their mastery of astronomy and astrology.

Chedorlaomer King of Elam, a country east of Babylonia on the Persian Gulf (Gen. 14).

Chemosh The national god of Moab to whom children were sacrificed as burnt offerings (Num. 21:29; Jer. 48:7, 13, 46). King Solomon erected an altar to Chemosh (1 Kings (11:7) that was not dismantled until Josiah's reforms more than three centuries later (2

Kings 23:13). Like the Israelites, the Moabites ("people of Chemosh") attributed their country's defeats and failures to their deity's anger.

Cherub, Cherubim (pl.) Mythological creatures—part animal, part bird, part human—that were placed in pairs at each side of the mercy seat of the tabernacle, and later in the innermost sanctuary of Solomon's temple, to protect the sacred relics in the Ark of the Covenant (Exod. 25:18–22). Their images were also embroidered on the veil of the temple (2 Chron. 3:14) and sculptured on a frieze around the temple walls and on the bases of the "Molten sea" (1 Kings 6:23; 7:29; 1 Chron. 28:18; Heb. 9:5). Such winged creatures, with a lion's or ox's body, eagle's wings, and human face, were common in ancient Near Eastern art and have been found in Byblos, Nineveh, and elsewhere. Originally the guardians of divine beings, they were later identified with the angels of Yahweh's heavenly court.

Christ From the Greek *Christos*, a translation of the Hebrew *Messiah*, meaning "anointed one," the term derives from the ancient practice of anointing kings at their coronation. The Messiah or Christ was to be a kingly descendant of David.

Christology The theological discipline that deals with the nature of Jesus Christ, particularly his divinity, relation to the Divine Father, and role in human redemption.

Church A term translating the Greek *ecclesia*, meaning "assembly of ones called out"; in New Testament usage, the community of believers in Jesus Christ. Individual churches or congregations make up the international Church, which is conceived as the visible part of Christ's spiritual body (Matt. 16:18; 18:17; Eph. 5:27; 1 Tim. 3:15; 1 Cor. 12:12–27; Col. 1:18).

Circumcision An ancient Semitic operation in which the foreskin of eight-day-old males is removed as a ceremony of initiation into the religion and community of Israel. Circumcision is represented as beginning with Abraham (Gen. 17:10–14) or Moses (Exod.

4:24–46; see also Lev. 1:59; 2:21; 12:3). The question of whether to circumcise Gentile converts to the early Christian Church was an important source of dissension (Acts 15; Gal. 2).

Claudius Fourth Roman emperor (41–54 C.E.), who expelled the Jews from Rome (Acts 11:28; 18:2).

Codex A manuscript book of an ancient biblical text, first used by Christians to replace the unwieldy scrolls on which the Scriptures were first recorded.

Colossae An ancient Phrygian city situated on the south bank of the Lycus River in central Asia Minor, important for its position on the trade route between Ephesus and Mesopotamia (Col. 1:1–2; 4:13).

Conquest of Canaan The gradual occupation of Palestine during the thirteenth and twelfth centuries B.C.E. by previously nomadic Israelites, an idealized account of which is given in Joshua 1–24.

Corinth A cosmopolitan center of trade and commerce in ancient Greece, destroyed by the Romans in 146 B.C.E. but later rebuilt. Home of a large population of Hellenistic Jews, Corinth was later a Christian center established by the Apostle Paul and his associates (Acts 18:24; 19:1; 1 and 2 Cor.).

Cornelius A Roman centurion associated with the Jewish synagogue in Caesarea who became the first Gentile convert to Christianity (Acts 10–11).

Covenant In Old Testament terms: (1) an agreement or compact between individuals, such as Abraham and Abimelech (Gen. 21: 27) or David and Jonathan (1 Sam. 18:3); (2) a promise Yahweh makes to certain people, such as Noah (Gen. 9:13) and Abraham (Gen. 15:18–21; 17:4–14); (3) a legal bond Yahweh forms with a chosen group, such as Israel, and the demands he makes in return. The Mosaic or Sinatic Covenant is that from which the Old "Testament" (a synonym for "covenant" or "contract") takes its name (Exod. 20–24; 34; Deut. 29; Josh. 24). In Christian terminology, Jesus introduced a "new cove-

nant" at the Last Supper (Mark 14:22–25; Matt. 26:26–29, etc.) that Christians believe superseded the Mosaic Covenant and embraced believers of all nations (1 Cor. 11:25).

Covenant Code A name given to the collection of ancient Hebrew laws found in Exodus 20:23–23:33, often called the book of the Covenant (Exod. 24:7).

Cult The formalized religious practices of a people, particularly its system of veneration, public rites, and liturgies.

Cuneiform A wedge-shaped writing that originated in ancient Sumer about 3000 B.C.E. and spread throughout Mesopotamia.

Cyrus II (the Great) Founder of the Persian Empire and conqueror of Babylon (539 B.C.E.) who liberated the Jews from captivity and decreed their return to Jerusalem to rebuild the temple (2 Chron. 36:22–23; Ezra 1:1–8). Second Isaiah calls him Yahweh's "shepherd" (Isa. 44:28) and his "Anointed" or "Messiah" (Isa. 45:1).

D *See* Deuteronomist.

Dagon An ancient Canaanite agricultural deity worshiped by the Philistines at Ashdod and Gaza (1 Sam. 5:1–7) and whose Gaza temple was reputedly destroyed by Samson (Judg. 16:23–30).

Damascus The capital of Syria and terminus of ancient caravan routes in the Fertile Crescent. Damascus was supposedly founded by Uz, grandson of Noah's son Shem (Gen. 5:32; 6:10; 10:23), and was visited by Abraham (Gen. 11:31; 12:4; 14:14). Paul's conversion to Christianity occurred near Damascus (Acts 9).

Dan (1) Son of Jacob and Rachel's servant, Bilhah (Gen. 30:1–6). (2) One of the twelve tribes of Israel, which first occupied a small territory between Judah and Ephraim (Josh. 19:40–48) but later migrated north to an area close to the Jordan's source (Josh. 19:47; Judg. 1:34; 18). (3) A Danite city formerly known as Laish, where Jeroboam I later established a cult center (1 Kings 12:26–30). As the phrase "from Dan to Beersheba" (Judg. 20:1; 2 Sam.

24:2; 1 Kings 4:25, etc.) indicates, it was regarded as the extreme northern boundary of Israel.

Daniel An ancient king whose name (Danel) appears in the *Ras Shamrah* epics and who was incorporated into the same tradition as Noah and Job (Ezek. 14:14; 28:3). He is not the same as the character in the Book of Daniel, who is referred to in no other canonical Old Testament work.

Darius The name of several Persian rulers mentioned in the Old Testament. (1) Darius I (522–486 B.C.E.), son of Hystaspes, was the emperor whose forces invaded Greece and were defeated at Marathon (490 B.C.E.). He continued Cyrus the Great's favorable treatment of the Jews (Ezra 5–6). (2) Darius "the Mede" (Dan. 5:31; 9:1), alleged to have condemned Daniel to the lion's den (Dan. 6:7–26), is unknown to history.

Dathan A Reubenite who rebelled with Korah against Moses and Aaron in the Sinai Desert (Num. 16:1–35; 26:7–11).

David Son of Jesse (Ruth 4:18–22), successor to Saul, and second king of the united twelve-tribe monarchy (1010–970 B.C.E.), David expanded Israel's boundaries to their greatest extent, founded a new administrative and religious capital at Jerusalem, and created a prosperous though short-lived Palestinian Empire. His story is told in 1 Samuel 16 through 1 Kings 2, while the Chronicler gives an often unreliable, idealized version of his cultic activities (1 Chron. 2, 3, 10–29). So great was David's effectiveness and popularity, especially in retrospect, that he became the prototype of the Messiah figure, who was prophesied to be his descendant (Isa. 9:5–7; 11:1–16; Jer. 23:5; 30:9, Ezek. 34:23–31, etc.).

Deacon Literally, a "servant," a term applied to one of the lower orders of the Christian ministry—in the early Church, probably to the bishop's assistant.

Dead Sea Known in biblical times as "the salt sea" (Gen. 14:3; Num. 34:3, 12; Josh. 3:16; 12:3), the "sea of the plain [Arabah]" (Josh. 3:16; 12:3), and "the east sea" (Ezek. 47:18;

Joel 2:20), this lake, forty-six miles long, was given its present name by Greeks in the second century B.C.E. Occupying a basin into which the Jordan River empties and located in a geological fault zone that extends from Syria to the Gulf of Aqabah and thence into East Africa, it lies 1,290 feet below sea level and has a depth of approximately 1,200 feet, making it the lowest body of water in the world. With a saline content five times that of the ocean, it supports no fish or other form of life.

Dead Sea Scrolls Biblical and other religious manuscripts dating from the second century B.C.E. to the first century C.E., found in caves near Qumran on the northwest shore of the Dead Sea.

Deborah A judge and prophetess who, with Barak, helped bring about Israel's victories over the Canaanite forces of Sisera (Judg. 4–5)

Decalogue *See* Ten Commandments.

Dedication, Feast of An eight-day Jewish celebration (now known as Hanukkah) instituted in 165 B.C.E. by Judas Maccabeus and held annually on the twenty-fifth day of Kislev (November–December) to commemorate the cleansing and rededication of the Jerusalem temple, which Antiochus IV had polluted. Referred to in John 10:22–38, it is also known as the Festival of Lights.

Delilah A woman from Sorek whom the Philistines bribed to discover and betray the secret of Samson's strength (Judg. 16). Her name means "coquette."

Deuterocanon The fourteen books of the Old Testament Apocrypha included in the Latin Vulgate but not in the Hebrew Bible. The Roman church regards these works as *deuterocanonical*, belonging to a second and later canon. (The term is sometimes applied to the Catholic Epistles and Book of Revelation in the New Testament.)

Deutero-Isaiah Also known as Second Isaiah, the name assigned to the anonymous prophet responsible for chapters 40–55 of the Book of Isaiah and also to the work itself.

Deuteronomic History The books of the Former Prophets (Joshua, Judges, Samuel, Kings) as compiled and revised from older sources by an anonymous author or editorial school deeply influenced by the historical philosophy of the Book of Deuteronomy. It was produced shortly before Jerusalem's destruction in 587 B.C.E. and perhaps further edited during the Babylonian exile.

Deuteronomic Reformation The label that biblical scholars apply to King Josiah's reforms of the Jewish religion following 621 B.C.E. The name derives from the assumption that the law book found during Josiah's repairs of the temple was a form of the Book of Deuteronomy (probably Deut. 12–26) and that the work's insistence on the centralization of Israel's cult at a single (undesignated) sanctuary inspired Josiah's sweeping destruction of all rival shrines (2 Kings 22–23).

Deuteronomist (1) The unknown writer who compiled and edited the present form of the Book of Deuteronomy. Some scholars believe that he added the introductory material (Deut. 1–11) and appendixes (Deut. 27–34) to the older Deuteronomic Code (Deut. 12–26). (2) The redactor or editorial school that produced the entire deuteronomic history in something resembling its present form.

Deutero-Pauline New testament books attributed to Paul but probably not written by him—e.g., Ephesians and the Pastorals.

Devil The English word commonly used to translate two Greek words with different meanings: (1) *diabolos*, "the accuser" (John 8:44); (2) *daimonion*, one of many evil spirits inhabiting the world, who were thought to cause disease, madness, and other afflictions (see Matt. 10:25; Mark 3:22; Luke 8; 11:14–16, etc.) In Revelation 12:9 the Devil is identified with the Hebrew Satan and the serpent of Genesis.

Diana of the Ephesians The Near Eastern form of the Greek goddess Artemis (whom the Romans identified with Diana) worshiped in Ephesus, which in Paul's time was the capital of the Roman province of Asia (Acts 19).

Diaspora Literally, a "scattering," the term refers to the distribution of Jews outside their Palestinian homeland, such as the many Jewish communities established throughout the Greco-Roman world.

Disciple From the Greek word meaning "learner," the term is applied in the New Testament to followers of particular religious figures, such as Moses (John 9:28), John the Baptist (Luke 11:1; John 1:35), the Pharisees (Mark 2:18), or Jesus. Although it applies especially to the Twelve (Matt. 20:17), it also designates others who associated with Jesus (Matt. 14:26). Paul made numerous disciples "for Christ" (Acts 20:1, 7; 21:16).

Documentary Hypothesis A scholarly theory associated with Julius Wellhausen which argues that the Pentateuch is not the work of one author but the result of many generations of anonymous writers, revisers, and editors (redactors) who produced the four main literary strands or components found in these five books: J (the Yahwist, about 950 B.C.E.); E (the Elohist, about 850 B.C.E.); D (the Deuteronomist, about 650–621 B.C.E.); and P (the Priestly component, about 550–450 B.C.E.).

Doublet A literary term denoting two or more versions, from different sources, of the same material (cf. Gen. 12:10–20; 20:1–18; 26:6–11; Exod. 3:1–20; 6:2–13; 20; Deut. 5, etc.).

Doxology In a religious writing or service, the formal concluding expression of praise or formula ritually ascribing glory to God.

Dragon A symbolic reptile derived from ancient Near Eastern mythology, related to the serpent in Eden (Gen. 3) and identified with the Devil and Satan (Rev. 12). *See* Leviathan.

E *See* Elohist.

Ebedmelech The Ethiopian (Cushite) eunuch who rescued Jeremiah from the cistern where the prophet's enemies had left him to die (Jer. 38:1–13; 39:15–18).

Eber The legendary ancestor of various Hebrew, Arab, and Aramean tribes (Gen. 10:24–30; 11:15; 1 Chron. 1:18); listed in the New Testament as an ancestor of Jesus (Luke 3:35).

Eden The gardenlike first home of humankind (Gen. 2:8); an earthly paradise from which the first couple was expelled (Gen 3:24). See also Ezekiel 28:13, where the "king of Tyre" enjoyed an "Eden," possibly a lush forested region (Ezek. 31:18; 36:25; Isa. 51:3; Joel 2:3).

Edom In Old Testament times, a region or country extending southward from the Dead Sea to the Gulf of Aqabah, bordered on the north by Moab, on the northwest by Judah, on the east and southeast by the Sinai desert (Num. 20:14–21; 2 Kings 3:20, etc.). It was also called "Seir" (Gen. 32:3; Num. 24:18; Judg. 5:4), identified with Esau (Gen. 36:1), and thought to be Yahweh's original homeland (Deut. 33:2; Judg. 5:4–5; Hab. 3:3). Famous for its wisdom tradition (Obad. 8; Jer. 49:7), Edom is the setting for the Job story and may have contributed the central ideas of that philosophical work.

Edomites According to Genesis, descendants of Jacob's twin brother, Esau, "who is Edom" (Gen. 36:1); a Semitic people who occupied the territory southeast of Judah and were among Israel's bitterest enemies (Judg. 11; 2 Kings 8:20–22; Ps. 137:7; Amos 1–2; 9; Ezek. 25:12–14; 35:1–15). The Edomites later infiltrated southern Judea, which in Hellenistic times was called Idumea (Mark 3:8).

Egypt Ancient nation centered along the Nile River southwest of Palestine, visited by Abraham (Gen. 12:10–20) and settled in by his Israelite descendants (Gen. 41–50) for a reputed 430 years (Exod. 12:40). Moses, raised at the Egyptian court, led the enslaved Israelites from Egypt about 1280–1250 B.C.E. (Exod. 1–15). Many of Israel's classical prophets advised against turning to Egypt for political or military help (Isa. 30:1–7; 31:1; 36; Jer. 46; Hos. 7:11), although King Solomon had once made an alliance with the pharaohs (1 Kings 9:16–18, 24). Egyptian attempts to restore its hegemony in Palestine were finally ended at the battle of Carchemish (605 B.C.E.), when Nebuchadnezzar of Babylon defeated Pharaoh Necho's troops.

El, Elohim (pl.) A Semitic term for a divine being. In Canaanite religion, El was the high god, father of lesser deities. In the Hebrew Bible, El, when used as a name for the Israelite deity, typically occurs as part of a phrase, such as El Shaddai ("God of the Mountain"), El Bethel ("God of the House of God"), or El Elyon ("God Most High"). In its plural form, the Hebrew generic term for deity applied to both their national god (Gen. 1:1; 2:5, etc.) and foreign deities (Exod. 15:2, 11).

Elam An ancient civilized center across the Persian Gulf from Sumer (now in Iran), supposedly founded by Elam, son of Shem (Gen. 10:22). Chedorlaomer, king of Elam, headed several Babylonian states (Gen. 14:1–11). Elamites later helped Assyria invade Judah (Isa. 11:11; 22:6).

Eleazar (1) The third son of Aaron, a chief of the Levites, who succeeded his father as high priest (Exod. 6:23; Num. 3:2, 32; 20:25–29; Josh. 14:1). (2) In 2 Maccabees, the aged "teacher of the Law" who was bludgeoned to death for refusing to eat pig's flesh (2 Macc. 6:18–31).

Eli In 1 Samuel 2:22–4:18, an ineffectual judge and priest at Shiloh under whose jurisdiction young Samuel served (1 Sam. 3:1).

Elihu A young man who condemns Job's alleged self-righteousness (Job 32–37).

Elijah Literally, "Yahweh is my God"; a fiercely Yahwist prophet from the northern kingdom whose anti-Baalism and attacks on Ahab's dynasty had a tremendous impact on Israel's political course during the ninth century B.C.E. and who shaped his nation's prophetic traditions for centuries thereafter (1 Kings 17–19; 21; 2 Kings 1–2). Reportedly carried to heaven in a fiery chariot (2 Kings 2:1–13), he was expected to reappear shortly before the Day of Yahweh arrived (Mal. 4:5–6). Although some Christian writers identified

John the Baptist with Elijah (Luke 1:17; Mark 9:12–13), some contemporaries viewed Jesus as Elijah returned (Mark 9:28; 16:14). Along with Moses, Elijah appears in Jesus' transfiguration (Mark 9:4; Matt. 17:3; Luke 9:30).

Eliphaz The most moderate and restrained of Job's critics (Job 3–8; 15; 22–24, etc.).

Elisabeth A Levite, wife of the prophet Zechariah, and mother of John the Baptist (Luke 1).

Elisha A ninth-century prophet in the northern kingdom, successor to Elijah (1 Kings 19:15–21; 2 Kings 2:1–15). Like his predecessor, Elisha was a clairvoyant who worked numerous miracles, including the resuscitation of a dead child (2 Kings 4:18–37; 6:32–7:2; 8:7–13; 13:14–19). So great was his prestige that he not only brought an end to the Omri-Ahab-Jezebel dynasty in Israel by having the upstart Jehu anointed king (2 Kings 9:1–13) but also made Hazael king of Syria (2 Kings 8:7–15).

Elohist The scholarly term designating the anonymous author or compiler responsible for the E document or tradition in the Pentateuch. The name arose from his characteristic use of *Elohim* to denote the Hebrew deity.

El Shaddai Although commonly translated "God Almighty," this term probably means "God of the Mountain," referring to the Mesopotamian cosmic "mountain" inhabited by divine beings. One of the patriarchal names for the Mesopotamian tribal god, it is identified with Yahweh in the Mosaic revelation (Exod. 6:3). Except for a few occurrences in Job (5:17, 8:5, etc.), Isaiah (13.6), and Ezekiel (10:5), it appears chiefly in the Pentateuch (Gen. 17:1; 28:3; 35:11; 43:14; 48:3; Exod. 6:3, etc.). *Shaddai* alone appears in Ruth 1:20–21 and Job 13:3; 20:15–20; 31:2; 40:2, etc.

Emmaus A village (site unknown) near Jerusalem, along the road to which the resurrected Jesus appeared to several disciples (Luke 24:13–32).

Endor Literally, "fountain of habitation"; a small town southeast of Nazareth, remembered for its witch whom King Saul solicited (1 Sam. 28:7–25).

Enoch A son of Cain (Gen. 4:17, J's account) or of Jared (Gen. 5:18, P's version) and father of Methuselah (Gen. 5:21). P's statement that "God took him" (Gen. 5:24)—apparently to heaven and without death—strongly influenced later Hebrew notions of immortality and gave rise to a whole body of pseudepigraphal literature in which Enoch is a model of divine wisdom.

Enuma Elish The Babylonian creation epic that takes its name from the opening phrase (in Akkadian), "When above."

Epaphras An early Christian of Colossae who reported on the Colossian church to the imprisoned Paul (Col. 1:7; 4:12; Philem. 23).

Epaphroditus A Macedonian Christian from Philippi who assisted Paul in prison (Phil. 2:25–27).

Ephesus A wealthy Hellenistic city, later capital of the Roman province of Asia, site of the famous temple of Artemis (Diana) (Acts 19–20). Ephesus is frequently mentioned in various Pauline and Deutero-Pauline letters (1 Cor. 16:19; 2 Cor. 12:14; 13:1; 1 Tim. 3:1; 2 Tim. 4:12, etc.). The author of Revelation (Rev. 2:1–7) judged the church there favorably. Later Christian traditions made it the site of the Virgin's assumption to heaven and the final ministry of the Apostle John.

Ephod An apronlike garment worn by the High Priest Aaron and his successors (Exod. 28).

Ephraim (1) Son of Joseph and Asenath (daughter of the priest Potipherah) and adopted by Jacob (Gen. 48:1–20). (2) The Israelite territory occupied by the tribe of Ephraim, bordered on the south by Dan and Benjamin, on the west by the Mediterranean, on the north by Manasseh, and on the east by the Jordan Rift Valley. Shechem (Josh. 21:20) was its most important city and served as an early capital of the northern kingdom (1 Kings 12:1). (3) The half-tribe of Ephraim, along with Manesseh, was one of the twelve tribes. After the ten northern tribes seceded

(922 B.C.E.) from the Davidic union, Ephraim became dominant in Israel and was commonly used as a synonym for the whole ten-tribe nation.

Epiphany An appearance or manifestation, particularly of a divine being; typically sudden and accompanied by dramatic natural effects (Exod. 3; 6; 19; 24; Isa. 6; Job. 38–42, etc.).

Epistle A formal letter intended for a wide public audience rather than for a specific group or individual.

Eponym The person from whom a people or group is reputed to have taken its name (Gen. 36:1).

Erech (Uruk) An ancient Sumerian city, home of the legendary King Gilgamesh.

Esarhaddon Son of the Assyrian Emperor Sennacherib, Esarhaddon ruled from about 680 to 669 B.C.E., despoiled Tyre and Sidon, colonized Samaria, and reputedly took Manasseh, king of Judah, captive to Babylon (2 Kings 19:37; Isa. 37:38; 2 Chron. 33:11; Ezra 4:2).

Esau First-born son of Isaac and Rebekah, twin brother of Jacob (Gen. 25:25–34), Esau gave up his birthright to his cleverer sibling (Gen. 27–28), thus becoming the prototype of the person who is insensitive to his heritage (Heb. 12:16). He was thought of as the progenitor of the Edomites, traditional enemies of Jacob's descendants (Israel) (Gen. 36).

Eschatology From the Greek, meaning a "study of last things," eschatology is a doctrine or theological concept about the ultimate destiny of humankind and the universe. Having both a personal and general application, it can refer to (1) beliefs about the individual soul following death, including divine judgment, heaven, hell, and resurrection; or (2) larger concerns about the fate of the cosmos, such as events leading to the Day of Yahweh, the final battle between supernatural good and evil, judgment of the nations, and the establishment of the deity's universal sovereignty. In Christian terms, it

involves the *Parousia* (return of Christ), the chaining of Satan, introduction of the Millennium, etc. Apocalyptic works like Daniel, Revelation, 2 Esdras, and the books of Enoch typically stress eschatological matters.

Essenes According to Josephus, one of the three major sects of first-century C.E. Judaism. Semiascetic in nature, the Essenes were spiritual descendants of the Hasidim ("pious") who had resisted Antiochus IV's attempts to destroy the Jewish religion. Their apocalyptic convictions and certain of their rituals akin to baptism have suggested to some scholars that they were an influence on such representative pre-Christian figures as John the Baptist. They are commonly identified with the Qumran community, which produced the Dead Sea Scrolls.

Esther Heroine of the canonical book bearing her name, cousin and adopted daughter of Mordecai (Esther 2:15), queen of Persia under Xerxes (Esther 1:1–2:18), Esther became a national heroine by delivering her people from a mass slaughter planned by Haman (Esther 2:19–4:17). The Book of Esther commemorates the Feast of Purim (Esther 9:17–10:3).

Ethiopia An area of northeast Africa (Abyssinia), which the Hebrews called Cush or Kush, supposedly settled by a son of Ham (Gen. 10:6–8). Classical writers mention a line of Ethiopian queens named Candace, one of whom is cited in Acts 8:27.

Etiology Literally, a statement of causes or origins; in literary terms, a narrative created to explain the origin or meaning of a social practice, topographical feature, ritual, or other factor that arouses the storyteller's interest.

Eucharist From the Greek word for "gratitude" or "thanksgiving," Eucharist is a name for the Christian ceremony of consecrated bread and wine that Jesus initiated at the Last Supper (Mark 14:22–25; Matt. 26:26–29, etc.).

Euphrates The longest river of southwest Asia, one of the four streams of Eden (Gen.

2:14), the Euphrates was the extreme northeastern border of Israel's kingdom at its height (2 Sam. 8:3; 10:16; 1 Kings 4:24).

Evangelist The New Testament name for a Christian who traveled from place to place proclaiming the Gospel (Acts 6:1–5; Eph. 4:11; 2 Tim. 4:5). The term is also used for the authors of the four Gospels and means "one who proclaims good news."

Eve The first woman, wife of Adam, who derived her name from the Hebrew verb "to live" because she was "the mother of all those who live" (Gen. 3:30). Paul's interpretation of her role in the fall of humankind is given in 2 Corinthians 11:3 and 1 Timothy 2:11–15.

Evil-merodach Son and successor of Nebuchadnezzar who reputedly treated well Judah's captive monarch Jehoiachin (2 Kings 25:27–30; Jer. 52:31–34). The name means "man of Marduk."

Exegesis A literary term denoting close analysis and interpretation of a text to discover the original author's exact intent and meaning. Once this has been established, later interpretations may also be considered.

Exile Period during which the Jews were captive in Babylon (587–538 B.C.E.).

Exodus A Greek term meaning "a going out" or "departure." In the Old Testament it refers to the escape of Israelite slaves from Egypt under Moses' leadership (about 1280–1250 B.C.E.), an event the Hebrews regarded as Yahweh's crucial saving act in their history (Exod. 15; 20:1–2; Deut. 5:6; Josh. 24:1–13; Ps. 105:26–39; Amos 2:10, etc.).

Exorcism The act or practice of expelling a demon or evil spirit from a person or place (Tob. 8:1–3; Mark 1:23–27, 32–34; 5:1–20; Matt. 8:28–34; Acts 19:13–19, etc.).

Expiation In religious terms, the act of making atonement for sin, usually by offering a sacrifice to appease divine wrath (Lev. 16).

Ezekiel A major prophet of the sixth century B.C.E., exiled to Babylon, who was distinguished by his strange visions and priestly concerns. The name means "God strengthens."

Ezra (Esdras) A postexilic Jewish priest who returned to Jerusalem from Babylon during the reign of the Persian Emperor Artaxerxes (Ezra 7:1) to promulgate the Mosaic Torah and supervise a reformation of the Jewish religion (Neh. 8–10; Ezra 7–10). His influence on later Judaism was so great that he was conceived as the recreator of the Hebrew Bible and author of several pseudohistorical and apocalyptic works (1 Esd. 8–9; 2 Esd. 14).

Fall, The Humankind's loss of innocence and divine favor through Adam's sin of disobedience (Gen. 3), which, according to some interpretations of Pauline thought (Rom. 5:12–21; 1 Cor. 15:45–49), resulted in the transmission of death and a proclivity toward sin, depravity, and evil to the entire human race. As a medieval rhyme expressed it, "In Adam's fall, we sinned all."

Felix, Antonius The Roman procurator or governor of Judea before whom Paul was tried at Caesarea about 60 C.E. (Acts 23:23–24:27).

Fertile Crescent The name by which James H. Breasted designated the arch or semicircle of fertile territory stretching from the Persian Gulf on the northeast to Egypt on the southwest and including Mesopotamia, Syria, and Palestine.

Festus, Porcius The procurator of Judea whom Nero appointed to succeed Felix and through whom Paul appealed to be tried by Caesar's court in Rome (Acts 24:27–26:32).

Firmament The Old Testament term for the vault or arch of the sky that separated the earthly oceans from the heavenly ocean of rain-giving clouds and in which Elohim placed the sun, moon, and stars (Gen. 1:6–8, 16–20, 7:11; 2 Sam. 22:8; 2 Kings 7:2; Pss. 24:2; 78:23; 104:2, 5; Job 26:11; 27:18).

Flood, The The global deluge of Noah's day (Gen. 6:5–8:22), based on ancient Mesopotamian flood stories akin to that found in the *Epic of Gilgamesh* and later used as a prototype of world judgment and destruction

(Matt. 24:36–41; Luke 17:26–30; 2 Pet. 2:5; 3:5–7).

Form Criticism An English rendition of the German *Formsgeschichte*, a method of biblical criticism that attempts to isolate, classify, and analyze individual units or characteristic forms contained in a literary text and to identify the probable preliterary form of these units before their incorporation into the written text. Form criticism also attempts to discover the setting in life (*Sitz-im-Leben*) of each unit—i.e., the historical, social, religious, and cultural environment from which it developed—and to trace or reconstruct the process by which various traditions evolved from their original oral state to their final literary form.

Gabriel In the Hebrew angelic hierarchy, one of the seven archangels whose duty it was to convey the deity's messages. Gabriel explained Daniel's visions to him (Dan. 8:15–26; 9:20–27) and, in the New Testament, announced the births of John the Baptist and Jesus (Luke 1:5–17; 26–38). The name may mean "person of God" or "God has shown himself mighty."

Gad (1) Firstborn son of Jacob and Zilpah (Gen. 30:1–11; 35:26), Gad was the eponymous ancestor of the Israelite tribe of Gad (Num. 2:14) whose territory was located northeast of the Dead Sea, east of the Jordan River (Num. 32; Deut. 3:16–20). Gad joined the revolt against Rehoboam and was part of the ten-tribe northern kingdom. (2) A prophet at David's court (1 Sam. 22:5; 2 Sam. 24; 1 Chron. 21; 2 Chron. 29:25, 29).

Gadara A Hellenistic city belonging to the Decapolis (ten-member league of Greek cities in Palestine), where Jesus exorcised a demoniac (Mark 5:1–20; Matt. 8:28–34; Luke 8:26–39).

Galatia A region in the interior of Asia Minor (Turkey) settled by Gauls; in New Testament times, a Roman province visited by Paul and his associates (Acts 16:6; 18:23; 1 Cor. 16:1; Gal. 1:2; 1 Pet. 1:1).

Galilee From the Hebrew term *Glil ha-goyim*, meaning "circle of the Gentiles," the name given northern Palestine lying west of the Jordan, an area originally assigned to the tribes of Ashur, Zebulun, and Naphtali, who failed to evict the Canaanites living there (Josh. 19; Judg. 1; 4; 5). The region where Jesus grew up (Matt. 2:23; Luke 2), Galilee was then under Roman control but administered by the Tetrarch Herod Antipas (4 B.C.E.–39 C.E.) (Luke 23:5–7).

Galilee, Sea of The major body of fresh water in northern Palestine and source of livelihood to many Galilean fishermen, such as Peter, Andrew, and John (Matt. 4:18–22). The towns and fields along its shores were the site of many of Jesus' public discourses and miracles (Mark 6:30–52, etc.) and of a resurrection appearance as well (John 21:1–14).

Gallio A proconsul of Achaia (the Roman province of Greece) who dismissed charges brought against Paul by Corinthian Jews (Acts 18:12–17), Gallio was a brother of Seneca, the Stoic philosopher.

Gamaliel A leading Pharisee, scholar, member of the Sanhedrin (Acts 5:34), reputed teacher of Paul (Acts 22:3), and exponent of the liberal wing of the Pharisaic party developed by his grandfather Hillel, Gamaliel persuasively argued for a policy of toleration toward the new religion preached by Peter and other apostles (Acts 5:38–40).

Gath Of the Philistines' five major cities, the one nearest to Hebrew territory (Josh. 13:3; 1 Sam. 17; 27, etc.).

Gaza The southernmost of the Philistines' five principal cities (Josh. 13:3) where Samson destroyed the temple of Dagon (Judg. 16). During the Israelite monarchy, Gaza marked the southernmost boundary of Judah (1 Kings 4:24).

Gehenna New Testament name for the "Valley of the Son [or Children] of Hinnom" that bordered Jerusalem on the south and west and had been the site of human sacrifices to Molech and other pagan gods (Jer. 7:32; Lev.

18:21; 1 Kings 11:7; 2 Chron. 28:3; 33:6). Later used as a dump in which to burn garbage, it became a symbol of punishment in the afterlife and is cited as such by Jesus (Matt. 5:22; 10:28–29; 18:8; 25:30, 46, etc.).

Gemara   The second part of the Talmud; an extensive commentary, in Aramaic, on the Hebrew Mishnah.

Gentile   Someone who is not a Jew, an uncircumcised person, one belonging to "the nations" (Ps. 9:17; Isa. 2:2; Zeph. 2:1; Hag. 2:7; Matt. 1:11; 12:21; Luke 21:24, etc.).

Gethsemane   The site of a garden or orchard on the Mount of Olives where Jesus took his disciples after the Last Supper; the place where he was arrested (Matt. 26:36–56; Mark 14:32–52; Luke 22:39–53; John 18:1–14).

Gibeah   A small hill town in the territory of Benjamin, prominent in the eleventh century B.C.E. because it was the home of Saul (1 Sam. 10:26) and the first capital of the united monarchy (1 Sam. 13–14; 2 Sam. 21:6).

Gibeon   A city of the Hivites ("Horites") (Josh. 9:17; 11:19), whose people deceived Joshua into making a treaty of protection with them (Josh. 9–10), Gibeon became an Israelite cult center (2 Sam. 21:1–9; 1 Kings 3:4–5; 1 Chron. 16:39–40; 2 Chron. 1:3, 13, etc.).

Gideon   Also called Jurubbaal ("contender against Baal"), a military judge who delivered Israel from the Midianites (Judg. 6–8). Although Gideon refused to accept a crown (Judg. 8:22–32), his son Abimelech reigned for three years at Shechem (Judg. 9).

Gilead   A rugged highland in central Transjordan located between the Yarmuk and Arnon rivers (Josh. 13; Jer. 8:22; 46:11).

Gilgal   The name of several Old Testament towns, including one located southeast of Jericho where Joshua erected twelve stones symbolic of Israel's twelve tribes (Josh. 4:1–9, 20); the site of the confirmation of Saul's kingship (1 Sam. 11:15; 13:4–15); and a cultic center in southwest Samaria associated with

a school of prophets, particularly Elijah and Elisha (2 Kings 2:1–4; 4:38).

Gnosticism   A movement in early Christianity which taught that salvation was gained through special knowledge (*gnosis*) revealed through a spiritual savior (presumably Jesus) and was the property of an elite few who had been initiated into its mysteries. Gnosticism became a major heresy in the primitive Church, though little is now known about its precise tenets.

Gog   The term Ezekiel uses to depict a future leader of Israel's enemies (Ezek. 38) whose attack on the Jerusalem sanctuary will precipitate Yahweh's intervention and the ultimate destruction of the wicked (Rev. 20:8).

Goliath   The Philistine giant from Gath whom the young David defeated with a slingshot (1 Sam. 17; 2 Sam. 21:19).

Goshen   An area in northeastern Egypt where Jacob and his clan settled to escape a Near Eastern famine (Gen. 46:28–34; 47:5–12).

Gospel   (1) The Christian message—literally, "good news." (2) The name applied to the literary form of the religious biographies of Jesus, especially Matthew, Mark, Luke, and John.

Gospel of St. Thomas   A Gnostic collection of approximately 114 sayings attributed to Jesus and allegedly the work of his disciple Didymus Judas Thomas. Although found in Egypt in 1945 as part of a thirteen-volume work containing forty-nine Coptic-language books dating from the fourth and fifth centuries C.E., it may have been written as early as 140 C.E.

Habakkuk   A prophet of the late seventh or early sixth century B.C.E., perhaps a Levitical temple musician (Hab. 1:1; 3:1, 19), and presumed author of the book bearing his name.

Habiru   An ancient Near Eastern term designating people or clans who were outside the urban social and legal structure. The Habiru appear to have been nomads who raided the settled populations during the Amarna

Period (fourteenth century B.C.E.) in Palestine. The biblical Hebrews may have been related to this group.

Hades The Greek term for the Underworld, abode of the dead, named for Zeus' brother Hades, god of the nether regions. In the Septuagint Bible, it is used to translate *Sheol*, the Hebrew word for the gloomy subterranean place where all the dead, good and evil alike, were eternally housed (Gen. 42:38; 1 Sam. 2:6; Job 7:9; Ps. 6:5; Prov. 27:20; Eccles. 9:10; Isa. 38:18, etc.). In the New Testament, *Hades* is also the usual term for the Underworld, although *Gehenna* (often translated "Hell") is cited as the place of punishment (Matt. 5:22, 29, 30; 16:18; Mark 9:43, 45, 47; Luke 12:5; Acts 2:31; Rev. 1:18; 20:14, etc.).

Hagar In Genesis 16, Sarah's Egyptian handmaiden, who bears Abraham's first son, Ishmael. In Genesis 21, the jealous Sarah persuades Abraham to drive Hagar and Ishmael into the wilderness, whence an angel rescues them.

Haggadah Jewish narrative writings dating from the first Christian centuries that illustrate and interpret the nonlegal portions of the Torah (Law).

Haggai A postexilic prophet who, with his contemporary Zechariah, urged the restored community of Jerusalem to rebuild the temple (520 B.C.E.).

Hagiographa A Greek term, meaning "sacred writings," which applies to the third major division of the Hebrew Bible (the *Kethuvi'im*), encompassing books of poetry, wisdom, late historical books (Chronicles-Ezra), and the apocalypse of Daniel.

Halakah A collection of Jewish interpretations and applications of the Mosaic law dating from the early Christian period; a part of the legal sections of the Talmud.

Ham According to Genesis, a son of Noah (Gen. 5:32; 6:10; 7:13; 9:18, 22) and the father of Canaan (Gen. 9:22), Ham was considered the progenitor of various nations in Phoenicia, Africa, and West Arabia (1 Chron. 8).

"The land of Ham" is usually taken to be Egypt (Pss. 78:51; 105:23, etc.).

Haman An official at Ahasuerus' (Xerxes') court who attempted to engineer the mass extermination of the Jews (Esther 3, 7).

Hammurabi Sixth king of Babylon's First Dynasty (1728–1686 B.C.E.) and founder of the first Amorite Empire in Mesopotamia. Hammurabi is best remembered for his law code, inscribed on an eight-foot stone monument in Akkadian cuneiform, whose legal forms resemble those of Hebraic covenant law.

Hannah Wife of Elkanah and mother of Samuel (1 Sam. 1). Hannah's lyric prayer (1 Sam. 2:1–10) anticipates the Magnificat of Mary (Luke 1:42–45).

Hanukkah *See* Dedication, Feast of.

Haran An ancient trade center in northwestern Mesopotamia, about sixty miles above the confluence of the Belikh and Euphrates rivers, Haran was the site of an important moon cult and of Abraham's call to follow Yahweh (Gen. 11:28–12:5, 24). The last refuge of the Assyrians, it was destroyed by the Medes about 606 B.C.E. (Zeph. 2:13–15; Nah. 3:1–3).

Hasidim Devout Jews who refused to forsake their religion during the persecutions of the Syrian monarch Antiochus Epiphanes (second century B.C.E.).

Hasmoneans The Jewish royal dynasty founded by the Maccabees and named for Hasmon, an ancestor of Mattathias. The Roman conquest of Palestine in 63 B.C.E. brought Hasmonean rulership and Jewish independence to an end.

Hazael An Aramean official of Damascus who murdered his king, Ben-hadad II, at the prophet Elisha's instigation (2 Kings 8:7–15; see also 1 Kings 19:15–18), usurped the Syrian kingship, and despoiled parts of Israel and Judah (Amos 1:3; 2 Kings 12; 2 Chron. 22). The name means "God sees."

Hebrew (1) A member or descendant of one of a group of northwestern Semitic peoples, including the Israelites, Edomites, Moabites, and Ammonites. According to Genesis 10:21–31 and 11:15, the Hebrews were descended from Eber, great-grandson of Shem (1 Chron. 1:18; Luke 3:35), and apparently belonged to an Aramean (ancient Syrian) branch of Semites who had originally migrated from Arabia. The Israelites' Aramean ancestry is referred to in the famous creed of Deuteronomy 26:5 (see also Gen. 25:20; 28:5). (2) The Semitic language spoken by the Israelites.

Hebron An ancient city nineteen miles southwest of Jerusalem (Num. 13:22), located near the sacred oaks of Mamre associated with Abraham (Gen. 13:18; 18; 35:27), and one of the oldest continuously inhabited sites in Palestine.

Heilsgeschicte A term from German biblical scholarship, usually translated as "sacred history" or "salvation history," which refers to the fact that Old Testament writers told Israel's story not as an objective series of events but as a confession of faith that their god was operating through the history of his chosen people, directing events in order to save them, or at least those faithful to their covenant relationship.

Hellenism The influence and adoption of Greek thought, language, values, and culture that began with Alexander the Great's conquest of the eastern Mediterranean world and intensified under his Hellenistic successors and various Roman emperors.

Hellenists Jews living outside Palestine who adopted the Greek language and, to varying degrees, Greek customs and ideas (Acts 6:1; 9:29).

Heresy Holding or teaching a religious opinion contrary to Church dogma. Applied to Christianity by its detractors (Acts 24:14), the term was not generally used in its modern sense during New Testament times except in the Pastoral Epistles (1 Tim. 1:3; 2; Titus 3:10).

Hermeneutics Study of the methodology of applying the principles and rules of interpreting a biblical text; especially, applying the results of such analysis to a contemporary situation, as one might apply the message of Hosea to modern problems of monogamy and religious faith.

Herod The name of seven Palestinian rulers.

(1) Herod I (the Great), the Idumean Roman-appointed king of Judea (40–4 B.C.E.), was ruling when Jesus was born (Matt. 2:1). An able administrator who completely reconstructed the Jerusalem temple, he was notorious for reputed cruelty and almost universally hated by the Jews.

(2) Herod Antipas, son of Herod I, tetrarch of Galilee (Luke 3:1) and Perea (4 B.C.E.– 39 C.E.), is frequently mentioned in the New Testament. Jesus, who called him "that fox" (Luke 13:31–32) and regarded him as a malign influence (Mark 8:15), was tried before him (Luke 9:7, 9; 23:7–15). Antipas was also responsible for executing John the Baptist (Matt. 14:1–12).

(3) Herod Archelaus, ethnarch of Judea, Samaria, so misruled his territory that he was recalled to Rome, an event to which Jesus apparently refers in Luke 19:12–27. Archelaus' evil reputation caused Joseph and Mary to avoid Judea and settle in Nazareth (Matt. 2:22–23).

(4) Herod, a son of Herod the Great and half-brother to Herod Antipas (Matt. 14:3; Mark 6:17).

(5) Herod Philip II, son of Herod the Great and half-brother of Herod Antipas, ruled portions of northeastern Palestine and rebuilt the city of Caesarea Philipi near Mount Hermon (Luke 3:1).

(6) Herod Agrippa I, son of Aristobulus and grandson of Herod the Great, ingratiated himself at the imperial court in Rome and, under Claudius, was made king over most of Palestine (41–44 C.E.). A persecutor of Christians, he reportedly died a horrible death immediately after accepting divine honors (Acts 12:1–23).

(7) Herod Agrippa II, son of Herod Agrippa I and great-grandson of Herod the Great,

was first king of Chalcis (50 C.E.) and then of the territory formerly ruled by Philip the Tetrarch, as well as of the adjoining area east of Galilee and the Upper Jordan. This was the Herod, together with his sister Bernice, before whom Paul appeared at Caesarea (Acts 25:13–26:32).

Herodians The name applied to members of an influential political movement in first-century C.E. Judaism who supported Herod's dynasty, particularly that of Herod Antipas. Opposing messianic hopes (Mark 3:6), they conspired with the Pharisees to implicate Jesus in disloyalty to Rome (Mark 12:13; Matt. 22:16).

Herodias Granddaughter of Herod the Great, daughter of Aristobulus, and half-sister of Herod Agrippa I, Herodias was criticized by John the Baptist for having deserted her first husband for her second, Herod Antipas, who divorced his wife to marry her. In revenge, she demanded the head of John the Baptist (Mark 6:17–29; Matt. 14:1–12; Luke 2:19–20).

Hexateuch A term meaning "six scrolls" that scholars use to denote the first six books of the Old Testament—the Torah plus the conquest narrative in Joshua—which some experts believe once formed a continuous account (J).

Hezekiah Son of Ahaz and fourteenth king of Judah (about 715–686 B.C.E.), Hazekiah ruled during the Assyrian crisis when Sargon II and then Sennacherib overran Palestine. His reign was notable for the prophetic careers of Isaiah and Micah and for sweeping religious reforms, which included purging the Jerusalem temple of non-Yahwistic elements (2 Kings 18–20; Isa. 22:15–25; 36–39; 2 Chron. 29–32).

Hierocracy A form of government controlled and administered by religious authorities, the term characterizes Jerusalem and Judah following the return from exile and the rebuilding of the temple in the late sixth century B.C.E. and after.

Higher Criticism The branch of biblical scholarship that attempts to analyze biblical writings for the purpose of determining their origins, their literary history, and their authors' purpose and meaning. Unlike lower criticism, which confines itself to studying the written texts to discover (if possible) the authentic words of the original writers or their redactors, higher criticism endeavors to isolate and interpret the religious, political, and historical forces that produced a given book and caused it in many cases to be revised and reedited by later hands. *See* Textual Criticism.

Hinnom, Valley of A topographical depression lying south and west of Jerusalem; also called "the Valley of the [Children] of Hinnom" (Jer. 7:32; 2 Chron. 28:3; 2 Kings 23:10, etc.). *See also* Gehenna (a corruption of *Ge-Hinnom*).

Hiram (1) The name of a series of rulers of Tyre, an ancient Phoenician seaport, with whom David and Solomon engaged in trade and commerce (2 Sam. 5:11; 1 Kings 5:1; 9: 11; 1 Chron. 14:1; 2 Chron. 3; Ezek. 26–28). (2) A half-Tyrian half-Israelite architect and craftsman whom King Hiram sent from Tyre to cast the bronze or copper fixtures and decorations of Solomon's temple (1 Kings 7:13–51; 2 Chron. 2:13–14; 4:16).

Historical Criticism Analyzing a written work by taking into consideration its time and place of composition in order to comprehend the events, dates, personages, and other factual elements mentioned in or influencing the text.

Hittites Mentioned forty-seven times in the Old Testament either by this name or as descendants of Heth (a grandson of Ham, son of Noah), the Hittites were among the most powerful people in the ancient Near East. A non-Semitic Indo-European group, they formed an older kingdom (about 1700–1400 B.C.E.) contemporaneous with the Hebrew patriarchal period (Gen. 23), as well as a later "new kingdom" (about 1400–1200 B.C.E.). Archaeologists have found remains of their cities in Asia Minor (central Anatolia), northern Mesopotamia, Syria, and Palestine, where the Pentateuch and Joshua list them among the nations occupying Canaan (Gen. 15:20; Exod. 3:8; Deut. 7:1; 20:17; Josh. 3:10, 11:3; 24:11).

The Hebrews from Abraham to Solomon had various commercial and political relations with the Hittites (Gen. 23:1–18; 26:34; Josh. 1:4; Judg. 3:5–6; 2 Sam. 11:2–27; 1 Kings 9:20–22; 11:1; 2 Kings 7:6; 2 Chron. 1:17; 8: 7–9; Ezek. 16:3, 45). About 1200 B.C.E., however, the Hittite Kingdom in Asia Minor fell to an invading Aegean people, probably Thracians and Phrygians. The Hittites centered near Carchemish in northern Syria were defeated by Sargon II in 717 B.C.E. and absorbed into the Assyrian Empire.

Holiness Code   The name given to the body of laws and regulations set forth in Leviticus 17–26 derives from the code's emphasis on holiness (separateness, religious purity) of behavior, which was to distinguish Israel and set its people apart from the rest of the world.

Holy of Holies   In Hebrew, a superlative referring to the Most Holy Place, the innermost room of the tabernacle and temple, where Yahweh was believed to be invisibly present.

Holy Spirit, The   The presence of God active in human life, a concept most explicitly set forth in John 14:16–26 and in the Pentecost miracle depicted in Acts 2. The Old Testament speaks of "the spirit of God" (based on the Hebrew word for "wind" or "breath") as the force that created the universe (Gen. 1: 2; Job 26:13; Ps. 104:29–30) and that inspires humans to prophesy and otherwise carry out the divine will (Exod. 31:3; Judg. 3:10; 1 Sam. 16:13–14; Isa. 61:1–3; Joel 2:28–30). In post-New Testament times, the Holy Spirit was declared to be the Third Person in the Trinity (Matt. 28:19–20).

Horeb, Mount   The name that the E and D traditions use for the mountain in the Sinai Desert at which Moses received Yahweh's law (Exod. 17:6; 33:6; Deut. 1:2, 6, 19; 4:10, 15; also Ps. 106:19). Called Sinai in the J and P sources, its exact location is unknown. According to 1 Kings 19:1–21, Elijah fled there to renew his prophetic inspiration.

Hosea   An eighth-century prophet active in the northern kingdom from before the death of Jeroboam II (d. about 746 B.C.E.) until shortly before its fall to Assyria in 721 B.C.E.; the source of the Book of Hosea, first in the printed list of Minor Prophets.

Hoshea (Hosea)   Last king of Israel (732–724 B.C.E.).

Hyksos   The Egyptian name (perhaps meaning "rulers of foreign lands") for a racially mixed but largely Semitic group that infiltrated and overran Egypt about 1720–1570 B.C.E., establishing the Fifteenth and Sixteenth dynasties; themselves expelled by the Theban kings Kamose and Ahmose I, who founded the native Egyptian Eighteenth Dynasty. Some scholars believe that the Hebrews entered Egypt during the friendly rule of the Semitic Hyksos and were enslaved when the native Egyptians returned to power.

Hyrcanus   Name of John I, son of Simon Maccabeus, Hasmonean king and high priest of Judah (134–104 B.C.E.). John II (63–40 B.C.E.), a high priest and puppet ruler installed by Rome, was succeeded by Herod the Great.

Idumea   The name, meaning "pertaining to Edom," that the Greeks and Romans applied to the country of Edom, Judah's southern neighbor; the home of Herod the Great (Mark 3:8; 1 Macc. 4:29; 5:65).

Immanuel   The name ("God is with us") that Isaiah gave to a child whose birth he predicted as a sign to King Ahaz during the Syro-Ephraimite War (late eighth century B.C.E.). Although not presented as a messianic prophecy, it was nevertheless interpreted as such (Mic. 5:3; Matt. 1:22–23).

Incarnation, The   The Christian doctrine asserting that the prehuman Son of God became flesh, the man Jesus of Nazareth, to reveal the divine will to humankind—a doctrine based largely on the Logos hymn that opens the Fourth Gospel (John 1:1–18, especially 1:14. See also Col. 1:15–20; 2:9–15; Phil. 2:5–11; Heb. 1:1–4; 2:14–18).

Isaac Son of Abraham and Sarah (Gen. 21:1–7), child of the covenant promise by which Abraham's descendants would bring a blessing to all the earth's families (Gen. 17:15–22; 18:1–15) but whom Yahweh commanded to be sacrificed to him (Gen. 18:1–18). Reprieved by an angel, Isaac marries Rebekah (Gen. 24:1–67), who bears him twin sons, Esau and Jacob (Gen. 25:19–26), the latter of whom tricks his dying father into bestowing the firstborn's birthright on him (Gen. 27:1–45). Paul interprets the near-sacrifice of Isaac as an allegory of Christ (Gal. 4:21–31).

Isaiah An eighth-century prophet and counselor of Judean kings, Isaiah of Jerusalem was active during the reigns of Uzziah, Jothan, Ahaz, and Hezekiah (collectively, 783–687 B.C.E.) (Isa. 1:1; 6:1; 7:1–12; 38:1–6). Oracles attributed to this historical figure are found in Isaiah 1–39, particularly in chapters 1–11, 20, 22, and 28–31 (chapters 24–27, 33–35, and 36–39 are thought to be by other hands). Second Isaiah, who lived during the Babylonian exile (587–538 B.C.E.), contributed chapters 40–55. Third Isaiah, whose work is found in chapters 56–66, lived during the postexilic period. A complete text of Isaiah, possibly dating from the second century B.C.E., was found among the Dea Sea Scrolls.

Ishmael The son of Abraham and Sarah's Egyptian handmaiden Hagar (Gen. 16), Ishmael and his mother were exiled to the desert, where an angel rescued them (Gen. 21). Cited as the eponymous ancestor of twelve princes (Gen. 25:12–16), he is also regarded as the progenitor of the Arabs and a forefather of Mohammed, founder of Islam. In Galatians 4:21–31, Ishmael, son of a slave woman, is compared to the Jerusalem of Paul's day.

Ishtar Goddess of love and war in the Assyrian and Babylonian religions; prototype of later fertility and erotic deities such as Ashtoreth, Aphrodite, and Venus (Jer. 44).

Ismaelites The name the J sources apply to caravan merchants trading with Egypt (Gen. 37:25–28; 39:1) but whom the E document calls Midianites (Gen. 37:28, 36). Although the twelve tribes of Ismael were a populous nation (Gen 17:20), the biblical record seldom refers to them.

Israel (1) The name given Jacob by an angel in Transjordan (Gen. 32:28, J source) and by Yahweh at Bethel (Gen. 35:10, P source). Although interpreted as "he has been strong against God" (Gen. 32:28), it probably means "may God show his strength" or "may God rule." (2) The Israelite nation descended from the twelve sons of Jacob (Israel); the covenant people chosen at Sinai. (3) The northern kingdom as opposed to the southern state of Judah during the period of the divided monarchies (922–721 B.C.E.).

Issachar Son of Jacob and Leah (Gen. 30:14–18), the eponymous progenitor of the inland tribe bearing his name (Gen. 49:14–15; Josh. 19:17–23; Deut. 33:18–19; Num. 1:29; 26:25; 1 Chron. 7:2).

J *See* Yahwist.

Jabal According to Genesis 4:20, a son of Lamech and Adah whom the J source regards as the progenitor of itinerant tent dwellers and keepers of livestock.

Jabesh-gilead An Old Testament city built in the rugged country east of the Jordan River, destroyed by Israelites who resented the town's failure to send representatives to a tribal assembly at Mizpah (Judg. 21:8–14). Men from this city rescued the decapitated body of Saul from the Philistines (1 Sam. 11; 31:12; 1 Chron. 10:11–12), for which courageous feat David rewarded them (2 Sam. 2:5–7).

Jachin and Boaz Names that Hiram, a half-Phoenician craftsman, gave to the twin pillars of copper decorating the entrance to Solomon's temple (1 Kings 7:13–22; 2 Chron. 3:17). Their exact appearance, religious function and significance, and the meaning of their names are conjectural.

Jacob The younger of twin sons born to Isaac and Rebekah (Gen. 25:21–26), Jacob is famous for his shrewdness, opportunism, and craftiness. He stole his brother Esau's birthright and Isaac's blessing (Gen. 25:29–34; 27:1–29), acquired great wealth in stock breeding (Gen. 29–30), and absconded with his father-in-law's household gods (Gen. 31:1–21) but later concluded a covenant with him (Gen. 31:22–25). Jacob was also the recipient of several divine visitations: the dream vision of a ladder to heaven at Bethel (Gen. 28) and wrestling with a divine being at Jabbok, Transjordan, after which his name was changed to Israel (Gen. 32:24–32; 33:4), a revelation renewed at Bethel (Gen. 35:1–15).

Father of twelve sons, eponymous ancestors of Israel's twelve tribes (Gen. 46:1–27), Jacob suffered in old age largely because of the temporary loss of his favorite children, Joseph (Gen. 37:2–36) and Benjamin (Gen. 43:1–14), and other filial problems reflected in his deathbed blessings (Gen. 49:1–28). In accordance with his wishes, he was buried in a cave near Mamre, which his grandfather Abraham had purchased from a Hittite (Gen. 49:29–33; 50:7–13).

Jael Wife of Heber the Kenite (member of a nomadic tribe of metal workers), who offered hospitality to Sisera, the Canaanite general, and then murdered him, thus becoming a national heroine in Israel (Judg. 4:11–22; 5:24–31).

Jairus The head of a synogogue in Galilee who asked Jesus to heal his dying child, for which act of faith he was rewarded with the girl's miraculous cure (Luke 8:41–42, 49–56; Mark 5:35–43; Matt. 9:18–20, 23–26).

James

(1) Son of Zebedee, brother of John, and one of the twelve apostles (Mark 1:19–20; 3:17; Matt. 4:21–22; 10:2; Luke 5:10; 6:14). A Galilean fisherman, he left his trade to follow Jesus and, with John and Peter, became a member of his inner circle. He was among the three disciples present at the transfiguration (Mark 9:2–10; Matt. 17:1–9; Luke 9:28–36) and was at Jesus' side during the last hours before his arrest (Mark 14:32–42, Matt. 26:36–45). James and John used their intimacy to request a favored place in the messianic kingdom, thus arousing the other apostles' indignation (Mark 10:35–45). James was beheaded when Herod Agrippa I persecuted the Jerusalem church (41–44 C.E.) (Acts 12:2).

(2) James, son of Alphaeus and Mary (Acts 1:13; Mark 16:1), one of the Twelve (Matt. 10:3–4), called "the less" or "the younger" (Mark 15:40).

(3) James, the eldest of Jesus' three "brothers" (or close male relatives) named in the gospels (Mark 6:3; Matt. 13:55), first opposed Jesus' work (Matt. 12:46–50; Mark 3:31–35; Luke 8:19–21; John 7:3–5) but was apparently converted by one of Jesus' postresurrection appearances (1 Cor. 15:7) and became a leader in the Jerusalem church (Acts 15:13–34; 21:18–26). According to legend a Nazirite and upholder of the Mosaic law, he apparently clashed with Paul over the latter's policy of absolving Gentile converts from circumcision and other legalistic requirements (Gal. 1:18–2:12). The reputed author of the New Testament Epistle of James, he was martyred at Jerusalem in the early 60s C.E.

Jamnia, Academy of An assembly of eminent Palestinian rabbis and Pharisees held about 90 C.E. in the coastal village of Jamnia (Yabneh) to define and guide Judaism following the Roman destruction of Jerusalem and its temple. According to tradition, a leading Pharisee named Yohanan ben Zakkai had escaped from the besieged city by simulating death and being carried out in a coffin by his disciples. Yohanan, who had argued that saving human lives was more important than success in the national rebellion against Rome, was given Roman support to set up an academy to study the Jewish law. Under his direction, the Pharisees not only preserved the Torah traditions but apparently formulated what was to become the official biblical canon of Palestinian Judaism. Out of the deliberations at Jamnia came the authoritative list of books in the Writings, the third major division of the Hebrew Bible.

Japheth According to Genesis 5:32; 6:10; 9: 18, and 10:1, one of Noah's three sons, the eponymous ancestor of various Indo-European nations, especially Aegean Sea peoples, including the Greeks (Ionians) and Philistines (Gen. 10:1–5).

Jashar, Book of Apparently a collection of Hebrew poetry (since lost), quoted in Joshua 10:12–13; 2 Samuel 1:18, and 1 Kings 8.53 (Septuagint version only).

Javan According to Genesis 10:4–5, the fourth son of Japheth and progenitor of the Ionian Greeks and other coastal and island peoples of the northeastern Mediterranean (1 Chron. 1:5, 7).

Jebus The city held by Jebusites, an ancient Canaanite tribe (Gen. 10:16; Josh. 11:3; 1 Chron. 1:14; Ezek. 16:3), which later became Jerusalem, it may have been the same town called Urusalim ("city of peace") in the Amarna Letters and called Salem, city of Melchizedek, in Genesis 14:18–20 (see also Josh. 18:16, 28; Judg. 19:10; 1 Chron. 11:4). David captured the city and made it his capital (2 Sam. 5:7–9; 6–10; 1 Chron. 11:4–9), placed the Ark of the Covenant there (2 Sam. 6:4–5), and purchased from a Jebusite an ancient stone threshing floor (2 Sam. 24:16–24; 1 Chron. 21:15–28) that became the site of Solomon's temple (1 Kings 6:1–8:66).

Jeduthun The representative leader or eponymous founder of a guild of temple singers and musicians (1 Chron. 25:1, 3, 6; 16:40–42) who provided music for services at the Jerusalem sanctuary. This group officiated during the reigns of Solomon (1 Chron. 5:12–13), Hezekiah (2 Chron. 29:14), and Josiah, whose magnificent revival of the Passover liturgies they helped celebrate (2 Chron. 35:15–16). Jeduthun's name appears in the superscriptions of Psalms 39, 62, and 77 and among the list of exiles returned to Jerusalem from Babylon (Neh. 11:17).

Jehoiachin King of Judah (598/597 B.C.E.), son and successor of Jehoiakim. After inheriting the throne at age eight and reigning for only three months and ten days, he was taken captive to Babylon (2 Kings 24:10–12; 2 Chron. 36:9–10), where he remained the rest of his life. Babylonian records indicate that he was at first accorded favored status but later imprisoned until Nebuchadnezzar's successor, Evil-merodach (Amel-Marduk), released him (562 B.C.E.) and honored him above other captive kings (2 Kings 25:27–30; Jer. 52:31–34).

Jehoiakim Second son of Josiah, Jehoiakim was made king of Judah about 609 B.C.E., when Pharaoh Necho of Egypt placed him on the throne, deposing his brother Jehoahaz who had reigned only three months (2 Kings 23:34; 2 Chron. 36:4). Another brother, Zedekiah, replaced Jehoiakim's heir, Jehoiachin, to become Judah's last Davidic monarch. The deuteronomist historians, the Chronicler, and the prophet Jeremiah all denounced his religious apostasy and misguided attempts to combat Babylonian domination with Egyptian alliances (2 Kings 23:36–24:6; 2 Chron. 36:5–8; Jer. 25–26; 36). Ignoring Jeremiah's advice (Jer. 36:1–26), Jehoiakim died or was assassinated before paying the consequences of his rebellion against Babylon (2 Kings 24:6). The Chronicler states that he was chained and carried off to Babylon (2 Chron. 36:6–7), but this was the fate of his son and heir, Jehoiachin (2 Kings 24:12–16; 2 Chron. 36:10).

Jehonadab Son of Rechab the Kenite (1 Chron. 2:55), he assisted Jehu in massacring King Ahab's family and slaughtering Baal worshipers in Israel (2 Kings 10:14–27). According to Jeremiah 35:1–19, he was a nomadic ascetic who condemned drinking wine, planting vineyards, cultivating fields, or building cities. His support of Jehu's fanatical Yahwism may have been in part a revolt against Ahab's urban culture.

Jehoram (1) A son of Ahab and king of Israel (849–842 B.C.E.) who enlisted King Jehoshaphat's help in quelling Moab's rebellion against paying Israel tribute (2 Kings 3:1–27). Jehu later murdered him (2 Kings 8:25–29; 9:22–26). (2) Son of Jehoshaphat and king of Judah (849–842 B.C.E.), he married Ahab's daughter Athaliah and fostered the religion of Baal in Judah (2 Kings 8:16–24; 2 Chron. 21:1–20). His reign was marked by wars with the Arabs and Philistines and by the loss of Judah's control of Edom. The name means "Yahweh is exalted."

Jehoshaphat Son of Asa and king of Judah (873–849 B.C.E.), his name means "Yahweh judges." Although the deuteronomist historians give him short shrift (1 Kings 15:24; 22:41–51), the Chronicler emphasizes the general success of his twenty-four-year reign (2 Chron. 17:1–21:1), which was marked by important religious reforms, effective wars against Edom, Moab, and Ammon (2 Chron. 20:1–30), and the achievement of relative political security and prosperity for his people.

Jehovah An English rendering of the divine name created by adding the vowels of *Elohim* and *Adonai* to the four consonants (YHWH) of the Tetragrammaton, the term entered the language via a Roman-Catholic Latin translation about 1518 C.E., though the name *Yahweh* is considered a more accurate rendition of the Hebrew original.

Jehu A son of Jehoshaphat (not the king of Judah) whom the prophet Elisha had anointed king of Israel in 842 B.C.E. (2 Kings 9:1–3), fulfilling an earlier command of Elijah (1 Kings 19:16–17). Thus commissioned by Israel's prophetic guild, Jehu proceeded to slaughter Ahab's family and all connected with it (2 Kings 9:14–10:27), including King Jehoram, King Ahaziah of Judah and his forty-two sons, Queen Jezebel, Ahab's seventy sons, and numerous other Israelites who worshiped Baal. Jehu's long reign (842–815 B.C.E.) saw Israel's territory shrink to a fraction of what it had been under Omri and Ahab (2 Kings 10:32–33). Although he murdered in Yahweh's name, his actions were condemned by the prophet Hosea (Hos. 1:3–5). Nor was he a wholehearted Yahwist (2 Kings 10:31), though his name means "Yahweh is He."

Jephthah The son of Gilead and a harlot, Jephthah was driven as a youth from the area of Gilead by his legitimate brothers (Judg. 11:1–3) but was recalled by Gilead's elders when the Ammonites attacked Israel. An effective military leader, he defeated the Ammonites and was judge (general) in Israel for six years (Judg. 12:7). Best known for vowing to make a burnt offering of the first person he met after the battle if Yahweh would grant him victory, he presumably immolated his own daughter, who had come to congratulate him on his success (Judg. 11:29–40; see 2 Kings 3:27). The author of Hebrews praises him for his faith (Heb. 11:32).

Jeremiah One of Israel's greatest prophets, Jeremiah warned Jerusalem and its kings of their misdeeds and of coming doom by the Babylonians for approximately forty years (about 627–587 B.C.E.) (Jer. 1:1–3). Beginning in the thirteenth year of Josiah's reign (640–609 B.C.E.), he also prophesied during the reigns of Jehoiakim (609–598 B.C.E.), Jehoiachin (598/597 B.C.E.), and Zedekiah (597–587 B.C.E.), continuing after Jerusalem's fall (587 B.C.E.) and during a forced exile in Egypt (Jer. 40–44).

Although usually ignored by the royal family, persecuted both by government officials and his compatriots for his unpopular (and seemingly treasonous) message that Yahweh had forsaken Judah and determined its annihilation, Jeremiah persisted in attacking official policy and denouncing those who trusted in the temple (Jer. 1:11; 15; 21–22; 25–28; 36–38). After Jerusalem's fall, he was treated well by the Babylonians (Jer. 39–40), but his fellow survivors forcibly transported him to Egypt (Jer. 42–44). His message is known for its promise of a new covenant and a restoration of Judah (Jer. 30–33).

Jericho One of the world's oldest cities, Jericho's ruins lie near an oasis on the west side of the south Jordan River Valley. Partly excavated by archaeologists, its earliest occupation dates to about 7800 B.C.E. Although according to Joshua 2 and 5:13–6:26 its fortified walls crumbled when the Israelites marched around the city, radiocarbon dating indicates that the site was already abandoned at the time of the conquest (thirteenth century B.C.E.). Jericho was partly rebuilt by Hiel of Bethel during Ahab's reign (869–850 B.C.E.) (1 Kings 16:34), but no evidence of this occupation remains. It was extensively rebuilt during Herod's day (40–4 B.C.E.) and is mentioned several times in the New Testament (Matt. 20:29; Mark 10:46; Luke 10:30; 18:35; 19:1; Heb. 11:30).

Jeroboam I An Ephraimite who led the ten northern tribes' secession from the Davidic monarchy and became the first ruler of the northern kingdom (1 Kings 11:26–12:33), Jeroboam I reigned from approximately 922 to 901 B.C.E. His first capital was Shechem, site of the old tribal confederacy (Josh. 24), but he later moved his administration to Tirzah, his former home and an ancient Canaanite royal sanctuary (1 Kings 12:24–25). The deuteronomist historians condemned him for establishing rival Yahwist shrines at Bethel and Dan to compete with the Yahwist temple at Jerusalem and for tolerating the worship of such foreign deities as Chemosh, Ashtoreth, and the Ammonite Milcom (1 Kings 11:33; 12:26–13:34).

Jeroboam II A descendant of Jehu, son of King Jehonash, and ruler of Israel (786–746 B.C.E.) whose long reign brought relative peace and material prosperity to the northern kingdom, Jeroboam II won major victories over Ben-hadad, king of Syria, and extended Israel's territory so that it included almost all the territory over which David and Solomon had ruled, except Judah. The Deuteronomist's brief account of his reign (2 Kings 14:23–29) gives no indication of its importance. The prophets Amos and Hosea, who were active during the time of Jeroboam II, denounced the country's economic oppression of the poor as well as its widespread materialism.

Jerusalem An ancient Palestinian holy city, sometimes identified with the Salem of Genesis 14:17–20 but more often with Jebus, a city of the Jebusite tribe (Josh. 18:28; Judg. 19:10), Jerusalem became King David's capital after he had captured it from the Jebu-

sites (2 Sam. 5:6–10; 2 Chron. 4:5). Solomon centralized the worship of Yahweh on a hill called Zion there (1 Kings 5–7; 2 Chron. 2–4), and Jerusalem remained the capital of Judah after the secession of the northern tribes (922 B.C.E.). The city suffered three major destructions: in 587 B.C.E. when the Babylonians razed Solomon's temple; in 70 C.E. when the Romans destroyed the city and its Herodian temple; and in 135 C.E. when the Romans decimated the city for the last time.

Jesse The son of Obed and grandson of Ruth and Boaz (Ruth 4:17, 22), Jesse was a Judean shepherd and father of seven or eight sons, including David (1 Sam. 16:10–11; 17:12; 1 Chron. 2:12–17) who became king of Israel. He is mentioned in the messianic prophecies of Isaiah 11:1, 10, and in Matthew's and Luke's genealogies of Jesus (Matt. 1:5–6; Luke 3:32; see also Rom. 15:12).

Jesus The English form of a Latin name derived from the Greek *Iesous*, which translated the Hebrew *Jeshua*, a late version of *Jehoshua* or *Joshua*, meaning "Yahweh is salvation." The name was borne by several biblical figures, including Joshua, leader of the conquest of Canaan; an ancestor of Jesus Christ (Luke 3:29); and a Jewish Christian, also called Justus (Col. 4:11). It appears several times in the Apocrypha, notably as the name of the author of Ecclesiasticus, Jesus Ben Sirach.

Jesus Christ The name and title given the firstborn son of Mary and Joseph (the child's legal father), the one whom Christians regard as the Spirit-begotten Son of God and savior of the world. According to Matthew 1:21 and Luke 1:31, he received the name Jesus because he was to "save his people from their sins." The term *Christ* is not a proper name but the English version of the Greek *Christos*, a translation of the Aramaic *Meshiha* and the Hebrew *Mashiah* ("Messiah," "the Anointed One"). While we know almost nothing about the historical Jesus, the New Testament presents a thorough documentation of what the early Christian community believed about the historical Christ.

Jethro A shepherd and priest of the Kenites, a Midianite tribe of coppersmiths, with whom Moses took refuge during his flight from Egypt and whose daughter Zipporah he married (Exod. 2:15–22; 18:1–12). Moses apparently identified Jethro's god, El Shaddai, with Yahweh, god of the Israelites (Exod. 3; 6; 18).

Jew Originally a member of the tribe or kingdom of Judah (2 Kings 16:6; 25:25), the term later included any Hebrew who returned from Babylonian captivity and finally encompassed Hebrews scattered throughout the world (Esther 2:5; Matt. 2:2). Certain New Testament writers refer to "the Jews" as any Israelites opposing Christianity (John 1:19; 5:16; 18:20; Acts 14:19; 16:20; 1 Cor. 1:23; Rev. 2:9).

Jezebel Daughter of King Ethbaal of Tyre and wife of King Ahab, Jezebel promulgated Baal worship in Israel and presecuted Yahweh's prophets (1 Kings 16:29–33; 18:4, 19; 19:1–3). After she perverted the Mosaic law to confiscate Naboth's vineyard (1 Kings 21:1–16), Elijah predicted her shameful death (1 Kings 21:24–26), a prophecy fulfilled when Jehu threw her body for dogs to eat during his bloody purge of Ahab's dynasty (2 Kings 9:30–37). In Revelation 2:20 she is a symbol of false religion.

Jezreel (1) A fertile valley, known as the Plain of Esdraelon, extending southeast across Palestine from north of Mount Carmel to the Jordan River. (2) A fortified city and the site of Naboth's vineyard (1 Kings 21:1–24) and of Jehu's murders of King Joram, of the Queen-mother Jezebel (2 Kings 9:24, 30–37), and of all Ahab's heirs (2 Kings 10:1–11).

Joab A son of Zeruiah, half-sister of David (2 Sam. 2:18), Joab was the cruelly efficient commander-in-chief of David's armies who managed the capture of Jerusalem (2 Sam. 5:8; 1 Chron. 11:6–8) and successful wars against the Syrians, Ammonites, and Edomites (2 Sam. 12:26–31; 1 Kings 11:15–17). He murdered Abner, general of the northern tribes under Saul's heir, Ishbaal (2 Sam. 2:18–23; 3:22–30); arranged Uriah's death so that David could marry Bathsheba (2 Sam. 11:6–21); reconciled David and Absalom (2 Sam. 14:28–33) but later murdered David's rebellious son (2 Sam. 18:9–17); and supported the wrong contender for David's throne (1 Kings 1:5–33), for which he was executed early in Solomon's reign (1 Kings 2:28–34), supposedly on David's deathbed advice (1 Kings 2:5–6).

Joanna Wife of Chuza, an administrator in Herod Antipas' Jerusalem household, who became a follower of Jesus (Luke 8:3) and was among the women who discovered his empty tomb (Luke 23:55–24:11).

Joash (Jehoash) The name of several Old Testament figures. (1) Judge Gideon's father (Judg. 6:11, 31–32). (2) A son of King Ahab (1 Kings 22:26–27; 2 Chron. 18:25–26). (3) The eighth king of Judah (about 837–800 B.C.E.), a son of Ahaziah, who reduced Baal worship and repaired the temple but later had to forfeit some of its treasures to pay Hazael, king of Aram, who besieged Jerusalem. Joash's reign, including the machinations of his grandmother, the Queen-regent Athaliah, is recorded in 2 Kings 11–12; 13:10–13; and 2 Chronicles 22:11–24:27. (4) The twelfth king of Israel, third of the Jehu dynasty, who recovered some of the Israelite territory that his predecessors had lost to Syria, defeated King Amaziah of Judah, and transported some of the temple's treasures from Jerusalem to Samaria (2 Kings 13:1–25; 14:8–16; 2 Chron. 25:18–19).

Job The name apparently dates from the second millennium B.C.E. and may mean "one who comes back to God," a penitent. It may derive from the Hebrew *ayab*, "to be hostile," denoting one whom God makes his enemy. The central character of the wisdom book bearing his name, Job is linked with Noah and Daniel as a person of exemplary righteousness (Ezek. 14:14, 20).

Joel Although numerous biblical figures bore this name (meaning "Yahweh is God"), the best known is the son of Pethuel (Joel 1:1), a prophet of postexilic Judah (perhaps about 350 B.C.E.).

John the Apostle A son of Zebedee and brother of the Apostle James, John was a Galilean fisherman whom Jesus called to be among his twelve most intimate followers (Mark 1:19–20; Matt. 4:21–22). Jesus called James and John *Boanerges* ("sons of thunder"), possibly because of their impetuous temperaments (Mark 3:17; 9:38; Luke 9:52–56). Always among the first four in the Gospel lists of the Twelve (Mark 3:14–17; Matt. 10:2; Luke 6:3–14), John was present at the transfiguration (Matt. 17:1; Mark 9:2; Luke 9:28) and at Gethsemane (Matt. 26:37; Mark 14:33). Tradition identifies him with the "beloved disciple" (John 13:23; 21:20) and as the author of the Gospel of John, a premise that most scholars believe is impossible to prove. Along with Peter and James, he was one of the triple "pillars" of the Jerusalem church (Acts 1:13; 3:1–4:22; 8:14–17; Gal. 2:9). He may have been martyred under Herod Agrippa, although a late second-century tradition states that he lived to old age in Ephesus.

John the Baptist The son of Zecharias, a priest, and Elisabeth (Luke 1:5–24, 56–80), John was an ascetic who preached the imminence of judgment and baptized converts in the Jordan River as a symbol of their repentance from sin (Matt. 3:1–12; Mark 1:2–8; Luke 3:1–18). The Gospel writers viewed him as an Elijah figure and forerunner of the Messiah (Luke 1:17; Matt. 11:12–14; John 1:15, 9–34; 3:22–36) who baptized Jesus but also recognized his superiority (Matt. 3:13–17; Mark 1:9–11; Luke 3:21–22). When imprisoned by Herod Antipas, he inquired whether Jesus were the expected "one who is to come." Jesus' answer was equivocal but he praised John's work as fulfilling prophecy (Matt. 11:2–19; Luke 7:24–35). At his stepdaughter Salome's request, Herod had John beheaded (Matt. 14:6–12; Mark 6:17–29). Some of John's disciples later became Christians (John 1:37; Acts 18:25).

Jonah A son of Amittai, a Zebulunite from Gath-hepher whom Yahweh sent as a prophet to warn Nineveh of its impending doom (Jon. 1:1–16). The "sign of Jonah," who was reputedly delivered from death inside a sea monster (Jon. 1:17–2:10), is cited in the Synoptics as prophetic of Jesus' death and resurrection (Matt. 12:40; 16:4; Luke 11:29–30).

Jonathan Son and heir of King Saul (1 Sam. 13:16; 14:49; 1 Chron. 8:33) and famous for his unselfish devotion to young David (1 Sam. 18:1–5; 19:1–7; 20:1–21:1; 23:15–18). Along with his father, Jonathan was killed by the Philistines at the Battle of Gilboa (1 Sam. 31:1; 2 Sam. 1:16), a loss David lamented in one of his most moving psalms (2 Sam. 1:17–27).

Joppa An important harbor of ancient Palestine, located on the Mediterranean coast about thirty-five miles northwest of Jerusalem and now a suburb of Tel Aviv (1 Macc. 10:76; 12:33–34; 13:11; 14:5, 34; 2 Macc. 12:3–4). It was in Joppa that Peter resurrected Tabitha (Acts 9:43) and experienced his vision welcoming Gentiles into the Church (Acts 10:1–48).

Jordan The main river of Palestine, which occupies a deep north-south rift valley connecting the Sea of Galilee with the Dead Sea (a distance of about sixty-five miles) and forms the boundary between east and west Palestine. The Jordan is mentioned in the narratives concerning Lot, Abraham, and Jacob (Gen. 13:10; 14:12–16; 32:10) but is best known as the last barrier Israel crossed before entering Canaan—an event marked by a miraculous stopping of the river's flow (Josh. 3:1–5:1)—and as the site of John the Baptist's activity (Matt. 3:5; Mark 1:5; Luke 3:3), including the baptism of Jesus (Matt. 3:13–17; Mark 1:9–11; Luke 13:21–22). Naaman was cured of leprosy by bathing in the Jordan (2 Kings 5:10–14).

Joseph

(1) The son of Jacob and Rachel, who aroused his ten brothers' jealousy, was sold into slavery, and taken to Egypt where, aided by his ability to interpret dreams, he rose to power second only to that of pharaoh himself. His story is told in Genesis 30:22–24 and Genesis 37–50. The name Joseph is used to represent the combined tribes of Ephraim and Manasseh

(Josh. 16:1–4) and the northern kingdom (Ps. 80).

(2) The husband of Mary and legal father of Jesus, a descendant of the Bethlehemite David (Matt. 1:20) but who lived in Nazareth (Luke 2:4) where he was a carpenter (Matt. 13:55). Little is known of him except for his piety (Luke 2:21–24, 41–42) and his wish to protect his betrothed wife from scandal (Luke 2:1–5). Since he does not appear among Jesus' family members during his (supposed) son's public ministry, it is assumed that he died before Jesus began his preaching career (Matt. 1:18–2:23; 13:55–56).

(3) Joseph of Arimathea, a wealthy member of the Sanhedrin and, according to John 19:38, a secret follower of Jesus who claimed Jesus' crucified body from Pilate for burial in his private garden tomb (Matt. 27:57–60; Mark 15:42–46; Luke 23:50–53; John 19:38–42).

Josephus, Flavius An important Jewish historian (about 37–100 C.E.) whose two major works—*Antiquities of the Jews* and *The Jewish Wars* (covering the revolt against Rome, 66–70 C.E.)—provide valuable background material for first-century Judaism and the early Christian period.

Joshua The son of Nun, an Ephraimite, Joshua ("Yahweh is salvation") was Moses' military assistant (Exod. 17:8–13), in charge of the tabernacle (Exod. 33:11), one of the two spies optimistic about Israel's prospects of conquering Canaan (Num. 13:1–16; 14:6–9), and chosen to succeed Moses (Num. 27:18–23; Deut. 3:28; 31:23; 34:9). He led the Israelites across the Jordan (Josh. 3), captured Jericho (Josh. 6) and Ai (Josh. 7–8), warred against the Canaanite kings (Josh. 10–12), allotted the land to various tribes (Josh. 13:1–22:8), and made a covenant with Yahweh and the people (Josh. 24).

Josiah Son of Amon (642–640 B.C.E.), Josiah ("Yahweh heals") became king of Judah after his father's murder. The outstanding event of his reign (640–609 B.C.E.) was the discovery of a Book of the Law (probably an early edition of Deuteronomy) and the subsequent religious reform it inspired (following 621 B.C.E.). Josiah purged Judah and part of Israel's old territory of their rural shrines and "high places," centering all worship at the Jerusalem temple (2 Kings 23:27). He was killed at Megiddo attempting to intercept Pharaoh Necho's army on its way to support the collapsing Assyrian Empire (609 B.C.E.) (2 Kings 22:1–23:30; 2 Chron. 34:1–35:27).

Jotham (1) The youngest son of Jerubbaal (Gideon) (Judg. 9:5), who denounced his brother Abimelech to the people of Shechem for the latter's murder of Jerubbaal's seventy sons (Judg. 9:7–21). (2) Son of Uzziah, who was king of Judah as regent for his father (about 750–742 B.C.E.) and later in his own right (742–735 B.C.E.) (2 Kings 15:32–38; 2 Chron. 27:1–9). The name means "Yahweh is perfect."

Jubilee Derived from the Hebrew word for "ram's horn" or "trumpet," the term refers to the sabbatical year described in Leviticus 25:8–24 to be kept every half-century and proclaimed by a trumpet blast on the Day of Atonement. During a Jubilee year, all debts were to be canceled and private property returned to its rightful owners.

Judah (1) The fourth son of Jacob and Leah (Gen. 29:35) who, according to the J account, received his father's most powerful blessing (Gen. 49:8) and became the progenitor of the tribe of Judah, which along with that of Ephraim was the most important in Israel's history. David was of this populous tribe, which loyally supported his dynasty (2 Sam. 2:4; 1 Kings 12:20). (2) The kingdom of Judah, the southern kingdom of the divided monarchy, was composed chiefly of the tribes of Judah and Benjamin, which supported the Davidic dynasty when the northern ten tribes seceded from the union (922 B.C.E.). It was destroyed by the Babylonians in 587 B.C.E.

Judaism The name applied to the religion of the people of Judah ("the Jews") after the northern kingdom of Israel fell (721 B.C.E.) and particularly after the Babylonian exile (587–538 B.C.E.).

Judas A late form of the name Judah, popular after the time of Judas ("the Jew") Maccabeus and borne by several New Testament figures: (1) the brother (or son) of James, one of the twelve apostles (Luke 6:16), who is sometimes identified with the Thaddeus of Matthew 10:3 or the Judas of John 14:22; (2) the "brother" or kinsman of Jesus (Mark 6:3; Matt. 13:55); (3) Judas Iscariot ("Judas the man of Kerioth"), son of Simon Iscariot (John 6:71; 13:26), the apostle who betrayed Jesus to the priests and Romans for thirty pieces of silver (Mark 3:19; 14:10; Luke 6:16; Matt. 26:14–16, 47; John 18:3) but later returned the blood money and committed suicide (Matt. 27:3–5; Acts 1:18–20). The Gospel writers little understood Judas' motives, attributing them to simple greed or to the influence of Satan (Luke 22:3; John 6:71; 12:1–8; 13:11, 27–29).

Jude An Anglicized form of the name Judah or Judas; one of Jesus' "brothers" (or a close male relative) (Mark 6:3; Matt. 13:55), perhaps a son born to Joseph before his marriage to Mary. Jude is less prominent in the early Christian community than his brother James (Jude 1:1) and is the traditional author of the Epistle of Jude, though most scholars doubt this claim.

Judea The Greco-Roman designation for territory comprising the old kingdom of Judah, the name first occurs in Ezra 5:8, a reference to the "province of Judea." In the time of Jesus, Judea was the southernmost of the three divisions of the Roman province of Western Palestine, the other two of which were Samaria and Galilee (Neh. 2:7; Luke 1:39; John 3:22; 11:7; Acts 1:1; Gal. 1:22).

Judge (1) In the Old Testament, a civil magistrate (Exod. 21:22; Deut. 16:18), administrator of a judiciary system traditionally organized by Moses (Exod. 18:13–26; Deut. 1:15–17; 16:18–20; 17:2–13; 19:15–20). Under the monarchy, the king became the supreme civil judge (2 Sam. 15:2; 1 Kings 3:9, 28; 7:7). (2) In the Book of Judges, the term refers primarily to people of God who led military revolts against Israel's foreign oppressors. There were twelve officially designated as

such: Othniel of Judah, Ehud, Shamgar, Deborah, Gideon, Tola, Jair, Jephthah, Ibzan, Elon, Abdon, and Samson, though Eli and Samuel were also spoken of as judges (1 Sam. 4:18; 7:15).

Judgment, Day of A theological concept deriving from the ancient Hebrew belief that the Day of Yahweh would see Israel's triumph and the destruction of its enemies, a confidence the prophet Amos shattered by proclaiming that it would mean calamity for Israel as for all who broke Yahweh's laws (Amos 5:18–20). This view prevails in Zephaniah 1:1–2; 3 and Malachi 3:1–6; 4:1–6. Isaiah also refers to "that day" of coming retribution (Isa. 11:10–16; 13:9, 13), while it is given an apocalyptic setting in Daniel 7:9–14, an idea developed in several apocryphal and pseudepigraphal books as well as in the New Testament (Matt. 25; Rev. 20).

Jupiter Latin name of the chief Roman deity, counterpart of the Greek Zeus, king of the Olympian gods for whom some ignorant men of Lycaonia mistook Paul's companion Barnabas (Acts 14:12–18).

Kadesh The central campsite of the Israelites during their wanderings through the Sinai wilderness (Num. 13:26–33; 20:1–11; 32:8; Deut. 1:19–25).

Kenite Hypothesis A theory arguing that Yahweh was originally the tribal god of the Kenite clan from which Moses and his Hebrew followers borrowed and adapted their religion (Exod. 18:1–12).

Kenites A Midianite clan of nomadic coppersmiths and metalworkers to which Jethro, Moses' father-in-law, belonged (Exod. 18:1–12; Num. 10:29–32; Judg. 1:16; 4:11; 1 Sam. 15:6).

Kethuvim (*Ketubim* or *Kethubim*) The Hebrew term designating the Writings, the third division of the Hebrew Bible: Psalms, Job, Proverbs, Song of Songs, Ecclesiastes, Esther, Ruth, Lamentations, Daniel, Ezra, Nehemiah, 1 and 2 Chronicles.

Kittim Originally an Old Testament name for the Island of Cyprus and its inhabitants (Gen.

10:4), thought to be descendants of Noah's grandson Javan, it was later applied to Macedonian Greeks (1 Macc. 1:1) and others (Dan. 11:30).

KJV Abbreviation for the King James Version of the Bible, published in 1611.

Koheleth (Qoheleth) The title—meaning "the president" or "the preacher" of an assembly or church (*qahal*)—that the otherwise anonymous author of Ecclesiastes (the Greek equivalent of the term) gives himself (Eccles. 1:1; 12:9–10).

Korah The son of Izhar who rebelled against Moses' leadership during the Sinai wanderings (Num. 16–17).

Laban A descendant of Nahor, brother of Rebekah (Gen. 24:29; 25:20), father of Leah and Rachel, and thus father-in-law of Jacob. An Aramean living in Haran, Laban was noted for his duplicity and greed (Gen. 24:29–31:55).

Lachish A major fortified city in Judah about thirty miles southwest of Jerusalem and twenty miles from the Mediterranean coast (2 Kings 14:19; 2 Chron. 11:5–12; 14:6; 32:9; Jer. 34:7).

Lamech According to J, the son of Methusael and father of Tubal and Jubal (Gen. 4:1–24); according to P, the son of Methuselah and father of Noah (Gen. 5:25–31). His boastful song of vengeance is given in Genesis 4:23–24.

Laodicea A commercial city on the Lycus River in Asia Minor and one of the seven churches of Asia (Col. 4:15–16; Rev. 3:14–22).

Latter Prophets Also known as the "writing prophets," the term refers to the books of Isaiah, Jeremiah, Ezekiel, and the twelve Minor Prophets.

Law The Torah ("teaching," "instruction") or Pentateuch, the first five books of the Bible containing the legal material traditionally ascribed to Moses.

Lazarus (1) The brother of Mary and Martha, a resident of Bethany whom Jesus resurrected (John 11:1–12:10). (2) The beggar in Jesus' parable of rewards and punishments in the afterlife (Luke 16:20–25).

Leah Laban's older daughter, whom he married to Jacob by trickery after the latter had worked seven years for her younger sister, Rachel (Gen. 29:16–30:21; 31:14). Although Jacob disliked Leah, she bore him six sons and a daughter: Reuben, Simeon, Levi, Judah, Issachar, Zebulun, and Dinah (Ruth 4:11).

Lebanons, The Two generally parallel mountain ranges 100 miles long, extending north-northeast to south-southwest from the Taurus Mountains in Asia Minor through Syria and Palestine and culminating in limestone cliffs at the Gulf of Suez. Between the two ranges lies El-Beka, a fertile plain 30 by 10 miles in dimension. The Lebanons marked the northwest boundary of Canaan (Deut. 1:17; 11:24; Josh. 1:4; 11:17). Their snow-capped peaks and cedar forests inspired Israel's poets and prophets (Pss. 80:10; 92:12; Song of Sol. 1:17; 4:14; 5:15; Amos 2:9; Jer. 22:7; Ezek. 27:5; 31:3–8). David and Solomon utilized the famed cedars of Lebanon in their building programs (2 Sam. 5:11; 1 Chron. 22:4–10).

Legend A term denoting unverifiable stories or narrative cycles about celebrated people or places of the past. Legends grow as the popular oral literature of a people. Their purpose is not to provide historical accuracy but entertainment, to illustrate cherished beliefs, expectations, and moral principles. Scholars consider much of the material associated with the stories of the patriarchs, Moses, and prophets as legendary.

Levi The third son of Jacob and Leah (Gen. 29:34; 35:23), Levi earned his father's disapproval for his violence in slaughtering tribal neighbors (Gen. 34:30; 49:5–7). He was the eponymous ancestor of the tribe of Levi to which Moses, Aaron, and Miriam belonged (Exod. 6:16; Num. 3:1–39).

Leviathan A mythical sea monster, the ancient Near Eastern dragon of chaos and symbol of evil which Yahweh defeated in creating the universe (Ps. 74:14; Dan. 7:2; Isa. 27:1; Job. 41:1–34. See also Rev. 11:7; 12:3; 13:1–8).

Levites The Israelite tribe descended from Levi, son of Jacob (Num. 3; 1 Chron. 5:27–6:81) that was given priestly duties in lieu of land holdings when Israel conquered Canaan (Deut. 18:1–8). According to P, only descendants of Aaron were to be priests (Exod. 28:1; Num. 18:7); the Levites were regarded as their assistants and servants (Num. 18:2–7; 20–32). They served as priests of secondary rank and as temple functionaries during the postexilic period, which was dominated by a priestly hierarchy (1 Chron. 24–26). Other stories involving Levites appear in Judges 19–21 and Luke 10:32.

Literary Criticism A form of literary analysis that attempts to isolate and define literary types, the sources behind them, the stages of composition from oral to written form with their characteristic rhetorical features, and the stages and degree of redaction (editing) of a text.

Logos A Greek term meaning both "word" and "reason," used by Greek philosophers to denote the rational principle that creates and informs the universe. Amplified by Philo Judaeus of Alexandria, Egypt, to represent the mediator between God and his material creation, as Wisdom had been in Proverbs 8:22–31, the term found its most famous expression in the prologue to the Fourth Gospel to denote the prehuman Jesus—"the Word became flesh and dwelt among us" (John 1:14).

Lord's Supper, The The ritual meal that Jesus held with his closest disciples the night before his death. Here he introduced the new covenant and shared the bread and wine that symbolized his body and blood about to be sacrificed on behalf of humankind (Mark 14:22–25; Matt. 26:26–29; Luke 22:14–20). Paul first calls the Christian "love feast" (*agapé*) or Communion by this name in 1 Corinthians 11:20, where he describes the ceremony of the Eucharist (1 Cor. 11:23–26). John's version of the event (John 13:1–35) differs strikingly from that in the Synoptics.

Lot Nephew of Abraham, with whom he migrated from Ur to Haran and finally to Canaan (Gen. 11:31; 12:5), Lot separated from his uncle, who rescued him from kidnappers (Gen. 13:1–14:16). Lot later entertained angels come to destroy Sodom (Gen. 19:1–29), who directed his escape from the doomed city. He reputedly fathered the nations of Moab and Ammon by incest with his two daughters (Gen. 19:30–38). Jesus referred to Lot's experience in Sodom (Luke 17:28–30), as did the author of 2 Peter 2:6–8.

Lucifer A term meaning "light bearer" and referring to the planet Venus when it is the morning star, the English name Lucifer translates the Hebrew word for "shining one" (Isaiah 14:12). An epithet applied to the king of Babylon, it was later mistakenly taken as a name for Satan before his expulsion from heaven.

Luke A physician and traveling companion of Paul (Col. 4:14; Philem. 24; 2 Tim. 4:11) to whom a late second-century tradition ascribes the Gospel of Luke and Book of Acts.

LXX A common abbreviation for the Septuagint, the Greek translation of the Hebrew Bible made in Alexandria, Egypt, during the last three centuries B.C.E.

Lycaonia A district in Asia Minor added to the Roman Empire around 25 B.C.E., where Paul endured persecution (Acts 13:50; 14:6–19).

Lycia A small province in southwestern Asia Minor, bordering the Mediterranean, which Paul visited on his missionary travels (Acts 21:1; 27:5–7).

Lydia A once powerful kingdom of western Asia Minor with its capital at Sardis, Lydia (Lud) is mentioned in Jeremiah 46:9 and Ezekiel 30:5.

Lystra A city in the Roman province of Galatia where Paul and Barnabas performed such successful healings that they were identified as Zeus and Hermes (Jupiter and Mercury) (Acts 14:6–19; 16:1; 18:23).

Maccabees A name bestowed upon the family that won religious and political independence for the Jews from their Greek-Syrian oppressors. Judas, called Maccabeus ("the hammerer"), son of the aged priest Mattathias, led his brothers and other faithful Jews against the armies of Antiochus IV (Epiphanes) (175–163 B.C.E.). The dynasty his brothers established was called Hasmonean (after an ancestor named Hashmon) and ruled Judea until 63 B.C.E., when the Romans occupied Palestine.

Macedonia The large mountainous district in northern Greece ruled by Philip of Macedon (359–336 B.C.E.), whose son Alexander the Great (356–323 B.C.E.) extended the Macedonian Empire over the entire ancient Near East as far as western India, incorporating all of the earlier Persian Empire. Conquered by Rome (168 B.C.E.) and annexed as a province (146 B.C.E.), Macedonia was the first part of Europe to be Christianized (Acts 16:10–17:9; 18:5; 19:29; 20:1–3).

Magdala A town on the northwest shore of the Sea of Galilee and home of Mary Magdalene ("of Magdala") (Matt. 15:39).

Magnificat Mary's beautiful hymn of praise, recorded in Luke 1:46–55.

Malachi The title of the last book of the Minor Prophets, the word means "my messenger" (Mal. 3:1) and may have been affixed by an editor (Mal. 1:1) who mistook it for a proper name.

Mamre A plain near what later became the city of Hebron in southern Palestine, where Abraham temporarily settled under its ancient oaks (Gen. 13:18) and where angels on the way to Sodom visited him (Gen. 18). From a Hittite, Abraham bought a cave near Mamre in which his wife Sarah (Gen. 23:17, 19) and then he himself (Gen. 50:13) were buried.

Manesseh

(1) The elder son of Joseph and the Egyptian Asenath, daughter of a high priest at On, who received a lesser blessing from the dying Jacob than his full brother Ephraim (Gen. 48:1–20), reflecting the tribe of Ephraim's greater importance in the later history of Israel.

(2) One of Israel's twelve tribes, divided into two sections and occupying land east and west of the Jordan River (Josh. 17:1–18).

(3) A son of Hezekiah and Hephzibah who was king of Judah longer than any other Davidic monarch (about 687–642 B.C.E.). In spite of the Deuteronomist's condemnation of him as the most evil ruler of Judah for his encouragement of Baalism, astrology, and human sacrifice, he proved an effective king, maintaining his country's relative independence during troubled times (2 Kings 21:1–18; 2 Chron. 33:1–20). The historicity of his supposed deportation to and return from Babylon has been questioned. In 2 Kings 23:26–27 Judah's final destruction is attributed to Manasseh's wickedness.

Manna The food miraculously supplied the Israelites during their wanderings in the Sinai wilderness (Exod. 16:1–36). Described in Numbers 11:7–9 and commonly referred to as "bread" from heaven (Deut. 8:3; Nah. 9:20; Ps. 78:24; John 6:31–35; Heb. 9:4; Rev. 2:17), its appearances ceased when Israel entered Canaan (Josh. 5:12).

Manoah A pious member of the tribe of Dan and father of Samson, Israel's Herculean judge (Judg. 13:2–25; 14:2–10; 16:31).

Mark (John Mark) Son of Mary, a Jerusalem Jew who accompanied Barnabas (his cousin) and Paul on an early missionary journey (Acts 12:12–25; 13:5, 13; 15:37). For reasons unstated, he left them at Perga (Acts 13:13), which so angered Paul that he refused to allow Mark to join a later preaching campaign (Acts 15:38), though he and the Apostle were later reconciled (Col. 4:10; Philem. 24). Some identify Mark with the youth who ran away naked at the time of Jesus' arrest (Mark 14:51–52). An early tradition ascribes authorship of the Gospel of Mark to him, as Papias and Eusebius (*Ecclesiastical Histories* 3.39.15) testify.

Martha The sister of Mary and Lazarus of Bethany (Luke 10:38–42; John 11:1–12:2), whose home Jesus frequently visited.

Martyr A "witness" for Christ who prefers to die rather than relinquish his faith. Stephen, at whose stoning Saul of Tarsus assisted, is known as the first Christian martyr (Acts 22:20; Rev. 2:13; 17:6).

Mary From the Latin and Greek *Maria*, from the Hebrew *Miryam* (Miriam), a name borne by six women in the New Testament.

(1) Mary the virgin, wife of Joseph and mother of Jesus, who, the angel Gabriel informed her, was conceived by Holy Spirit (Matt. 1:18–25; Luke 1:26–56; 2:21). From her home in Nazareth, Mary traveled to Bethlehem, where her first son was born (Luke 2:1–18), and thence into Egypt to escape Herod's persecution (Matt. 2:1–18), returning to Nazareth in Galilee after Herod's death (4 B.C.E.) (Matt. 2:19–23). She had one sister (John 18:25), probably Salome, wife of Zebedee, mother of James and John (Matt. 27:56), and was also related to Elisabeth, mother of John the Baptist (Luke 1:36). Gabriel's annunciation of the Messiah's birth occurs in Luke 1:26–36; the Magnificat, in Luke 1:46–55.

Mary visited Jerusalem annually for the Passover (Luke 2:41) and reprimanded the twelve-year-old Jesus for lingering behind at the temple (Luke 2: 46–50). She may have been among family members convinced that Jesus' early preaching showed mental instability (Mark 3:21) and apparently humored his requests during the wedding celebration at Cana (John 2:1–12). Although Jesus showed his mother little deference during his ministry (Mark 3:31–35; Luke 11:27–28; John 2:4), on the cross he entrusted her care to his "beloved disciple" (John 19:25–27). Mary last appears in the upper room praying with the disciples just before Pentecost (Acts 1:13–14).

(2) Mary Magdalene, a woman from Magdala, from whom Jesus cast out seven demons (Luke 8:1–2) and who became

his follower. A common tradition asserts that she had been a prostitute whom Jesus had rescued from her former life (Mark 16:9; Luke 7:37–50), but this is by no means certain. She was present at the crucifixion (Mark 15:40; Matt. 15:47), visited Jesus' tomb early Sunday morning (Matt 28:1; Mark 16:1; Luke 24:10; John 20:1), and was one of the first to see the risen Jesus (Matt. 28:9; Mark 16:9; John 20:11–18), although the male disciples refused to believe her (Luke 24:9–11).

(3) Mary, sister of Lazarus and Martha, whose home at Bethany Jesus frequented (Luke 10:38–42; John 11:1–12:8).

(4) Mary, wife of Cleophas, mother of James the Less and Joseph (Joses), was a witness of Jesus' crucifixion, burial, and resurrection (Matt. 27:56–61; 28:1; Mark 15:40, 47; 16:1; Luke 24:10; John 19:25).

(5) Mary, sister of Barnabas and mother of John Mark, provided her Jerusalem home as a meeting place for the disciples (Acts 12:12; Col. 4:10).

(6) An otherwise anonymous Mary mentioned in Romans 16:6.

Masada A stronghold built by Herod the Great on a fortified plateau 800 feet above the Dead Sea, Masada was captured by Zealots during the revolt against Rome (66 C.E.). When the attacking Romans finally entered Masada (73 C.E.), they found only 7 women and children alive, 953 others having died in a suicide pact.

Masoretes From a Hebrew term meaning "tradition," the name given to medieval Jewish scholars who copied, annotated, and added vowels to the text of the Hebrew Bible.

Masoretic Text (MT) The standard text of the Hebrew Bible as given final form by the Masoretes in the seventh through the ninth centuries C.E.

Mattathias A Jewish priest who, with his sons John, Simon, Judas, Eleazar, and Jonathan, led a revolt against the oppressions of Antiochus IV (about 168–167 B.C.E.) (1 Macc. 2:1–70).

Matthew A Jewish tax collector working for Rome whom Jesus called to be one of the twelve apostles (Matt. 9:9; 10:3; Mark 2:13–17; 3:18; Luke 5:27–32; 6:15; Acts 1:13), Matthew (also called Levi) is the traditional author of the Gospel of Matthew, an attribution contested by most scholars.

Matthias The early Christian elected to replace Judas among the Twelve (Acts 1:23–26). The name means "gift of Yahweh."

Medes An ancient Ayrian (Iranian) Indo-European people occupying mountainous country south of the Caspian Sea who established a kingdom that by 600 B.C.E. extended from near the Persian Gulf to the Black Sea. In 612 B.C.E. they joined the Neo-Babylonians and Scythians to destroy Nineveh and terminate the Assyrian Empire. They were subdued by Cyrus the Great (549 B.C.E.), whose dominion was commonly known as the Medo-Persian Empire (Nah. 2:3–3:19; Esther 1:19; Dan. 5:28). The "law of the Medes and Persians" was traditionally immutable (Esther 1:19; Dan. 6:8, 15) and once given could not be rescinded, a factor that plays an important part in the Book of Esther (Esther 8:7–12).

Megiddo An old Palestinian city overlooking the Valley of Jezreel (Plain of Esdraelon), the site of numerous decisive battles in biblical history (Josh. 12:21; 2 Kings 9:27; 23:29–30; 2 Chron. 35:20–24; Zech. 12:11) and symbolic location of the climactic War of Armageddon (Rev. 16:16).

Megillot A Hebrew word meaning "scrolls"; the five Old Testament books—Song of Songs, Ruth, Lamentations, Ecclesiastes, and Esther—each of which was read publicly at one of Israel's annual religious festivals.

Melchizedek The king-priest of Canaanite Salem (probably the site of Jerusalem) to whom Abraham paid a tenth of his spoils of war (Gen. 14:17–20); cited by the author of Hebrews as foreshadowing Jesus Christ (Ps. 110:4; Heb. 5:6–10; 7:1–25).

Mercury Roman name for Hermes, Greek god of persuasion, business, trade, and messenger of Zeus, for whom Paul was mistaken in Lystra (Acts 14:12).

Merodach A Hebrew form of the Akkadian Marduk (also called Bel), the chief Babylonian god, ridiculed by Second Isaiah (Isa. 46:1–4) and Jeremiah (Jer. 51:44–45).

Mesopotamia The territory between the Euphrates and Tigris rivers at the head of the Persian Gulf (modern Iraq); cradle of the Sumerian, Akkadian, Assyrian, and Neo-Babylonian civilizations (Gen. 24:10; Judg. 3:8–10; 1 Chron. 19:6; Acts 2:9; 7:2).

Messiah A Hebrew term meaning "anointed one," designating a king or priest of ancient Israel who had been consecrated by having his head smeared with holy oil, marking him as set apart for a special role. King David is the model of Yahweh's anointed ruler; all his descendants who ruled over Judah were Yahweh's messiahs (2 Sam. 7:1–29; Ps. 89:3–45). After the end of the Davidic monarchy (587 B.C.E.), various Hebrew prophets applied the promises made to the Davidic dynasty to a future heir who would eventually restore the kingdom of David (Pss. 2; 110; Dan. 9:25–26). Christians believe that Jesus of Nazareth was the promised Messiah (Christ) as expressed in Peter's "confession" (Matt. 16:13–20; Mark 8:27–30; Luke 9:18–22, etc.).

Methuselah According to Genesis 5:21–27, an antediluvian patriarch descended from Seth and Enoch who attained an age of 969 years. He appears as Methushael in Genesis 4:18 and in Luke's genealogical list (Luke 3:37).

Micah A Judean prophet of the late eighth century B.C.E. and younger contemporary of Isaiah of Jerusalem (Isa. 2:2–4; Mic. 4:1–3). A rural figure who denounced the evils of urban life (Mic. 1:5) and predicted Jerusalem's fall (Mic. 3:12; cited in Jer. 26:18–19), his oracles form most of the present Book of Micah in the Minor Prophets. His name means "Who is like Yahweh?"

Micaiah An eighth-century prophet who predicted Ahab's defeat and death at the Battle of Ramoth-gilead (1 Kings 22:8–28; 2 Chron. 18:6–27).

Michael The angel whom the Book of Daniel represents as being the spirit prince, guardian, and protector of Israel (Dan. 10:13, 21; 12:1). Jude 9 depicts him as an archangel fighting with Satan for Moses' body. In Revelation 12:7 he leads the war against the Dragon (Satan) and casts him from heaven. His name means "Who is like God?"

Michal A daughter of Saul (1 Sam. 14:49) who was offered to David as his wife for his exploits against the Philistines (1 Sam. 18:20–27). Michal helped David escape Saul's wrath (1 Sam. 19:11–17), only to be rejected when she criticized his dancing naked before the Ark (2 Sam. 6:14–23).

Midianites An ancient nomadic people inhabiting an area in the northwest Arabian Desert, east of the Gulf of Aqabah, opposite the Sinai Peninsula, and south of Moab. According to Genesis 25:1–4, they were descended from Abraham and his wife Keturah. Judges 8:24 identifies them in Gideon's time as Ishmaelites, the name given in Genesis 37:25 to the merchants to whom Joseph was sold. Moses took refuge with the Kenites, a Midianite group (Exod. 2:15–3:1; 18:1–15) into which he married. The judge Gideon defeated some Midianites who encroached upon Israel's territory (Judg. 1:16; 4:1; 6–8).

Midrash From a Hebrew word meaning "to search out," Midrash refers to a commentary on or interpretation of Scripture. Collections of such haggadic or halakic expositions of the significance of the biblical text are called Midrashim.

Millennium A thousand-year epoch, particularly the period of Christ's universal reign (Rev. 20:1–8) during which Satan will be chained and the dead resurrected.

Minor Prophets Twelve prophetic books short enough to be recorded together on a single scroll: Hosea, Joel, Amos, Obadiah, Jonah, Micah, Nahum, Habakkuk, Zephaniah, Haggai, Zechariah, and Malachi.

Miriam The daughter of Amram and Jochebed, older sister of Aaron and Moses, who brought her mother to nurse the infant Moses after he was found and adopted by pharaoh's daughter (Exod. 2:4–8; Num. 26:59; 1 Chron. 6:3). Miriam led the victory celebration after the crossing of the Sea of Reeds (Exod. 15:20–21). Although later stricken with leprosy for criticizing Moses, she was cured and readmitted to Yahweh's favor after her brother interceded for her (Num. 12:2–15).

Mishnah From the Hebrew verb "to repeat," a collection of Pharisaic oral interpretations (Halakah) of the Torah compiled and edited by Rabbi Judah ha-Nasi about 200 C.E.

Mizpah The name of several Old Testament sites, the most important of which was located in the territory of Benjamin (Josh. 18:26) near the border of Judah and Israel, perhaps a cult site (Judg. 20:1–11) on Samuel's prophetic circuit (1 Sam. 7:5–16; 10:17–24) and the temporary center of Jews remaining in Palestine after Nebuchadnezzar's deportations (2 Kings 25:23; Jer. 40–41).

Mizraim According to Genesis 10:6, a son of Noah's son Ham and the progenitor of the Hamatic nations of Lower Egypt, North Africa, and Canaan. It is also the Hebrew name of Egypt.

Moab An ancient neighbor-state of Israel located in the Jordan highlands east of the Dead Sea and north of Edom. Supposedly descended from Lot's incestuous union with his daughter (Gen. 19:30–38), the Moabites were Israel's traditional enemies (Num. 22:3; 24:17; Judg. 3:12–20; 11:15; 2 Kings 1:1; 3:4–27) and frequently denounced by the prophets (Isa. 15:16; 25:10; Jer. 9:26; 25:26; 48; Ezek. 28:8–11; Amos 2:12; Zech. 2:8–11; Ps. 60:8). Yet both David and Jesus were descended from Ruth, a Moabite (Ruth 4:13–22; Luke 3:31–32). In extreme emergencies, the national god Chemosh was sometimes worshiped with human sacrifice (2 Kings 3:27; 13:20).

Molech (Moloch) The national god of Ammon whose worship characteristically involved human sacrifice, an act specifically forbidden the Hebrews (Lev. 18:21; 20:2; Amos 5:26) but allegedly introduced by King Manasseh (2 Kings 21:6; 2 Chron. 33), rooted out by Josiah (2 Kings 23:10), and denounced by the prophets Jeremiah (Jer. 7:29–34; 19:1–13) and Ezekiel (Ezek 16:20–21; 20:26, 31).

Money   In early biblical times, before coins were first minted, value in business transactions was determined by weighing quantities of precious metals. In the early period, the term *shekel* does not refer to a coin but a certain weight of silver. The use of coinage was first introduced into Palestine during the Persian era when the daric or dram, named for Darius I (521–486 B.C.E.), appeared. After Alexander's conquest of Persia, Greek coinage became the standard. The silver drachma (Luke 15:8), a coin of small value, was equivalent to the Roman denarius. The lepton was a small copper coin (Luke 12:59; 21:2), the least valuable in circulation, and one of the denominations coined by the Jews for use in the temple. This was the "widow's mite" (Mark 12:42). The talent (Matt. 18:24) was not a coin but money of account; it was divided into smaller units—60 minas or 6,000 drachmas—and was worth at least $2,000. The denarius (Matt. 18:28), the basic unit in the New Testament, was a silver coin, the day's wage of a rural laborer (Matt. 20:2).

Monotheism   Belief in the existence of one god, a major theme of Second Isaiah (Isa. 40–46).

Mordecai   His name derived from Marduk or Merodach (the chief Babylonian deity), Mordecai was the cousin and foster father of Esther, who according to the book bearing her name, was the Jew married to Ahasuerus, emperor of Persia. Representing the typically devout but politically ambitious Jew living in the diaspora, Mordecai saved his sovereign's life (Esther 2:21–23) and outwitted Haman, who attempted to exterminate him and all Jews throughout the Persian domain (Esther 3:6–15), a plot he employed his beautiful cousin to foil so that, by his as-

tuteness, he became second in power to the emperor (Esther 8–10).

Moses   The great Hebrew lawgiver, religious reformer, founder of the Israelite nation, and central figure of the Pentateuch was the son of Amram (a Levite) and Jochebed and brother to Aaron and Miriam (Exod. 2:1–4). Adopted by pharaoh's daughter and raised at the Egyptian royal court (Exod. 2:5–10; Acts 7:22), he fled Egypt after killing an Egyptian bully and settled in Midian among the Kenites, where he married Jethro's daughter Zipporah (Exod. 2:11–22).

After an encounter with Yahweh at the burning bush (Exod. 3:1–4:17), he returned to Egypt (Exod. 4:18–31), interceded with pharaoh during the ten plagues (Exod. 5–11), led the Israelites across the Reed Sea (Exod. 14–15) to Sinai where he mediated the law covenant between Yahweh and Israel (Exod. 19–31), pled for his people (Exod. 33–34; Num. 14), directed their migration through the Sinai wilderness (Num. 11–14; 20–25), appointed Joshua as his successor (Num. 27:18–23), and died in Moab (Deut. 34:1–7; Acts 7:20–44). He is also credited with building the tabernacle (Exod. 35–40), organizing Israel (Exod. 18:13–26), restating Israel's law code shortly before his death (Deut. 1–31), and composing several hymns (Deut. 32–33; Ps. 90).

Although Moses' name became synonymous with the covenant concept and Israel's traditions (Pss. 77:20; 103:7; 105:26; 106:23; Isa. 63:12; Mic. 6:4; Matt. 17:3; Luke 16:29; John 1:17; 3:14; 5:46; 7:19; 9:29; Acts 3:22; 21:21), modern scholars have concluded that much of the material in the Pentateuch dates from post-Mosaic times (*see* Documentary Hypothesis). Moses also figured prominently in Paul's theology (Rom. 5:14; 10:5; 1 Cor. 10:2; 2 Cor. 3:7; 3:15) and that of the author of Hebrews (Heb. 3:2; 7:14; 9:19; 11:23). Jude preserves an old tradition, probably derived from the pseudepigraphal Assumption of Moses, that the Devil disputed the angel Michael for Moses' body (Jude 9; Rev. 15:3).

Mystery   Derived from a Greek word meaning "to initiate" or "to shut the eyes or mouth," probably referring to the secrets of Hellenistic "mystery religions," the term is used variously in the New Testament. Jesus speaks at least once of the "mystery" of the Kingdom (Matt. 13:11; Mark 4:11; Luke 8:10), but Paul employs the term frequently as if the profounder aspects of Christianity were a religious secret into which the Spirit-directed believer becomes initiated (Rom. 11:5; 16:25; 1 Cor. 2:7; 4:1; 13:2; 14:2; 15:51; Col. 1:26; 2:2; 4:3; 2 Thess. 2:7; 1 Tim. 3:9; 3:16. See also Rev. 1:20; 10:7; 17:5–7).

Myth From the Greek *mythos*, a "story," the term denotes a narrative expressing a profound psychological or religious truth that cannot be verified by historical inquiry or other scientific means. When scholars speak of the "myth of Eden," for example, it is not to denigrate the tale's historicity but to emphasize the Eden story's archetypal expression of humankind's sense of alienation from the spirit world. Myths typically feature stories about gods and goddesses who represent natural or psychological forces that deeply influence humans but that they cannot control. The psychologist Carl Jung interpreted myth as humankind's inherited concept of a primeval event that persists in the unconscious mind and finds expression through repeated reenactments in ritual worship and other cultic practices. Israel's covenant-renewal ceremonies and retellings of Yahweh's saving acts during the exodus are examples of such cultic myths.

Mythology A system or cycle of myths, such as those featuring the deities of ancient Greece or Rome. Once the embodiment of living religious beliefs, Greco-Roman and other mythologies are now seen as archetypal symbols that give philosophic meaning to universal human experiences. Mythologies are thus "falsehoods" only in the narrowest literal sense. They are probably akin to dreams in revealing persistent images and attitudes hidden in the human subconscious.

Naaman The Syrian commander-in-chief of Ben-hadad, king of Damascus and an enemy of Israel, whom the prophet Elisha bathes in the Jordan River to cure his leprosy (2 Kings 5:1–27).

Nabal An epithet meaning "fool," the name applied to the rich shepherd, husband of Abigail, who refused to feed David's band of outlaw guerrillas (1 Sam. 25:2–42).

Nabi The Hebrew word for "prophet," a spokesperson for Yahweh who delivered his god's judgments on contemporary society and expressed his intentions toward the world (Deut. 13:1–5; 18:9–22; Amos 3:7, etc.).

Nabonidus Son of Nabu-balatsuikbi, father of Belshazzar, and last ruler of the Neo-Babylonian Empire (556–539 B.C.E.).

Nabopolassar The name means "son of a nobody." Nabopolassar founded the Neo-Babylonian Empire by revolting against Assyria, a move that enabled King Josiah of Israel to carry out his religious reforms without Assyrian interference and to regain much of the old territory of the northern kingdom. Allied with the Medes, Nabopolassar destroyed Nineveh (612 B.C.E.) and was succeeded by his son Nebuchadnezzar II (Nah. 3:1–3; Zeph. 2:12–14; Jer. 46). *See also* Josiah.

Naboth A landowner in the city of Jezreel whose vineyard King Ahab coveted, Naboth was illegally executed through Queen Jezebel's machinations (1 Kings 21:1–16). This crime, denounced by the prophet Elijah, became the focal point of resistance to Ahab's royal dynasty and culminated in its extermination by Jehu (1 Kings 21:17–29; 2 Kings 9:1–10:11).

Nahor According to Genesis 11:27–30, the son of Terah, brother of Abraham and Haran. By Milcah (and a concubine) Nahor fathered twelve sons, eponymous ancestors of the North-Semitic Aramean tribes (Gen. 21:33; 24:24; 29:5–6).

Nahum A prophet from Elkosh (Nah. 1:1) who delivered poems rejoicing in Nineveh's fall and the destruction of the Assyrian Empire (612 B.C.E.).

Naomi Wife of Elimelech of Bethlehem (Ruth 1:2) and mother-in-law to Ruth, whose marriage she arranged to her Jewish kinsman Boaz (Ruth 3–4). Her name means "my pleasantness."

Naphtali (1) According to Genesis 30:7–8, Naphtali was the son of Jacob and Rachel's handmaid Bilhah and compared to a wild hind in his father's blessing (Gen. 49:21); the eponymous ancestor of one of the northern tribes of Israel (1 Chron. 7:13; Exod. 1:4; Num. 1:15, 42; 26:50). (2) The tribe of Naphtali was assigned territory north of Megiddo along the upper Jordan and western shores of the Sea of Galilee (Josh. 19:32–39; Judg. 1:33). It supported King David (1 Chron. 12:34–40) but became part of the northern kingdom after 922 B.C.E. (1 Kings 15:20) and was dispersed by the Assyrians in 722–721 B.C.E. (2 Kings 15:29).

Nathan (1) A son of David (2 Sam. 5:14; Zech. 12:12; Luke 3:31). (2) A prophet and political counselor at David's court who enunciated the concept of an everlasting Davidic dynasty (2 Sam. 7), denounced the king for his adultery with Bathsheba (2 Sam. 12:1–23), revealed Adonijah's plan to seize power (1 Kings 1:5–8), helped Solomon succeed to David's throne (1 Kings 1:8–45), and is credited with writing a history of David and Solomon's reigns (1 Chron. 29:29; 2 Chron. 9:29).

Nazarenes A name applied to early Christians (Acts 24:5).

Nazareth A town in Lower Galilee above the Plain of Esdraelon (Megiddo) where Jesus spent his youth and began his ministry (Matt. 2:23; Luke 1:26; 4:16; John 1:46).

Nazirites From the Hebrew *nazar* ("to dedicate"), referring to a group in ancient Israel that rigorously observed ascetic principles, including refusing to drink wine, cut their hair, come in contact with the dead, or eat religiously "unclean" food (Num. 6:1–21). Samson, in spite of his ill-fated love affairs, belonged to this sect (Judg. 13–16).

Nebuchadnezzar (1) A Fourth-Dynasty king of the Old Babylonian Empire (twelfth century B.C.E.). (2) Son of Nabopolassar and the most powerful ruler of the Neo-Babylonian Empire (605–562 B.C.E.), Nebuchadnezzar II defeated Pharaoh Necho at the Battle of Carchemish (605 B.C.E.) (2 Kings 24:1–7; Jer. 46:2) and brought much of the Near East under his control. He attacked Judah and deported many of its upper classes in 598–597 B.C.E., besieged and destroyed Jerusalem in 587 B.C.E., and took much of its population captive to Babylon (2 Kings 24:10–25; 25:11–21; 2 Chron. 26:6–21; Jer. 39:1–10; 52:1–30). The portrait of him in Daniel is probably not historical (Dan. 2:1–13; 3:1–7; 4:4–37).

Nebuzaradan Commander of the Babylonian guard under Nebuchadnezzar who was sent to oversee the destruction of Jerusalem (587 B.C.E.) and the deportation to Babylon of Judah's population (2 Kings 25:8–20).

Necho Pharaoh Necho II, son of Psammetichus I (Psamtik), second king of the Twenty-sixth Egyptian Dynasty (610–594 B.C.E.), defeated and killed King Josiah of Judah at Megiddo (609 B.C.E.), thus ending Josiah's religious reforms and Judah's political renaissance (2 Kings 23:29–35; 2 Chron. 35:20–24; 36:4). His plans to reassert Egyptian hegemony in the Near East were permanently thwarted when Nebuchadnezzar of Babylon defeated Egyptian forces at Carchemish (605 B.C.E.) (2 Kings 24:7; Jer. 46).

Negeb, The The largely desert territory south of Beersheba in Judah (Deut. 1:42–46; Josh. 10:40; 15:21–32; 19:1–9; Judg. 6:3; 1 Sam. 27:5–10, etc.).

Nehemiah A Jewish court official (cupbearer) living at the Persian capital in Susa who persuaded Emperor Artaxerxes I (465–423 B.C.E.) to commission him to go to Judea and rebuild Jerusalem's walls (Neh. 1:1–2:20). Although he encountered resistance from Judah's jealous neighbors, Nehemiah finished the rebuilding in record time (Neh. 3:33–6:19) and, with the priest Ezra, effected numerous social and religious reforms among the returned exiles (Neh. 8:1–9:3; 11:1–3; 12:27–13:3).

Nergal-sharezer A high Babylonian official present at the capture of Jerusalem who at

King Nebuchadnezzar's orders helped protect the prophet Jeremiah (Jer. 39:1–14). He later became king of Babylon (560–556 B.C.E.) after murdering Amel-Marduk (the Evil-merodach of 2 Kings 25:27).

Nero   Nero Claudius Caesar Augustus Germanicus, emperor of Rome (54–68 C.E.), the Caesar by whom Paul wishes to be tried in Acts 25:11 and under whose persecution Paul was probably beheaded (64–65 C.E.). A first-century superstition held that Nero, slain during a palace revolt, would return at the head of an army. Regarded by some Christians as the Antichrist, Nero's reappearance is apparently suggested in Revelation 13:4–18.

Nethinim   A group of temple servants who performed such menial tasks as carrying wood and water (Ezra 7:7, 24; 8:20; Neh. 3: 26–31; 10:28–31).

New Year Festival   (*Rosh Hashanah*) Also called the Feast of Trumpets (Lev. 23:23–25), this was a time when work ceased and the Israelites assembled together (Num. 29:1–6). Before the exile (587–538 B.C.E.) the Jews observed the festival in the autumn, but afterward they adopted the Babylonian celebration held in the spring, the first day of the month of Nisan (March–April). With a new emphasis on atonement, it became the first of Ten Days of Penitence, a solemn introduction to the Day of Atonement (*Yom Kippur*) (Lev. 16). Ezekiel urged the keeping of both New Years (Ezek. 40–48).

Nicanor   (1) A general of Antiochus IV whom the Maccabees defeated (1 Macc. 3:38; 7:26–32). (2) A deacon in the Jerusalem church (Acts 6:1, 5).

Nicodemus   A leading Pharisee and member of the Sanhedrin (John 3:1; 7:50; 19:39) who discussed spiritual rebirth with Jesus (John 3:1–21), visited him by night and defended him against other Pharisees (John 7:45–52), and with Joseph of Arimathea, helped entomb his body (John 19:38–42).

Nimrod   According to J, the great-grandson of Noah, grandson of Ham, son of Cush, and a legendary hunter and founder of cities in Mesopotamia (Gen. 9:19; 10:8–12). Several ruined sites in Iraq preserve his name.

Nineveh   The last capital of the Assyrian Empire, located on the east bank of the Tigris River, and supposedly founded by Nimrod (Gen. 10:11), Nineveh was one of the greatest cities in the ancient Near East (Jon. 1:2; 3: 2–4; 4:11). Several Judean kings, including Hezekiah, sent tribute there (2 Kings 18:13–16). Its destruction was foretold by the prophets (2 Kings 19:5–37; Zeph. 2:13) and celebrated by Nahum (Nah. 1–3). Assyria's last major ruler, Ashurbanipal (668–627 B.C.E.), was an antiquarian who collected thousands of literary works on clay tablets—including the *Epic of Gilgamesh* and the *Enuma Elish*—for the royal library at Nineveh. After a three-month siege, the city was destroyed in 612 B.C.E. by a coalition of Medes, Babylonians, and Scythians. Jesus ironically refers to the "men of Nineveh" as more spiritually receptive than his contemporaries (Matt. 12:41).

Noah   The son of Lamech (Gen. 5:28–30), father of Ham, Shem, and Japheth (Gen. 4:32), whom Yahweh chose to build a wooden houseboat containing pairs of all living creatures to survive the flood (Gen. 6:13–8:19) and with whom Yahweh made an "everlasting" covenant (Gen. 8:20–9:17). In another story (Gen. 5:29; 9:18–27), Noah is the first vinegrower and a victim of excessive drinking. Infrequently mentioned elsewhere in the Old Testament (Isa. 54:9; Ezek. 14:14), he and the flood are often cited in the New Testament as examples of divine judgment (Matt. 24:37–39; Luke 17:26–28; Heb. 11:7; 1 Pet. 3:20; 2 Pet. 2:5; 3:5–6).

Obadiah   (1) One of Ahab's stewards who hid 100 Yahwist prophets in caves during Jezebel's persecutions and who arranged the meeting between Ahab and Elijah (1 Kings 18:3–16) that resulted in a contest between Yahweh and Baal on Mount Carmel (1 Kings 18:17–46). (2) Traditional author of the Book of Obadiah, about whom nothing is known. His book is fourth and shortest among the Minor Prophets.

Obed Son of Ruth and Boaz and father of Jesse, father of David (Ruth 4:17–22; 1 Chron. 2:12; 11:47).

Obed-edom (1) A citizen of Gath in whose house David placed the Ark of the Covenant before taking it to Jerusalem (2 Sam. 6:10–12; 1 Chron. 13:13–14). (2) The founder of a group of singers at the second temple (1 Chron. 15:21; 16:5).

Olives, Mount of (Olivet) A mile-long limestone ridge with several distinct summits paralleling the eastern section of Jerusalem, from which it is separated by the narrow Kidron Valley. Here David fled during Absalom's rebellion (2 Sam. 15:30–32), and according to Zechariah 14:3–5, here Yahweh will stand at the final eschatological battle, when the mountain will be torn asunder from east to west. From its summit, with its panoramic view of Jerusalem, Jesus delivered his apocalyptic judgment on the city that had rejected him (Matt. 24–25). He often retreated to its shady groves in the evening (John 7:53; 8:1), including the night before his death (Matt. 26:30–56; Mark 14:26; Luke 22:39; see also Matt. 21:1; Mark 11:1; Luke 19:29; Acts 1:12).

Omega The last letter in the Greek alphabet, used with Alpha (the first letter) as a symbol of the eternity of God (Rev. 1:8; 21:6) and Jesus (Rev. 1:17; 22:13), probably echoing Isaiah's description of Yahweh as "the first and the last" (Isa. 44:6; 48:12).

Omri Sixth ruler of the northern kingdom (876–869 B.C.E.) and founder of a dynasty that included his son Ahab (869–850 B.C.E.), his grandson Ahaziah (850–849 B.C.E.), and a younger son Jehoram (849–842 B.C.E.), whose important military, political, and economic successes are minimized by the deuteronomist historians (2 Kings 16:23–28). Omri's leadership raised Israel to a power and prestige considerably above that of Judah. Even a century after his death and the extinction of his dynasty, Assyrian records referred to Israel as "the land of the House of Omri."

Onesimus The runaway slave of Philemon of Colossae whom Paul converted to Christianity and reconciled to his master (Philem. 8–21; Col. 4:7–9).

Ophel The southern end of Jerusalem's eastern or temple hill, the site of David's city (2 Chron. 27:3; 33:14; Neh. 3:26–27; 11:31).

Oracle (1) A divine message or utterance (Rom. 3:2; Heb. 5:12; 1 Pet. 4:11) or the person through whom it is conveyed (Acts 7:38). (2) An authoritative communication, such as that from a wise person (Prov. 31:1; 2 Sam. 16:23). (3) The inner sanctum of the Jerusalem temple (1 Kings 6:5–6; 7:49; 8:6–8; Ps. 28:2). (4) The supposedly inspired words of a priest or priestess at such shrines as Delphi in ancient Greece and Cumae in Italy.

Oral Tradition Material passed from generation to generation by word of mouth before finding written form. Scholars believe that much of Israel's early history, customs, and beliefs about its origins, such as the stories about the patriarchs and Moses in the Pentateuch, were so transmitted before J first committed them to writing about 950 B.C.E..

P *See* Priestly Document.

Palestine A strip of land bordering the eastern Mediterranean Sea, lying south of Syria, north of the Sinai Peninsula, and west of the Arabian Desert. During the patriarchal period, it was known as Canaan (Gen. 12:6–7; 15:18–21). Named for the Philistines, it was first called Palestine by the Greek historian Herodotus about 450 B.C.E.

Pamphylia A small area (after 74 C.E., a Roman province) along the southern coast of Asia Minor where Paul broke with Barnabas and John Mark (Acts 13:13; 14:24–25; 15:38; 27:5).

Parable From the Greek *parabole* ("a placing beside," "a comparison"), a short fictional narrative that compares something familiar to an unexpected spiritual value. Using a commonplace object or event to illustrate a religious principle was Jesus' typical method of teaching in the Synoptic Gospels (Matt. 13:3–53; 22:1; 24:32; Mark 4:2–3; 13:28; Luke 8:4–18; 13:18–21; 21:29). Yet a recurrent tradition held that Jesus used parables to prevent most of his hearers from understanding his message (Mark 4:10–12; Matt. 13:10–15; Luke 8:9–10). Famous Old Testament parables or fables include Nathan's (2 Sam. 12:1–14), Isaiah's (Isa. 5:1–7), Jotham's (Judg. 9:7–21). Jehoash's (2 Kings 14:8–10), and Ezekiel's (Ezek. 17:22–24; 24:1–14), the last two of which are allegories.

Paraclete A Greek term (meaning "an advocate" or "intercessor summoned to aid") that the Gospel of John uses to denote the Holy Spirit, Paraclete is variously translated "Comforter," "Helper," "Advocate," or "Spirit of Truth" (John 7:39; 14:12, 16–18; 15:26; 16:7; see also 1 John 2:1).

Paradise Literally, a "park" or walled garden, Paradise is the name applied to Eden (Gen. 2:8–17) and in post-Old Testament times to the abode of the righteous dead, of which the lower part housed souls awaiting the resurrection and the higher was the permanent home of the just. It is possible that Jesus referred to the lower paradise in his words to the thief on the cross (Luke 23:43). Paul's reference to being "caught up" into paradise may refer to the third of the seven heavens postulated in later Jewish eschatology (as in the books of Enoch) (2 Cor. 12:2–5). John's vision of the tree of life in "the garden of God" (Rev. 2:7; 22:1–3) depicts an earthlike heaven.

Parallelism A structural feature typical of Hebrew poetry, consisting of the repetition of similar or antithetical thoughts in similar phrasing: "The wicked will not stand firm when Judgment comes nor sinners when the virtuous assemble" (Ps. 1:5).

Parousia A Greek term (meaning "being by" or "being near") used to denote the second coming or appearance of Christ, commonly regarded as his return to judge the world, punish the wicked, and redeem the saved. It is a major concept in apocalyptic Christianity (Mark 13; Matt. 24–25; Luke 21; 1 and 2 Thess.; 2 Pet. 2–3; Rev.); but see also John 14:25–29, which emphasizes Jesus' continued spiritual presence rather than an eschatological apparition.

Passion The term commonly used to denote Jesus' suffering and death (Acts 1:3).

Passover, The An annual Jewish observance commemorating Israel's last night of bondage in Egypt when the Angel of Death "passed over" Israelite homes marked with the blood of a sacrificial lamb to destroy the firstborn of every Egyptian household (Exod. 12:1–51). Beginning the seven-day Feast of Unleavened Bread, it is a ritual meal eaten on Nisan 14 (March–April) and includes roast lamb, unleavened bread, and bitter herbs (Exod. 12:15–20; 13:3–10; Lev. 23:5; Num. 9:5; 28:16; Deut. 16:1). The Passover was scrupulously observed by Israel's great leaders, including Joshua (Josh. 5:10), Hezekiah (2 Chron. 30:1), Josiah (2 Kings 23:21–23, 2 Chron. 35:1–18), and the returned exiles (Ezra 6:19), as well as by Jesus and his disciples (Matt. 26:2, 17–29: Mark 14:1–16; Luke 22:1–13; John 13:1; 18:39). According to the Synoptics, Jesus' Last Supper with the Twelve was a Passover celebration (Matt. 26; Mark 14; Luke 22) and the model for Christian Communion (the Eucharist) (1 Cor. 11:17–27).

Pastoral Epistles The name applied to the New Testament books of 1 and 2 Timothy and Titus, presumably written by the Apostle Paul to two of his fellow ministers (pastors) but that modern scholars believe were composed by an anonyous disciple of Pauline thought living near the mid-second century c.e.

Patmos A small Aegean island off the coast of western Asia Minor (Turkey) where John, author of Revelation, was exiled by the Emperor Domitian about 95 c.e. (Rev. 1:9).

Patriarch The male head (father) of an ancient family line, a venerable tribal founder or leader, especially: (1) the early ancestors of humanity listed in Genesis 4–5, known as the "antediluvian patriarchs"; (2) prominent "fathers" living after the flood to the time of Abraham (Gen. 11); (3) the immediate progenitors of the Israelites: Abraham, Isaac, and Jacob (Gen. 12–50; Exod. 3:6; 6:2–8). Acts 7:8–9 includes Jacob's twelve sons among the patriarchs.

Paul The most influential apostle and missionary of the mid-first-century Church and author of nine or ten New Testament letters, Saul of Tarsus was born in the capital of the Asia Minor province of Cilicia (Acts 9:11; 21:39; 22:3) into a family of Pharisees (Acts 23:6) of the tribe of Benjamin (Phil. 3:5) and had both Roman and Taurean citizenship (Acts 22:28). Suddenly converted to Christianity after persecuting early Christians (Acts 7:55–8:3; 9:1–30; 22:1–21; 26:1–23; 1 Cor. 9:1; 15:8; Gal. 1:11–24; Eph. 3:3; Phil. 3:12), he undertook at least three international missionary tours, presenting defenses of the new faith before Jewish and Gentile authorities (Acts 13:1–28:31). His emphasis on the insufficiency of the Mosaic law for salvation (Gal. 3–5; Rom. 4–11) and the superiority of faith to law (Rom. 4–11) and his insistence that Gentiles be admitted to the Church without observing Jewish legal restrictions (Gal. 2; 5; Rom. 7–8) were decisive in determining the future development of the new religion. He was probably martyred in Rome about 64–65 C.E.

Pella A Gentile city in Palestine east of the Jordan River, to which tradition says that Jesus' family and other Jewish Christians fled during the Jewish revolt against Rome (66–70 C.E.). Before this time Jerusalem had been the center of the Palestinian Jewish Christian church. References in Acts and Paul's letters indicate that Palestinian Christian teachings differed significantly from those Paul stressed in the churches of Gentile Christianity. No writings from the Palestinian Christians survive, so the fate of the Pella community is not known.

Pentateuch From a Greek word meaning "five scrolls," the term denotes the first five books of the Hebrew Bible, the Torah.

Pentecost (1) Also known as the Feast of Weeks (Exod. 34:22; Deut. 16:10), the Feast of Harvest (Exod. 23:16), and the Day of the First Fruits (Num. 28:26), Pentecost was a one-day celebration held fifty days after Passover at the juncture of May and June. (2) The occasion of the outpouring of Holy Spirit on early Christians assembled in Jerusalem (Acts 2:1–41), regarded as the spiritual baptism of the Church.

Peniel A site on the Jabbok River in Jordan where Jacob wrestled with El (God) and thereby won a blessing (Gen. 32:22–33).

Peor A mountain in Moab on which King Balak commanded the prophet Balaam to build seven altars (Num. 23:28–30), Peor may also have been the place where Israel sinned by worshiping Baal (Num. 25:1–18; Josh. 22:17).

Peraea (Perea) A name the historian Josephus gave the area that the Old Testament called the land "beyond" or "across" (east of) the Jordan River (Gen. 50:10; Num. 22:1; Matt. 4:14; 19:1; John 10:40). Both John the Baptist and Jesus retreated to this rugged territory (John 1:28; 10:40–42; 11:3).

Pergamum A major Hellenistic city in western Asia Minor (modern Bergama in west Anatolian Turkey), site of a magnificent temple of Zeus, which some commentators believe is referred to as "Satan's Throne" in Revelation 2:13, Pergamum is one of the seven churches the Revelator addresses (Rev. 1:11; 2:12–17).

Pericope A term used in form criticism to describe a literary unit (a saying, anecdote, parable, or brief narrative) that forms a complete entity in itself and is attached to its context by later editorial commentary. Many of Jesus' pronouncements probably circulated independently as pericopes before they were incorporated into the written Gospel records.

Persepolis A capital of the Persian Empire established by Darius I (522–486 B.C.E.) and burned by Alexander the Great (330 B.C.E.) (2 Macc. 9:2).

Persia A large Asian territory southeast of Elam inhabited by Indo-European (Ayrian, hence "Iran") peoples, Persia became a world power under Cyrus the Great, who united Media and Persia (549 B.C.E.), conquered Lydia (546 B.C.E.) and Babylon (539 B.C.E.), including its former dominion, Palestine, then permitted the formerly captive Jews to return to their homeland (2 Chron. 36:20–22; Ezra 1). Under Emperor Darius I (522–486 B.C.E.) the Jerusalem temple was rebuilt (Ezra 3–6). A son of Darius, Xerxes I (486–465 B.C.E.) was probably the Ahasuerus of the Book of Esther (Esther 1:2; 2:1; 3:1; 8:1). Artaxerxes I (465–423 B.C.E.) decreed the return of two other exile groups under Ezra and Nehemiah.

Pesher   A Hebrew word denoting an analysis or interpretation of Scripture, it is applied to the commentaries (*persherim*) found among the Dead Sea Scrolls.

Peshitta   A version of the Old Testament translated for Christian churches in Syria during the fifth century C.E.

Peter   The most prominent of Jesus' twelve chief disciples, Peter was also known as Simon (probably his surname), Simeon (Symeon), and Cephas (the Aramaic equivalent of *petros*, meaning "the rock" or "stone") (John 1:40–42). The son of Jonas or John (Matt. 16:17; John 1:42; 21:15–17), brother of the Apostle Andrew, and a native of Bethsaida, a fishing village on the Sea of Galilee (John 1:44), he was called by Jesus to be "a fisher of men" (Matt. 4:18–20; Mark 1:16–18; Luke 5:1–11). The first to recognize Jesus as the Messiah (Matt. 16:13–20; Mark 8:27–30; Luke 9:18–22), Peter later denied him three times (Matt. 26:69–75; Mark 14:66–72; Luke 22:54–62; John 18:15–18).

Commanded to "feed [the resurrected Jesus'] sheep" (John 21:15–19), Peter became a leader of the Jerusalem church (Acts 1:15–26; 2:14–42; 15:6–12) and miracle worker (Acts 3:1–10) and was instrumental in bringing the first Gentiles into the Church (Acts 10–11), although Paul regarded him as a conservative obstacle to this movement (Gal. 2:11–14). He appeared before the Sanhedrin (Acts 4:1–12) and was miraculously rescued from at least one imprisonment (Acts 5:17–42; 12:1–19). A married man (Matt. 8:14; Mark 1:30; Luke 4:8; 1 Cor. 9:5), Peter was to be the "rock" on which Jesus' Church was built (Matt. 16:16–20). Although some scholars regard him as the source of 1 Peter, virtually all experts deny Petrine authorship to the second epistle bearing his name. He was martyred under Nero about 64–65 C.E.

Pharaoh   The title of Egypt's king, commonly used in place of a ruler's proper name in the Old Testament. Thus the pharaohs who confiscated Abraham's wife (Gen. 12:14–20), rewarded Joseph (Gen. 41:37–57), enslaved the Israelites (Exod. 1:8–22), and opposed Moses (Exod. 5:1–6:1; 6:27–15:19) are all anonymous, although many scholars believe that the pharaoh of the exodus was Rameses II (c. 1290–1224 B.C.E.). Solomon later made Egyptian pharaohs his allies (1 Kings 3:1; 7:8). Pharaoh Shishak (Sheshonk I) sacked the Jerusalem temple during King Rehoboam's time (c. 922–915 B.C.E.) (1 Kings 14:25–28; 2 Chron. 12:2–9). Pharaoh Necho killed King Josiah at Megiddo but was later defeated by Nebuchadnezzar at Carchemish (2 Kings 23:29–34; 24:7; 2 Chron. 35:20–36:4).

Pharisees   A leading religious movement or sect in Judaism during the last two centuries B.C.E. and the two first centuries C.E., the Pharisees were probably descendants of the Hasidim who opposed Antiochus IV's attempts to destroy the Mosaic faith. Their name may derive from the Hebrew *parush* ("separated") because their rigorous observance of the law bred a separatist view toward common life. Although the New Testament typically presents them as Jesus' opponents, their views on resurrection and the afterlife anticipated Christian teachings. The "seven woes" against the Pharisees appear in Matthew 23:13–32. Paul was a Pharisee (Acts 23:6; 26:5; Phil. 3:5).

Philadelphia   A city in Lydia (modern Turkey) about twenty-eight miles from Sardis, one of the seven churches in Revelation 3:7–13.

Philemon   A citizen of Colossae whose runaway slave, Onesimus, Paul converted to Christianity (Philem. 5, 10, 16, 19).

Philip   (1) King of Macedonia (359–336 B.C.E.), father of Alexander the Great (1 Macc. 1:1;

6:2). (2) One of the Twelve, a man of Bethsaida in Galilee (Matt. 10:3; Mark 3:18; Luke 6:14; John 1:43–49; 12:21–22; 14:8–9; Acts 1:12–14). (3) An evangelist of the Jerusalem church who was an administrator (Acts 6:1–6) and preacher (Acts 8:4–8), the convertor of Simon the sorcerer (Acts 8:9–13) and of an Ethiopian eunuch (Acts 8:26–39). Paul visited him at Caesarea (Acts 21:8–15). (4) A son of Herod the Great and Palestinian tetrarch (4 B.C.E.–34 C.E.) (Luke 3:1).

Philippi A city of eastern Macedonia, the first European center to receive the Christian message (Acts 16:10–40), Philippi became the Apostle Paul's favorite church (Acts 20:6; Phil. 4:16; 2 Cor. 11:9) and the one to which his letter to the Philippians is addressed.

Philistines A people from Aegean Sea islands (called Caphtor in Amos 9:7) who settled along the southern coast of Palestine during the twelfth century B.C.E. to become the Israelites' chief rivals during the period of the judges and early monarchy (about 1200–1000 B.C.E.) (Josh. 13:2–4; Judg. 1:18–19; 13:1–16:31; 1 Sam. 4:2–7:14; 13:1–14:46; 17:1–54; 2 Sam. 5:17–25; 8:1–2; 21:15–18; see also Jer. 47:1–7; Zeph. 2:4–7).

Philo Judaeus The most influential philosopher of Hellenistic Judaism, Philo was a Greek-educated Jew living in Alexandria, Egypt (about 20 B.C.E.–50 C.E.), who promoted a method of interpreting the Hebrew Bible allegorically (which may have influenced Paul in such passages as 1 Corinthians 10:4 and Galatians 4:24, as well as the authors of the Fourth Gospel and Hebrews). His doctrine of the Logos (the divine creative Word) shaped the prologue to the Gospel of John.

Phinehas Grandson of Aaron, son of Eleazar, Israel's third high priest (Num. 10:8–10; 25:6–13; Josh. 22:13, 30–32; 24:33).

Phoebe A servant or deaconess of the church at Cenchrae, a port of Corinth, whose good works Paul commends in Romans 16:1–2.

Phoenicia A narrow coastal territory along the northeast Mediterranean, lying between the Lebanon range on the east and the sea on the west. It included the ports of Tyre and Sidon. Notable Old Testament Phoenicians are Ethbaal, king of Tyre (1 Kings 16:21); his daughter Jezebel, wife of Ahab (1 Kings 18:19); Hiram, king of Tyre (2 Sam. 5:11; 1 Kings 5:1–12; 2 Chron. 2:3–16); and Hiram, the architect-decorator of Solomon's temple (1 Kings 7:13–47; 2 Chron. 2:13). Jesus visited the area, where he healed the daughter of a Syro-Phoenician woman (Matt. 15:21; Mark 7:24, 31; Acts 15:3; 21:2–7).

Phylacteries One of two small leather pouches containing copies of four scriptural passages (Exod. 13:1–10, 11–16; Deut. 6:4–9; 11:13–21), worn on the left arm and forehead by Jewish men during weekday prayers (Exod. 13:9, 16; Deut. 6:8; 11:18; Matt. 23:5).

Pilate, Pontius The Roman prefect (also called a procurator) of Judea (26–36 C.E.) who presided at Jesus' trial for sedition against Rome and sentenced him to be crucified (Luke 3:1; 13:1; 23:1–25; Matt. 27:1–26; Mark 15:1–15; John 18:28–19:22; Acts 3:13; 13:28; 1 Tim. 6:13).

Polytheism Belief in more than one god, the most common form of religion in the ancient world.

Potiphar The head of pharaoh's bodyguard who placed Joseph in charge of his household but later threw him in prison when the Hebrew slave was accused of seducing Potiphar's wife (Gen. 37:36; 39:1).

Priestly Document Also called the Priestly Code or P, this is the final written addition to the Pentateuch, consisting largely of genealogical, statistical, and legal material compiled during and after the Babylonian exile (about 550–450 B.C.E.). Major blocks of P occur in Exodus 25–31; 35–40; Leviticus 1–27; and Numbers 1–10. P incorporated the earlier J and E sources and provided an editorial framework for the entire Torah.

Prisca (Priscilla) The wife of Aquila and a leading member of the early Church (Acts 18:18; Rom. 16:3; 2 Tim. 4:19).

Proconsul A Roman governor or administrator of a province or territory, such as Gallio, proconsul of Achaia, before whom Paul appeared (Acts 18:12).

Procurator The Roman title of the governor of a region before it became an administrative province. During the reigns of Augustus and Tiberius, Judea was governed by a prefect, the most famous of whom was Pontius Pilate. The office was upgraded to the level of procurator under Claudius.

Prophet One who preaches or proclaims the word or will of his or her deity (Amos 3:7–8: Deut. 18:9–22). A true prophet in Israel was regarded as divinely inspired. *See* Nabi.

Prophets, The The second major division of the Hebrew Bible, including Joshua through 2 Kings, Isaiah, Jeremiah, Ezekiel, and the twelve Minor Prophets.

Proverb A brief saying that memorably expresses a familiar or useful bit of folk wisdom, usually of a practical or prudential nature.

Providence A quasi-religious concept in which God is viewed as the force sustaining and guiding human destiny. It assumes that events occur as part of a divine plan or purpose working for the ultimate triumph of good.

Psalm A sacred song or poem used in praise or worship of the deity, particularly those in the Book of Psalms.

Pseudepigrapha (1) Literally, books falsely ascribed to eminent biblical figures of the past, such as Enoch, Noah, Moses, and Isaiah. (2) A collection of religious books outside the Hebrew Bible canon or Apocrypha that were composed in Hebrew, Aramaic, and Greek from about 200 B.C.E. to 200 C.E.

Pseudonymity A literary practice, common among Jewish writers of the last two centuries B.C.E. and the first two centuries C.E., of writing or publishing a book in the name of a famous religious figure of the past. Thus an anonymous author of about 168 B.C.E. ascribed his work to Daniel, who supposedly lived during the 500s B.C.E. The Pastorals, 2 Peter, James, and Jude are thought to be pseudonymous books written in the mid-second century C.E. but attributed to eminent disciples connected with the first-century Jerusalem church.

Ptolemy (1) Ptolemy I (323–285 B.C.E.) was a Macedonian general who assumed rulership of Egypt after the death of Alexander the Great. The Ptolemaic dynasty controlled Egypt and its dominions until 31 B.C.E., when the Romans came to power. (2) Ptolemy II (285–246 B.C.E.) supposedly authorized the translation of the Hebrew Bible into Greek (the Septuagint).

Publican In the New Testament, petty tax collectors for Rome, despised by the Jews from whom they typically extorted money (Matt. 9:10–13; 18:17; 21:31). Jesus dined with these "sinners" (Matt. 9:9–13) and called one, Levi (Matthew), to apostleship (Matt. 9:9–13; Luke 5:27–31). He also painted a publican as more virtuous than a Pharisee (Luke 18:9–14).

Purim A Jewish nationalistic festival held on the fourteenth and fifteenth days of Adar (February–March) and based on events in the Book of Esther.

Q An abbreviation for *Quelle*, the German term for "source," a hypothetical document that many scholars believe contained a collection of Jesus' sayings (*loggia*). The theory of its existence was formed to explain material common to both Matthew and Luke but absent from Mark's Gospel. It is assumed that Matthew and Luke drew on a single source (Q), assembled about 50 C.E., for this shared material.

Queen of Heaven A Semitic goddess of love and fertility worshiped in various forms throughout the ancient Near East. Known as Ishtar to the Babylonians, she was denounced by Jeremiah but worshiped by Jewish refugees in Egypt after the fall of Jerusalem (Jer. 7:18; 44:17–19, 25).

Qumran, Khirbet Ruins of a community (perhaps of Essenes) near the northwest corner of the Dead Sea, where the Dead Sea Scrolls were produced.

Rabbi A Jewish title (meaning "master" or "teacher") given to scholars learned in the Torah. Jesus was frequently addressed by this title (Matt. 23:8; 26:25, 49; Mark 8:5; 10:51; 11:21; 14:45; John 1:38, 49; 3:2; 4:31; 6:25; 9:2; 11:8; 20:16), as was John the Baptist (John 3:26), although Jesus supposedly forbade his followers to be so called (Matt. 23:7–8).

Rachel Daughter of Laban, second and favorite wife of Jacob, mother of Joseph and Benjamin (Gen. 29:6–30; 30:1–24; 35:16–19). When Rachel fled her father's house with Jacob, she stole Laban's household gods (Gen. 31:32–35). Jeremiah prophesied that Rachael (Israel) would "weep for her children," which the author of Matthew's Gospel regarded as fulfilled when Herod slaughtered the children of Bethlehem (Jer. 31:15; Matt. 2:18; see also Ruth 4:11).

Rahab (1) A woman of Jericho, possibly a priestess in a Canaanite fertility cult, who hid Israelite spies and was spared her city's destruction (Josh. 2:1–24; 6:25; Ps. 87:4; Heb. 11:31). (2) A mythological sea monster, the dragon of chaos, whom Yahweh subdued before his creation of the universe (Ps. 89:10); also a symbol of Egypt (Ps. 87:4; Isa. 30:7).

Rameses (Raamses) One of the two "store cities" that the enslaved Israelites built for pharaoh (probably Rameses II) (Exod. 1:11; 12:37; Num. 33:3–5).

Rameses II Ruler of Egypt (c. 1290–1224 B.C.E.) who many scholars think was the pharaoh of the exodus.

Ramoth-gilead A town in Gilead, east of Jordan near the Syrian border, that was a city of refuge (Deut. 4:43; Josh. 20:8) and a Levitical center (Josh. 21:38; 1 Chron. 6:80) for the tribe of Gad. Ahab of Israel (869–850 B.C.E.) was killed trying to recapture it from Aram (Syria) (1 Kings 22:1–38; 2 Chron. 18:1–34), and the usurper Jehu was anointed there (2 Kings 9:1–21).

Rebekah (Rebecca) The daughter of Milcah and Bethuel, son of Abraham's brother Nahor (Gen. 24:15, 47), and sister of Laban (Gen. 25:20), whom Abraham's representative found at Haran and brought back to Canaan as a bride for Isaac (Gen. 24). Of Esau and Jacob, the twin sons she bore Isaac, she preferred Jacob and helped him to trick her dying husband into giving him the paternal blessing (Gen. 25:21–28; 27:5–30; see also Rom. 9:10).

Rechab The father of Jehonadab (Jonadab), who assisted Jehu in exterminating Ahab's entire household and associates (2 Kings 10:1–28). The Rechabites were a group of ascetics who abstained from wine, settled dwellings, and other aspects of what they considered urban corruption.

Redaction Criticism A method of analyzing written texts that tries to define the purpose and literary procedures of editors (redactors) who compile and edit older documents, transforming shorter works into longer ones, as did the redactor who collected and ordered the words of the prophets into their present biblical form.

Reed Sea A body of water or swampland bordering the Red Sea that the Israelites miraculously crossed during their flight from Egypt (Exod. 14:5–15:21). The origin of the name is uncertain as there are no reeds in the Red Sea, which is more than 7,200 feet deep.

Rehoboam A son of Solomon and Naamah (an Ammonite princess), the last ruler of the united kingdom (922–915 B.C.E.), whose harsh policies resulted in the ten northern tribes' deserting the Davidic monarchy in Judah and forming the independent northern kingdom of Israel (922 B.C.E.) (1 Kings 11:43; 12:1–24; 14:21–31; 2 Chron. 9:31–12:16) and in Pharaoh Shishak's (Sheshonk I) despoiling the Jerusalem temple (1 Kings 14:25–28).

Resurrection The returning of the dead to life, a late Old Testament belief (Isa. 26:19; Dan. 12:2–3, 13) that first became prevalent in Judaism during the time of the Maccabees (after 168 B.C.E.) and became a part of the

Pharisees' doctrine. Like the prophets Elijah and Elisha (1 Kings 17:17–24; 2 Kings 4:18–37), Jesus performed several temporal resurrections: of the widow of Nain's son (Luke 7:11–17), the daughter of Jarius (Mark 5:21–43), and Lazarus (John 11:1–44). Unlike these personages, however, Jesus ascended to heaven after his own resurrection (Acts 1:7–8). Paul gives the fullest discussion of the resurrection in the New Testament (1 Thess. 4; 1 Cor. 15), although he leaves many questions unanswered (see also Matt. 25:31–46 and Rev. 20:13).

Reuben (1) The son of Jacob and Leah, eldest of his father's twelve sons (Gen. 29:32; Num. 26:5), Reuben slept with his father's concubine (Gen. 35:22), which cost him a paternal blessing (Gen. 49:3–4), but defended Joseph against his brothers (Gen. 37:21–30). (2) The northern Israelite tribe supposedly descended from Reuben (Num. 32:1–38) that along with Gad settled in the highlands east of the Jordan River.

Rhetorical Criticism A method of textual analysis that studies not only the form and structure of a given literary work but the distinctive style of the author.

Roman Empire The international, interracial government centered in Rome, Italy, that conquered and administered the entire Mediterranean region from Gaul (France and southern Germany) in the northwest to Egypt in the southeast and ruled the Jews of Palestine from 63 B.C.E. until Hadrian's destruction of Jerusalem during the second Roman War (132–135 C.E.).

Ruth A widow from Moab who married Boaz of Bethlehem and became an ancestress of King David (Ruth 4:17).

Saba (Sheba) A Semitic kingdom in western Arabia noted for its merchants and luxury trade but best known for the visit of one of its queens to Solomon's court (1 Kings 10:1–13; 2 Chron. 9:1–12; Matt. 12:42; Luke 11:31).

Sabbath The seventh day of the Jewish week, sacred to Yahweh and dedicated to rest and worship. Enjoined upon Israel as a sign of Yahweh's covenant (Exod. 20:8–11; 23:12; 31:12–17; Lev. 23:3; 24:1–9; Deut. 5:12–15) and a memorial of Yahweh's repose after six days of creation, the Sabbath was strictly observed by leaders of the returned exiles (Neh. 13:15–22; Isa. 56:2–6; Ezek. 46:1–7). Jesus was frequently criticized for his liberal attitude toward the Sabbath, which he contended was made for humankind's benefit (Matt. 12:1–12; Mark 2:23–28; Luke 6:1–9; John 5:18).

Sabbatical Year According to the Torah, every seventh year was to be a Sabbath among years, a time when fields were left fallow, native-born slaves freed, and outstanding debts cancelled (Exod. 21:2–6; 23:10–13; Lev. 25:1–19; Deut. 15:1–6).

Sacrifice In ancient religion, something precious—usually an unblemished animal, fruit, or grain—offered to a god and thereby made sacred. The Mosaic law required the regular ritual slaughter of sacrificial animals and birds (Lev. 1:1–7:38; 16:1–17:14; Deut. 15:19–23, etc.).

Sadducees An ultraconservative Jewish sect of the first century B.C.E. and first century C.E. composed largely of wealthy and politically influential landowners. Unlike the Pharisees, the Sadducees recognized only the Torah as binding and rejected the Prophets and Writings, denying both resurrection and a judgment in the afterlife. An aristocracy controlling the priesthood and temple, they cooperated with Roman rule of Palestine, a collusion that made them unpopular with the common people (Matt. 3:7; 16:1; 22:23; Mark 12:18; Luke 20:27; Acts 4:1; 5:17; 23:6).

Saints Holy ones, persons of exceptional virtue and sanctity, believers outstandingly faithful despite persecution (Dan. 7:18–21; 8:13; Matt. 27:52; Acts 9:13; 26:10; Rom. 8:27; 1 Cor. 6:2; 1 Thess. 3:13; 2 Thess. 1:10; Heb. 13:24; Rev. 5:8; 13:7–10; 17:6; 20:9).

Salome (1) Daughter of Herodias and Herod (son of Herod the Great) and niece of Herod Antipas, before whom she danced to secure the head of John the Baptist (Matt. 14:3–11; Mark 6:17–28). Anonymous in the New Testament, her name is given by Josephus (*Antiquities* 18.5.4). (2) A woman present at Jesus' crucifixion (Matt. 27:56; Mark 15:40) and at the empty tomb (Mark 16:1).

Samaria Capital of the northern kingdom (Israel), Samaria was founded by Omri (c. 876–869 B.C.E.) (1 Kings 16:24–25) and included a temple and altar of Baal (1 Kings 16:32). The Assyrians destroyed it in 721 B.C.E. (2 Kings 17), a fate the prophets warned awaited Jerusalem (Isa. 8:4; 10:9–11; Mic. 1:1–7).

Samaritans Inhabitants of the city or territory of Samaria, the central region of Palestine lying west of the Jordan River. According to a probably biased southern account in 2 Kings 17, the Samaritans were regarded by orthodox Jews as descendants of foreigners who had intermarried with survivors of the northern kingdom's fall to Assyria (721 B.C.E.). Separated from the rest of Judaism after about 400 B.C.E., they had a Bible consisting of their own edition of the Pentateuch (Torah) and a temple on Mount Gerizim, which was later destroyed by John Hyrcanus (128 B.C.E.) (Matt. 10:5; Luke 9:52; John 4:20–21). Jesus discussed correct worship with a woman at Jacob's well in Samaria (John 4:5–42) and made a "good Samaritan" the hero of a famous parable (Luke 10:29–37).

Samson Son of Manoah of the tribe of Dan, Samson was a Nazirite judge of Israel famous for his supernatural strength, abortive love affair with Delilah, and spectacular destruction of the Philistine temple of Dagon (Judg. 13–16).

Samuel The son of Hannah and Elkanah, an Ephraimite (1 Sam. 1:1–2), Samuel was Israel's last judge (1 Sam. 7:15; Acts 13:20), a prophet and seer (1 Sam. 9:9) who also performed priestly functions (1 Sam. 2:18, 27, 35; 7:9–12). Trained by the high priest Eli at Shiloh (1 Sam. 2:11–21; 3:1–10), he became the single greatest influence in Israel's transition from the tribal confederacy to monarchy under Saul, whom he anointed king (1 Sam. 8:1–10:27) but later rejected in favor of David (1 Sam. 13:8–15; 15:10–35).

Sanctuary A holy place dedicated to the worship of a god and believed to confer personal security to those who took refuge in it. Solomon's temple on Mount Zion in Jerusalem was such a sacred edifice, although Jeremiah denounced those who trusted in its power to save a disobedient people from punishment (Jer. 7; 26).

Sanhedrin The supreme judicial council of the Jews from about the third century B.C.E. until the Romans destroyed Jerusalem in 70 C.E., its deliberations were led by the high priest (2 Chron. 19:5–11). Jesus was tried before the Sanhedrin and condemned on charges of blasphemy (Matt. 26:59; Mark 14:55; 15:1; Luke 22:66; John 11:47). Stephen was stoned as a result of its verdict (Acts 6:12–15). Peter, John, and other disciples were hailed before its court (Acts 4:5–21; 5:17–41), and Paul was charged there with violating the Mosaic Torah (Acts 22).

Sarah The wife and half-sister of Abraham (Gen. 11:29; 16:1; 20:12), Sarah traveled with him from Ur to Haran and ultimately to Canaan and after a long period of barrenness bore him a single son, Isaac (Gen. 18:9–15; 21:1–21). She died in Hebron (Gen. 23:2) and was buried at Machpelah in Canaan (Gen. 23:19; see also Rom. 4:9; Heb. 11:11; 1 Pet. 3:6).

Sardis Capital of the kingdom of Lydia (modern Turkey), captured by Cyrus the Great (546 B.C.E.); later part of the Roman province of Asia and the site of a cult of Cybele, a pagan fertility goddess (Rev. 3:1–6).

Sargon I The Semitic founder of a Mesopotamian Empire incorporating ancient Sumer and Akkad and stretching from Elam to the Mediterranean (about 2360 B.C.E.).

Sargon II Successor of Shalmaneser V and king of Assyria (722–705 B.C.E.) who completed his predecessor's three-year siege of Samaria and captured the city, bringing the northern kingdom (Israel) to an end in 721 B.C.E. (Isa. 20:1; 2 Kings 17).

Satan In the Old Testament "the satan" appears as a prosecutor in the heavenly court among "the sons of God" (Job 1–2; Zech. 3:1–3) and only later as a tempter (1 Chron. 21:1; cf. 2 Sam. 24:1). Although the Hebrew Bible says virtually nothing about Satan's origin, the pseudepigraphal writings contain much legendary material about his fall from heaven and the establishment of a hierarchy of demons and devils. By the time the New Testament was written, he was believed to head a kingdom of evil and to seek the corruption of all people, including the Messiah (Matt. 4:1–11; Luke 4:1–13). Satan (the "opposer" or "adversary") is also "the evil one" (Matt. 6:13; 13:19; Eph. 6:16; 1 John 2:13; 5:18–19), "the devil" (Matt. 4:1; 13:39; 25:41; John 8:44; Eph. 4:27), and the primordial serpent who tempted Adam (Rev. 12:9).

Saul Son of Kish, a Benjaminite, and the first king of Israel (about 1020–1000 B.C.E.), Saul was anointed by Samuel to meet the Philistine crisis, which demanded a strong centralized leadership (1 Sam. 9:1–10:27). He defeated the Ammonites (1 Sam. 11:1–11) and Philistines at Geba and Michmash but rapidly lost support after antagonizing Samuel (1 Sam. 13:8–15) and refusing to kill the Amalekite king (1 Sam. 15:7–35). He was also upstaged by David, of whom he became intensely jealous (1 Sam. 18:6–24:23). Saul and his son Jonathan were killed by the Philistines at the Battle of Gilboa (1 Sam. 31) and commemorated by one of David's most beautiful psalms (2 Sam 1:17–27).

Savior One who saves from danger or destruction, a term applied to Yahweh in the Old Testament (Ps. 106:21; Isa. 43:1–13; 63:7–9; Hos. 13:4) and to Jesus in the New (Luke 2:11; John 4:42; Acts 5:31; 13:23; Phil. 3:20; 1 Tim. 4:10; 2 Tim. 1:10; 1 John 4:14).

Scapegoat According to Leviticus 16, a sacrificial goat upon whose head Israel's high priest placed the people's collective sins on the Day of Antonement, after which the goat was sent out into the desert to Azazel (possibly a demon). The term has come to signify anyone who bears the blame for others (see Isa. 53).

Scribes Professional copyists who recorded commercial, royal, and religious texts and served as clerks, secretaries and archivists at Israel's royal court and temple (2 Kings 12:10; 19:2; Ezra 4:8; 2 Chron. 34:8; Jer. 36:18). After the Jews' return from exile, professional teachers or "wise men" preserved and interpreted the Mosaic Torah (Ezra 7:6; Neh. 7:73–8:18). In the New Testament, scribes are often linked with Pharisees as Jesus' opponents (Matt. 7:29; 23:2, 13; Luke 11:44) who conspired to kill him (Mark 14:43; 15:1; Luke 22:2; 23:10), although some became his followers (Matt. 8:19; see also Acts 6:12; 23:9; 1 Cor. 1:20).

Scroll A roll of papyrus, leather, or parchment such as those upon which the Hebrew Bible and New Testament were written. The rolls were made of sheets about nine to eleven inches high and five or six inches wide, sewed together to make a strip up to twenty-five or thirty feet long, which was wound around a stick and unrolled when read (Isa. 34:4; Rev. 6:14; Jer. 36).

Scythians A fierce nomadic people from north and east of the Black Sea who swept southward toward Egypt and Judah about 626 B.C.E. Jeremiah prophesied that Judah would be devastated (Jer. 4:5–31; 5:15–17; 6:1–8, 22–26), and Zephaniah saw the invasion as a sign that the Day of Yahweh had arrived (Zeph. 1:7–8, 14–18); but the Scythians were bribed by Pharaoh Psammetichus I (664–610 B.C.E.) and returned north by the coastal route without attacking Palestine.

Seer A clairvoyant or diviner who experiences ecstatic visions (1 Sam. 9:9–11); forerunner of the prophets.

Seir A mountain range running through Edom almost to the Gulf of Aqabah through which the Israelites passed during their desert wanderings (Deut. 2:1; 33:2). Seir was regarded as the home of the Esau tribes, rivals of Israel (Gen. 36:8, 20–21; Josh. 24:4), and was also an early name for Edom (Gen. 32:3; 35:20–21, 30; Num. 14:18).

Seleucids The Macedonian Greek dynasty founded by Alexander's general Seleucis (ruled 312–280 B.C.E.), centered in Syria with Antioch as its capital. After defeating the Ptolemies of Egypt, it controlled Palestine from 198 to 165 B.C.E., after which the Maccabean revolt defeated the forces of Antiochus IV and eventually drove the Syrians from Judea (142 B.C.E.) (1 and 2 Macc.).

Semites According to Genesis 10:21–31, peoples descended from Noah's son Shem, whose progeny included Elam, Asshur, Arpacshad (Hebrews and Arabs), Lud (Lydians), and Aram (Syrians) (Gen. 10:22). In modern usage, the term applies to linguistic rather than to racial groups, such as those who employ one of a common family of inflectional languages, including Akkadian, Aramaic, Hebrew, and Arabic.

Sennacherib Son of Sargon II and king of Assyria (704–681 B.C.E.). In 701 B.C.E. Sennacherib devastated Tyre and besieged Jerusalem, after which he levied heavy tribute upon King Hezekiah of Judah (2 Kings 18). A clay prism recording Sennacherib's version of the Judean campaign tallies well with 2 Kings 18:14–16 but strikingly diverges from the story of 185,000 Assyrian soldiers slain by Yahweh's angel in a single night (2 Kings 19:10–35; Isa. 37:9–36).

Septuagint (LXX) A Greek translation of the Old Testament traditionally attributed to seventy or seventy-two Palestinian scholars during the reign of Ptolemy II (285–246 B.C.E.), the Septuagint was actually the work of several generations of Alexandrine translators, begun about 250 B.C.E. and not complete until the first century C.E. The later additions to the Septuagint were deleted from the standard Hebrew Bible (Masoretic Text) but included in the Christian Scriptures as the Apocrypha.

Seraphim Heavenly beings, usually depicted with six wings (Isa. 6), who attended the throne of God; perhaps derived from Assyrian or Egyptian mythology.

Serpent A common symbol in Near Eastern fertility cults, a snake was the original tempter of humankind (Gen. 3–4) and a symbol of Assyria, Babylon (Isa. 27:1), and the Israelite tribe of Dan (Gen. 49:17). A bronze image of a snake that was used to heal the Israelites during a plague of snakes in the wilderness (Num. 21:4–9) was later destroyed by King Hezekiah (2 Kings 18:4). Revelation 12:9 identifies the serpent with the Devil and Satan (the primordial dragon).

Seth The third son of Adam and Eve (Gen. 4:25–26; 5:2–8), cited as the first man to invoke Yahweh's sacred name.

Shadrach The name the leading eunuch of Babylon gave the Hebrew boy Hananiah (Dan. 1:7; 2:49). Along with Abednego and Meshach, he survived incarceration in a fiery furnace (Dan. 3:1–30).

Shalmaneser The name of five Assyrian kings, two of whom appear in the Old Testament. (1) Shalmaneser III (859–824 B.C.E.), one of Assyria's most effective rulers, defeated a coalition of Syrian and Palestinian states led by Ben-hadad (Hadadezer) of Damascus and King Ahab of Israel, a defense league that disintegrated largely because of Elijah's and Elisha's interference in Israelite and Syrian politics (2 Kings 8:7–15, 9–10). Shalmaneser's Black Obelisk shows either Jehu, who overthrew Ahab's dynasty, or one of his representatives groveling at the Assyrian king's feet and paying him tribute. (2) Shalmaneser V (726–722 B.C.E.), successor to Tiglath-Pileser, extorted tribute from Hoshea, last ruler of the northern kingdom (732–724 B.C.E.). When Hoshea later refused payment, Shalmaneser captured him and laid siege to Israel's capital, Samaria, for three years but died before taking the city (2 Kings 17:3–5; 18:9).

Shaphan Scribal secretary of state for King Josiah (640–609 B.C.E.), to whom Hilkiah the priest entrusted the "lost" Book of the Law (probably Deuteronomy) found during repairs on the Jerusalem temple. After reading it to Josiah, Shaphan was sent to ask the prophetess Huldah what Yahweh wished done with the book. He may have been instrumental in the subsequent religious reforms (2 Kings 22:3–20).

Sharon, Plain of The most fertile part of the coastal plain of Palestine, stretching about fifty miles north to the headland of Mount Carmel, belonged to the northern kingdom after 922 B.C.E. Its desirable fields became an image of the messianic bounty (Isa. 35:2).

Sheba, Queen of *See* Saba.

Shechem (1) The son of Hamor the Hivite from whom Jacob bought land in Canaan and who later raped and wished to marry Jacob's daughter Dinah (Gen. 33:18–20; 34:1–31). In spite of Hamor's friendly wish to ally his clan with Jacob's, Simon and Levi led Jacob's sons in a murderous attack on Shechem's clan to avenge their sister's dishonor. (2) An ancient Canaanite city located about forty-one miles north of Jerusalem in the hill country later allocated to the tribe of Ephraim, Shechem was the first site in Canaan that Abraham visited (Gen. 12:6) and the first place where the Hebrews came in touch with Canaanite culture (Gen. 33:18–20; 34:1–31). Here Joshua held a covenant-renewal ceremony uniting the Israelite tribes under Yahweh and, according to some scholars, including native tribes friendly to the Israelites. Abimelech attempted to make himself king here (Judg. 9), and here Rehoboam came to be crowned (1 Kings 12), only to be divested of his northern territories by Jeroboam I, who made Shechem his capital. Although the Deuteronomists mention its religious importance (Deut. 11:26–32; 17:1–26; Josh. 8:30–37), Shechem fell into obscurity until the mid-fourth century B.C.E. when the Samaritans built a temple on Mount Gerizim. The city was destroyed by John Hyrcanus in the late second century B.C.E. but rebuilt as Flavia Neapolis.

Shem Noah's oldest son, brother of Ham and Japheth, the eponymous ancestor of the Semites, including the Arameans, Hebrews, Akkadians, and Arabs (Gen. 5:32; 9:21–27; 10:1).

Shema Judaism's supreme declaration of monotheistic faith, expressed in the words of Deuteronomy 6:4–9 beginning "Listen (Hebrew *shema*, "hear"), Israel, Yahweh our God is the one Yahweh." It also includes Deuteronomy 11:13–21 and Numbers 14:37–41 (cf. Mark 12:29–34).

Sheol According to the Old Testament, the subterranean region to which the "shades" of all the dead descended, a place of intense gloom, hopelessness, and virtual unconsciousness for its inhabitants. The term was translated *Hades* in the Greek Septuagint and in later Hellenistic times was regarded as an abode of the dead awaiting resurrection (Gen. 42:38; 1 Sam. 2:6; Job 7:9; 14:13–14; 26:6; Pss. 6:5; 16:10; 55:15; 139:8; Prov. 27:20; Eccles. 9:10; Isa. 14:15; 28:15; 38:10, 18; Hos. 13:14; Jon. 2:2; cf. references to Hades in Matt. 16:18; Luke 10:15; Acts 2:31; Rev. 1:18; 20:15). It is not the same theological concept as Hell or Gehenna (Matt. 10:28; 23:33; Mark 9:43; Luke 12:5).

Shephelah The low hills east of Palestine's coastal plain situated between Philistia and the hills of southern Judah (1 Macc. 12:38).

Shewbread The term the King James Version uses for the twelve loaves of consecrated unleavened bread placed in the Holy Place of the tabernacle and temple (Exod. 25:30; Lev. 24:5–9; 1 Sam. 21:2–6).

Shibboleth The password Jephthah used to determine whether fugitives from a battle between the Ephraimites and his own Gileadites were his people or the enemy's. The Ephraimites could not pronounce *sh* but said *s* instead (Judg. 12:4–6). In contemporary usage, the term refers to the slogans or distinctive values of a party or class.

Shiloh A prominent town and religious center that the Israelites established in the highlands of Ephraim, where Joshua assigned the tribes of Israel their territorial allotments (Josh. 18). Apparently a headquarters for the tribal confederacy during the time of the judges (Josh. 21:2; 22:9; Judg. 21:15–24; 1 Sam. 2; 12–17; 3:30), the Ark of the Covenant was kept there until the Philistine war, when it was taken to a camp at Ebenezer, where the Philistines captured it (1 Sam. 4). Returned, it was not again placed in Shiloh (1 Sam. 6:21–7:2), possibly because the Philistines had devastated the site. Jeremiah predicted that Yahweh would deal with Jerusalem as he had with Shiloh (Jer. 7:12–15; 26:6–9).

Shinar, Plain of An alluvial lowland between the Tigris and Euphrates rivers at the head of the Persian Gulf. Settled by Sumerians about 4000 B.C.E., it was later known as Babylonia after the principal city in the area (Gen. 11:2; 14:1, 9). This region is the traditional homeland of Abraham, ancestor of the Israelites (Gen. 11:31; see also Isa. 11:11; Zech. 5:11; Dan. 1:2).

Shishak An Egyptian pharaoh (Sheshonk or Sheshonq I) (935–914 B.C.E.), founder of the Twenty-second Dynasty, who during Solomon's reign gave asylum to the rebellious Jeroboam (1 Kings 11:40) but later invaded Judah and stripped the temple of many of its treasures (1 Kings 14:25–28; 2 Chron. 12:2–9).

Shittim Site of the Israelites' encampment in Moab, opposite Jericho, prior to their crossing the Jordan River into Canaan (Num. 24–36).

Shrine A sacred place or altar at which a god is worshiped, usually with ritual sacrifices. The discovery of Deuteronomy (621 B.C.E.), which prohibited sacrifice at any but a designated central sanctuary (assumed to be the Jerusalem temple), inspired Josiah's sweeping destruction of all rival shrines in Judah and Samaria (2 Kings 22–23; 2 Chron. 34–35).

Shunammite The "Shulamite" bride who is praised in the Song of Solomon 6:13; the origin and meaning of the name are uncertain.

Sidon A wealthy Phoenician port city (Gen. 10:15, 19; 1 Chron. 1:13) that suffered repeated destructions during the Assyrian,

Babylonian, and Persian periods (Jer. 25:22; 27:3; Ezek. 27:8; 28:21–23) but was rebuilt and visited by Jesus and Paul during Roman times (Mark 7:24–31; Acts 27:3). *Siddonians* is a common biblical term for Phoenicians.

Silas The Semitic, perhaps Aramean, name of an early Christian prophet (Acts 15:32), otherwise called Silvanus, who accompanied Barnabas and Paul to Antioch with decrees from the Jerusalem council (Acts 15:1–35) and who joined Paul on his second missionary journey (Acts 16–18; 1 Thess. 1:1; 2 Thess. 1:1). He may have been the author of 1 Peter (1 Pet. 5:12).

Simeon (1) The second son of Jacob and Leah (Gen. 29:33) who helped avenge his sister's rape upon the people of Shechem (Gen. 34). The tribal group named after him, the Simeonites, was probably absorbed by Judah and is seldom mentioned in the Old Testament (Deut. 27:12). (2) Another name for Simon Peter (Acts 15:14; 2 Pet. 1:1). (3) The devout old man who recognized the infant Jesus as the promised Messiah (Luke 2:22–34).

Simile A comparison, usually to illustrate an unexpected resemblance between a familiar object and novel idea. Jesus' parables about the Kingdom of God are typically cast as similes (Matt. 13:31–35, 44–50; Mark 4:26–32; Luke 13:18–19).

Simon The name of several New Testament figures. (1) Simon Peter (Matt. 4:18; 10:2). (2) One of the twelve apostles, Simon the Canaanite (Matt. 10:4; Mark 3:18), a nationalist Zealot (Luke 6:15; Acts 1:13). (3) One of Jesus' "brothers" (Matt. 13:55; Mark 6:3). (4) A leper whom Jesus cured (Mark 14:3–9). (5) The man from North Africa who was forced to carry Jesus' cross (Mark 15:21). (6) A Pharisee who entertained Jesus in his home (Luke 7:36–50). (7) Simon Iscariot, father of Judas the traitor (John 6:71; 13:26). (8) A leather tanner of Joppa with whom Peter stayed (Acts 9:43; 10).

Simon Magus A Samaritan sorcerer ("magus") who tried to buy the power of the Holy

Spirit from Peter (Acts 8:9–24); thought by some to be the forerunner of the Faust figure. The sale of church office is known as *simony*.

Sin, Wilderness of A desert plain on the Sinai Peninsula through which the Israelites passed on their way to Mount Sinai (Exod. 16:1; 17:1; Num. 33:11–12).

Sinai (1) A peninsula at whose southern apex the Gulf of Aqabah joins the Gulf of Suez at the head of the Red Sea. Its 150-mile inverted base borders the Mediterranean, forming the boundary between Egypt and Palestine. (2) According to the J and P accounts, Mount Sinai, the sacred mountain in the wilderness where Moses experienced Yahweh's call (Exod. 3; 6) and to which he led the Israelites from Egypt for Yahweh's revelation of the Torah (Exod. 19–24; 34:4). This site, which has never been positively identified, is called Horeb by E and D (Exod. 3:1; 17:6; Deut. 1:6; 4:10).

Sisera The Canaanite leader whose forces Deborah and Barak defeated and whom Jael, wife of Heber the Kenite, murdered in her tent (Judg. 4–5).

Sitz-im-Leben German term used in form criticism to denote the social and cultural environment out of which a particular biblical unit grew and developed.

Smyrna An Aegean port city of western Asia Minor (Turkey), site of an early Christian church that the author of Revelation praises for its poverty and faithfulness (Rev. 1:11; 2:8–10).

Sodom Along with Gomorrah, Admah, Zebolim, and Zoar (Gen. 13:10–12; 14:2; Deut. 29:23), one of the "five cities of the plain" (near the south shore of the Dead Sea) destroyed by a great cataclysm attributed to Yahweh (Gen. 19:1–29). Abraham, who had been royally welcomed by Sodom's king (Gen. 14:13–24), pleaded for it to be spared (Gen. 18:16–32). Contrary to legend, its sins were regarded as violence and inhospitality to strangers rather than homosexuality. Later Bible writers cite it as a symbol of divine judgment upon wickedness (Isa. 3:9; Lam. 4:6; Matt. 10:15; 2 Pet. 2:6; Jude 7; Rev. 11:8).

Solomon Son of David and Bathsheba and Israel's third king (c. 961–922 B.C.E.) (2 Sam. 12:24–25), who inherited the throne through David's fondness and the intrigues of his mother and the prophet Nathan (1 Kings 1:9–2:25). He became famous for his wisdom (1 Kings 3:5–28); allied himself with Hiram of Tyre (1 Kings 5); built and dedicated Yahweh's temple in Jerusalem (1 Kings 6, 8); built a huge palace for himself (1 Kings 7:1–12); received Yahweh's renewal of the Davidic Covenant (1 Kings 9:1–9); was visited by the Queen of Sheba (1 Kings 10:1–13); worshiped other gods than Yahweh, presumably because of his foreign wives' influence (1 Kings 11:1–40); and died leaving his people financially exhausted and politically discontented (1 Kings 11:41–12:25). An idealized account of his reign is given in 2 Chronicles 1–9.

Solomon's Porch A magnificent covered colonnade built along the east side of Herod's temple in Jerusalem in which Jesus walked (John 10:23); the site of several apostolic miracles (Acts 3:11; 5:12).

Son of Man

(1) An Old Testament phrase used to denote a human being (Pss. 8:4; 80:17; 144:3; 146:3; Isa. 56:2; Jer. 51:43), including a plural usage (Pss. 31:19; 33:13; Prov. 8:4; Eccles. 3:18–19; 8:11; 9:12). The phrase is characteristic of the Book of Ezekiel, where it is commonly used to indicate the prophet himself (Ezek. 2:1).

(2) In Daniel 7:12–14 "one like a son of man" refers to Israel itself or to a divinely appointed future ruler of Israel, although this figure is not given specific messianic significance.

(3) In certain pseudepigraphal writings, particularly the Similitudes of the Book of Enoch, he who serves as Yahweh's agent in the coming Day of Judgment is variously called "the Elect One," "the Anointed One," and "the Son of man."

(4) In the Gospels the phrase is always spoken by Jesus and in most cases applied to himself (Matt. 8:20; 9:6; 11:19; 12:8; 16:27–28; 19:28; 24:30; 28:31; Mark 2:28; 8:38; 9:31; 10:45; 13:26; Luke 12:8–10; 18:8; 21:27; 22:22; John 3:14). Outside the Gospels it is used only once (Acts 7:56), although the author of Revelation echoes Daniel 7:13 (Rev. 14:14).

Sopherim The name applied to Jewish scribes, from the time of Ezra and after, who copied and transmitted the manuscripts of the Hebrew Bible.

Soul In Hebrew, *nephesh* ("breath"), applied to both humans and animals as living beings (Gen. 1:20; 2:7; 2:19; 9:4; Exod. 1:5; 1 Chron. 5:21). It was translated *psyche* in the Greek Septuagint, the same term used (commonly for "life" rather than the immortal personality) in the New Testament (Matt. 10:28; 16:26; Acts 2:27; 3:23; Phil. 1:27; Rev. 20:4).

Source Criticism Analysis of a biblical document to discover the sources, written or oral, that the author(s) incorporated into it. Close study of the Pentateuch has led scholars to conclude that at least four main literary units—J, E, D, and P—were blended in its composition.

Stele (Stela) An upright slab or pillar inscribed with a commemorative message, such as those bearing the law code of Hammurabi (early seventeenth century B.C.E.) or that of King Mesha of Moab (about 835 B.C.E.) who commemorated his victory over Israel following Jehu's revolution.

Stephen A Hellenistic Jew of Jerusalem who was stoned for his Christian heresy (Acts 6:8–60), thus becoming the first martyr of the early Church. The name means "royal" or "crown."

Stoicism A Greek philosophy that became popular among the upper classes in Roman times; Stoicism emphasized duty, endurance, self-control, and service to the gods, the family, and the state. Its adherents believed in the soul's immortality, rewards and punishments after death, and in a divine force (providence) that directs human destiny. Paul encountered Stoics when preaching in Athens (Acts 17:18–34), and Stoic ideas appear in Ecclesiastes, the Wisdom of Solomon, Proverbs, John 4:23 and 5:30, James 1:10, and 1 Peter 2:17.

Succoth An Old Testament term meaning "booths." (1) A town east of the Jordan River in the area allotted to Gad (Josh. 13:27), where Jacob had erected booths (Gen. 33:17). (2) An Egyptian site in the Nile Delta given as the first Israelite camp during the exodus (Exod. 12:37; 13:20).

Sukkoth *See* Booths, Feast of.

Sumer The land at the head of the Persian Gulf between the Tigris and Euphrates rivers, site of the oldest high civilization in the ancient Near East, and traditional homeland of Abraham and his ancestors. Its cities include Erech (Uruk), Ur (Gen. 10:10; 11:10–27; 15:7), and Calah (Nimrud). While Sumer occupied southernmost Mesopotamia, Akkad lay to the north (Gen. 10:11–12); the two regions together were later known as Babylonia.

Symbol From the Greek *symbolon*, a "token" or "sign," and *symballein*, to "throw together" or "compare." In its broadest usage it means anything that stands for something else, as the star of David signifies Judaism and the cross represents Christianity. The use of symbols characterizes prophetic and apocalyptic writing. In Daniel, for example, wild beasts symbolize pagan nations; in Ezekiel, Yahweh's presence is symbolized by his radiant "glory."

Synagogue In Judaism, a gathering of no fewer than ten adult males assembled for worship, scriptural instruction, and administration of local Jewish affairs. Synagogues probably began forming during the Babylonian exile when the Jerusalem temple no longer existed. Organization of such religious centers throughout the diaspora played an important role in the faith's transmission and survival. The synagogue liturgy included lessons from the Torah, the Prophets, the Shema, Psalms, and eighteen prayers.

Syncretism The blending of different religions, a term Bible scholars typically apply to the mingling of Canaanite rites and customs (Baalism) with the Israelites' Mosaic faith. Although a practice repeatedly denounced by the prophets (Judg. 2:13; 3:7; 6:31; 8:33; 1 Kings 16:31; 18:26; 2 Kings 10:18; Jer. 2:8; 7:9; 19:5; 23:13; Hos. 2:8), Judaism borrowed many of its characteristic forms, psalms, concepts, and religious rituals from earlier Canaanite models.

Synoptics The first three Gospels, so named because they share a large quantity of material in common, allowing their texts to be viewed together "with one eye."

Syria (1) The territory extending from the upper Euphrates River to northern Palestine. (2) The kingdom of Aram, with its capital at Damascus (Isa. 7:8). As the creed in Deuteronomy 26:5 states, the Israelites regarded themselves as descended from Arameans (Syrians). Isaiah 7 refers to the Syro-Ephraimite coalition against Assyria.

Syro-Phoenician The name applied to a woman living near the Phoenician cities of Tyre and Sidon whose daughter Jesus healed (Mark 7:24–30; Matt. 15:21–28).

Tabernacle The portable tent-shrine, elaborately decorated, that housed the Ark of the Covenant (Exod. 25–31; 35–40; Num. 7–9) from the exodus to the building of Solomon's temple (1 Kings 6–8); used in both Old and New Testaments as a symbol of God's presence with humankind (Num. 9:5; Deut. 31:15; Pss. 15:1; 43:3; 61:4; 132:7; Isa. 4:6; 33:20; Hos. 12:9; Acts 7:46; Heb. 8:2; 9:11; 2 Pet. 1:14; Rev. 21:3).

Tabernacles, Feast of *See* Booths, Feast of.

Tables (Tablets) of the Law The stone slabs upon which the Ten Commandments were inscribed (Exod. 24:12; 32:15–20).

Tabor A prominent limestone hill in Galilee (Deut. 33:19; Josh. 19–22; Judg. 4:6; 5:15–21; Ps. 89:12–13; Jer. 46:18).

Talmud A huge collection of Jewish religious traditions consisting of two parts: (1) the Mishnah (written editions of ancient oral interpretations of the Torah), published in Palestine by Judah ha-Nasi (died about 220 C.E.) and his disciples; (2) the Gemara, extensive commentaries on the Mishnah. The Palestinian version of the Talmud, which is incomplete, was produced about 450 C.E.; the Babylonian Talmud, nearly four times as long, was finished about 500 C.E. Both Talmuds contain Mishnah and Gemara.

Tamar (1) The wife of Er, son of Judah (Gen. 38:6), who when widowed posed as a prostitute to trick her father-in-law into begetting children (the twins Pharez and Zerah) by her (Gen. 38:6–30). (2) Absalom's sister who was raped by her half-brother Amnon, whom Absalom later killed (2 Sam. 13:1–32; 1 Chron. 3:9).

Tammuz An ancient Near Eastern fertility god, a counterpart to the Semitic-Greek Adonis, at whose mythic death women ritually wept (Jer. 22:18; Amos 8:10; Ezek 8:14).

Targum Interpretative translations of the Hebrew Bible into Aramaic, such as that made by Ezra after the Jews' return from the Babylonian exile (Neh. 8:1–18). The practice may have begun in the postexilic synagogues, where Hebrew passages were read aloud and then translated into Aramaic with interpretative comments added.

Tarshish (1) A son of Javan (Greece, Aegean peoples) (Gen. 10:4; 1 Chron. 1:7). (2) An Old Testament term used to designate ships and ports, particularly the Phoenician variety (1 Kings 10:22; 22:48; Jon. 1:3; 2 Chron. 20:36).

Tarsus Capital of the Roman province of Cilicia (southeastern Turkey) and birthplace of Paul (Saul) (Acts 9:11; 11:25; 21:39; 22:3); a thriving commercial center in New Testament times.

Tell Flat-topped artificial mounds consisting of the ruins of ancient cities that dot the landscape of Mesopotamia, Syria, and Palestine.

Temple, The

(1) The imposing structure built by King Solomon (using Phoenician architects and craftsmen) on Mount Zion in Jerusalem to house the Ark of the Covenant in its innermost room (the Holy of Holies) (1 Kings 5:15–9:25). Later recognized as the only authorized center for sacrifice and worship of Yahweh, it was destroyed by Nebuchadnezzar's troops in 587 B.C.E. (2 Kings 25:8–17; 2 Chron. 36:18–19).

(2) The second temple, rebuilt by Jews returned from the Babylonian exile under Governor Zerubbabel, was dedicated about 515 B.C.E. (Ezra 1:1–11; 3:1–13; 4:24–6:22; Hag. 1–2; Zech. 1:1–8:13).

(3) Herod's splendid temple replaced the inferior edifice of Zerubbabel's time and took nearly a half-century to complete (John 2:20).

Jesus, who visited the temple as a child (Luke 2:22–38; 41–50) and often taught there (Matt. 21:23–24:1; Luke 20:1; John 7:14–52; 10:22–39), cleansed it of its money changers (Matt. 21:12–17; Mark 11:15–19; Luke 19:45–46; John 2:13–22) and prophesied its destruction (Matt. 24:1–2; Mark 13:1–4; Luke 21:5–7), which was fulfilled when the Romans sacked Jerusalem in 70 C.E. Until that event, the apostles continued to preach and worship there (Acts 3:1–26; 5:42; 21:26–22:29).

Ten Commandments (Decalogue) The set of ten religious and moral laws that Yahweh inscribed on stone tablets and gave Moses (Exod. 20:1–17; repeated in Deut. 5:6–21). Some scholars believe that a ritual Decalogue is contained in Exodus 34:1–16 and 22:29b–30; 23:12, 15–19 (see also Exod. 31:18–32:16).

Tent of Meeting *See* Tabernacle.

Terah A son of Nahor, father of Abraham, a younger Nahor, and Haran (Gen. 11:26; 1 Chron. 1:26–27), Terah migrated from the Sumerian city of Ur to Haran in northwest Mesopotamia (Gen. 11:27–32).

Teraphim Household gods, probably in the form of human figurines, perhaps representing a family's guardian spirit or ancestors and thought to confer good luck on their possessor. When secretly absconding with her husband Jacob, Rachel stole and hid her father's teraphim (Gen. 31:30–35). Even as late as the monarchy, owning such domestic idols was not necessarily viewed as conflicting with Yahweh's worship (Judg. 17:4–13; Hos. 3:4), although Samuel likened their use to idolatry (1 Sam. 15:23) and King Josiah outlawed them (2 Kings 23:24). They may have been used in fortunetelling.

Testament From the Latin for "covenant," this is the term used for the two main divisions of the Bible—the Old Testament (canonical Hebrew Scriptures) and the New Testament (Christian Greek Scriptures).

Tetragrammaton The four consonants (YHWH) comprising the sacred name Yahweh, the god of Israel. Although the name appears nearly 7,000 times in the canonical Old Testament, some modern Bible translations continue the Jewish practice of inaccurately rendering it as "the Lord."

Tetrateuch A critical term for the first four books of the Bible. Genesis through Numbers are composed primarily of J, E, and P material, with little or no discernible contribution from the Deuteronomist (D), who is responsible for Deuteronomy, the fifth book of the Torah.

Textual Criticism Comparison and analysis of ancient manuscripts to discover copyists' errors and, if possible, to reconstruct the true or original form of the document; also known as "lower criticism."

Thaddeus One of the most obscure of Jesus' apostles, he is listed among the Twelve in Matthew 10:3 and Mark 3:18 but not in Luke 7:16 or Acts 1:13.

Theodicy From a Greek term combining "god" and "justice," theodicy denotes a rational attempt to understand how an all-good all-powerful god can permit the existence of evil and undeserved suffering. Job, Habak-kuk, and 2 Esdras contain notable theodicies.

Theophany From the Greek, meaning an ap-pearance of a god to a person, as when El wrestled with Jacob (Gen. 32:26–32), Yahweh appeared to Moses (Exod. 3:1–4:17; 6:2–13) and the elders of Israel (Exod. 24:9–11), or the resurrected Jesus revealed himself to Thomas (John 20:24–29) and Paul (Acts 9:3–9).

Theophilus The otherwise unknown man to whom the Gospel of Luke and Book of Acts are addressed. He may have been a Roman official who became a Christian.

Thessalonica A major Macedonian city (modern Salonika) where Paul and Silas con-verted "some" Jews, "many" Greeks and "God-fearers," as well as numerous "rich women" to Christianity (Acts 17:1–9). Paul later revis-ited it (1 Cor. 16:5) and wrote two of his ear-liest surviving letters to its congregation (1 and 2 Thess.).

Thigh, Under the A euphemistic expression for the grasping of another's male organs during the conclusion of a vow, oath, or cov-enant (Gen. 24:2, 9; 47:29; see also Judg. 8:30).

Thomas One of the twelve apostles (Matt. 10:3; Mark 3:18; Luke 6:15; Acts 1:13), seldom mentioned in the Synoptics but relatively prominent in the Fourth Gospel, where he is called Didymus ("twin") (John 11:16; 20:24; 21:2). Unable to believe the other disciples' report of Jesus' resurrection, Thomas is sud-denly confronted with the risen Jesus and pronounces the strongest confession of faith in the Gospel (John 20:24–29).

Thunder, Sons of An epithet (*Boanerges*) applied to the apostles James and John (Mark 3:17), possibly because of their impulsive temperaments (Luke 9:52–56).

Thyatira A city of ancient Lydia in Asia Mi-nor (modern Turkey), original home of Lydia, Paul's first European convert (Acts 16:14) and one of the seven churches of Asia in Reve-lation 2:18–29.

Tiberias A city on the western shore of the Sea of Galilee founded by Herod Antipas and named after the Emperor Tiberius; a well-known spa in Jesus' day.

Tiberius (Tiberius Claudius Nero) Stepson of Augustus and second emperor of Rome (14–37 C.E.). According to Luke 3:1, Jesus came to John for baptism in the fifteenth year of Tiberius' reign. Except for Luke 2:1, he is the Caesar referred to in the Gospels (Matt. 22:17; Mark 12:14; Luke 20:22; John 19:12).

Tiglath-Pileser III Emperor of Assyria (745–727 B.C.E.), the biblical "Pul" (2 Kings 15:19) who captured Damascus in 732 B.C.E. and coerced tribute from kings Menahem of Is-rael and Ahaz of Judah (2 Kings 16:7–18; 2 Chron. 28:20–25). Ahaz's stripping of the Je-rusalem temple and sponsoring of pagan cults were probably done to placate Assyria's king.

Tigris According to Genesis 2:14 (where it is called the Hiddekel), the Tigris was the third of four rivers that watered Eden (see Dan. 10:4). Approximately 1,146 miles long, it forms the eastern boundary of Mesopotamia (the land between the Tigris and Euphrates). On its banks rose the ancient cities of Nineveh, Asshur, and Calah (Gen. 10:11), centers of the Assyrian Empire.

Timothy Younger friend and fellow mission-ary of Paul, who called him "beloved son" (1 Cor. 4:17; 1 Tim. 1:2–28; 2 Tim. 1:2), Timothy was the son of a Greek father and devout Jewish mother (Acts 16:1; 2 Tim. 1:5). To please the Jews, Paul circumcised Timothy before taking him on his second evangelical tour (Acts 16:1–4; 20:1–4). Paul later sent him to Macedonia (1 Thess. 3:6) and thence to Corinth to quiet the dissension there (Acts 19:22; 1 Cor. 4:17; 16:11), which he failed to do (2 Cor. 7:6, 13–14; 8:6, 16, 23; 12:18). The picture of Timothy in the Pastoral Epistles seems irreconcilable with what is known of him from Acts and Paul's genuine letters.

Tirzah A Canaanite city that Joshua cap-tured (Josh. 12:24), later the home of King Jeroboam (1 Kings 14:17), and the northern kingdom's capital during the reigns of Baasha (about 900–877 B.C.E.), Elah (877–876 B.C.E.), Zimri (seven days in about 876 B.C.E.), and Omri (about 876–869 B.C.E.), who took it by siege and ruled there for six years until he transferred the capital to Samaria (1 Kings 15:33–16:28).

Tishbite A term used to describe the prophet Elijah (1 Kings 17:1; 21:17; 2 Kings 1:3, 8; 9:36), its origin and meaning are uncertain.

Tithe Paying a tenth of one's income in money, crops, or animals to support a government (1 Sam. 8:15–17) or religion (Lev. 27:30–33; Num. 18:24–28; Deut. 12:17–19; 14:22–29; Neh. 10:36–38). In Israel, the high priest, Levites, and temple upkeep were supported by required levies. Abraham is reported to have paid Melchizedek tithes (Gen. 14:20; see also Heb. 7:2–6). Jesus regarded tithing as an obligation of his people (Luke 11:42; 12:13–21 18:12).

Titus A Greek whom Paul converted and who became a companion on his missionary journeys (2 Cor. 8:23; Gal. 2:1–3; Titus 1:4), Titus effected a reconciliation between Paul and the Corinthians (2 Cor. 7:5–7; 8:16–24; 12:18). A post-Pauline writer makes him the type of the Christian pastor (Titus 1–3).

Titus, Flavius Sabinius Vespasianus Son and successor of Vespasian and emperor of Rome (79–81 C.E.), he directed the siege of Jerusalem, which culminated in the destruction of the city and Herodian temple in 70 C.E. His carrying of the temple treasures to Rome is commemorated in the triumphal Arch of Titus that still stands in the Roman Forum.

Tobiah A partly Jewish Ammonite who occupied a storeroom in the rebuilt temple area after the exile and whom Nehemiah threw out of his lodgings (Neh. 13:6–9). Tobiah allied himself with Sanballat the Samaritan in opposing Nehemiah's reconstruction of Jerusalem's walls (Neh. 2:10; 4:3, 7; 6:1–19).

Tongues, Speaking in An ecstatic phenomenon of the early Church (Acts 2:1–45), presented at first as a miraculous and intelligible speaking and understanding of foreign languages by those who did not know these tongues (Acts 2:5–12) but later criticized by Paul as an inferior spiritual gift (1 Cor. 12–14).

Torah A Hebrew term usually translated "law," "instruction," or "teaching," it refers primarily to the Pentateuch, the first five books of the Hebrew Bible, and in a general sense to all the canonical writings, which are traditionally regarded as a direct oracle or revelation from Yahweh.

Tradition (1) Collections of stories and interpretations transmitted orally from generation to generation and embodying the religious history and beliefs of a people or community. Traditions of the patriarch were eventually included in the J and E sagas and finally incorporated into the first book of the Torah. (2) Oral explanations, interpretations, and applications of the written Torah (1 Chron. 4:22; Mark 7:5, 9; Matt. 15:2; Gal. 1:15), many of which were eventually compiled in the Mishnah. (3) Recollections and interpretations concerning Jesus that circulated orally through various early Christian churches and some of which were included in the Gospel narratives (1 Cor. 15:1–8; 2 Thess. 2:15).

Tradition Criticism Analysis of the origin and development of specific biblical themes—such as the exodus motif in the Old Testament and the eschatology of the Kingdom of God in the New—as presented by different Bible writers. In some cases, tradition criticism emphasizes the early and oral stages of development.

Trajan (Marcus Ulpius Nerva Trajanus) Emperor of Rome (98–117 C.E.) who was born in Spain about 53 C.E., became a successful military leader, and brought the Roman Empire to its greatest extent, annexing Dacia, Armenia, Mesopotamia, Assyria, and Arabia. Probably following the policies of Vespasian (69–79 C.E.), he conducted a persecution of Christians, although he wrote to Pliny the Younger, governor of Bithynia, that they were not to be sought out or denounced anonymously.

Transfiguration A supernatural happening that Jesus' three closest disciples—Peter, James, and John—experienced when, alone with him on an isolated mountaintop, they saw Jesus transformed into a being of light accompanied by Elijah (symbolizing the Hebrew prophetic tradition) and Moses (symbolizing the Torah) (Matt. 17:1–13; Mark 9:2–13; Luke 9:28–36). A heavenly voice identified Jesus as his "beloved son," thus revealing Jesus as the culmination of, and superior to, the Law and Prophets.

Transjordan The rugged plateau area east of the Jordan River, a region Joshua assigned to the tribes of Reuben, Gad, and half of Manasseh (Josh. 13) but which they failed to wrest from other Semites living there.

Tree of Life An ancient Mesopotamian symbol of rejuvenation or immortality (as in the *Epic of Gilgamesh*), the J (Yahwist) author places it in the Garden of Eden, humankind's original home, where its fruit would confer everlasting life on the eater (Gen. 2:9; 3:22–24). Yahweh's express motive for expelling the first human couple from Eden was to prevent their rivaling him further by eating from the Tree of Life (Gen. 3:22–24). It is often referred to in apocalyptic literature (En. 24:4; 25:4–6; Asmp. M. [Life of Adam and Eve] 19:2; 22:3; 28:2–4; XII P.: Levi 18:11), where it is usually reserved for the righteous to eat after the Day of Judgment (2 Esd. 8:52; cf. Rev. 2:7 and 22:2, 24).

Tribes of Israel, Twelve In ancient Israel, tribes were confederations of clans, which in turn were composed of families related by blood, adoption, or long asssociation, all forming a corporate community with a distinct social, religious, or ethnic identity. Traditionally believed to have descended from the twelve sons of Jacob (Israel) (Gen. 49:2–28; a parallel list, Moses' Blessing, mentions only eleven, omitting Simeon; Deut. 33:6–25), the tribes were Reuben, Simeon, Levi, Judah, Issachar, Zebulun (born of Jacob's wife Leah), Joseph (later divided into the tribes of Ephraim and Manasseh) and Benjamin (both born of Jacob's favorite wife, Rachel), Gad and Asher (by the slave girl Zilpah), Dan and Naphtali (by another concubine, Bilhah).

The apportionment of tribal territories in Palestine is described in Joshua 13–19. Ezekiel foresaw an idealized tribal state in Israel (Ezek. 48), and the author of Revelation multiplied the traditional twelve tribes by 12,000 to symbolize the number of Jews redeemed in Christ (Rev. 7:4–8). (See also Matt. 19:28; Luke 22:30; James 1:1, where the twelve tribes represent "spiritual Israel," the Christian community.) The so-called ten lost tribes were those of the northern kingdom assimilated into the Assyrian Empire after 721 B.C.E. (2 Kings 17).

Trinity A post–New Testament doctrine which holds that God exists as three divine Persons in One, although he manifests himself on different occasions as Father, Son, or Holy Spirit. After generations of ecclesiastical debate on the subject had seriously divided the Church, Constantine, the first Christian emperor of Rome but then unbaptized, called a council of church leaders in Nicea to settle the issue (325 C.E.). The council decreed the orthodoxy of the trinitarian formula, so that the mystery of trinity in unity henceforth became central to the Christian faith (Matt. 28:19–20; 2 Cor. 13:14; Gal. 1:1–5).

Trumpets, Feast of The Hebrew month began with a new moon. On the first day of the seventh (sabbatical) month, a festival, assembly, and sacrifice were to be held (Lev. 13:23–25; Num. 29:1–7).

Tubal-cain According to J, the son of Lamech and Zillah and the ancestor of all metalworkers in bronze and iron (Gen. 4:19–26). He may have been regarded as the eponymous progenitor of the Kenites.

Twelve, Book of the The twelve books of the Minor Prophets—Hosea to Malachi—originally compiled on a single scroll.

Twelve, The The twelve apostles whom Jesus specifically chose to follow him. Different names appear on different New Testament lists of the Twelve (Matt. 10:1–5; Mark 3:16–19; Luke 6:12–16 Acts 1:13–14).

Tychicus A loyal helper and companion of Paul who accompanied him through the Roman province of Asia on his third missionary journey (Acts 20:4), Tychicus delivered Paul's letters to the Colossians (Col. 4:7–9) and Ephesians (Eph. 6:21).

Tyre An ancient Phoenician seaport famous for its commerce and wealth, Tyre was originally built on a small offshore island about twenty-five miles south of Sidon. King Solomon made an alliance with its ruler, Hiram, the skills of whose architects and craftsmen he utilized in constructing the Jerusalem temple (1 Kings 5:15–32; 7:13–51). Its power and luxury were later denounced by the prophets (Isa. 23; Ezek. 26–28; Amos 1:9–10; Zech. 9:3–4). Alexander the Great sacked the city in 332 B.C.E., although it had been rebuilt by Jesus' day (Mark 7:24–31; Luke 3:8).

Ur One of the world's oldest cities, in Sumer, Ur was the ancestral homeland (Gen. 11:28–31) from which Abraham and his family migrated to Haran, although some scholars have suggested a northern location for the Abrahamic Ur. Archaeologically, the Sumerian Ur is notable for its well-preserved ziggurat and "royal Cemetery," whose tombs have yielded a number of beautifully crafted artworks, furniture, jewelry, and other sophisticated artifacts (mid-third millennium B.C.E.).

Uriah (1) A Hittite practicer of Yahwism and soldier of David whose wife Bathsheba the Israelite king seduced and wished to marry. David ordered him exposed in the front lines of battle so that he was inevitably killed, a crime the prophet Nathan denounced to the king's face (2 Sam. 11–12). (2) A priest whom King Ahaz of Judah (about 735-716 B.C.E.) commissioned to remodel the temple area and construct an altar modeled on that which Ahaz had seen in Assyrian-dominated Damascus (2 Kings 16:10–16). (3) A Judean prophet who predicted the Babylonian destruction of Jerusalem, fled to Egypt to escape King Jehoiakim's wrath, but was murdered and his body returned to Judah where it was buried in a common grave (Jer. 26:20–23).

Urim and Thummim Undescribed objects (whose names may mean "oracle" and "truth") that were used by Israel's priests in casting lots to determine Yahweh's will on a specific matter. They could apparently indicate only yes or no responses (Exod. 28:29–30; Num. 27:21; 1 Sam. 28:6; Ezra 2:63; Neh. 7:65).

Uz Job's unidentified homeland, which various scholars have suggested to be Edom, Arabia, or a location east of the Jordan River.

Uzziah (Azariah) Son of Amaziah, king of Judah (783–742 B.C.E.), and a contemporary of King Jeroboam II of Israel (786–746 B.C.E.) (2 Kings 14:22; 15:1–7; 2 Chron. 26:1–23), Uzziah fortified Jerusalem, defeated the Philistines, Ammonites, and Arabs, and greatly extended Judah's political jurisdiction. Both the Deuteronomist and Chronicler rate him as "pleasing" Yahweh, although the latter attributes the king's leprosy to his usurping priestly functions in the temple.

Vashti The empress of Persia (unknown to history) who refused to exhibit herself to the male friends of her husband, Ahasuerus (Xerxes I), and whom Esther replaced as queen (Esther 1:9–2:18.)

Veil, The The elaborately decorated curtain separating the Holy Place from the Most Holy Place in the tabernacle and Jerusalem temple (Exod. 26:31–37), which was reputedly rent in two at Jesus' crucifixion (Matt. 27:51; Heb. 6:19; 9–10).

Vespasian Emperor of Rome (69–79 C.E.) who led Roman legions into Judea during the Jewish revolt (66–70 C.E.), the siege of Jerusalem passing to his son Titus when Vespasian became emperor.

Vulgate Jerome's Latin translation of the Bible (late fourth century C.E.), including the Apocrypha, which became the official version of Roman Catholicism.

Weeks, Feast of *See* Pentecost.

Wisdom Literature Biblical works dealing primarily with practical and ethical behavior and ultimate religious questions, such as the problem of evil. The books include Proverbs, Job, Ecclesiastes, Ecclesiasticus, and the Wisdom of Solomon. Habakkuk, 2 Esdras, and the New Testament Book of James also have characteristics of wisdom writing.

Woes, The Seven Messianic The series of seven condemnations of scribes and Pharisees attributed to Jesus when he was rejected by official Judaism (Matt. 23:13–32).

Word, The (1) The "word" or "oracle" of Yahweh, a phrase characteristic of the Hebrew prophets, typically referring to a divine pronouncement, judgment, or statement of purpose that the prophet delivers in his god's name. (2) The preincarnate Jesus (John 1:1–3). *See* Logos.

Writings, The *See* Kethuvim.

Xerxes I (486–465 B.C.E.); thought to be the biblical Ahasuerus, emperor of Persia (Esther; Ezra 4:6).

Yahweh A translation of the sacred name of Israel's god, represented almost 7,000 times in the canonical Old Testament by the four consonants of the Tetragrammaton (YHWH). According to Exodus 6:2–4, it was revealed for the first time to Moses at the burning bush; according to J, it was used from the time of Enosh before the flood (Gen. 4:26). Scholars have offered various interpretations of the origin and meaning of the divine name. According to one accepted theory, it is derived from the Hebrew verb "to be" and means "He is" or "He causes to be," implying that Yahweh is the maker of events and shaper of history.

Yahwist The name scholars give the anonymous writer or compiler who produced the J document, the oldest stratum in the Pentateuch (about 950 B.C.E.).

Yom Kippur *See* Atonement, Day of.

Zadok A priest officiating during the reigns of David and Solomon who supported the latter's claim to the throne and was rewarded by being made chief priest at the temple (2 Sam. 15:24–29; 17:15; 19:11; 20:25; 1 Kings 1:7–8, 32–39, 45; 2:35; 1 Chron. 6:4–15, 50–52; 12:28). Ezekiel regarded Zadok's descendants as the only legitimate priests (Ezek. 40:46; 43:19; 44:15; 48:11). After the exile they apparently enjoyed a monopoly in the second temple (1 Chron. 24:2–19; 27:17; 29:22).

Zaphenath-paneah According to Genesis 41:45, the Egyptian name given Joseph, son of Jacob. It has been variously translated as "Says the God: he will live," "revealer of secrets," and "minister of agriculture."

Zarephath According to 1 Kings 17:8–24, a Phoenician town near Sidon where Elijah befriended a widow during a famine and resuscitated her son (Luke 4:25–27).

Zealots An extremely nationalistic party in first-century Judaism dedicated to freeing Judea from foreign domination by armed revolt if necessary. Their militarism and fanatical patriotism generated several uprisings, culminating in the great rebellion against Rome (66–70 C.E.). According to Josephus' possibly biased account, their intransigence led to the destruction of Jerusalem and the temple. The Simon of Luke 6:15 and Acts 1:13 is called a "zealot."

Zebedee A Galilean fisherman, husband of Salome, father of the apostles James and John (Matt. 27:56; Mark 1:19–20; 3:17; 14:33; 15:40).

Zebulun (1) The sixth son of Jacob and Leah, full brother of Reuben, Simeon, Levi, Judah, and Issachar (Gen. 30:20; 35:23). (2) The tribe of Zebulun, represented in Jacob's blessing (Gen. 49:13) as a seagoing group located near the Phoenician port of Sidon, actually settled in a landlocked farming area of northern Palestine (Josh. 19:10–16), although they were on a main trading route with coastal cities. Except for their failure to expel the Canaanites from their allotted territory and their joining Barak and Deborah against Sisera (Judg. 1:27–30; 4:10–16; 5:18), they are seldom mentioned in the Old Testament.

Zechariah

(1) The son of Jehoiada the priest, Zechariah was stoned to death for denouncing Judah's idolatry (late ninth century B.C.E.) (2 Chron. 25:20–22; he is usually identified with Zacharias in Matt. 23:35 and Luke 11:51).

(2) The son of Jeroboam II and the last king of Jehu's dynasty in Israel, who reigned only six months (about 746/745 B.C.E.) before he was murdered (2 Kings 10:30).

(3) The son of Berechiah or the priest Iddo (Zech. 1:1, 8; Ezra 5:1; Neh. 12:16), a Judean prophet whose message is contained in the book of the Minor Prophets bearing his name.

The latter, a contemporary of Haggai (about 520–515 B.C.E.), urged the returned exiles to rebuild Yahweh's temple in Jerusalem. Although Judah was then part of the Persian Empire ruled by Darius, he apparently regarded the Jewish governor, Zerubbabel, a descendant of David, as a potential messianic king (Zech. 4:6–15; 6:9–14). His work is characterized by strange imagery and apocalyptic visions. Chapters 9–14 are thought to have been appended by a later author.

Zecharias (1) A Judean priest married to Elisabeth, a descendant of Aaron, whose long childless marriage was blessed in his old age by the birth of the future John the Baptist (Luke 1:5–25, 57–80; 3:2). A vision foretelling the birth rendered him temporarily paralyzed, but he recovered his speech in time to name the child and to utter a prayer of thanksgiving—the Benedictus (Luke 1:67–79). (2) A Jewish martyr mentioned in Jesus' phrase "from Abel to Zecharias" (Matt. 23:35; Luke 11:51), usually identified with Zechariah, son of Jehoiada in 2 Chronicles 24:20–24.

Zedekiah A son of Josiah and the last king of Judah (about 597–587 B.C.E.), Zedekiah reigned as a tribute-paying vassal of Nebuchadnezzar (2 Chron. 36:13; Jer. 29:3–7; Ezek. 17:15–18). A weak ruler, he consulted the prophet Jeremiah (Jer. 21:1–7) but acceded to his advisers' pressures to seek help from Egypt in overthrowing Babylon's yoke (Jer. 27:12–22; 37:6–21; 38:7–28). When he rebelled against Babylon, Nebuchadnezzar laid siege to and destroyed Jerusalem (587 B.C.E.). Zedekiah tried to escape but was captured, tried, and condemned to having his sons slain before his eyes and his own eyes put out, after which he was imprisoned in Babylon, where he died (2 Kings 24:17–25:7; 2 Chron. 36:10–21; Jer. 39:6–14; 52:1–27).

Zephaniah (1) Son of Maaseiah and second-ranking priest under King Zedekiah who acted as go-between for the king in his consultations with Jeremiah (2 Kings 25:18; Jer. 21:1; 29:25–32; 37:3–4; 52:24–27). After Jerusalem's fall, he was executed by the Babylonians. (2) A seventh-century Judean prophet whose pronouncements of judgment are collected in the book bearing his name (Zeph. 1:1). Virtually nothing is known of his life.

Zerubbabel A son of Shealtiel or Salathiel (Ezra 3:2, 8; Hag. 1:1; Matt. 1:12) or of Pedaiah (1) Chron. 3:19), Zerubbabel (meaning "begotten in Babylon") was a grandson of Jehoiachin, the king of Judah imprisoned in Babylon (1 Chron. 3:17), and therefore a legitimate heir to the Davidic throne. Appointed governor of the restored Jewish community in Jerusalem (Ezra 3; Hag. 1:1, 14), he returned from Babylon with the first group of exiles and, with Joshua, the high priest, set up an altar to Yahweh and made arrangements to rebuild the temple. Between the time the work began and the temple's dedication in 515 B.C.E. (Ezra 6), however, Zerubbabel disappeared from history. The prophets Haggai and Zechariah, who had urged the rebuilding, had both regarded him as a potential messianic king (Hag. 2:20–23; Zech. 4:6b–10a; 6:9–15—the latter passage reworked by later scribes). When these political expectations failed to materialize, hopes were focused on a priestly hierarchy represented by Joshua (Zech. 3:1–4; 6:11–12).

Zeus In Greek mythology, the son of Cronus and Rhea, king of the Olympian gods, and patron of civic order. A personification of storm and other heavenly powers, he ruled by wielding the lightning bolt. The Romans identified him with Jupiter (Jove). Some people of Lystra compared Barnabas to Zeus and Paul to Hermes (Acts 14:12). The erection of his statue in the Jerusalem temple courts helped spark the Maccabean revolt (about 168 B.C.E.).

Ziggurat A characteristic architectural form of Sumerian and Babylonian temples, the ziggurat was a multileveled tower resembling a stepped or recessed pyramid consisting of succeedingly smaller platforms built one atop the other. At its apex was a chapel dedicated to a major civic god. Broad ceremonial staircases used for liturgical processions led to the ziggurat's summit, to which it was believed the gods invisibly descended. The story of the Tower of Babel in Genesis 11:1–9 is probably based on a misunderstanding of the ziggurat's function.

Zilpah The handmaid of Leah by whom Jacob begot Gad and Asher (Gen. 29:24; 30:9–13, 35:26.)

Zimri A chariot captain who murdered King Elah and seized Israel's throne, which he held for only seven days (876 B.C.E.). When Omri, leader of the military, attacked him at Tirzah, Zimri set the palace on fire and per-ished in the ruins, after which Omri became king (1 Kings 16:8–20).

Zion The name, probably meaning "citadel," for a rocky hill in old Jerusalem, it was originally a Jebusite acropolis that David captured and upon which he built his palace and housed the Ark of the Covenant (Judg. 19:11–12; 2 Sam. 5:6–12; 6:12–17; 1 Chron. 11:5–8). David purchased a threshing floor in Zion (2 Sam. 24:18–25) upon which Solomon later built the temple. In time, the term referred either to the hill on which the temple stood or to the surrounding city of Jerusalem (Pss. 2:6; 9:11; 76:2; 127:3; Isa. 1:26–27; 10:24; 30:19; 64:10; Jer. 31:6; Amos 1:2; Mic. 3:12).

Zipporah A daughter of Jethro, a Midianite shepherd and priest, Zipporah became Moses' wife (Exod. 2:11–22) and bore him at least two sons, Gershom (Exod. 2:22) and Eliezer (Exod. 18:3–4), saving the latter from Yahweh's wrath by circumcising him with a flint stone (Exod. 4:18–26).

Zoar One of the five "cities of the plain" on the eastern shore of the Dead Sea (Gen. 13:10; 14:2, 8) that Lot reached as Sodom was being destroyed (Gen. 19:20–23). Since it is referred to by the prophets, it may have survived the catastrophe (Isa. 15:5; Jer. 48:34).

Zophar A Naamathite, one of Job's three companions (Job 2:11; 11:1; 20:1; 42:9).

GENERAL BIBLIOGRAPHY

This bibliography provides a representative list of important scholarly works on the Old and New Testaments. Many additional references on specific topics and individual biblical books are included in Recommended Reading sections appended to particular units throughout the text.

BIBLE COMMENTARIES, DICTIONARIES, AND OLD TESTAMENT INTRODUCTIONS

Ackroyd, P. R., et al., eds. *The Cambridge Bible Commentary.* Cambridge, England: Cambridge University Press, 1972—.

Anderson, Bernhard. *Understanding the Old Testament,* 3rd ed. Englewood Cliffs, N. J.: Prentice-Hall, 1975.

Black, Matthew, and Rowley, H. H., eds. *Peake's Commentary on the Bible,* rev. ed. New York: Thomas Nelson, 1962.

Brown, Raymond E., Fitzmyer, Joseph A., and Murphy, Roland E. *The Jerome Biblical Commentary.* Englewood Cliffs, N. J.: Prentice-Hall, 1968.

Buttrick, George, et al., eds. *The Interpreter's Dictionary of the Bible.* 5 vols. Nashville: Abingdon Press, 1962, 1976.

Childs, Brevard S. *Introduction to the Old Testament as Scripture.* Philadelphia: Fortress Press, 1979.

Eissfeldt, Otto. *The Old Testament: An Introduction.* New York: Harper & Row, 1965.

Fohrer, Georg. *Introduction to the Old Testament.* Nashville: Abingdon Press, 1968.

Gunneweg, A. H. J. *Understanding the Old Testament.* Philadelphia: Westminster Press, 1978.

Hayes, John H. *An Introduction to Old Testament Study.* Nashville: Abingdon Press, 1979.

Humphreys, W. Lee. *Crisis and Story: Introduction to the Old Testament.* Palo Alto, Calif.: Mayfield Publishing Co., 1979.

Laymon, Charles M., ed. *The Interpreter's One-Volume Commentary on the Bible.* Nashville: Abingdon Press, 1971.

May, Herbert G., and Metzger, Bruce M. *The Oxford Annotated Bible with the Apocrypha, Revised Standard Edition.* New York: Oxford University Press, 1965.

Pfeiffer, Robert H. *Introduction to the Old Testament,* rev. ed. New York: Harper & Row, 1949.

Sandmel, Samuel. *The Hebrew Scriptures: An Introduction to Their Literature and Religious Ideas.* New York: Alfred A. Knopf, 1963.

Soggin, J. Alberto. *Introduction to the Old Testament.* Philadelphia: Westminster Press, 1976.

ANCIENT TEXTS RELATING TO THE OLD TESTAMENT

Beyerlin, Walter, ed. *Near Eastern Religious Texts Relating to the Old Testament.* Translated by John Bowden. Philadelphia: Westminster Press, 1978.

Coogan, Michael David. *Stories from Ancient Canaan.* Philadelphia: Westminster Press, 1978. A paperback collection of Canaanite myths and their biblical parallels.

Cross, Frank M. *Canaanite Myth and Hebrew Epic.* Cambridge, Mass.: Harvard University Press, 1973.

Gaster, Theodor H. *Myth, Legend, and Custom in the Old Testament.* New York: Harper & Row, 1969.

Heidel, Alexander. *The Gilgamesh Epic and Old Testament Parallels.* Chicago: University of Chicago Press, 1949.

_____. *The Babylonian Genesis,* 2nd ed. Chicago: University of Chicago Press, 1951. A paperback translation of the *Enuma Elish* with commentary.

Pritchard, James B. *The Ancient Near East: An Anthology of Texts and Pictures.* Princeton, N. J.: Princeton University Press, 1965. A less expensive work containing excerpts from the following two books.

_____. *The Ancient Near East in Pictures Relating to the Old Testament.* Princeton, N. J.: Princeton University Press, 1965.

Pritchard, James B., ed. *Ancient Near East Texts Relating to the Old Testament.* 3rd ed. supp. Princeton, N. J.: Princeton University Press, 1969. Translations of relevant Egyptian, Babylonian, Canaanite, and other ancient literatures—the standard work.

Sanders, N. K. *The Epic of Gilgamesh.* Baltimore: Penguin Books, 1972. A readable translation of the *Epic of Gigamesh* with a scholarly introduction.

BIBLICAL ARCHAEOLOGY

Albright, William F. *Archaeology and the Religion of Israel.* Garden City, N. Y.: Doubleday Anchor Books, 1960.

_____. *The Archaeology of Palestine*, rev. ed. New York: Penguin Books, 1961.

_____. *Yahweh and the Gods of Canaan*. Garden City, N. Y.: Doubleday Anchor Books, 1969.

Burrows, Millar. *What Mean These Stones?* New York: Meridian, 1957.

Cornfield, Gaalyah, and Freedman, David N., eds. *Archaeology of the Bible: Book by Book*. New York: Harper & Row, 1976.

Frank, Harry T. *Bible, Archaeology, and Faith*. Nashville: Abingdon Press, 1971.

_____. *Discovering the Biblical World*. New York: Harper & Row, 1975.

Freedman, David N., and Campbell, Edward F., Jr. *The Biblical Archaeologist Reader, 2 and 3*. Garden City, N. Y.: Doubleday Anchor Books, 1964.

Freedman, David N., and Greenfield, J. C., eds. *New Directions in Biblical Archaeology*. Garden City, N. Y.: Doubleday, 1969.

Kenyon, Kathleen. *Archaeology in the Holy Land*, 3rd ed. New York: Praeger Publishers, 1970.

Landay, Jerry M. *Silent Cities, Sacred Stones*. London: Weidenfeld and Nicolson, 1971.

Magnusson, Magnus. *Archaeology of the Bible*. New York: Simon & Schuster, 1977.

Mazar, Benjamin. *The Mountain of the Lord*. Garden City, N. Y.: Doubleday, 1975.

Moscati, Sabatino. *The Face of the Ancient Orient*. Garden City, N. Y.: Doubleday Anchor Books, 1962.

Pritchard, James B. *Archaeology and the Old Testament*. Princeton, N. J.: Princeton University Press, 1958.

_____. *Gibeon, Where the Sun Stood Still*. Princeton, N. J.: Princeton University Press, 1962.

Shanks, Hershel. *The City of David*. Washington, D. C.: The Biblical Archaeology Society, 1973.

Winton, Thomas D., ed. *Archaeology and Old Testament Study*. Oxford: Clarendon Press, 1967.

Wright, George E. *Biblical Archaeology*, rev. ed. Philadelphia: Westminster Press, 1962.

Wright, George E., ed. *The Bible and the Ancient Near East*. Garden City, N. Y.: Doubleday Anchor Books, 1965.

OLD TESTAMENT HISTORY, THEOLOGY, AND INTERPRETATION

Ackroyd, Peter R. *Exile and Restoration: A Study of Hebrew Thought in the Sixth Century B.C.E.* Philadelphia: Westminster Press, 1968.

Albrektson, Bertil. *History and the Gods*. Lund, Sweden: C. W. K. Gleerup, 1967.

Albright, W. F. *From the Stone Age to Christianity*. Garden City, N. Y.: Doubleday, 1957.

————. *The Biblical Period from Abraham to Ezra*. New York: Harper & Row, 1963.

Alonso-Schokel, Luis, S. J. *Understanding Biblical Research*. New York: Herder and Herder, 1963.

Alt, Albrecht. *Essays on Old Testament History and Religion*. Translated by R. A. Wilson. New York: Doubleday, 1967.

Anderson, Bernhard W., ed. *The Old Testament and Christian Faith*. New York: Harper & Row, 1963.

Anderson, G. W. "Some Aspects of the Uppsala School of Old Testament Study." *Harvard Theological Review* 43 (1950): 239–56.

Anderson, G. W., ed. *Tradition and Interpretation*. Oxford: Clarendon Press, 1979.

Avi-Yonah, Michael, ed. *A History of the Holy Land*. New York: Macmillan, 1969.

Barr, James. *The Bible in the Modern World*. New York: Harper & Row, 1973.

Boman, Thorlief. *Hebrew Thought Compared with Greek*. Translated by Jules L. Moreau. Philadelphia: Westminster Press, 1960.

Bright, John. *Early Israel in Recent History Writing*. London: SCM Press, 1956.

————. *A History of Israel*. Philadelphia: Westminster Press, 1972.

Bruce, F. F. *Israel and the Nations: From the Exodus to the Fall of the Second Temple*. Grand Rapids, Mich.: Wm. B. Eerdmans, 1963.

Childs, Brevard S. *Biblical Theology in Crisis*. Philadelphia: Westminster Press, 1970.

Clements, Ronald E. *God's Chosen People: A Theological Interpretation of the Book of Deuteronomy*. London: SCM Press, 1968.

————. *A Century of Old Testament Study*. London: Lutterworth Press, 1976.

Cross, Frank Moore. *The Ancient Library of Qumran and Modern Biblical Studies*. Garden City, N. Y.: Doubleday, 1961.

Denton, Robert C. *The Knowledge of God in Ancient Israel*. New York: Seabury Press, 1968.

de Vaux, Roland. *Ancient Israel: Its Life and Institutions*. Translated by David Smith. New York: McGraw-Hill, 1961.

————. *The Early History of Israel: To the Period of the Judges*. Philadelphia: Westminster Press, 1976.

————. *The Early History of Israel*. Translated by David Smith. Philadelphia: Westminster Press, 1978.

Eichrodt, Walther. *Theology of the Old Testament*. Vol. 1, translated by J. A. Baker. Philadelphia: Westminster Press, 1961.

————. *Theology of the Old Testament*. Vol. 2, translated by J. A. Baker. Philadelphia: Westminster Press, 1967.

Eliade, Mircea. *Cosmos and History: The Myth of the Eternal Return.* New York: Harper Torchbooks, 1954.

———. *The Sacred and the Profane: The Nature of Religion.* New York: Harper Torchbooks, 1961.

Ellis, Peter. *The Yahwist: The Bible's First Theologian.* Notre Dame, Ind.: Fides, 1968.

Fohrer, Georg. *History of Israelite Religion.* Translated by David Green. Nashville: Abingdon Press, 1972. Traces the development of Israel's characteristic religious concepts and traditions.

Frankfurt, H., et al., eds. *The Intellectual Adventure of Ancient Man.* Chicago: University of Chicago Press, 1946.

Freedman, David Noel. "Canon of the O.T." In *The Interpreter's Dictionary of the Bible: Supplementary Volume,* pp. 130–36. Nashville: Abingdon Press, 1976. A good introduction.

Fromm, Erich. *You Shall Be as Gods.* Greenwich, Conn.: Fawcett Publications, 1966.

Gaster, Theodor H. *Thespis: Ritual, Myth, and Drama in the Ancient Near East.* New York: Abelard-Schuman, 1950.

———. *Myth, Legend, and Custom in the Old Testament.* New York: Harper & Row, 1969.

———. *The Dead Sea Scriptures in English Translation.* Garden City, N. Y.: Doubleday, 1976.

Gelin, Albert. *The Religion of Israel.* Twentieth Century Encyclopedia of Catholicism, translated by J. R. Foster, New York: Hawthorn Books, 1959.

Gottwald, Norman K. *The Tribes of Yahweh: A Sociology of the Religion of Liberated Israel, 1250–1050 B.C.E.* Maryknoll, N. Y.: Orbis Books, 1979.

Grant, Robert M. *A Short History of the Interpretation of the Bible,* rev. ed. New York: Macmillan, 1963.

Habel, Norman. *Literary Criticism of the Old Testament.* Philadelphia: Fortress Press, 1971.

Hahn, Herbert F. *The Old Testament in Modern Research.* Philadelphia: Fortress Press, 1966.

Hasel, Gerhard F. *Old Testament Theology: Basic Issues in the Current Debate,* rev. ed. Grand Rapids, Mich.: Wm. B. Eerdmans, 1975.

Hayes, John H., and Miller, J. Maxwell, eds. *Israelite and Judaean History.* Philadelphia: Westminster Press, 1977.

Hermann, Siegfried. *A History of Israel in Old Testament Times.* Philadelphia: Fortress Press, 1981.

Hillers, Delbert R. *Covenant: The History of a Biblical Idea.* Baltimore: Johns Hopkins University Press, 1969.

Irwin, W. A. *The Old Testament: Keystone of Human Culture.* New York: Abelard-Schuman, 1952.

Jagersma, Henk. *A History of Israel in the Old Testament Period.* Philadelphia: Fortress Press, 1983.

Kaufmann, Yehezkel. *The Religion of Israel.* Translated by Moshe Greenberg. Chicago: University of Chicago Press, 1960.

Klein, Ralph W. *Textual Criticism of the Old Testament: The Septuagint after Qumram.* Philadelphia: Fortress Press, 1974.

Koch, Klaus. *The Growth of the Biblical Tradition: The Form-Critical Method.* Translated by S. M. Cupitt. New York: Charles Scribner's Sons, 1969.

_____. *The Prophets.* vol. I, *The Assyrian Age,* translated by Margaret Kohl. Philadelphia: Fortress Press, 1982.

Kohler, Ludwig. *Old Testament Theology.* Translated by A. S. Todd. Philadelphia: Westminster Press, 1958.

Kuntz, Kenneth J. *The People of Ancient Israel.* New York: Harper & Row, 1974.

Levie, Jeann, S. J. *The Bible, Word of God in Words of Men.* New York: P. J. Kennedy & Sons, 1961.

Lindblom, Johannes. *Prophecy in Ancient Israel.* Philadelphia: Fortress Press, 1963.

Maier, John, and Tollers, Vincent, eds. *The Bible in Its Literary Milieu: Contemporary Essays.* Grand Rapids, Mich.: Wm. B. Eerdmans, 1979.

McCarthy, Dennis J. *Old Testament Covenant: A Survey of Current Opinions.* Oxford: Basil Blackwell, 1972.

McCurley, Foster R. *Ancient Myths and Biblical Faith: Scriptural Transformations.* Philadelphia: Fortress Press, 1983.

McKenzie, John L. *A Theology of the Old Testament.* Garden City, N. Y.: Doubleday, 1974.

Mendenhall, George. "Biblical History in Transition." In *The Bible and the Ancient Near East,* edited by G. E. Wright. New York: Doubleday Anchor Books, 1965.

_____. "Covenant." In *The Interpreter's Dictionary of the Bible,* vol. 2, pp. 714–23. New York and Nashville: Abingdon Press, 1962.

_____. *Law and Covenant in Israel and the Ancient Near East.* Pittsburgh: Biblical Colloquium, 1955.

Miller, J. Maxwell. *The Old Testament and the Historian.* Guides to Biblical Scholarship. Philadelphia: Fortress Press, 1976.

Muilenburg, James. *The Way of Israel.* New York: Harper & Row, 1961.

Newman, Murray. *The People of the Covenant.* Nashville: Abingdon Press, 1962.

Nielsen, Edward. *Oral Tradition: Studies in Biblical Theology,* no. 11. Naperville, Ill.: Alex R. Allenson.

Noth, Martin. *The History of Israel.* New York: Harper & Row, 1960.

_____. *A History of Pentateuchal Traditions.* Englewood Cliffs, N. J.: Prentice-Hall, 1972.

Orlinsky, Harry M. *Ancient Israel.* Ithaca, N. Y.: Cornell University Press, 1960.

Pfeiffer, Robert H. "Canon of the O.T." In *The Interpreter's Dictionary of the Bible*, vol. 1, pp. 498–520. New York and Nashville: Abingdon Press, 1962.

Raitt, Thomas M. *A Theology of Exile.* Philadelphia: Fortress Press, 1977.

Ringgren, Helmer. *The Faith of Qumran.* Philadelphia: Fortress Press, 1961.

_____. *Israelite Religion.* Translated by David E. Green. Philadelphia: Fortress Press, 1966.

_____. *Religions of the Ancient Near East.* Translated by John Sturdy. Philadelphia: Westminster Press, 1973.

Robertson, David. *The Old Testament and the Literary Critic.* Guides to Biblical Scholarship. Philadelphia: Fortress Press, 1977.

Robinson, H. Wheeler. *Inspiration and Revelation in the Old Testament.* Oxford: Clarendon Press, 1946.

_____. *Worship in Ancient Israel: Its Forms and Meaning.* Philadelphia: Fortress Press, 1967.

Rowley, Harold H., ed. *The Old Testament and Modern Study.* New York: Oxford University Press, 1951.

Sanders, James A. *Torah and Canon.* Philadelphia: Fortress Press, 1972. A concise and helpful introduction to canon information.

Soulen, Richard N. *Handbook of Biblical Criticism.* Atlanta: John Knox Press, 1976.

Tucker, Gene M. *Form Criticism of the Old Testament.* Guides to Biblical Scholarship. Philadelphia: Fortress Press, 1971.

von Rad, Gerhard. *The Theology of Israel's Historical Traditions.* Translated by M. G. Stalker. New York: Harper & Row, 1962.

_____. *The Theology of Israel's Prophetic Traditions.* Translated by M. G. Stalker. New York: Harper & Row, 1965.

_____. *God at Work in Israel.* Translated by John Marks. Nashville: Abingdon Press, 1980.

Vriezen, Thomas. *An Outline of Old Testament Theology.* Translated by S. Neuijen. Oxford: Basil Blackwell, 1958.

Westermann, Claus, ed. *Essays on Old Testament Hermenuetics.* Translated and edited by James Luther Mays. Richmond, Va.: John Knox Press, 1963.

_____. *The Promises to the Fathers: Studies on the Patriarchal Narratives.* Translated by David E. Green. Philadelphia: Fortress Press, 1980.

Wolff, Hans Walter. *Anthropology of the Old Testament.* Translated by Margaret Kohl. Philadelphia: Fortress Press, 1981.

_____. *Confrontations with Prophets.* Philadelphia: Fortress Press, 1983.

Wright, G. Ernest. *The Old Testament and Theology.* New York: Harper & Row, 1969.

Zimmerli, Walther. *Man and His Hope in the Old Testament: Studies in Biblical Theology*, 2nd series. Naperville, Ill.: Alec R. Allenon, 1968.

_____. *Old Testament Theology in Outline.* Translated by David E. Green. Atlanta: John Knox Press, 1978.

OLD TESTAMENT APOCYPHA, PSEUDEPIGRAPHA, AND APOCALYPTIC WRITINGS

Becker, Joachim. *Messianic Expectation in the Old Testament.* Translated by David E. Green. Philadelphia: Fortress Press, 1980.

Charles, R. H., ed. *The Apocrypha and Pseudepigrapha of the Old Testament in English.* 2 vols. New York: Oxford University Press, 1913, 1963.

Charlesworth, J. H., ed., *The Old Testament Pseudepigrapha,* vol. 1. Garden City, N. Y.: Doubleday Anchor Books, 1982.

Hanson, Paul D. *The Dawn of Apocalyptic: The Historical and Sociological Roots of Jewish Eschatology.* Philadelphia: Fortress Press, 1979.

Mowinckel, Sigmund. *He That Cometh.* Translated by G. W. Anderson. Nashville: Abingdon Press, 1956.

Nickelsburg, George W. E. *Jewish Literature Between the Bible and the Mishnah: A Historical and Literary Introduction.* Philadelphia: Fortress Press, 1981.

Ringgren, Helmer. *The Messiah in the Old Testament: Studies in Biblical Theology,* no. 18. Chicago: Alec R. Allenson, 1956.

Rost, Leonard. *Judaism outside the Hebrew Canon: An Introduction to the Documents.* Nashville: Abingdon Press, 1976.

Russell, D. S. *The Method and Message of Jewish Apocalyptic: 200 B.C.–A.D. 100.* Philadelphia: Westminster Press, 1964. A useful review of apocalyptic literature of the Greco-Roman period.

_____. *Apocalyptic: Ancient and Modern.* Philadelphia: Fortress Press, 1978.

NEW TESTAMENT INTRODUCTIONS, THEOLOGY, CRITICISM, AND INTERPRETATION

Connick, C. Milo. *The New Testament: An Introduction.* 2nd ed. Belmont, Calif.: Dickenson Publishing Co., 1978. A college-level textbook offering a clear analysis of the New Testament.

Goodspeed, Edgar M. *A History of Early Christian Literature,* rev. ed. by R. M. Grant. Chicago: University of Chicago Press, 1966. Concentrates on noncanonical literature.

Goppelt, Leonhard. *Theology of the New Testament.* 2 vols. Translated by John E. Alsup and edited by Jurgen Roloff. Grand Rapids, Mich.: Wm. B. Eerdmans, 1981.

Guthrie, Donald. *New Testament Theology.* Downers Grove, Ill.: Inter-Varsity Press, 1981.

Hahn, Ferdinand. *Historical Imagination and New Testament Faith: Two Essays.* Philadelphia: Fortress Press, 1983.

Kee, Howard C. *Understanding the New Testament,* 4th ed. Englewood Cliffs, N. J.: Prentice-Hall, 1983. A scholarly, analytical approach to New Testament study.

Koester, Helmut. *Introduction to the New Testament.* 2 vols. Philadelphia: Fortress Press, 1982.

Kummel, W. G. *Introduction to the New Testament.* Translated by H. C. Kee. Nashville: Abingdon Press, 1975.

Perrin, Norman, and Duling, Dennis C. *The New Testament: An Introduction,* 2nd. ed. New York: Harcourt Brace Jovanovich, 1982.

Pfeiffer, Robert. *History of New Testament Times: With an Introduction to the Apocrypha.* New York: Harper & Row, 1949. Covers Roman rule from Pompey's conquest (63 B.C.E.) to outbreak of Jewish revolt (66 C.E.).

Spivey, Robert A., and Smith, D. M. *Anatomy of the New Testament,* 3rd ed. New York: Macmillan, 1982.

Tyson, Joseph B. *The New Testament and Early Christianity.* New York: Macmillan, 1984. An introduction that places early Christian literature, including non-canonical Gospels, in its historical Jewish-Hellenistic context.

BIRTH, TRIAL, AND RESURRECTION NARRATIVES

Brown, Raymond E. *The Birth of the Messiah: A Commentary on the Infancy Narratives in Matthew and Luke.* New York: Doubleday, 1977. A comprehensive analysis of the historicity and theological implications of the infancy narratives.

Brown, Raymond E., Donfried, K. P., Fitzmyer, S. J., and Reumann, John, eds. *Mary in the New Testament: A Collaborative Assessment by Protestant and Roman Catholic Scholars.* Philadelphia: Fortress Press, 1978.

Catchpole, David R. *The Trial of Jesus.* Leiden: Brill, 1971. Argues that Jesus was executed for religious offenses.

Denielou, Jean. *The Infancy Narratives.* Translated by Rosemary Sheed. New York: Herder and Herder, 1968. Attempts to discern historical worth of the birth stories.

Fuller, Reginald H. *The Formation of the Resurrection Narratives.* Philadelphia: Fortress Press, 1980.

Marxsen, Willi. *The Resurrection of Jesus of Nazareth.* Translated by Margaret Kohl. Philadelphia: Fortress Press, 1970.

Perrin, Norman. *The Resurrection According to Matthew, Mark, and Luke.* Philadelphia: Fortress Press, 1977.

Rivkin, Ellis. *What Crucified Jesus? The Political Execution of a Charismatic.* Nashville: Abingdon Press, 1984. Presents Jesus as a victim of "the system," a Roman-Jewish establishment devoted to preserving the political status quo.

Winter, Paul. *On the Trial of Jesus.* Berlin: Walter de Gruyter, 1977. Emphasizes the political charges against Jesus.

WOMEN AND THE BIBLE

Daly, Mary. *Beyond God the Father: Toward a Philosophy of Women's Liberation.* New York: Harper & Row, 1980.

Gerstenberger, Erhard S., and Schrage, Wolfgang. *Woman and Man.* Translated by D. W. Scott. Nashville: Abingdon Press, 1982.

Otwell, John H. *And Sarah Laughed.* Philadelphia: Westminster Press, 1977.

Ruether, Rosemary R. *Sexism and God-Talk.* New York: Harper & Row, 1982.

Wolkstein, Diane, and Kramer, Samuel N. *Inanna, Queen of Heaven and Earth.* New York: Harper & Row, 1980.

INDEX

Anti-Semitism, and Esther, 179
Antithetical parallelism, 160–161
'Apiru (Habiru), 20
Apocalypse, 179; Christian, 358–361
Apocalypse of Baruch: Greek, 238–239; Syriac, 237–238
Apocalypse of Peter, 365
Apocalyptic elements: in Apocrypha and Pseudepigrapha, 226, 231, 233, 234–238; in Dead Sea Scrolls, 243–244; in New Testament, 250, 290, 293–294, 338–340, 362–364; in Old Testament, 115, 118, 120, 126, 130, 134–135, 149–150, 151
Apocalyptic literature, 179–187
Apocrypha: 1, 11, 18, 197–201, 246; Christian, 18–19, 365; Old Testament, 197–223
Apoditic law, 67
Apollo, 231, 239
Apollos, 326, 347
Apostles: Acts of the, 309–315; list of the Twelve, 288
Apostolic tradition and New Testament canon, 16, 18
Aramaic language, 5
Arameans, 19
Archaeological discoveries pertaining to Bible, 36–39
Aristeas, Letter of, 6, 224–225
Aristobulus, 11, 246
Ark of the Covenant, 65, 82, 83, 90, 92, 94, 98
Armageddon, 42, 134, 254, 361
Arses, 107
Artaxerxes, 107, 188, 189, 191, 206
Asa, 195
Ascension of Isaiah, 227
Ashdod, 117
Asher, 240
Ashurbanipal IV, 101; library of, 3
Asia Minor, 317, 331, 360
Asmodeus, 202
Assumption of Moses, 236, 358
Assurnasirpal II, 35
Assyria, 35, 44, 100, 101, 104–105, 110, 118 (map), 140, 202; as divine instrument of punishment, 143; in Isaiah's time, 115–117
Assyrian Empire, 114, 118 (map), 202
Astronomy, in I Enoch, 233
Astyages (Cyrus), 214
Athaliah, 100
Athanasius, 16, 18, 364
Athens, 326
Atonement, Day of, 21, 69, 348
Augustus, 264
Authorized Version of the Bible, 8, 21
Ave Maria, 298
Azariah (Abednego), 213
Azariah (Uzziah), 115
Azazel, 69

Baal, 4; worship by Israelites, 73, 84, 85, 99, 104, 132
Babel, Tower of, 54
Babylon, 3–4, 32, 34, 39, 118, 119, 130, 143, 144, 164, 175, 195, 199, 200, 214, 237, 352; as divine instrument of punishment, 122, 124; as symbol, 212, 213, 352, 360, 361
Babylonian exile, 96, 98, 110, 111, 115, 125, 127, 212; and Jewish theology, 155–156, 164; and Pentateuch, 49; return from, 118–119, 129–130, 189
Babylonian Genesis. See *Enuma Elish*
Balaam's blessing, 73
Balak, 73
Barabbas, 295, 300
Barak, 86
Bar Kochba Letters, 39
Barnabas, 312, 313, 317, 347; Epistle of, 18, 364
Bartholomew, 288
Baruch, 121–123; Book of, 211–213; Greek Apocalypse of (3 Baruch), 238–239; Syriac Apocalypse of (2 Baruch), 237–238
Bassha, 100
Bathsheba, 93, 98, 193
Beatitudes, 278
Bechira, 227
Bede, Venerable, 7
Beersheba, Valley of, 42
Bel (Marduk), 212, 214
Bel and the Dragon, 214–215
Belial, 227
Belshazzar, 183, 184
Benjamin, 91, 99, 240, 336; war against, 88–89
Bethany, 283
Bethel, 4, 58, 99, 109, 137
Bethlehem, 142, 169, 299
Bethulia, 204
Bible: archaeological discoveries pertaining to, 33, 36–40; authorship and date, 2–4; Christian, 16–19, 364–365; contents of, 12–13; English versions of, 7–9; manuscripts, 6–7; original languages, 5–6; sources, 3–4, 22, 37, 38, 47–50, 52–53, 61; translations of, 5–6; versions of. *See individual translations*
Biblical history, events in Near East related to, 34–35
Bildad, 157, 159
Bishop's Bible, 8
Bishops, duties of, 344
Bithynia, 255
Blessing of Moses, 77
Blessings, psalms of, 163–164
Blood: and covenant ratification, 56, 57, 66; and forgiveness, in Hebrews, 348
Boaz, 169
Book of Adam and Eve, 241–242
Book of the Covenant, 64, 83

Judah, 99–104; events and rulers, 44–45, 90–98; 100–101; fall to Assyrians, 104

Israelite confederacy, 35, 87 (map)

Israelite Empire, of David and Solomon, 35, 97 (map), 98

Israelites, origin of, 19–20, 56, 59, 61–64

Issachar, 240

J (Yahwist) document, 2–3, 47–48, 53, 61, 82, 85, 90

Jacob, 20, 44, 58–59, 239

Jael, 86

James (kinsman of Jesus), 317, 331, 350, 357

James (son of Alphaeus), 288

James (son of Zebedee), 264, 288, 293, 302

James, Letter of, 265, 350–351

Jamnia, Academy at, 10, 197, 265

Japheth, 55

Jashar, Book of, 82

Jason (high priest), 222

Jason of Cyrene, 221

JE source, 48–49, 61, 71, 73, 82, 90

Jehoahaz (king of Israel), 100

Jehoahaz (king of Judah), 101

Jehoash, 100

Jehoiachin, 101, 106, 127

Jehoiakim, 101, 106, 121, 124

Jehonadab, 104

Jehoram, 100

Jehoshaphat, 103, 195

Jehovah, 21

Jehu, 100, 103–104

Jephthah, 86

Jeremiah, 93, 101, 108, 112, 186, 212, 276, 278, 330; Book of, 121–126; and Daniel, 186; Letter of, 212–213

Jericho, 82–83, 109; excavations at, 38

Jeroboam I, 99, 100, 104

Jeroboam II, 100, 104, 132, 136

Jerome, Saint, 6, 11, 192, 197

Jerusalem, 4, 42, 81; Babylonian conquest of, 80, 106, 107, 124–125, 129, 130, 144, 175–176, 200, 212, 238; belief in invincibility of, 93, 98, 116, 117, 122, 124; David's conquest of, 92, 93; early Christian church at, 311–314, 317, 324, 329, 330–333, 346; heavenly, 332, 348, 349, 361; Jesus' entry into, 293–294; Jesus' ministry in, 303, 306, 307; Roman destruction of, 199, 200, 232, 237, 247, 281–282, 287, 293, 294; and second temple, 147, 149; and Solomon's temple in, 98, 105, 115, 124, 128, 130, 195; as universal religious center in Zecheriah, 149

Jerusalem Bible, 8, 16, 21, 134, 170, 205

Jerusalem Conference, First, 264, 313–314, 320

Jerusalem ministry of Jesus, 283, 291–292, 293–295, 300, 303, 308, 310

Jesse, 169

Jesus: ascension of, 311; baptism of, 277, 288; birth of, 274–276, 298–299; crucifixion and death of, 283–284, 294–295, 300, 310; divinity of, 256, 268, 304, 305–306, 336, 337, 348; genealogy of, 270, 271, 274, 298; historical, 255–258; as Messiah, 274–278, 283, 287–288, 292–293, 348; ministry of, 270–271, 278–280, 281–283, 287–294, 299–300, 306–307; miracles performed by, 287–290, 306–307; and other religious groups, 251, 252, 258, 291–292; postresurrection appearances by, 272–273, 284, 300–301; resurrection of, 284, 296, 300, 310; teachings of, 266, 267, 268, 278–280, 281–283, 287–294, 299–300, 304, 307, 310; temptation of, 270, 271, 275, 288; transfiguration of, 293; trial of, 283, 287, 294–295, 300, 310

Jesus Ben Sirach, 10; wisdom of, 153, 209–211

Jewish Bible, order of books in, 9–10, 12–13. *See also* Hebrew Bible; Old Testament

Jewish literature, in intertestamental period, 249–250. *See also* Extracanonical works

Jewish political autonomy, 220, 246–247

Jewish revolt against Rome, 45, 247, 251, 253, 254, 265, 281–282; second, 39, 265

Jewish social customs, in Tobit, 202–203

Jews: attitudes toward, in Gospels, 281, 284, 287–288, 291–292; and early Christian church, 311–315, 323; Hellenistic, 207, 212–213, 224, 229–231; in Roman Empire, 246–247

Jezebel, 103

Jezreel, Valley of, 42

Joanna, 300

Joash, 100

Job, 153, 154, 182, 207, 239; Book of, 155–159; compared to Ecclesiastes, 154, 171

Joel, 113, 312; Book of, 133–135

John (disciple), 288, 293, 302, 331, 355, 359, 365

John, Gospel of, 209, 265, 266, 268, 302–310, 355; authorship and date, 302–303; compared to Synoptics, 268, 271, 273, 303, 304; Logos in, 305–306; purpose and themes of, 304–305; sources of, 303

John, Letters of, 355–357; authorship and date of, 355; First, 355–356; Second, 356–357; Third, 357

John Hyrcanus, 220

John Hyrcanus II, 246

John of Patmos, 359

John the Baptist, 244, 254, 264, 275, 286, 288, 292, 298, 303, 304

John the Elder, 302, 355, 357, 359

Jonah, 113; Book of, 139–141

Jonathan (Maccabee), 220

Jonathan (son of Saul), 91, 92

Jordan River, 42, 277, 288; crossing of, 82

Joseph (son of Jacob), 59, 182, 240

Joseph of Arimathea, 295

Josephus, 15, 251, 253, 254, 350

Joshua (high priest), 149, 189

Joshua (son of Nun), 44, 72, 79, 236; Book of, 67, 81–84

Marcion, 17

Mardochaeus (Mordecai), 205

Marduk, 52–53, 178, 361

Mari, 32, 36–37

Mark, Gospel of, 266, 285–296; authorship and date of, 265, 266, 273, 285–286; concept of Messiah in, 287; purpose of, 285–286; as source, 266, 267–268, 273, 277, 281, 285, 297, 300, 303–304

Marriage: Paul's view on, 326; in Hosea, 132

Martha, 300, 303

Martyrdom of Isaiah, 227

Mary (mother of James the younger), 295, 309

Mary (mother of Jesus), 274, 275, 276, 298, 299

Mary (sister of Martha), 300, 303

Mary Magdalene, 295, 300, 308, 309

Masoretic Text (M. T.), 6, 12–13, 244

Mattathias, 217, 218

Matthew (disciple), 272

Matthew, Gospel of, 266, 267–268, 270, 272–284; authorship and date of, 273–274; purpose of, 273–274, 278; use of Old Testament in, 267, 273, 274–275, 276–278

Matthew's Bible, 8

Matthias, 311

Medes, 143

Media, 184, 204

Meditation, psalms of, 164

Megiddo, plain of, 42, 43, 105, 361

Megillot (Festival Scrolls), 167–179

Melchizedek, 348

Menahem, 100

Menelaus (high priest), 222

Menzaleh, Lake, 64

Meribah, 77

Meshach, 183, 213

Mesopotamia, 3–4, 19, 31–37, 44, 52, 55, 58, 100–101. See also Babylon

Messiah: defined, 94, 116; and Abrahamic covenant, 56, 57; in Apocrypha, 200; in Daniel, 185; and Davidic covenant, 92–93, 94–95; and Essenes, 243, 254; Jesus as, 256, 263, 273, 274–278, 287–288, 292–293, 299, 304, 326, 348; in Prophets, 116–117, 119, 149, 151; in Pseudepigrapha, 227, 232, 233, 237, 238; in Revelation, 361; and Zerubbabel as, 147–148

Messianic banquet, 290

Messianic psalms, 163

Messianic secret, 287

Methuselah, 54

Micah, 100, 112, 274, 276; Book of, 141–142

Mical, 91

Michael, 236, 239, 242, 361

Midian, 62

Midianites, 73

Midrash, 225

Millennium, 361

Minor Prophets, 109–113; Books of, 131–151. See also names of individual prophets

Miriam, 72, 74, 109; song of, 3, 63–64

Mishna, 252

Missionary journeys, of Paul, 313, 314–315, 317, 318–319 (maps)

Moab, 74, 146, 169

Moabite Stone, 39

Moabite women, 73

Monarchy, 86, 89, 90–91, 100–101. See also Divided Kingdom

Monotheism, 24, 73, 119, 158–159, 226

Moral distinctions, in apocalyptic literature, 181

Moral responsibility: of Christians, 323–324, 332, 338, 349, 350, 352–353, 356; in Ezekiel, 128–129

Mordecai, 177, 178

Moresheth, 141

Mosaic Covenant, 16, 46–47, 64, 66–67, 110, 122, 142, 156

Mosaic law, 46–47, 64; in Apocrypha and Pseudepigrapha, 198, 210, 212, 217, 226; in early Christian church, 313; in Gospels, 268, 278–279, 291, 307; in Old Testament, 66–67, 80, 103, 151, 190, 191; Paul's view of, 316, 322–324, 331–332; and Pharisees and Sadducees, 252, 253. See also Religious observance

Moses, 2, 3, 21; Assumption of, 236; biography of, 61–62; parallels to, in Akkadian legend, 31; in Pentateuch, 61–67 passim, 72–78 passim; in Pseudepigrapha, 225, 226; relation of, to Pentateuch, 46–47, 66

Muratorian Canon, 17

Mysticism, Hebrew (in 2 Enoch), 235

Mythical elements: in Genesis, 52, 53, 55; in Revelation, 360–361

Nabonidus, 184

Nabopolassar, 107

Naboth, 103

Nadab, 100

Nahum, 101, 112; Book of, 142–143

Naomi, 169

Naphtali, 240

Nathan, 92, 93, 98, 106

Nathanael, 304

Nature: in Ecclesiastes, 174–175; Jesus' power over, 256, 289; in Job, 158–159; in Romans, 322

Nazareth, 42, 288

Nazarites, 86, 88, 276

Near East: ancient civilizations of, 31–33; ancient literature of, compared to Bible, 3–4, 37, 52–53, 54; events related to Biblical history, 34–35; Hellenistic events of, 182–186; 216–218

Nebuchadnezzar, 101, 105–106, 107, 110, 124, 125, 129, 155, 175, 176, 180, 183, 184, 203, 238

Necho, Pharaoh, 105, 110, 124, 143

Nehemiah, 44, 107, 188, 189; Book of, 190–192

Nephesh (soul), 24

Nephilim, 55

Neriglissar, 107

Nero, 265, 317, 347, 352, 361

Nevi'im (prophets), 108–109

New American Bible, 8

New covenant, 16; in Jeremiah, 125–127

New English Bible, 8, 21, 205, 266

New heavens, 355, 361

New Testament, 1, 2, 5, 16–18; authorship of, 2; books of, 263, 264–265, 266; canon, 16–18; extracanonical works, 18–19, 364–365; history, events in, 264–265; language and literature, 249–250; manuscripts of, 7, 302; sources and growth of, 266–268. *See also names of individual books*

Nicanor, 218, 222

Nicodemus, 306

Nineveh, 105, 124, 140, 143, 202

Ninth of Ab, Feast of, 168

Noachan covenant, 55, 57

Noadiah, 109

Noah, 55, 182, 354; Book of, 233

Numbers, Book of, 67, 71–73, 77

Nunc Dimittis, 299

Nuzi Tablets, 37

Obadiah, 112; Book of, 139

Old Testament, 1, 5–6; apocalyptic elements in, 120, 134–135, 149–150, 179–181; Apocrypha, authorship and date of, 11, 14, 197; canon, 9–10; and Gospels, 267–268, 273–275, 276–278, 282, 293; history, major events of, 34–35; manuscripts of, 5–7, 14–15; order of books in, 12, 13–14; and Revelation, 359; Satan in, 26–28. *See also names of individual books*

Olives, Mount of, 150

Omri, 99, 100

Onesimus, 345–346

Oracles: in the Prophets, 108, 113, 114, 115, 121, 131, 136, 146, 150; Sibylline, 231–232

Oral elements: in Gospels, 257, 267, 285, 286, 294; in Haggadah, 241; in Old Testament, 2–3, 23, 47, 50, 82, 89

Oral law, 252

Original sin, 200, 322–323

Orpha, 169

Orthodoxy, early Christian, 341–342, 343, 344, 355–358

P (priestly document), 48–50, 52–53, 61, 68, 71, 82, 191

Palestine, 40, 42–43, 56, 88, 92, 150, 246; climate and geography, 40–43; events in, 44–45; maps of, 41, 87, 97, 102, 186, 219, 248. *See also* Canaan

Palm Sunday, 293

Papias, 267, 285, 286, 302

Parables: in 1 Enoch, 233; not found in Gospel of John, 304; in Luke, 298, 299; in Mark, 287, 290; in Matthew, 280–281, 282–283

Paraclete, 304, 310

Paradise, 242, 300

Paradox, in Ecclesiastes, 174

Paralipomena (Chronicles), 192

Parallelism, in Hebrew poetry, 160–161

Parity covenant, 57

Parousia: in Gospels, 281–282, 290, 292–294; Paul's view of, 338–340, 344; problem of delayed, 354–355; in Revelation, 359–361; response of Christian church to disappointment in, 362–364

Passion, in Gospels, 286, 292, 294–295, 300, 307–308

Passover, 63, 105, 168; and Christian communion, 286, 294, 300, 303

Pastoral Epistles, 340–345; authorship and date of, 340–341

Patriarchs, 2, 32, 34, 36, 44, 51, 55–59; Testament of the Twelve, 239–240

Paul, 2, 3, 16–17, 250, 264–265, 347, 354, 355; apostleship of, 331; imprisonment of, 315, 333, 335, 345–346; and Jews, 313–315, 317; letters ascribed to, 333–334, 340–345; letters of, 316–332, 335–340, 345–346, 354, 355; missionary activities of, 313, 314–315, 317, 318, 320; opposition to, 314–315, 331–332; and Pharisees, 315, 317, 336; travels and correspondence, 318–319 (maps), 320 (table)

Peace, universal: in Isaiah, 112, 117, 120; in Micah, 142; in Revelation, 361

Pekah, 100

Pekahiah, 100

Pentateuch, 46–50, 224, 252; authorship of, 2–3, 47–50; books of, 51–78; canonization of, 9–10; sources of, 47–50. *See also* Mosaic law

Pentecost, 135, 168, 312

Penuel, 59

Perea, 247

Persecution: by Antiochus IV, 182–183, 213, 216–217, 221–222, 230; and apocalyptic literature, 179–186, 358–361; of Christians by Romans, 255–256, 352–356, 358–359; meaning and effects of, in New Testament, 283, 287, 295, 300, 312, 314, 347, 352–353, 359

Persian Empire, 107, 147, 177, 178, 184–185, 188, 205, 250

Persian religion: influence of, in Old Testament, 27–28, 250

Peter (apostle), 267, 288, 317, 322, 326, 331, 352–354, 363; authority of, 281; in Gospels, 264, 265, 285, 286, 293, 294

Peter, Apocalypse of, 365

Peter, Letters of, 352–353, 354–355, 358

Petition, psalms of, 163

Sirbonis, Lake, 64

Sisera, 86

Slavery, Paul's attitude toward, 345–346

Slavonic Book of Enoch (2 Enoch), 234–235

Social justice, 110, 137, 141, 351; in Luke, 298; in Pentateuch, 70, 74; in Prophets, 111–112, 115–116, 131, 136–137, 141–142

Sodom, 42, 56, 358

Solomon, 98, 153, 165, 170, 171, 194, 195, 207; Psalms of, 228–229; Song of, 168, 170; temple of, 98, 162; Wisdom of, 24, 153, 206–209

Son: relation of, to Father (in Gospel of John), 305–306, 307

Son of Man: in 1 Enoch, 233; in Daniel, 185; in Gospels, 283, 285, 292–294

Song of Moses, 75, 77

Song of Songs, Book of, 167, 168, 170

Song of the Suffering Servant, 119–120

Song of the Three Holy Children, 213–214

Sons of the prophets, 109

Sophia, 167

Soul: in Apocrypha, 200, 207, 230, 235; Greek influence on Pharisaic and Christian beliefs about, 250, 252; Judaeo-Christian beliefs about, 24, 173, 364; in Paul's view, 328, 330

Spirit, the Holy, 275, 288, 304, 310, 326, 332; in Acts, 312; in Ephesians, 333–334; in Gospel of John, 310

Spirit mediums, 108

Spiritual body, Paul's doctrine of, 328, 330

Stephen (martyr), 312, 317

Stoic philosophy: influence of, on Bible writers, 172, 173, 305

Succession Narrative, in Samuel, 93

Suetonius, 256

Suffering: in New Testament, 287–288, 291, 294–295, 352–353; in Old Testament, 69, 119–120; redemptive value of, 120

Sumerian civilization, 3–4, 31

Sumero-Babylonian literature, and the Bible, 3–4, 31, 52–53, 55, 361

Susa, 185

Susanna, 214

Suzerainty Covenant, 66

Sylvanus, 352. See Silas

Symbolism: in apocalyptic literature, 126, 180–181, 183, 185; in Revelation, 358–360

Synagogues, expulsion of Christians from, 252

Synonymous parallelism, 160

Synoptic Gospels, 266–268, 270–304. See also Luke; Mark; Matthew

Synoptic Problem, 266

Synthetic parallelism, 161

Syntyche, 336

Syria, 19, 32, 33, 36, 182, 216, 217, 218, 220, 246; rule of Palestine, 216–222

Syriac Apocalypse of Baruch (2 Baruch), 237–238

Syro-Ephraimite crisis, in Isaiah, 115–116

Tabernacles (Booths), Feast of, 168, 191, 307

Tacitus, 256

Talmud, 252, 256

Tamar, 59

Tammuz, 128

Tarsus, 317

Teacher of Righteousness, 244

Tekoa, 136

Temple, 130, 141, 142, 150, 193, 194, 295; Herod's, 246–247; Jesus' attack on, 291, 303, 306; Jesus' presentation at, 299; Roman destruction of, 254; second, 80, 147, 148, 185–186, 189, 211, 213, 253; second, pollution of, 217; Solomon's, 95, 98, 117, 122, 124, 125, 128, 147, 217; worship at, 75–76, 348–349

Ten Commandments, 46, 64, 75

Ten plagues, on Egypt, 62–63

Ten Weeks Apocalypse, 233

Teraphim, 58

Testament, 16, 250

Testaments of the Twelve Patriarchs, 239–241

Tetragrammaton, 21

Thaddeus, 288

Thanksgiving, psalms of, 163

Theodicy, 155–156, 199–200. See also Justice, divine

Theophany, 64, 82, 103, 158–159, 310

Theophilus, 298, 311

Thessalonians, Letters to, 264, 338–340; First, 338–339, 362; Second, 339–340

Thessalonica, 338

Third Isaiah, 113, 115, 120

Thomas (disciple), 288, 310; Gospel of, 17, 19, 365

Tiamat, 52–53, 361

Tiberius, 247, 264

Tiglath-Pileser, 35, 100

Tigris, River, 242

Timothy, 317, 329, 335, 347; First, 341–342; Letters to, 341–344; Second, 343–344

Titus, 329; Letter to, 344–345

Titus (emperor), 265

Tobia, 190

Tobias, 202

Tobit, Book of, 201–203

Tongues, speaking in: Paul's attitude toward, 327–328

Torah, 10, 66–67, 109, 224, 252, 253; authorship of, 47–50; books of, 51–78; revised by Ezra, 107, 191

Tradition, Christian, 342, 343

Trajan, 255, 265
Transfiguration of Jesus, 293, 354
Transjordan, 42
Tribes, Israelite, 19–20, 59, 83; and twelve disciples, 288
Triumvirate, second, 232
Trust, psalms of, 163
Twelve (disciples), 279, 288
Tyndale, William, 6, 7–8
Tyre, 32; King of, 129

Ugarit, 183
Ugaritic texts, 32, 38
Unity, in Christian church, 327–328, 333–338, 341–342
Universe, final consummation of, 355
Ur, 19
Uriah, 93
Uriel, 200
Ur-Zababa, 31
Utnapishtim, 3, 55
Uz, 156
Uzziah (in Judith), 204
Uzziah (king), 100, 115

Vashti, 177, 178
Vespasian, 265
Vices, catalogue of, in 2 Timothy, 343
Virgin birth of Jesus, 274–275, 276, 298–299
Virgin conception, in Isaiah, 116
Virtues, four cardinal, 230; in Wisdom of Solomon, 208
Visions: in 2 Esdras, 200; in prophets, 115, 127–128, 130, 137–138, 185; in Pseudepigrapha, 233, 235, 238–239; in Revelation, 359–361
Vulgate, 6, 7, 18, 197, 199, 205, 212

Watchers, in 1 Enoch, 233
Wealth, biblical attitudes toward: Essene, 254; in Gospels, 290, 299, 300; in Letter of James, 351; in 1 Timothy, 342
Wife, in Proverbs, 167
Wine: in ceremonial meal of Essenes, 254; at Last Supper, 283, 294; in miracle at Cana, 306; in Pauline churches, 327
Wisdom: in Ecclesiastes, 208–211; in Job, 155; in New Testament, 305, 350; in Paul's view, 326–327; in Pseudepigrapha, 230; as Yahweh's agent, 153, 166–167, 208
Wisdom, psalms of, 164, 207
Wisdom literature, 152–159, 165–167, 171–174, 206–211
Wisdom of Jesus Ben Sirach, 10, 209–211
Wisdom of Solomon, 24, 153, 206–209, 305
Witch of Endor, 193

Wives, in Ezra, 190
Women: in New Testament, 299–300, 342; in Old Testament, 52–54, 58, 167, 177–178, 203–204, 210; Paul's views on, 327
Word (Logos), 167, 208, 250, 304–306
Work, value of (in 2 Thessalonians), 340
Works, in James' doctrine, 351
Worship: in early Christian church, 327; Israel's, 69–70, 75–76, 84, 98, 105, 141–142, 162–164, 211
Wrath, day of (in Zephaniah), 145–146
Writings, 152–196, 252; canonization, 10. See also names of individual books
Wycliffe, John, 7

Xerxes I, 107, 177–178
Xerxes II, 107

Yahweh: as name of God, 2, 21–24, 62, 130, 211; and Abraham, 56, 57; and Baal worship, 84, 85, 99; as Creator, 53–54; and Davidic covenant, 92–95; Day of, 134–135, 137–138, 145–146; and the exodus, 61–64; and foreign nations, 116, 130; glory of, 127–128; in Job, 155–159; in Leviticus, 69–71; not named in Ecclesiastes, 175; in Numbers, 72; as Old Testament deity, 77, 84, 85, 88, 128, 130, 140, 144, 145, 156, 166, 176, 186; and Satan, 26–28, 156–157; varying depictions of, 21–26; 119; worship of, 137, 141–142, 189. See also Elohim; God
Yahwist (J) document, 2, 47–48, 53–54, 61, 82, 85, 90
Yahwist supporters of Jehu, 104
Yom Kippur, 69

Zadok, 130, 253
Zadokite Document, 243, 249
Zadokites, 130
Zealots, 254
Zebedee, 288, 302
Zebulun, 240
Zechariah, 113, 189; Book of, 145–147
Zechariah (father of the Baptist), 295
Zedekiah, 94, 101, 106, 124
Zeno the Stoic, 172
Zephaniah, 112; Book of, 145–147
Zerubbabel, 113, 147, 148–149, 189, 198, 199
Zeus, 217
Zion, 94, 142, 162
Zion, Mount, 139
Zophar, 157, 159
Zoroastrianism: influence of, on Tobit, 203; as origin of Satan concept, 27–28